RECONCEPTUALISING THE RULE OF LAW IN GLOBAL GOVERNANCE, RESOURCES, INVESTMENT AND TRADE

The relevance and importance of the rule of law to the international legal order cannot be doubted. Its significance was recently reaffirmed by the Declaration of the High-level Meeting of the General Assembly on the Rule of Law at the National and International Level, which made a solemn commitment to the rule of law on behalf of states and international organisations. In this edited collection, leading scholars and practitioners from the fields of global governance, resources, investment and trade examine how the commitment to the rule of law manifests itself in their respective fields. The book looks at cutting-edge issues within each field and examines the questions arising from the interplay between them. With a clear three-part structure, it explores each area in detail and addresses contemporary challenges while trying to ensure a commitment to the rule of law. The contributions also consider how the rule of law has been or should be reconceptualised. Taking a multidisciplinary approach, the book will appeal to international lawyers from across the spectrum, including practitioners in the field of international investment and trade law.

Reconceptualising the Rule of Law in Global Governance, Resources, Investment and Trade

Edited by
Photini Pazartzis and Maria Gavouneli
with
Anastasios Gourgourinis and Matina Papadaki

• HART •
OXFORD • LONDON • NEW YORK • NEW DELHI • SYDNEY

HART PUBLISHING
Bloomsbury Publishing Plc
Kemp House, Chawley Park, Cumnor Hill, Oxford, OX2 9PH, UK

HART PUBLISHING, the Hart/Stag logo, BLOOMSBURY and the Diana logo are trademarks of Bloomsbury Publishing Plc
First published in Great Britain 2016

First published in hardback, 2016
Paperback edition, 2018

A catalogue record for this book is available from the British Library.

ISBN: PB: 978-1-50992-474-5
HB: 978-1-84946-880-0
ePDF: 978-1-50990-178-4
ePub: 978-1-50990-179-1

Typeset by Forewords, Oxford

Preface

THIS BOOK BRINGS together papers presented at the very successful 2013 ILA Regional Conference held in Sounion, Athens on 29–31 August 2013.

The Conference took place against the backdrop of political, social and economic stability, despite the pervasive underlying problems, and resulted in a successful exchange of views and knowledge. It also served as a meeting point of both people and ideas. Lawyers and academics from all over the world, both established figures as well as young researchers, came together and discussed a great variety of issues ranging from philosophical aspects of the rule of law in relation to international law to technical rules of trade law.

The quality of all the papers presented was of such a high level that the need was felt to publish not only the proceedings of the conference but a book. Thirty conference participants revised and submitted their papers for publication, making contributions of great value, and closing a gap in the existing literature. The book addresses important current and cross-cutting issues that have not been adequately dealt with together or in an interdisciplinary manner. Moreover, all of the issues are of relevance both academically as well as to practitioners of public and private international law.

The contributions are organised into three main parts. The first addresses the contemporary challenges of global governance, shedding light both on the actors and processes as well as on the structures and factors of the international community. The second deals with resources in a novel way, approaching it both from the viewpoint of the preservation of the past, looking into cultural heritage, while also according the requisite importance to sharing and maintaining the future through a disciplined approach to natural resources. Finally, the last part explores investment and trade from various angles.

It is hoped that this book will help map out interactions of interrelated topics that are slowly coming to occupy the centre stage of the international law discourse.

Professor Christos Gortsos
Vice President Hellenic Branch ILA
Chairman, Organising Committee

Contents

Introduction

ON 24 SEPTEMBER 2012, the Heads of State and Government attending the High-Level meeting of the UN General Assembly on 'The Rule of Law at the National and International Levels' reaffirmed in a solemn Declaration their 'commitment to the rule of law', encompassing States and international organisations on the international level and all persons, institutions and entities, public and private, on the national level, and agreed that any 'collective response to the challenges and opportunities arising from the many complex political, social and economic transformations . . . must be guided by the rule of law, as it is the foundation of friendly and equitable relations between States and the basis on which just and fair societies are built'.

This collection of essays stems from papers originally presented during the 2013 International Law Association (ILA) Regional Conference held in Greece. The high quality and thought-provoking interconnections among the presentations led us to invite the participants to revisit their papers and present them as book chapters. The contributions received are aptly situated at the crossroads between the developed and the emerging world in times of global crisis and concentrate on various manifestations of the international rule of law with a view to portraying its different nuances. In this volume we attempted to put together, in a coherent framework, contributions from distinct perspectives, striking a balance between views expressed by renowned scholars and practitioners and newer voices.

The book is structured around three distinct axes: global governance, resources, and investment and trade. In this context, the authors explore cutting-edge issues within each field but also answer or ask questions arising from the interplay between them.

The purpose of this Introduction is to serve as a compass for navigating through the different but tightly connected contributions. To achieve this, instead of offering a summary of each chapter, we explain, in broad strokes, the overarching themes that comprise the backbone of the book's structure. We believe that the organisation of the topics as well as the substance of the contributions will give the readers a *tour d'horizon* of issues of global concern and their interaction with and effects on international law norms and mechanisms.

The chapters included in Part I under the general theme of *Global Governance* provide both a background discussion on the architecture of international law as well as an examination of the prospects for further development. This part examines how crises, challenges and developments in the international arena fit into or challenge the current structure of international law. More specifically, in the first section, the contributions shed light on the role assigned to actors on the international scene and their respective impact on international processes. They offer fresh perspectives in relation to the transparency of global governance, aspects of domestic and international adjudication as well as the contribution of non-state entities in either shaping the law or challenging the limits of law-creation as traditionally conceived. In the second section, the contributions engage in an evaluation of current challenges, including addressing natural disasters, statelessness, protection of minorities and an assessment of the effects of financial crises and debt. The result leads to a concise mapping of the changing patterns of authority and responsibility at the international level.

The general theme of Part II is *Resources*. The chapters of this part address topical issues pertaining to the management of shared resources, including marine resources, fresh water and indeed cultural resources. As the demand for resources in the global markets increases, so does the role they are called to play in world affairs – and commensurably their significance and normative impact as well. The race towards resources, currently operating in a rather under-regulated environment, displays great potential for the concurrent application of different, often widely diverse and occasionally contradictory, sets of rules. Thus, while the protection of the past drives the evolution of the global regulation on cultural heritage, it is the willingness (or need?) to share and safeguard the present and future that characterises the discourse on marine resources and water, occasionally stranded between the concepts of sovereignty and responsibility. In an effort to reflect this struggle, this part also consists of two sections. The first focuses on the safeguarding of the past, namely on the legal framework concerning the protection of cultural heritage. In the second and most extensive section the authors elaborate on different issues, which nevertheless share the same concern, that of allocation and sharing of resources while touching upon issues of protection and preservation.

Finally, Part III concentrates on two ever-topical areas: *International Investment* and *Trade*. The first section includes contributions by both investment law scholars and practitioners, who provide current insights on a wide variety of cross-cutting issues from the rule of law in arbitration to public policy concerns, abuse of rights in international arbitration and issues pertaining to the interpretation of the relevant contractual arrangements. The contributions not only depict the current status of the field but also go further to discuss its future potential. The second section moves to address the modern challenges faced at the level of the multilateral trading system. The WTO offers an excellent example of a regime encompassing a wide array of activities within a single institutional framework, complete with its own dispute settlement system. However, often there are challenges set by trade regionalism, as well as by other regimes, such as international investment, or intergovernmental organisations, such as OPEC, that cast doubt on its self-contained nature. Thus, naturally, the ambit of the contributions of this part includes the manner in which these two facets of modern international economic law project into a more comprehensive system of international economic regulation. Including both narrow and wide-ranging topics, the contributions address issues at the heart of the debate between regionalism and global approaches, the interface between different systems and fields of law, as well as issues of state responsibility.

This collection should prove of great interest to readers who want to focus on contemporary challenges while at the same time keeping in mind the constant interaction between the different thematic fields of international law. Most importantly, it highlights cross-cutting issues fitting in the same narrative, namely how and if international law responds to challenges and newly created needs.

We are particularly grateful to Anastasios Gourgourinis, Lecturer in International Economic Law at the Faculty of Law, National & Kapodistrian University of Athens and Matina Papadaki, doctoral student in the same University, for their valuable contribution to the preparation of this volume. Thanks are also due to a wider group of young scholars and graduate and doctoral students, who were instrumental in the organisation and the eventual success of the Conference that gave rise to the present publication.

Photini Pazartzis
National and Kapodistrian
University of Athens
President Hellenic Branch ILA

Maria Gavouneli
National and Kapodistrian
University of Athens
Treasurer Hellenic Branch ILA

Part I

Contemporary Challenges of Global Governance in the Spotlight

Section 1

Actors and Processes Revisited

1

The Transparency of Global Governance

ANNE PETERS*

I. *PROBLÉMATIQUE* AND CONCEPTS

IN AUGUST 2013, the US military officer Bradley (Chelsea) Manning, who had transmitted information about war crimes committed by members of the US army during the Iraq war to WikiLeaks, was condemned to a 35 year prison sentence for violation of the Espionage Act.[1] Another individual who has become a globally relevant actor in the context of transparency is Edward Snowden, an employee of the US secret service CIA, who revealed to the public and to foreign governments the existence of a secret internet surveillance programme conducted by the United States, PRISM.

PRISM and other surveillance activities of the US National Security Agency, spying on private and inter-agency telephone and internet communication in numerous European states, illustrate the *problématique* of this paper: in a liberal system of governance, the ideal is that the governors themselves should be transparent about the measures they take or not, while the citizens' sphere of privacy should be respected. Citizens are under no prima facie-transparency obligation—quite the contrary. PRISM reversed this order: all users of the internet, mostly private individuals, were rendered transparent through the surveillance programme. However, that fact was completely concealed to outsiders—the measure itself was intransparent. Snowden rendered the surveillance programme partly transparent. He did this by breaching his obligations under his employment contract, and by committing a crime under US law.

Could this action, which is illegal under the domestic law of a state, be justified or excusable under some higher principles, perhaps under international

* Prof Dr iur, Director at the Max Planck Institute for Comparative Public Law and International Law, Heidelberg (Germany), adjunct professor at the University of Basel; honorary professor at the University of Heidelberg and Freie Universität Berlin.

[1] *United States v Private First Class Bradley Manning*, Military Judge Colonel Denise Lind (court-martial Fort Meade, sentence of 21 August 2013).

legal obligations of transparency vis-à-vis foreign states and foreign citizens? The answer to this question depends on the existence of transparency or publicity principles under international law.

'Publicity' is a traditional term of political theory (and political practice). Publicity (δγμοσιότγτα) contains the word δγμος, the people. This etymology shows that the ancient Greeks had already realized the inner link between publicness or publicity and democracy. In contrast, 'transparency' has become a more recent buzzword, also in the field of international law and governance. In this chapter, both terms are used interchangeably. By 'transparency', I understand a culture or scheme in which relevant information (on law and politics) is available.

In all major fields of international law—eg environmental law, trade and investment law, human rights law, international humanitarian law, health law, peace-and-security law—demands for more transparent institutions and procedures have recently been voiced by civil-society actors, by states and within international institutions, and have to a large extent also been honoured. We have called this the transparency turn in global governance.[2]

The turn concerns, first, transparency *for* governance,[3] ie requirements imposed by international law on states. Examples are found in the Aarhus Convention[4] and the Council of Europe Convention on Access to Official Documents (No 205) of 2009.[5] A recent example in the field of international security law are the UN Human Rights Council's Framework Principles for Securing the Human Rights of Victims of Terrorism of 2012. One of these principles is the imperative to conduct an effective official investigation of lethal incidents under 'public scrutiny'.[6]

The Human Rights Committee's General Comment No 34 on Article 19

[2] See A Peters, 'Towards Transparency as a Global Norm' in A Bianchi and A Peters (eds), *Transparency in International Law* (Cambridge University Press, 2013) 607. This contribution builds on the findings set out in more detail in our book.

[3] For the distinction between transparency *for* governance and transparency *of* governance see RB Mitchell, 'Transparency for Governance: The Mechanisms and Effectiveness of Disclosure-based and Education-based Transparency Policies' (2011) 70 *Ecological Economics* 1882, 1882.

[4] UN Economic Commission for Europe, Convention on Access to Information, Public Participation in Decision-Making and Access to Justice in Environmental Matters 2161 UNTS 447 (adopted 25 June 1998, entered into force 30 October 2001).

[5] Not yet in force (it needs 10 ratifications but as of 11 February 2016 has six, mostly by Eastern European states and Sweden).

[6] The states' obligation to protect life obliges them to conduct an effective official investigation whenever individuals have been seriously harmed through the use of lethal or potentially lethal force in a terrorist context (through terrorist acts or through governmental anti-terrorist measures), notably after targeted killing and drone strikes. Ben Emmerson, in the Report of the Special Rapporteur on the Promotion and Protection of Human Rights and Fundamental Freedoms while Countering Terrorism: Framework Principles for Securing the Human Rights of Victims of Terrorism, UN Human Rights Council 12th Session, Doc A/HRC/20/14, para 36 (4 June 2012), mentions as one of the 'minimum requirements' that 'there must be a sufficient element of public scrutiny of the investigation and its results to secure public accountability. This is essential to maintaining public confidence in the authorities' adherence to the rule of law, and prevents any appearance of collusion in, or tolerance of, unlawful acts or omissions.'

ICCPR of 2011[7] offered an important, extended reading of the human right to information, and understood it as encompassing a right to access to official documents held by states, and to those held by functionally public actors. I submit that international organizations might be counted among those actors which exercise public functions.

This leads us to the second dimension of the transparency turn, the increasing demands on the transparency *of* (global) governance actors themselves. Transparency requirements are imposed, for example, on the EU in the EU Transparency Regulation of 2001.[8] With regard to the World Trade Organization (WTO), the Sutherland Report devoted an entire section to the debate on improving the transparency of the WTO and civil society involvement.[9] An example of transparency of an international conference is the conference/meeting of the parties of the UN Framework Convention on Climate Change and Kyoto Protocol (COP 16/CMP 6), held in Cancún in 2010, which was explicitly conducted under the heading of transparency.[10] Furthermore, in 2010, the World Bank issued its 'World Bank Policy on Access to Information'.[11] A final example is the initiative of the 'Small 5' (a group of small states) of 2012, which suggested a draft resolution 'Enhancing the Accountability, Transparency and Effectiveness of the Security Council',[12] though this was ultimately not adopted by the UN General Assembly.

II. THE NORMATIVE QUALITY OF TRANSPARENCY

Currently, no general international transparency treaty exists, and such a codification would probably be neither feasible nor desirable. The question is whether a customary international law principle of transparency exists, or a general principle of law in that sense. In order to be 'legalizable' under these

[7] UN Human Rights Committee, International Covenant on Civil and Political Rights CCPR/C/GC/34 General Comment No 34 (12 September 2011).

[8] Regulation of the European Parliament and of the Council (EC) 1049/2001 of 30 May 2001 regarding Public Access to European Parliament, Council and Commission Documents [2001] OJ L145/43.

[9] P Sutherland et al (eds), *The Future of the WTO: Addressing Institutional Challenges in the New Millennium* (WTO, 2004) 45, paras 183–205.

[10] The Mexican conference's President gave 'full commitment to the principles of transparency and inclusiveness. There will be no parallel or overlapping discussions and I will continue ensuring that all positions are taken into account' (UNFCCC Informal Stocktaking Plenary, Statement by Her Excellency Mrs Patricia Espinosa, COP 16/CMP 6 President (8 December 2010)). In the same sense, see the informal meeting of the President, statement of 5 December 2010: '[t]he Mexican Presidency will continue to work with full transparency and according to established United Nations procedures'. See also UNFCCC Subsidiary Body for Implementation, Synthesis Report on Ways to Enhance the Engagement of Observer Organizations, FCCC/SBI/2010/16 (19 October 2010), with a view to the 33rd session in Cancún, 30 November to 4 December 2010, with proposals for 'ensuring transparency, accountability and information-sharing' (paras 16–17 and 26–28).

[11] World Bank, 'Policy on Access to Information' (1 July 2010), available at http://documents.worldbank.org (accessed on 3 February 2014).

[12] UN General Assembly Doc A/66 L.42/Rev.1 (3 May 2012).

two headings, a concept 'must meet two fundamental structural preconditions: it must be sufficiently precise to generate an obligation and to assess its implementation, and it must have an obligor and an obligee'.[13] Both conditions are not easily fulfillable with regard to the transparency buzzword. As a result, it would seem difficult to argue that transparency as such is a norm of hard international law—and maybe it can never become one.[14] This finding may, however, be of little relevance. It is possible that the classic boxes, the 'sources' in terms of Article 38 ICJ Statute, do not tell us much about the state of international law and its power to influence the behaviour of internationally relevant actors.

III. THE VALUE AND FUNCTIONS OF TRANSPARENCY

In international law and governance, we can discern three clusters of functions: (i) good governance and the rule of law, including foreseeability, accessibility and legal clarity; (ii) accountability, participation and democracy; (iii) effectiveness and efficiency, notably in the financial sector. Here, I will discuss only the second cluster.

Democracy needs transparency. The classic statement in this regard was tendered by James Madison:

> [a] popular Government, without popular information, or the means of acquiring it, is but a prologue to a Farce or a Tragedy; or perhaps both. Knowledge will forever govern ignorance: [a]nd a people who mean to be their own Governors must arm themselves with the power which knowledge gives.[15]

Transparency is obviously a *conditio sine qua non* for the informed consent of the governed. It is critical for uncovering abuses and defending interests. Transparency can arguably alleviate the democratic deficit of global governance. But transparency in itself does not bring about democracy—it is solely a precondition for democratic procedures.

Transparency facilitates control and scrutiny, and can thus help to improve accountability. The question is to whom the accountability of international law and policy-makers, notably the international organizations, should extend—to

[13] B Rudolf, 'Is "Good Governance" a Norm of International Law?' in P-M Dupuy et al (eds), *Völkerrecht als Wertordnung: Festschrift für Christian Tomuschat* (Engel, 2006) 1007, 1026.

[14] See J Ebbesson, 'Global or European Only? International Law on Transparency in Environmental Matters for Members of the Public' in Bianchi and Peters (n 2) 49, 73, who sees only 'normative fragments' which give only limited support for international law on transparency vis-à-vis members of the public. Alan Boyle and Kasey McCall-Smith find 'remarkably little identifiable international law underpinning at this rather significant' transparency practice of international organizations and treaty bodies (A Boyle and K McCall-Smith, 'Transparency in International Law-Making' in Bianchi and Peters (n 2) 419, 435).

[15] J Madison, 'James Madison to WT Barry' in PB Kurland and R Lerner (eds), *The Founders' Constitution* (University of Chicago Press, 1987) ch 18, document 35, writings 9, 103–09. This remark was made in the context of establishing a state-funded educational system (I thank Roy Peled for this information).

member states of specific organizations, to all states, or to a global citizenry? Who are the relevant and legitimate actors, who should the recipients of the accounts be?

In this context, Allen Buchanan and Robert O Keohane usefully distinguish between 'narrow' and 'broad' accountability.[16] Broad accountability means not only allowing those who presently receive the accounts (the states, notably the member states of specific organizations) or also others (such as NGOs and populations) who might wish to contest the very terms of accountability. The gist is that 'broad transparency is needed for critical revision of the terms of accountability'.[17] Seen in this way, transparency becomes even more important for accountability because it can address the accountability mismatch.

Here an objection can be raised: is not transparency merely a surrogate, replacing the much more difficult substantive issues of democracy, good governance, economic efficiency, social justice and the rule of law?[18] Indeed, there exists the danger that certain types of transparency will degenerate to 'empty titles of legitimacy'.[19] The debate on transparency masks other issues behind it, but the gist is that, while transparency is indeed a substitute, it is a necessary one, because it replaces, in a global and pluralistic political space, the unattainable certitude and conviction about the 'right' international law and policy through a procedural device allowing everyone to form their own opinion on matters of global governance.

To conclude, while transparency policies to a certain degree generate only an ersatz legitimacy and may even at times be counterproductive, they more often seem to be 'a reasonable initial step'[20] towards improving the accountability and legitimacy of international law and governance. Still, transparency has its drawbacks, to which I now turn.

IV. DRAWBACKS OF TRANSPARENCY

First, there are intrinsically negative effects of transparency, notably the dangers posed to the quality of deliberations.[21] Secondly, there are countervailing

[16] A Buchanan and RO Keohane, 'The Legitimacy of Global Governance Institutions' (2006) 20 *Ethics & International Affairs* 405, especially 427, with a link to transparency.

[17] Ibid, 428.

[18] V Haufler, 'Disclosure as Governance: The Extractive Industry Transparency Initiative and Resource Management in the Developing World' (2010) 10 *Global Environmental Politics* 53, 70 on transparency as a 'default option'.

[19] L Hölscher, *Öffentlichkeit und Geheimnis: Eine begriffsgeschichtliche Untersuchung zur Entstehung der Öffentlichkeit in der frühen Neuzeit* (Klett-Cotta, 1979) 170.

[20] Haufler (n 18) 70.

[21] For a classic critique see H Morgenthau, *Politics among Nations* (Alfred A Knopf, 1950) 431–33.

legitimate interests, such as security,[22] privacy and business or trade secrets,[23] which must be balanced against the benefits of transparency. Thirdly, as is the case with basically all policies, transparency measures have their financial costs and in simple practical terms may be unfeasible due to time and space constraints. Fourthly, transparency may only be simulated through data flooding ('drowning in disclosure'),[24] disinformation and propaganda. This has traditionally played an important role in international relations.[25]

Another point is that transparency measures can be circumvented: the legal and political actors might hold conclave behind the façade of the public meeting, keep secret files apart from those that are public, or minimize record keeping altogether. If such are the foreseeable or inevitable consequences of transparency or of too much transparency in a certain context, the entire policy will ultimately be rendered ineffective or even counterproductive, and thus creating yet more intransparency. This very brief overview about the pros and cons of transparency or of more transparency in global governance leads to some policy recommendations.

V. POLICY RECOMMENDATIONS

De lege ferenda, international law and institutions should be rendered more transparent, ie the current trend should be basically continued and reinforced. However, because of the mixed effects of transparency, any move in this direction must be qualified.

First, total transparency of international law is neither appropriate nor realistic. International law- and policy-makers should treat transparency as a variable of institutional and legal design. They need to balance the potential negative effects against the positive ones.

[22] A Peters, 'Transparency, Secrecy, and Security: Liaisons Dangereuses' in J Iliopoulos-Strangas et al (eds), *Rechtsstaat, Freiheit und Sicherheit in Europa/Rule of Law, Freedom and Security in Europe/Etat de droit, liberté et sécurité en Europe* (Nomos, 2010) 183. For a powerful argument in favour of disclosure obligations even in matters sensitive for national security deriving from 'the principle of transparency' in combination with an 'emerging positive right to receive information' see E Lieblich, 'Show us the Films: Transparency, National Security and Disclosure of Information collected by Advanced Weapon Systems under International Law' (2012) 45 *Israel Law Reports* 459.

[23] See eg WTO, Agreement on Trade-related Aspects of Intellectual Property Rights 1869, UNTS 299 Art 39 (15 April 1994). IAEA, Model Protocol Additional to the Agreement(s) between State(s) and the International Atomic Energy Agency for the Application of Safeguards, INFCIRC/540 (Corrected) (September 1997). Art 15 requires the International Atomic Energy Agency to 'maintain a stringent regime to ensure effective protection against disclosure of commercial, technological and industrial secrets and other confidential information coming to its knowledge'.

[24] A Gupta, 'Transparency under Scrutiny: Information Disclosure in Global Environmental Governance' (2008) 8 *Global Environmental Politics* 1, 4.

[25] Holzner and Holzner quote a senior official of the EU: '[t]he impression of transparency is that it is a straight ray of light. But it can be simulated by a thousand mirrors' (B Holzner and L Holzner, *Transparency in Global Change: The Vanguard of Open Society* (University of Pittsburgh Press, 2006) 102).

Secondly, a (legal) presumption of transparency should be acknowledged.[26] A presumption of transparency means that the non-release of documents and the closure of meetings to the public must be specifically justified on the basis of legal exceptions which have been clearly defined and circumscribed prior to the fact. These exceptions can only be granted by stating the reasons for them publicly. The burden of explaining and of proving the need for secrecy is thereby placed on the institution itself—not on those outsiders who request access.

Thirdly, intransparency is rendered the more acceptable the more it is embedded in what Thore Neumann and Bruno Simma have called 'meta-transparency'.[27] Meta-transparency means that the reasons for the intransparency (ie whether it is necessary at all) and its substantive and temporal scope must be made transparent. In other words, the questions as to whether, how much and for how long intransparency is warranted (eg the need for a closed-door debate, the circumscription of exceptions, possible reform of the policy) must be subject to public debate.[28] Thereby an 'element of public accountability for the secrecy itself' is introduced.[29] In the end, only meta-transparency provides the necessary means for transcending the limits of transparency.[30]

VI. CONCLUSIONS

My conclusion is that the rise of transparency demands and their satisfaction in the international sphere, which I call the transparency turn of global governance, manifests a paradigm shift. It is international law's shifting character from a 'private' law to a 'public' law character. Traditional international law (being mainly inter-state law) has long been conceived as 'private law writ large'.[31] My claim is that international law has been made public in three senses.

[26] See A Gutmann and D Thompson, *Democracy and Disagreement* (Belknap, 1996) 96, explaining the basis 'for a presumption in favor of publicity and the authority of claims of secrecy and other values that could rebut the presumption'; J Stiglitz, 'On Liberty, the Right to Know, and Public Discourse: The Role of Transparency in Public Life' in MJ Gibney (ed), *Globalizing Rights, The Oxford Amnesty Lectures 1999* (Oxford University Press, 1999) 115, 152: '[b]ecause of these limitations of legalistic approaches, emphasis must be placed on creating a culture of openness, where the presumption is that the public should know about and participate in all collective decisions'. Buchanan and Keohane (n 16) 431: '[t]here should be a very strong but rebuttable presumption of transparency'. O Ben-Naftali and R Peled, 'How Much Secrecy Does Warfare Need?' in Bianchi and Peters (n 2) 321, 323, argue that 'the presumption in favour of secrecy during wartime should be reversed, requiring government officials to shoulder the burden of proof to justify why secrecy is necessary in any particular matter'.

[27] T Neumann and B Simma, 'Transparency in International Adjudication' in Bianchi and Peters (n 2) 436, 472.

[28] Stiglitz (n 26) 152.

[29] Gutmann and Thompson (n 26) 104.

[30] Ibid, 127, on publicity.

[31] T Holland, *Studies in International Law* (Clarendon Press, 1898) 152. Montesquieu described international law as '*le droit civil de l'univers dans le sens que chaque peuple est un citoyen*'

Understanding the first sense requires of us to recall the traditional public law/private law distinction. This distinction ultimately stems from the different logics of *iustitia distributiva* (to be realized through distributive, public policies) and *iustitia compensativa* (as realized in the private sphere and through the market).[32] The emerging transparency norm within international law—with its quality as an enabler and to some extent a proxy for accountability, participation and global democracy—is currently strengthening the element of global distributive justice in international law. International law has in that first sense been rendered more like 'public' law, a law in the global public interest ('for' the public).

Secondly, international law is becoming 'public' law in another sense: a law which constrains political authority, and which seeks to reconcile the exercise of global political authority with individual autonomy.

Finally, international law is becoming international public law in a third sense: it is made—if and to the extent that it is transparent—under scrutiny of the public ('through' the public) even if not fully made 'by' a global public.

In the end, the transparency of governance is only a necessary, but not a sufficient, condition for bringing about accountability, and possibly democracy in the global sphere; there is no automatic progress from global transparency to democratic global governance. Moreover, the theoretical conceptualization and practical implementation of fair global governance mechanisms, procedures and institutions will depend on further research into additional juridical building blocks, such as participation, contestation and solidarity, to name but a few.

(Charles de Secondat, Baron de Montesquieu, *De l'esprit des lois* (Barrilot & Fils, 1748): '*des lois dans le rapport qu'elles doivent avoir avec l'ordre des choses sur lesquelles elles statuent; chapitre premier—idée de ce livre*').

[32] N Jansen and R Michaels, 'Private Law and the State' (2007) 71 *Rabels Zeitschrift für Ausländisches und Internationales Privatrecht* 345, reprinted in N Jansen and R Michaels (eds), *Beyond the State: Rethinking Private Law* (Mohr Siebeck, 2008) 15, 62.

2

Between Flexibility and Stability: Ad Hoc Procedures and/or Judicial Institutions?

CHIARA GIORGETTI*

I. INTRODUCTION

THE CHOICE BETWEEN the flexibility offered by ad hoc procedures and the stability proper of established judicial institutions poses many interesting questions for those interested in international dispute resolution. This chapter seeks to assess some of these questions and, possibly, to offer suggestions to future parties and their counsel on how to select the most appropriate resolution mechanism to resolve their international inter-state dispute.[1]

To begin with, it is worth noting two important and related trends that characterize contemporary international dispute resolution: first, the increased use of international litigation by diverse international actors, and second, the multiplication of dispute resolution mechanisms.

Indeed, there has been a proliferation of judicial bodies in the international community. More, and more diverse international forums are available to parties. Recently created international judicial bodies include the International Criminal Court, the International Tribunal of the Law of the Sea (ITLOS) and the African Court of Justice and Human Rights. At the same time, more of these forums have a very specialized jurisdiction, including the dispute

* Associate Professor of Law, Richmond Law School. The author would like to thank the organizers and the participants to the 2013 Regional Conference of the Hellenic Branch of the International Law Association for their support and comments. I am also grateful to Saud Aldawsari of Richmond Law School for his research and editorial assistance. Email: cgiorget@richmond.edu.

[1] In general, see C Giorgetti (ed), *The Rules, Practice and Jurisprudence of International Courts and Tribunals* (Martinus Nijhoff Publishers, 2012). See also L Malintoppi, 'Methods of Dispute Resolution in Inter-state Litigation: When States Go to Arbitration rather than Adjudication' (2006) 5(1) *Law and Practice of International Courts and Tribunals* 133.

mechanism of the World Trade Organization, the European Court of Human Rights and the arbitration mechanism under the International Convention for Settlement of Investment Disputes (ICSID Convention).

States, the principal actors in the international legal community, are increasingly involved in international litigations. This can be explained simply by observing that, as a result of post-cold war fragmentation, there are more states that have ever growing reciprocal obligations and responsibilities, which in turn create more opportunities for disputes.[2]

In many instances, states act as respondents in international litigation—for example, in investment arbitration or human rights litigation—and so do not have a choice on the forum at the time of each dispute—the choice having been made (usually by treaty) beforehand. However, in inter-state situations, where states are in a position to choose between different forums, how should they decide where to go?

The classic dichotomy is between the flexibility that ad hoc arbitral tribunals offer and the stability provided by standing judicial institutions, like the International Court of Justice (ICJ, the Court).

Ad hoc bodies and judicial institutions include a variety of diverse bodies, including:

- judicial bodies that are permanent structures, like the ICJ and ITLOS, which have a variety of subject matter jurisdictions;
- quasi-judicial bodies, including institutionalized and non-institutionalized arbitral tribunals. The Slovenia/Croatia maritime boundary arbitration presently litigated under the auspices of the Permanent Court of Arbitration (PCA) is an example of the first,[3] the boundary dispute resolved by the Taba arbitration between Egypt and Israel an example of the second;[4] and
- other diverse ad hoc bodies, like the United Nations Claims Commission (UNCC),[5] the Eritrea–Ethiopia Boundaries and Claims Commissions[6] and

[2] See T Buergenthal, 'Proliferation of International Courts and Tribunals: Is it Good or Bad?' (2001) 14 *Leiden Journal of International Law* 267.

[3] Arbitration between the Republic of Croatia and the Republic of Slovenia, Arbitration Agreement of 4 November 2009, available at http://www.pcacases.com/web/view/3 (accessed 10 February 2016).

[4] Award in Boundary Dispute Concerning the Taba Area (Egypt/Isr) (1988) 27 ILM 1421; see CS Copeland, 'The Use of Arbitration to Settle Territorial Disputes' (1999) 67 *Fordham Law Review* 3073, available at http://ir.lawnet.fordham.edu/cgi/viewcontent.cgi?article=3585&context=flr (accessed on 12 February 2016).

[5] The UN Claims Commission was created by the UN Security Council for claims for compensation arising out of the invasion of Kuwait by Iraq and brought by individuals, private companies, international organizations and states against Iraq. See, in general, TJ Feighery, 'The United Nations Compensation Commission; in Giorgetti (n 1 above).

[6] Eritrea and Ethiopia agreed in August 2000 to resolve their boundary dispute and claims arising from the 1998–2000 war by binding international arbitration. The PCA served as registry to both arbitrations. See BD Daly, 'Permanent Court of Arbitration' in Giorgetti (n 1 above); see also the PCA Case Repository, at http://www.pcacases.com/web/ (accessed on 12 February 2016).

the Iran–US Claims Tribunal, created to address and resolve a specific dispute.[7]

When states decide to litigate their legal differences, different factors come into play that can move the balance in favour of arbitration or judicial institution. This chapter aims to highlight some of the factors that should be taken into consideration when choosing an international dispute settlement mechanism.

II. FLEXIBILITY V STABILITY: THE ABILITY TO CHOOSE THE ARBITRAL TRIBUNAL

One of the main differences between permanent judicial bodies and ad hoc institutions is the ability of the parties in ad hoc arbitrations to directly choose members of the adjudicative body charged to hear their dispute.

At the ICJ, the principal judicial organ of the United Nations and the paramount example of an international judicial body, judges are elected by the UN General Assembly and the Security Council for a renewable term of nine years. The 15 judges who make up the Court are recognized international law experts and represent different legal cultures, as well as geographical and (increasingly) gender diversity.[8]

The method of selection can be mitigated. Occasionally, parties also have the possibility of choosing their judge at the ICJ. This can happen when there is no judge of the same nationality of the parties. In that case, the state that does not have a 'national judge' can select an ad hoc judge to hear the case and join the other members of the Court. Similarly, parties can ask to have their case heard by a five-member chamber. In that—rare—occasion, parties can suggest certain members of the Court and their opinion carry considerable weight in the final decision.

Conversely, in arbitration, parties always choose at least some of the members of the tribunal. Generally, arbitration panels are constituted by three arbitrators, each party selecting one arbitrator and the third—and presiding—arbitrator being selected either by the two parties themselves or by an appointing authority. In more complex cases, such as many boundary disputes, the arbitral tribunal may be constituted of five members, and the mechanism for selection generally does not change. Each party selects two arbitrators, and the presiding arbitrator is chosen either by agreement between the two parties or by a designated appointing authority. This selection process affords

[7] The Iran–US Claims Tribunals was created in 1981 by agreement of the parties through the mediation of Algeria to hear individual and sovereign claims between Iran and the US. See, in general, JK Sharpe, 'Iran–United States Claims Tribunal' in Giorgetti (n 1 above).

[8] See ICJ Statute, available at http://www.icj-cij.org/documents/?p1=4&p2=2&p3=0 (accessed 12 February 2016). On the ICJ in general see also SD Murphy, 'The International Court of Justice' in Giorgetti (n 1 above).

parties the possibility of choosing arbitrators with specific qualities, including expertise, legal background and languages spoken.

The ability to choose arbitrators is consistently seen by parties as a fundamental feature in favour of arbitration. Parties consistently report that the ability to appoint an arbitrator in international arbitration is a key reason for them to choose that mechanism.

III. FLEXIBILITY ON RULES OF PROCEDURES

A particular advantage of arbitration over international judicial institutions is that parties can choose their own rules of procedures if they so wish, and tailor them to the specific needs of a specific case.

To a certain extent, this can also be done at the ICJ with a *compromis*—but some rules would still apply in ICJ proceedings (including, for example, Articles 62 and 63 ICJ Statute on third-party intervention, and Article 41 Statute on provisional measures[9]).

At the same time, drafting detailed procedural rules is time consuming and complex, and requires expert counsel. Parties and their counsel need to consider many issues, including schedule, possible bi- or tri-furcation of proceedings, sequence and timing of pleadings, organization of proceedings, rules of evidence (including those applying to witnesses), logistical aspects, language, translation of documents and challenges of arbitrators.

Most often, parties in ad hoc proceedings apply the UNCITRAL Rules.[10] The paragraphs below highlight some of the procedural issues in which the choice of the parties in respect of a specific forum matters most.

A. Length of Proceedings

The ICJ is often criticized because of the length of its proceedings. The practice of the court has been to fix fairly long time limits for the filing of written pleadings. For example, in the *Oil Platforms* case[11]—filed by Iran in 1992 against the United States—the hearings were held in 2002 and the judgment on the merits rendered in 2003 (11 years after the case was initially filed). One important consideration is that even at the ICJ the parties can, to a large extent, decide the timetable of the proceedings. There are, however, more procedural constraints, for example third party intervention.

Conversely, parties can really speed up proceedings if they so choose. This

[9] All available at http://www.icj-cij.org/documents/?p1=4&p2=2&p3=0.

[10] Available at http://pca-cpa.org/showpage.asp?pag_id=1064.

[11] *Oil Platforms (Islamic Republic of Iran v United States of America)*, a timeline of the case, as well as all the decisions, is available at http://www.icj-cij.org/docket/?p1=3&p2=3&case=90&code=op&p3=4.

happened in the Eritrea/Yemen maritime dispute and Eritrea/Ethiopia boundary proceedings, in which the parties opted for a particularly expedite schedule:

1. Eritrea/Yemen: 11 months for simultaneous exchange of memorials, two months for the replies, three months after that oral proceedings were held. The tribunal was asked to, as far as possible, deliver the award within three months from the end of the oral proceedings. The entire arbitration took only three years.[12]
2. The Eritrea/Ethiopia Boundary Commission was also organized on a tight schedule, which the parties respected—three months to file simultaneous memorials, three months for an exchange of counter-memorials and one month for replies. The award was issued by the tribunal equally expeditiously.[13]

In other cases the parties have also decided to request the tribunal to issue the award within a limited amount of time and have imposed specific time limits on the tribunal.

B. Terms of Reference of the Tribunal

In ad hoc proceedings, parties can agree on specific terms of reference for the arbitral tribunal, which establish the issues to be decided by the tribunal. At the ICJ, this can be done at the time when the parties submit their dispute to the ICJ through a mutually agreed *compromis*.

C. Number and Types of Parties

Ad hoc proceedings allow unique flexibility in terms of the number of parties that can be brought into proceedings. For example, at the UNCC, Iraq was a *sui generis* respondent in cases brought by individuals, international organizations and states, and cases involved mass claims as well as single and multi-party claims.

IV. CHOOSING BETWEEN CONFIDENTIALITY AND PUBLICITY

One important difference between international ad hoc proceedings and proceedings in judicial institutions is confidentiality of proceedings. At the ICJ and in other established proceedings, hearings are open to the public and all submissions—written and oral—as well as all of the Court's decisions, are

[12] In general, see PCA Past Cases (n 6 above).
[13] Ibid.

published and readily available from the ICJ website once the hearings are finished.

Conversely, in ad hoc proceedings, parties can choose to keep some (eg written pleadings or oral pleadings) or all of the proceedings confidential. Indeed, the existence of the entire dispute could be kept confidential. This could be of interest especially for politically sensitive issues or to limit possible drawbacks for payments of any future award.

Thus, in sensitive cases, arbitration may be preferable. Parties can decide if and what to open to the public—like the parties choose to do in the Abey Arbitration between Sudan and the Sudan's People Liberation Movement/Army.[14] In a recent arbitration between the US and Ecuador, the parties agreed to make the pleadings public, but not the award.[15]

V. FLEXIBILITY ON APPLICABLE LAW

Parties in ad hoc proceedings also have a certain flexibility to determine the applicable law to their dispute.

Article 38 of the ICJ Statute provides the generally recognized enumeration of sources of law for international disputes. It provides that:

> The Court, whose function is to decide in accordance with international law such disputes as are submitted to it, shall apply:
> a. international conventions, whether general or particular, establishing rules expressly recognized by the contesting states;
> b. international custom, as evidence of a general practice accepted as law;
> c. the general principles of law recognized by civilized nations;
> d. subject to the provisions of Article 59, judicial decisions and the teachings of the most highly qualified publicists of the various nations, as subsidiary means for the determination of rules of law.[16]

In special cases, parties can direct the tribunal to use a specific body of law. For example, in the Eritrea/Ethiopia boundary dispute, the parties asked the tribunal to delimit and demarcate the colonial treaty borders between them based on the pertinent colonial treaties (1900, 1902 and 1908) and applicable international law.[17]

The flexibility to determine the applicable law can be an important argument in favour of ad hoc arbitration in certain cases in which the parties have a predetermined and agreed body of law that they wish to apply. However, choosing the applicable law is no simple matter, and may not be preferable in many other contests.

[14] Ibid.

[15] Documents for both proceedings are available at the website of the PCA, ibid, which acted as registry in both cases.

[16] Art 38, ICJ Statute, available at: http://www.icj-cij.org/documents/?p1=4&p2=2&p3=0

[17] For the award and arbitration agreement see PCA Past Cases (n 6 above).

VI. FLEXIBILITY V. STABILITY: THE BINDING NATURE OF THE AWARD, ENFORCEABILITY AND POST-JUDGMENT REMEDIES

Judgments and awards are always final and binding for the parties. Critics, however, point out that international law lacks an enforcement mechanism similar to the police force found in domestic law. The truth is that, as Louis Henkin famously wrote in 1979, 'almost all nations observe almost all principles of international law and almost all of their obligations almost all of the time'.[18] Equally, parties to international disputes respect and apply the final decisions rendered by an international court or tribunal almost of all the time. All parties have a mutual advantage in respecting international judicial decisions. They are, of course, also legally obligated to do so by international law, whether as members of the United Nation or by the agreement they signed to go to arbitration. Failure to comply, therefore, can result in state responsibility for international law violation.

The UN Charter provides at Article 94 that parties must 'comply with the decision of the ICJ' and

> if any party to a case fails to perform the obligations incumbent upon it under the ICJ judgment, the other party may have recourse to the Security Council, which may, if it deems necessary, make recommendation or decide upon measures to be taken to give effect to the judgment.[19]

Thus, the Security Council can be called upon to play a role in enforcing an ICJ judgment. An important problem, however, is the exercise of a veto by one of the veto-holding members of the Security Council, which could block any enforcement effort. Famously, for example, the US used its veto power to block the enforcement of an ICJ judgment in a case that Nicaragua brought against the US.[20]

This is more problematic in arbitration, which lacks an immediate link to the Security Council. A reference to an enforcing role of the United Nations could, and should, be included in the terms of reference of the tribunal.

Where enforceability may be problematic from the start, established judicial bodies like the ICJ may thus present an advantage.

Established judicial bodies are also preferable when tribunals are needed after the judgment is issued, for example if a clarification, correction or interpretation is needed by the parties. In arbitration, the arbitral tribunal ceases to exist after the award is issued, making it difficult for it to reconvene to hear a post-award request. Differently, the statute of the ICJ includes specific provisions for such situations, thus providing added stability.

[18] L Henkin, *How Nations Behave* (Columbia University Press, 1979).

[19] Art 94, UN Charter, available at http://www.un.org.

[20] *Military and Paramilitary Activities in and against Nicaragua (Nic v USA)*—ICJ Judgment of 27 June 1986. For the exercise of the veto power, see UN Security Council, draft resolution, UN Doc S/18428, 28 October 1986, vetoed by the US; UN Security Council meeting 2718, verbatim record, in UN Doc S/PV.2718, 28 October 1986.

VII. CONCLUSION

International dispute resolution nowadays offers a real menu of options to prospective litigants. The choice of forum in international litigation is a fundamental decision, with important repercussions for the parties. Any such decision must therefore be carefully considered by the parties.

Different forums have different functions and may appeal to different litigants. In general, international dispute resolution is quite flexible and parties have substantial freedom.

Flexibility can play an important role when parties agree to settle their dispute by a binding international law mechanism, and parties can choose specific rules of procedures and applicable law, and—most importantly—have a say on who decides their dispute by selecting members of the tribunal directly. To go to arbitration, states must recognize the existence of a legal dispute and be willing to have it resolved through arbitration.

Standing tribunals like the ICJ have important and unique functions: they provide for compulsory jurisdiction and their public forum may validate decisions for domestic constituencies. Judgments of standing tribunals may also result in better enforceability.

Sometimes, of course, there is no choice, as there is no standing forum that has jurisdiction over the specific dispute. Also, sometimes (albeit rarely) there is only limited choice—a dispute resolution clause may only allow for one forum. In certain situations, arbitration may also be the only option. For example, Article 287 UNCLOS provides that if a party has not chosen by a written statement one of the three settlement methods listed or if the parties have not chosen the same method, the dispute will be resolved by arbitration.

Cost is also always an important consideration, as arbitration can be much more costly then the ICJ, where the cost of the court and the registry is not paid by the parties.

3

Domestic Courts as Compliance Enforcers

MIZUSHIMA TOMONORI*

I. INTRODUCTION

DOMESTIC COURTS SETTLE disputes by applying international law, where appropriate, but do not settle international disputes in the sense of inter-state disputes. Such inter-state disputes have been settled through other mechanisms, including the International Court of Justice (ICJ). One role of domestic courts in this context may be described as that of preventing a private person's claim against a state from developing into an inter-state dispute. The traditional principle of the exhaustion of local remedies is the basis for this role. If a domestic court grants remedies to the private person, there no longer exists any need for the state of his/her nationality to take up his/her claim and exercise diplomatic protection against the forum state. A dispute between the two states is thus prevented from arising. In this way, the domestic court has played the role of inter-state dispute preventer under traditional international law.

Today, with the dramatic increase in international investment agreements, this role of inter-state dispute preventer in the area of investment has mostly, if not entirely, been passed from domestic courts to investor-state arbitral tribunals. Most of the parties to investor-state arbitration—virtually all of the relevant parties in this context being host states—have complied with awards and, as a result, 'the role of diplomatic protection has somewhat faded'.[1] However, in the rare cases in which an award has not been complied with, domestic courts may reappear on the scene in the new role of compliance enforcers. When the investor seeks to enforce the award in the state of his/her nationality or in a third state, the state may be obligated to recognize and enforce it.

* Professor of International Law, Graduate School of Law, Nagoya University, Japan. Email: t.mizushima@law.nagoya-u.ac.jp.

[1] *Ahmadou Sadio Diallo (Republic of Guinea v Democratic Republic of Congo)* [2007] ICJ Reports 582, 614 (para 88).

In this chapter, I first examine the expected role of domestic courts as compliance enforcers in the context of investment arbitration (section II). I then take up and analyse a couple of recent problems concerning the principle of sovereign immunity from execution, which has apparently prevented domestic courts from effectively performing this role (section III).

II. ENFORCEMENT OF INVESTMENT ARBITRAL AWARDS BY DOMESTIC COURTS

For the purposes of this chapter, it is useful to deal separately with ICSID arbitral awards (subsection A) and other investment arbitral awards (subsection B). As will be seen, Article 54 of the ICSID Convention provides for the recognition and enforcement of ICSID awards by the courts of a contracting state, and this enforcement provision is considered to be 'a distinctive feature of the ICSID Convention'.[2]

A. ICSID Arbitral Awards

Article 53, paragraph 1 of the ICSID Convention provides:

> The award shall be binding on the parties and shall not be subject to any appeal or to any other remedy except those provided for in this Convention. Each party shall abide by and comply with the terms of the award except to the extent that enforcement shall have been stayed pursuant to the relevant provisions of this Convention.[3]

If any of the parties—usually the host state—does not comply with the award despite its binding force, the other party—usually the investor—may seek the enforcement of the award in a contracting state of the ICSID Convention. Article 54, which then comes into play, provides:

> (1) Each contracting state shall recognize an award rendered pursuant to this Convention as binding and enforce the pecuniary obligations imposed by that award within its territories as if it were a final judgment of a court in that state . . .
>
> (2) . . .
>
> (3) Execution of the award shall be governed by the laws concerning the execution of judgments in force in the state in whose territories such execution is sought.

This provision applies not only to the host state, but to all contracting states

[2] CH Schreuer et al, *The ICSID Convention: A Commentary*, 2nd edn (Cambridge University Press, 2009) 1117.

[3] The relevant provisions are those concerning interpretation, revision and annulment of the award (Arts 50–52).

of the ICSID Convention.[4] Given the number of contracting states, ie 152, the enforcement system under the ICSID Convention might be assumed to be effective. However, Article 55 should also be taken into account because it provides: 'Nothing in Article 54 shall be construed as derogating from the law in force in any contracting state relating to immunity . . . of any foreign state from execution.'

As is well known, under international law, the property—or certain property, at least—of a foreign state enjoys sovereign immunity from execution in the forum state.[5] The domestic law of some states contains provisions which reflect this principle. Thus, the ICSID Convention on the one hand obligates contracting states to recognize and enforce ICSID awards, but on the other hand it leaves the rules regarding sovereign immunity from execution, which may prevent the enforcement of awards, intact. In other words, the drafters of the ICSID Convention did not abolish sovereign immunity from execution even for the limited purposes of the enforcement of ICSID awards.[6]

In some cases,[7] host states have not voluntarily complied with ICSID awards and investors have sought the enforcement of the awards in third states that are contracting states of the ICSID Convention. Although some courts have recognized ICSID awards and issued *exequaturs*, no enforcement measures have actually been taken.[8] The application of sovereign immunity from execution has resulted in such a situation. Most investors would consider the recognition of an award in their favour which does not lead to actual enforcement to be a Pyrrhic victory. The role of domestic courts as compliance enforcers under the ICSID Convention is therefore not as effective as it might first appear.

B. Other Investment Arbitral Awards

The compliance mechanism of the ICSID Convention does not apply to other investment arbitral awards. For instance, under the UNCITRAL Arbitration

[4] See also Schreuer et al (n 2 above), 1123–24.

[5] See generally H Fox and P Webb, *The Law of State Immunity*, 3rd edn (Oxford University Press, 2013) 479–508.

[6] See also A Broches, 'The Convention on the Settlement of Investment Disputes between States and Nationals of Other States' (1972) 136 *Recueil des Cours* 331, 403.

[7] *Benvenuti and Bonfant Srl v Government of the People's Republic of Congo* (ICSID Case No ARB/77/2), Award, 8 August 1980, translated in 1 ICSID Reports 330; *Société Ouest Africaine des Bétons Industriels [SOABI] v State of Senegal* (ICSID Case No ARB/82/1), Award, 25 February 1988, (1991) 6 ICSID Review 125, translated in 2 ICSID Reports 190; *Liberian Eastern Timber Corp [LETCO] v Government of the Republic of Liberia* (ICSID Case No ARB/83/2), Award, 31 March 1986, 2 ICSID Reports 343; *AIG Capital Partners Inc v Republic of Kazakhstan* (ICSID Case No ARB/01/6), Award, 7 October 2003, 11 ICSID Reports 3.

[8] *Benvenuti* (1988) 115 Journal du droit international 108; *SOABI* (1991) 118 Journal du droit international 1005; *LETCO*, 2 ICSID Reports 383; *AIG Capital Partners* [2005] EWHC 2239 (Comm), 129 Intl L Rep 589.

Rules (as revised in 2010),[9] '[a]ll awards . . . shall be final and binding on the parties. The parties shall carry out all awards without delay.' However, these rules, which are not provided for in a treaty, cannot obligate a third state to recognize and enforce an UNCITRAL arbitral award. An international investment agreement may impose such an obligation upon contracting states,[10] but by no means upon a non-contracting state.[11]

Thus, some legal framework is required for the purpose of enforcing investment arbitral awards other than ICSID awards. The New York Convention on the Recognition and Enforcement of Foreign Arbitral Awards is an instrument that serves such a purpose. Article 3 of this convention provides: 'Each contracting state shall recognize arbitral awards as binding and enforce them in accordance with the rules of procedure of the territory where the award is relied upon'. As a commentator explains, 'New York Convention awards are enforceable in [156] countries and are often more readily enforceable than municipal court judgments from other states'.[12] Although the New York Convention mainly deals with awards to which private persons are parties, it has also been applied to awards to which a state is a party, such as investment arbitral awards.[13]

One feature of the enforcement mechanism under the New York Convention is that it enumerates several grounds for refusing the enforcement of awards in Article 5, as distinct from the ICSID Convention. It is true that cases of ultra vires of an arbitral tribunal, for instance, are treated similarly under the ICSID Convention.[14] However, a public policy exception, such as that contained in the New York Convention, according to which a contracting state may refuse the enforcement of an arbitral award if 'enforcement of the award would be contrary to the public policy of that country [where enforcement is sought]' (Article 5, paragraph 2(b)), is not provided for in the ICSID Con-

[9] Available at www.uncitral.org/pdf/english/texts/arbitration/arb-rules-revised/arb-rules-revised-2010-e.pdf.

[10] See, eg the 2003 Agreement between Japan and the Socialist Republic of Viet Nam for the Liberalization, Promotion and Protection of Investment, Art 14, para 5, which provides: 'The decision of arbitration shall be final and binding upon both parties to the investment dispute. This decision shall be executed by the applicable laws and regulations concerning the execution of decision in force in the country in whose [territory] such execution is sought.'

[11] Vienna Convention on the Law of Treaties, Arts 34 and 35.

[12] AK Bjorklund, 'State Immunity and the Enforcement of Investor-state Arbitral Awards' in C Binder et al (eds), *International Investment Law for the 21st Century: Essays in Honour of Christoph Schreuer* (Oxford University Press, 2009) 304.

[13] See, eg AJ van den Berg, 'Some Recent Problems in the Practice of Enforcement under the New York and ICSID Conventions' (1987) 2 *ICSID Review* 439, 447–48; Bjorklund (ibid) 308.

[14] The New York Convention, Art 5, para 1(c), provides: 'Recognition and enforcement of the award may be refused, at the request of the party against whom it is invoked', if '[t]he awards deals with a difference not contemplated by or not falling within the terms of the submission to arbitration, or it contains decisions on matters beyond the scope of the submission to arbitration'. Likewise, under the ICSID Convention, an ad hoc committee may stay enforcement of the award pending its decision if either party requests annulment of the award on the grounds that 'the Tribunal has manifestly exceeded its powers' (Art 52, paras 1(b) and 5).

vention.[15] Thus, it is pointed out that '[t]he applicability of the New York Convention does not give the same degree of enforceability as Art[icle] 54 of the ICSID Convention'.[16]

On the other hand, the New York Convention does not contain a provision which expressly refers to sovereign immunity, perhaps because the convention was not necessarily intended to deal with investment arbitral awards to which a state is a party. The absence of a provision on sovereign immunity does not, however, mean that immunity constitutes no obstacle to the enforcement of an arbitral award under the New York Convention. Sovereign immunity from execution could be applied either through the above-mentioned public policy exception or through Article 3, which obligates a contracting state to enforce an arbitral award 'in accordance with the rules of procedure of the territory where the award is relied upon'.[17] As pointed out above, what has barred the enforcement of ICSID awards is, in most cases, sovereign immunity from execution. Essentially, then, there is no significant difference between ICSID awards and other awards insofar as their enforcement is concerned. For instance, in the *Sedelmayer* case, the German Federal Supreme Court did not enforce an investment arbitral award, which was not an ICSID award,[18] on the grounds of sovereign immunity from execution.[19]

III. SOVEREIGN IMMUNITY FROM EXECUTION AS APPLIED BY DOMESTIC COURTS

As pointed out above, sovereign immunity from execution may prevent, and has prevented, the enforcement of investment arbitral awards. In other words, sovereign immunity from execution prevents domestic courts from effectively performing their role as compliance enforcers. In this context, it may be appropriate to note what Broches has to say on the matter:

> The express provision of Article 55 [of the ICSID Convention] has been regretted by some. These critics overlook the fact that Article 55 does no more than acknowledge state practice as regards immunity from execution. Accordingly, the scope of Article 54 will evolve along with state practice.[20]

The same comment also applies to other investment arbitral awards. Thus, if the rules of sovereign immunity from execution were to evolve and the scope of immunity were restricted, the possibility of the enforcement of investment

[15] See Broches (n 6 above) 402–03.

[16] Schreuer et al (n 2 above) 1121.

[17] See Bjorklund (n 12 above) 308–09.

[18] *Sedelmayer v Russian Federation*, Stockholm Chamber of Commerce, Award, 7 July 1998, available at www.italaw.com/sites/default/files/case-documents/ita0757.pdf.

[19] BGH, VII ZB 8/05, NJW-Rechtsprechungs-Report Zivilrecht 2006, 425; BGH, VII ZB 9/05, NJW-Rechtsprechungs-Report Zivilrecht 2006, 198. See also P Wrange, '*Sedelmayer v Russian Federation*' (2012) 106 *American Journal of International Law* 347 (note).

[20] Broches (n 6 above) 404.

arbitral awards would increase accordingly. Indeed, it is generally accepted that the international law of sovereign immunity has changed from absolute to restrictive immunity, not only in terms of immunity from adjudication (immunity from jurisdiction *sensu stricto*), but also in terms of immunity from execution.

Problems of sovereign immunity from execution have been discussed mainly in the context of the enforcement of judgments of the forum state against a foreign state. However, in principle, the same rules would apply to the enforcement of judgments of another state and that of arbitral awards.[21] The United Nations Convention on Jurisdictional Immunities of States and Their Property, which was adopted in 2004, could be a starting point for discussion about sovereign immunity from execution, although this convention has not yet entered into force. In particular, Articles 19 and 21 are relevant to this matter.

Article 19: State immunity from post-judgment measures of constraint

No post-judgment measures of constraint, such as attachment, arrest or execution, against property of a State may be taken in connection with a proceeding before a court of another State unless and except to the extent that:

(a) the State has expressly consented to the taking of such measures as indicated:
  (i) by international agreement;
  (ii) by an arbitration agreement or in a written contract; or
  (iii) by a declaration before the court or by a written communication after a dispute between the parties has arisen; or
(b) the State has allocated or earmarked property for the satisfaction of the claim which is the object of that proceeding; or
(c) it has been established that the property is specifically in use or intended for use by the State for other than government non-commercial purposes and is in the territory of the State of the forum, provided that post-judgment measures of constraint may only be taken against property that has a connection with the entity against which the proceeding was directed.

Article 21: Specific categories of property

(1) The following categories, in particular, of property of a State shall not be considered as property specifically in use or intended for use by the State for other than government non-commercial purposes under article 19, subparagraph (c):

(a) property, including any bank account, which is used or intended for use in the performance of the functions of the diplomatic mission of the State . . . ;
(b) property of a military character or used or intended for use in the performance of military functions;
(c) property of the central bank or other monetary authority of the State;

[21] See also R O'Keefe and CJ Tams (eds), *The United Nations Convention on Jurisdictional Immunities of States and Their Property: A Commentary* (Oxford University Press, 2013) 317–18 (C Brown and R O'Keefe).

(d) property forming part of the cultural heritage of the State or part of its archives and not placed or intended to be placed on sale;
(e) property forming part of an exhibition of objects of scientific, cultural or historic interest and not placed or intended to be placed on sale.
(2) Paragraph 1 is without prejudice to . . . article 19, subparagraphs (a) and (b).

The UN Convention was drafted on the basis of the Draft Articles on Jurisdictional Immunities of States and Their Property, which were adopted by the International Law Commission (ILC) in 1991.[22] It should be noted that ILC Draft Article 18, paragraph 1(c), which corresponds to Article 19, subparagraph (c) of the UN Convention, provides:

(1) No measures of constraint . . . against property of a State may be taken in connection with a proceeding before a court of another State unless and except to the extent that: . . .
(c) the property is specifically in use or intended for use by the State for other than government non-commercial purposes and is in the territory of the State of the forum *and has a connection with the claim which is the object of the proceeding* . . . .[23]

This italicized requirement would have significantly diminished the prospects of investment arbitral awards being enforced, because it is very unlikely that the host state would have property that has a connection with the investment in its territory but that is located in a third state where enforcement is sought.[24] Therefore, Article 19 of the UN Convention, in which this requirement has been deleted, can be considered to be more favourable to investors who seek the enforcement of an arbitral award than ILC Draft Article 18.[25]

On the other hand, recent practice suggests that there has been an expansion rather than a restriction of the scope of sovereign immunity from execution in two respects. The first concerns an expansive interpretation of what constitutes sovereign property that is immune from execution (subsection A) and the second concerns a restrictive interpretation of a waiver of sovereign immunity (subsection B). Needless to say, in the context of the enforcement of investment arbitral awards, such practice works to the disadvantage of investors.

A. Expansive Interpretation of Sovereign Property

In a state which adopts the absolute theory of sovereign immunity from execution, there is no possibility that investment arbitral awards would be enforced there unless the host state were to waive its immunity. In other words, the courts of such a state are not expected to perform the role as compliance enforcers. In a series of judgments in 2011 concerning the enforcement of a

[22] [1991] 2-ii *Yearbook of the International Law Commission* 13.
[23] Emphasis added.
[24] See also Schreuer et al (n 2 above) 1160, 1166.
[25] See also ibid 1166.

foreign arbitral award, the Court of Final Appeal of the Hong Kong Special Administrative Region of the People's Republic of China adopted the absolute theory of sovereign immunity.[26] Given that China had signed the UN Convention in 2005, some may consider the adoption of the absolute theory by China to defeat the object and purpose of the UN Convention, which is based on the restrictive theory.[27] In any event, it is unlikely that courts of other states would follow such a practice of absolute immunity today. Moreover, investors would not expect that arbitral awards would be enforced in a state that adopts the absolute theory of sovereign immunity from execution. Thus, in such a situation, the problem does not arise that such a practice is contrary to the investor's expectations.

Rather, this problem arises when a state ostensibly follows the restrictive theory of sovereign immunity from execution. Investors would expect that arbitral awards in their favour would be enforced in such a state against the commercial (non-sovereign) property, if any, of the host state. In such a situation, if a court of the forum state considers the property at issue as sovereign (non-commercial) property and does not take enforcement measures on the grounds of sovereign immunity, that would be contrary to the investor's expectations.

It may be appropriate to make reference to the 2012 judgment of the ICJ in *Jurisdictional Immunities of States (Germany v Italy)*,[28] in which the ICJ stated:

> It is clear in the present case that the property which was the subject of the measure of constraint at issue is being used for governmental purposes that are entirely non-commercial, and hence for purposes falling within Germany's sovereign functions. Villa Vigoni is in fact the seat of a cultural centre intended to promote cultural exchanges between Germany and Italy. This cultural centre is organized and administered on the basis of an agreement between the two Governments concluded in the form of an exchange of notes dated 21 April 1986. Before the Court, Italy described the activities in question as a 'centre of excellence for the Italian-German co-operation in the fields of research, culture and education', and recognized that Italy was directly involved in 'its peculiar bi-national . . . managing structure'.[29]

In my view, it is far from clear that property which is used as the seat of a cultural centre is sovereign property and thus immune from execution, especially when compared with those categories of property that are listed in Article 21

[26] *Democratic Republic of Congo v FG Hemisphere Associates LLC (No 1)*, 147 Intl L Rep 376 (Hong Kong Special Administrative Region of the People's Republic of China, Court of Final Appeal, 2011); *Democratic Republic of Congo v FG Hemisphere Associates LLC (No 2)*, 150 Intl L Rep 684 (Court of Final Appeal, 8 September 2011). See also S Wei, 'FG Hemisphere Associates v Democratic Republic of the Congo' (2014) 108 *American Journal of International Law* 776 (note).

[27] See Vienna Convention on the Law of Treaties, Art 18, which provides: 'A state is obliged to refrain from acts which would defeat the object and purpose of a treaty when . . . it has signed the treaty . . . subject to ratification, acceptance or approval'.

[28] *Jurisdictional Immunities of the State (Germany v Italy: Greece Intervening)* [2012] *ICJ Reports* 99.

[29] Ibid, 148, para 119.

of the UN Convention. I would take this part of the ICJ's judgment as an example of an expansive interpretation of what constitutes sovereign property. Even if domestic courts may not follow the practice of absolute immunity that China has adopted, they are likely to follow the ICJ in its expansive interpretation of sovereign property. If such an interpretation is adopted in the context of the enforcement of investment arbitral awards, clearly it is contrary to the investor's expectations.

B. Restrictive Interpretation of a Waiver of Sovereign Immunity

If such an expansive interpretation of sovereign property were adopted, it would become more important for investors that they obtain a waiver of sovereign immunity from execution.[30] However, it is pointed out that

> In many situations the investor will never have the chance to negotiate a waiver of immunity. This is particularly so if consent to jurisdiction is not based on a direct agreement between the parties but on host state legislation or on a bilateral or multilateral treaty.[31]

Moreover, even if an investor successfully obtains a waiver of sovereign immunity from execution, that is not the end of the matter. There are some recent cases in which domestic courts interpret such waivers restrictively and consider that immunity has not been waived. Such an interpretation is also contrary to the investor's expectations.

In a series of judgments in *NML Capital v Argentina*, the French Court of Cassation recently held that, with regard to sovereign property, the waiver of sovereign immunity from execution must not only be explicit but must also specify the sovereign property against which enforcement measures may be taken.[32] Likewise, in *The 'ARA Libertad'* case before the International Tribunal for the Law of the Sea (ITLOS),[33] which originates from the *NML Capital* case, Argentina argued that 'this waiver [of immunity from execution] should be explicit and specific to the related military asset at stake',[34] although the

[30] See also van den Berg (n 13 above) 451, 456.

[31] Schreuer et al (n 2 above) 1173.

[32] *Sté NML Capital Ltd c République argentine* (2012) 139 Journal du droit international 668 (bank accounts used for the diplomatic mission of Argentina); *Sté NML Capital c République argentine* (2013) 140 Journal du droit international 899 (labour and corporate taxes and oil royalties debts).

[33] *The 'ARA Libertad' Case (Argentina v Ghana)*, ITLOS, Order (Request for the Prescription of Provisional Measures), 15 December 2012, available at www.itlos.org. See also J Kraska, '*The "ARA Libertad" (Argentina v Ghana)*' (2013) 107 *American Journal of International Law* 404 (note).

[34] *The "ARA Libertad" Case (Argentina v Ghana)*, Argentina, Request for Provisional Measures under Art 290, Para 5, of the United Nations Convention on the Law of the Sea, 14 November 2012, para 41, available at www.itlos.org.

ITLOS did not deal with the problem of the waiver.[35] The Federal Constitutional Court of Germany took a similar position and considered that a general waiver of sovereign immunity from execution does not suffice.[36]

Such a requirement of a specific waiver is problematic because, when drafting a waiver clause, it is almost impossible for private persons, including investors, to anticipate which property will be available for enforcement.[37] Moreover, it is arguable that the UN Convention does not contain this requirement of specificity.[38] Given that such a specific waiver, if any, would fall within the scope of Article 19, subparagraph (b) of the UN Convention, the requirement of specificity, or the idea that a general waiver does not suffice, would deprive Article 19, subparagraph (a) of its meaning. A commentary of the ILC also suggests that a general waiver would suffice in order to allow enforcement measures against sovereign property, except for those categories of property that are listed in Article 21, paragraph 1.[39] Thus, except for these limited categories of property, the requirement of a specific waiver is unacceptable not only from the viewpoint of private persons but also as a matter of interpretation of the UN Convention.[40]

IV. CONCLUDING REMARKS

Under contemporary international law, the traditional role of domestic courts as inter-state dispute preventers has diminished and, in the area of inter-

[35] After the ITLOS gave its order of 15 December 2012, the Supreme Court of Ghana held in the judgment of 20 June 2013 that '[a] waiver of immunity has no effect in relation to military assets in Ghana' and that '[t]here should . . . be no further seizures of military assets of sovereign states by Ghanaian courts in execution of foreign judgments, even if the sovereign concerned has waived its immunity'. Subsequent to this judgment, which Argentina considered constitutes sufficient satisfaction, Argentina and Ghana reached an agreement on 27 September 2013 and requested the Arbitral Tribunal to issue an order for the termination of the arbitral proceedings. On 11 November 2013, the Arbitral Tribunal issued a Termination Order. *The ARA Libertad Arbitration (Argentina v Ghana)*, available at www.pca-cpa.org/showpage.asp?pag_id=1526 (accessed on 1 December 2013). It should be noted that the Supreme Court of Ghana considered a waiver of immunity to have no effect in relation to military assets in Ghana for public policy reasons. It was not because the waiver did not specify the property at issue. See also S Blanchard, '*Republic v High Court Accra, ex p Attorney General*' (2014) 108 *American Journal of International Law* 73 (note).

[36] BVerfG, 2 BvM 9/03, BVerfGE 117, 141.

[37] See also Schreuer et al (n 2 above) 1179.

[38] See also A Blumrosen and F Malet-Deraedt, '*NML Capital Ltd v Republic of Argentina*' (2013) 107 *American Journal of International Law* 638 (note) 643–44; G Cuniberti, '*Sté NML Capital c République argentine*' (2013) 140 *Journal du droit international* 899 (note) 921–23.

[39] 'Notwithstanding the provision of paragraph 1, the state may waive immunity in respect of any property belonging to one of the specific categories listed . . . by specifically consenting to the taking of measures of constraint in respect of that category of its property . . . A general waiver or a waiver in respect of all property in the territory of the state of the forum, without mention of any of the specific categories, would not be sufficient to allow measures of constraint against property in the categories listed in paragraph 1.' [1991] 2-ii *Yearbook of the International Law Commission* 59 (para 8) (commentary on Art 19, para 2). The ILC draft Art 19 corresponds to Art 21 of the UN Convention.

[40] See also O'Keefe and Tams (eds) (n 21 above) 346 (C Brown and R O'Keefe).

national investment law, their role may be considered as that of compliance enforcers under the ICSID Convention and the New York Convention. However, as pointed out above, the effective performance of this role as compliance enforcers has been prevented by the application of sovereign immunity from execution. The oft-quoted comment that '[i]mmunity from execution may be viewed . . . as the last bastion of state immunity'[41] still applies in this context.

Recent practice concerning sovereign immunity from execution indicates that there is an expansive interpretation of sovereign property and a restrictive interpretation of a waiver of sovereign immunity. This is not a desirable development in international law because it is contrary to the expectations of private persons, including investors. From a broader perspective of governance in international law, we may consider such a situation concerning the role of domestic courts in the context of dispute settlement and compliance mechanisms to be a kind of governance deficit.

This governance deficit in dispute settlement and compliance mechanisms might originate from the asymmetrical character of the international law of sovereign immunity.[42] On the one hand, the granting of any broader immunity by domestic courts cannot constitute a violation of international law, including the ICSID Convention[43] and the New York Convention. On the other hand, a denial of immunity can be internationally wrongful conduct, which may give rise to an inter-state dispute. This asymmetry in the law could incline domestic courts to err on the side of granting immunity in borderline cases. It is necessary to change this situation by putting stress on the interests of private persons.

[41] [1991] 2-ii *Yearbook of the International Law Commission* 56 (para 2) (commentary on Art 18).

[42] See Mizushima T, *Shuken Menjo no Kokusaihō [Public International Law Aspects of Foreign State Immunity]* (Nagoya, The University of Nagoya Press, 2012) 26, 48.

[43] See also Schreuer et al (n 2 above), 1154.

4

Towards Reinforcing or Contesting the Vision of the Rule of Law?

MYRIAM SENN*

I. INTRODUCTION

CONSIDERING NORMATIVE GOVERNANCE, this chapter points to the issue of either reinforcing or contesting the vision of the rule of law. Why this issue? Indeed, the Declaration of the UN General Assembly on the Rule of Law on 24 September 2012 (the Declaration)[1] solemnly reaffirming the commitment of heads of state and government to the rule of law and its continuous efforts to enforce it[2] can be interpreted as reflecting the current uneasiness accompanying the implementation of the concept of the rule of law.[3] It is a concept of fundamental importance for political dialogue and cooperation between states. A range of issues arise with regard

* University of St Gallen, Switzerland. Email: myriam.senn@unisg.ch. This contribution extends aspects of an article of mine published under the title: 'Transnationales Recht und öffentliches Recht zwischen Konvergenz und Divergenz' in G-P Calliess (ed), *Transnationales Recht, Stand und Perspektiven* (Mohr Siebeck, 2014) 353–68. It was first prepared for and presented at the Regional Conference of the International Law Association, Imperium juris: Governance, Trade, Resources, Athens, August 2013.

[1] Declaration of the High-level Meeting of the General Assembly on the Rule of Law at the National and International Levels, 24 September 2012, United Nations, Resolution adopted by the General Assembly, A/RES/67/1.

[2] United Nations Rule of Law, available at http://www.unrol.org/ (accessed on 6 October 2014).

[3] The UN General Assembly has considered the rule of law as an agenda item since 1992, with renewed interest since 2006. It has adopted resolutions at its last three sessions: A/RES/61/39, A/RES/62/70 and A/RES/63/128. The Security Council too has held a number of thematic debates on the rule of law. See S/PRST/2003/15, S/PRST/2004/2, S/PRST/2004/32, S/PRST/2005/30, S/PRST/2006/28. It has also adopted resolutions emphasizing the importance of the issue in the context of women, peace and security (SC res1325, SC res 1820), children in armed conflict (eg SC res 1612) and the protection of civilians in armed conflict (eg SC res 1674). On its side, the Peacebuilding Commission has regularly put rule of law issues with respect to countries on its agenda. See United Nations Peacebuilding Commission, available at http://www.un.org/en/peacebuilding/ (accessed on 6 October 2014).

to the Declaration. The main points focused on here are the issue of its worldwide understanding, in particular the historical aspects—that is, the emergence and development of the concept—and the role played by transnational regulatory regimes, notably their possible linkage to state and international law.[4] This chapter will cover the following aspects: first, the characteristics of the rule of law; secondly, the issues; and thirdly, the prospects regarding governance towards a reinforced or a contested rule of law.

II. CHARACTERISTICS OF THE RULE OF LAW

In characterizing the rule of law, it should be noted that the title of this chapter uses the word 'vision' with regard to the rule of law.[5] Here, 'vision' is used to indicate that there is no generally accepted definition of what the rule of law is. Similarly to legal science, the concept of the rule of law is a construction. It represents an idealistic model,[6] which should be appropriate and adaptable to real situations. However, in practice, as a model, it is a constituent part of a system.[7] As such, it is not complete, but evolves in accordance with the system—in other words, with its environment. Hence, its meaning and interpretation are subject to changes and adaptations.

Basically, the rule of law implies that everyone—individuals, the state, legal actors, public institutions and entities—is accountable to just, fair and equitable laws. Hence, at the state level, the common requirements for an understanding of the rule of law include the regulation of government power, equality before the law and the availability of an independent judicial process.[8] An objective of the rule of law is that it should be applied by all states

[4] Within this chapter, the focus is placed on the concept of transnational regimes pursuing business activities and their attitude towards the rule of law. Hence, it points to an aspect the UN did not specifically address in the Declaration. Indeed, the implementation of the rule of law by these regimes plays an important role both with regard to the role of the institutions involved as well as in relation to the issue of linkage with state and international law regulatory regimes.

[5] This term is also used by other authors, such as M Koskenniemi, *Politics of International Law* (Hart Publishing, 2011) 37.

[6] A von Bogdandy, *Gubernative Rechtssetzung, Eine Neubestimmung der Rechtsetzung und des Regierungssystems unter dem Grundgesetz in der Perspektive gemeineuropäischer Dogmatik* (Mohr Siebeck, 2000) 19–22; M Senn, 'Transnationales Recht und öffentliches Recht zwischen Konvergenz und Divergenz' in G-P Calliess (ed), *Transnationales Recht, Stand und Perspektiven* (Mohr Siebeck, 2014) 355–56.

[7] Bogdandy (ibid), 19–22; Senn (ibid), 355–56; N Luhmann *Soziale Systeme, Grundriss einer allgemeinen Theorie* (Suhrkamp 1987) 15–28, 32–34; H Willke, *Systemtheorie I: Grundlagen, Eine Einführung in die Grundprobleme der Theorie sozialer Systeme*, 6th edn (Lucius & Lucius, 2000) 7–8, 51–53.

[8] On the rule of law see S Chesterman, 'An International Rule of Law?' (2008) 56 *American Journal of Comparative Law* 331; AV Dicey, *An Introduction to the Study of the Law of the Constitution*, 10th edn (Palgrave Macmillan, 1985); T Bingham, *The Rule of Law* (Penguin, 2011); see also G Teubner, *Verfassungsfragmente, Gesellschaftlicher Konstitutionalismus in der Globalisierung* (Suhrkamp, 2012); BS Chimni, 'Legitimating the International Rule of Law' in J Crawford and M Koskenniemi (eds), *The Cambridge Companion to International Law* (Cambridge University Press, 2012) 290–93.

equally, and by international organizations too. Establishing respect for the rule of law is considered by the UN to be fundamental to achieving a durable peace in the aftermath of conflict, to the effective protection of human rights, and to sustained economic progress and development.[9]

Both the delineation and the objective of realizing the rule of law are originally linked to the concept of the state and state law. The rule of law requires the consistent application of the basic principles of law in a state. At the international level, as embedded in the Charter of the United Nations, it is primarily understood as encompassing elements relevant to the conducting of state-to-state relations.[10] Currently, though, the concept of the rule of law at both the national and international levels appears to be undermined by current societal developments, which is confirmed by the need of the UN General Assembly to reaffirm the commitment of the UN Member States to an international order based solely on the rule of law.[11] The Declaration was supported not only by the Member States, but also by non-governmental organizations and civil society, as represented at the highest level. It underlines the importance of international cooperation. According to the Declaration, donors, regional, subregional and other intergovernmental organizations, as well as relevant civil society actors, including non-governmental organizations, are invited to provide technical assistance and capacity building on rule-of-law-related issues, as well as to share practices and lessons learned from the rule of law at the international and national levels.[12] Moreover, the necessity to 'strengthen engagement on the rule of law at the national and international level' was also specifically addressed in the Secretary-General's Annual Report on Strengthening and Coordinating United Nations Rule of Law Activities.[13]

III. THE ISSUES

With a view to the above situation, this chapter argues that two issues are not sufficiently considered within the debate on the rule of law and the challenges its realization poses. These are (i) the emergence and development of the concept itself in the context of international law; and (ii) the role played by the dominating political system in a state in relation to transnational regulatory regimes.

[9] United Nations and the Rule of Law, available at http://www.un.org/en/ruleoflaw/ (accessed on 6 October 2014).

[10] Charter of the United Nations, Preamble, Chapter I: Purposes and Principles; Koskenniemi (n 5 above), 37.

[11] Declaration (n 1 above).

[12] Point 38 of the Declaration (ibid).

[13] Annual Report on Strengthening and Coordinating United Nations Rule of Law Activities, UN Doc A/64/298, 17 August 2009; see also A Peters, 'Are We Moving towards Constitutionalization of the World Community?' in A Cassese (ed), *Realizing Utopia, The Future of International Law* (Oxford University Press, 2012) 124; critically: U Mattei and M de Morpurgo 'The Dark Side of the Rule of Law: Reassessing Global Law and Its Legitimacy' [1/2010] *Juridikum* 15–23.

A. Rule of Law as a Concept of the West

An important issue is that the rule of law is based on the concept of the state, and there is an uncritical assumption that the legal principles and mechanisms applied by states can be transposed directly to the international level or the global sphere.[14] In reality, however, the architecture, content and role of national or domestic laws are not comparable to those of international law. The classical state approach to regulation—a command and control[15] mode of regulation—is not transferable per se to the international level.[16]

This is the case even though international law has expanded, deepened and diversified greatly over the course of the last 20 years[17] and thus exercises even more influence on states. It has also superseded state laws in many cases. Nowadays, international law is a quasi-omnipresent field of law. However, as argued by some academicians, one should not overlook the fact that the architecture and substantive content of international law were first shaped by Western culture. Although international law pursues the overall goal of realizing human rights worldwide, it remains primarily a model representing the values and interests of Western countries. At its origins, it was imposed on other—often former colonial—countries.[18]

Accordingly, the current international law model is primarily understood as an instrument of power of the West. It is still not understood or implemented as a world order providing justice and realizing the same goals everywhere.[19] Up to now, this model has been applied to other countries and regions without sufficiently taking their own traditions, values and interests into account. In reality, the power relationships between countries and regions are evolving, and the concept of international law is losing some of its preponderance and significance as far as the influence of Western countries is concerned.[20] This, in turn, influences the understanding of and commitment to the rule of law. This ongoing power and ideological struggle weakens the recognition of the role and acceptance of the rule of law in practice. In addition, it should not be ignored that, due to their international law character, the international law rules laid down lack monitoring and compliance mechanisms similar to

[14] Koskenniemi (n 5 above), 36.

[15] R Baldwin, M Cave and M Lodge, *Understanding Regulation, Theory, Strategy, and Practice*, 2nd edn (Springer, 2012) 106–11.

[16] It should be noted that the UN now differentiates between the promotion of the rule of law at the international level and an approach to the rule of law at the national level. See 'Strengthening and Coordinating United Nations Rule of Law Activities', Report of the Secretary-General, 29 July 2013, United Nations General Assembly, A/68/213, 3–9.

[17] Peters (n 13 above).

[18] M Koskenniemi, 'International Law in the World of Ideas' in Crawford and Koskenniemi (n 8 above), 47–61; G Simpson, 'International Law in Diplomatic History' in Crawford and Koskenniemi (n 8 above), 25–45; Koskenniemi (n 5 above), 35–38; Chesterman (n 8 above), 333–40.

[19] Koskenniemi in Crawford and Koskenniemi (ibid), 47–61; B Fassbender, 'Das Völkerrecht als Ordnung des Westens', *Neue Zürcher Zeitung*, 15 July 2013, no 161, 13.

[20] In that sense see Koskenniemi in Crawford and Koskenniemi (n 18 above), 47–61; Fassbender (ibid).

those of states,[21] and this renders the implementation of the rule of law even more challenging.

Furthermore, accompanying the process of globalization, regulation is no longer the prerogative of the state. Besides international law as understood as law defined by states or a legitimate authority, a number of alternative regulatory regimes have emerged. Non-state and private actors, networks and epistemic communities are the new standard-setters.[22] They now play an influential role and have the capabilities[23] to define regulation. Their regulatory activities have led to the emergence of a third level of regulation besides the traditional divide between national and international regulation. Indeed, it breaks this divide. This regulation is functionally orientated and, contrary to state law or public international law, is not based on political rationales. It applies to determined policy issues at the national, international or global level. As a body of rules, it is commonly subsumed under the term 'transnational regulation'.[24] Currently, transnational regulatory regimes abound in all sectors. They also can present diverse grades of crystallization.

At this point, it should be noted that the UN does not consider transnational regulation as a proper third level of regulation. In its work on the rule of law, the UN recognizes a transnational dimension—that is, one which permeates national borders and affects entire regions and ultimately the international community as a whole—but it subsumes and includes it under the concept of international law. The UN concentrates on the subject of transnational threats. According to the UN, the threats are transnational organized crime and terrorism, which in its view represent some of the greatest challenges to peace and security.[25] In this chapter, transnational regulatory regimes are understood in a broader sense than in the case of the UN, which is as autonomous regulatory regimes to be encountered in any sector as far as they break the traditional divide between national and international law.[26] How far these non-state regimes are or can be committed to the rule of law is still the subject of lively debate.

[21] A van Aaken, 'Behavioral International Law and Economics' (2014) 55 *Harvard International Law Journal* 453, 464 et seq; Koskenniemi in Crawford and Koskenniemi (n 18 above), 60–61.

[22] From the large amount of literature on the topic see, eg A Fischer-Lescano and G Teubner, *Regime-Kollisionen, Zur Fragmentierung des globalen Rechts* (Suhrkamp, 2006); P Schiff Berman, 'From International Law to Law and Globalization' (2005) 43 *Columbia Journal of Transnational Law* 485.

[23] F Cafaggi and K Pistor, 'Regulatory Capabilities: A Normative Framework for Assessing the Distributional Effects of Regulation' (2015) 9(2) *Regulation & Governance* 95.

[24] On the concept see PC Jessup, *Transnational Law* (Yale University Press, 1956); G-P Calliess, 'Law, Transnational' in HK Anheier and M Juergensmeyer (eds), *The Encyclopedia of Global Studies*, vol 3 (Sage, 2012) 1035 et seq; Fischer-Lescano and Teubner (n 22 above); F Cafaggi, *The Challenge of Transnational Private Regulations: Conceptual and Constitutional Debates* (Wiley-Blackwell, 2011).

[25] See 'Strengthening and Coordinating United Nations Rule of Law Activities', Report of the Secretary-General, 11 July 2014, United Nations, General Assembly, A/68213/Add.1, 9–10; 'Strengthening and Coordinating United Nations Rule of Law Activities', A/68/213 (n 16 above), 3–9.

[26] See, eg Fischer-Lescano and Teubner (n 22 above); Calliess (n 24 above).

B. Role of the Political System

A further, major challenge arises out of the political system of states. Overall, the rule of law should contribute to the creation of welfare and to achieving sustained economic progress and development.[27] This implies that sovereign states are in a position to protect and enhance the exercise of their citizens' liberties, supporting their free development. As such, the rule of law is linked to the concept of the democratic state.[28] In democratic states, the exercise of activities is based on a multilateral consensus among the citizens, state institutions and politics. Democratic states are committed to liberalism. The word 'liberal' comes from the Latin language. It means that there are no frontiers, but liberty. Taking the political regime of democratic states into account, these states do not pursue the goal of effectuating an all-encompassing and controlling power within their territory over their citizens or over everything. Rather, they adopt a liberal attitude, which follows the principles of freedom, equality and the rule of law.[29] In contrast, dictatorships and totalitarian states are characterized by their all-encompassing exercise of power. They claim to exercise complete control over their citizens and over everything within their territory.

Liberalism also includes the openness of the state towards changes,[30] and therefore, in the context of this chapter, towards the emergence of alternative regimes. Thus, it is the concept of the liberal democratic state that determines which values are protected and which interests are pursued.[31] Actually—an important assertion of this chapter—it is this concept itself which leads to, allows and supports the emergence of the alternative, private, self-regulatory, transnational and non-state regulatory regimes that are causing a shift within the prevailing institutional order of state law and international law. Contrary to state and international law, the emergence of these regimes is spontaneous and not hierarchical, but heterarchical. They do not fit into the approach applied by states or international organizations when opting for policy and regulatory measures. This approach typically consists of the following steps: first, the definition of a short-, medium- and long-term strategy; second, the introduction of the subsequent regulatory measures; and third, their implementation and enforcement.[32] In contrast, these regimes can represent either a fragmentation or a dispersion of rules.[33] They can both deviate from the state or international law framework and fragment it, or they may emerge from outside of the framework.

[27] Chesterman (n 8 above), 56, 331–61; Dicey (n 8 above); Bingham (n 8 above); Chimni (n 8 above), 290–93.

[28] Democratic means a government in which the supreme power is vested in the people.

[29] Koskenniemi (n 5 above), 36.

[30] In that sense see also Koskenniemi (ibid), 35–37.

[31] Teubner (n 8 above), 33–41.

[32] M Senn, *Non-State Regulatory Regimes, Understanding Institutional Transformation* (Springer, 2011) 11–20.

[33] Regarding the concepts see Section IV below.

In other words, transnational developments basically can and do take place in democratic states. The autonomy of these regimes is supported and boosted by the constitutional order of democratic states and their institutional structures. As a result, the emergence of alternative transnational regulatory regimes is just the confirmation and evidence of an effectively functioning democratic liberal state. It can be interpreted as a reflection of the dominating political system. At the same time, however, it is a paradox that these distinctive non-politically, but functionally orientated regimes are a 'product' or emerge out of the political, democratic structures of states.[34] In that regard, it is interesting to note that Jessup, who delimited the concept of transnational regulation as understood nowadays, used the concept just to designate the continuation of cooperation between Eastern and Western countries or between democracies and dictatorships during the cold war,[35] ie as a consequence of the dominating political systems.

As a consequence, these non-state, transnational regulatory regimes raise a valid issue regarding the application of the rule of law. The challenge is to find ways to either integrate or link them to the state and international law regimes or to commit them to respect and implement the rule of law.

IV. PROSPECTS FOR GOVERNANCE

In order to determine a governance approach, I focus first on two determining structural aspects of the framework just delineated. Then, I briefly elaborate on the critical aspects that provide insight into the delimitation of a governance path towards linkages that might be supportive of the implementation of the rule of law. The issue of linkage of the rule of law to other challenges, such as sustainable development and inclusive economies, that is, including institutions and encompassing activities exercised by diverse regulatory regimes, is a declared goal of the UN.[36]

[34] In that sense see also Teubner (n 8 above), 35–36.

[35] Jessup (n 24 above).

[36] Within its work, the UN and in particular the discussions of its General Assembly on the rule of law have repeatedly underlined the necessity to develop further the linkages between the rule of law and the three main pillars of the United Nations, namely peace and security, human rights and development, and especially the inter-relationship between the rule of law and sustainable development in the post-2015 international development agenda. It reaffirmed the essential role of the rule of law in promoting sustainable development and inclusive economies. The General Assembly also requested the Secretary-General to propose ways and means of developing, with wide stakeholder participation, further such linkages. UN Sixty-Eighth Session—The Rule of Law at the National and International Levels (Agenda item 85); see Report of the Secretary-General to the General Assembly: Strengthening and Coordinating United Nations Rule of Law Activities, 24 July 2014, A/69/181; http://www.un.org/en/ga/sixth/68/RuleOfLaw.shtml (accessed on 6 October 2014); Declaration (n 1 above), note 41.

A. Structural Aspects

Taking the divide between national and international law regimes as well as the emergence of transnational regulatory regimes into account, it is interesting to consider whether the structural characteristics of these regimes offer any clues that might be useful for governance matters. Two basic characteristics can be made out: on the one side, there is a fragmentation of regulation; on the other side, there is a dispersion of regulation.

In legal terms, *fragmentation* is used to indicate that the state and international legal orders break or separate themselves into fragments.[37] Parts detach themselves from the whole or from the centre, the state. Although their origin remains the same, the legal order of the state is divided and in the process of getting even more divided. Fragmentation of regulation is the result of a process of specialization and delegation of power by states. Since the 1980s, for instance, there is in the emergence of a large number of specialized, functionally orientated agencies based on the delegation of power by the states themselves.[38] These agencies—first of all at the national, but also at the international, level—possess proper regulatory competencies. As a result, the legal order is no longer unified, but is fragmented. At this point, it is important to underline once again that with fragmentation, the origin of the rules remains the same. It is centred towards the national or state law and/or international law.[39]

The second aspect is *dispersion*.[40] Dispersion is a more open and broader notion than fragmentation. It designates forms or regulations that emerge without being linked to national or international law. They are decentred and constitute autonomous regulatory regimes. There is no definite source from where these regimes are initiated. They represent a scattering of orders.[41] In particular, states cannot cope adequately with all issues and in all cases. Developments such as the rise of new technologies or the realization of business interests, for instance, often necessitate prompt, adequate regulatory interventions and worldwide coordination. They encompass both institutional issues and issues regarding the substantive aspects of regulation. Often, there is an institutional vacuum either at the national or state and at the international

[37] For a basic reference see M Koskenniemi, 'Fragmentation of International Law: Difficulties Arising from the Diversification and Expansion of International Law', Report of the Study Group of the International Law Commission, United Nations, A/CN.4/L.682, 13 April 2006; for a definition of fragmentation see Senn (n 32 above), 182–84; see further A Fischer-Lescano and G Teubner, 'Fragmentierung des Weltrechts: Vernetzung globaler Regimes statt etatistischer Rechtseinheit' in M Albert and R Stichweh (eds), *Weltstaat und Weltstaatlichkeit, Beobachtungen globaler politischer Strukturbildung nach der Globalisierung* (VS Verlag für Sozialwissenschaften, 2007) 37–61.

[38] J Jacint, D Levi-Faur and X Fernández, 'Global Diffusion of Regulatory Agencies: Channels of Transfer and Stages of Diffusion' (2011) 44 *Comparative Political Studies* 1343.

[39] Senn (n 32 above), 184.

[40] On the definition of 'dispersion' see Senn (n 32 above), 183–84.

[41] Senn (ibid), 184.

levels. The states might not always be in a position to introduce regulatory solutions within a reasonable time frame or to take adequate measures, not least due to political rationales and the lengthiness of the state regulatory process. Private businesses or groups may also regulate themselves, thus developing transnational regulatory regimes. In addition, transnational threats such as those defined by the UN, encompassing terrorist activities and transnational organized crime in such diverse areas as human trafficking and environmental crimes, and the activities of criminal networks also emerge independently from the national or international legal regimes.[42]

Altogether, there is an acephalous system of regimes.[43] National and international regulatory regimes coexist with third, non-state orders, or orders emerging outside of the state.

B. Elements of a Governance Approach

With regard to this situation, the issue now arising is which governance approach should be adopted and which may either reinforce or contest the rule of law? Indeed, issues concerning the legitimacy, implementation and distributional effects of these diverse regulatory regimes have been subjects of lively debate. Up to now, however, less emphasis has been placed on the cutting-edge issue of governance in relation to national, international and transnational regulation and its role with reference to the implementation of the rule of law.

To delimit a governance approach and determine the corresponding governance principles, it should first be noted that the development of these regimes is neither linear nor systematic. Thus, taking the issue of effectively implementing the rule of law into account, an approach should primarily aim at finding connections and complementarities among these national, international and transnational regulatory regimes. It should not enhance the divide among them, thereby leading to an even more fragmented or dispersed regulatory framework. A possible interplay between these regimes must be identified, together with behavioural rituals and mechanisms of potential coordination and co-operation of their interactions. A first aspect to consider is whether these regimes present elements of convergence among each other, whereupon the main focus is placed on the relationship between the national and international regulatory regimes on the one side and transnational regulatory regimes on the other side. Specifically, the issue is if and how far the transnational regulatory regimes—as autonomous regulatory regimes—apply general principles of law and whether they are committed to respecting the rule of law.

[42] A/68213/Add.1 (n 25 above), 9–10; A/68/213 (n 16 above), 9; see also Fischer-Lescano and Teubner (n 22 above), 158–69, with regard to transnational cybercrime.

[43] Senn (n 32 above), 182–84.

In this chapter, it is argued that prima facie there is an inherent convergence among these regimes as far as their institutional structure is concerned. This applies even though transnational regulatory regimes are not political regimes. On the one hand, a transnational regulatory regime may take shape because state political authorities have decided not to intervene in a specific case. A prominent example is represented by the decision adopted by the community of states to refrain from creating and maintaining their own standard-setting organization since this would qualify as an international organization under international law.[44] Rather, they decided deliberately to respect the private character of the International Organization for Standardization (ISO).[45] Hence, the institutional non-state structure of that organization is a consequence of a political decision of states in which the public policy debate played a determining role. The main rationale for this policy of states not to intervene directly is due predominantly to the specific technical work of the ISO. Unlike state activities, it requires highly specialized expert knowledge to define standards. Such work is largely dominated by commercial, business and trade interests. ISO operations, moreover, are conducted in a professional, serious and successful manner.[46] Thus, with regard to the commitment to the rule of law, it should not be ignored that independent regimes such as the ISO constitute parts of a system and are interdependent. While transnational regulatory regimes emerge where there is either a voluntary or involuntary institutional vacuum within the architecture of state law or international law, at the same time they complement these bodies of law. Thus, there is an innate institutional convergence, which offers opportunities to promote the establishment of respect for the rule of law by all regimes.

It must also be noted, however, that there is a fundamental divergence as far as the interests pursued are concerned.[47] While state law and international law are motivated by the pursuance of the public interest, the emergence of transnational regulatory regimes is motivated by particular interests, mainly the economic and business interests of private groups or networks. It is generally acknowledged that the role of states as well as of international organizations is to both represent and defend the collective interest. States and international organizations should act and steer the interests of the community. Thus, contrary to transnational regimes, they operate based on a commonly defined medium- and long-term strategy. To implement that strategy, they will then take adequate regulatory measures. Finally, they will have to implement the measures adopted.

[44] For criteria applying to the definition of an international organization in the sense of international law see I Seidl-Hohenveldern and G Loibl, *Das Recht der Internationalen Organisationen einschliesslich der Supranationalen Gemeinschaften*, 7th edn (Carl Heymanns Verlag KG, 2000) 1–7.

[45] Available at http://www.iso.org/iso/home.html (accessed on 6 October 2014).

[46] Ibid; J Braithwaite and P Drahos, *Global Business Regulation* (Cambridge University Press, 2000) 503.

[47] Senn (n 6 above), 365–68.

In contrast, non-state, transnational regulatory regimes do not follow any predefined strategy. Rather, they operate on a case-by-case basis. Their behaviour is determined by the logic of competition. They adopt ad hoc measures based on the opportunities of the moment. They will also concentrate on realizing the interests of the groups they represent. Common rules to and for a group emerge and shape themselves over the course of time, and their implementation remains voluntary. However, these regimes cause externalities. As an example, the protection of the environment as regulated by states in the public interest is opposed to the interests pursued by the construction industry, which has at its disposal a strong network and a proper transnational regulatory regime. Taking the public interest into account, these externalities have to be internalized. Hence, the divergence of interests might lead to the contestation of the rule of law, or at least some of its aspects. Consequently, a governance approach should include determining common principles and rules to master these issues in a way that is acceptable to all the regimes involved. The point is to commit transnational regulatory regimes to a shared responsibility.

Besides this brief mention of seminal elements applying to the distinction of these regimes and their interactions, the existence of a range of hybrid forms of regulatory regimes should not be ignored either. In practice, their delimitation does not operate according to a strict scheme; indeed, there are a number of regulatory arrangements.[48] From a holistic point of view, this situation of regimes coalescing, interacting and pursuing their own goals depending on the circumstances can be interpreted as a struggle between normativity and factuality.[49]

V. CONCLUSION

Taking into account that state, international and transnational regulatory regimes are all constituent parts of a system, it should be possible to apply a model which is in line or can adapt itself to developments occurring within the system, leading to a reinforcement of the rule of law. An approach based on the analysis of convergence or divergence elements among state, international and transnational regulatory regimes offers a valuable starting point from which to study their contours and relationships, base on which a governance approach can be refined.

[48] Teubner (n 8 above), 62 et seq.

[49] In a similar sense, Koskenniemi uses the distinction between concreteness and normativity to explain the role of international law as an objective body of rules. International law should ensure concreteness by distancing itself from theories of natural justice. It should guarantee its normativity by creating distance between itself and actual state behaviour, will or interest. Koskenniemi (n 5 above), 38–40. In a similar sense see also M Foucault, *Naissance de la biopolitique. Cours au Collège de France 1978–79* (Gallimard/Seuil, 2004) 280–81.

5

Formation of International Custom and the Role of Non-State Actors

GEORGE D KYRIAKOPOULOS*

'Identification of State practice. What counts as 'state practice'? . . . Beyond the State, whose acts?' (Michael Wood, Special Rapporteur, ILC)

TRADITIONALLY, INTERNATIONAL CUSTOM is considered to be one of the main sources of international law, pursuant to the famous wording of Article 38, paragraph 1 of the Statute of the International Court of Justice ('evidence of a general practice accepted as law'). According to this definition, the cumulative constituent elements of custom are (i) a repeated and uniform state practice and (ii) the credo that said practice is based on a sense of legal obligation (*opinio juris*). This two-element-based formation of international customary rules has been repeatedly asserted by the international jurisprudence, mainly of the Permanent Court of International Justice and its successor, the International Court of Justice (ICJ, the Court).[1]

In the relevant cases of the ICJ, practice—as a prerequisite of customary rule creation—was state practice, although in the *Nicaragua* case the Court stated that practice of states against certain resolutions of the UN General Assembly could be of importance regarding the emergence of an *opinio juris*. This position of the ICJ gave rise to a doctrinal, reformative, 'modern' approach to international custom, which minimized the importance of the 'practice' element in favour of the *opinio juris* element, thus giving priority to the identification of customary rules through the instant crystallization of

* Lecturer in International Law, National and Kapodistrian University of Athens.

[1] *The Case of SS 'Lotus' (France v Turkey)* [1927] PCIJ Rep Series A no 10 (Official Case No 9); *North Sea Continental Shelf (Federal Republic of Germany v Denmark, Federal Republic of Germany v Netherlands)* [1969] ICJ Reports 3; *Delimitation of the Maritime Boundary in the Gulf of Maine Area (Canada v United States)* [1984] ICJ Reports 246; *Military and Paramilitary Activities in and against Nicaragua (Nicaragua v United States) (Merits)* [1986] ICJ Reports 14.

norms instead of the traditional slow (and evolutional in nature) approach of measuring state practice through time.

Meanwhile, international law is no longer the same, since new entities have come to the fore: as has gradually become accepted, the so-called 'non-state actors' (such as multinational corporations, NGOs, armed groups, etc) claim a role in the creation of international law—an evolution which constitutes a real challenge to traditional approaches to the international law-making process. It has to be questioned if the practice of such entities can also contribute to the creation of new rules in the context of international customary law and, if so, under what conditions.

In view of the above, the purpose of this chapter can be posed as the following question: provided that the element of practice remains critical for the creation of customary rules, may the practice of non-state entities be validly counted for this purpose?

It should be mentioned that the importance of shedding more light on the oldest form of international norms, such as the customary ones, wass demonstrated perfectly in the decision of the International Law Commission, during its 64th session (2012), to include in its programme of work the topic: 'formation and evidence of customary international law'.[2]

I. THE IMPORTANCE OF STATE PRACTICE IN THE FORMATION OF INTERNATIONAL CUSTOMARY LAW

Article 38 of the Statute of the ICJ, referring to the sources of international law, describes custom as 'evidence of a general practice accepted as law'. As already noted, the custom requires two elements: state practice and legal conviction (*opinio juris*). State practice refers to general and consistent practice by states, while *opinio juris* means that the practice is followed out of a belief of legal obligation. The distinction between the two elements of the custom has been shown in the literature to be problematic, since it is not always easy to discern exactly which state activity is part of the practice and which is evidence of the *opinio juris*. In this respect, it has been mentioned that treaties and declarations 'represent *opinio juris* because they are statements about the legality of action, rather than examples of that action'.[3]

[2] ILC, 'Report of the Sixty-Fourth Session' (2012) UN Doc A/67/10. The ILC decided to appoint Mr Michael Wood as Special Rapporteur for the topic. At its sixty-fifth session in 2013, the title of the topic was changed to 'Identification of Customary International Law': ILC, 'Report of the Sixty-Fifth Session' (2013) UN Doc A/68/10, para 65.

[3] AE Roberts, 'Traditional and Modern Approaches to Customary International Law: A Reconciliation' (2001) 95 *American Journal of International Law* 757, based on a distinction of D'Amato, according to which actions of states constitute practice, whereas statements are evidence of *opinio juris*: A D'Amato, *The Concept of Custom in International Law* (Cornell University Press, 1971).

A. Formation and Evidence of International Customary Law

In order to shed light on a number of terms, I should mention that, as Michael Wood, Special Rapporteur of the International Law Commission, has pointed it out, the term 'formation' describes the process by which rules of customary international law develop, while 'evidence' has to do with the identification of such rules.[4] However, it appears that this distinction is of limited value, since it has been held that the process of the formation of customary international law and that of its consolidation as a rule of positive international law are two sides of the same coin, which is suggested by the fact that the concept of 'custom' refers to both the law-making process and the end result of that process—a legally binding norm at the universal or, more rarely, the regional level.[5]

(i) Both Elements (Practice, Opinio Juris*) Are Necessary . . .*

Over time, international justice has consistently stressed the need for the cumulative existence of both the material (practice) and psychological (*opinio juris*) elements in order to determine the existence of a customary rule: in the old *Lotus* case, the Permanent Court had noted that 'the rules of law binding upon states therefore emanate from their own free will as expressed in conventions or by usages generally accepted as expressing principles of law'.[6] However, it is in the context of the *North Sea Continental Shelf* case that the ICJ thoroughly analysed the two components of international custom:

> Not only must the acts concerned amount to a settled practice, but they must also be such, or be carried out in such a way, as to be evidence of a belief that this practice is rendered obligatory by the existence of a rule of law requiring it. The need for such a belief, ie the existence of a subjective element, is implicit in the very notion of the *opinio juris sive necessitatis*. The States concerned must therefore feel that they are conforming to what amounts to a legal obligation. The frequency, or even habitual character of the acts is not in itself enough. There are many international acts, eg, in the field of ceremonial and protocol, which are performed almost invariably, but which are motivated only by considerations of courtesy, convenience or tradition, and not by any sense of legal duty.[7]

[4] ILC, 'First Report on Formation and Evidence of Customary International Law' (Sixty-Fifth Session, 2013) UN Doc A/CN.4/663, paras 13 et seq.

[5] P-M Dupuy, 'Formation of Customary International Law and General Principles' in D Bodansky, J Brunnée and E Hey (eds), *The Oxford Handbook of International Environmental Law* (Oxford University Press, 2008) 451.

[6] PCIJ Rep A no 10, 18.

[7] [1969] ICJ Reports, para 77. Similar considerations were expressed by the Court in the *Nicaragua* (para 207) and *Gulf of Maine* (para 111) cases. As Treves observes, in the *North Sea Case* and the *Gulf of Maine Case* 'the references to the *opinio juris* seem to indicate that what is referred to is more belief than consent': T Treves, 'Customary International Law' in *Max Planck Encyclopedia of Public International Law* (Oxford University Press, 2012) 18.

(ii) . . . But Which is the Most Important One?

Despite the general recognition of the cumulative contribution of the elements of international custom, the question was raised, in the literature, about which of these two elements may be of greatest importance for the creation of customary rules. In other words, which of the two factors—practice and *opinio juris*—is the most decisive in the context of the customary process?[8]

In this context, the traditional approach, considering that practice was the most important element, focused on the value of state actions and deeds, while a modern approach, by seeking manifestations of the legal conviction of states, assessed the overarching importance of *opinio juris*.[9]

(a) The Traditional Approach

In the context of the traditional conception on the formation of international custom—which is mainly reflected in the reasoning of the *Lotus* case—the existence of a general and consistent state practice prevails over *opinio juris*. As was pointed out, 'practice had priority over *opinio juris;* deeds were what counted, not just words'.[10]

For A Roberts, 'traditional custom is evolutionary and is identified through an *inductive* process in which a general custom is derived from specific instances of state practice'.[11] This means that specific actions and operations of states—of a domestic or transnational nature—provide, through time, a general state attitude towards international relations. Thus, specific and concrete deeds are likely to lead to state positions of a general significance. In this regard, it is evident that *opinio juris* does not constitute the decisive factor in the creation of custom, since it is virtually limited to the legal assessment of the actions undertaken.

This traditional approach still has its proponents. For instance, B Simma and Ph Alston note that the

> rules of customary law . . . firmly established through inductive reasoning based on deeds rather than words may have been, and still are, limited in scope, but they had, and continue to have, several undoubted advantages. They are hard and solid; they have been carefully hammered out on the anvil of actual, tangible interaction among states; and they allow reasonably reliable predictions as to future state behavior.

(b) The Modern Approach

The modern approach on the formation of international customary rules is ideally reflected in the merits decision of the ICJ in the *Nicaragua* case. In just two paragraphs, the Court not only downplayed the contribution of state

[8] Treves (n 7 above), 20.

[9] Roberts (n 3 above), 759.

[10] B Simma and P Alston, 'The Sources of Human Rights Law: Custom, Jus Cogens and General Principles' (1988–89) 12 *Australian Yearbook on International Law* 88.

[11] Roberts (n 3 above), 757 (emphasis in the original).

practice in the creation of customary rules, but also considered that a decisive *opinio juris* can emerge through important resolutions of the General Assembly of the United Nations:

> The Court does not consider that, for a rule to be established as customary, the corresponding practice must be in absolutely rigorous conformity with the rule. In order to deduce the existence of customary rules, the Court deems it sufficient that the conduct of States should, in general, be consistent with such rules, and that instances of State conduct inconsistent with a given rule should generally have been treated as breaches of that rule, not as indications of the recognition of a new rule . . .[12]

As regards *opinio juris*,

> [it] may . . . be deduced from, *inter alia*, the attitude of the Parties and the attitude of States towards certain General Assembly resolutions, and particularly resolution 2625 (XXV) . . . The effect of consent to the text of such resolutions . . . may be understood as an acceptance of the validity of the rule or set of rules declared by the resolution by themselves.[13]

In other words, statements such as those contained in General Assembly resolutions are becoming more important in the context of detecting the existence of a customary rule, while actions of states must be in line with those statements.

Regarding the legal value of the General Assembly resolutions, the Court was more enlightening in its advisory opinion on the *Legality of the Threat or Use of Nuclear Weapons*, emphasizing that

> General Assembly resolutions, even if they are not binding, may sometimes have normative value. They can, in certain circumstances, provide evidence important for establishing the existence of a rule or the emergence of an *opinio juris*. To establish whether this is true of a given General Assembly resolution, it is necessary to look at its content and the conditions of its adoption; it is also necessary to see whether an *opinio juris* exists as to its normative character. Or a series of resolutions may show the gradual evolution of the *opinio juris* required for the establishment of a new rule.[14]

In the same line, the Trial Chamber of the International Criminal Tribunal for the former Yugoslavia (ICTY, the Tribunal), judging in the *Kupreskic* case, underlined that:

> Admittedly, there does not seem to have emerged recently a body of state practice consistently supporting the proposition that one of the elements of custom, namely *usus* or *diuturnitas* has taken shape. This is however an area where *opinio iuris sive necessitates* may play a much greater role than *usus*, as a result of the . . .

[12] *Military and Paramilitary Activities in and against Nicaragua (Nicaragua v United States of America) (Merits)* [1986] ICJ Reports 186.

[13] Ibid, para 188.

[14] *Legality of the Threat or Use of Nuclear Weapons (Advisory Opinion)* [1996] ICJ Reports 70.

> Martens Clause. In the light of the way states and courts have implemented it, this Clause clearly shows that principles of international humanitarian law may emerge through a customary process under the pressure of the demands of humanity or the dictates of public conscience, even where state practice is scant or inconsistent.[15]

It is obvious that this modern approach to international custom kept away from any voluntarist considerations inherent in the traditional approach, which focused mainly on state practice, somehow emphasizing the expression of a collective unconscious in international society. As Roberts points out

> modern custom is derived by a *deductive* process that begins with general statements of rules rather than particular instances of practice . . . Modern custom can develop quickly because it is deduced from multilateral treaties and declarations by international *fora* such as the General Assembly, which can declare existing customs, crystallize emerging customs, and generate new customs . . .[16]

It was the time of the *coutume sauvage*:[17] the role of international practice was limited to establishing a consensus to a legal conviction, which sprang from the participation of states in international fora such as the General Assembly of the United Nations. Simma and Alston consider, as a good example of this approach,

> the elevation of the Universal Declaration of 1948 and of the documents that have built upon its foundations to the status of customary law, in a world where it is still customary for a depressingly large number of States to trample upon the human rights of their nationals.[18]

It should be noted, at this point, that this modern approach to the creation of international custom, by assigning particular importance to the *opinio juris* and its tracing through the participation of states in international institutions, facilitated the assumption that entities other than states can participate in the creation of international customary rules. As I Gunning pointed out, 'in order to accommodate all of the desired human rights principles', this modern view of customary international law is combined with 'the ability to create custom' of non-state actors such as international organizations and 'certain

[15] *Prosecutor v Kupreskic (Judgment)* ICTY-IT-95-16-T (14 January 2000), para 527, available at http://www.icty.org/x/cases/kupreskic/tjug/en/kup-tj000114e.pdf (accessed on 1 December 2014). This case is also mentioned by Michael Wood in his first report to the ILC (para 70).

[16] Roberts (n 3 above), 758–59 (emphasis in the original). Similarly, Simma and Alston point out that 'the approach now used is *deductive*: rules or principles proclaimed, for instance, by the General Assembly . . . are taken not only as the starting points for the possible development of customary law in the event that State practice eventually happens to lock on these proclamations, but as a law-making process which is more or less complete in itself, even in the face of contrasting "external" facts' (n 10 above, 89–90).

[17] Term used by R-J Dupuy, 'Coutume sage et coutume sauvage' in *La Communauté internationale—Mélanges offerts à Charles Rousseau* (A Pedone, 1974) 76: 'Certes, il existe des coutumes sages qui se sont lentement dégagées de faits immémoriaux, établis sur une tradition mentale, mais on voit aussi, spécialement de nos jours, des coutumes sauvages dont l'excroissance soudaine puise sa racine plus dans les volontés alertées que dans des esprits assouplis par une longue habitude'.

[18] Simma and Alston (n 10 above), 90.

non-governmental organizations [that] have a distinct, measurable impact on international affairs'.[19]

B. The 'Modern' Approach Weakness: The Evaluation of Negative or Controversial Practice

One of the main weak points of the modern approach is the mode of evaluation of a negative, opposite state practice, especially in the field of the international protection of human rights.

Some scholars tend to minimize the importance of this phenomenon, considering it a violation of a customary rule that has already been formed. In this respect, it is worth remembering the dictum of the Court in the *Nicaragua* case, according to which

> it [is] sufficient that the conduct of States should, in general, be consistent with such rules, and that instances of State conduct inconsistent with a given rule should generally have been treated as breaches of that rule, not as indications of the recognition of a new rule.[20]

Similarly, in relation to the protection of fundamental human rights, such as, for instance, the prohibition of torture, the ICTY, in its judgment in the *Furundzija* case, stressed the importance of the fact that 'no State ha[d] ever claimed that it was authorised to practice torture in time of armed conflict, nor ha[d] any State shown or manifested opposition to the implementation of treaty provisions against torture'. For the Tribunal, this fact was sufficient for the formation of customary rule, despite any contrary manifested practice.[21]

However, other scholars, such as O Schachter, are more cautious about the unconditional deletion of a contrary practice: in the field of protection of human rights in particular, Schachter feels that any contrary practice cannot be dismissed in any case, especially since human rights violations are 'widespread, often gross and generally tolerated by the international community'.[22] What Schachter proposes is a two-tier approach: taking as an example the Universal Declaration of Human Rights, he distinguishes between human rights for which state practice is not consistent with the assumption of the existence of a customary rule and 'hard core' human rights (such as against genocide, torture, etc), in respect of which the sense of the existence of a customary rule is particularly pronounced, since 'this can be shown not so much by apply-

[19] I Gunning, 'Modernizing Customary International Law: The Challenge of Human Rights' (1991) 31 *Virginia Journal of International Law* 212, cited by Simma and Alston (n 10 above), 84–85.

[20] [1986] ICJ Reports 186.

[21] *Prosecutor v Anto Furundzija (Judgment)* ICTY-IT-95-17/1-T (10 December 1998), available at http://www.icty.org/x/cases/furundzija/tjug/en/fur-tj981210e.pdf (accessed on 1 December 2014).

[22] O Schachter, 'International Law in Theory and Practice: General Course in Public International Law' (1982) 178 *Recueil des Cours de l'Académie de Droit International* 21, 335.

ing formal criteria of customary law as by considering conduct that has been universally condemned as violative of the basic concept of human dignity'.[23]

C. A 'Gordian' Solution: Resorting to General Principles of International Law Rather Than to International Customary Rules

According to Simma and Alston, the so-called modern approach has created an identity crisis for custom, and relevant rules would be better understood as general principles of international law.[24] This crisis is due to the de-emphasizing of material practice as a constitutive element combined with the tendency to count the articulation of a rule 'twice, so to speak', 'not only as an expression of *opinio juris* but also as state practice itself'.[25]

Under this consideration, said scholars believe that the position of the ICJ about the evaluation of negative practice 'appears less convincing, in instances where the inconsistency between words and factual behavior has been glaring from the very beginning'.[26]

The Report of the Committee on the Formation of Customary Law, established in 1986 by the American Branch of the International Law Association (the ABILA Report), is in line with that position: the committee considered that:

> Where the rule in question is admittedly neither 'old' nor 'established', however, the approach of looking first to articulated rules and only secondarily to practice in support of those rules, coupled with a broader definition of and diminished requirements for practice, may result in a sort of 'instant' customary international law of dubious relationship to the actual behavior and interests of states.[27]

On the other hand,

> it is difficult to distinguish 'general principles' from 'international custom' when both are viewed in their broader senses. In the former case, one has general principles of law which are 'recognized' by some groups, of states; in the latter case, one has, effectively, rules which states generally apply, or claim as applying, in practice.

[23] Ibid, 336. In relation to the criticism of the 'modern' approach, see also P Weil, 'Vers une normativité relative en droit international?' [1982] *Revue Générale de Droit International Public* 5, 40: 'L'équilibre classique sur lequel reposait la théorie classique de la coutume est rompu, puisque aussi bien l'opinio juris se dissout dans un consentement majoritaire mal define et se réduit plus ou moins à un vague "consensus"'. On the same line, Stern notes that 'est règle coutumière international celle qui est considérée comme telle par la volonté d'Etats pouvan imposer leur point de vue': B Stern, 'La Coutume au coeur du droit international—Quelques réflexions' [1981] *Mélanges Reuter* 479, 498.

[24] Simma and Alston (n 10 above), 96.

[25] Ibid.

[26] Ibid, 97.

[27] Committee on the Formation of Customary International Law, American Branch of the International Law Association, 'The Role of State Practice in the Formation of Customary an *Jus Cogens* Norms of International Law' [1987–88] *Proceedings of the American Branch of the Law Association* 109.

> One may posit distinctions between the two, but it is difficult to reconcile these distinctions with any consistent usage.[28]

What is the advantage of the 'general principle' conception? A general principle, in the sense of Article 38 of the Statute of the ICJ,

> clearly appears to be a normative standard, unrelated either to the quantity of states or to their interests in a given dispute or rule. Moreover, the concept of a 'recognized' general principle seems to conform more closely than the concept of 'custom' to the situation where a norm is widely accepted even though widely violated.[29]

It seems that, at least implicitly or subconsciously, the Trial Chamber of the ICTY, in the *Kupreskic* case, accepted the above considerations, as it stated that

> the precedents may constitute evidence of customary rule in that they are indicative of the existence of *opinio juris* and international practice on a certain matter, *or else they may be indicative of the emergence of a general principle of law*.[30]

Finally, in his First Report to the International Law Commission, Special Rapporteur M Wood adopted a similar view, noting that 'the ICJ itself may have recourse to general principles of international law in circumstances when the criteria for customary international law are not present'. In this respect, Wood quoted a dictum of G Gaja:

> The relatively frequent reference by the ICJ to principles that are not part of municipal laws is explained, at least in part, by the narrow definition of customary international law that is provided in Art. 38 (1) (b) ICJ Statute. Should custom be regarded, as stated in that provision, as 'evidence of a general practice accepted as law', given the insufficiency of practice, several rules of international law which are not based on treaties would not fit in the definition of custom. Hence the reference to principles or general principles.[31]

[28] Ibid, 111. The ABILA Report cites Bin Cheng, who has stated: 'While conventions can easily be distinguished from the two other sources of international law, the line of demarcation between custom and general principles of law recognized by civilized nations is often not very clear, since international custom or customary international law, understood in a broad sense, may include all that is unwritten in international law, *ie,* both custom and general principles of law': B Cheng, *General Principles of Law as Applied by International Courts and Tribunals* (reprinted Cambridge, 1987) 23.

[29] ABILA Report, 112.

[30] Above n 15, para 540 (emphasis added).

[31] G Gaja, 'General Principles of Law' in *Max Planck Encyclopedia of Public International Law* (2012). See 1 ILC Report 36.

II. BEYOND STATE PRACTICE: IS IT TIME TO TAKE INTO CONSIDERATION WHAT NON-STATE ACTORS DO?

Diverse contemporary issues, such as international terrorism activity, the global business expansion of multinational corporations, the proliferation of separatist movements, the phenomenon of globalization and the steadily increasing influence of the banking sector in international affairs, have so radically changed international relations that we are now questioning who are today's makers of international law. In this regard, current scholarship is attempting to determine whether the sources of international law have fundamentally changed.

It is in the context of this quest that the issue of non-state actors (NSAs) comes into play.

We define a 'non-state actor' as any entity that is not a state under international law.

Broadly speaking, an NSA typology comprises intergovernmental organizations, NGOs, multinational corporations and groups such as rebel groups, terrorist organizations, religious groups, civil society organizations, corporations and individuals.[32] DB Hollis classifies these entities into three broad groups: sub-state actors, supranational actors and extra-national actors.[33]

Hollis defines 'sub-state actors' as 'semi-autonomous territorial entities that are legally dependent upon, or associated with, independent sovereign states, such as sub-national components of federal states, overseas territories and other dependent territories of existing states'. The criterion for an NSA to be considered as a 'supranational actor' resides in the combination of two elements: 'first, states must transfer to the entity powers that they themselves previously exercised over their nationals. Second, in exercising these previously national powers, a supranational actor must have independent authority from its member states.' In this respect, the reference actor, according to Hollis, is the European Union. Finally, the 'extra-national actors' exist 'separate from nation-state systems' and include 'international organizations and other international institutions created by states for a particular purpose'.[34]

[32] See N Arajärvi, 'From State-Centricism to Where? The Formation of (Customary) International Law and Non-State Actors', available at http://papers.ssrn.com/sol3/papers.cfm?abstract_id=1599679 (accessed on 1 December 2014); DB Hollis, 'Why State Consent Still Matters—Non-State Actors, Treaties, and the Changing Sources of International Law' (2005) 23 *Berkeley Journal of International Law* 138.

[33] Hollis (ibid), 146.

[34] Ibid, 146 et seq.

A. Non-state Actors' Participation in the Formation of International Custom: Behind the Scenes of State Practice

Some proponents of the modern approach about the formation of international custom suggest (in my opinion, without much success) that the existence of an NSA practice is a decisive factor for the creation of customary rules.

They mainly stress that a textual interpretation of Article 38(1)(b) of the Statute of the ICJ would not obstruct the practice of NSAs as a contributory factor to the formation of customary international law, as states are not explicitly mentioned in the definition of international custom. Moreover, they suggest that UN General Assembly resolutions can be seen as international practice arising from an NSA, the international organization here 'acting not as a vehicle of its member states but as an individual entity'.[35]

They generally believe that international organizations and other non-state entities 'have taken over functions traditionally conceived as the prerogative of states', and through their actions 'influence increasingly what can be understood as international practice'.[36] Additionally, they have a strong implicit impact on the practice of states in both unilateral and multilateral actions.

However, although the implicit impact of NSAs on state policies and decisions cannot be denied, their role, until now, has been behind the scenes of state practice:

As Treves justifiably points out,

> practice is what the subjects of international law do and say, what they want (or consent to), and what they believe. Such practice may in some cases be attributable to States taken singularly and in other cases to States taken in groups. In order to determine the existence of customary international rules, a broader notion of practice seems useful, however. Such broader notion also includes acts by non-subjects of international law which, because of the authority that subjects of international law have conferred upon them, or because of their influence on the relations between such subjects, *indirectly* provide elements to assess the existence of customary international rules or the relevance of the various elements of the practice of the subjects of international law.[37]

According to this line of thinking, non-state actors' activities cannot be regarded as falling within the substance of 'practice' as meant in Article 38 of the Statute of the Court. However, their implicit influence cannot be denied: '[t]he perception of these actors of what is permitted and of what is prohibited to States in their relationship with other States, and their impact on public

[35] Arajärvi (n 32 above), 11.

[36] N Arajärvi, *The Changing Nature of Customary International Law: Methods of Interpreting the Concept of Custom in International Criminal Tribunals* (Routledge, 2014) 18.

[37] Treves (n 7 above), 5–6.

opinion, nevertheless influences the perception of governments and ultimately their *opinio iuris*'.[38]

In this respect, it is notable that C Ryngaert, despite being in favour of including NSA practice in the formation of customary international law in the context of international humanitarian law, is very sceptical about the impact of this practice on international law, declaring that

> one should however also be willing to accept the consequence that the content of the customary rules thus formed may not as a matter of course be a humanitarian's dream. Armed opposition groups, and *a fortiori* transnational armed groups with a religious-ideological agenda such as Al Qaeda, are not known for their respect for IHL, quite on the contrary. Accordingly, including non-State actors in the process of customary law formation may possibly lead to *regression*.[39]

Regarding the impact of armed groups in the context of international humanitarian law, A Roberts and S Sivakumaran are essentially sceptical of the assessment of their practice. Although the authors confirm that, in some case, such groups have publicized codes of military conduct, internal orders or drafted constitutions, they consider that 'the legal status of these materials remains contentious'.[40] What could be done, in their opinion, is the elaboration of a theory of 'quasi-custom', under which the practice of entities such as armed groups would have an impact.[41]

Regarding individuals, although they are regarded, at least in some branches of international law, as subjects of it, it is less certain, according to an expression of M Akehurst,

> whether the practice of private individuals can create rules of customary law. All the same, there are few, if any, examples of individuals performing this function in fact… Of course, the reactions of States to the acts of individuals (eg by prosecuting or failing to prosecute them for assaulting diplomats) can give rise to customary law, but that is not the same as saying that the acts of individuals give rise to customary law. Individuals may form pressure groups to campaign for changes in the law, but the change is made by States and not by individuals. It is arguable that even writers on international law, who exercise more influence on international law

[38] Ibid, 7. Treves also notes: 'Certain rules of customary international law have been considered as applicable to non-State actors: the rule on self-defence has been invoked against terrorists, rules of international humanitarian law have been considered applicable to irregular armed formations. The impact of such applicability on the practice of the non-State actors concerned may have an impact on the scope of application of the customary rules concerned'.

[39] C Ryngaert, 'Non-State Actors and International Humanitarian Law', working paper (Katholieke Universiteit Leuven, Faculty of Law, Institute for International Law, 2008) 8 (emphasis in the original), available at https://www.law.kuleuven.be/iir/nl/onderzoek/wp/WP146e.pdf (accessed on 1 December 2014).

[40] A Roberts and S Sivakumaran, 'Lawmaking by Nonstate Actors: Engaging Armed Groups in the Creation of International Humanitarian Law' [2012] 37 *Yale Journal of International Law* 109, 150.

[41] Ibid.

than other individuals, have no effect unless or until their views are accepted by States or by international courts.[42]

B. Towards a Limited Acceptance of the Role of Non-state Actors in the Formation of International Custom

In any case, it seems that international jurisprudence tends, in some exceptional cases, to accept the contribution of the practice of non-state entities in the formation and crystallization of customary rules. These cases seem to have one thing in common: they pertain to the action of collective entities which were either created by states or their function is acceptable and desired by the states—such as international organizations of all kinds.

In the *Tadic* case, the ICTY referred to the contribution of the International Committee of the Red Cross (ICRC) to the development and implementation of international humanitarian law. The ICTY, having considered that, regarding 'the emergence of customary rules on internal armed conflict, the ICRC has made a remarkable contribution by appealing to the parties to armed conflicts to respect international humanitarian law', further stated that

> the practical results the ICRC has thus achieved in inducing compliance with international humanitarian law *ought therefore to be regarded as an element of actual international practice; this is an element that has been conspicuously instrumental in the emergence or crystallization of customary rules.*[43]

In this respect, Arajärvi notes that

> the Court did not discuss whether the reports or the practical functions carried out by the ICRC affect the formation of customary norms as such, or whether they are relevant merely through their influence on the states. Nonetheless, by referring to the ICRC, the Court paves the way for custom formation beyond state-dominated law creation.[44]

Further, the ICJ, in the *Reservations to the Genocide Convention* case, took into consideration the practice of the UN Secretary-General as depositary of the instruments of ratification of and accession to the Genocide Convention.[45] The Final Report of the ILA Committee on Formation of Customary (Gen-

[42] M Akehurst, 'Custom as a Source of International Law' (1974–75) 47 *British Yearbook on International Law* 11.

[43] *Prosecutor v Tadic (Decision on the Defence Motion for Interlocutory Appeal on Jurisdiction)* Case No IT-94-1-A1C Appeals Chamber, 2 October 1995, para 109 (emphasis added), at www.icty.org/x/cases/tadic/tdec/en/100895.htm.

[44] Arajärvi (n 32 above), 17.

[45] 'It may, however, be asked whether the General Assembly of the United Nations, in approving the Genocide Convention, had in mind the practice according to which the Secretary-General, in exercising his functions as a depositary, did not regard a reservation as definitively accepted until it had been established that none of the other contracting States objected to it': Reservations to the Convention of Genocide (Advisory Opinion) [1951] ICJ Reports 15.

eral) International Law (London Report) referred to this case in the context of the 11th Principle, according to which 'the practice of intergovernmental organizations in their own right is a form of "state practice"'.[46]

As far as certain resolutions of United Nations Organs are concerned, reference has already been made[47] to the legal significance of certain important resolutions of the UN General Assembly, regarding the verification of the *opinio juris* of states. Nevertheless, as rightly pointed out by Treves,

> in assessing their significance, caution is particularly necessary, as States often participate in the adoption of these resolutions in view of the fact that they are not binding. Declarations made upon adoption may also give indications relevant for assessing their significance. Caution is also necessary to distinguish provisions that can be considered as evidence of *opinio iuris* from those expressing the will to introduce new rules.[48]

However, the London Report made an important clarification, in relation to the identity of the practice that can emerge from a resolution of the United Nations:

> Organs of international organizations, and notably the UN General Assembly, also from time to time adopt resolutions containing Statements about customary international law. *Formally*, since the decision is recorded as a resolution of (the organ of the) organization, its adoption is a piece of practice *by the organization;* and some writers treat it in this way. However, in the context of the formation of customary international law, it is probably best regarded as a series of verbal acts by the individual member States participating in that organ. If so, it would add little or nothing to the weight of such practice *by the member States themselves* to treat the resolution itself (as distinct from voting for it) as a *further* piece of practice, this time on the part of the organization.[49]

The importance of the UN General Assembly resolutions for the formation of international custom was also recognized by international arbitration. The Iran–United States Claims Tribunal expressed its view on the matter in the *Sedco* case, stating that

> United Nations General Assembly resolutions are not as such binding upon states and generally are not evidence of customary law. Nevertheless, it is generally accepted that such resolutions in certain specified circumstances may be regarded as evidence of customary international law or can contribute—among other factors—to the creation of such law.[50]

[46] International Law Association, Committee on Formation of Customary (General) International Law, London Conference (2000), 'Final Report of the Committee, Statement of Principles Applicable to the Formation of General Customary International Law', 11.

[47] Section I(2)(b) above.

[48] Treves (n 7 above), 8.

[49] London Report, 19 (emphasis in the original).

[50] *Case concerning Sedco, Inc and National Iranian Oil Company and Iran (Interlocutory Award)* (27 March 1986) Iran-USCTR 25 ILM 33, available at http://www.iusct.net/ (accessed on 1 December 2014).

In the context of the work of the International Law Commission on the identification of international customary law, the Rapporteur M Wood approached the issue of the practice of international organizations in his Second Report.[51] Although the Rapporteur admitted that 'the acts of international organizations on which States have conferred authority may also contribute or attest to the formation of a general practice in the fields in which those organizations operate', he stressed the importance of the distinction 'between practice relating to the internal affairs of the organization on the one hand, and the practice of the organization in its relations with States, international organizations, etc., on the other'. On the basis of this distinction, he underlined that

> it is the latter practice that is relevant for present purposes, and which mostly consists of 'operational activities', defined . . . as 'the programmatic work of international organizations carried out as part of their overall mission or in fulfillment of a specific mandate'.[52]

The Rapporteur also draws our attention to further distinctions, which he considers necessary in order to measure accurately the role of the practice of international organizations:

> Another important distinction should be drawn . . . between the practice of organs or other bodies composed of the representatives of states and that of organs composed of individuals serving in their personal capacity, as the latter cannot be said to represent states. A distinction should, moreover, be made between products of the secretariats of international organizations and products of the intergovernmental organs of international organizations. While both can provide materials that can be consulted . . . the greater weight . . . [is] to be given to the products of the latter, whose authors are also the primary authors of state practice.[53]

Obviously these reservations finally led the Rapporteur to conclude that

> while it has been suggested that 'IOs provide shortcuts to finding custom', considerable caution is required in assessing their practice. Considerations that apply to the practice of states may also be relevant to the practice of international organizations, and the present report should be read in that light.[54]

III. CONCLUDING REMARKS

There is no doubt that international custom, as an equivalent source to treaties, is formed, in accordance with Article 38 of the Statute of the ICJ, through

[51] ILC, 'Second Report on Identification of Customary International Law' (Sixty-Sixth Session, Geneva 5 May–6 June and 7 July–8 August 2014) UN Doc A/CN.4/672.

[52] Ibid, para 43.

[53] Ibid.

[54] Ibid. The Rapporteur further notes that 'the practice of those international organizations (such as the European Union) to which Member States sometimes have transferred exclusive competences, may be equated with that of States, since in particular fields such organizations act in place of the Member States' (para 44).

the interaction of two elements, the material element of practice and the psychological element of the *opinio juris*.

Through time, regarding the importance and primacy of the two components of the customary rule, two opposing trends have developed, in the literature as well as international jurisprudence. The so-called traditional view—according to which international custom was mainly based on state practice—reflected voluntarist considerations, implementing the position of the Permanent Court of International Justice in the *Lotus* case, namely that 'the rules of law binding upon states . . . emanate from their own free will as expressed . . . by usages generally accepted as expressing principles of law'. The diametrically opposite view, mainly inspired by the ICJ's position in the *Nicaragua* case, focused on exploring the existence of an *opinio juris* through certain resolutions of the General Assembly of the United Nations, from which it could be diagnosed as a sort of consensus of the international community on specific issues.

This modern approach of international custom, despite meeting strong criticism due to the incompatibility of an 'instant' crystallization of *opinio juris* with the existence of a contrary, or even contradictory, practice, led part of the relevant doctrine and jurisprudence to instead resort, against such cases, to the concept of general principles of international law.

In any case, this same modern approach gave room for the emergence of the theoretical view that non-state entities, whose action in international affairs has now multiplied, can contribute, through their actions, to the creation of international customary rules.

Nevertheless, in most cases, the action of non-state actors has only an indirect or implicit effect on the practice of states, which thus remain the ultimate actors in international law, from a legal standpoint. Even in the context of international humanitarian law—where non-state actors such as armed groups have demonstrated a strong and powerful practice—scholars remained sceptical of the effective contribution of this practice to the creation of international custom, because of the often brutal nature of the NSAs' operations.

All of the above result in a limited acceptance of the role of non-state actors in the creation of international custom, mainly through the action and practice developed by international organizations. However, even in this case, major research projects—such as the relevant studies of the International Law Association and the reports already drawn up by the Rapporteur of the International Law Commission—insist that any effective acceptance of such practice must be based on the fact that relative action was undertaken by the organization per se and should not be credited to its member states.

In the light of these considerations, a final conclusion must be reached:so far, only state practice, as opposed to non-state actor practice, appears to be, formally and directly, taken into account for the formation and identification of international customary law.

Section 2

Factors and Structures Reconsidered

6

Disaster Relief in International Law

GABRIELLA VENTURINI*

I. DISASTER RELIEF AND INTERNATIONAL ORGANIZATION

THE DRAFT ARTICLES on the Protection of Persons in the Event of Disasters, as provisionally adopted by the International Law Commission (ILC), define *disaster* as 'a calamitous event or series of events resulting in widespread loss of life, great human suffering and distress, or large-scale material or environmental damage, thereby seriously disrupting the functioning of society'.[1] Both natural and human-made disasters are included in this definition; however, armed conflicts are excluded.[2] *Relief* includes all those actions which are aimed at meeting the immediate needs of disaster victims. Given the serious disruption of the functioning of society, national resources often prove inadequate to provide effective relief to disaster victims. Thus the international community has striven to promote cooperation in disaster relief since 1927, when the International Relief Union (IRU) was established and mandated with the coordination of international assistance in case of disaster. However, partly because no major disaster occurred in the following years, the IRU did not take any operational action during its existence. After World War II, Member States progressively abandoned the Union, and its secretariat officially closed in 1982: a rare example of an international organization which was shut down. But the promotion of cooperation in disaster relief had been taken up by the United Nations in 1971, when the Office

* This contribution is based on the results of a research project carried out by the Scuola Superiore Sant'Anna (Pisa), the University of Milan and the University of Modena and Reggio Emilia (A de Guttry. M Gestri and G Venturini (eds), *International Disaster Response Law*, (TMC Asser Press–Springer 2012), hereinafter: *IDRL* 2012). Further literature is included in Vol 55 of the *German Yearbook of International Law, Focus Disaster Preparedness and Response*, hereinafter: *GYIL* 2012.

[1] Art 3, Definition of disaster (A/CN.4/L.758).

[2] Art 4, Relationship with international humanitarian law (ibid).

of the United Nations Disaster Relief Coordinator (UNDRO) was established.[3] The UNDRO was subsequently merged with other emergency structures into the Department of Humanitarian Affairs and eventually transformed into the Office for the Coordination of Humanitarian Affairs (OCHA).[4] The coordination of humanitarian responses in disasters and emergencies is one of OCHA's key areas, which also include policy development and humanitarian advocacy.

II. THE ACTORS AND THE LAW OF DISASTER RELIEF

During the last decades, the realm of humanitarian assistance has been populated with a multitude of actors—states, intergovernmental and non-governmental organizations—increasing the difficulty of coordinating humanitarian actions and leading to the duplication and waste of resources.[5] At the same time, treaty law has flourished. A great number of bilateral, regional and sub-regional agreements have been concluded, often as a reaction to the occurrence of specific disasters. In several universal treaties regulating matters such as the transport of goods by sea or air, customs, health regulations, human rights, waste management and the protection of the environment, specific rules have been included stipulating states parties' obligations in the event of a natural or human-made disaster.[6] Moreover, a number of universal treaties regulate particular issues related to emergency situations, such as industrial or nuclear accidents, or the use of specific assets in disaster relief.[7]

[3] General Assembly Res 2816 (XXVI) of 14 December 1971.

[4] See http://www.unocha.org/about-us/who-we-are/history (accessed on 22 July 2013).

[5] See C-A Hofmann, 'NGO Certification: Time to Bite the Bullet?' (October 2011) 52 *Humanitarian Exchange Magazine*, available at http://www.odihpn.org/humanitarian-exchange-magazine/issue-52/ngo-certification-time-to-bite-the-bullet, 13–14 (accessed on 22 July 2013).

[6] Among these are the 1965 London Convention on Facilitation of International Maritime Traffic (section F); the International Standards and Recommended Practices, Facilitation, Annex 9 of 1997 to the Convention on International Civil Aviation (Chapter 8, letter C); the 1961 Customs Convention on the Temporary Importation of professional equipment; the 1973 International Convention on the simplification and harmonization of Customs procedures (Kyoto Convention, Revised 2000; the 1990 Istanbul Convention on Temporary Admission; the International Health Regulations 2005; the 1966 International Covenant on Civil and Political Rights (Art 4); the 1989 Basel Convention on the Control of Transboundary Movement of Hazardous Wastes and Their Disposal; the 1969 Bruxelles International Convention Relating to Intervention on the High Seas in Cases of Oil Pollution Casualties Intervention; the 1990 International Convention on Oil Pollution Preparedness, Response and Cooperation; and the 2000 London Protocol on Preparedness, Response and Cooperation to Pollution Incidents by Hazardous and Noxious Substances. See A de Guttry, 'Surveying the Law' [2012] *IDRL* 3, 34–35.

[7] See, eg the 1986 Convention on Early Notification of a Nuclear Accident; the 1986 Convention on Assistance in the Case of Nuclear Accident or Radiological Emergency; the 1992 Convention on the Transboundary Effects of Industrial Incidents; the 1992 United Nations Framework Convention on Climate Change and the 1997 Kyoto protocol thereto; the 1999 Tampere Convention on the Provision of Telecommunication Resources for Disaster Mitigation and Relief Operations; the 1999 Food Aid Convention; the 2000 Framework Convention in Civil Defence Assistance; the 2005 Revision of the International Health Regulations; and the 2005 Optional Protocol to the 1994 Convention on the Safety of United Nations and Associated Personnel. See de Guttry (ibid).

This fragmentation inevitably entails many incongruities among the various treaty levels, which considerably strain the legal discipline. Although the general principles on inter-temporal application of treaties[8] may help solve the legal problems, in practice, normative inconsistencies risk hampering the effectiveness of disaster relief.

Finally, disaster relief is currently managed in accordance with a multitude of soft law instruments adopted either by international organizations and intergovernmental conferences, or by NGOs in cooperation with states. These instruments have a proven record of great importance in influencing the behaviour of international actors, but in some cases they risk blurring the borders between soft law and positive law, and downgrading the status of certain obligations and rights which are already established by customary or treaty law.[9] Thus the need for a better synchronization and coordination of the codification activities regarding disaster relief is dramatically emerging in the international community.

III. SOVEREIGNTY V COOPERATION IN DISASTER RELIEF

Since disaster relief is the primary responsibility and falls within the jurisdiction of the state in whose territory the catastrophic event has occurred, any assistance from foreign states or international organizations is subject to the principle of consent. Therefore, the affected state is free to admit or prohibit entrance to persons providing assistance, as well as to related materials and services. Nevertheless, cases where assistance from abroad has been refused have been widely condemned by the international community.[10] Furthermore, a considerable number of bilateral and multilateral treaties concluded within the framework of regional organizations establish a duty of the parties to accept assistance. Customary international law is also moving in this direction. The ILC Draft Articles (as provisionally adopted) put the state affected by a disaster under the obligation to seek assistance where its national response capacity is inadequate.[11] Although the provision of external assistance requires the consent of the affected state, a right to offer assistance is recognized by states and international organizations, and consent must not be refused

[8] See Art 30 VCLT on Application of successive treaties relating to the same subject matter.

[9] See G Venturini, 'International Disaster Response Law in Relation with other Branches of International Law' [2012] *IDRL* 45, 53–56.

[10] In 2008, despite widespread destruction and severe human suffering caused by the Cyclone Nargis to the population of Myanmar, the government did not immediately allow international aid to access the affected areas. Intense pressure by the international community through the UN Secretary-General's good offices and the involvement of ASEAN eventually led to an effective humanitarian response. See M Costas Trascasas, 'Access to the Territory of a Disaster-Affected State' [2012] *IDRL* 220, 236–39.

[11] Art 10, Duty of the affected state to seek assistance (A/CN.4/L.794).

arbitrarily.[12] States are called upon to cooperate with each other, with the UN and with intergovernmental as well as non-governmental organizations in the provision of assistance.[13] The traditional principle of state sovereignty is thus being challenged by the duty to cooperate in providing relief to disaster victims, but it may be difficult to achieve a reasonable balance between the two.

Access to victims often proves difficult, and not only where consent is denied by the affected state. External emergency workers as well as foreign relief consignments encounter a vast array of obstacles, including administrative regulations, customs procedures and restrictions to the movement of persons, goods and services. A considerable body of law has been developed to deal with these issues, where soft law plays a central role: the present strategy of the United Nations recommends that states incorporate international non-governmental guidelines in their national legislation to facilitate emergency relief.[14]

IV. WHAT IS THE ROLE OF 'RESPONSIBILITY TO PROTECT'?

A controversial issue concerns the role of the 'Responsibility to Protect' (R2P) doctrine in relation to disaster situations. This has been discussed particularly with reference to the Myanmar events.[15] The current position within the United Nations holds that

> The responsibility to protect applies, until Member states decide otherwise, only to the four specified crimes and violations: genocide, war crimes, ethnic cleansing and crimes against humanity. To try to extend it to cover other calamities, such as HIV/AIDS, climate change or the *response to natural disasters*, would undermine the 2005 consensus and *stretch the concept* beyond recognition or operational utility.[16]

As far as diplomatic, humanitarian and other peaceful means are concerned, however, there is no reason why the R2P should not be extended to disaster victims; indeed, international practice is consistent with this assumption. It is also fair to say that the role of the United Nations and regional organizations is pivotal in ensuring the provision of protection and immediate relief to the victims of catastrophic events. In extreme cases, the Security Council could use its power to decide or authorize coercive action under Chapter VII of the UN Charter when it finds that a disaster triggers a threat to inter-

[12] Art 11, Consent of the affected state to external assistance, paras 1–2; Art 12, Offers of Assistance (A/CN.4/L.794).

[13] Art 5, Duty to cooperate (A/CN.4/L.758).

[14] See, inter alia, General Assembly Res 66/227 of 15 March 2012 on 'International cooperation on humanitarian assistance in the field of natural disasters, from relief to development', para 7; Res 67/87 of 7 December 2012 on 'Strengthening the coordination of emergency humanitarian assistance of the United Nations', para 17.

[15] Above n 10.

[16] 'Implementing the Responsibility to Protect', Report of the Secretary-General, A/63/677 of 12 January 2009, para 10(b) (emphasis added). See SE Davies, 'Natural Disasters and the Responsibility to Protect' [2012] *German Yearbook of International Law* 149.

national peace and security (eg causing massive cross-border flows of people). Unilateral coercive (let alone military) intervention would most likely worsen the situation of the victims and for this reason it should not be endorsed.

V. THE EMERGING RIGHT TO HUMANITARIAN ASSISTANCE

Disaster relief must be implemented in conformity with the international obligations established, inter alia, by human rights law, refugee law and global health law. Although a right to humanitarian assistance is not explicitly mentioned by the core human rights treaties, these (in particular the International Covenant on Civil and Political Rights and the International Covenant on Economic, Social and Cultural Rights) stipulate a number of rights relevant to disaster relief, such as the rights to life, food and water, housing, clothing, health, livelihood and freedom from discrimination.[17] International humanitarian law also applies when a disaster occurs during an armed conflict. More generally, international humanitarian law contains the basic foundational principles governing humanitarian assistance, ie humanity, impartiality and neutrality. Within this framework, a crucial question is whether individuals have a right to humanitarian assistance—ie to relief in the case of disaster. Such a right would result in a legal entitlement of certain persons, being identified as the victims of a disaster, to receive certain services, as set out in the appropriate legal instruments. The question is: who would be the corresponding duty bearers? Obviously, the territorial government has specific obligations to ensure the rights of all persons under its jurisdiction, including assistance in the case of disaster. But what if its national response capacity is inadequate? Does the duty to cooperate include an obligation owed to disaster victims by third states, international organizations or the international community as a whole? Such an interpretation would certainly excessively strain the realm of international law, and it is not currently supported by state practice. Obligations stipulated in bilateral and multilateral treaties covering disaster relief are typically owed to other states, not to individuals. Nevertheless, in the future, international law should develop in a different direction, ie towards recognizing that disaster victims have a right to request and receive humanitarian assistance not only from their government, but also from third states and international organizations. This path is already traced by a few international agreements concerning the protection of internally displaced persons, as well as by a number of soft law instruments.[18] The more a true right-based

[17] See A Creta, 'A (Human) Right to Humanitarian Assistance in Disaster Situations? Surveying Public International Law' [2012] *IDRL* 353; W Kälin, 'The Human Rights Dimension of Natural or Human-Made Disasters' [2012] *German Yearbook of International Law* 119.

[18] See D Fisher, 'The Right to Humanitarian Assistance' in W Kälin, RC Williams, K Koser and A Solomon (eds), *The Guiding Principles on Internal Displacement into Domestic Law: Issues and Challenges* (The American Society of International Law and The Brookings Institution, 2010) 47–128, 70.

approach focusing on the situation and the needs of individual victims is adopted, the more all institutions and entities will be held accountable towards those who are vulnerable to and affected by disasters.[19]

VI. THE FUTURE OF DISASTER RESPONSE

Although improving relief could help considerably to alleviate the situation of disaster victims, this is not the only way to enhance disaster response. Equally, and possibly even more, important are prevention, mitigation, preparedness and resilience in respect of disasters, which are embraced by the concept of disaster risk reduction (DRR), in respect of which international environmental law and the law of international development play an essential role.[20] In 2000, the United Nations Member States adopted the International Strategy for Disaster Reduction as a strategic framework to guide and coordinate the efforts of a wide range of partners to achieve a substantial reduction in disaster losses, aimed at building resilient nations and communities as an essential condition for sustainable development.[21] While states are the main actors in DRR, intergovernmental and non-governmental organizations and civil society itself are called upon to work together to reduce disaster risk. DRR policies contribute to the avoidance of health emergencies and environmental harm, thus making relief actions easier. Likewise, the sixth report on the protection of persons in the event of disasters by the ILC Special Rapporteur, Mr Eduardo Valencia-Ospina, emphasizes the duty of states to reduce the risk of disasters by adopting appropriate measures such as multi-hazard risk assessments, the collection and dissemination of loss and risk information, and the installation and operation of early warning systems.[22]

[19] In elaborating over the positive obligations that Art 2 of the ECHR poses on states to take appropriate steps to safeguards the lives of those under their jurisdiction, the European Court of Human Rights has also considered situations of disaster. See *Öneryildiz v Turkey* (ECtHR 48939/99, 30 November 2004) and *Budayeva and Others v Russia* (ECtHR 15339/02, 20 March 2008).

[20] For a definition of key terms see United Nations Office for Disaster Risk Reduction (UNISDR), *Living with Risk: A Global Review of Disaster Reduction Initiatives*, vol 2 (UNISDR, 2004), available at http://www.unisdr.org/files/657_lwr21.pdf, 1–9 (accessed on 3 February 2016).

[21] See http://www.unisdr.org/who-we-are/international-strategy-for-disaster-reduction (accessed on 28 July 2013). See also A La Vaccara, 'An Enabling Environment for Disaster Risk Reduction' [2012] *IDRL* 199; D Fisher, The Future of International Disaster Response Law' [2012] *German Yearbook of International Law* 87.

[22] A/CN.4/662, 3 May 2013.

7

After 60 Years: The International Legal Regime Protecting Stateless Persons—Stocktaking and New Tendencies

TAMÁS MOLNÁR*

I. SETTING THE SCENE

STATELESSNESS UNDER INTERNATIONAL law has not traditionally been at the forefront of academic research or the writings of legal scholars. Only a few monographs have been published on statelessness and nationality since World War II.[1] This chapter aims to present an overview of the legal status of stateless persons under international law, shedding light onto the rather sporadic but noteworthy legal developments after the adoption of the 1954 New York Convention on the Status of Stateless Persons, which celebrated its 60th anniversary in 2014.[2] It is thus timely to explore both the current legal framework on the universal and regional levels (*de lege lata*) and new tendencies in legal developments (*de lege ferenda*).

* Adjunct Professor, Corvinus University of Budapest, Institute of International Studies.

[1] Eg HF van Panhuys, *The Role of Nationality in International Law* (AW Sijthoff 1959); P Weis, *Nationality and Statelessness in International Law* (Sijthoff & Noordhoff, 1979); L van Waas, *Nationality Matters: Statelessness under International Law* (Intersentia, 2008); R Likibi, *Le droit de l'apatridie, pratiques et controversies* (Publibook, 2013). The newest reference book devoted to the topic is a collected volume edited by L van Waas and A Edwards (*Nationality and Statelessness under International Law*, Cambridge University Press, 2014, 306 pages).

[2] For example, the First Global Forum on Statelessness, held in The Hague on 15–17 September 2014 (co-organized by Tilburg University and UNHCR), was devoted to this occasion. At the end of November 2014, UNHCR started its 10-year campaign to eradicate statelessness by 2024 in the context of this commemoration. See http://www.unhcr.org/pages/53174c306.html (last accessed on 12 January 2015).

II. INTRODUCTION INTO THE WORLD OF 'LEGAL GHOSTS'

According to a recent estimate of the Office of the United Nations High Commissioner for Refugees (UNHCR), 10 million people continue to be denied the right to a nationality,[3] and the existence of such 'legal ghosts' is likely to persist for a long time. The biggest stateless populations can be found in the Middle East, Asia and the Caribbean,[4] but it is also noteworthy in Europe (with around 640,000 stateless individuals[5]).

1. Statelessness can occur in the migratory context (typically in European countries), though there are also large in situ stateless populations (eg in Burma, Nepal, Thailand, Syria). Many factors can lead to statelessness, such as: state successions (the most common reason since the 1990s); conflicting nationality laws leading to the non-acquisition or loss of nationality; arbitrary deprivation of nationality as an extreme form of discriminatory state policy; lack of birth registration; extremely burdensome administrative practices with regard to naturalization procedures; and the trafficking of human beings.[6] In the future, statelessness may even occur as a result of the sinking of small island states due to a rise in the ocean level induced by climate

[3] UNHCR, '2012 Global Trends. Displacement: The New 21th Century Challenge' (2013) 2, 7, 41, available at http://unhcr.org/globaltrendsjune2013/UNHCR%20GLOBAL%20TRENDS%20 2012_V05.pdf (last accessed on 12 January 2015). By the end of 2012, UNHCR had identified some 3.34 million stateless persons in 72 countries. However, UNHCR estimated that the overall number of stateless persons worldwide, given the hidden character of the phenomenon, could be far higher—about 10 million people. According to estimates of the Open Society Institute, being recently involved in the advocacy activities related to statelessness, this number is even higher, around 15 million (http://www.opensocietyfoundations.org/projects/statelessness (last accessed on 12 January 2015)).

[4] K Southwick and M Lynch, *Nationality Rights for All: A Progress Report and Global Survey on Statelessness* (Refugees International, 2009) 28–53, available at http://www.refintl.org/sites/default/files/RI%20stateless%20Report_FINAL_031109.pdf (last accessed on 12 January 2015); see also UNHCR Global Appeal 2014–2015, 'Addressing Statelessness', available at http://www.unhcr.org/528a0a1316.html (last accessed on 15 October 2014); http://www.opensocietyfoundations.org/projects/stateless/where-does-statelessness-happen (last accessed on 12 January 2015); http://www.state.gov/documents/organization/181258.pdf (last accessed on 12 January 2015).

[5] Viewpoint of 9 June 2008 of the Council of Europe Commissioner for Human Rights: 'No One Should Have to Be Stateless in Today's Europe', available at http://www.coe.int/t/commissioner/viewpoints/080609_EN.asp (last accessed on 12 January 2015). See also: 'The Rights of Stateless Persons must be Protected', statement by Thomas Hammarberg, Commissioner for Human Rights of the Council of Europe, at the 4th Council of Europe Conference on Nationality 'Concepts of Nationality in the Globalised World' (CommDH/Speech(2010)13), Strasbourg, 17 December 2010.

[6] For more see, eg M Verwilghen, 'Conflits des nationalités. Plurinationalité et apatridie' (1999) 277 *Recueil des Cours de l'Academie de Droit International de la Haye* 122; M Achiron, *Nationality and Statelessness. A Handbook for Parliamentarians* (Inter-Parliamentary Union—United Nations High Commissioner for Refugees, 2005) 27–42; van Waas (n 1 above), chs IV–VII; K Southwick and M Lynch (n 4 above) 2–3; BK Blitz and M Lynch, 'Statelessness and the Deprivation of Nationality' in BK Blitz and M Lynch (eds), *Statelessness and Citizenship. A Comparative Study on the Benefits of Nationality* (Edward Elgar 2012) 5–10; Likibi (n 1 above), 72–99.

change.[7] Because of their lack of nationality, stateless people are a particularly vulnerable group, often marginalized and legally invisible ('legal ghosts'). Given its specific nature, statelessness remains a largely hidden phenomenon, especially with regard to government recognition. Therefore, identification and mapping are major challenges, as highlighted and promoted by the UNHCR as the principal UN agency responsible for the identification and protection of stateless people. Projects mapping statelessness have recently been conducted in a number of countries, including the United Kingdom,[8] Belgium,[9] the Netherlands,[10] Slovenia,[11] Poland[12] and Malta.[13]

2. The international legal regime governing the protection of stateless persons currently in force was created in the 1950s; since then the issue was practically forgotten for decades, and was largely absent from the global human rights agenda, too.[14] A turning point came in the 1990s, due to a number of factors. First, the UNHCR's mandate was expanded in 1995 by the UN General Assembly, as a result of which the UNHCR was given a specific and global mandate to prevent and reduce statelessness as well as to protect non-refugee stateless persons[15] (it is important to note that this mandate is not limited to state parties to the statelessness conventions, but gives a global authorization to act).[16] Secondly, the dissolution of states and the creation of new ones following the

[7] For more see J McAdam, 'Disappearing States, Statelessness and the Boundaries of International Law', UNSW Law Research Paper No 2010-2; J McAdam, *Climate Change, Forced Migration, and International Law* (Oxford University Press, 2012) 119–60.

[8] UNHCR, 'Mapping Statelessness in The United Kingdom' (November 2011), available at http://www.refworld.org/docid/4ecb6a192.html (last accessed on 12 January 2015).

[9] UNHCR, 'Mapping Statelessness in Belgium' (October 2012), available at http://www.refworld.org/docid/5100f4b22.html (last accessed on 12 January 2015).

[10] UNHCR, 'Mapping Statelessness in the Netherlands' (November 2011), available at http://www.refworld.org/docid/4eef65da2.html (last accessed on 12 January 2015).

[11] UNHCR, 'Statelessness in Slovenia: The Identification and Protection of Stateless Persons in Slovenia' (November 2013) (manuscript with the author).

[12] The Halina Niec Legal Aid Center, 'The Invisible. Stateless Persons in Poland (Executive Summary)' (December 2013), available at http://www.pomocprawna.org/images/stories/Pomoc_migrantom/The_Insvisible_stateless_Persons_in_Poland_2013_Summary.pdf (last accessed on 12 January 2015).

[13] UNHCR, 'Mapping Statelessness in Malta' (August 2014), available at http://www.unhcr.org.mt/news-and-views/press-releases/774 (last accessed on 12 January 2015).

[14] See also, eg M Fullerton, 'Without Protection: Refugees and Statelessness. A Commentary and Challenge', Brooklyn Law School Legal Studies Research Paper No 351 (August 2013), 2.

[15] The UNHCR's role in the field of statelessness dates back to 1974, when the UNGA entrusted the UNHCR with a specific role under Article 11 of the 1961 Convention on the Reduction of Statelessness (*cf* UNGA Resolution 3274 (XXIV) of 10 December 1974). Since then the UNHCR has been given a broader and horizontal mandate in this regard by a series of UNGA resolutions (most importantly by UNGA RES/50/152, 21 December 1995), ie the agency was asked to continue its activities on behalf of stateless persons, to promote accession to and implementation of the 1954 and 1961 UN conventions, and to provide relevant technical and advisory services pertaining to the preparation and implementation of nationality legislation to interested states: UNHCR, 'Self-Study Module on Statelessness' (1 October 2012) 12–13, available at http://www.refworld.org/docid/50b899602.html (last accessed on 12 January 2015).

[16] *Cf* M Manly and L van Waas, 'The Value of the Human Security Framework in Addressing Statelessness' in A Edwards and C Ferstman, *Human Security and Non-Citizens* (Cambridge University Press, 2010) 58, fn 30.

end of the cold war was also a major cause of new stateless populations (eg in the former Soviet and Yugoslav republics, Eritrea), and shed more light on this phenomenon which had started to re-emerge on the international political and human rights agenda. Thirdly, the UNHCR launched a global campaign in 1996 to increase the number of ratifications of the two major universal legal instruments on statelessness and to promote this cause worldwide, along with the widespread dissemination of information.[17] Finally, the latest symbolic event highlighting all these efforts and developments, as well as paving the way for the mid-term future, was the December 2011 Intergovernmental Ministerial Event in Geneva, organized by the UNHCR on the occasion of the 60th anniversary of the 1951 Refugee Convention and the 50th anniversary of the 1961 Statelessness Convention, where over 60 states made statelessness-related pledges (these included accession to the statelessness conventions, law reform to prevent or reduce statelessness, and improvement of civil registration systems).[18] This breakthrough was described by the then UN High Commissioner for Refugees, Mr Antonio Guterres, as a quantum leap forward in relation to the protection of stateless people, contributing also to significantly expanding awareness of the problem of statelessness in all regions.[19]

III. RESPONSES OF THE INTERNATIONAL COMMUNITY TO TACKLE STATELESSNESS

1. After the creation of the UN, when statelessness was a major cause for concern as an aftermath of World War II, two parallel approaches were formulated by the international community in order to tackle this negative phenomenon. The first focuses on preventing future statelessness and reducing the existing number of stateless persons as much as possible. This attempt is marked principally by the 1961 UN Convention on the Reduction of Statelessness[20] being the universally recognized general instrument in this matter and, as a specific instrument with a limited scope, by the 1957 UN Convention on the Nationality of Married Women.[21] In addition, a number of other, not so comprehensive, treaties appeared on the regional (European) level, elaborated under the aegis of the Commission Internationale de l'Etat Civil (CIEC) and

[17] The legal basis and authorization for UNHCR's global campaign was Conclusion No 78 of Executive Committee of the High Commissioner's Programme on Prevention and Reduction of Statelessness and the Protection of Stateless Persons [ExCom Conclusion No 78 (XLVI), points (c)–(d)].

[18] UNHCR, 'Ministerial Intergovernmental Event on Refugees and Stateless Persons—Pledges 2011' (October 2012) 32–36, available at http://www.refworld.org/docid/50aca6112.html (last accessed on 12 January 2015).

[19] Ibid, 8.

[20] Convention on the Reduction of Statelessness of 30 August 1961 (UNTS No 14458, vol 989, 175.).

[21] Convention on the Nationality of Married Women of 20 February 1957 (UNTS No 4468, vol 309, 65).

the Council of Europe (CoE).[22] This specific legal framework is embedded in the general international human rights law, completed and strengthened by provisions relating to the right to a nationality as a human right[23] ('the right to have rights').[24]

2. Nevertheless, despite all these efforts, the number of stateless persons will never reach zero. Therefore, representing the other approach, a new, autonomous legal status was created by virtue of the 1954 New York Convention relating to the Status of Stateless Persons,[25] aimed at providing an appropriate standard of international protection, a status comparable to other forms of international protection, such as refugee status. In today's international law, it is still the 1954 New York Convention alone, more than 60 years after its adoption, under which stateless people enjoy specific international legal protection, as it contains the basic rights determining their legal status.

Besides the 1954 New York Convention as a *lex specialis*, certain core human rights treaties are also applicable to stateless persons, notably those human rights contained in these instruments which are applicable to everyone, irrespective of nationality (eg the majority of civil and political rights, and some economic, cultural and social rights). The rationale behind this logic is that 'the rights of the individual do not spring from the fact that he is a citizen of a given state, but from the fact that he is a member of the human family'.[26] A great illustration of this approach is provided by General Comment No 15 of the Human Rights Committee on the position of non-nationals: 'the rights set forth in the Covenant apply to everyone, irrespective of reciprocity, and irrespective of his or her nationality or statelessness'.[27] The

[22] See, in chronological order, the 1973 CIEC Convention No 13 to Reduce the Number of Cases of Statelessness; then two Council of Europe instruments: the 1997 European Convention on Nationality (CETS No 166), ch VI and the 2006 Council of Europe Convention on the Avoidance of Statelessness in relation to State Succession (CETS No 200).

[23] See, first, the 1948 Universal Declaration of Human Rights (Art 15); then a series of subsequent universal treaties: 1965 Convention on the Elimination of All Forms of Racial Discrimination (Art 5); the 1966 International Covenant on Civil and Political Rights (Art 24); the 1979 Convention on the Elimination of All Forms of Discrimination against Women (Art 9); the 1989 Convention on the Rights of the Child (Arts 7 and 8); the 2006 Convention on the Rights of Persons with Disabilities (Art 18) or other regional human rights treaties, such as the 1969 American Convention on Human Rights; the 1990 African Charter on the Rights and Welfare of the Child; the 1995 Commonwealth of Independent States Convention on Human Rights and Fundamental Freedoms; or the 2004 Revised Arab Charter on Human Rights.

[24] 'Citizenship is man's basic right for it is nothing less than the right to have rights' (United States Supreme Court Chief Justice Earl Warren, in *Trop v Dulles, Secretary of State et al*, 356 US 86, 1958).

[25] Convention relating to the Status of Stateless Persons of 28 September 1954 (UNTS No 5158, vol 360, 117).

[26] UN, 'Our Rights as Human Beings: A Discussion Guide on the Universal Declaration of Human Rights' (New York, 1949) 13. Quoted by van Waas (n 1 above), 221.

[27] Human Rights Committee, 'CCPR General Comment No 15: The Position of Aliens under the Covenant' (Geneva, 11 April 1986). See also Human Rights Committee, General Comment 31: Nature of the General Legal Obligation Imposed on States Parties to the Covenant, CCPR/C/21/Rev.1/Add.13 (Geneva, 26 May 2004) para 10. In the legal literature, see, eg D Weissbrodt and C Collins, 'The Human Rights of Stateless Persons' (2006) 28 *Human Rights Quarterly* 254.

1954 New York Convention itself refers to and establishes links with general human rights law, serving as the 'legal safety net' behind the specific status and protection created by the Convention when reaffirming in its preamble 'the principle that human beings shall enjoy fundamental rights and freedoms without discrimination'; nevertheless 'it is desirable to regulate and improve the status of stateless persons by an international agreement' and 'to assure stateless persons the widest possible exercise of these fundamental rights and freedoms'.[28]

3. Historically, after a number of unsuccessful attempts under the auspices of the League of Nations,[29] the origins of the current international law framework protecting stateless people can be found in the 1951 Geneva Convention on the Status of Refugees[30] and its *travaux préparatoires*. The story began in 1948, when the United Nations Economic and Social Council requested of the UN Secretary General that a study be undertaken and recommendations made on the situation of stateless persons.[31] This 'Study on Statelessness', finished in 1949, led to the formation of an ad hoc committee to consider, amongst others, the desirability of an international convention relating to the status and protection of both refugees and stateless persons.[32] In February 1950, a Draft Convention relating to the Status of Refugees was elaborated, accompanied by a Draft Protocol relating to the Status of Stateless Persons. As a result, the United Nations General Assembly (UNGA) decided to convene a diplomatic conference, which adopted in 1951 Refugee Convention; however, the Draft Protocol relating to the Status of Stateless Persons was not adopted (it was referred back to the UNGA). In 1954, a new conference of plenipotentiaries was convened in New York to revise the Draft Protocol on the Status of Stateless Persons.[33] During the Conference, however, the delegates decided to make a separate instrument from the 1951 Convention, thus setting aside the protocol approach and adopted a distinct, self-standing Statelessness Convention that was completely independent from the 1951 Convention.[34] The text of

[28] See also, in a different context, van Waas (n 1 above), 226.

[29] *Cf* the 1930 Hague Convention on Certain Questions relating to the Conflict of Nationality Laws (No 4137, 179 LNTS 89) and its 1930 Protocol on a Certain Case of Statelessness (No 4138, 179 LNTS 115); then the 1930 Special Protocol concerning Statelessness (C.27.M.16.1931.V—never entered into force). For more on this see, eg UN, 'A Study of Statelessness' (New York, August 1949) E/1112; E1112/Add.1, 128–30; M Stiller, 'Statelessness in International Law: A Historic Overview', *DAJV Newsletter*, 3/2012, 97–98. It is worth mentioning that during the interwar period, after the above Conference for the Codification of International Law in The Hague, the Institute of International Law elaborated a resolution to the attention of states on the desired legal status of stateless persons (*Statut juridique des apatrides et des réfugiés* (rapporteur: M. Arnold Raestad), Institut de Droit International, Session de Bruxelles—1936, le 24 avril 1936).

[30] Convention Relating to the Status of Refugees of 28 July 1951 (UNTS No 2545, vol 189, 137).

[31] UN, 'A Study of Statelessness' (n 29 above).

[32] N Robinson, *Convention Relating to the Status of Stateless Persons: Its History and Interpretation* (Institute of Jewish Affairs, 1955; reprinted by UNHCR, 1997) 1–2.

[33] Conference of Plenipotentiaries on the Status of Stateless Persons convened by Economic and Social Council resolution 526 A (XVII) of 26 April 1954.

[34] C Batchelor, 'The 1954 Convention Relating to the Status of Stateless Persons: Implementation within the European Union Member States and Recommendations for Harmonisation' (2004)

the 1954 Convention in large part mirrors that of the 1951 Geneva Convention (eg the set of rights provided for in the 1954 Statelessness Convention is similar to those in the 1951 Refugee Convention).[35] Nonetheless, despite the common roots and needs to be fulfilled, the overall protection regime of the stateless is much less well developed than international refugee law.

IV. SCOPE AND CONTENT OF THE 1954 NEW YORK CONVENTION: AN OVERVIEW

According to the UNHCR, the 1954 New York Convention is 'the primary international instrument adopted to date to regulate and improve the legal status of stateless persons and to ensure to stateless persons fundamental rights and freedoms without discrimination'.[36] One can only fully agree with this, since the 1954 New York Convention establishes a specific, autonomous legal status for stateless individuals, with accompanying civil, political, economic, cultural and social rights. It is the only international legal instrument to do so.[37] It therefore goes without saying that any investigation into the protection regime of stateless persons under international law should start by analysing the scope, concept and main provisions of the Convention.

1. With regard to its scope *ratione personae*, the 1954 New York Convention applies to non-refugee stateless persons (stateless refugees are covered by the 1951 Geneva Convention[38]) and its definition strictly covers so-called *de iure* stateless persons. It stipulates that '[f]or the purpose of this Convention, the term "stateless person" means a person who is not considered as a national by any State under the operation of its law'.[39] The International

22 *Refuge* 34; *Statelessness: The Quiet Torture of Belonging Nowhere* (Coventry Peace House, 2008) 15–16; van Waas (n 1 above), 226–27; GS Goodwin-Gill, 'Introductory Note, Convention Relating to the Status of Stateless Persons, New York, 28 September 1954' (UN Audiovisual Library of International Law, 1954), available at http://legal.un.org/avl/ha/cssp/cssp.html.

35 As Robinson (n 32 above), 25, notes, 'the prevailing view of the conference was that for a practical consideration (time) they should not engage in rewording the text of the 1951 Refugee Convention, except when this was justified by the difference between the two groups (refugees vs. Stateless persons)'. See also P Weis, 'The Convention Relating to the Status of Stateless Persons' (1961) 10 *International and Comparative Law Quarterly* 255; van Waas (n 1 above), 227.

36 UNHCR, 'Information and Accession Package: The 1954 Convention relating to the Status of Stateless Persons and the 1961 Convention on the Reduction of Statelessness' (Geneva, January 1999) 10. Quoted by van Waas (n 1 above), 228.

37 Manly and van Waas (n 16 above), 54. Similarly, but in the context of criticizing the 1954 Convention, see van Waas (n 1 above), 393–94.

38 Convention relating to the Status of Refugees of 28 June 1951, Art 1A(2).

39 For a thorough analysis and interpretation of this seemingly straightforward but, if one deconstructs it, actually complex and difficult definition, see UNHCR, 'Expert Meeting—The Concept of Stateless Persons under International Law ("Prato Conclusions")' (May 2010), available at http://www.refworld.org/docid/4ca1ae002.html (last accessed on 12 January 2015); UNHCR, 'Guidelines on Statelessness No 1: The Definition of "Stateless Person" in Article 1(1) of the 1954 Convention relating to the Status of Stateless Persons' (20 February 2012), HCR/GS/12/01, available at http://www.refworld.org/docid/4f4371b82.html (last accessed on 12 January 2015). The

Law Commission (ILC) has observed that the definition in Article 1(1) of the New York Convention is now part of customary international law.[40] It should be noted, however, that not all stateless persons falling under the definition of Article 1(1) are entitled to benefit from this protection regime. According to the exclusion clause, the New York Convention shall not apply to: (i) persons receiving from UN agencies other than the UNHCR (eg United Nations Relief and Works Agency) protection or assistance so long as they are receiving it; (ii) persons recognized by the competent authorities of the country of residence as having the rights and obligations which are attached to the possession of the nationality of that country; and (iii) persons having committed a crime against peace, a war crime, a crime against humanity or a serious non-political crime outside the country of their residence prior to their admission to that country or having been guilty of acts contrary to the purposes and principles of the UN.[41]

2. The set of rights provided for in the New York Convention is similar to those in the 1951 Geneva Convention. Some 30 provisions of the New York Convention set out a minimum standard of treatment for stateless persons, without discrimination, beyond which states are free to extend additional protection and rights.[42] Three different levels of protection are established: first, treatment at least as favourable as that accorded to aliens generally; secondly, treatment on a par with nationals; and thirdly, the absolute rights which are not contingent upon the treatment of any other group, but are guaranteed directly.[43] The rights in respect to which treatment at least as favourable as that accorded to aliens generally in the same circumstances applies are, inter alia: the acquisition of movable and immovable property; the right of association; the right to engage in wage-earning employment; the right to self-employment; the right to housing; and the right to choose the place of residence and to move freely within the country.[44] Regarding the next, higher level of legal protection, stateless persons shall enjoy the same protection as is accorded to nationals of the country of residence with respect to: freedom of religion; access to courts, including legal assistance; elementary education; public relief and assistance; remuneration, hours of work, minimum age of employment, etc. and social security; and duties, charges or taxes, etc. The absolute rights reflecting their special needs are: the right to non-discrimination; the issuance

latter may be conceived as the authentic interpretation of this key provision in the 1954 Convention in the light of the rules on the interpretation of treaties of the 1969 VCLT.

[40] 'Draft Articles on Diplomatic Protection with Commentaries' (2006) II-ii *Yearbook of the International Law Commission* 49.

[41] Art 1(2) of the 1954 New York Convention.

[42] Ibid, Art 5.

[43] See also van Waas (n 1 above), 230–31; UNHCR, 'Guidelines No 3: The Status of Stateless Persons at the National Level' (17 July 2012), HCR/GS/12/03, point 11, available at http://www.refworld.org/docid/5005520f2.html (last accessed on 12 January 2015).

[44] For a comprehensive analysis of protecting civil, political, economic, cultural and social rights of stateless persons under the 1954 New York Convention and general human rights law see van Waas (n 1 above), chs X–XII.

of identity papers (if the person does not possess a valid travel document); the issuance of travel documents; and facilitated naturalization. It should be emphasized that, since there is no element of persecution (risk of persecution) in the case of statelessness, no similar protection against refoulement like in the 1951 Geneva Convention is provided for stateless persons. However, the 1954 Convention sets forth in Article 31 that the contracting states shall not expel a stateless person lawfully from their territory save on grounds of national security or public order, and such expulsion shall be only in pursuance of a decision reached in accordance with the due process of law. On the other hand, in return for giving the above entitlements to the stateless, 'the responsibility placed on states to respect, protect and fulfil 1954 Convention rights is balanced by the obligation in Article 2 of the same treaty that stateless persons abide by the laws of the country in which they find themselves'.[45]

3. Another classification for the rights enshrined in the 1954 Convention is the level of attachment of the stateless person with the state concerned.[46] First, in order to benefit from certain provisions, the mere physical presence[47] of the individual, satisfying the 'stateless person' definition, is sufficient (eg in relation to non-discrimination, status, property, access to courts, rationing, public education or administrative assistance). Secondly, some other rights are conferred on those stateless persons who are 'lawfully in' or 'lawfully staying in' the territory of a contracting party (this set of rights includes, amongst others: the right of association; the right to work; the right to engage in self-employment; the right to public relief; labour and social security rights; the freedom of movement; and the right to a travel document or the protection from expulsion). Thirdly, further rights are only given to stateless persons who are 'habitually resident' in the territory of a given state (eg exemption from legislative reciprocity, artistic rights and industrial property).

4. The international protection regime of stateless persons cannot be compared to international refugee law, where, in addition to the 1951 Refugee Convention, the UNHCR ExCom and other bodies (non-judicial and judicial ones) have developed detailed conventional rules and interpreted on several occasions the meaning of different concepts, such as the act of persecution and the principle of non-refoulement. International refugee law has been constantly evolving since its creation, while the only international instrument for the protection of stateless people is the 1954 New York Convention; and we have not witnessed such a rich and constantly growing soft law and jurispru-

[45] UNHCR, 'Guidelines No 3' (n 43 above), point 12.

[46] van Waas (n 1 above), 229-30; L van Waas, 'Nationality and Rights' in Blitz and Lynch (n 6 above) 29–30; UNHCR, 'Guidelines No 3' (ibid), points 13–20.

[47] Other scholars differentiate between the terms 'being subject to the state's jurisdiction' and the 'physical presence' according to the wording of the Convention (although neither of these expressions is used in its text). See van Waas (n 1 above), 229–30; van Waas (ibid) 29. I treat these situations as the same since I cannot see any real difference in the formulae contained in the relevant articles of the 1954 Convention; the common feature is that the stateless person must be present on the territory of a given contracting party in order to benefit from those entitlements.

dence in this field either. Further, as mentioned above, no supervisory body has been set up for a long time to monitor the situation of stateless persons under the jurisdiction of the contracting states. This is in contrast to the 1951 Refugee Convention, in relation to which the UNHCR had always played a major monitoring and implementing role since its adoption. Another weakness of the system is that the 1954 New York Convention is not, by its substance, a self-executing treaty. Not only do its content and broad, insufficiently precise formulation of the rights suggest, but Article 33 also explicitly stipulates that states have to adopt domestic legislation to make it effective, and they are obliged to communicate those domestic laws to the UN Secretary General. Moreover, the New York Convention does not contain provisions for the procedure to determine statelessness either (it is up to the individual states to establish such legal channels), which omission makes claiming those rights more difficult if one cannot officially obtain that status.[48] To sum up, international statelessness law has been all but forgotten for long decades.

V. SUBSEQUENT DEVELOPMENTS OF THE PROTECTION REGIME UNDER INTERNATIONAL LAW

A. Horizontal Issues

Despite having hitherto been forgotten, statelessness has recently reappeared on the mainstream international human rights agenda.[49] The gradual growth in importance of this issue is evidenced, first, in the recurring appearance of the topic in the activities of various international institutions and bodies, such

[48] On the need to establish such procedures, see: UNHCR, 'Guidelines on Statelessness No 2: Procedures for Determining Whether an Individual is a Stateless Person' (5 April 2012), HCR/GS/12/02, available at http://www.refworld.org/docid/4f7dafb52.html (last accessed on 12 January 2015); G Gyulai, 'Statelessness Determination and the Protection Status of Stateless Persons. A Summary Guide of Good Practices and Factors to Consider when Designing National Determination and Protection Mechanisms' (European Network on Statelessness 2013), available at http://www.statelessness.eu/resources/ens-good-practice-guide-statelessness-determination-and-protection-status-stateless (last accessed on 12 January 2015).

[49] See, eg BK Blitz, 'Policy Responses and Global Discourses on the Rights of Non-citizens and Stateless People' in BK Blitz and C Sawyer (eds), *Statelessness in the European Union. Displaced, Undocumented, Unwanted* (Cambridge University Press, 2011) 118–23; L Kingston, 'Moving Statelessness Forward on the International Human Rights Agenda', available at http://www.statelessness.eu/blog/moving-statelessness-forward-international-human-rights agenda#sthash.Ml6IGcbe.dpuf (last accessed on 12 January 2015); L Kingston, '"A Forgotten Human Rights Crisis": Statelessness and Issue (Non)Emergence' (2013) 14 *Human Rights Review* 73; L Kingston, 'Statelessness and Issue (Non-)Emergence' (2012) 40 *Forced Migration Review* 50. Generally on the emergence studies see, eg CR Carpenter, 'Setting the Advocacy Agenda: Theorizing Issue Emergence and Nonemergence in Transnational Advocacy Networks' (2007) 51 *International Studies Quarterly* 99.

as the UNHCR, the UNGA,[50] the UN Human Rights Council[51] and different treaty bodies.[52] Secondly, in the last few years the number of accessions to the 1954 New York Convention has increased continually (18 new state parties since December 2011), and even more new accessions are to come as a result of the pledges state made at the December 2011 Intergovernmental Ministerial Conference. Thirdly, topics related to statelessness have attracted greater academic interest, too, as a result of which there has been much wider academic research and more scholarly writings (legal, political, sociological and interdisciplinary), policy-oriented study (eg the Open Society Institute's initiative[53] and that of the International Observatory on Statelessness[54]) and institutionalized networking (eg the creation of the European Network on Statelessness).[55] On the international policy-making level, all these positive developments and newly acquired attention have culminated in the elaboration and adoption of a series of UNHCR soft law instruments (guidelines) interpreting and explaining in greater depth the main features, concepts, logic and provisions of the major international treaty instruments on statelessness.[56] Another significant development is the mushrooming of national statelessness determination procedures throughout the world (most of which have been introduced in Europe, but the Americas and Asia are also on the map).[57] Thus, despite the silence of the 1954 Statelessness Convention on this matter, individual states, cooperating with each other, took their own positive steps

[50] For the statelessness-related UNGA resolutions see 'United Nations General Assembly Resolutions of Particular Relevance to Statelessness and Nationality' (25 March 2013), available at http://www.refworld.org/docid/4c49a02c2.html (last accessed on 12 January 2015).

[51] Mainly from the point of view of the right to a nationality and the prohibition of arbitrary deprivation of nationality see UNHCR, 'Human Rights Council Resolutions Relating to Nationality and Statelessness', available at http://www.refworld.org/statelessness.html (last accessed on 12 January 2014). In the framework of the Universal Periodic Review see UNHCR, 'Compilation of Recommendations relating to Statelessness Made during the First Cycle (1st–12th Sessions) of the Human Rights Council's Universal Periodic Review' (11 July 2013), available at http://www.refworld.org/docid/51dfaf484.html (last accessed on 12 January 2015); UNHCR, 'Compilation of Recommendations relating to Statelessness Made during the Second Cycle (13th–16th Sessions) of the Human Rights Council's Universal Periodic Review' (11 July 2013), available at http://www.refworld.org/docid/51dfb0ee4.html (last accessed on 12 January 2015).

[52] For the relevant texts produced by these treaty bodies see UNHCR, 'Extracts of Selected General Comments and Recommendations of the United Nations Human Rights Treaty Bodies relating to Nationality and Statelessness', available at http://www.unhcr.org/4517ab402.html (last accessed on 12 January 2015).

[53] See http://www.opensocietyfoundations.org/projects/statelessness.

[54] See http://www.nationalityforall.org/.

[55] On the renaissance of social science scholarship on statelessness see Manly and van Waas (n 16 above), 50; BK Blitz and C Sawyer, 'Statelessness in the European Union' in Blitz and Sawyer (n 50 above), 7–14; L van Waas and M Manly, 'The State of Statelessness Research. A Human Rights Imperative' (2014) 19 *Tilburg Law Review* 3.

[56] After expert consultations, UNHCR has published four sets of guidelines, relating to the definition of stateless person, the national statelessness determination procedures, the legal status of recognized stateless persons at the national level and children's right to acquire nationality (see the references below). A fifth set of guidelines, concerning loss/deprivation of nationality under the 1961 Convention on the Reduction of Statelessness, is in preparation.

[57] In order to get a general picture about these procedures see, eg Gyulai (n 48 above).

to fill this gap and to grant effective access to the rights offered via the 1954 Convention for the 'legal ghosts' by officially identifying them.

B. Specific Domains

Progressive developments on specific issues of law related to statelessness have sporadically been made and are enshrined in a number of subsequently adopted international instruments.

1. Considering these thematically, the progress made in the field of consular protection of stateless persons is worthy of attention first. The starting point is the Schedule to Article 28 of the 1954 Convention, which declares that the delivery of travel document 'does not in any way entitle the holder to the protection of the diplomatic or consular authorities of the country of issue, and does not ipso facto confer on these authorities a right to protection'.[58]

The 1967 Council of Europe Convention on Consular Functions took a different approach,[59] its Article 46(1) stipulating:

> [a] consular officer of the state where a stateless person has his habitual residence, may protect such a person as if [the consular officer is entitled to protect the nationals of the sending state], provided that the person concerned is not a former national of the receiving state.

Thus the Council of Europe Convention, applying the same definition as introduced by the 1954 Convention (referring to the latter in Article 46(2)), takes a significant step forward, and this rule can be considered as a progressive development of international law in this domain since, according to the classical standpoint of public international law, states are entitled to grant consular protection only to their own nationals. Hence, habitual residence of the stateless person concerned is a precondition for the state to exercise this function. What makes the picture less clear, however, is that the 1967 Convention has only entered into force recently, due to the low number of ratifications.[60] This right is not a widely shared treaty law rule, but shows the tendencies of legal developments in this regard.

Summing up, it can be stated that consular protection operates as an additional element of a state's protection abroad, even if the rules only become legally binding a short time ago and only apply in relation to a limited number of states, but they clearly indicate the developments of the international community and its will to move forward.

[58] Para 16 of the Schedule to Art 28.

[59] 1967 European Convention on Consular Functions (CETS No 061). For a recent analysis of the convention made by the Council of Europe Secretariat, see Examination of the European Convention on Consular Functions (ETS No 61), CAHDI (2014) 18, available at http://www.coe.int/en/web/cahdi/48th-meeting-meeting-documents (last accessed on 12 January 2015).

[60] As of 1 January 2015, five states have ratified it (most recently Georgia in March 2011) and an additional four states have signed it without ratifying it yet (source http://conventions.coe.int).

2. There are virtually no domains or set of rights extended to *de iure* stateless by quasi-universal international treaties other than intellectual property rights. From a human rights perspective, the right to intellectual property is one element of a cluster of rights broadly referred to as 'cultural rights'. For the stateless, a cultural identity distinct from that of the majority of the population is often a contributing factor to their plight; similarly, difficulties in enjoying that distinct cultural life are not uncommon.[61] In 1971, Protocol No 1 was annexed to the Universal Copyright Convention[62] as revised in Paris on 24 July 1971. This assimilated stateless persons having habitual residence in a state to the nationals of that state (paragraph 1). By doing so, the protocol builds upon the provisions of the 1954 New York Convention. Article 14 of the latter sets forth the rights concerning artistic rights (which is a synonym for copyright) and industrial property, stating that stateless persons shall be accorded, in the country in which they have the habitual residence, the same protection as accorded to nationals of that country. However, they also enjoy protection in any other contracting party: they shall be accorded the same protection as provided for the nationals of their country of habitual residence in the territory of that contracting party. Protocol No 1 to the Universal Copyright Convention determines the same level of protection (stateless persons are on an equal footing with nationals) and the same condition for benefiting from this right (habitual residence in a contracting party). The purpose of these rules is to provide protection of the 'totality of creations of the human mind'.[63] Although the 1954 New York Convention does not specify the type of protection and it can thus be assumed that all aspects of protection are covered, the Universal Copyright Convention as revised in Paris on 24 June 1971 lays down specific rules in this regard. Even if the scope *ratione materiae* of the two provisions are roughly the same, the two treaties have significantly different numbers of state parties. While Protocol No 1 has only 38, the 1954 New York Convention currently has 84 state parties.[64] Moreover, the geographical coverage is different as well, since, despite the lower number of ratifications, Protocol No 1 also applies to India, Russia and the United States, which are not parties to the 1954 New York Convention.

3. Thirdly, two treaties on the equal treatment of nationals and non-nationals in social security matters develop the related provisions of the 1954 New York Convention. One treaty, which was universally acclaimed though not widely ratified,[65] was elaborated by the International Labour Organiza-

[61] van Waas (n 1 above), 346–47.

[62] Protocol 1 annexed for Universal Copyright Convention as revised at Paris on 24 July 1971 concerning the application of that Convention to works of stateless persons and refugees 1971 (UNTS No 13444).

[63] Robinson (n 32 above), 55, in relation to Art 14 of the 1954 New York Convention.

[64] See http://treaties.un.org.

[65] As of 1 January 2015, it has only 37 state parties (the Netherlands denounced it in 2004). However, it is in force in relation to important countries of concern such as Bangladesh, Iraq or Pakistan. See http://www.ilo.org/ilolex/cgi-lex/ratifce.pl?C118 (last accessed on 12 January 2015).

tion (ILO) in 1962 (Convention No 118 concerning Equality of Treatment of Nationals and Non-Nationals in Social Security). Convention No 118 refers to the 1954 New York Convention definition of 'stateless person'[66] and applies it to them 'without any condition of reciprocity'[67] and without the requirement of residence. It prescribes equal treatment between nationals and stateless persons in different branches of social security (eg medical care, sickness benefit, maternity benefit, old-age benefit, unemployment benefit and family benefit). However, the scope of the obligations varies from state to state, since 'each Member shall specify in its ratification in respect of which branch or branches of social security it accepts the obligations of this Convention'.[68]

The second, similar regional instrument, the 1972 European Convention on Social Security,[69] is also worth mentioning briefly. After the European Interim Agreements on Social Security made in 1953 under the aegis of the CoE, the CoE Member States left open the possibility of extending the agreements to give non-nationals and migrants more complete and effective protection. Thus, in 1959, it was decided to draft a multilateral convention to co-ordinate the social security legislations of the CoE Member States.[70] This convention, using the 1954 New York Convention definition of 'stateless person', covers stateless persons resident in the territory of a contracting party[71] who have been subject to the legislation of the contracting parties, together with the members of their families and their survivors. It affirms the principle of equality of treatment with nationals in the fields of application of the convention, such as general and special schemes and whether contributory or non-contributory, including employers' liability schemes providing benefits. This instrument can be considered as building upon, for a limited number of states in Europe, the provisions relating to social security of the 1954 New York Convention, without prejudice to the provisions of the 1962 ILO Convention.[72]

4. Fourthly, noteworthy developments have occurred in relation to the facilitated naturalization of stateless people, for whom acquisition of nationality is the ultimate legal channel to put an end to this legal anomaly. Despite the expansion of the concept advocating that universal human rights determine one's legal status irrespective of one's nationality or lack of it ('denationalization of rights'), in practical terms nationality still holds its importance as 'the right to have rights'. As Sir Lauterpacht opined, nationality 'is now increasingly regarded as an instrument for securing the rights of the individual in the national and international spheres'.[73] Naturalization is the best and most

[66] Ibid, Art 1 lit (h).
[67] Ibid.
[68] Ibid, Art 2(3).
[69] 1972 European Convention on Social Security (CETS No 078). It is not a widely ratified convention, with only eight state parties as of 1 January 2015.
[70] Explanatory Report to the 1972 European Convention on Social Security, para 7.
[71] Ibid, Art 4.
[72] Ibid, Art 6(1).
[73] H Lauterpacht, 'Foreword to the First Edition' in Weis (n 1 above), xi.

durable solution for stateless people, since it addresses what is really missing for them: nationality. However, one cannot find a comprehensive international legal framework concerning facilitated naturalization of stateless individuals. On the global level, the only legally binding provision is Article 32 of the 1954 New York Convention. If we take a close look at the text of the article, it is not an individual right of persons lacking nationality but, rather, an opportunity for them to enjoy naturalization. The addressees are the contracting states, which are urged to facilitate stateless persons' access to nationality, but it remains within their discretion to do so. In other words, Article 32 contains a 'shall clause', but content-wise this obligation is much softer, since it is does no more than prescribe that states make every effort in this regard.[74] This is quite vague, with no further details on the conditions listed therein (expedition of proceedings and reduction of related charges and costs). After deconstructing this provision, some preliminary remarks can be made. First, the term 'expedition of proceedings' can mean two things: (i) shortening the waiting period; or (ii) issuing the decision in a speedy manner or in a non-time-consuming procedure.[75] In understanding the other conditions, the *travaux préparatoires* of the New York Convention give guidance. Manley O Hudson, the first rapporteur of the topic for the ILC, identified a number of issues that were impairing naturalization, for instance complicated and expensive procedures, and stringent requirements as to the possession of property.[76]Although hesitantly dealing with the question of naturalization,[77] the strength of this treaty provision lies in the fact that Article 32 applies to all stateless people, irrespective of the lawfulness of their stay in a given state (but which is not reflected in state practice[78]).

Richer soft law has subsequently blossomed, driven by the UNHCR ExCom trying to set global standards (many ExCom conclusions between 2006 and 2008 called for states to take action on the matter).[79] The need for facilitated acquisition of nationality for the stateless has also been propelled by certain regional instruments, namely the 1997 European Convention on Nationality (ECN), the CoE Committee of Ministers Recommendation R (1999) 18 on the Avoidance and Reduction of Statelessness and the 2006 CoE Convention on the Avoidance of Statelessness in relation to State Succession (with specific focus on situations of state succession). The above CoE conventions laid down more detailed binding rules and a concrete, more precise obligation to facilitate the

[74] van Waas (n 1 above), 365.

[75] See also J Hathaway, *The Rights of Refugees under International Law* (Cambridge University Press, 2005) 986.

[76] MO Hudson, 'Nationality, Including Statelessness, Annex III—Statelessness' (1952) II *Yearbook of the International Law Commission* document A/CN.4/50, 22.

[77] van Waas (n 1 above), 385.

[78] According to the UNHCR Final Report concerning the Questionnaire on Statelessness Pursuant to the Agenda for Protection (2004), only 59.5% of the responding states provide for facilitated naturalization of stateless persons.

[79] UNHCR ExCom conclusions No 106 (LVII) 2006, No 107 (LVIII) 2007, No 108 (LIX) 2008, available at http://www.refworld.org/docid/4b28bf1f2.html (last accessed on 12 January 2015).

naturalization of stateless persons.[80] It is worth noting that the ECN is currently the only international convention setting a maximum waiting period (10 years) that a state can require before lawful and habitual residents (including stateless individuals) become eligible to apply for naturalization.[81] Furthermore, the Explanatory Report to the ECN indicates the required favourable conditions (eg reduction of the length of required residence, less stringent language requirements, easier procedure and lower procedural fees).[82] A similar approach is taken in the 1999 Committee of Ministers Recommendation, which also adds that criminal offences should not unreasonably prevent stateless persons seeking naturalization.[83] The question now arises whether there already exists a 'right to be considered for naturalization' for stateless persons as an emerging human right related to reducing existing statelessness. The emergence of such a human right, a form of *ius connectionis*, has been advocated by scholars in this field,[84] and the concept is implicitly supported by the practice of certain treaty bodies, notably the Human Rights Committee and the Committee on the Elimination of Racial Discrimination.[85]

All in all, what we have seen as regards naturalization is the strengthening of the norm obliging states to grant facilitated access to nationality for those lacking it; and it has become a more sophisticated and self-standing rule than at the time of the drafting of the 1954 Statelessness Convention. Nonetheless, regional human rights law developments appear to require an additional element not present in Article 32 of the 1954 New York Convention, ie the establishment of lawful and habitual residence in the territory of a given state, in order for stateless persons to be able to acquire the new nationality in a simplified way.

5. Finally, in the years 2000, facilitation was made in favour of stateless persons concerning their right to international travel in a regional setting, within the European Union (EU). The reason behind this was that the EU enlargement with 10 new Member States on 1 May 2004 had the paradoxical effect of reducing the scope of the possibility of granting a visa exemption, since the EU Visa Regulation (Regulation No 539/2001/EC) did not provide for a visa exemption for stateless persons residing in a Member State that does not yet fully apply the Schengen acquis, who have to cross an external Schengen border when entering into the Schengen zone or other non-Schengen Member

[80] Art 6(4) lit g) of the ECN; Art 9 of the 2006 CoE Convention.

[81] Art 6(3) of the ECN. See also L van Waas, 'Fighting Statelessness and Discriminatory Nationality Laws in Europe' (2012) 14 *European Journal of Migration and Law* 248.

[82] Para 52, available at http://conventions.coe.int/Treaty/en/Reports/Html/166.htm (last accessed on 12 January 2015).

[83] Point II.B.d, available at http://www.refworld.org/docid/510101e02.html (last accessed on 12 January 2015).

[84] Eg van Waas (n 1 above), 362, 366, 369–70.

[85] Human Rights Committee, *Individual complaint of Stewart v Canada*, case number 538/1993, A/52/40, vol II, 1 November 1996, para 12.4; CERD General Recommendation 30: Discrimination against Non-Citizens, 2004, para 13.

State. To remedy this situation,[86] Regulation (EC) No 1932/2006, modifying the EU Visa Regulation, included a new type of automatic visa exemption for stateless persons recognized by the EU Member States. Article 1(1) lit b) of the modifying regulation says that 'stateless persons and other persons who do not hold the nationality of any country who reside in a Member State and are holders of a travel document issued by that Member State' shall be exempt from the visa requirement. This means that stateless persons residing in a Member State in possession of a valid travel document (not necessarily that prescribed in the Schedule annexed to the 1954 New York Convention) are not required to have a visa in order to enter other Member States and reside in their territory for up to 90 days within any 180 day period (intra-EU short-term stay). Besides this automatic (compulsory) visa exemption category, the Regulation goes even further in giving to Member States the discretion to exempt those stateless persons from the visa requirement who reside in a third country, listed in Annex II ('the white list') of the EU Visa Regulation, having issued their travel document. The latest modification of the EU Visa Regulation further expanded the intra-EU visa free travel to those stateless persons 'and other persons who do not hold the nationality of any country' who reside in two non-Schengen Member States, ie the United Kingdom and Ireland,[87] since their travel conditions within the EU have not hitherto been clarified. The newly introduced rules leave Member States free to decide on the exemption from the visa requirement for that category of persons in compliance with their international obligations ('may clause'). For the sake of transparency, Member States should notify such decisions to the European Commission. It is an innovative element in these rules on visa-free travel that they cover all stateless persons, both those who come under the 1954 New York Convention and those outside of its scope. For example, non-citizens of Latvia are given a special passport (not the one according to the 1954 New York Convention) which not only grants them the constitutional right to belong to the state, but has also been recognized by the EU as valid for visa-free travel.[88] This is thus the first time in EU legislation where a larger personal scope (including eventually the de facto stateless as well) applies than that defined in the 1954 New York Convention.

In addition, although it is a technical norm, a further EU legislative innovation makes the international travel of stateless people easier in practice,

[86] The European Commission has been expressly asked to do so by the European Parliament and the Council in the course of the negotiations on the proposal of the Schengen Borders Code (Regulation No 562/2006/EC). This exemption was mainly aimed at resolving the situation of 'Latvian non-citizens' (see COM 2006(4) final, 5).

[87] Regulation (EU) No 1289/2013 of the European Parliament and of the Council of 11 December 2013 amending Council Regulation (EC) No 539/2001 listing the third countries whose nationals must be in possession of visas when crossing the external borders and those whose nationals are exempt from that requirement [2013] OJ L347, 74–80, recital (9), Art 1(3) lit b).

[88] R Bauböck, B Perchinig and W Sievers (eds), *Citizenship Policies in the New Europe: Expanded and Updated Edition* (Amsterdam University Press, 2009) 73.

creating legal certainty and transparency. This is the reformed Table of Travel Documents recognized by Member States, which consists of travel documents issued by Member States, third countries and international organizations.[89] The new EU-wide Table of Travel Documents, which is available to the public,[90] includes in Part II 'travel documents issued to stateless persons under the United Nations Convention relating to the Status of Stateless Persons of 28 September 1954' as well as 'travel documents issued to persons who do not hold the nationality of any country and who reside in a Member State'.[91] It is a promising sign, showing the mutual trust between them, that Member States recognize each other's travel documents issued for the above two categories of stateless individuals, as well as some Member States recognizing stateless travel documents issued by third countries even beyond the contracting parties of the 1954 New York Convention.

VI. *DE LEGE FERENDA* PROPOSALS: NEW TENDENCIES

This section is devoted to the way forward and examines what the future holds for enhancing the protection regime offered to this highly vulnerable group of people. Two topics will be discussed: diplomatic protection and the protection of the stateless from expulsion.

1. One had to wait a couple of decades after the 1967 CoE Convention on Consular Functions until the issue of protecting stateless persons abroad was put again on the international law-making agenda, this time at the global level (within the UN system). The ILC included the topic of diplomatic protection on its agenda in 1995 and adopted the Draft Articles on Diplomatic Protection in 2006, endorsed by the UNGA,[92] which is of interest from the perspective of stateless people, since this mechanism could offer them fair and proper treatment abroad.[93]As draft article 1 is definitional by nature, it does not mention stateless persons. Article 3, on the other hand, makes it clear that diplomatic protection may be exercised in respect of such persons.[94] Draft article 3(2) opens the door generally for certain categories of persons not being nationals of the state concerned,[95] including stateless persons. This

[89] Decision No 1105/2011/EU of the European Parliament and of the Council of 25 October 2011 on the list of travel documents which entitle the holder to cross the external borders and which may be endorsed with a visa and on setting up a mechanism for establishing this list [2011] OJ L287, 9–12, and, based on this, Commission Implementing Decision C(2013) 4914 of 2 August 2013 establishing the list of travel documents which entitle the holder to cross the external borders and which may be endorsed with a visa.

[90] Available at http://ec.europa.eu/dgs/home-affairs/what-we-do/policies/borders-and-visas/document-security/index_en.htm (last accessed on 12 January 2015).

[91] Art 3(3) lit c)–d), Decision No 1105/2011/EU.

[92] A/RES/62/67.*Diplomatic Protection* (General Assembly of the United Nations).

[93] See also van Waas (n 1 above), 380–85; van Waas (n 46 above), 39–40.

[94] Above n 40, 26.

[95] Draft art 3(2) reads: 'Notwithstanding paragraph 1, diplomatic protection may be exercised by a state in respect of a person that is not its national in accordance with draft article 8'.

is explicitly expressed in draft article 8, which relates to stateless persons and refugees. By virtue of paragraph 1 of this article, 'a state may exercise diplomatic protection in respect of a stateless person who, at the date of injury and at the date of the official presentation of the claim, is lawfully and habitually resident in that state'.

This is clearly an attempt for progressive development of international law, because traditionally the general rule was that a state might exercise diplomatic protection only on behalf of its nationals. This is well illustrated in the *Dickson Car Wheel Company v United Mexican States* case (1931), when the United States–Mexican Claims Commission held that a stateless person could not be the beneficiary of diplomatic protection: '[a] state . . . does not commit an international delinquency in inflicting an injury upon an individual lacking nationality, and consequently, no state is empowered to intervene or complain on his behalf either before or after the injury'.[96] As the ILC found, this dictum no longer reflects the accurate position of international law for stateless persons. Contemporary international law reflects a concern for the status of this category of persons, evidenced by specific conventions on statelessness.[97] In line with these efforts, according to draft article 8(1), a state may exercise diplomatic protection in respect of a stateless person, regardless of how he/she became stateless, provided that the person was lawfully and habitually resident in that state both at the time of injury and at the date of the official presentation of the claim. The requirement of both lawful residence and habitual residence sets a high threshold, notions borrowed from the 1997 ECN.[98] Habitual residence in this context is intended to convey continuous residence. Although this threshold is high and may lead to a lack of effective protection for some individuals, the combination of lawful residence and habitual residence is, as pointed out by the ILC in the Commentaries, justified in the case of an exceptional measure introduced *de lege ferenda*,[99] since states are more likely to accept such a new rule if enlarging the scope *ratione personae* of diplomatic protection is not without limitations and conditions. I also draw attention to the temporal requirement for the bringing of a claim: the stateless person must be a lawful and habitual resident of the claimant state both at the time of the injury and at the date of the official presentation of the claim, even if quite a long time has already elapsed between the two acts. Finally, it is to be noted that the 'may clause' contained in draft article 8(1) emphasizes the discretionary nature of the right. In other words, it is not an obligation of states to include legally and habitually residing stateless individuals within the sphere of diplomatic protection; rather, states have discretion about whether to extend such protection to a stateless person. The fate and

[96] UNRIAA, vol IV, 669, 678. See also Weis (n 1 above), 162; and Draft Articles (n 40 above), 48.
[97] Draft Articles (n 40 above), 48.
[98] Art 6 (4), point (g), where they are used in connection with the acquisition of nationality.
[99] Draft Articles (n 40 above), 49.

the normative character of the ILC Draft Articles on Diplomatic Protection is still uncertain eight years after its adoption.

2. As far as the protection of stateless persons against expulsion is concerned, it is again the ILC that has been the driving force behind the codification of the general principles related to this matter. The ILC adopted Draft Articles on the Expulsion of Aliens in August 2014 on second reading,[100] which were then referred to the UNGA for further consideration (either to take note of the draft articles in a resolution and to encourage their widest possible dissemination, or to consider, at a later stage, the elaboration of a convention on the basis of the draft articles).[101] Draft article 7, entitled 'Rules relating to the expulsion of stateless persons', is of particular relevance in this regard. However, its content is disappointing. This provision does not even echo Article 31 of the 1954 New York Convention; it is merely a 'without prejudice clause'. Therefore neither substantial requirements nor the procedural safeguards articulated in paragraphs (1)–(3) of the same article are incorporated in the draft. Draft article 7 stipulates that

> [t]he present draft articles are without prejudice to the rules of international law relating to stateless persons, and in particular to the rule that a state shall not expel a stateless person lawfully in its territory save on grounds of national security or public order.

The Commentaries laconically state as follows: '[d]raft article 7 consists of a "without prejudice" clause aimed at ensuring the continued application to stateless persons of the rules concerning their expulsion'.[102] There is not much explanation about the intentions of the drafters or the reasons behind such a minimalist approach. As a prima facie observation, one can conclude that draft article 7 has no added value, which is evidence of the lack of consensus between the ILC members on this matter. I regret this missed opportunity to consolidate and develop the law.

VII. CONCLUSIONS

Having analysed the stateless-specific protection regime under international law, I will now make some general concluding remarks. Since the establishment of the UN, international action on statelessness, notwithstanding the oscillating attention to the issue, has been a good example of the normative power of the law of the nations. Public international law created a new legal category, an abstract and autonomous *de iure* stateless status, with its

[100] Report of the International Law Commission, Sixty-sixth session (5 May–6 June and 7 July–8 August 2014), GAOR, Sixty-ninth session, Supplement No 10, A/69/10, Ch IV.

[101] Ibid, para 42.

[102] 'Expulsion of Aliens—Text of the Draft Articles and Commentaries Thereto', Report of the International Law Commission, Sixty-sixth session (5 May–6 June and 7 July–8 August 2014), GAOR, Sixty-ninth session, Supplement No 10, A/69/10, 32.

own terminology—all with a view to establishing a coherent, logically closed legal architecture and to offering a self-standing protection status for those having been denied the basic right of belonging to a state. This approach is embodied first and foremost in the 1954 New York Convention, which is universal in its acclaim. This *lex specialis* instrument and the other various human rights treaties and documents presented in the foregoing have been designed to ensure that those not enjoying the right to a nationality are not unreasonably disadvantaged by their plight (protection of stateless persons).[103] We could observe some significant developments and improvements in the international law 'safety net' offering them protection and attaching rights and entitlements to the stateless status. Nevertheless, there are still serious gaps and shortcomings in the relevant international legal framework, and the existing norms also face limited effectiveness (eg the relatively low overall number of ratifications of the 1954 Convention and other global or regional conventions, the challenges of identifying stateless populations and the unclear character of customary law of certain stateless-specific treaty rules). What is positive is the growing attention to the cause of statelessness from international institutions and the international community as a whole, alongside the changing attitudes of states (enough to mention the remarkable increase of new accessions to the 1954 Convention in the last few years and the number of statelessness-related state pledges).

My academic evaluation of this re-emerging, old–new domain of international law is rather positive. It is undoubtedly a significant achievement that there is a theoretically well-elaborated concept employed by public international law to protect the individual in his/her transnational engagements. This is a specific example of creating a new substantive legal category of individuals under international law. International statelessness law is now in transition into 'adulthood', with richer, more robust and more sophisticated legal foundations, backed up with soft and hard enforcement mechanisms, the most important of which should be domestic authorities and domestic courts. In my assessment, the perspectives and potential in this field of law are promising enough to soon falsify Judge Abi-Saab's brilliant bon mot, describing international law as a 'normative giant, but an institutional dwarf'.[104]

[103] van Waas (n 1 above), 436.

[104] G Abi-Saab, 'The International Judicial Function' (UN Audiovisual Library of International Law), available at http://legal.un.org/avl/ls/Abi-Saab_CT_video_1.html (last accessed on 12 January 2015).

8

Responsibility to Protect (R2P) and Minorities

VASSILIOS GRAMMATIKAS*

I. INTRODUCTION

IN 1999, DURING the NATO bombings of Yugoslavia over the issue of Kosovo, the former UN Secretary General Kofi Annan said that 'Emerging slowly, but I believe surely, is an international norm against the violent repression of minorities that will and must take precedence over concerns of sovereignty'.[1]

The subsequent development of the concept of 'responsibility to protect' (R2P) by the International Commission on Intervention and State Sovereignty (ICISS) created the single most discussed/debated modern annotation regarding human rights both among states, at the UN level, and among scholars. While the R2P concept acquired official status as part of the UN World Summit Outcome Document, it also attracted severe criticism, being seen by many states as a way to legalize so-called humanitarian intervention.

The present chapter attempts to explore the modern parameters of R2P, address the relevant criticism and determine whether R2P is applicable as a tool of minority protection worldwide, as Kofi Annan advocated.

* Assistant Professor of International Law, Democritus University of Thrace, Komotini, Greece. Email: bgramm@bscc.duth.gr. All websites/links used were checked on 22 November 2014.

[1] UN Secretary General Kofi Annan addressing the Commission of Human Rights in Geneva on 7 April 1999. UN Doc E/CN.4/1999/SR.19, p 4, para 8. Several years later, however, in a 2005 report entitled 'In Larger Freedom' Mr Annan advocated for the application of the Responsibility to Protect (R2P) concept for 'populations of states, citizens, civilians', but without explicit reference to minorities (UN Doc A/59/2005, paras 133, 135).

II. THE EVOLUTION OF R2P

A. The Concept of Humanitarian Intervention

(i) State Practice Linked to Humanitarian Intervention

The idea of unilateral military action to protect fundamental human rights is definitely not new. It was invoked several times during the nineteenth century by the great powers to justify military interventions abroad. There is a general agreement among scholars that such a right existed as customary international law before the Charter of the United Nations (the Charter) was signed in 1945.[2]

One of the most frequently quoted definitions of humanitarian intervention is that which Rougier defined as

> The theory of intervention on the ground of humanity is properly that which recognizes the right of one state to exercise an international control by military force over the acts of another in regard to its internal sovereignty when contrary to the law of humanity.[3]

Amongst the most illustrative cases of this type are the battle of Navarino of 1827—the intervention of the fleets of Britain, France and Russia against the Ottoman fleet in order to stop atrocities of the latter against the Greek population, which was explicitly justified on humanitarian grounds[4]—and the French armed action in Syria (1860–61) to stop massacres against the Christian population.[5]

No state practice invoking this right occurred during the League of Nations period. It did, however, re-emerge, through various forcible state activities, after the adoption of the UN Charter. The first action of this type was the Indian invasion of East Pakistan in 1971, in response to atrocities committed

[2] See inter alia I Brownlie, *International Law and the Use of Force by States* (Clarendon Press, 1963) 340; H Wheaton, *Elements of International Law* (1866) 95 (para 69); H Lauterpacht (ed), *Oppenheim's International Law. Vol I. Peace*, 8th edn (Longmans Green, 1955) 312; R Lillich, 'Humanitarian Intervention through the United Nations' (1993) 53 *Zeitschrift für ausländisches öffentliches Recht und Völkerrecht* 557, 559; DJ Scheffer, 'Toward a Modern Doctrine of Humanitarian Intervention' (1992) 23 *University of Toledo Law Review* 253, 258–59; B Benjamin, 'Unilateral Humanitarian Intervention: Legalizing the Use of Force to Prevent Human Rights Atrocities' (1992–93) 16 *Fordham Journal of International Law* 120, 128–29.

[3] A Rougier, 'La théorie de l'intervention d'humanité' (1910) 17 *Revue Générale de Droit International Public* 468. The authentic French text reads as follows: 'La théorie de l'intervention d'humanité est proprement celle qui reconnaît pour un droit l'exercice du contrôle international d'un État sur les actes de souveraineté intérieure d'un autre État contraires "aux lois de l'humanité", et qui prétend en organiser juridiquement le fonctionnement'.

[4] In the Treaty between Great Britain, Russia and France for the Pacification of Greece, signed in London on 6 July 1827, the three powers were motivated 'no less by sentiments of humanity than by interests for the tranquility of Europe' (1826–27) 14 *British and Foreign State Papers* 632, 633, while Art V of the Treaty emphasizes that the three powers do not have any territorial or commercial interest (ibid, 636).

[5] See I Pogany, 'Humanitarian Intervention in International Law: The French Intervention in Syria Reexamined' (1986) 35 *International and Comparative Law Quarterly* 182.

by the Pakistani troops against the local population, which secured secession of this territory and the eventual independence of Bangladesh as a state.[6] Several other military actions in the 1970s, 1980s and 1990s bear characteristics that could classify them as humanitarian interventions, namely, the French intervention in the Central African Republic (1979),[7] the intervention of Tanzania in Uganda (1979),[8] the invasion of Vietnam in Cambodia to overthrow the Khmer Rouge regime (1978–79)[9] and the ECOWAS interventions in Liberia and Sierra Leone in the 1990s, partly due to humanitarian concerns, which were retrospectively commended by the Security Council.[10]

Separate mention should be made of the Israeli operation in Uganda (1976) to rescue the passengers of an El-Al aircraft, which was hijacked and taken to Entebbe Airport,[11] but the 'humanitarian concern' behind the operation was limited to the protection of nationals, with Israel relying on the right of self-defence.[12]

(ii) Humanitarian Intervention as a Doctrine in the UN Period

The starting point of the modern debate on the legality of humanitarian intervention was the 1999 NATO air campaign against Yugoslavia over the issue of Kosovo. In a NATO seminar in the Netherlands,[13] a few months after the

[6] It should be noted, however, that, before the UNSC, while India invoked humanitarian reasons, its principal argument was self-defence due to previous Pakistani bombings of Indian airfields. For a detailed account of the conflict see S Ganguly, *Conflict Unending: India-Pakistan Tensions since 1947* (Columbia University Press, 2001) 51–78.

[7] For an account of the basic facts of the case see C Rousseau, 'Chronique des faits internationaux' (1980) 83 *Revue Générale de Droit International Public* 351, 365; S Chesterman, *Just War or Just Peace? Humanitarian Intervention and International Law* (Oxford University Press, 2001), 82.

[8] See W Rosenberger and HC Tobin, *Keesing's Contemporary Archives 1979* (Keesing's Publications, 1979), 29669–72; SK Chatterjee, 'Some Legal Problems of Support Role in International Law: Tanzania and Uganda' (1981) 30 *International and Comparative Law Quarterly* 755, 755–58; F Hassan, 'Realpolitik in International Law: After Tanzanian-Ugandan Conflict Humanitarian Intervention Reexamined' (1980–81) 17 *Willamette Law Review* 859, 865–82.

[9] SJ Morris, *Why Vietnam Invaded Cambodia: Political Culture and Causes of War* (Stanford, CA, 1999) 108–12.

[10] UNSC Resolution 788 (1992), which, in para 1 'commends ECOWAS for its efforts to restore peace, security and stability in Liberia', and UNSC Resolution 1162 (1998), which also commented the ECOWAS for restoring peace and security in Sierra Leone.

[11] M Knisbacher, 'The Entebbe Operation: A Legal Analysis of Israel's Rescue Action' (1977–78) 12 *Journal of International Law & Economics* 57, 68–70.

[12] 31 UNSCOR (1941st meeting) para 32, UN Doc S/PV 1941 (1976), where the American representative stated that: 'Israel's action in rescuing the hostages necessarily involved a temporary breach of the territorial integrity of Uganda. Normally, such a breach would be impermissible under the Charter. However, there was a well established right to use limited force for the protection of one's own nationals from an imminent threat of injury or death in a situation where the State in whose territory they were located was either unwilling or unable to protect them. The right, flowing from the right of self-defence, was limited to such use of force as was necessary and appropriate to protect threatened nationals from injury. The requirements of that right to protect nationals were clearly met in the Entebbe case.'

[13] NATO Seminar in Scheveningen, November 1999. Source: 'Humanitarian Intervention: Definitions and Criteria' (June 2000) 3(1) *CSS Strategic Papers* 1.

bombings, the following definition of humanitarian intervention was adopted: 'A Humanitarian Intervention is an armed intervention in another state, without the agreement of that state, to address [the threat of] a humanitarian disaster, in particular caused by grave and large-scale violations of fundamental human rights'.

This particular definition was chosen because it represents the NATO perception of its own action in the former Yugoslavia. Essentially, all other definitions provided, whether by individual authors or organizations, are variations on this basic structure.

The protagonists of the Yugoslavia campaign referred to the humanitarian nature of their actions on numerous occasions. Thus, during the debate in the Security Council (SC), the British representative explicitly stated that 'In these circumstances, and as an exceptional measure on grounds of overwhelming humanitarian necessity, military intervention is legally justifiable'.[14]

However, the only NATO member that formulated a legal construction to support the action as humanitarian intervention was Belgium, which, during the hearings of the case brought before the International Court of Justice (ICJ) by Yugoslavia against the NATO countries that participated in the bombing campaign, stated that:

> The Kingdom of Belgium in particular, felt obliged to intervene to forestall an ongoing humanitarian catastrophe . . . The purpose of NATO's intervention is to rescue a people in peril, in deep distress. For this reason the kingdom of Belgium takes the view that this is an armed humanitarian intervention, compatible with Art. 2, § 4 of the Charter, which covers only intervention against the territorial integrity or political independence of a state.[15]

The aforementioned and other similar efforts to assert the legality of humanitarian intervention in the UN period are based upon three lines of argumentation: (i) that it is compatible with the UN Charter, as it is not directed against the territorial integrity and political independence of states; (ii) that it is legal, as it is customary international law; and (iii) since the promotion of human rights is a purpose of the UN (Article 1, § 3) and universal respect for human rights and fundamental freedoms is set as a condition necessary for the peaceful and friendly relations between states (Articles 55 and 56), military action to safeguard fundamental human rights is both moral and legal.

However, it should be noted that this kind of argument is neither new nor original. It had been used by the UK before the ICJ in the *Corfu Channel* case, where, during the pleadings, the UK claimed that 'our action . . . threatened neither the territorial integrity no the political independence of Albania.

[14] Speech of Sir Jeremy Greenstock at the 988th SC Meeting, 24 March 1999, UN Doc S/PV/3988.

[15] Available at http://icj-cij.org; see also DJ Harris, *Cases and Materials on International Law*, 6th edn (Sweet & Maxwell, 2004) 956.

Albania suffered thereby neither territorial loss nor any part of its political independence'.[16] The ICJ rejected this argument, stating that

> The Court can only regard that the alleged right of intervention as a policy of force, such as has, in the past, given rise to the most serious abuses and such as cannot, whatever be the present defects in international organization, find a place in international law . . . to ensure respect for international law, of which it is the organ, the Court must declare that the action of the British Navy constituted a violation of Albanian sovereignty.[17]

Moreover, it is highly problematic to fit humanitarian intervention into the permissible uses of force under the UN Charter and this is accepted by many of its supporters, as it does not amount to self-defence (in the absence of an armed attack), while action through regional organizations (Chapter VIII of the Charter) has to conform to the Charter principles.

In general, theories on humanitarian intervention, regardless of their legal basis, tend to focus on the just and moral cause that is served through the military action taken and, while there is no uniform approach to the exact characteristics and content of humanitarian intervention, it is endorsed—in principle—by many scholars of various disciplines,[18] as well as by an increasing number of states.

B. From Humanitarian Intervention to R2P

In September 2000, the Canadian government established an international body of experts called the International Commission on Intervention and State Sovereignty (ICISS) to discuss all the legal and political questions related to humanitarian intervention. Its outcome is described in a straightforward manner:

[16] *Corfu Channel Case (Albania v UK)* [1949] III ICJ Pleadings 296. The action the UK referred to was the dispatch of military vessels to gather mines from Albanian territorial water, despite the express objection by the Albanian government, after a British ship had hit a mine during a passage through the Corfu Channel.

[17] *Corfu Channel Case (Decision)* [1949] ICJ Reports, 35. It should be noted that in the *Nicaragua Case* the ICJ cited the *Corfu Channel Case* in support of a general principle of non-intervention: *Nicaragua Case (Merits)* [1986] ICJ Reports 106–07, para 202.

[18] See inter alia 'Humanitarian Intervention' (n 13 above), 2; C Chinkin, 'The Legality of NATO's Action in the Former Republic of Yugoslavia (FRY) under International Law' (2000) 49 *International and Comparative Law Quarterly* 910, 920–21; C Greenwood, 'International Law and the NATO Intervention in Kosovo' (2000) 49 *International and Comparative Law Quarterly* 926, 926–34; JJ Merriam, 'Kosovo and the Law of Humanitarian Intervention' (2001) 33 *Case Western Reserve Journal of International Law* 111, 127–35; P Hilpold, 'Humanitarian Intervention: Is There a Need for a Legal Reappraisal?' (2001) 12 *European Journal of International Law* 437, 467, where the author distinguishes between the morality and legality of humanitarian intervention; F Harhoff, 'Unauthorized Humanitarian Interventions: Armed Violence in the Name of Humanity?' (2001) 70 *Nordic Journal of International Law* 65; J Pattison, *Humanitarian Intervention and the Responsibility to Protect: Who Should Intervene?* (Oxford University Press, 2010), 13, 72.

> This report is about the so-called 'right of humanitarian intervention': the question of when, if ever, it is appropriate for states to take coercive—and in particular military—action, against another state for the purpose of protecting people at risk in that other state.[19]

It thus directly connects its outcome to the concept of humanitarian intervention and its potential 'legitimization'.

The conclusion of the ICISS was the formulation of the responsibility to protect (R2P) along three basic propositions:

- *The responsibility to prevent*: to address the causes of internal conflict and other man-made crises putting populations at risk.
- *The responsibility to react:* to use appropriate measures to respond in situations of compelling human need, which may include various coercive measures like sanctions, international prosecution for acts that amount to crimes against humanity and, in special cases, military humanitarian intervention.
- *The responsibility to rebuild:* this is the stage after the intervention has taken place and includes the provision of assistance through recovery, reconstruction and reconciliation, addressing the causes of the situation that triggered the intervention.

The introduction of R2P as a new concept towards the protection of human rights and its holistic approach in three phases has been very influential in the rhetoric of states and the practice of UN organs, and was officially accepted as a concept of universal application by the UNGA in the World Summit Outcome Document (WSOD) of 2005.[20] Paragraphs 138 and 139 endorse the responsibility to protect,[21] but not to the extent proposed by the ICISS report.

[19] ICISS, *The Responsibility to Protect: Report of the International Commission on Intervention and State Sovereignty* (International Development Research Centre, 2001) vii.

[20] UN Doc A/RES/60/1, 28 October 2005.

[21] The relevant paragraphs read as follows: '138. Each individual State has the responsibility to protect its populations from genocide, war crimes, ethnic cleansing and crimes against humanity. This responsibility entails the prevention of such crimes, including their incitement, through appropriate and necessary means. We accept that responsibility and will act in accordance with it. The international community should, as appropriate, encourage and help States to exercise this responsibility and support the United Nations in establishing an early warning capability.

139. The international community, through the United Nations, also has the responsibility to use appropriate diplomatic, humanitarian and other peaceful means, in accordance with Chapters VI and VIII of the Charter, to help to protect populations from genocide, war crimes, ethnic cleansing and crimes against humanity. In this context, we are prepared to take collective action, in a timely and decisive manner, through the Security Council, in accordance with the Charter, including Chapter VII, on a case-by-case basis and in cooperation with relevant regional organizations as appropriate, should peaceful means be inadequate and national authorities are manifestly failing to protect their populations from genocide, war crimes, ethnic cleansing and crimes against humanity. We stress the need for the General Assembly to continue consideration of the responsibility to protect populations from genocide, war crimes, ethnic cleansing and crimes against humanity and its implications, bearing in mind the principles of the Charter and international law . . .'

The main distinctive lines between the two versions of R2P can be summarized as follows:

The ICISS report explicitly sanctions the unilateral use of force in enforcing R2P, while the WSOD renders any such possibility subject to the authorization of the SC (paragraph 139), thus retaining the Charter framework regarding the permissible uses of force.

The WSOD limits the application of R2P to genocide, war crimes, ethnic cleansing and crimes against humanity. On the other hand, the ICISS report refers to a more general concept of 'human security', also using the terms 'crimes and atrocities' without any further qualifications.

In order to support its proposal, the ICISS report puts forward a series of moral justifications in favour of forcible humanitarian intervention, in contrast to the WSOD, which puts emphasis upon the UN Charter principles and procedures.

The WSOD focuses on the prevention phase (paragraph 138) whereas the ICISS report focuses mainly on the responsibility to react.

Despite the above differences, the whole discussion is focused on the possibility of using military force to implement the R2P and whether this should be unilateral or through the SC. In fact, it is this particular, fundamental, difference of opinions that led some authors to characterize the WSOD as 'R2P lite'.[22]

However, the 'heavy R2P' version failed to attract the acceptance of the majority of states, as its most controversial feature (ie the possibility of unilateral armed action) was rejected in the sense that any such possibility was explicitly made subject to the authorization of the SC, thus leaving the Charter regime concerning the use of force virtually unchanged. This attitude of the UNGA has attracted some criticism from scholars who support the ICISS version of R2P for not being effective in dealing with the situations that R2P is supposed to counter.[23]

There is no doubt that the WSOD represents a compromise between a smaller number of states that would like to see R2P, as it was formulated in the ICISS report, incorporated therein (eg most NATO Member States) and the vast majority of states that either hesitated to endorse or explicitly

[22] The rather ironical phrase was first used by Thomas Weiss, who was heading the research team of the ICISS during their work. Weiss considered the R2P version that emerged from the WSOD as 'R2P lite' because it fell short of accepting the possibility of unilateral, unauthorized military intervention. T Weiss, *Humanitarian Intervention: Ideas in Action* (Polity Press, 2007), 116–117.

[23] See inter alia A Bellamy, 'Realizing the Responsibility to Protect' (2009) 10 *International Studies Perspectives* 111, 111; A Bellamy, *Responsibility to Protect: The Global Effort to End Mass Atrocities* (Polity Press, 2009) 91–93; C Badescu and L Bergholm, 'The Responsibility to Protect and the Conflict in Darfur: The Big Let-Down' (2009) 40 *Security Dialogue* 287, 291; Weiss, ibid.

rejected[24] any idea of unilateral armed action sanctioned by a UN document.[25] Nevertheless, the unanimous adoption of the WSOD as a political document represents the degree of consensus of all UN Member States and, even though certain states and scholars do not like it, it set the R2P limits regarding the potential uses of force.

The outward reference to paragraphs 138 and 139 of the WSOD by UNSC Resolution 1674 (2006)[26] (which was adopted unanimously) could also be interpreted as reflecting the position of the major Western powers (namely USA, UK and France) vis-à-vis the content of the R2P in the sense that they implicitly accepted the limits set in the WSOD (as they did by adopting the WSOD in 2005 as individual UN members as well), although their political attitude and state practice are clearly in the opposite direction. Resolution 1706 (2006) on Darfour (Sudan) recalls the R2P reference of SC Resolution 1674.[27]

C. The UN Secretary General's Contribution towards the Development of R2P

Both of the UN Secretary Generals who have served since 1999 have been keen supporters of the various R2P ideas. Kofi Annan became a 'partisan' of the humanitarian intervention concept, supporting the possibility of unilateral intervention, despite the fact that these practices undermined the foundations of his own organization. In 2000 he wondered: 'If humanitarian intervention is, indeed, an unacceptable assault on sovereignty, how should we respond to

[24] See the statement of India's permanent representative to the UN Nirupam Sen who said that 'We have studied carefully the Secretary-General's views on the issue of "responsibility to protect". This is an issue of utmost importance and needs to be addressed with necessary caution and responsibility. We do not believe that discussions on the question should be used as a cover for conferring any legitimacy on the so-called "right of humanitarian intervention" or making it the ideology of some kind of "military humanism"' during the discussions of the UN Secretary General's report entitled 'In Larger Freedom' in 2005 (UN Doc A/59/2005, 21 March 2005), available at http://www.un.int/india/2005/ind1085.pdf. Also, the former Russian Prime Minister Yevgeny Primakov, in an often quoted statement, said that 'UN process, not humanitarian intervention is world's new hope', *New Perspectives Quarterly*, 2 September 2004, available at http://www.digitalnpq.org/global_services/ global%20viewpoint/02-09-04primakov.html.

[25] See JM Welsh, 'Conclusion: Humanitarian Intervention after 11 September' in JM Welsh (ed), *Humanitarian Intervention and International Relations* (Oxford University Press, 2004) 176–88, where the author records the negative attitude of many states vis-à-vis the existence or emergence of a right of humanitarian intervention through the R2P. China's steady position against any possibility of unilateral humanitarian intervention has also been evident since the case of Kosovo in 1999: see JE Davis, 'China's Position on Humanitarian Intervention' (2011) 44 *Vanderbilt Journal of Transnational Law* 217, 273–77, esp at 277.

[26] UN Doc S/RES/1674 (2006), entitled 'Protection of Civilians in Armed Conflict', states in operative para 4 that '[The SC] [*r*]*eaffirms* the provisions of paragraphs 138 and 139 of the 2005 World Summit Outcome Document regarding the responsibility to protect populations from genocide, war crimes, ethnic cleansing and crimes against humanity'. The same phrase is repeated in the preamble of UNSC Resolution 1894 (2009), 11 November 2009, which also deals with the protection of civilians.

[27] UN Doc S/RES/1706 (2006), 31 August 2006, preamble, § 2.

a Rwanda, to a Srebrenica, to gross and systematic violation of human rights that offend every precept of our common humanity?'[28] In his 2005 report 'In Larger Freedom' he addressed the issue, again referring to the R2P, which was not yet an official UN policy, probably relying in the ICISS R2P concept without specifying the bearer of this right.[29]

Mr Ban Ki-moon, the successor of Kofi Annan and the current Secretary General of the UN, was even more enthusiastic in endorsing R2P, but under a solid basis: the WSOD. Building up on the provisions of the latter, his perception of R2P was presented in detail in his 2009 report on the R2P,[30] in the form of three pillars:

- the protection responsibilities of the state;
- international assistance and capacity-building; and
- timely and decisive response.

In the words of Ban Ki-moon, the approach to R2P 'has been defined by the provisions of paragraphs 138 and 139 of the Summit Outcome',[31] and they

> are to be undertaken only in conformity with the provisions, purposes and principles of the Charter of the United Nations. In that regard, the responsibility to protect does not alter, indeed it reinforces, the legal obligations of Member States to refrain from the use of force except in conformity with the Charter.[32]

Thus, unlike his predecessor, he is departing from the ICISS approach. In contrast, Ban's report supported that the WSOD R2P provisions 'are firmly anchored in well-established principles of international law' and that states should 'seek to give a doctrinal, policy and institutional life to the R2P'.[33]

In his follow-up 2012 report, entitled 'The Role of Regional and Subregional Arrangements in Implementing the R2P',[34] Ban Ki-moon supports a

[28] K Annan, 'We the Peoples—The Role of the United Nations in the 21st Century' (2000), 48, available at http://www.un.org/en/events/pastevents/pdfs/We_The_Peoples.pdf. An adviser to Mr Annan on UN reform claimed that Annan's agenda included endorsement of humanitarian intervention through the R2P and that the WSOD succeeded in legalizing humanitarian intervention: SJ Stedman, 'UN Transformation in an Era of Soft Balancing' (2007) 83 *International Affairs* 933, 938.

[29] UN Doc A/59/2005, para 132 (also paras 125–26). It should be noted that his report was based on the 2004 Report of the High-level Panel on Threats, Challenges and Change (UN Doc A/59/565, 2 December 2004), which was set up by Mr Annan himself and endorsed R2P in principle, accepting that there is a collective international responsibility, 'exercisable by the Security Council authorizing military intervention as a last resort, in the event of genocide and other large-scale killing, ethnic cleansing and serious violations of humanitarian law which sovereign governments have proved powerless or unwilling to prevent' (para 203), and presented a number of criteria that would be used by the SC in order to decide the use of force (para 207). Apparently, however, Mr Annan did not follow the conclusions of the High-level Panel.

[30] Ban K-m, 'Implementing the Responsibility to Protect', UN Doc A/63/677, 12 January 2009.

[31] Ibid, para 10.

[32] Ibid, para 3.

[33] Ibid, para 2. Implicitly, the UN Secretary General admits that the WSOD is a document of predominantly political nature and that, in order to acquire a more solid binding force, it should be transformed or upgraded to an international treaty.

[34] UN Doc A/65/877, 27 June 2011.

more active—and more independent—role for regional organizations in implementing R2P. Finally, in his 2013 report, entitled 'R2P: State Responsibility and Prevention', Ban Ki-moon puts emphasis upon prevention, describing a range of preventive measures that had been proposed to governments.[35]

D. Behaviour of States towards R2P after the WSOD

One might have expected that the adoption of R2P as a concept of universal acceptance would have fostered its development and that states would have been willing to engage in its further promotion. However, this was not going to be the case. The initial enthusiasm over the evolution of this new concept was soon transformed into scepticism as to the potential abuse of this principle, which would introduce humanitarian intervention 'through the back door'. This fear is reinforced by many scholars, who attach a unilateralism aspect to the WSOD[36] or directly link R2P with the legalization of humanitarian intervention.[37]

Since the initial phase of R2P's existence, some states have tried to use it in order to secure authorization for the use of force in situations clearly falling outside the limits of the WSOD. Thus, France tried to use R2P in order to persuade the SC to authorize the forcible distribution of humanitarian assistance to the victims of the cyclone Nargis in Myanmar (Burma).[38] The attempt was met with strong opposition from China and Russia, but also from Panama, Slovenia and Japan. In the end, a statement by the President of SC (UK) repeated that R2P covers only war crimes, genocide, crimes against humanity and serious violations of international humanitarian law.[39]

Professor Alex Bellamy, one of the keen supporters of R2P, observes that, 'Given all this, it is not hard to see why many governments continue to suspect that R2P is simply a "Trojan horse" for the legitimization of unilateral intervention'.[40]

The subsequent adventures of R2P within the UN did not help its establish-

[35] UN Doc A/67/929, 9 July 2013.

[36] See inter alia S Bernstein, 'The Responsibility to Protect after Libya: Humanitarian Prevention as a Rule of Customary International Law' (2012) 38 *Brooklyn Journal of International Law* 305, 309–10; G Shaffer and M Pollack, 'Hard versus Soft Law in International Security' (2011) 52 *Boston College Law Review* 1147, 1211; M Saxer, 'The Politics of Responsibility to Protect', Friedrich Ebert Stiftung Briefing Paper No 2 (April 2008) 4, 5, available at http://library.fes.de/pdf-files/iez/global/05313–20080414.pdf.

[37] See A Bannon, 'The Responsibility to Protect: The UN World Summit and the Question of Unilateralism' (2006) 115 *Yale Law Journal* 1157, 1158, 1162; R Morningstar and C Blacker, 'World Orders: Unilateralism vs Multilateralism' (2004) 26 *Harvard International Review* 74, 74.

[38] See inter alia http://www.ambafrance-uk.org/Bernard-Kouchner-on-Burma-disaster.html, http://www.responsibilitytoprotect.org/index.php/crises/crisis-in-burma.

[39] UN Doc S/PRST/2008/18.

[40] AJ Bellamy, 'The Responsibility to Protect and the Problem of Military Intervention' (2008) 84 *International Affairs* 615, 617. Another champion of R2P, Thomas Weiss, considers that the US action in Iraq (2003) and the humanitarian concerns raised by President Bush contaminated

ment as a principle of universal acceptance. In the years that followed, despite the systematic efforts by the UN Secretary General and the inclusion of R2P as an item in the General Assembly's agenda (2009), nothing was added, clarified or improved.[41] As an author has recently—correctly—observed: 'As it stands, R2P is actually less likely to be implemented by the United Nations now than it was between 2001 and 2005'.[42]

The most significant recent development regarding R2P was SC Resolution 1973 (2011), which authorized military action in Libya to protect civilians, directly invoking Libya's responsibility to protect its population, which was seen by several authors as a triumph of R2P[43] since not only was it incorporated in an SC resolution, but it also authorized the use of force to protect civilians. It should be noted, however, that the resolution was passed by 10 positive votes and five important abstentions, namely China, Russia, India, Brazil and Germany,[44] while the resolution itself considered the situation as 'a threat to international peace and security'.[45] The phrasing of the latter resolution was repeated in SC Resolution 1975 (2011) on the post-election situation in Cote d'Ivoire,[46] and the same or similar language has frequently been used since by the SC in resolutions on post-Qaddafi Libya,[47] Yemen,[48] Mali,[49] South Sudan[50] and the Central African Republic.[51]

However, despite R2P-type language becoming frequent in the course of SC decision making, the outcome of the Libyan case was rather negative for R2P,[52] basically due to the misuse/abuse of the SC mandate (forcible protection of

the concept of R2P. T Weiss, 'R2P after 9/11 and the World Summit' (2006) 24 *Wisconsin International Law Journal* 740, 749.

[41] The resolution that was unanimously adopted, UN Doc A/RES/63/308, 7 October 2009, merely reaffirmed the 2005 WSOD commitments.

[42] RW Murray, 'Challenges Facing R2P Implementation' in WA Knight and F Egerton (eds), *The Routledge Handbook of the Responsibility to Protect* (Routledge, 2012), 72.

[43] See A Garwood-Gowers, 'China and the "Responsibility to Protect": The Implications of the Libyan Intervention' (2012) 2 *Asian Journal of International Law* 375, 375; T Weiss, 'R2P Alive and Well after Libya' (2011) 25 *Ethics and International Affairs* 1, 1.

[44] http://www.un.org/News/Press/docs/2011/sc10200.doc.htm.

[45] On the nature of SC Resolution 1973 see H Gärtner, *The Responsibility to Protect (R2P) and Libya* (Östereichisches Institut für Internationale Politik, 2011) 7.

[46] UN Doc S/RES/1975 (2011), 30 March 2011. According to Bellamy and Williams, although the abstaining states had serious doubts about the potential of military action in Libya, partly due to severe criticism, they 'abstained because they believed that they could not legitimize inaction in the face of mass atrocities': A Bellamy and P Williams, 'The New Politics of Protection? Cote d'Ivoire, Libya and the Responsibility to Protect' (2011) 87 *International Affairs* 825, 840.

[47] UN Docs S/RES/2016 (2011), 27 October 2011, and S/RES/2040 (2012), 12 March 2012, which repeated the same language as SC Resolution 1973, though after the military action, undertaken by virtue of the latter, had succeeded in defeating the brutal Qaddafi regime, with him killed and, supposedly, the source of all atrocities against the Libyan population removed.

[48] UN Doc S/RES/2014 (2011), 21 October 2011.

[49] UN Docs S/RES/2085 (2012), 19 December 2012, and S/RES/2100 (2013), 25 April 2013.

[50] UN Docs S/RES/1996 (2011), 8 July 2011 and S/RES/2109 (2013), 11 July 2013.

[51] UN Docs S/RES/2121 (2013), 10 October 2013, S/RES/2127 (2013), 5 December 2013, and S/RES/2134 (2014), 28 January 2014.

[52] See Garwood-Gowers (n 43 above), 376.

civilians) and the use of air power in order to destroy Qaddafi and secure an otherwise impossible victory for the rebels. This became evident during the various phases of the Syrian crisis, where all drafts that were proposed and involved Chapter VII measures against the Assad regime, mainly by Western powers, were blocked by Russia and China.[53]

F. Responsibility while Protecting (RWP)

Seen by some as the final blow to the R2P, the concept of 'responsibility while protecting' (RWP) was developed by a 2011 Brazilian initiative.[54] Its content, however, is not about destroying R2P, but about setting stricter and more detailed rules to be applied during the exercise of R2P, especially concerning the use of force.[55] Although most recent articles dealing with R2P tend to neglect this initiative, the evolution of RWP can be attributed to a necessity on behalf of many states to clarify and set the specific limits of R2P and the course of action by the SC in exercising R2P.

Ban Ki-moon implicitly acknowledged that RWP could serve as a useful addition to R2P by stating that

> The essence of 'responsibility while protecting' is doing the right thing, in the right place, at the right time and for the right reasons. Timely and decisive action puts a premium on assessment, on understanding what is happening, why it is happening, and how the international community can help keep a difficult situation from becoming worse.[56]

[53] UN Doc S/2012/538, 19 July 2012, which was a British draft resolution on UNSMIS that invoked Chapter VII and was vetoed by Russia and China; UN Doc S/2012/77, 4 February 2012, which was a draft resolution that promoted an Arab League plan for transition in Syria, which was also vetoed by Russia and China; and UN Doc S/2011/612, 4 October 2011, a draft resolution that condemned the Syrian crackdown on protestors and referred to Chapter VII measures, which was vetoed by Russia and China, while Brazil, India and South Africa abstained.

[54] UN Doc A/66/551, 11 November 2011.

[55] The relevant paragraphs read as follows: '(c) The use of force, including in the exercise of the responsibility to protect, must always be authorized by the Security Council, in accordance with Chapter VII of the Charter, or, in exceptional circumstances, by the General Assembly, in line with its resolution 377 (V);

(d) The authorization for the use of force must be limited in its legal, operational and temporal elements and the scope of military action must abide by the letter and the spirit of the mandate conferred by the Security Council or the General Assembly, and be carried out in strict conformity with international law, in particular international humanitarian law and the international law of armed conflict;

(e) The use of force must produce as little violence and instability as possible and under no circumstance can it generate more harm than it was authorized to prevent;

(f) In the event that the use of force is contemplated, action must be judicious, proportionate and limited to the objectives established by the Security Council;

(g) These guidelines must be observed throughout the entire length of the authorization, from the adoption of the resolution to the suspension of the authorization by a new resolution;'

[56] Ban K-m, 'Responsibility to Protect: Timely and Decisive Response', UN Doc A/66/874, 25 July 2012, para 53.

Western governments were less enthusiastic about the introduction and timing of this concept as it was considered to be a distraction from the events in Syria and the efforts of several Western powers to persuade the SC to authorize the use of force against the Syrian regime.[57] Regardless of the reaction of various stakeholders, RWP has been established as an addition to R2P and will certainly play a role in the further clarification or codification of the concept.[58] Moreover, the introduction of RWP signalled a clear message against the abuse of R2P to facilitate regime change or other concerns raised by adversaries of military intervention.[59]

III. R2P AND MINORITIES

A. Why Minorities?

It might seem a bit awkward for Kofi Annan to refer to minorities as recipients of humanitarian action, especially because the concept of minorities itself has never been granted a universally accepted definition, despite numerous efforts, during the last 40–50 years.[60] Nevertheless, the use of the concept of minorities by Kofi Annan in order to develop his argument was justified for a number of reasons.

While minorities have not been defined per se, they still constitute the most recognizable group in the eyes of general audiences. In the words of the first OSCE High Commissioner on Minorities Max van Der Stoel, 'Even though I may not have a definition of what constitutes a minority, I would dare to say that I know a minority when I see one'.[61]

[57] T Benner, 'Brazil as a Norm Entrepreneur: The "Responsibility while Protecting" Initiative', (Global Public Policy Institute, Berlin, 2013) 6. See also the remarks made by the US during the informal discussion of the concept, available at http://usun.state.gov/briefing/statements/184487.htm.

[58] P Wojcikiewicz Almeida, 'From Non-indifference to Responsibility while Protecting: Brazil's Diplomacy and the Search for Global Norms', Occasional Paper No 138 (South African Institute of International Affairs, 2013) 19, available at http://www.saiia.org.za/occasional-papers/from-non-indifference-to-responsibility-while-protecting-brazils-diplomacy-and-the-search-for-global-norms; J Pattison, 'The Ethics of "Responsibility while Protecting": Brazil, the Responsibility to Protect, and Guidelines for Humanitarian Intervention', Denver University Human Rights & Human Welfare Working Paper No 71 (2013) 21 available at http://www.du.edu/ korbel/hrhw/working/2013/71-pattison-2013.pdf.

[59] G Zyberi (ed), *An Institutional Approach to the Responsibility to Protect* (Cambridge University Press, 2013) 285.

[60] On the progressive development of minority rights and the issue of definition see, inter alia, F Capotorti, 'Study on the Rights of Persons belonging to Ethnic, Religious and Linguistic Minorities', UN Doc E/CN.4/Sub.2/384/Rev.1/1979; V Grammatikas, 'The definition of Minorities in International Law: A Problem Still Looking for a Solution' (1999) 52 *Revue Hellénique de Droit International* 321.

[61] Max van der Stoel, addressing the OSCE Human Dimension Seminar on Minorities, Warsaw, 24–28 May 1993, 5, available at http://www.osce.org/odihr/19660.

In contrast to other terms that are used (populations, civilians, citizens, residents, etc) which are neutral, the term 'minorities' bares significant emotional weight, thus attracting more attention.

As minorities have frequently been subjected to oppressive policies and ethnic cleansing, particularly in the former Soviet Union and Yugoslavia, public opinion is more sympathetic to the concept. Consequently, it is easier to 'sell' R2P (or humanitarian intervention) to Western audiences by reference to its application to minorities.

B. WSOD Crimes vis-à-vis Minorities

The WSOD applies R2P to four categories of crimes: genocide, war crimes, crimes against humanity and ethnic cleansing.[62] The ICISS report makes a more general reference to crimes and atrocities,[63] specifying several individual behaviours throughout the text.

If we stick to the WSOD list of crimes, as the one endorsed by all states, the first three are well established in international law. Genocide is prohibited by virtue of the UN Genocide Convention of 1948,[64] crimes against humanity are defined by the Statute of the International Criminal Court,[65] and war crimes constitute grave breaches of the 1949 Geneva Conventions and a series of other violations, codified in Article 8 of the ICC Statute.

Ethnic cleansing is a relatively new concept (albeit an old practice), meaning the forcible removal of a population from a certain geographical region, with a view to creating an ethnically homogeneous area. In contrast to genocide, ethnic cleansing does not involve the destruction of the group per se. It was first used to describe similar tactics that were employed during the Yugoslav wars.[66] It was added as a crime in Article 5 of the ICTY Statute, as well as a crime against humanity, in Article 7, § 1(d) of the ICC Statute.

In recent years, minorities have been subjected to similar treatment. The ICJ found that the Srebrenica massacre amounted to genocide, about 500,000 Serbs of Krajna (Kroatia) were ethnically cleansed during the 1995 operation storm of the Croatian military and several hundred thousand were forcibly removed from their homes during the Armenia–Azerbaijan war over Nagorno

[62] WSOD, para 138.

[63] ICISS report (n 19 above), para 2.29.

[64] Convention on the Prevention and Punishment of the Crime of Genocide, Paris, 9 December 1948, 78 UNTS 277. As of today, 144 states are parties to it.

[65] Rome Statute of the International Criminal Court, Rome, 17 July 1998, 2187 UNTS 3, Art 7, available at http://legal.un.org/icc/statute/romefra.htm. As of today, 122 states are parties to it (not including, among others, the US, Russia, China, Turkey, Israel and Egypt).

[66] As a practice, it was condemned by the UNGA Resolution A/RES/47/80 of 16 December 1992 as incompatible to universally recognized human rights. It was properly defined by a group of experts constituted by virtue of UN SC Resolution 780 (1992) in a document entitled 'Report of the Commission of Experts Established Pursuant to United Nations Security Council Resolution 780 (1992)' (UN Doc S/1994/674, 27 May 1994, para 130). They classified practices related to ethnic cleansing as a crime against humanity.

Karabakh, while in Karabakh itself all Azeris were cleansed. After Kosovo was 'liberated', in 2004, an organized circle of violence, the so-called March riots, cleansed Kosovo almost entirely of the remaining Serb and Roma populations.[67] Also, many political and military officers of all parties were convicted by the ICTY for war crimes and crimes against humanity. The catalogue of similar behaviours during the 1990s and even more recently is rather lengthy.

While several of the above actions targeted minorities, in most cases the framework was not formulated in the context of majority–minority relations. In Srebrenica, for example, the mass killings were committed against the majority group (the Bosniacs), while ethnic cleansing between Armenia and Azerbaijan was a generalized policy directed against all nationals of the other party residing in the 'wrong' territory. The Rwandan genocide was also not committed in terms of majority–minority relations.

In light of the above, it is submitted that R2P (in any of its versions) was not created with the intention of protecting minorities; crimes of this kind can be committed against anybody. Minorities may be more vulnerable as groups (in the majority of cases), but the general idea of R2P (the reaction phase) is to protect people against mass atrocities and not against any violation of human rights.

The wording of the WSOD itself refers to 'populations', thus extending the basis of its application far beyond the concept of minorities, in order to achieve a more generalized protective regime. On the other hand, the ICISS report contains a number of references to minorities, not as subjects of R2P, but as groups to be protected in the context of the responsibility to rebuild (the post-intervention phase).[68] Thus, it may reasonably be concluded that, when formulating the basic parameters of R2P, the ICISS did not intend to apply R2P to minority groups.

Moreover, the scale and effects criterion, also applied in the theories of humanitarian intervention, is rarely met in cases involving minorities. Even if one takes the landmark case of modern humanitarian intervention, Kosovo, the magnitude and type of violations were comparably very small in comparison to their effect, military campaign and assisted secession.[69]

[67] See A Hehir, 'Microcosm, Guinea Pig or *sui generis*? Assessing International Engagement with Kosovo' in A Hehir (ed), *Kosovo, Intervention and Statetbuilding* (Routledge, 2010), 190, 192.

[68] ICISS report (n 19 above), paras 5.8, 5.14, 5.15.

[69] According to Alex Bellamy, the level of violence in Kosovo prior to 1998 was not alarming at all: A Bellamy, *Kosovo and International Society* (New Hampshire, 2002) 24–26. General Clark, the NATO Commander-in-Chief during the Kosovo campaign, said 'What Milosevic never really understood was this wasn't a conflict strictly about Kosovo. It wasn't even a conflict ultimately about ethnic cleansing. It was a battle about the future of NATO, about the credibility of the US as a force in world affairs' (quoted in M Prokopijevic, 'Humanitarian Intervention' in G Meggle (ed), *Ethics of Humanitarian Intervention* (Ontos Verlag, 2004), 187). Finally, Noam Chomsky emphasized that 'Operation Allied Force was not designed as a means of blocking Serb ethnic cleansing. It was not designed as a means of waging war against the Serb and MUP forces in Kosovo. Not in any way. There was never any intend to do that' (N Chomsky, *The New Military Humanism: Lessons from Kosovo* (Pluto Press, 1999) 36).

IV. FUTURE OF R2P

The ultimate question to be asked is whether there is any and what kind of future for R2P. As the concept has already been abused several times before it is even properly established as a legal principle, and given the retreat of many states from the initial 2005 agreement (in terms of their subsequent attitude), its course in the international political arena appears uncertain.[70]

Syria could be used as a study case on the limits of R2P. Even if one accepted that R2P is a well-established principle of universal acceptance, Syria would probably be *the* case for the application of R2P. Many parts of its population face various types of atrocities, there are more than a million refugees in neighbouring states and the situation on the ground keeps deteriorating. The question, though, is rather simple: who should be protected from whom? The people in the rebellious cities, like Homs and Hama, from Assad? The civilians belonging to other Muslim denominations (Shias, Alawites) from the jihadist Sunni rebels and mercenaries? The Christian population of Syria, who are being systematically exterminated, including the oldest Christian communities in the world? And how should we treat civilians who cheer when the heads of their neighbours are cut off and footage is uploaded onto YouTube? A simple response would provide for an all-out war in Syria by an international force against all warring parties, in order to secure the lives and fundamental rights of civilians. Is this possible? Did the drafters of R2P (in any of its versions) conceive of such a situation? And are states willing to go that far to save the lives of innocent people, no matter what the cost and the implications of such an operation?

Despite the above considerations, the introduction of R2P as a protective principle of universal acceptance through the WSOD constitutes an important innovation towards the more effective protection of fundamental human rights before the UN. If and when R2P is dissociated from controversial applications (such as humanitarian intervention) and stops being used as a mere excuse for the legalization of the use of force (like in Libya), it could have a significant impact towards the formation of a new human rights world order within the only competent international forum, the United Nations.

As Anne Orford commented,

> the significance of the responsibility to protect lies not in its capacity to transform promise into practice, but rather in its capacity to transform practice into promise, or deeds into words. The project of developing and seeking to implement the R2P concept engages with the way in which the UN thinks.[71]

[70] For similar concerns over the future of R2P see M Serrano, 'The Responsibility to Protect and its Critics: Explaining the Consensus' (2011) 3 *Global Responsibility to Protect* 1, 13.

[71] A Orford, *International Authority and the Responsibility to Protect* (Cambridge University Press, 2011) 2–3.

9

Governance of Financial Crises: A Role for the International Protection of Economic and Social Rights?

LORENZA MOLA*

I. INTRODUCTORY REMARKS

AS HIGHLIGHTED THROUGHOUT different crisis periods, financial and economic hardship has an adverse impact on the enjoyment of human rights, particularly on the realization of economic and social rights (ESRs), and falls most heavily on the most vulnerable.[1] It has also been stated that austerity measures foreseen in adjustment programmes to cope with sovereign debt crises exacerbate the negative consequences of the difficult economic situation.[2] Indeed, the criticism raised in the past, on

* PhD, Associate Professor of International Law, Università degli Studi di Torino, Italy.

[1] As regards the serious crisis ongoing since 2007/2008, see United Nations Human Rights Council (HRC) Resolution on the Impact of the Global Economic and Financial Crises on the Universal Realization and Effective Enjoyment of Human Rights, S-10/1 (10th Special Session, 20 February 2009), UN Doc A/HRC/S-10/L1; Council of Europe Commissioner for Human Rights, 'Safeguarding Human Rights in Times of Economic Crisis', Issue Paper (Council of Europe, November 2013); European Union Fundamental Rights Agency (FRA), 'Protecting Fundamental Rights During the Economic Crisis', working paper (Publication Office of the European Union, 2010), available at http://fra.europa.eu/en/publication/2011/protecting-fundamental-rights-during-economic-crisis (accessed on 30 September 2014). It is a shared consideration that this crisis has had an adverse impact on all human rights and on all countries: Office of the UN High Commissioner for Human Rights (OHCHR), Report on the Impact of the Global Economic and Financial Crises on the Realization of All Human Rights and on Possible Actions to Alleviate it, submitted to the HRC in response to a request by the HRC following its 10th special session dedicated to this issue (17th session, 18 February 2010), UN Doc A/HRC/13/88.

[2] On 'the adverse impact of the debt burden and of the relevant adjustment measures on the enjoyment of economic, social and cultural rights in many countries' see Committee on Economic, Social and Cultural Rights (CESCR), 'General Comment No 2: International Technical Assistance Measures (Article 22)', E/1990/23, 2 February 1990, para 9, where the Committee 'recognizes that adjustment programmes will often be unavoidable and that these will frequently

the insensibility of inter-governmental financial institutions to human rights issues,[3] is echoed in many respects with regard to the crisis that has been ongoing since 2007/2008. This occurs especially in the debate on the austerity response pursued—at least initially—by several European countries, together with international and European institutions, namely the International Monetary Fund (IMF) and the European Union (EU). As observed by the Fundamental Rights Agency of the European Union, the EU has been facing a crisis which transcends issues of finance and 'has implication for democratic legitimacy and the rule of law, and therefore also for the respect of fundamental rights'.[4]

During the recent global crisis, another broad question has arisen, namely, whether the course of events has affected the global economic governance based on the international institutions that were created after the Second World War.[5] 'Global governance' has recently been described in terms of pluralism of actors, channels and forms, including 'the profusion within many domains of international organizations with partially complementary, but also partially competing purposes, representing differing values and accountable to distinct sets of authorizing actors . . . [in] novel forms of regulation'.[6] There is a trend at the global and European levels seeking to reform not only the macroeconomic approach to tackling serious debt crises but also the international financial architecture. In regard to both issues, an ever-increasing role

involve a major element of austerity', but it also warns that '[u]nder such circumstances . . . endeavours to protect the most basic economic, social and cultural rights become more, rather than less, urgent'. Referring to the crises in the early 1990s, see the Second Progress Report prepared by Danilo Türk, Special Rapporteur, Subcommission for the Prevention of Discrimination and Protection of Minorities (43rd session, 18 July 1991), UN Doc E/CN4/Sub2/1991/17, and his Final Report (49th session, 3 July 1992), UN Doc E/CN4/Sub.2/1992/16. For references to the literature developing such an argument regarding the crises in the 1980s see M Darrow, *Between Light and Shadow: The World Bank, The International Monetary Fund and International Human Rights Law* (Hart Publishing, 2003) 69. On the current crisis, see the report by Chepas Lumina, the then independent expert on the effects of foreign debt and other related international financial obligations of states on the full enjoyment of all human rights, particularly economic, social and cultural rights, submitted to the UN General Assembly (67th session, 13 August 2012), UN Doc A/67/304.

3 References to documents and literature on the issue are too numerous to list here. See Darrow's (ibid) analysis and the literature quoted therein.

4 FRA, *The European Union as a Community of Values: Safeguarding Fundamental Rights in Times of Crises* (Publication Office of the European Union, 2013) 5, available at http://fra.europa.eu/sites/default/files/fra-2013-safeguarding-fundamental-rights-in-crisis_en.pdf (accessed on 30 September 2014).

5 With a focus on the international, inter-institutional architecture of global economic governance, see M Vellano, 'La cooperazione tra le principali organizzazioni economiche internazionali' in A Comba (ed), *Neoliberismo e global economic governance* (Giappichelli, 2008) 283.

6 G De Burca, RO Kehoane and CF Sabel, 'New Modes of Pluralist Global Governance' NYU School of Law, Public Law Research Paper No 13-08/Columbia Law and Economics Working Paper No 448 (2013), available at http://ssrn.com/abstract=2225603 (accessed on 30 September 2014).

has been played by states gathered in such informal settings as the G20,[7] as well as by non-state actors.

With these perspectives in mind, the international protection of human rights in the wake of a serious economic crisis deserves specific attention. The present chapter intends to provide a review of international settings, at both the universal and regional levels, where the protection of human rights against the negative consequences of the recent crisis, and as part of its policy response, has been taken into account. The focus is on aspects of governance, rather than on international obligations to protect and promote human rights or on responsibility under international law. It is, however, worth recalling some basic points relating to international organizations.[8] As the International Court of Justice held in 1980, 'international organizations are subjects of international law and, as such, are bound by any obligations incumbent upon them under general rules of international law, under their constitutions or under international agreements to which they are parties'.[9] It could hardly be claimed that any human right standards, other than gross violations, have acquired the status of customary law. As regards treaty law, some authors have argued that international organizations, especially UN agencies, by virtue of the requirement to interpret their constitutive agreement consistently with regard to the UN Charter principles and in light of the agreements concluded with the UN, may be considered as being committed to not violate human rights principles and to 'prevent adverse human rights impacts'.[10]

The review is premised on the observation that the recent experience involving European countries provides both a special and a privileged field of study. In Europe, states' action in the face of the crisis has been shaped by strong international bounds stemming from membership of the EU. Some of these

[7] On the second issue, which is at the core of the G20's 'role and legacy' (www.g20.org), see M Giovanoli, 'The International Financial Architecture and its Reform after the Global Crisis' in M Giovanoli and D Devos (eds), *International Monetary and Financial Law: the Global Crisis* (Oxford University Press, 2010) 3.

[8] The literature has long concentrated on the question of whether international organizations may have any legal obligations to respect, prevent and fulfil human rights in the implementation of their mandate and be held responsible internationally directly, or whether international obligations are incumbent upon, and responsibility ultimately lies with, the member states. With specific reference to international financial institutions, S Skogly, *The Human Rights Obligations of the World Bank and the International Monetary Fund* (Cavendish Publishing, 2001); M Darrow (n 2 above), esp 124–33; B Ghazi, *The IMF, the World Bank and the Question of Human Rights* (Brill, 2005); P De Sena, 'International Monetary Fund, World Bank and Respect for Human Rights: A Critical Point of View' (2010) 10 *Italian Yearbook of International Law* 247.

[9] 'Interpretation of the Agreement of 25 March 1951 between the WHO and Egypt' [1980] ICJ Reports 1980, 73, 89–90.

[10] Darrow (n 2 above), 124–25, 132, referring to CESCR, General Comment No 2 (n 2 above), paras 6, 8–9. For a confutation of these theses, see De Sena (n 8 above), who also argues that international norms on the attribution of illicit acts to international organizations are hardly met when it comes to international financial institutions' activities, including policy conditionality on adjustment programmes. In principle, international organizations can be held internationally responsible for obliging their member states to commit human rights violations.

countries—notably, but not only, Greece[11]—have received financial assistance to support their increasingly unsustainable sovereign debts from other European states, EU institutions and the IMF acting in coordination through the 'troika' (ie the European Commission, the European Central Bank and the IMF). All these initiatives have been biased towards fiscal consolidation pursued through the adoption of austerity measures. The conditionality policy that has usually been implemented by the IMF in the past has thus been perpetuated within the European context, and was even given EU-treaty status with regard to the permanent crisis mechanism to safeguard the financial stability of the euro area as a whole.[12] Here, too, international and regional bodies devoted to the protection of human rights, particularly ESRs, have had a say on such policies. The review will thus be aimed at analysing how a plurality of actors has been engaged in the management of the crisis and its consequences on ESRs. In other words, actions that seek respect for the international obligations on the protection of ESRs are examined with a view to assessing whether they have or would have an impact on the governance of economic and financial crises, at both the national and supranational levels. This is done with the awareness that much more insightful analytical study on the relevant practice is required for such purposes.

Two main channels, involving a plurality of actors, can be detected in recent European practice. On the one hand, review mechanisms have been activated by institutional bodies or non-state actors that call into question the respect of human rights obligations by states enacting certain austerity measures. The case of Greece is a major example of where governmental decisions are assessed through, and partly reshaped after, the intervention of multiple actors and procedures for the protection of human rights. These aspects cannot be properly examined within the limits of this chapter, but some relevant decisions will be mentioned.[13] On the other hand, initiatives to strengthen coherence between human rights and financial concerns at the European and international institutional levels have also been undertaken. These initiatives accommodate new forms of interaction, although they also relate to the traditional problem of coordination between international institutions (Part II). All these instances have raised significant considerations about the substantial

[11] Summaries of the evolution of the Greek crisis and of the measures adopted pursuant to the adjustment programmes requested in exchange for international financial assistance or under EU procedures can be found in K Featherstone, 'The Greek Sovereign Debt Crisis and EMU: A Failing State in a Skewed Regime' (2010) 48 *Journal of Common Market Studies* 193; J Pagones, 'The European Union's Response to the Sovereign Debt Crisis: Its Effect on Labor Relations in Greece' (2013) 36 *Fordham International Law Journal* 1517.

[12] European Council Decision 2011/199/EU of 25 March 2011 amending Article 136 of the Treaty on the Functioning of the European Union with regard to a stability mechanism for Member States whose currency is the euro [2011] OJ L91/1.

[13] References to the decisions issued by several judicial bodies, such as national supreme courts, the European Court of Human Rights and the European Committee of Social Rights, as well as to related literature may be found in L Mola, 'The Margin of Appreciation Accorded to States in Times of Economic Crisis' (2015) 5(1) *Lex Social*.

aspects of the protection of ESRs in times of financial and economic crisis, clarifying the scope of minimum thresholds of protection. Most relevantly for the purposes of this chapter, they have also contributed to identifying the procedural aspects involved in several ESRs themselves—for example, the right to collective bargaining. The impact on governance is also clear: social dialogue and civil society participation have to be enhanced by governmental authorities in the determination of policy responses to the crisis, and international institutions should take account of this (Part III). However, although some progress can be found towards better integration of concerns relating to the realization of ESRs, recent experience also shows weaknesses of this aspect, in the emerging redefinition of governance of economic crises (Part IV).

II. COOPERATION AND COHERENCE AMONG INSTITUTIONS DEALING WITH HUMAN RIGHTS AND WITH FINANCIAL ISSUES IN CRISIS MANAGEMENT

On a number of occasions and in different settings, actors involved in managing the development of financial stability on the one hand and of human rights on the other hand have sought to coordinate their actions with a view to providing coherent and legitimate responses to the crisis that broke out in 2007. This part of the chapter presents an overview of the coordination mechanisms or instances activated among inter-governmental institutional actors at the universal and regional levels. A framework of existing statutory obligations and mechanisms is briefly outlined, and an analysis of initiatives relating to the crisis is carried out, both within the 'UN family', including specialized agencies, particularly the International Labour Organization (ILO) and the IMF, and through the regional/universal dimension.

The UN Charter provides norms on cooperation in the economic and social fields and in human rights matters (that is, the UN Organization's purposes set out in Articles 1, paragraph 3, and 55), addressing states (Article 56) and with regard to specialized agencies through coordination of their policies and activities (Article 58). As regards states' action within international institutions, the Economic and Social Council (ECOSOC) in particular may address recommendations to the Members of the United Nations with a view to coordinating the activities of the specialized agencies (Article 63, paragraph 2).

Moreover, the International Covenant on Economic, Social and Cultural Rights (ICESCR) provides an obligation upon state parties 'to take steps, individually and through international assistance and cooperation, especially economic and technical', to progressively realize the rights recognized therein (Article 2, paragraph 1). However, this has mainly been intended in relation to international cooperation for development.[14] The UN Committee on Eco-

[14] CESCR, 'General Comment No 3: The Nature of States Parties' Obligations (Art 2, Para 1, of the Covenant)', UN Doc E/1991/23, 14 December 1990, para 14; MS Carmona, 'The Obligation

nomic, Social and Cultural Rights (CESCR), in its General Comment No 18: The Right to Work, states as follows:

> *State Parties that are members of international financial institutions*, in particular the International Monetary Fund, the World Bank and regional development banks, should pay greater attention to protection of the right to work in *influencing* the lending policies, credit agreements, structural adjustment programmes and international measures of these institutions. These strategies, programmes and policies adopted by states parties under structural adjustment programmes should not interfere with their core obligations in relation to the right to work . . .[15]

Some comments on the above-quoted passage may inspire more general reflections. First of all, such a document aims to assist and promote the implementation of the covenant by clarifying its normative content on the basis of experience gained by the CESCR through the examination of states' reports.[16] Secondly, it addresses states and does not envisage similar obligations directly towards specialized agencies. Conversely, arguably, in the General Comment No 11: Plans of Action for Primary Education, the committee refers to the obligation of the 'international community' to assist and specifically mentions specialized agencies, including the ILO, the IMF and the World Bank.[17] Thirdly, at the same time, the extract above suggests that integration of human rights concerns into the activities of international financial institutions may be achieved precisely through the obligations of states that are parties to both treaties (the ICESCR and the treaty establishing the economic institution). This can be compared with the amplified version offered by the 1997 Maastricht Guidelines on Violations of Economic, Social and Cultural Rights, where it is stated that:

> The obligations of states to protect economic, social and cultural rights *extend also to their participation in international organizations, where they act collectively* . . . Member States of such organizations, individually or through the governing bodies, as well as the secretariat *and nongovernmental organizations* should encourage and generalized the trend of several such organizations to revise their policies and programmes to take into account issues of economic, social and cultural rights, especially when these policies and programmes are implemented in *countries that lack the resources to resist the pressure brought by international institutions on their decision-making affecting economic, social and cultural rights*.[18]

Fourthly, however, in General Comment No 18, quoted above, the influence to be exercised by state parties in international financial institutions is given

of "International Assistance and Cooperation" under the International Covenant on Economic, Social and Cultural Rights. A Possible Entry Point to Human Rights Based Approach to Millennium Development Goal' (2009) 13 *International Journal of Human Rights* 86.

[15] UN Doc E/C.12/GC/18, 6 February 2006, para 30 (emphasis added).

[16] Carmona (n 14 above), ft 25.

[17] UN Doc E/C12/1999/4, 10 May 1999, paras 9 and 11. See Carmona (n 14 above), 92.

[18] (1998) 28 HRQ 691 (emphasis added) and also the comment by V Dnakwa, C Flinterman and S Leckie at 705.

content in somewhat weak terms, as states 'should' pay attention to the right to work therein. Fifthly, states are addressed also in relation to their internal policy, when adopting measures within adjustment and structural programmes. This commitment was restated by the Chairperson of the CESCR at the 67th Session of the UN General Assembly in 2012, with reference to a letter addressed to state parties in May 2012, where he recalled 'their obligations to protect economic, social and cultural rights in times of economic and financial crisis'. This was in light of the fact that 'taking retrogressive steps in relation to economic, social and cultural rights is not only contrary to one's obligations under the Covenant', but also acts as a disincentive for growth and can have a disproportionate impact on the most vulnerable groups in society.[19]

As regards the relationships within the UN system—namely, the General Assembly and the ECOSOC according to Article 60 of the UN Charter on the one hand and the specialized agencies on the other hand—the view is commonly shared that the Charter's design has resulted in functional decentralization rather than in a framework for coordination.[20] Indeed, these institutions interact on a parity footing through relationship agreements between independent international organizations (Articles 57 and 63, paragraph 1).[21] Coordination of the activities of the specialized agencies is directly pursued by the UN through recommendations addressed to, as well as consultation with, them (Articles 58 and 63, paragraph 1). The centre for coordination is the Chief Executives Board for Coordination (CEB), which brings together the UN, specialized agencies (including the ILO, the IMF and the World Bank), other international organizations, such as the World Trade Organization (WTO), and funds and programmes established by the UN General Assembly. The CEB provides coordination and directions on social, economic and related matters for the UN system as a whole, focusing on inter-agency priorities and initiatives under the chairmanship of the Secretary General. In 2009, the Executive Heads of the CEB issued a communiqué on the UN System's response to the financial and economic crisis, which commits the inter-agency system to policy coherence and international policy coordination.[22]

On a general note, it is worth recalling that the IMF and the World Bank distinguish themselves from other specialized agencies by looser coordination and stronger autonomy safeguards,[23] while the ILO figures among the organ-

[19] Statement by Mr AG Pillay, UN General Assembly, 67th Session, Item 69(a), 23 October 2012.

[20] NM Blokker describes this 'coordination problem' as 'a time-honoured paradox of the UN system: the wish to combine the autonomy of the parts of the system with greater coherence', 'Explanatory Introduction' in NM Blokker and HG Schermers (eds), *Proliferation of International Organizations. Legal Issues* (Brill, 2001) 1, 43.

[21] MR Saulle, *Lezioni di Organizzazione Internazionale*, 2nd edn (Edizioni Scientifiche Italiane, 2002) 195, 197.

[22] CEB, 'The Global Financial Crisis and its Impact on the Work of the UN System', CEB Issue Paper (April 2009), available at http://www.unsceb.org/CEBPublicFiles/Global%20Financial%20Crisis.pdf (accessed on 15 October 2014).

[23] Relationship agreement between the UN and the IMF of 15 November 1947, Art I, para 2 specifies that '[b]y reason of the nature of its international responsibilities and the terms of its

izations which cooperate most actively with the UN.[24] Arguably, this has also emerged in the current crisis period.

Two bodies monitoring the realization of ESRs within the UN and the ILO—namely the CESCR, and the Committee of Experts on the Application of Conventions and Recommendations—have held informal meetings since 2002, hosted by the Friedrich Ebert Foundation, with the aim of enhancing cooperation and exchanging views on issues of mutual interest.[25] At the seventh meeting, in 2009, representatives of the European Committee of Social Rights (the monitoring body of the European Social Charter within the Council of Europe (CoE))[26] were also present, as in 2008 all three bodies had engaged in studies on social security especially in the time of global financial crisis. In 2012, in reporting on the point to the UN General Assembly, the CESCR stressed once again the importance it gave to 'promoting coherent and mutually reinforcing approaches'.[27] Similar meetings have not taken place between the UN organs and the IMF, apart from the one-day meetings between ECOSOC, the IMF and the World Bank, which have been running annually since 1998. However, and more generally, such meetings do not convincingly deal with the coordination problem.[28]

Another prominent ILO initiative vis-à-vis the global crisis is the Global Jobs Pact, which was adopted by the International Labour Conference in June 2009[29] and endorsed by ECOSOC.[30] The pact outlines policy measures which countries are encouraged to adopt in order to ease the impact of the crisis and accelerate recovery in employment. In addition, it requires policy coherence and international cooperation for the effective implementation of these policies.[31] The pact is one of the nine Joint Crisis Initiatives agreed upon by the CEB during the spring session in April 2009.[32]

With regard to cooperation on an inter-institutional level between specialized

Articles of Agreement, the Fund is, and is required to function as, an independent international organization' (similarly, UN/World Bank agreement, Art 1, para 2). The cooperation envisaged in this agreement takes the forms of reciprocal representation, proposal of agenda items, consultation and recommendations, and exchange of information. On this point, see Skogly (n 8 above), 103–04; A Di Blase, *Nazioni Unite e istituti specializzati. La rilevanza giuridica del coordinamento* (Jovene, 1982).

24 Agreement between the UN and the ILO, signed on 30 May 1946, [1946] XXIX(4) Official Bulletin.

25 CESCR, Report on the Forty-sixth and Forty-seventh Sessions, UN Docs E/2012/22 and E/C.12/2011/3 (2012), paras 444–45.

26 See n 51 below.

27 Report on the Forty-second and Forty-third Sessions, UN Doc E/2010/22 (2012), para 492.

28 Blokker (n 20 above), 39.

29 International Labour Conference, 'Recovering from the Crisis: A Global Jobs Pact', adopted at the 98th Session, 19 June 2009, available at http://www.ilo.org/wcmsp5/groups/public/---ed_norm/---relconf/documents/meetingdocument/wcms_115076.pdf (accessed on 30 November 2014).

30 ECOSOC Resolution 2010/25, 23 June 2010, UN Doc E/2010/INF/2/Add.1, 129–30.

31 See also the UN Secretary General Report, UN Doc E/2011/92, 28 April 2011, prepared by the ILO, and ECOSOC Resolution 2011/37, 28 July 2011, UN Doc E/2011/L21/Rev1, paras 6–8.

32 See n 22 above.

agencies,[33] the crisis brought about a number of instances where coherence and convergence were sought. Focusing on the relations between the ILO and the IMF, which are not based on a bilateral agreement, the jointly held 2010 Oslo Conference assumed a prominent role in promoting their cooperation efforts in face of the current economic and financial crisis. In a discussion paper drafted for discussion at the conference,[34] the two international organizations acknowledged that since 1945 there has been 'increasing policy specialization and even contradiction', in contrast to the envisaged architecture for global governance and the requirement it implied for 'policy coherence across the responsibilities of different ministries and international organizations'.[35] The drafters then highlighted the strong need for cooperation. However, they left this to the mutual commitment by countries, such as recognized by the G20 summits and the G20 process of mutual assessment and multilateral consultations launched in 2009.[36] This is certainly interesting for the purposes of this analysis and in light of the general comments made above on the role of states, and is discussed further in Part IV below. Overall, this initiative does not seem to add any significant innovative inter-institutional elements to the policy dialogue developed between the ILO and the Bretton Wood financial institutions since the 1995 Copenhagen Summit for Social Development and the East Asian financial crisis.[37]

Since the 2010 Oslo Conference, meetings between the ILO and the IMF have taken place at country level. On the occasion of the 9th ILO Regional Meeting, which took place in Oslo in April 2013, a high-level tripartite ILO/IMF/European Commission (EC) panel discussion dealt, inter alia, with the question whether there is 'an opportunity for enhanced international policy

[33] For example, according to Art X of the Articles of Agreement of the IMF, this organization 'shall cooperate within the terms of this Agreement with any general international organization and with public international organizations having specialized responsibilities in related fields'. In 1989, the IMF and the World Bank concluded an agreement fixing the modalities of the cooperation which had developed so far (the IMF–World Bank Concordat, SM/89/54).

[34] IMF/ILO, 'The Challenges of Growth, Employment and Social Cohesion', discussion paper for the Joint ILO–IMF Conference in cooperation with the office of the Prime Minister of Norway (Oslo, 13 September 2010), available at http://www.osloconference2010.org/discussionpaper.pdf (accessed on 15 October 2014).

[35] As regards international economic institutions, a shortfall of cohesion often reflects a lack of coherence between the ideological approaches (P Juillard, 'Les organisations internationales économiques' in R-J Dupuy (ed), *Manuel sur les organisations internationales*, 2nd edn (Martinus Nijhoff, 1998) 649–701), while these institutions all pursue the same ultimate objectives (Vellano, n 5 above).

[36] IMF/ILO (n 34 above), Concluding observations.

[37] A detailed overview is outlined by the former ILO Deputy Director-General for External Relations from 1994 to 1998 and Executive Director for Social Dialogue from 1998 to 2000, KA Hagen, 'Policy Dialogue Between the International Labour Organization and the International Financial Institutions: The Search for Convergence' (2003) 9 *Friedrich Ebert Stiftung Dialogue on Globalization Occasional Papers*, available at http://library.fes.de/pdf-files/bueros/genf/50035.pdf. As for legal documents, see in particular IMF, 'Communiqué of the Interim Committee of the Board of Governors of the International Monetary Fund', IMF Press Release No 95/51 (Washington, October 1995), available at www.imf.org/external/np/sec/pr/1995/pr9551.htm (accessed on 15 October 2014).

coherence based on analysis, research and policy cooperation between the ILO, the IMF and the European Commission'.[38] High-level officials from the ILO expressed the urgent need for closer cooperation and coherence between the ILO, the IMF and the EU. Their IMF counterparts also declared their awareness that international organizations have shared responsibilities, notwithstanding their different mandates. In the final 2013 Oslo Declaration, the ILO's means of actions are identified as promoting synergies and policy coherence with international and regional organizations and institutions (reference being made to the IMF, the OECD, the World Bank, the EU and the Eurasian Economic Commission) and through fora such as the G20.[39]

Inter-level institutional meetings have also occurred within missions undertaken by human rights monitoring bodies to some of the European countries that were severely hit by the crisis, in particular Greece. The ILO Conference Committee requested a high-level mission of the ILO to visit Greece and also to meet the European Commission and the IMF; these took place in Athens, Brussels and Washington in autumn 2011. These inter-organizational meetings provided an exchange of views on the situation in Greece and on the policy measures adopted to cope with the crisis. However, they ended quite poorly, with the EU acknowledging that there is room for the ILO to provide assistance within its sphere of competences and with the IMF declaring its readiness to stay in touch.[40] It seems that the consideration made by the European Parliament, that the ILO should be involved in the EU–IMF financial assistance programmes, has still not been satisfied to date.[41] Also Mr Lumina, the independent expert on the effects of foreign debt and other international financial obligations of states on the full enjoyment of all human rights, particularly ESRs, undertook an official visit to Greece in April 2013. There he met national institutions as well as representatives of international institutions (the IMF, the European Commission and the UN High Commissioner for Refugees in Greece), along with academics and civil society organizations.[42]

[38] ILO, 'Recovery from Crisis—Coherent Policies for Growth and Jobs', background paper for the high-level tripartite ILO/IMF/EC panel discussion (2013), available at http://www.ilo.org/global/meetings-and-events/regional-meetings/europe-and-central-asia/erm-9/lang--en/index.htm (accessed on 15 October 2014).

[39] ILO, 'The Oslo Declaration: Restoring Confidence in Jobs and Growth' Ninth European Regional Meeting, Oslo, ERM.9/D7 (2013) 3.

[40] ILO Report on the High Level Mission to Greece (Athens, 19–23 September 2011) (Geneva, December 2011), available at http://www.ilo.org/wcmsp5/groups/public/@ed_norm/@normes/documents/missionreport/wcms_170433.pdf (accessed on 15 October 2014) esp 50–57.

[41] European Parliament Resolution on the Financial, Economic and Social Crisis: Recommendations concerning the Measures and Initiatives to be Taken (6 July 2011) [2013] OJ C33E/140.

[42] C Lumina, 'End of Mission Statement. Mission to Greece, 22–26 April 2013' (26 April 2013). See also 'Mission to Latvia (14–18 May 2012)', Addendum to Report 2013, UN Doc A/HRC/23/37/Add1, 27 May 2013, available at www.ohchr.org (accessed on 18 August 2013). Inconsistency with the obligations undertaken by the countries through ratification of core international human rights treaties is evoked, albeit indirectly. It is also noticed that 'there are viable alternatives to rigid austerity'.

III. CRISIS GOVERNANCE THROUGH SOCIAL DIALOGUE AND CIVIL SOCIETY PARTICIPATION

The activation of human rights bodies during the recent economic crisis[43] has outlined a major implication in terms of governance, at least within states. Emphasis has constantly been placed on the involvement of collective interest representations and civil society in the policy responses to the crisis. As the European experience itself has recently demonstrated, two threats may occur to participatory rights when national governments act under pressure within an economic crisis. One regards the way in which policy measures are decided and the other concerns the content of such measures. Both attenuate the forms of representation and consultation that were previously put in place.[44]

Almost all institutional and non-governmental actors concerned with the respect for human rights in this economic crisis, at all levels, have called for 'ensuring the full participation of all segments of society in decision-making processes'.[45] In particular, protecting and enhancing the role of collective bargaining, tripartite consultations and more generally social dialogue is important as it allows the social consequences of the crisis to be fully taken into account.[46] Social dialogue constitutes one of the sets of measures envisaged by the ILO's Global Jobs Pact.

Similarly, a general assumption stems from the monitoring bodies of the ILO and the CoE that are dealing with the ESRs that are under threat during this economic crisis. The rights to organize and to collectively bargain and the space for democratic participation should be preserved and enhanced in the determination of measures affecting human rights in times of economic hardship. In its 2013 report, with specific regard to Greece, the ILO Committee of Experts on the Application of Conventions and Recommendations commented that governments should assure that social partners be 'fully involved in the determination of any further alterations [of labour relations] within the framework of the agreements with the EC, the International Monetary Fund . . . and the European Central Bank', and that their views be fully taken into account.[47] This was also pointed out by the ILO Committee on Freedom of Association within the complaint on the Spanish measure suspending a

[43] See n 13 above, 48–51, 57.

[44] J Sarkin and M Koenig, 'Developing the Right to Work: Intersecting and Dialoguing Human Rights and Economic Policies' (2011) 33 *Human Rights Quarterly* 1.

[45] Lumina, 'End of Mission Statement' (n 42 above).

[46] ILO (n 38 above); IMF/ILO (n 34 above).

[47] ILO Committee of Experts on the Application of Conventions and Recommendations, Report III (Part 1A) (2013) ILO Doc ILC/201/III1(A) 107. Similarly, in its Report 2014 (ILO Doc ILC103/III/1B, 118), the Committee of Experts reiterated that full consultation of the social partners and their direct participation in the operation of minimum wage systems is a fundamental principle. It also stated that, as noted vis-à-vis Portugal's legislation on minimum wages in its Report 2013, this principle 'assumes particular importance in periods of economic and social crisis, owing to the considerable repercussions that decisions relating to the fixing and periodic adjustment of minimum wages are likely to have on economic policy, including employment policy, and the purchasing power of workers. Open and constructive social dialogue facilitates

collective agreement relating to an increase in remuneration throughout the public administration.[48] The committee recalled that the right to collective bargaining is a fundamental right. Accordingly, it specified that, in the context of economic stabilization, collective bargaining should be given priority over the adoption of legislation as a means of determining conditions of employment. As a consequence, although a decision by the government that the conditions of employment cannot be settled freely through collective bargaining was not precluded, it should be considered an exceptional measure, satisfying conditions on necessity and temporariness, and providing safeguards to protect workers' living standards. Moreover, the government should make efforts to convince the social partners to voluntarily adapt the collective agreements to the new economic policy instead of imposing their renegotiation.[49]

At the regional level, within the CoE, the Parliamentary Assembly called for enhanced democratic structures and processes by means of parliamentary participation, and new forms of participation and consultation of citizens in economic policy making at the national and EU levels.[50] The European Committee of Social Rights expressed a similar position with respect to the restrictive content of the measures impinging on labour rights. According to this body, the European Social Charter aims to provide guarantees in times when the beneficiaries need the protection most.[51]

the adoption of balanced measures to ensure a fair division of the efforts to be made to overcome the crisis, thereby promoting support for reforms and the maintenance of social cohesion.'

[48] Case No 2918, *Citizens' Service Federation of the Trade Union Confederation of Workers' Commissions (FSC-CCOO), Report No 368, para 362*. This special procedure, which supplements the general procedures for the supervision of the application of ILO standards, was established in 1950–51; governments or organizations of workers and of employers can submit complaints concerning violations of trade union rights by states even when the Conventions on Freedom of Association and Collective Bargaining have not been ratified. For more information see ILO, *Freedom of Association. Digest of Decisions and Principles of the Freedom of Association Committee of the Governing Body of the ILO*, 5th rev edn (International Labour Office, 2006).

[49] Case No 2820, *Greek General Confederation of Labour (GSEE), Civil Servants' Confederation (ADEDY), General Federation of Employees of the National Electric Power Corporation (GENOP–DEI–KIE) and Greek Federation of Private Employees (OIYE) supported by the International Confederation of Trade Unions (ITUC)*, Report No 365, para 995.

[50] Resolution on 'Austerity Measures—A Danger for Democracy and Social Rights', 21st and 22nd Sittings (26 June 2012) Res 1884 (2012).

[51] *General Federation of Employees of the National Electric Power Corporation (GENOP-DEI) / Confederation of Greek Civil Servants' Trade Unions (ADEDY) v Greece*, Complaint Nos 65/2011 and 66/2011, decisions on the merits of 18 June 2012, para 18. The European Committee of Social Rights examined the situation in single European countries within the state reporting procedure since 2009, and adopted an interpretative statement on the guarantee of ESR in times of economic crisis in its Conclusions of 2009 ('Comment on the Application of the Charter in the Context of the Global Economic Crisis', *European Social Charter (Revised)—Conclusions 2009, vol. 1* and *European Social Charter—Conclusions XIX-2 (2009)*, in both documents at paras 15 and 17). It also received complaints against Greece by Greek trade unions within the optional collective complaints procedure. The complainants were the same trade unions as those addressing the ILO bodies plus several others claiming the violation of similar rights envisaged by the respective treaty instruments, through the same austerity measures designed to implement the Memoranda of Understanding signed by the 'troika'. On the collective complaint procedure provided in the optional Additional Protocol of 1995, entered into force in 1998 (signed by

The EU has been subjected to severe criticism, from a human rights perspective, with regard to the legitimacy and accountability of its procedures and austerity approach in reaction to the crisis. As a result, some progress has then been made on involving social partners and civil society in the decision-making process when dealing with financial stabilization. This is especially laid down in the Regulation on the strengthening of economic and budgetary surveillance of Member States in the euro area experiencing or being threatened with serious difficulties with regard to their financial stability.[52] For the first time in a piece of legislation aimed at contrasting financial instability, following amendments introduced by the European Parliament, legal obligations are imposed on the EU and on the Member States to take human rights and democratic participation into account. First of all, explicit reference is made to the so-called 'social clause' inserted by the Lisbon Treaty at TFEU, Article 9.[53] Secondly, consideration is given to the need for rules enhancing dialogue between EU institutions, improving transparency and accountability, and informing the European Parliament of a Member State that is subject to a macroeconomic adjustment programme or enhanced surveillance.[54] It also states that Member States 'should involve the social partners and civil society organizations in the preparation, implementation, monitoring and evaluation of financial assistance programmes, in accordance with national rules and practice'.[55] Thirdly, 'full' observance is imposed on EU institutions and Member States of the treaty provision on the role of social parties and the social tripartite summit at the EU level (TFEU, Article 152) and of the right to collective bargaining and action recognized by the Charter of Fundamental Rights of the European Union.[56] This specification may appear pleonastic, as it refers to the respect of primary EU law in implementing secondary law, unless it implies the intention to exclude the possibility of applying derogations or at least of applying them very restrictively. Indeed, the most stringent interpretation would go beyond the determinations by the human rights moni-

Greece and entered into force for that country in 1998), and more generally on the European Social Charter and its control procedures, see O De Schutter (ed), *The European Social Charter: A Social Constitution for Europe* (Bruylant, 2010).

52 Regulation (EU) 472/2013 of the European Parliament and of the Council of 21 May 2013 [2013] OJ L140/1.

53 Ibid, recital 2.

54 Ibid, recital 10.

55 Ibid, recital 11.

56 Ibid, Art 1, para 4. According to Art 51, para 1 of the Charter ([2012] OJ C236/391), the Charter's provisions are addressed to the institutions, bodies, offices and agencies of the Union, which shall abide by it within the exercise of their powers and EU competences. Following this, the European Commission and the Council have adopted internal guidelines and resolutions on the mainstreaming of human rights in their activities: see I Butler, 'Ensuring Compliance with the Charter of Fundamental Rights in Legislative Drafting: The Practice of the European Commission' [2012] *European Law Review* 397. The Charter also binds Member States when they are implementing EU law.

toring bodies themselves.[57] Finally, Member States are required to ('shall') seek the views of, and pursue consensus by, social partners and civil society organizations during the preparatory phase of their macroeconomic adjustment programmes.[58]

IV. CONCLUDING OBSERVATIONS

This chapter has sought to provide a broad overview of the instances that have occurred at the international institutional level during the recent financial and economic crisis that could have an impact on global governance by the integration of human rights concerns into macroeconomic policy responses. From the above examination, the following conclusions are drawn.

First of all, in terms of 'governance', as mentioned at the beginning of the paper, at least as far as Europe is concerned, recent developments show increased pluralism and complexity. Regarding the plurality of 'actors', social parties, national judges, regional parliamentary assemblies, and regional and international human rights, monitoring bodies have actively interacted with governments and among themselves to seek respect for ESRs within the economic policy reactions to the crisis. However, the interplay between these actors and regional and universal institutions dealing with financial stability is limited. As regards 'channels', alongside judicial, collective complaint and review mechanisms dealing with human rights, inter-policy cooperation has been pursued mainly through institutional informal meetings and official visits. Conversely, the EU has undertaken legislative process which pursues the integration of some social rights into the preparation, implementation, monitoring and evaluation of macroeconomic adjustment programmes. Finally, the outcomes of such initiatives are in different 'forms'. They consist mainly of reports, resolutions, joint background papers, discussion papers and press releases, while binding commitments appear only within the EU legal order. At the inter-institutional level, it appears that the involvement of human rights-

[57] In particular, the European Court of Human Rights accorded states such as Greece a wide margin of appreciation as regards limitations to the rights enshrined in the European Convention on Human Rights for fiscal consolidation purposes in times of serious economic and financial crisis. It significantly relied on the national supreme courts' assessment of the general interests at stake, also taking account of the observation that the national interest at the time corresponded to the general interest of the Member States of the euro area in light of the EU obligations on fiscal consolidation. See *Koufaki and ADEDY v Greece* App Nos 57665/12 and 57657/12 (ECtHR, 7 May 2013), esp paras 12, 31, 37–38, 44; *da Conceição Mateus and Santos Januário v Portugal*, App nos 62235/12 and 57725/12 (ECtHR, 13 October 2013), esp paras 22, 25.

[58] Regulation (EU) 472/2013 (n 52 sbove), Art 8. It is worth mentioning the most recent meetings of the Tripartite Social Summit: see European Commission, Communication to the European Parliament and the Council, Strengthening the Social Dimension of the Economic and Monetary Union, COM(2013) 690 (Brussels, 2 October 2013). The Tripartite Social Summit for Growth and Employment was established by Council Decision 2003/174/EC of 6 March 2003 [2003] OJ L70/31. It brings together the Council 'troika', the European Commission, 10 workers' representatives and 10 employers' representatives from the European and national levels.

related bodies in the elaboration of the economic policy response to the crisis has not been shaped in formal settings and procedures.

Secondly, with specific reference to the broad UN family, in face of the recent financial and economic crisis, it does not seem that the current framework for global governance has overcome the problems of cooperation that have occurred in the past. One may think of the lack of institutionalization of coordination meetings between international bodies. The acknowledged need for policy coherence across the responsibilities of different international organizations has not so far been integrated into the follow-up practice of each institution. Even in highly structured and binding institutional and normative settings among states, such as the EU, the widespread recourse to mechanisms outside the Treaties risks hampering attempts at coordinating and balancing pursuance of financial stabilization with respect for human rights (including the right to collective bargaining and those other rights having procedural, participatory aspects as their core element).[59]

Thirdly, as well as the procedures put in place within the post-1945 international institutional architecture, the new fora, informal settings and novel configurations that group together different actors should be noted. In general, stress has increasingly been put on states and their obligations and commitments to act unilaterally and collectively within international institutions and the G20. This attenuates the pressure of addressing the issue of international organizations' commitments vis-à-vis the protection of human rights in economic crisis contexts. However, it also calls for an enhanced role of the human rights monitoring mechanisms available within regional and universal institutions, even though the outcomes of most procedures are not binding. The trend towards crisis management centred in states at the global level is strongly reflected in the growing importance gained by the G20 since 2008. Although it was founded as long ago as 1999, its recent revival was intended to provide a centre from which to face the global financial and economic crisis. The G20 brings together the G8 members, emerging countries and the EU, which is represented by the presidents of the European Council and the European Central Bank. It has been defined as a contemporary version of the concert system consisting of multilateral, high-level, political conferences of Westphalian memory.[60] Indeed, it has described itself as 'the premier forum

[59] Treaty establishing the European Stability Mechanism, concluded by the euro area Member States, available at http://www.esm.europa.eu/pdf/esm_treaty_en.pdf, and the Treaty on Stability, Coordination and Governance in the Economic and Monetary Union, concluded by all EU Member States with the exception of the United Kingdom and the Czech Republic, available at http://www.consilium.europa.eu/media/1478399/07_-_tscg.en12.pdf (accessed on 30 September 2014).

[60] C Ku, *International Law, International Relations and Global Governance* (Routledge, 2012) 46.

for international cooperation on the most important issues of the global economic and financial agenda'.[61]

Thus, the question arises whether the persistent coordination problem among the international organizations which were designed to provide global governance post-1945 has contributed to the shift in the core settings from where to address the crisis. Furthermore, one may ask whether this current framework enhances the integration of human rights concerns within global economic governance. To answer these questions, evidence may be found in the kind of interactions that exist between formal international organizations and the G20. With reference to the issues outlined in the previous analysis, economic-related organizations such as the IMF, the World Bank, the Financial Stability Board, the OECD and the WTO, as well as the UN and the ILO, regularly attend G20 meetings. Several documents are prepared or addressed by international institutions to the G20. This was the case with the ILO's dossier for the G20 Employment and Labour Ministers meeting in Washington DC in April 2010.[62] As well as providing technical support or advice, international organizations are also involved in drafting reports, position papers and proposals on the agenda, and they take into account the outcomes of the meetings in their subsequent activity. It is against such a background and ongoing developments that the first ever G20 Finance and Labour Ministers meeting took place in Russia in July 2013. The final document[63] is clearly based on the assumption that the social dimension of economy is beginning to play an increasingly important role, and it elaborates on labour-fostering and labour-market policies, including collective bargaining and social dialogue. However, one cannot single out any explicit reference to human rights, particularly ESRs; nor is any mention made of international coordination and coherence other than within the G20 itself. Again, and overall, some advance may be found in the recent economic and financial crisis, towards the redesigning of socially responsible global economic governance, but general propositions have not been implemented (so far).

[61] The citation comes from http://www.g20.org/docs/about/about_G20.html (accessed on 31 July 2013). Interestingly, as of November 2013, the presentation read slightly differently, as follows: 'the premier forum for its members' international economic cooperation and decision-making . . . G20 leaders meet annually, additionally during the year Finance Ministers and Central Bank Governors meet regularly to discuss ways to strengthen the global economy, reform international financial institutions, improve financial regulation, and discuss the key economic reforms that are needed in each of the member countries'.

[62] The dossier and other information are available at http://www.ilo.org/dyn/jobcrisis/f?p=11105:12:0 (no longer updated) (accessed on 30 November 2014).

[63] G20 Labour and Employment and Finance Ministers' Communiqué (Moscow, 19 July 2013), esp point 8, available at http://www.voltairenet.org/Article179531.html (accessed on 30 November 2014).

10

Recent Regulatory Initiatives in the Ratings Industry: CRA III and the ESMA Proposals on Structured Finance, the Performance of Agencies and their Fee Arrangements

EMMANUEL P MASTROMANOLIS*

I. INTRODUCTION

FOR A NUMBER of years, the status and the activities of credit rating agencies had remained unregulated; the agencies were only directed to follow a set of seminal and non-binding conduct guidelines released by IOSCO,[1] touching upon such fundamental issues as the quality and integrity of the rating process, the avoidance of conflict of interest situations and the agencies' disclosure obligations towards the investing public.[2] Many theorists

* Assistant Professor of Commercial Law, Faculty of Law, National & Kapodistrian University of Athens.

[1] The initial version of the IOSCO Code of Conduct Fundamentals for Credit Rating Agencies issued by the Technical Committee of the International Organization of Securities Commission (December 2004) is available at http://www.iosco.org/library/pubdocs/pdf/IOSCOPD180.pdf; its revised version (May 2008) is available at http://www.iosco.org/library/pubdocs/pdf/IOSCOPD271.pdf. According to the guidelines, agencies had to 'comply or explain' any instances of deviation of their own code of conduct from such guidelines.

[2] See, in particular, Arts 1.1 (adoption, implementation and enforcement of written procedures), 1.2 (use of rigorous and systematic rating methodologies), 1.9 (regular review of issuers' creditworthiness), 2.4 (dissociation of the ratings from business relationships of the rating agency and the rated issuer), 2.5 (operational separation of the rating business and other businesses of the rating agency), 2.7 (disclosure of actual and potential conflicts of interest of the agency), 2.9 (no engagement in securities or derivatives trading presenting conflicts of interest for the rating activities of the agency), 2.13 (handling of conflicts of interests at the level of the agencies' employees), 3.1 (distribution of ratings in a timely manner), 3.5 (publication of sufficient

partly attributed the outburst and expansion of the worldwide financial crisis of year 2008 to this very legislative lacuna.[3] In the context of the crisis, the agencies were considered to have considerably contributed to the lenient, and largely unconstrained, assessment of the credit risk arising from the novel financial products that had been widely distributed in the financial markets during the period that preceded the crisis, and thus to have endorsed those products. In the aftermath of the crisis, the European Union, acting alongside parallel United States legislative initiatives,[4] promptly developed a two-stage regulatory response, reflected in two regulations that entered into force in 2009 and 2011.[5] These regulations mostly address such issues as the licensing specifications of the agencies wishing to have their ratings equipped with regulatory licenses in the European Union; the agencies' internal governance; the handling of conflicts of interest within the agencies, including those arising from the 'issuer pays' remuneration pattern; the transparency of several aspects of the agencies' status and operations; and the sanctions imposed on the agencies in case of their failure to abide by the provisions of the regulations.[6]

information on methodologies and assumptions underlying the ratings), 3.8 (publication of information regarding the historical default rates of each rating category) of the initial Code of 2004 and Arts 1.7-1 (establishment of a review function within the rating agency), 2.8 (disclosure of the agency's compensation arrangements, compensation derived from non-rating activities and identity of clients from which the agency derives more than 10% of its annual revenue) and 3.5 (provision of information of loss and cash-flow analysis for structured finance products and distinguished presentation of the ratings of such products) of the revised codes of 2008.

[3] See, eg J Coffee, 'What Went Wrong? An Initial Inquiry into the Causes of the 2008 Financial Crisis' (2009) 9 *Journal of Corporate Law Studies* 1; D Darcy, 'Credit Rating Agencies and the Credit Crisis: How the "Issuer Pays" Conflict Contributed and What Can Regulators Do About It' (2009) *Columbia Business Law Review* 604; K Dennis, 'The Ratings Game: Explaining Rating Agency Failures in the Build Up to the Financial Crisis' (2008–09) 63 *University of Miami Law Review* 1112; C Hill, 'Why Did Rating Agencies Do Such a Bad Job Rating Subprime Securities?' (2009–10) 71 *University of Pittsburgh Law Review* 585; JP Hunt, 'Credit Rating Agencies and the "Worldwide Credit Crisis": The Limits of Reputation, the Insufficiency of Reform, and a Proposal for Improvement' (2009) *Columbia Business Law Review* 109; F Partnoy, 'Perspectives on the Financial Crisis: Ivan Kreuger, the Credit-Rating Agencies, and the Two Theories About the Function, and Dysfunction, of Markets' (2009) 26 *Yale Journal on Regulation* 431; L White, 'Credit-Rating Agencies and the Financial Crisis: Less Regulation of CRAs is a Better Response' (2010) 4 *Journal of International Banking Law and Regulation* 170.

[4] Credit Rating Agency Reform Act of 2006, 15 USC 78o-7 (27 September 2006); Title IX, Subtitle C of the Dodd-Frank Wall Street Reform and Consumer Protection Act, ss 931–39H, Publ No 111-203, 124 Stat 1376 (2010); Securities Exchange Act of 1934 (as amended), Rules 17g-1–17g-7.

[5] Regulation (EC) No 1060/2009 of 16 September 2009 on credit rating agencies [2009] OJ L30/1 and Regulation (EU) No 513/2011 of 11 May 2011 amending Regulation (EC) No 1060/2009 on credit rating agencies [2011] OJ L145/30, commonly referred to as CRA I and CRA II, respectively. The entry into force of the regulations had been preceded by a Communication of the European Commission, [2006] OJ C59/2.

[6] See, in particular, Art 4 (permitted regulatory use of credit ratings of registered agencies and endorsement of ratings), Art 5 (certification on the basis of equivalence of agencies established in third countries outside the European Union), Art 6 and Annex I, Sections A and B (avoidance of conflicts of interest), Art 9 (rating methodologies, models and key assumption of credit rating agencies), Art 10 and Annex I Section D (mode of presentation of ratings), Art 11 and Annex I Section E (disclosures of rating agencies) and Arts 14–20 (registration of credit rating agencies) of CRA I; and Arts 36a and 36b and Annex III (fines and periodic payments for infringements of CRA I and CRA II) of CRA II.

Less than two years after CRA II, a third regulation (CRA III)[7] was adopted to complement the existing framework. In contrast to the two previous regulations, which focused mainly on such internal matters as the organization and operations of the credit rating agencies, and the manner in which these should be disclosed to the public, Regulation 462/2013 follows a more macroscopic approach, aspiring, inter alia, to remedy the structural inefficiencies of the rating market, to water down the systemic importance of the rating agencies by reducing over-reliance of investors on the ratings and to set out the practicalities of the communication of sovereign ratings to investors.[8]

II. THE IDENTITY OF THE RATINGS MARKET

The legislative initiative behind the novelties introduced by CRA III is connected to, and necessitated by, the idiosyncrasies of the ratings market: the latter is a highly concentrated market, in which, at least during the era that preceded the worldwide financial crisis, competition among the major agencies only triggered a race to the bottom with regard to the quality of the ratings; it is a market which, due to the applicable regulatory specifications and the widespread belief in the value of ratings, is marked by an over-reliance of financial intermediaries, entities offering financial services and investors in such ratings; in this market, the basic service providers (namely, the rating agencies) for a long time operated under conditions of severe conflicts of interest, and their remuneration mode was itself grounded on a conflict of interest; and the operation of this market may develop a systemic impact on the economies of the countries directly or indirectly concerned by the ratings, especially when they relate to the assessment of the credit risk of sovereign states, regional and local authorities or financial instruments issued by them (as reflected in sovereign ratings), or of structured finance instruments.

A. A Highly Concentrated Market

In all material respects, taking into account the number of agencies, and the total numbers of ratings and of customers served, the ratings market is a

[7] Regulation (EU) No 462/2013 of 21 May 2013 amending Regulation (EC) No 1060/2009 on credit rating agencies [2013] OJ L146/1.

[8] U Blaurock, 'Neuer Regulierungsrahmen für Ratingagenturen' (2013) 16 *Europaische Zeitschrift fur Wirtschaftsrecht* 608, with a discussion and a commentary of the novelties introduced by CRA III; and further references to Wagner, in *Festschrift für Blaurock* (Mohr Siebeck, 2013) 467; U Blaurock, "Verantwortlichkeit von Ratingagenturen—Steuerung durch Privat-oder Aufsichtsrecht?" [2007] *Zeitschrift fur Unternehmens- und Gesellschaftsrecht* 603; C Lequesne-Roth and A van Waeyenberge, 'La Réglementation Européenne: De la Négligence à l'Impuissance?', *Les Agences de Notation Financière: Entre Marchés et Etats* (Larcier, 2013) 111, 125.

highly concentrated one, dominated by only a few powerful players.[9] Theorists note that the concentration in the ratings industry is explained by historical, natural and regulatory barriers to entry that impede the development of activities of players other than the incumbents. Historical barriers are designated as those that are created by the long and traditional operation of the incumbents and the accumulation of a solid reputational capital, making customers unwilling to shift their business to alternative small or niche competitors. Natural barriers to entry are, in turn, heightened by the fact that there is general demand for general-purpose rating agencies; powerful agencies offer diverse services, while their rivals may not attain the requisite economies of scale that would permit them to compete with these agencies on an equal footing. Finally, barriers to entry are raised by regulatory requirements for the recognition of agencies, which partly relate to the wide use of ratings by the market, a criterion that favours already reputed agencies.[10]

At the same time, mainly for reasons of regulatory compliance,[11] the norm has recently become that an increasing number of customers seek ratings by more than one rating agency for the same entities or issues. At first glance, such proliferation should imply that competition among the agencies is vigorous; in reality, however, this has not been reported to contribute to a significant decrease in the level of concentration, or to give rise to either lower rating fees or an improvement in the quality or accuracy of the ratings.[12]

Indeed, regardless of these structural aspects, price and non-price competition among rating agencies was distorted during the years before the crisis.

[9] G Mattarocci, *The Independence of Credit Rating Agencies* (Elsevier Academic Press, 2014), 37 et seq (according to the author, the three major rating agencies, Moody's Investors Services, Standard & Poor's and Fitch Ratings, account for more than 60% of the ratings available and evaluate more than 73% of the customers, although, during the last decade, their market shares appear to have been eroded in favour of smaller agencies; this all the more true for certain countries in which fringe agencies have a vigorous national reputation and therefore enjoy a considerable local market share).

[10] A Darbellay, *Regulating Credit Rating Agencies* (Edward Elgar Publishing, 2013) 167, 168. With regard to the credibility and market acceptance criterion for the recognition of ECAIs in the context of the standardized approach under Directive 2006/48 of 14 June 2006 relating to the taking up and pursuit of the business of credit institutions, [2006] OJ L177/1 (repealed since 1 January 2014), see the following excerpt of Annex VI, part 2:

'8. Competent authorities shall verify that ECAIs' individual credit assessments are recognised in the market as credible and reliable by the users of such credit assessments.

9. Credibility shall be assessed by competent authorities according to factors such as the following:

(a) market share of the ECAI;

(b) revenues generated by the ECAI, and more in general financial resources of the ECAI;

. . .

(d) at least two credit institutions use the ECAI's individual credit assessment for bond issuing and/or assessing credit risks.'

[11] For instance, the use of more than one ratings could be encouraged by virtue of the specifications of part 3 of Annex VI of Directive 2006/48.

[12] Mattarocci (n 9 above), 43–45 (for instance, in the case of multiple coverage of customers of a rating agency by two to five of its competitors, 62.5% of such coverage is undertaken by the agency's 'more representative' competitor; this usually signifies recourse to the services of the most powerful rating agencies).

The level of rating fees was set in a discriminatory manner, that is, depending on a successful rating outcome, or on the supply of ancillary or advisory services by the agency to the rated entity or issuer, rather than in response to competitive pressure from other agencies. Regarding the quality, accuracy and timeliness of the ratings, two principal reasons have been proffered as causes of the agencies' poor performance.

First, the fact that the agencies were remunerated directly by the rated entities and issuers, and that they offered ancillary non-rating services to them on a paid basis, built strong incentives for the agencies to divert their attention away from providing high-level services; the agencies were instead prompted to opt for a lax assessment of credit risk, of which customers willing to pay higher remunerations of the agencies took advantage. In essence, competition among the agencies was ill-conceived, as it triggered a race to the bottom in the quality of ratings and a distorted fee-setting mechanism.

Secondly, because of the knock-on consequences that at least some categories of ratings could develop (sovereign ratings, ratings of systemically important financial institutions, ratings of structural finance instruments), the agencies were eager to proceed to downgrades only at a very late stage, namely when the market itself had acknowledged the need to do so.[13] Therefore, the structure of the industry was not the only reason behind the poor quality of rating services. It has been advocated that, even had competition flourished, the over-reliance on ratings and the existing conflicts of interest would have prevented the agencies from substantially altering their conduct and performance.[14]

B. Over-reliance on Ratings

Over-reliance should be distinguished from reliance on ratings.[15] Reliance is principally explained by the informational value of ratings. More particularly, the asymmetry of information regarding the credit risk levels pertaining to legal entities or issues, often caused by the complex structure of some financial instruments, may prompt investors (including the sophisticated ones) to ground their placement decisions on ratings. Over-reliance, by contrast, is dissociated from the purely informational input of ratings; instead, it is connected mostly with their transactional value, in two respects.

[13] Darbellay (n 10 above), 183,184, 189, 190, 195.

[14] Ibid, 213 ('Competitive pressures can be counterproductive if they create wrong incentives'); JC Coffee, 'Ratings Reform: The Good, the Bad and the Ugly' (2011) *Harvard Business Law Review* 231.

[15] Over-reliance on ratings was first addressed by the Financial Stability Board in a set of principles published in October 2010, available at http://www.financialstabilityboard.org/publications/r_101027.pdf. Recital 10 of CRA I provides that: 'the users of credit ratings should not rely blindly on credit ratings but should take utmost care to perform own analysis and conduct appropriate due diligence at all times regarding their reliance on such credit ratings'.

At a first level, the ratings issued by agencies of recognized standing, such as external credit assessment institutions (ECAIs), are frequently equipped with specific regulatory weight,[16] and are admitted as proxies of appropriate credit risk evaluation, while, under certain circumstances, they may guarantee the regulatory compliance of banks and investors that include the rated instruments in their portfolios. The dependence of minimum capital requirements of credit institutions that follow the so-called standardized approach from ratings provides an illustration of how rating agencies may be granted a regulatory licence to make assessments of the credit risk, which is then used as an automatic reference by those credit institutions.[17] The eligibility of collateral offered to the European Central Bank in the context of marginal lending facilities and deposit facilities is also defined by taking into account the ratings of ECAIs.

At a second level, general market perception about the quality and accuracy of the ratings regularly drives investors to include them as benchmarks of the standing and performance of their contractual counterparties (usually in the form of 'contractual triggers'); in this sense, a downgrading by the agencies may bring about an acceleration in the performance of agreed obligations of the counterparties, cause the generation of additional obligations, necessitate the amendment of contractual terms (eg the level of interest rates) or even justify the termination of contracts.[18] As ratings are procyclical, downgrades may ultimately cause mass sales of downgraded financial instruments, liquidity problems and systemic crises.[19]

Proposals to tackle the problem of over-reliance on ratings are usually twofold, and include both a removal or replacement by the competent authorities of the references to ratings from standards, laws and regulations, and an obligation of banks and market participants to make their own credit analyses, without relying solely or mechanically on credit rating agency (CRA) ratings.[20] Enhanced disclosure by rated entities, issuers of rated financial instruments and the agencies alike may facilitate the making of informed decisions by investors, thus reducing their reliance on ratings.

[16] The regulatory weight is of direct concern to 'regulated entities', listed in Art 4, para 1 of CRA I (including credit institutions, investment firms, insurance undertakings, reinsurance undertakings and undertakings for collective investment in transferrable securities).

[17] Under the now repealed Directive 2006/48, in the context of the 'standardized approach', ratings of ECAIs were used for the calculation of the risk weights of their exposures and thus contributed to the calculation of their capital requirements. Credit institutions following the internal ratings based approach could still use external ratings (of ECAIs) as a primary factor for the determination of internal credit ratings, though after having taken into account other relevant information (Annex VII, part 4 of Directive 2006/48). R Garcia Alcubilla and J Ruiz del Pozo, *Credit Rating Agencies on the Watch List: Analysis of European Regulation* (Oxford University Press, 2012) 97–99.

[18] Darbellay (n 10 above), 175.

[19] Garcia Alcubilla and Ruiz del Pozo (n 17 above), 43.

[20] Financial Stability Board, Principles for Reducing Reliance on CRA Ratings (October 2010).

C. The Systemic Impact of Sovereign and Structured Finance Ratings

Over-reliance on ratings may contribute to their systemic impact.[21] Rating migration and rating downgrades of certain market participants may increase systemic risk, to the extent that they may develop knock-on effects on other participants to which the former are linked and ultimate consequences on the stability of the financial system.[22] In the context discussed here, linkages among market participants occur when a rating migration or downgrade relates to a systemically important market participant (eg a major credit institution), the failure or misconduct of which inevitably disrupts the credit risk status or operation of other entities in the same financial system; when it relates to financial instruments characterized by a high degree of correlation with other financial instruments or assets (eg structured finance assets and derivatives); or when it concerns a market or sector with strong correlations with other markets or sectors (eg the commercial loan market and the insurance market). But even with a lack of correlations, investors in instruments similar to those downgraded, due to their over-reliance on ratings, may seek to divest their holdings at the same time as the former, thereby fuelling a liquidity shortage and, ultimately, a financial crisis.

Systemic impact is furthermore reinforced because of the procyclical nature of ratings and of prudential regulation of financial institutions. Ratings are procyclical in the sense that the frequency and intensity of downgrades are increased under adverse economic conditions. Prudential regulation, especially regulation of credit institutions, is procyclical because it accentuates the accumulation of capital reserves in response to economic downturns, rather than requiring such accumulation in anticipation of such downturns.[23]

Systemic impact is particularly acute in the case of sovereign ratings and of ratings of structured finance instruments. Sovereign ratings concern the credit risk relating to state and regional authorities, and to financial instruments issued by them, and have an unavoidable bearing on a multitude of market participants connected to them.[24] Structured finance ratings may have

[21] R Syllas, 'An Historical Primer on the Business of Credit Ratings' in R Levich, G Majnoni and C Reinhart (eds), *Ratings, Rating Agencies and the Global Financial System* (Kluwer Academic Publishers, 2002) 29; ANR Sy, 'The Systemic Regulation of Credit Rating Agencies and Rated Markets', IMF Working Paper No 09/129 (2009), available at http://www.imf.org/external/pubs/ft/wp/2009/wp09129.pdf.

[22] Darbellay (n 10 above), 160.

[23] The recently enacted provisions of prudential supervision of credit institutions and investment firms, largely reflecting the global regulatory standards of Basel III, provide for capital buffers against procyclicality; these buffers are institution-specific, and may vary for groups, as also for systemically important institutions. In addition, a systemic risk buffer may be required to prevent and mitigate long-term non-cyclical systemic or macroprudential risks. Directive 2013/36/EU of 26 June 2013 on access to the activity of credit institutions and the prudential supervision of credit institutions and investment firms [2013] OJ L176/338, Arts 128–41.

[24] Sovereign ratings, grounded on such parameters as the monetary and fiscal policy of a sovereign state, are systemically important in a globalized economy, to the extent that a downgrade may develop a contagion effect on other countries connected with the sovereign state, or affect inter-

a knock-on effect on the financial instruments underlying them or correlated with them. As will be seen, CRA III introduces new rules of disclosure and communication of such ratings to the public, with a view to assisting investors to make informed placement decisions, reducing reliance on ratings and thereby minimizing the systemic consequences of ratings.

D. Conflicts of Interest and Survival of the 'Issuer Pays' Remuneration Model

Conflicts of interest have been a focal point of concern in the recent EU regulatory initiatives. Besides a catch-all provision, mandating the rating agencies to identify, eliminate, manage and disclose actual or potential conflicts of interest that may undermine their independence,[25] CRA I lists conflicts prohibiting agencies from taking any rating action (including those caused by ownership interests of the agency, its analysts or employees in the rated entity; by the participation of analysts or employees in the administrative or supervisory board of the rated entity; by existing business relationships of the analysts with the rated entity; by the provision of consultancy or advisory services to the rated entity; and by the participation of employees directly involved in rating activities in the negotiation of fees with the rated entity)[26] and permitted conflicts (caused inter alia by the compensation paid by rated entities to agencies for their ancillary or other non-rating services),[27] which are handled by the agencies concerned at their option and in various manners, for instance via the establishment of information barriers between their different functions or by raising other corporate firewalls.

The 'issuer pays' model itself constitutes perhaps the more fundamental and common conflict of interest underlying the agencies' operations. The basic flaw behind this model lies in the fact that the agencies' integrity may be easily compromised, since it is the rated entities themselves that pay for the assessment of the credit risk arising from their operations or the financial instruments they issue.[28] Along the same line, agencies are often compensated not only upon the delivery of a rating output palatable to their customers, but also for a non-transparent and discriminatory package of rating and non-rating services offered to the customers, discriminatory against those that contract only for rating services.

national investors having invested in financial instruments issued by the sovereign state. See RP Nye, *Understanding and Managing the Credit Rating Agencies* (Euromoney Books, 2014) 180–81.

[25] Art 6, para 1 of CRA I.

[26] Annex I.B.3 of CRA I.

[27] Annex I.B.6 of CRA I.

[28] Matarrocci (n 9 above), 67, 68 (noting that rating is a non-standardized service, customized to the needs of its individual recipients, especially the issuers, and that its value is measured on the basis of its contribution to lowering the user's/issuer's cost of capital, rather than on the degree of its objective accuracy).

In principle, however, the 'issuer pays' model had been endorsed by the agencies after the 1970s as a response to the technological changes that made the unimpeded dissemination of information possible and therefore threatened the agencies' financial viability. Under a persisting 'subscriber pays' model, critics argued, in the absence of restrictions, ratings would be communicated to and used by investors who were not subscribers and who would therefore be taking a free ride on those parties subscribing to the agencies' services.[29] Despite this criticism, even in the aftermath of the worldwide financial crisis, the 'issuer pays' model has survived under CRA I. This may be partly explained by the fact that the application of alternative remuneration patterns were not free from flaws that could impact on the integrity of the rating agencies and the efficiency of rating assessments.[30] Under the new EU regulations, the remuneration by rated parties does not in itself constitute a 'prohibited' conflict that would prevent the issuance of ratings. Instead, when endorsing this remuneration mode, agencies must follow a set of rules that are geared to guaranteeing their independence towards their customers and, hence, the issuance of unbiased, and therefore reliable, ratings. These rules govern the fee-setting mechanism and internal rewarding within the agency system, and mandate the disclosure of certain parameters regarding the fees.[31]

[29] Ibid, 71 (noting that the alternative 'user fee' pattern is suitable only if the users are able to pay fees that are high enough to cover the agency's cost of producing a rating and its profit; in view of the imminent free riding danger, the agencies may be prompted to charge excessively high fees to subscribing customers, which the latter could rarely afford, although the 'user fee' approach may be followed by niche or small agencies as a pitch for their integrity).

[30] For instance, these models, unlike the 'issuer pays', would result in ratings based on limited availability of informational input, and would not necessitate the co-operation of the issuer; the 'user pays' pattern would give rise to conflicts of interest in the case of subscribers holding securities positions they would not wish to see downgraded, or potential investors interested in low-rated high-yield placements; a 'public utility' model could lead to the indirect intervention of central banks in the determination of ratings, to the detriment of rating quality; and the 'payment upon results model' could prompt the agencies to manipulate their methodologies, with a view to achieving the desired performance results: Garcia Alcubilla and Ruiz del Pozo (n 17 above), 247–52.

[31] Art 7.5 CRA I (compensation and performance evaluation of analysts and persons approving the credit ratings not contingent on the amount of revenue generated by the rated entities); Art 7.2 (prohibition of participation of employees directly involved in credit rating activities in the negotiation of the agency's fees); point (b) of Annex I.B.7 (obligation to keep records of the persons having paid the agency as well as of the amounts paid); Annex IE I 4 (publication of the general nature of the agencies' compensation arrangements); Annex I.B2 (publication of the names of the rated entities or related third parties from which the agencies received more than 5% of its annual revenue); Annex IE (periodic disclosure of financial information on the revenue of the credit rating agencies divided into fees from rating activities and from non-rating activities).

III. THE RECENT REGULATORY NOVELTIES AND PROPOSALS

A. Invigorating Competition among the Rating Agencies

Invigoration of competition among the rating agencies remains one of the pillars of recent regulatory initiatives,[32] despite the fact that, in the past, considerable doubt has been cast on whether vigorous competition alone could guarantee a high quality in the agencies' performance, even with the over-reliance on ratings still persisting and the impact of conflicts of interests of the agencies not being closely monitored.[33]

CRA III contemplates three fundamental tools for reinforcing competition among the rating agencies.[34] First, it provides for a mechanism of mandatory rotation among the agencies in regular intervals, designed to smoothen the

[32] Among the additional novelties of CRA III, the following are also noteworthy: the provision of civil liability of rating agencies in the case of intentional or grossly negligent commitment of any of the infringements listed in Annex III of CRA I (as subsequently amended by CRA II) having an impact on credit ratings, with the burden of proof of the infringement and causal connection between the latter and the decision to invest, divest or hold onto a financial instrument falling on the plaintiff investor (Art 35a, inserted by CRA III); the regulatory treatment of rating outlooks (defined as opinions as to the likely direction of a credit rating in the short or medium term) in a manner that is similar to the ratings, especially in terms of the agencies' conflicts of interests (Art, 6 para 1 of CRA I, as amended by CRA III); the agencies' analysis of all information available to them, which should be of sufficient quality and should emanate from reliable sources, before the issuance of rating outlooks (Art 8, para 2 of CRA I, as amended by CRA III); and the disclosure of rating outlooks in a non-selective manner (Art 10, para 1 of CRA I, as amended by CRA III). Among the voluminous literature on the civil liability of rating agencies, see, in particular, P Calamari and P Schantz, 'Suing the Rating Agencies for Subprime Investment Losses: Recent Developments in the United States and a German Perspective' (2010) 3 *Deutsch-Amerikanische Juristen-Vereinigung Newsletter* 131; A Grunshteyn, 'Horseshoes and Hand Grenades: The Dodd-Frank Act's (Almost) Attack on Credit Rating Agencies' (2011) 39 *Hofstra Law Review* 937; C Schmitt, 'Holding the Enablers Responsible: Applying SEC Rule 10B-5 Liability to the Credit Rating Institutions' (2011) 13 *University of Pennsylvania Journal of Business Law* 1035; N Ellis, 'Is Imposing Liability on Credit Rating Agencies a Good Idea? Credit Rating Agency Reform in the Aftermath of the Global Financial Crisis' (2012) 17 *Stanford Journal of Law, Business & Finance* 175; E Mastromanolis, *Credit Rating Agencies of Trading Entities and Financial Instruments: Function, Regulation, Civil Liability* (Nomiki Vivliothiki, 2013, in Greek) 261–67.

[33] It has also been advocated that a main driver behind the issuance of ratings is 'mimetic conduct' ('comportement mimétique'); should this be the case, invigorating competition should not bring about better quality of ratings. See JM Gollier, 'Le Courage de la Vérité Dans un Monde Mimétique' in *Les Agences de Notation Financière: Entre Marchés et Etats* (Larcier, 2013) 157–59; according to this author 'l'anticipation mimétique est bien un réflexe type de spéculateur sur les marchés financiers. Au lieu de fonder sa decision sur sa propre conviction à propos de la valeur d' un actif, il doit anticiper ce que les autres pensent de cette valeur.'

[34] In addition to this three-level response to the oligopolistic structure of the ratings market, CRA III also provides for open-ended means of reinforcement of the role of small-scale agencies as follows: (i) through the appointment, at the discretion of entities or issuers considering the services of more than one agency as desirable, of at least one 'small' agency with a market share that does not exceed 10%, if its capacity to rate the relevant entity or issue is deemed adequate (Art 1 of CRA III, inserting Art 8c in CRA I, subsequently amended by CRA II; and recital 11 of the CRA III Preamble); and (ii) through the operation of a publicly funded network of small rating agencies, the feasibility of which will be assessed by the European Commission (Art 1 of CRA, inserting new Art 39b, para 3 in CRA, subsequently amended by CRA II, and recital 50 of the CRA II Preamble).

'lock-in effect' akin to relationships among the agencies and their long-standing clients, to facilitate already operating agencies to expand their activities in new sectors and to spur new entry.[35] It should be noted, however, that the application of this mechanism is introduced only on a test basis and, until further regulation on this issue is enacted,[36] it should be confined to a particular area of the rating services market, namely to ratings of re-securitization financial instruments. The rationale behind testing the efficiency of the rotation mechanism only in connection with re-securitization instruments is twofold: on the one hand, this segment has gravely underperformed, especially since the worldwide financial crisis, and therefore any benefits of the rotation mechanism will be more easily measurable in it; and on the other hand, credit risk in re-securitizations is transaction-specific (rather than issuer-specific), therefore rotation will not result in increased service costs for issuers and the agencies, due to the contemplated cross-agency shift.[37]

With regard to the rotation mechanism provided by the CRA III for re-securitization instruments, the following parameters apply:

(a) Rotation is centred around originators, rather than issuers of re-securitization instruments, since these issuers are most frequently vested in the form of one-off special-purpose entities which seldom develop long-term relationships, with the agencies liable to trigger 'lock-in' effects.[38]
(b) Rotation is made necessary because the maximum duration of issuer–agency contractual relationships for re-securitizations of underlying assets of the same originator may not exceed a period of four years.[39]
(c) A 'cool-off' period equal to the duration of the expired (four-year) contractual relationship and no longer than four years is provided in CRA III;

[35] At the same time, a minimum period of contractual relationship is necessary so that agencies may be permitted to recoup the costs required for the issuance of ratings, especially when a new financial instrument is rated; the period of four years is considered by CRA III as sufficient for this purpose (recitals 13 and 15 of the CRA III Preamble).

[36] Indeed, Art 39, para 3 is added by CRA III, according to which the European Commission shall assess, by 1 January 2016, (i) whether there is need for an extension of the application of the rotation mechanism to asset classes other than resecuritization, in which case it shall also indicate the length of period of rotation for each new asset class to which the application of the mechanism will be extended; and (ii) whether there is a need to implement measures additional to the ones introduced by CRA III, with a view to fostering competition and tackling the problems arising from oligopolistic structure of the ratings market.

[37] Recital 15 of the CRA III Preamble.

[38] It can also be credibly argued that the rotation mechanism could as successfully be centred around sponsors, since the latter may be equally considered as being the driving force behind resecuritizations, and therefore liable to build long-term relationships with the agencies rating the instruments they sponsor. According to CRA III, however, rotation around sponsors is necessitated by the fact that the latter are normally associated with a large number of agencies, therefore the four-agency exception would automatically apply and therefore the rotation mechanism would be rendered redundant (recital 16 of the CRA III Preamble).

[39] Art 6b, para 1, inserted in CRA I by CRA III.

during such 'cool-off' period a rating agency may not issue ratings from the same originator.[40]

(d) The application of the rotation mechanism is subject to two exceptions, which apply (i) when competition in the rating services is already intense due to the fragmentation of the market[41] and (ii) in the case of 'small' rating agencies that reasonably contribute to the fostering of competition but are not part of the 'big-three' oligopoly.[42]

A second tool relates only to structured finance instruments and consists in a requirement for issuers of such instruments to obtain ratings from at least two rating agencies, what will permit comparisons by investors and will incentivize the agencies to issue more accurate ratings.[43]

Finally, anticipated regulation, when enacted and put into force, will provide for enhanced transparency obligations of the agencies in relation to the ratings and to the agencies' performance records; more transparency, it is thought, may then permit issuers to opt for services of raters having good performance records and investors to invest in instruments rated by reliable agencies.[44] At the current stage, ESMA, responding to the mandate given to it by Articles 11a and 11, paragraph 2 of CRA III, has released a consultation paper dated 11 February 2014 which includes, inter alia, draft regulatory standards on the European Rating Platform, in the form of a draft Commission-delegated regulation that will repeal Regulations 446/2012 and 448/2012.[45] Under the contemplated standards, the European Rating Platform will display, in a public website available to investors, and updated whenever a credit

[40] Art 6b, para 3, inserted in CRA I by CRA III (this provision covering also rating agencies belonging to the same group of companies, or linked by shareholding participations).

[41] This will be the case when at least four agencies each rate more than 10% of the total number of outstanding rated resecuritizations of the same originator (Art 6b, para 2, inserted by CRA III in CRA I, subsequently amended by CRA II, and Preamble 15 of CRA III).

[42] This is the case of rating agencies having fewer than 50 employees or having an annual turnover generated from rating activities of less than euros 10 million at a group level (Art 6b, para 5, inserted in CRA I by CRA III, subsequently amended by CRA II, and Preamble 17 of CRA III).

[43] Art 8c, inserted in CRA I by CRA III, and recital 28 of the CRA III Preamble (it should be noted that the two rating agencies appointed must not be connected with each other by shareholding participations, voting rights, rights of appointment of members of their administrative supervisory bodies or dominant influence relationships). The two-agency measure is also intended to decrease over-reliance on the ratings of structured finance instruments.

[44] This will be made possible through a central repository established by ESMA, incorporated in the so-called 'European rating platform', which will include information on the historical performance of the agencies, the ratings transition frequency and information about changes of ratings in the past (Arts 11a and 11, para 2, inserted in CRA I by CRA III, subsequently amended by CRA II).

[45] Commission Delegated Regulation (EU) supplementing Regulation (EC) No 1060/2009 of the European Parliament and of the Council with regard to regulatory technical standards for the presentation of the information that credit rating agencies shall make available to the European Securities and Markets Authority for the purposes of displaying the rating data on a public platform, for the purpose of ongoing supervision and for the purpose of making available historical performance data and repealing Commission Delegated Regulation No 446/2012 and Commission Delegated Regulation No 448/2012 (draft EPR Delegated Regulation), (available at http://www.esma.europa.eu/content/Consultation-Paper-CRA3-Implementation).

rating or a credit outlook is issued or endorsed, such information as: rating and outlook of rated instruments; press releases accompanying rating actions; types of rating actions; date and hour of publication; and status of ratings as 'solicited', 'unsolicited with participation' and 'unsolicited without participation'. All the above rating information will be collected by all credit rating agencies and will be merged with a view to providing investors with a global view on the same instrument.[46] In addition, information to be included in the 'central repository' of Article 11, paragraph 2 of CRA I, regarding consequential rating actions and default[47] of the rated entity or issuer, will also appear in the platform, thus further facilitating the comparability of the ratings and enhancing the investors' understanding of the raters' performance.[48]

B. Paving the Way for Reducing Over-reliance on Ratings

The strategic initiatives enunciated by CRA III with a view to reducing over-reliance on credit ratings are twofold and are addressed to both the entities referred to in Article 4, paragraph 1 of CRA I (credit institutions, investment firms, insurance undertakings, reinsurance undertakings, institutions for occupational retirement provision, management companies, investment companies, alternative investment fund managers and central counterparties) and to the sectoral authorities entrusted under the relevant sectoral legislation with the duty to supervise those entities.

According to Article 5a, paragraph 1 of CRA III, the entities must make their own credit risk assessment and avoid relying solely or mechanically on credit ratings for this purpose. Sectoral authorities are mandated to encourage the entities, through appropriate legislation, to mitigate the impact of credit ratings issued by the agencies (Article 5a, paragraph 2 of CRA III). At the same time, EBA, EIOPA and ESMA, where appropriate, are bound not to refer to ratings in their new standards, guidelines and recommendations, as well as to remove similar existing references, where appropriate, by 31 December 2013; the European Commission must follow a similar path by 1 January 2020. In

[46] Recital 3, Arts 2 para 1 and 9 of the draft ERP Delegated Regulation.

[47] According to Art 3 of the draft ERP Delegated Regulation, reportable default is defined as (i) any event designated as such according to the rating agencies' definitions, (ii) the insolvency or debt restructuring of the rated entity or issuer, and (iii) any other instance considered by the agency as warranting default or material impairment of the entity, issuer or financial instrument.

[48] Art 2, 3 and Art 11 of the draft ERP Delegated Regulation (in essence, all data provided to ESMA in the context of the monthly reporting of the agencies will be used by it to extract useful performance information that will be posted at the European Rating Platform). For instance, in field 4 of Table 1 of Annex 1 of the draft ERP Delegated Regulation, the reasons for a change in ratings (correction of data? update of data?) should be reported to ESMA; and in field 6 of Table 3 of Annex 2 of the draft ERP Delegated Regulation, subsequent rating actions to an initial rating (upgrading, downgrading, withdrawal, affirmation, removal from default status, etc) should be reported to ESMA.

the context of complying with CRA III, references to ratings in prudential legislation of credit ratings have already been largely mitigated.[49]

The above-referenced initiatives are geared to only partly tackling the problem of over-reliance and only on the medium term, since they cover only sophisticated and institutional investors, while other investors, due to considerable information lag, will continue to rely on credit ratings, even if the agencies are deprived of their 'regulatory licenses'. It is submitted that, at least in the short run, investors that lack the capacity to analyse and digest the input already provided in CRA I and envisioned in the new technical standards, especially in the structured finance sector,[50] will continue to rely solely or mechanically on ratings, especially since no alternative benchmarks for the evaluation of credit risk have been widely accepted.[51]

C. Tackling the Systemic Importance of Sovereign Ratings and of Structured Finance Ratings

CRA III sets out rules on two types of ratings that, due to their interconnectedness with various economic segments, other financial instruments and assets, may, especially in the event of downgrading, develop important systemic impact, namely sovereign ratings[52] and ratings of structured finance instruments. The regulation of various aspects of those ratings is intended to

[49] Arts 5b and 5c inserted in CRA I by CRA III. Under Regulation 575/2013 (Art 136), the mapping of ratings shall be subject to the long-term default rate associated with all items assigned the same credit assessment; and (Art 268) the use of external credit ratings is subject to a number of conditions, including the alignment of payments taken into account for the rating with those to which the credit institution is contractually entitled, the publication of the loss and cash-flow analysis, and the sensitivity of ratings to ratings assumptions by the agencies, etc.

[50] Annex D of CRA I, setting out the particulars of presentation of credit ratings (and relating to the disclosure of material sources used to prepare the credit rating; the methodology used; the definition of rating categories; the date of the last update of the rating; the attributes and limitations of the credit rating; the key elements underlying the rating; indications about the solicited or unsolicited status of the rating; the level of due diligence performed by the agency; and the explanation of the assumptions, parameters, limits and uncertainty associated with the rating). See also the new proposed standards for structured finance instruments in Section III below.

[51] CDS spreads and credit spreads have been proposed as such alternatives, although they have been criticized as being susceptible to abuse by market participants. See Darbellay (n 10 above), 232, 233; M Flannery, J Houston and F Partnoy, 'Credit Default Swap Spreads as Viable Substitutes for Credit Ratings' (2010) *University of Pennsylvania Law Review* 2085.

[52] See ESMA, 'Credit Rating Agencies: Sovereign Ratings Investigation' (ESMA's assessment of governance, conflicts of interest, resourcing adequacy and confidentiality controls), available at http://www.esma.europa.eu/system/files/2013-1780_esma_identifies_deficiencies_in_cras_sovereign_ratings_processes.pdf, in which it is stated that 'Sovereign ratings are of crucial importance from a credit market and financial stability perspective. In particular, when a sovereign rating is changed, this invariably has an important cascade impact on other rated entities and products since a sovereign rating is usually a factor used in the determination of other types of ratings, eg bank ratings.' In this report, ESMA stresses the necessity of separating sovereign rating and commercial functions within agencies in order to avoid selective communications of sovereign ratings to subscribers of the commercial services and to prevent conflicts of interest that would touch upon the integrity of the sovereign ratings.

alleviate their possible systemic consequences. Whether this regulation will ultimately achieve the aims it purports to serve is highly contestable.[53] At the same time, doubt has been cast on the very use of sovereign ratings of EU Member States, the issuance of which is virtually conditional on the alignment of the states to US-inspired governance standards and the observance by the states of intense liberalization programmes.[54]

With regard to sovereign ratings, CRA III rules relate to:

(a) *a confined coverage of sovereign ratings by subject*: sovereign ratings should be characterized by individual specificity, and relate to states, regional or local authorities, or international financial institutions only on a stand-alone basis; by contrast, they should not relate to groups of states or authorities, especially when those have different attributes not warranting a unified risk assessment, in a manner that could dampen the accuracy of the ratings or artificially enhance their systemic influence;[55]

(b) *a notification mechanism of the sovereign ratings before their release to the public, with a view to attaining accuracy*:[56] rated entities should be notified of a projected rating or rating outlook at least a full working day before their public release, so that they have ample time to comment on them;

(c) *the factual substantiation of the ratings on reliable data:* ratings should be grounded either on publicly available data or on data which lies within the sphere of the rated entity, which has been released with the consent of the latter; hence the rated entity's accountability, as also the ratings' accuracy, shall be guaranteed to the maximum possible extent;[57]

(d) *enhanced disclosure obligations that will further the understanding of investors:* transparency relates to the research work underlying the ratings, the staff allocated to the preparation of the ratings and the underlying assumptions behind the ratings (included in a detailed research report), and should be complemented by analyses and indicators available to the European Commission in the context of its surveillance of the Member States; transparency should reduce over-reliance on credit ratings, and hence their systemic impact;[58]

[53] Some commentators have nevertheless criticized CRA III as inadequate in this respect, arguing that the suspension of sovereign ratings or the issuance of sovereign ratings by a European rating agency of universal acceptance would yield optimum results. See Lequesne-Roth and van Waeyenberge (n 8 above), 127; Blaurock, 'Neuer Regulierungsrahmen' (n 8 above), 611.

[54] G Lewkowicz, 'Les Agences de Notation Financière contre les Etats: Une Lutte Globale Pour le Droit à l'Issue Incertaine', *Les Agences de Notation Financière: Entre Marchés et Etats* (Larcier, 2013) 185, 195, 199.

[55] Art 8a, para 1, inserted in CRA I by CRA III.

[56] Recital 41 of the Preamble of CRA III.

[57] Art 8a, para 2, inserted in CRA I by CRA III; recital 44 of the Preamble of CRA III.

[58] Recital 39 of the Preamble of CRA III and the new part entitled 'Additional Obligations in Relation to Sovereign Ratings' in section D of Annex I of CRA I, inserted by CRA III. Most sovereign ratings are issued on an unsolicited basis, and this fact should be disclosed, with an indication of the extent to which the rated entities may have contributed to them by provid-

(e) *the timing of the publication of sovereign ratings in a manner that is not prejudicial for rated entities:* rating agencies shall be obliged to announce a short-term sovereign ratings schedule; they should publish on their website and submit to ESMA, on an annual basis, a calendar at the end of December of each year that will apply for the next 12 months and shall (i) set a maximum of three dates for the unsolicited sovereign ratings and related rating outlooks they plan to issue and (ii) set the dates (without restriction as to frequency) for their projected solicited sovereign rating and related rating outlook actions;[59] also, sovereign ratings should be published only after the close of business of trading venues, so that risk of volatility is reduced;[60] and

(f) *the dissociation of sovereign ratings and outlooks from the any recommendations, prescriptions or guidelines that the agencies could address to the rated states and authorities.*[61]

With regard to the ratings of structured finance instruments, of particular interest are the draft technical standards proposed by ESMA, which will ultimately be incorporated in a Commission-delegated regulation.[62] As part of the mandate to ESMA provided by Article 8b of CRA I, the technical standards specify what information should be made public in relation to structured finance instruments, contributing to the investors' due diligence and concurrently reducing the systemic impact in the event of downgrading. The information relates to the underlying assets of structured finance instruments, the structure of the securitization transactions, the cash flows and collateral supporting securitization exposures, and any other data permitting the performance of stress tests. The relevant publication obligation rests jointly on issuers, originators and sponsors of structured finance instruments, and develops extraterritorial effects, especially since it applies when at least one of these parties is established in the European Union,[63] regardless of whether the rated instruments are offered to the public or are admitted to trading in the Union, and of whether the agency assigning the rating of the structured finance instrument is established in the Union. In addition, any event that is likely to affect the creditworthiness or the risk characteristics of the underlying exposures

ing their input, so that investors may in turn attribute to the ratings or outlooks the value they deserve (Art 10, para 5 of CRA I, as amended by CRA III).

[59] Art 8a, para 3, inserted in CRA I by CRA III; recital 42 of the Preamble of CRA III.

[60] Point 3 of the part entitled 'Additional Obligations in Relation to Sovereign ratings' in section D of Annex I of CRA I, inserted by CRA III.

[61] Ibid, point 4.

[62] Commission Delegated Regulation supplementing Regulation (EC) No 1060/2009 with regard to regulatory technical standards on disclosure requirements for structured finance instruments, available at http://www.esma.europa.eu/content/Consultation-Paper-CRA3-Implementation.

[63] Art 2 of the Commission Delegated Regulation on disclosure requirements for structured finance instruments.

or to constitute a breach of the transaction documentation underlying the structured finance instrument must be disclosed to the public without delay.[64]

D. Expanding the Regulation of the Agencies' Conflicts of Interest

The regulation of rating agencies' conflicts of interest is expanded, by virtue of CRA III, in two principal ways: first, through the explicit prohibition of the issuance of ratings by agencies connected with rated entities via shareholding or other similar relationships;[65] and secondly, with the enactment of extensive disclosure obligations by the agencies with regard to their fee policies, which is designed to prevent distortions inherent in the 'issuer pays' remuneration model that still persists under CRA III.

According to the new rules,[66] the list of prohibited conflicts of interest is widened by provisions stipulating that no rating action can be taken with respect to a particular rated entity in the event of a shareholder of a rating agency holding, directly or indirectly, 10 per cent or more of its share capital or voting rights, or being otherwise in a position to exercise decisive influence on the business activities of the agency and simultaneously holding 10 per cent of either the share capital or the voting rights of the rated entity itself or any other party related to it, or a position on the administrative or supervisory board of the latter; likewise, the issuance of a rating is prohibited when it is the rated entity itself that holds a share capital participation or voting rights above such level in the rating agency. By contrast, shareholdings or similar participations by or in the rating agency exceeding 5 per cent but less than 10 per cent of the share capital do not prevent the possibility of the issue of ratings, but warrant a respective disclosure by the rating agency, so that investors may evaluate this fact when relying on ratings for their placement decisions.[67]

[64] According to Arts 4 and 6 of the Commission Delegated Regulation, the information to be published relates to: (i) the loan underlying the structured finance instrument, made available to investors on a quarterly basis; (ii) the structured finance instrument and the transaction pertaining to the instrument (including, but not limited to, the final offering document or prospectus, the asset sale agreement, the servicing agreement, inter-creditor agreements, asset characteristics, credit enhancement and liquidity support features, noteholders rights and transaction triggers), made available to investors upon issuance of the instrument; and (iii) investor reports and cash flow models, made available to investors on a monthly basis.

[65] Before its amendment by CRA III, CRA provided only for prohibited conflicts of interest under the following circumstances: (i) when the rating agency itself (rather than its shareholder) has direct or indirect ownership interest in the rated entity, or the latter is linked to the rating agency by control; and (ii) when a rating analyst, employee and any other natural person whose services are placed at the disposal or under the control of the agency (rather than the agency's shareholder) is a member of the administrative or supervisory board of the rated entity or any party related to it (Annex I, section B, point 3 of CRA I, before its amendment by CRA III).

[66] Annex I, section B, point 3 of CRA I, as amended by CRA III.

[67] Annex I, section B, point 3a of CRA I, inserted by CRA III.

of the ratings and the adverse impact of the still persisting remuneration pattern of the agencies ('issuer pays') on the integrity of their ratings. It is true that CRA III, rather than being confined to mere internal organization rules, as are CRA I and CRA II, introduces a more macroscopic regulatory approach in relation to the operation of the agencies. It is equally true, however, that CRA III, rather than providing one-stop-shop solutions, merely constitutes a first step towards remedying the structural problems of the ratings market that contributed greatly to the outburst of the recent worldwide financial crisis.

According to CRA III, the extent to which over-reliance on ratings will be decreased must be monitored in the long-run. This is largely contingent upon the parallel enactment of sectoral rules lifting the regulatory weight that is currently attributed to ratings, and certainly concerns only sophisticated and institutional investors. The handling of the systemic importance of ratings is likewise subject to similar constraints. The bias of agencies in favour of rated entities paying for their own ratings is hard to prevent, despite new disclosure obligations regarding the agencies' fee policies and arrangements. Finally, invigoration of competition on the merits may be difficult to achieve if it ultimately turns out that the other structural problems of the ratings industry (namely, over-reliance, systemic importance and conflicts of interest) are not successfully dealt with.

11

The Odious Debt Doctrine: The Past and the Challenges of the Present

GEORGIOS NIKOLAIDES-KRASSAS*

I. INTRODUCTION

THE ODIOUS DEBT Doctrine (the Doctrine) was originally developed and formulated by the émigré Russian jurist Alexander Nahum Sack[1] in a treatise he published in 1927, while lecturing in Paris on the effect of state transformations on public debt. In this treatise, entitled 'Les Effets des transformations des Etats sur leurs dettes publiques et autres obligations financiers',[2] Sack proposed that, following state succession, the new government could under certain circumstances renege on some debts of its predecessors, which he called odious debts (*dettes odieuses*). Of course, 'In a sense, all debts are odious; that is, to use dictionary definitions, "hateful; disgusting; offensive"'.[3] However, the debts which Sack was referring to had to fulfil three conditions in order to be defined as odious in the context of international law and allow the successor government to legally repudiate them,[4] namely:

(a) To have been incurred by a despotic regime, that is, without the people's consent.
(b) To have been without benefit to the people, its needs and its interest.

* MJur (Oxon), Attorney at Law (Athens Bar Association).

[1] On the life of AN Sack and the various inaccuracies usually associated with it and his work see S Ludington and M Gulati, 'A Convenient Untruth: Fact and Fantasy in the Doctrine of Odious Debts' (2008) 48 *Virginia Journal of International Law* 595.

[2] AN Sack, *Les Effets des transformations des États sur leurs dettes publiques et autres obligations financiers* (Recueil Sirey, 1927).

[3] JV Feinerman, 'Odious Debt, Old and New: The Legal Intellectual History of an Idea' (2007) 70(4) *Law & Contemporary Problems* 193.

[4] Sack (n 2 above), 157–65.

(c) At the time of paying out the loan, the creditors were aware of its odious nature.

Despite appearing radical at first sight, the formulation of the Odious Debt Doctrine by Sack seems to have been an attempt to support rather than undermine the interests and lending institutions of what today would be described as the developed world.[5] This it accomplished by 'sacrificing' the most outrageous cases of illegitimate debt, while establishing a restrictive framework that 'reaffirmed the core responsibility of states to repay the debt incurred by governments through a presumption of payment'[6] and shifted the burden of proof onto successor governments.

There is an additional implicit condition for invoking the Odious Debt Doctrine: state succession, or at least regime change. A general agreement exists that the Odious Debt Doctrine is applicable in the case of state succession; in any case, the nature of the sovereignty of the state having contracted the debt has been altered, and its international personality has been transformed or even eliminated.[7] Because state succession is the traditional context in which the odiousness of debts has initially arisen, it has been argued that the Odious Debt Doctrine applies exclusively in such cases and not in other kinds of political transition.[8] That would seem rather arbitrary, since the difference between the two is sometimes difficult to discern; they are 'levels of abstraction unfitted to dealing with specific issues'.[9] This could be the result of a misconception of the default rule that in cases of state succession the new state does not automatically assume the debts of its predecessor, while in cases of regime change there is no change of the legal personality of the state and thus its obligations remain.[10]

Regardless of the context in which the Doctrine is invoked, the legal consequence (*Rechtsfolge* in German) of a debt being determined as odious is that it does not entail a repayment obligation.[11] The creditor's right to payment and the debtor's obligation to pay are considered imperfect; in the words of Emer de Vattel, this means that, in contrast to a '*perfect obligation* . . . which gives to the opposite party the right of compulsion', an '*imperfect* gives him only a right to ask'.[12] The debt itself does not become invalid; it is the obli-

[5] On Sack's procreditor scholarship see Ludington and Gulati (n 1 above), 616–20.

[6] LC Backer, 'Odious Debt Wears Two Faces: Systemic Illegitimacy, Problems, and Opportunities in Traditional Odious Debt Conceptions in Globalized Economic Regimes' (2007) 70(4) *Law & Contemporary Problems* 1, 3.

[7] R Howse, 'The Concept of Odious Debt in Public International Law', UNCTAD Discussion Paper No 185 UNCTAD/OSG/DP/2007/4 (2007), 16.

[8] Ibid.

[9] Ian Brownlie, *Principles of Public International Law* (6th edn, Oxford University Press, 2003) 80.

[10] Howse (n 7 above), 17.

[11] CG Paulus, 'The Evolution of the "Concept of Odious Debts"' (2008) 68 *Zeitschrift für ausländisches öffentliches Recht und Völkerrecht* 391, 394.

[12] E de Vattel (B Kapossy and R Whatmore, eds), *The Law of Nations*, GG and J Robinson edn (The Liberty Fund, 2008) 75.

gation to pay it that is no longer enforceable. Thus no restitution under the principle of unjust enrichment can be sought for any amounts already paid.

II. CATEGORIES OF ODIOUS DEBTS

Although the Odious Debt Doctrine was formulated in the interwar period, its roots are much older. In Book II, chapter XIV, paragraphs XII and XIV of his classic work *De Jure Belli ac Pacis*, Hugo Grotius holds that the contracts of the Prince harmful to the People should not be honoured and that neither the People nor the legitimate Princes can be held liable for the debts of an usurper in excess of any benefit to them under the principle of unjust enrichment.[13] However, most of the examples of state practice quoted in relation to the Odious Debt Doctrine date from the late nineteenth and early twentieth centuries. Since these are interrelated with the categories of odious debt Sack acknowledged, it is important to examine them. Based on the writings of Sack, three categories of odious debts are generally recognized: war debts, subjugation debts and regime debts. In a useful analogy to biology, Mohammed Bedjaoui, in one of his reports as Special Rapporteur to the ILC, has described odious debts as the genus and the categories as the species within the genus.[14] It would be more accurate, however, to think of these categories not as conceptually distinct, but rather as indicative of the different contexts in which the Odious Debt Doctrine has been invoked.[15]

War debts are the debts incurred by a state in the context of its war effort against another state.[16] The successor state is excused from paying debts that were used for the preparation or prosecution of war against itself and possibly against other states.[17] Nonetheless, in the case of war debts, the first and/or second of the three prerequisites of odious debts, the benefit to and consent of the people, seem to be of minor importance.[18] In the case of the British annexation of the Boer Republics in 1900, the British government refused to assume debts of the Boer Republics closely related to their war effort against Great Britain without any particular argument;[19] it could be argued that this is a case of the old concept in international law, already acknowledged by

[13] H Grotius (R Tuck, ed), *The Rights of War and Peace*, Jean Barbeyrac edn (The Liberty Fund, 2005) 815–16.

[14] M Bedjaoui, 'Ninth Report on the Succession of States in Respect of Matters other than Treaties' [1977] 2-ii *Yearbook of the International Law Commission* 67.

[15] A Khalfan, J King and B Thomas, 'Advancing the Odious Debt Doctrine', CISDL working paper (2003) 14, available at www.dette2000.org/data/File/odious_debt_CISDL.pdf (accessed on 1 July 2013).

[16] Sack (n 2 above), 158.

[17] T-H Cheng, 'Renegotiating the Odious Debt Doctrine' (2007) 70(3) *Law & Contemporary Problems* 7, 13.

[18] Khalfan et al (n 15 above), 18–19.

[19] CP Abrahams, 'The Doctrine of "Odious Debts"', LLM Thesis (Rijks Universiteit Leiden, 2000) 29–34.

Grotius in Book III, chapter VIII, paragraph IV of *De Jure Belli ac Pacis*, that the rights and obligations of a conquered state belong to its conqueror to the extent that the latter accepts them.[20] So it would seem that the view that war debts need not always be odious is justified,[21] even though Sack expressly mentioned them as such. In the case of states seceding from the defeated state, however, war debts must be presumed without benefit to and without the consent of the successor state's people.[22] War debts are closely related to the next category of odious debts accepted by Sack, subjugation debts. Anyway, given the UN Charter prohibition on the use of force, the category of war debts, especially those in relation to the conquest of a state, appears to be of relatively limited importance nowadays.

Subjugation debts, also called by some authors 'hostile debts',[23] are the debts incurred by a state in order to keep the population of a part of its territory subjugated or for the colonization of such a part by members of the dominant nationality.[24] In this category there are a few more examples of state practice, mainly from the twentieth century, but the most famous one dates from the end of the nineteenth century: it is the repudiation by the US of debts contracted by Spain for its colonial empire and specifically secured upon Cuban revenues. In the aftermath of the Spanish–American War of 1898, during the peace negotiations in Paris, the US opposed the Spanish claim that these debts devolved to the US upon cession to it of the territory of Cuba, arguing that the debts had been contracted contrary to Cuban interests and had been imposed upon Cuba without its consent.[25] That is generally regarded as the first direct application of a doctrine of odious debts.[26] There are other examples, the most important ones including the repudiation in the Treaty of Versailles of certain Polish debts incurred by the Prussian and German governments for the colonization of Poland by German settlers (Article 255, § 2)[27] and the refusal of Indonesia to assume certain debts incurred by the Netherlands, particularly those resulting from Netherlands military operations against the Indonesian national liberation movement.[28] According to a minority view, even the debts incurred by the apartheid regime should be considered subjugation debts (rather than regime debts, as per the most orthodox view), such a regime being closer to colonial rule.[29]

[20] Grotius (n 13 above), 1379.

[21] DP O'Connell, *State Succession in Municipal and International Law. Vol 1. Internal Relations* (Cambridge University Press, 1967) 461.

[22] Howse (n 7 above), 8.

[23] Paulus (n 11 above), 398.

[24] Sack (n 2 above), 158.

[25] Abrahams (n 19 above), 35–41.

[26] Khalfan et al (n 15 above), 25.

[27] Ibid, 27.

[28] Bedjaoui (n 14 above), 73.

[29] Z Motala, 'Under International Law, Does the New Order in South Africa Assume the Obligations and Responsibilities of the Apartheid Order? An Argument for Realism over Formalism' (1997) 30 *Comparative and International Law Journal of Southern Africa* 287, 295.

Regime debts cover the rest of the odious debt cases, where no state succession is involved. Bedjaoui, who is of the opinion that regime debts is just another name for odious debts, focuses on war and subjugation debts, but reserves a third category for other cases.[30] In this category the *Tinoco* case[31] stands out, as it is the only judicial decision to have applied the Odious Debt Doctrine. For this reason, a closer examination is in order. José Federico Alberto de Jesús Tinoco Granados, Secretary of War for Costa Rica, overthrew its government with the assistance of his brother on the 27 January 1917. He later held an election to ratify the coup, in which there were several indications that his victory was legitimate. However, after two years, support for his government had evaporated. In July and August of 1919, the government of Costa Rica contracted debts through the Banco Internacional de Costa Rica with the Royal Bank of Canada for expenses of representation of President Tinoco, as well as expenses and four years' worth of salaries, to be paid in advance, for his brother, who had just been appointed ambassador to Italy. His brother was assassinated on 10 August, and three days later Tinoco himself fled the country. On 22 August, the Constitutional Congress of the restored Costa Rican government enacted a law invalidating, among others, the aforementioned debts. Great Britain's diplomatic protection resulted in arbitration by a sole arbitrator, William Taft, former president of the US and at the time Chief Justice of the US Supreme Court. The award is widely considered as having applied the Odious Debt Doctrine,[32] even though there is no explicit mention of the odiousness of the debts in the arguments of Costa Rica or in the award itself; the arbitrator ruled in favour of Costa Rica, accepting that the debts had been contracted for the personal enrichment of President Tinoco and his brother, and that the Royal Bank of Canada was well aware of the fact.[33] Another reason why the *Tinoco* case is considered such an important landmark is because it first applied the Odious Debt Doctrine in the context not of state succession, but of regime change.[34]

III. RECENT CASES FOR APPLYING THE ODIOUS DEBT DOCTRINE

In the last two decades there have been two other cases of state debt where it is widely accepted that the Odious Debt Doctrine would have been applicable: the debt of the apartheid regime of South Africa and the debt of Iraq under Saddam Hussein. In the case of South Africa, it was more than

[30] Bedjaoui (n 14 above), 67.

[31] *Tinoco Arbitration (GB v Costa Rica)*, 'Arbitration between Great Britain and Costa Rica, Opinion and Award of William H Taft, Sole Arbitrator' (1924) 18 AJIL 147.

[32] Abrahams (n 19 above), 46; LC Buchheit, GM Gulati and RB Thompson, 'The Dilemma of Odious Debt' (2006–07) 56 *Duke Law Journal* 1201, 1216; J Damle, 'The Odious Debt Doctrine after Iraq' (2007) 70(4) *Law & Contemporary Problems* 139, fn 3.

[33] *Tinoco Arbitration* (n 31 above), 167–68.

[34] Khalfan et al (n 15 above), 47.

evident that all three prerequisites for invoking the Doctrine were present: there was a clear lack of consent of the majority of the population, the debt had been predominantly incurred for the benefit of a small minority and the oppression of the rest of the population, and the creditors were well aware of both these facts in light of UN SC Resolution 181 of 1963 and a string of UN GA resolutions since the 1960s condemning the apartheid regime;[35] furthermore, the new regime had wide international support and both the intent and capacity to pay any newly incurred debts.[36] Nevertheless, and in spite of pressure on it at national and international level to repudiate the debt, the South African government decided to honour the obligations of the former regime.[37] In the case of Iraq, the conditions are also considered to have been met[38] and, although the new regime did not enjoy the wide international support that the African National Congress did, it had—more importantly, perhaps—the full weight of US diplomatic support behind it. However, despite extensive campaigning about the odiousness of Iraqi debt by the US,[39] ultimately the debt was not repudiated; instead, a major part of bilateral loans owed to states was restructured after negotiations within the framework of the Paris Club.[40] While in the case of South Africa the fear of the dangers to the country's reputation and credit of invoking the Odious Debt Doctrine seem to have been the main reasons behind its decision,[41] which may have been reinforced by the relatively limited amounts involved,[42] in the case of Iraq these reasons were not present: its reputation and credit would suffer at least as much from restructuring the debt, while the debt itself was massive.[43] However, invoking the Odious Debt Doctrine was deemed as a likely longer, more expensive and possibly less successful process,[44] while the debt restructuring agreement Iraq obtained via the Paris Club helped it avoid legal complications and quickly achieve a relative stability of its finances. So, even though there was a legal basis for invoking the Odious Debt Doctrine in the cases of both South Africa and Iraq, reasons of policy and expediency dictated against such an action.

[35] Abrahams (n 17 above), 53-62.

[36] Damle (n 32 above), 140.

[37] M Kremmer and S Jayachandran, 'Odious Debt', paper presented at IMF Conference on Macroeconomic Policies and Poverty Reduction, Washington, DC, March 2002, 8 available at www.imf.org/external/np/res/seminars/2002/poverty/mksj.pdf (accessed on 3 July 2013); Howse (n 7 above), 13–14; S Bonilla, *Odious Debt: Law-and-Economics Perspectives* (Gabler Verlag, 2011) 35.

[38] KH Anderson, 'International Law and State Succession: A Solution to the Iraqi Debt Crisis?' [2005] *Utah Law Review* 401, 436.

[39] O Ben-Shahar and M Gulati, 'Partially Odious Debts?' (2007) 70(4) *Law & Contemporary Problems* 47, 54.

[40] Damle (n 32 above), 147.

[41] Bonilla (n 37 above), 35–36.

[42] Less than 15 billion USD; Abrahams (n 17 above), 62.

[43] About 125 billion USD in loans alone, possibly up to 230 billion USD or roughly 10 times its 2004 GDP, Anderson (n 38 above), 431.

[44] Damle (n 32 above), 143–44.

IV. REASONS OF THE ODIOUS DEBT DOCTRINE'S IMPRACTICALITY

Besides the specific reasons of each of the two cases mentioned above, there are also generic ones that can be presumed to have played a part in judging the Odious Debt Doctrine to be impractical. They concern the three prerequisites required by it, as there are certain problematic aspects in applying each one of them.

A. Lack of the People's Consent

As a rule of thumb, this should be presumed in all dictatorial regimes (despotic, in the terminology of Sack), as they rule by definition without the people's consent,[45] although that should not necessarily mean that all debts incurred by such regimes are odious.[46] The main problem lies with quasi-democratic governments, where the outer trappings of democratic rule are maintained but extensive propaganda, monopolistic party systems, limited franchise and/or substantial unrepresented minorities undermine their claim to democratic rule.[47] Determining whether a certain regime is democratic enough to be considered as having the people's consent can be very challenging[48]—and, one might suspect, open to abuse and manipulation.

B. Lack of Benefit to the People

This requirement has two aspects, both of which must be present: that the purpose of the debt contracted is without benefit to the people and that the proceeds are actually spent without benefit to the people.[49] But what happens when the debt has been contracted supposedly in the people's benefit, but without any real benefit in the end (as in the case of the infamous nuclear power plant of the Philippines, built on a fault line in the vicinity of an active volcano)?[50] The strict application of the rule would mean that such a debt could not be repudiated, even though it was evident, from a certain point onwards, that it was just a government boondoggle. And whereas some purposes are self-evidently against the people's interest (personal enrichment of officials, procurement of arms to suppress popular uprisings or to fight aggressive wars, strengthening oppressive institutions, investment to the benefit of a defined advantaged minority), many other purposes and expenditures are

[45] Khalfan et al (n 15 above), 42.
[46] Damle (n 32 above), 148.
[47] Khalfan et al (n 15 above), 42–43.
[48] Bonilla (n 37 above), 85.
[49] Khalfan et al (n 15 above), 15.
[50] S Ambrose, 'Social Movements and the Politics of Debt Cancellation' (2005) 6 *Chicago Journal of International Law* 277.

neutral in this respect (maintenance of governmental equipment and offices, public enterprises, etc).[51]

C. Creditor's Awareness

The main question as far as creditor's awareness is concerned is whether it must be ascertained by a subjective or objective standard. Sack seemed to be in favour of the former,[52] but both options have their disadvantages. If the test were subjective, the creditor would simply strive to 'blindfold' himself in order to remain ignorant of the loan's purpose; if it were objective, it would mean an onerous burden on the creditor that could adversely affect the transaction costs of loans.[53]

A last issue to be dealt with, albeit briefly, is the legal foundation of the Odious Debt Doctrine. Even though the examples of state practice mentioned already are not the only ones,[54] they are the most important, and, notwithstanding the plain fact that state succession and regime change are infrequent phenomena, it is true that the cases where the Odious Debt Doctrine has been unambiguously confirmed are few, if any.[55] This has created doubts concerning its standing as part of international customary law.[56] As Anna Gelpern succinctly put it, 'the fact that Odious Debt's most fervent proponents to this day must cite an 1898 treaty and a 1923 arbitration as their best authorities suggests that the law-making project is in trouble'.[57] This argument, while sound, is misleading, because the validity of the Odious Debt Doctrine should

[51] Khalfan et al (n 15 above), 43ff.

[52] Sack (n 2 above), 157.

[53] Cheng (n 17 above), 21.

[54] Other examples quoted in relation to the Odious Debt Doctrine (although in many of those its application was not accepted) include (in chronological order): the US repudiation of debts of the Republic of Texas after its annexation in 1844; the Mexican repudiation of the debts of Emperor Maximilian after his overthrow in 1897; the Chilean conquest of Tarapaca from Peru in 1880; the Soviet repudiation of Tsarist debts after the Russian Revolution; the restoration of Ethiopia after WWII in the Treaty of Peace with Italy of 1947; the People's Republic of China repudiation of imperial debts; the odiousness defence raised by Iran in the *USA v Islamic Rebublic of Iran* case before the Iran–US Claims Tribunal, *United States v Iran*, 32 Iran–US CL Trib Rep (1996) 162, 175. Often mentioned as an example of (attempted) abuse of the Odious Debt Doctrine is the repudiation by Nazi Germany of Austrian debts after the 1938 *Anschluß*: Nazi Germany had claimed that all debts contracted by the Austrian government had been prejudicial to the people of Austria, whose interest lay with the annexation of that country by Germany.

[55] PB Stephan, 'The Institutionalist Implications of an Odious Debt Doctrine' (2007) 70(3) *Law & Contemporary Problems* 213; A Rheinisch, 'A History of the Doctrine of Odious Debts: Serving Individual/Bilateral or Community Interests?' in U Fastenrath et al (eds), *From Bilateralism to Community Interest: Essays in Honour of Bruno Simma* (Oxford University Press, 2011) 1225, 1231.

[56] CG Paulus, '"Odious Debts" vs Debt Trap: A Realistic Help?' (2005) 31 *Brooklyn Journal of International Law* 83, 91; Howse (n 7 above), 7.

[57] A Gelpern, 'What Iraq and Argentina Might Learn from Each Other' (2005) 6 *Chicago Journal of International Law* 391, 406.

be viewed as founded not in international custom, but rather in the general principles of law, the third primary source of international law alongside treaties and custom according to Article 38(1c) of the ICJ Statute.[58] These principles, common to a wide range of the world's legal systems, depending on the specific context in which the Odious Debt Doctrine is invoked, could include a wide range of concepts usually associated with the law of contracts and already accepted as being part of international law, like *bona fides*, the prohibition of abuse of rights, the 'clean hands' doctrine, the invalidity of acts *contra bonos mores*, fundamentally changed circumstances or the provisions on the corruption of the agent to the detriment of the contracting principal.[59] If the Odious Debt Doctrine is accepted as part of the general principles of law, the lack of sufficient examples of state practice becomes of limited relevance.

V. CONCLUSIONS

Despite its apparent recent revival, the Odious Debt Doctrine seems to remain confined within the limits of the historical context of its creation. The recent academic and political interest in it has offered much food for thought, but this seems to have left state actors largely unimpressed. South Africa and Iraq were two great, but missed, opportunities for the Doctrine's application, especially Iraq, considering the extensive rhetoric about the odiousness of the debts incurred by Saddam Hussein's regime;[60] in the end, the Iraqi arguments put forward before the members of the Paris Club were about security and oil prices.[61] One could argue that in this respect Iraq was a unique case, its situation having such a great potential impact on the world scene,[62] but then all cases of state succession or fundamental regime change tend to be so, to some degree at least. The problematic aspects of the Doctrine, the uncertainty not so much about its legal basis as about its exact content, not to mention the complications of modern financial institutions, such as the role of secondary markets in sovereign debt,[63] have drawn potential beneficiaries of the Doctrine away from it. Besides, it is not uncommon on the international scene for political approaches to be preferred over legal ones. It is obvious that the Doctrine is in urgent need of an extensive overhaul to bring it up to date, but the initiative seems to rest mostly with state actors, not academics.

[58] Howse (n 7 above), 6.

[59] Ibid; Rheinisch (n 55 above), 1231–34.

[60] As Paul Wolfowitz, at the time Undersecretary of Defence, had put it, the Iraqi people should not have to pay for the guns, palaces and (in reality nonexistent) weapons of mass destruction of Saddam Hussein: Ludington and Gulati (n 1 above), 701.

[61] Damle (n 32 above), 147.

[62] Gelpern (n 57 above), 400–02.

[63] An excellent analysis of secondary markets and the nature of transactions within their framework as assignment or novation is given in Khalfan et al (n 15 above), 97–99.

Part II

International Legal Facets of the Modern Race towards Resources

Section 1

Protecting the Past

12

'Return of Cultural Treasures to their Countries of Origin': Principle or Trend in Cultural Property Law?

IRINI STAMATOUDI*

I. INTRODUCTION

THE NOTION OF 'return' under cultural property law carries particular weight and works, in most cases, as a prerequisite for the preservation of the integrity of cultural contexts.[1] The term 'return' is also used interchangeably with the term 'restitution', although they typically bear different meanings. The term 'restitution' refers to any sort of restitution in the case of illegally alienated cultural objects in order for the 'wrong' committed to be rectified, even in cases where the object no longer exists. Restitution in this sense includes return, compensation or any other sort of rectification, which a court may consider appropriate in the circumstances. It is, however, only *restitutio in integrum*, which directly refers to the return of a cultural object to the place from which it has been illegally alienated, or else the re-establishment of the situation as it was before the removal of the cultural good. This type of restitution also comes close to the notion of 'compensation *in natura*', which means that, instead of being paid compensation, the dispossessed owner is entitled to the actual return of the object, which constitutes compensation in kind. The latter is borrowed from civil law[2] and applies to those cases where such a kind of restitution is possible, corresponds to what the claimant wants and requests from the court, and constitutes what

* Irini Stamatoudi LLM, PhD.

[1] For more information on principles and trends in cultural property law see I Stamatoudi, *Cultural Property Law and Restitution. A Commentary to International Conventions and European Union Law* (Edward Elgar Publishing, 2011).

[2] In fact, in civil law it is referred as compensation *in natura*.

the court considers more appropriate in the circumstances. *Restitutio in integrum* is recognized under international customary law.

Yet return in cultural property law is not an act initiated only under circumstances of commitment of a wrong in the narrow sense of the word, as this is specifically described in law (national or international), eg theft (or akin crimes) and illegal import/export. It may be initiated in other cases, too, where a 'wrongful' act in the wider sense of the word has been committed. The displacement of cultural property from its country of origin could have taken place on the basis of many instances. It could be the result of acts of war, hostilities, occupation, colonization or punitive raids (where a country cannot retain control of its heritage, as was the case with Benin (Nigeria)[3] and Ethiopia[4]), or by reason of exploitation of political, social or other circumstances (ie the weakness of a state or arrangements between other states which the state of origin could not prevent in the given circumstances).[5] In these cases, the physical return[6] of the object (or its preservation in situ)[7] is initiated on the basis of ethical, scientific, humanitarian or other grounds, and not necessarily for the rectification of a legal wrong. Here the notion of 'wrong' is generally linked to the displacement of an object from its cultural context without the country of origin's authorization or consent, and it is this 'wrong' which in many instances has been turned into a legal wrong.

The preservation of the integrity of a single monument or a cultural site is an aim which holds value in itself without the need to be linked to the methods or circumstances under which a cultural object has been detached from this cultural context. Once a cultural object is removed from its context, it can provide little information about the territory, history, culture or civilization to which it belongs.[8] A typical example in this respect is the Parthenon

[3] See the British Punitive Expedition against Benin in 1897, during which the famous Benin bronzes were plundered from the royal palace of the Kingdom of Benin.

[4] During the Second Italo-Ethiopian War (1935–36) and subsequently during Ethiopia's annexation into the newly created colony of Italian East Africa.

[5] L Prott, 'The Ethics and Law of Returns' (2009) 61(1–2) *Museum International* 101.

[6] See also the 34th UNESCO General Conference Recommendation 44 (2007), according to which digital access to cultural heritage cannot replace the enjoyment of the original in its authentic form. E Korka, 'Final Synthesis and Conclusions of the Athens Conference' (2009) 61(1–2) *Museum International* 153.

[7] Relevant in this respect is the Convention on the Protection of the Underwater Cultural Heritage, which was concluded in Paris in 2001. It is another international instrument which includes provisions concerning preservation in situ. The Convention provides that states parties must take measures for the seizure of underwater cultural heritage in their territory that has been recovered in a manner not in conformity with the Convention (Art 18, para 1). The seized cultural properties are subject to a special regime, based on the concept of public benefit, and the interests of states having 'a verifiable link' with the object are taken in special consideration. See also F Fechner, 'The Fundamental Aims of Cultural Property Law' (1998) 7 *International Journal of Cultural Property* 376; JH Merryman, 'Cultural Property Export Control' (1989) 111 *UFITA* 63; JH Merryman, 'Two Ways of Thinking About Cultural Property' (1986) 80 *American Journal of International Law* 831.

[8] See RJ Elia, 'Preventing Looting through the Return of Looted Archaeological Objects' (2009) 61(1–2) *Museum International*, 130; L Rosenbaum, 'Art History Meets Archaeology: Considering Cultural Context in American Museums' (2009) 61(1–2) *Museum International*, 132; N Brodie,

Marbles, and the fact that some of them are exhibited in the New Acropolis Museum whilst others are exhibited in the British Museum.[9] This is also the reason why archaeological evidence should be preserved in situ where possible.[10] This was stated in the conclusions of the International Conference on the Return of Cultural Objects to their Countries of Origin (Athens, 17–18 Match 2008)[11] and reaffirmed in the Recommendation adopted by the extraordinary session of the Intergovernmental Committee for Promoting the Return of Cultural Property to its Countries of Origin or its Restitution in Case of Illicit Appropriation (ICPRCP) commemorating its 30th anniversary in Seoul (25–28 November 2008)[12].[13]

'An Archaeological View of the Trade in Unprovenanced Antiquities' in BT Hoffman (ed), *Art and Cultural Heritage—Law, Policy and Practice* (Cambridge University Press, 2006) 52; Fechner (n 7 above), 379.

[9] See W St Clair, 'Imperial Appropriations of the Parthenon' in JH Merryman (ed), *Imperialism, Art and Restitution* (Cambridge University Press 2006) 65–82. The above author mentions that 'the Elgin Marbles were shown not only divorced from their Athenian geographical, climatic, historical, religious, and architectural context, and displayed as "works of art" in accordance with European post-romantic aesthetics, but incorporated into a metropolitan, "universal", museum that, by the sheer extent and miscelaneity of its collections, celebrated British national and imperial success'. For more information on the Parthenon Marbles see I Stamatoudi, 'Legal Issues Associated with the Return of the Parthenon Marbles' in M Marouli-Zilemenou (ed), *Ο Παρηενώμας Η Επιστροφή των Γλυπτών* [*The Parthenon. The Return of the Sculptures*] (I Sideris, 2004) 214; I Stamatoudi and E Korka, 'The Parthenon Marbles Issue: Legal, Ethical and Political Issues' in *Proceedings of the 3rd International Conference of Experts on the Return of Cultural Property* (Hellenic Ministry of Culture and Sports, 2014) 45; I Stamatoudi, 'The Law and the Ethics Deriving from the Parthenon Marbles Case' (1997) 3 *Web Journal of Current Legal Issues* 12, available at http://www.ncl.ac.uk/~nlawwww/; I Stamatoudi, 'Legal Grounds for the Return of the Parthenon Marbles' [2002] 2 *Revue Hellénique de droit International* 513.

[10] 'Integrity', intended as a measure of the wholeness and intactness of the heritage, is a condition for a property to be inscribed on the World Heritage List as established under the Convention Concerning the Protection of the World Cultural and Natural Heritage. The UNIDROIT Convention provides that a court or other competent authority of the state addressed shall order the return of an illegally exported cultural object if the requesting state establishes that the removal of the object from its territory significantly impairs, inter alia, the interest in 'the integrity of a complex object' (Art 5, para 3).

[11] '[C]ertain categories of cultural property are irrevocably identified by reference to the cultural context in which they were created (unique and exceptional artworks and monuments, ritual objects, national symbols, ancestral remains, dismembered pieces of outstanding works of art). It is their original context that gives them their authenticity and unique value.' 'Conclusions of the Athens International Conference on the Return of Cultural Objects to their Countries of Origin' (2009) 61(1–2) *Museum International* 158.

[12] 'Certain categories of cultural property fully reveal their authenticity and unique value only in the cultural context in which they were created.' See also the conclusions of the Non-governmental Expert Meeting Held in Commemoration of the 30th Anniversary of the ICPRCP (Seoul, 26 November 2008), where it was stated that 'it is an indissociable attribute of the sovereignty of every people that it should have access to, and enjoyment of, the irreplaceable symbols of its heritage'.

[13] 'The preservation of the integrity of cultural contexts can also be seen as a mean to ensure cultural diversity. The parties to the Convention on the Protection and Promotion of the Diversity of Cultural Expressions (Paris, 2005) recognize "the need to take measures to protect the diversity of cultural expressions, including their contents, especially in situations where cultural expressions may be threatened by the possibility of extinction or serious impairment"' (Preamble). They reaffirm 'the sovereign rights of states to maintain, adopt and implement policies and measures that they deem appropriate for the protection and promotion of the diversity of cultural expres-

II. GROUNDS FOR RETURN

A. Law and International Customary Rules

By law, we mean national law, regional law and international conventions. There are several national laws—especially those of source states—which provide for the inalienability of significant cultural objects and their return in case they are removed from the country.[14]

In the international conventions in the area there is a clear reference to the fact that restitution should mean return, since this is the most appropriate way of rectifying a situation where an object has been illegally removed (ie by reason of illegal export, theft and so on) from its country of origin. In addition, it is demonstrated that it is not so much the rectification of the wrong that is at issue as it is the return of the object to the country of origin in order for it to be reintegrated into its original cultural context. This 'return' in relation to stolen and illegally exported cultural objects is specifically mentioned (in relation to the notion of restitution) throughout the 1995 Unidroit Convention (see, for example, the Preamble to the Convention, Articles 3–5) and the 1970 UNESCO Convention (eg Article 7). Also, a number of regional, sub-regional and bilateral treaties or agreements (as well as memoranda of understanding), which have been concluded on the basis of Article 15 of the 1970 UNESCO Convention or Article 13, paragraph 1 of the 1995 Unidroit Convention, operate in the same spirit. Examples of regional and sub-regional agreements are the Convention on the Protection of the Archaeological, Historical and Artistic Heritage of the American Nations (San Salvador, 1976), in particular Articles 11 and 12, and the Centro-American Convention for the Restitution and the Return of Archaeological, Historical and Artistic Objects (Guatemala City, 1995), in particular Article 1.[15] Council Directive 93/7/EEC of 15 March 1993 on the return of cultural objects unlawfully removed from the territory of a Member State can also be added as a regional legal instrument, which provides for return and, though not enacted within the scope of the 1970 UNESCO Convention, has been largely affected by it.[16] Council

sions in their territory' (Art 1h). T Scovazzi, 'Diviser c'est détruire: ethical principles and legal rules in the field of return of cultural properties', papre presented at the 15th Session of the Intergovernmental Committee for Promoting the Return of Cultural Property to its Countries of Origin or its Restitution in case of illicit appropriation, UNESCO, Paris, 11–13 May 2009, 31.

[14] Such examples are Greece, Italy, Egypt, Peru, Bolivia and China.

[15] See also the Convention on the Protection of the Archaeological. Historical and Artistic Heritage of the American Nations of 16 June 1976 (also known as the Convention of San Salvador), which aims, amongst other issues, to prevent the unlawful exportation of the cultural heritage of the American Nations. Available at http://www.oas.org.jurdico/english/treaties/c16.html.

[16] [1993] OJ L/74, replaced by Directive 2014/60/EU of the European Parliament and of the Council of 15 May 2014 on the return of cultural objects unlawfully removed from the territory of a Member State and amending Regulation (EU) No 1024/2012 [1994] OJ 159/1.

Regulation 3911/92 of 9 December 1992 on the export of cultural goods[17] operates in the same spirit, since it establishes a common export policy for cultural goods leaving the European Union in order to secure their return to it. Some examples of bilateral agreements (some of them concluded by major destination states, eg the US and Switzerland) are those between the US and Mexico (1970), the US and Guatemala (1997), the US and Peru (1997), the US and Italy (2001), the US and Cyprus (2002), Switzerland and Italy (2006), Switzerland and Greece (2007), China and Italy (2006) and China and Greece (2008).[18] They all provide for the prevention of importation of designated

[17] Council Regulation 3911/92 on the export of cultural goods [1992] OJ L395/1 (Corrigendum [1996] OJ L267/30), as amended by Council Regulation 2469/96 [1996] OJ L335/9, Council Regulation 974/2001 [2001] OJ L137/10 and Council Regulation 806/2003 [2003] OJ L122/1. Regulation 3911/92 has been replaced by Regulation 116/2009 on the export of cultural goods [2009] OJ L39/1. See also First Report from the Commission to the Council, the European Parliament and the Economic and Social Committee on the Implementation of Council Regulation (EEC) No 3911/92 on the export of cultural goods and Council Directive 93/7/EEC on the return of cultural objects unlawfully removed from the territory of a Member state (COM(2000) 325 final).

[18] Interesting in this respect is the US case *United States of America v Frederick Schultz*, 333 F3d 393 (2nd Cir 2003), cert denied, *Schultz v US*, 157 L Ed 2d 891 (2004), which sets a precedent with regard to the enforcement by US courts of foreign cultural property laws. In the case at issue. the court enforced the 1983 Egyptian Law 117, which provides that 'all antiquities are considered to be public property . . . It is impermissible to own, possess or dispose of antiquities except pursuant to the conditions set forth in this law and its implementing regulations'. See also *US v McClain*, 545 F 2d 988 (5th Cir 1977), rehearing denied, 551 F 2d (5th Cir 1977), and appeal after remand, 593 F 2d 658 (5th Cir 1979) and *US v Hollinshead*, 495 F 2d 1154 (9th Cir 1974). All these cases, including the following, involved the enforcement of the National Stolen Property Act of 1948 (18 USC §§2314–15) *Peru v Johnson*, 720 F Supp 10 (CD Cal 1989), aff'd sub nom; *Peru v Wendt*, 933 F 2d 1013 (9th Cir 1991); *United States v Pre-Columbian Artifacts*, 845 F Supp 544 (N Dist III Lexis 14656, 1993); *United States v Portrait of Wally*, 99 Civ 9940 (MBM) (11 April 2002). See also J Hughes, 'The Trend toward Liberal Enforcement of Repatriation Claims in Cultural Property Disputes' (2000) 33 *George Washington International Law Review* 131. See also BT Hoffman, 'International Art Transactions and the Resolution of Art and Cultural Property Disputes: A United States Perspective' in BT Hoffman (ed), *Art and Cultural Heritage—Law, Policy and Practice* (Cambridge University Press, 2006) 159, where she mentions that US courts have become more sympathetic to foreign governments' claims for the return of stolen antiquities whilst the US government has aggressively and successfully brought forfeiture actions under the National Stolen Property Act, customs statutes and directives. See also page 164, where she refers to a number of US cases based on different legal bases for the return of cultural treasures to their original owners as well as to the legal issues these cases set: *United States v An Antique Platter of Gold*, 991 F Supp 222, 1997 US Dist Lexis 18899; *United States v Hollinshead*, 495 F 2d 1154 (9th Cir 1974); *United States v McClain*, 545 F 2d 998 (5th Cir) [*McClain I*], rehearing denied, 551 F 2d 52 (5th Cir 1977) (per curian); *US v McClain*, 593 F 2d 658 (5th Cir) [*McClain II*], cert denied, 444 US 918 (1979); *McClain III*, 593 F 2d, 658 (5th Cir 1979); *United States v Pre-Columbian Artifacts*, 845 F Supp 544 (N Dist Ill Lexis 14656, 1993); *United States of America v Frederick Schultz*, 178 F Supp 2d 445, 2002 US Dist Lexis 15; *United States of America v Portrait Wally*, 99 Civ 9940 (MBM) (11 April 2002); *Kunstsammlung zu Weimer v Elicofon*, 536 F Supp 829 (EDNY 1981) aff'd 678 F 2d 1150 (2d Cir 1982); *Autocephalous Greek-Orthodox Church of Cyprus and The Republic of Cyprus v Goldberg & Feldman Fine Arts, Inc*, 717 F Supp 1374 (SD Ind 1985), aff'd, 917 F 2d 278 (7th Cir 1990); *Republic of Croatia v The Trustee of the Marquess of Northampton*, 1987, Settlement 203 AD 2d 167, NYS 2d 263 (Dept 1994); *Solomon R Guggenheim Foundation v Lubell*, 153 AD 2d 143, 149, 550 NYS 2d 618, 621–22 (1st Dep't 1990), aff'd, 77 NY 2d 311, 567 NYS 2d 623, 569 NE 2d 426 (1999); *O'Keefe v Snyder*, 416A 2d 862 870 (NJ 1980); *Greek Orthodox Patriarchate of Jerusalem v Christie's, Inc*, 1999 US Dist Lexis 13257; *Warin v Wildenstein & Co*, 740 NYS 2d 331, 2002 NY App Div

objects from the aforementioned countries and co-operation for their immediate return, and they also contain provisions on cultural collaboration. Also relevant are the provisions of the Commonwealth Scheme for the Protection of the Material Cultural Heritage. According to this, a Commonwealth country can seek the return of unlawfully exported cultural objects that are found in another Commonwealth country that is part of the scheme. Although this scheme refers to unlawfully exported cultural objects only, in practice it covers stolen artifacts, too, in the sense that an artifact that is stolen will hardly ever be given formally permission to leave the country should its possessor ever apply for one.

In relation to cultural objects removed in times of war, a number of international instruments provide for their return (without any time limitations).[19] As these instruments are widely recognized, accepted and ratified (depending on the instrument), they are considered to constitute international customary rules.[20] Such instruments are: the Westphalia Treaties of 1648, concluded by 194 European states, providing for the reciprocal restitution of 'archives, writings and other movables'; the Regulations annexed to the Second Hague Convention on the Laws and Customs of War on Land 1899; and the Regulations annexed to the Fourth Hague Convention on the Laws and Customs on Land 1907, which prohibited the pillage of places[21] and the seizure of, destruction of and wilful damage done to institutions, monuments and works

Lexis 3835 (App Div 1st Dept. 2002); *Republic of Austria et al v Maria Altmann*, 124 S Ct 2240 (2004); *Bennigson v Alsdorf* (Cal Super Ct June 16, 2003) (unreported), aff'd, No B168200, 2004 WL 803616 (Cal Ct App April 15, 2004) (affirming that the defendant's contacts with California were insufficient to justify assertion of personal jurisdiction), review granted, S124828, 2004 Cal Lexis 6903 (Cal July 28, 2004), dismissed, S124828, 2005 Cal Lexis 13370 (Cal Nov 30, 2005) (dismissing the case pursuant to notice of settlement); see also *United States v One Oil Painting Entitled 'Femme En Blanc' by Pablo Picasso*, 362 F Supp 2d 1175 (CD Cal 2005); *Alsdorf v Bennigson*, No 04 C 5953, 2004 WL 2806301 (ND Ill 2004) (granting a six-month stay awaiting resolution of Bennigson v Alsdorf); *Claude Cassirer et al v Stephen Hahn* 01158698 (Santa Barbara Super Ct filed July 19, 2004); *Sarah-Rose Josepha Adler et al v Elizabeth Taylor* (CV 04-H472 February 2005); *Leonard Malewicz et al v City of Amsterdam*, 362 F Supp 298 (DC March 30 2005). For more case law see the site of the International Foundation for Art Research (IFAR) see http://www.ifar.org/home.php. See also the developments with regard to the UK law: A Parkhouse, 'The Illicit Trade in Cultural Objects: Recent Developments in the United Kingdom' in BT Hoffman (ed), *Art and Cultural Heritage. Law, Policy and Practice* (Cambridge University Press, 2006) 178. UK courts have also been sympathetic to such claims. See *Bumper Development Corporation v Commissioner of Police of the Metropolis and others* [1991] 1 WLR 1362 (CA), which concerned a stone object of religious worship that was stolen from India after 1976. In this case, the UK court recognized that the Hindu temple could sue in the English courts even though it would not be recognized as a legal entity under English law.

[19] This principle is thought to have been established at the beginning of the 19th century. See Scovazzi (n 13 above), 6 et seq.

[20] See Merryman (n 9 above), who refers to the fact that the 'seizure of works of art in the occupied countries violated an international law prohibition on the confiscation of private property by aggressive occupying powers. This was, by 1939, a customary international law norm that had been formalized in Art 46 of the 1907 Hague Convention (Hague IV) on the Laws of War and in the Kellog-Briand Pact of 1928', at 7–8 and fn 21.

[21] See Arts 28 and 47.

of art.[22] Return as *restitution in integrum* was followed in the Franco-German war of 1870–71 and included in the peace treaties that were concluded after World Wars I and II.[23] The Hague Convention for the Protection of Cultural Property in the Event of Armed Conflict 1954 and the First Protocol to it, by reason of the high number of ratifications (123 state parties to the Convention and 100 parties to the Protocol), are considered to constitute customary international law and dictate, in addition to the prohibition of seizure of cultural properties, an obligation for the return of any such properties to the country from which they were taken. The same applies to the Second Protocol to the 1954 Hague Convention.[24]

The fact that these rules constitute customary law was also affirmed in an Italian judgment of 28 February 2007 concerning the return of the statue of Venus of Cyrene to Libya, which was displaced from Libya by the Italians in 1915. In this decision, and although there was a joint declaration signed on 4 July 1998 between Italy and Libya, according to which Italy undertook to return all manuscripts, artifacts, documents and archaeological objects brought to Italy during and after the Italian colonization of Libya, pursuant to the 1970 UNESCO Convention on the Means of Prohibiting and Preventing the Illicit Import, Export and Transfer of Ownership of Cultural Property, the court mentioned that the return of Venus was also dictated by two customary rules of international law: the first one referred to the succession of states,[25] whilst the second one provided that cultural heritage removed in time of war should be restored to its original situation as provided by the 1899 and 1907 Hague Conventions.

Apart from the above prohibitions of removal and obligations for return, removal in times of war is also regarded as a crime. The Charter of the International Military Tribunal of Nuremberg, established under the agreement signed in 1945 by France, the Soviet Union, the UK and the US, included among the crimes of war the 'plunder of public and private property' (Article 6b). The same crime is also included among the crimes of war (together with the 'seizure of, destruction or willful damage done to institutions dedicated to religion, charity and education, the arts and sciences, historic monuments and works of art and science' (Article 3d)) according to Article 3e of the Statute of the International Criminal Tribunal for the Former Yugoslavia (Security

[22] See Art 56.

[23] For more details see Scovazzi (n 13 above), 6 et seq.

[24] See Art 15, paras 1c and e.

[25] The first rule according to the Italian court is that, in the case of a newly independent state, 'movable property, having belonged to the territory to which the succession of states relates and having become state property of the predecessor state during the period of dependence, shall pass to the successor state' and that 'movable state property of the predecessor state . . . to the creation of which the dependent territory has contributed, shall pass to the successor state in proportion to the contribution of the dependent territory' (Art 15, paras 1e and f of the Vienna Convention on Succession of States in Respect of State Property, Archives and Debts). This principle, derived from Art 15 of the 1983 Vienna Convention, was found to apply even though the Convention had not entered in force.

Council Resolution 827/25.5.1993). Equivalent to this is the Statute of the International Criminal Court,[26] established in Rome in 1998.[27]

Although the principle of return applies unequivocally in times of war, it is also considered to apply in times of occupation and colonization, as well as in times when a state does not have control over its cultural heritage and therefore such weakness can be exploited by another state in order to remove cultural properties from the former. In all those instances, as is the case in times of war, force is exercised by one state over another, or the latter state is incapable, because of the particular circumstances, of reacting to its exploitation and preventing the removal of its cultural property. A characteristic example in this respect is the 1991 Native American Graves Protection and Repatriation Act (NAGPRA), according to which a large number of US museums were asked to inventory their holdings of American Indian objects and return them.[28] Another example is the displacement of art during World War II.[29]

In relation to cultural objects displaced during colonial domination,[30] a considerable number of soft law instruments provide for the return of those objects to their countries of origin. These include: the United Nations General Assembly Declaration of Decolonization 1960;[31] the United Nations General Assembly Resolution 3187 (XXVIII) of 18 December 1973 (Restitution of Works of Art to Countries Victims of Expropriation);[32] the ICOM Reports in 1976 and 1980; the 'Plea for the Return of an Irreplaceable Cul-

[26] It provides for the 'extensive destruction and appropriation of property, not justified by military necessity and carried out unlawfully and wantonly' (Art 8, para 2a.iv) and for the 'destroying or seizing the enemy's property unless such destruction or seizure be imperatively demanded by the necessities of war' (Art 8, para 2b.xiii).

[27] Scovazzi (n 13 above), 9–10.

[28] NAGPRA 'vests title to cultural objects discovered on tribal lands in the individual descendant or tribe on whose tribal land the object was discovered, not in the US government. Native American cultural objects found on federal land become the property not of the government but of the tribe which has the "closest affiliation" with the object': *United States v Steinhardt*, 184 F 3d 131 (2d Cir 1999) (No 97-6319). See also MF Brown and MM Bruchac, 'NAGPRA from the Middle Distance: Legal Puzzles and Unintended Consequences' in Merryman (n 9 above), 193; DH Thomas, 'Finders Keepers and Deep American History: Some Lessons in Dispute Resolution' in Merryman (n 9 above), 218.

[29] See *Republic of Austria v Altmann*, 541 US 677 (2004), according to which Altmann claimed before the federal district court in Los Angeles six paintings by Gustav Klimt that were seized by the Nazis and found at the Austrian National Museum in Vienna. The US Supreme Court found that, under a provision of the Foreign Sovereign Immunities Act, Altmann could proceed with her case in the courts of Los Angeles. In the end, the case was settled before trial when the parties agreed to submit it to arbitration in Vienna.

[30] 'Seen as a sort of prolonged foreign occupation of a territory': Scovazzi (n 13 above), 17.

[31] UNGA Resolution 1514 of 14 December 1960. Declaration on the Granting of Independence to Colonial Countries and Peoples.

[32] This Resolution 'deplored "the wholesale removal, virtually without payment of objets d'art, from one country to another, frequently as a result of colonial or foreign occupation" and called for their prompt restitution. The General Assembly also recognized "the special obligations in this connection of those countries which had access to such valuable objects only as a result of colonial or foreign occupation" (para 2) and declared itself convinced that "the restitution of such works would make good the serious damage suffered by countries as a result of such removal"': Scovazzi (n 13 above), 17.

tural Heritage to Those Who Created It' by the Director General of UNESCO on 7 June 1978, which formulated an ethical basis for the return of cultural objects to their countries of origin;[33] and the 1995 Principles and Guidelines for the Protection of the Heritage of Indigenous Peoples developed by the UN Human Rights Committee.[34] From the above instruments, it can be derived that the same principle applies in relation to the return of cultural objects to indigenous communities, and it is also thought to apply to any sort of foreign occupation by another state in instances where the state of origin cannot exercise control over its cultural properties. Such an example also forms the Security Council Resolution mandating the return to Iraq of cultural objects displaced from the country in 2003.[35]

[33] Amadou-Mahtar M'Bow, 'A Plea for the Return of Irreplaceable Cultural Heritage to Those Who Created It' (1979) 31 *Museum* 58.

[34] Ibid, 104–05. The UNESCO Universal Declaration on Cultural Diversity and the UNESCO Convention on the Protection and Promotion of Cultural Expressions 2005 also function in the same spirit. See also Art 12 of the Draft Declaration on the Rights of Indigenous People (1994), available at http://www.unhchr.ch/huridocda/huridoca.nsf/(Symbol)/E.CN.4.SUB.2.RES.1994.45.En?OpenDocument.

[35] Even import countries such as the UK have progressively changed their attitude towards the protection of cultural property. For example, (i) the UK has enacted the Holocaust (Return of Cultural Objects) Act 2009, according to which (para 7) 'Where two conditions are met the Act gives the governing bodies of the national institutions named in the Act a power to transfer an object from their collection and return it to the person who claims it. The first condition is that the Advisory Panel recommends that the object should be returned to the claimant. The second condition is that the Secretary of State approves the Panel's recommendation. Scottish Ministers must give their consent before the Secretary of State can approve a recommendation that relates to an object in the collection of one of the Scottish bodies specified in the Act. The Act will expire on the tenth anniversary of the day on which it received Royal Assent' (that is, 12 November 2019). (ii) See also the Tribunals, Courts and Enforcement Act 2007, Chapter 4, part 6, which provides for the 'protection of cultural objects on loan'. (iii) In October 2006, the British Museum and the Museums, Libraries and Archives Council (MLA) formed a partnership with eBay.co.uk to ensure that antiquities found in the UK are sold legally on the latter's website. In order to prevent illegal sales of treasures, the Portable Antiquities Scheme (PAS, which is managed by the British Museum on behalf of the MLA and is a voluntary scheme to record archaeological objects found by members of the public in England and Wales) set up a team to monitor antiquities sold on eBay.co.uk and to ensure that sellers have the right to trade them. Where the listing is illegal, PAS reports it to the Art and Antiques Unit of the Metropolitan Police, and eBay.co.uk has committed to end illegal listings. In 2007, 144 cases were investigated. (iv) There are also the Crime International Co-operation Act 2003 and the Crime Act 2002, which facilitate mutual legal assistance on criminal matters. (v) See also the guidelines published by the Department for Culture, Media and Sport (Cultural Property Unit), 'Combating Illicit Trade: Due Diligence Guidelines for Museums, Libraries and Archives on Collecting and Borrowing Cultural Material' (2005–10), which aim to assist museums, libraries and archives when considering the acquisition by purchase, gift or bequest of items of cultural property originating outside the UK. (vi) The Cultural Property Advice site (http://www.culturalpropertyadvice.gov.uk/) was launched in February 2007 by the British government with the aim of assisting the collecting, buying and selling of art, antiques and antiquities. (vii) See also the Export of Objects of Cultural Interest (Control) Order 2003, according to which objects are prohibited from being exported to any destination except under the authority of a licence in writing granted by the Secretary of State, and in accordance with all the conditions attached to the licence. (viii) See further the Dealing in Cultural Objects (Offences) Act 2003, according to which a person is guilty of an offence if he dishonestly deals in a cultural object that is tainted, knowing or believing that the object is tainted. (ix) Also, the UK Border Agency, on the basis of the Customs and Excise Management Act 1979, may confiscate any (cultural) object for which a false statement is submitted and a process for its return to its country of origin may be initiated.

As Vrdoljak[36] mentions in a 'colonization context', the first rationale behind the restitution of cultural objects is the restoration of the 'sacred' link between people, land and cultural heritage; the second rationale is the reversal of internationally wrongful acts, including discrimination and genocide; while the third rationale is intimately tied to the broader notion of the right to self-determination that evolved following decolonization. There should be no discrimination between the various instances of the illegal movement of art. It is the movement itself which renders the artifact inoperative, by depriving it from its cultural context. This act can only be restituted by the return of the object itself. If another form of restitution were provided: (i) it would not form a considerable disincentive for traders and purchasers of illegal objects; and (ii) it would not serve the aim of the preservation of cultural contexts.

B. Ethics

Return is also mentioned in Articles 3 and 4 of the UNESCO International Code of Ethics for Dealers in Cultural Property in relation to cultural objects that have been the product of a clandestine excavation or have been acquired illegally or dishonestly from an official excavation site or monument, as well as cultural objects which have been illegally exported. The ICOM Code of Ethics for Museums 2004 also refers to return. Article 6.3 of the ICOM Code provides that:

> when a country or people of origin seeks the restitution of an object or specimen that can be demonstrated to have been exported or otherwise transferred in violation of the principles of international and national conventions, and shown to be part of that country's or people's cultural or natural heritage, the museum concerned should, if legally free to do so, take prompt and responsible steps to co-operate in its return.

Article 6.2 provides that:

> Museums should be prepared to initiate dialogues for the return of cultural property to a country or people of origin. This should be undertaken in an impartial manner, based on scientific, professional and humanitarian principles as well as applicable local, national and international legislation, in preference to action at a governmental or political level'.[37]

[36] AF Vrdoljak, *International Law, Museums and the Return of Cultural Objects* (Cambridge University Press, 2008) 2.

[37] See also P Gerstenblith, 'Acquisition and Deacquisition of Museum Collections and the Fiduciary Obligations of Museums to the Public' [2003] *Cardozo Journal of International and Comparative Law* 11, who argues that in the US museum trustees by law have a fiduciary responsibility towards the institution they serve to ensure acquisitions policies and diligence procedures.

C. Practice and Public Feeling

The increasing number of return cases demonstrates the practice in the area and reflects public feeling. Some examples are:

- The reunification and return to Great Zimbabwe of the soapstone birds, a national symbol, the lower part of which was exhibited in 1997–98 at the Royal Museum for Central Africa in Tervuren (Belgium), coming from the Museum für Völkerkunde in Berlin, while the upper part remained at the National Museums and Monuments of Zimbabwe in Harare.[38]
- The return from Denmark (ie the National Museum of Denmark) to Greenland (ie the Nunatta Katersugaasivia Allagaateqarfialu—the Greenland National Museum and Archives), between 1982 and 2001, of approximately 35,000 archaeological and ethnographic artifacts within the Utimut (meaning 'return' in Greenlandic) project.[39]
- The repatriation of Ngarrindjeri Old People (human remains) from the University of Edinburgh in 1991 and from Manchester Museum to Tasmania (Australia) in 2005 to the Ngarrindjeri country in South Australia. These human remains had been subjects of scientific study during the colonization of Australia by the British in 1788.[40]
- The return of the Axum Obelisk from Italy to Ethiopia in 2005. This obelisk (the second largest stele of the site) originated from the town of Axum in Ethiopia, which is included in UNESCO's World Heritage List. The obelisk was created during the height of the Kingdom of Axum (first to third centuries AD) and was removed in 1937 following the annexation of Ethiopia by Italy (1935–36).[41]
- The return of the Kwakwaka'wakw mask in 2005 as a long-term loan from the British Musum in London to Alert Bay, British Columbia, Canada, from where it was removed in 1921.[42]

[38] D Munjeri, 'The Reunification of a National Symbol' (2009) 61(1–2) *Museum International* 12; C Tytgat, 'The 1997 Exhibition and the Reunification Process' (2009) 61(1–2) *Museum International* 22.

[39] D Thorleifsen, 'The Repatriation of Greenland's Cultural Heritage' (2009) 61(1–2) *Museum International* 25; M Gabriel, 'The Return of Cultural Heritage from Denmark to Greenland' (2009) 61(1–2) *Museum International* 30. One should note that Greenland was a Danish colony for more than 200 years (1721–1953), during which there was extensive collecting activity on the part of the Danish.

[40] C Wilson, 'Implications and Challenges of Repatriating and Reburying Ngarrindjeri Old People from the "Edinburgh Collection"' (2009) 61(1–2) *Museum International* 37; C Fforde, 'From Edinburgh University to the Ngarrinjeri Nation, South Australia' (2009) 61(1–2) *Museum International* 41; T Besternam, 'Returning a Stolen Generation' (2009) 61(1–2) *Museum International* 107.

[41] H Mariam, 'The Cultural Benefits of the Return of the Axum Obelisk' (2009) 61(1–2) *Museum International* 48; T Scovazzi, 'Legal Aspects of the Axum Obelisk Case' (2009) 61(1–2) *Museum International* 52; G Croci, 'From Italy to Ethiopia: the Dismantling, Transportation and Re-erection of the Axum Obelisk' (2009) 31(1–2) *Museum International* 61.

[42] A Sanborn, 'The Reunification of the Kwakwaka´wakw Mask with its Cultural Soul' (2009) 61(1–2) *Museum International* 81. Other cultural objects were also repatriated to this region by

- The return of 67 masterpieces to Italy from the JP Getty Museum in Los Angeles (California), the Metropolitan Museum of Art in New York, the Museum of Fine Arts in Boston and the Princeton University Museum, which had left Italy and been acquired under suspicious circumstances.
- The return from the Louvre Museum in Paris to Egypt in 2009 of a painted wall fragment taken from a Luxor tomb.[43]
- The return of six masterpieces to Greece, four from the JP Getty Museum in Los Angeles and two masterpieces from the L Levy and Sh White Private Collection in New York, which had left Greece and been acquired under suspicious circumstances.
- Other cases of repatriation of cultural objects back to Greece are the return of: a fragment from the Parthenon's sculptural decoration from the University of Heidelberg (2006); a collection of 48 ancient Greek coins from Sweden (2006); a fragment of an ancient Greek marble relief portraying Athens from a Danish citizen after 110 years (2007); six ceramic oinochoe from a British professor of archaeology (2007); a stolen statue of Apollonas Lykeios from Gortyna in Crete from Switzerland (2007); and 90 stolen antiquities from the Theodoropoulos collection from Germany (2007).[44]
- Hundreds of cultural objects in 2007 and 2008 have been repatriated back to Peru from the US, Uruguay, Germany, New Zealand,[45] UK and Colombia.[46]

The aforementioned cases comprise only a small fraction of all the returns that have taken place in recent years on the basis of law, ethics and public feeling.[47] Public feeling is either sensed by the states or institutions themselves, which act on their own initiative, or after a request has been submitted to them; public feeling is also proven by opinion polls run by cultural institutions, non-governmental organizations or even private companies. Such examples are those run in Britain in 1998 and 2002[48], which demonstrated that public opinion was in favour of the return of the Parthenon Marbles to Greece, one of

the Smithsonian's National Museum of the American Indian in New York, from the André Breton Collection in Paris, France, amongst others.

[43] http://www.google.com/hostednews/afp/Art/ALeqM5gQVU1X-7yM469ItXJ3PxYfOXMnVA.

[44] I Stamatoudi, 'Mediation and Cultural Diplomacy' (2009) 61(1–2) *Museum International* 116.

[45] New Zealand has also returned artifacts on the basis of law. See *Tupuna Maori*, P580/88 High Court of New Zealand, Wellington, 19 May 1988, in relation to the return of a Maori head to Maori people (the New Zealand Maori Council) and *Department of Affairs v The Poverty Bay Club Inc* [1989] DCR 481 in relation to a 1776 letter written by Captain James Cook to Captain Charles Clerke, which was sent to Sotheby's in London for auction. The letter was ultimately returned to the New Zealand government. See I Barker, 'The Protection of Cultural Heritage Items in New Zealand' in Hoffman (n 18 above), 145.

[46] BA Guerrero, 'Repatriation of Cultural Properties: the Peruvian Experience' (2009) 61(1–2) *Museum International* 145.

[47] For more cases see http://portal.unesco.org/culture/en/ev.php-URL_ID=36505&URL_DO=DO_TOPIC&URL_SECTION=201.html:.

[48] 25 September 1998, Mori poll; 18 January 2002, CNN.com. Both at odysseus.culture.gr/a/1/12/ea128.html.

the most famous cases in the area of repatriation of cultural objects to their country of origin pending before the ICPRCP since 1984.

The ICPRCP, which was set up to serve claims for return not falling within the ambit and scope of the 1970 UNESCO Convention, formed and transformed the ethics in the area. The ICPRCP has been entrusted with the responsibility of seeking ways and means of facilitating bilateral negotiations for the return of cultural property to its country of origin and the promotion of multilateral and bilateral co-operation with a view to this aim (Article 4, paragraph 1 and 2, of the ICPRCP Statutes).

Cases of return have also taken place on the basis of agreements between states and cultural institutions (museums or other) or individual collectors. Examples are the agreements referred to above between Italy and various American museums, and between Greece and American museums and collectors.

III. TIME LIMITATIONS

The return of cultural objects of particular significance should not be subject to time limitations. When the international conventions in the area of illicit trade in art were adopted, this principle was regarded as a breakthrough view, which would impinge on many countries' national legislation regarding time limitations for chattels. Yet law and ethics have been transformed since then, and countries have become friendlier towards the idea of repatriation. The first seeds of this concept are found—apart from national laws (some of them incorporating the principle to its full extent by providing for the imprescriptibility of such objects[49] or their inalienability,[50] categorizing them as *res extra commercium*[51] or *res sacrae*, for which the only legitimate possessor is the state, which preserves them for the common interest and benefit)—in international conventions. The 1970 UNESCO Convention contains no provisions on time limitations, leaving Member States free to apply the time limitations they consider appropriate. The 1995 UNIDROIT Convention, which is more specialized, in the area of international claims for the return of cultural objects, provides, apart from the general time limitations, extended

[49] According to Art 18(1) of the French law for historical monuments of 1993, 'all the movable objects listed are imprescriptible'.

[50] Ie Mexico; Spain, in its Law on Historical Patrimony 1985 and the Law on National Patrimony 1982; and Greece, in its Acts 3028 of 2002 and 3658 of 2008. See also Art 28 of the relevant Portuguese law, which does not allow for any private ownership of works of art listed in a national registry.

[51] See, eg the Greek Act 3028 of 2002, which provides that 'movable ancient monuments up to 1453 belong to the state in terms of ownership and possession, are imprescriptible and extra commercium according to Art 966 of the Civil Code'. This was also explained by Prof Mussgnug at the 1990 Heidelberg Symposium with reference to the German administrative law and to the broadly accepted concept of *res sacrae*.

time limitations for a special category of cultural objects. Specifically, Article 3(4) provides that:

> [C]ultural object[s] forming an *integral part of an identified monument or archaeological site, or belonging to a public collection*, shall not be subject to time limitations other than a period of three years from the time when the claimant knew the location of the cultural object and the identity of the possessor'.[52]

Member States can, however, provide for a fixed time limitation of 75 years[53] on a reciprocal basis.[54] The Commonwealth Scheme provides for a five-year time limitation for making a claim for the return of an unlawfully exported cultural object, calculated from the time the country of export had knowledge of the whereabouts of the item in the country of location (ie subjective knowledge is required). No absolute time limitations are provided which would bar such claims.[55]

There have also been legal instruments that do not provide for any time limitations at all, especially in the area of cultural property alienated in times of armed conflict, such as the Treaty of Westphalia in 1648, the 1907 Hague Convention on the Laws of War, the post-First World War settlements, the Declaration of London of 1943 concerning the restitution of cultural property taken under the Nazi occupation, the Hague Convention on the Protection of Cultural Property in the Event of Armed Conflict and the First Protocol to the Convention of 1954, the Second Protocol of 1999 and the Security Council Resolution mandating the return to Iraq of cultural objects displaced from the country in 2003.[56] In the same spirit with respect to cultural objects taken in colonial circumstances are the United Nations General Assembly Declaration on Decolonization 1960[57] and the practice of return of such items from

[52] Emphasis added.

[53] See also Art 3(6).

[54] Art 9(1).

[55] Interesting in this respect are the time limitations provided by some of the US states. For example, in New York, on actions for recovery of stolen art according to the demand and refusal rule developed in *Menzel v List* in 1938, the three year time limitation governing a cause of action for replevin against a good faith purchaser does not begin to run until the true owner makes a demand for return of the chattel and the possessor (current owner) refuses to return it. See *Solomon R Guggenheim v Lubell*, 153 AD 2d 143, 149, 550 NYS 2d 618, 621–22 (1st Dept 1990), aff'd, 77 NY 2d 311, 567 NYS 2d 623, 569 NE 2d 426 (1999). In *O'Keefe v Snyder* 416A 2d 862 870 (NJ 1980) it was mentioned that the cause of action does not begin to accrue until the true owner first knew, or reasonably should have known through the exercise of due diligence, of the cause of action, including the identity of the possessor.

[56] Italy returned the Axum Obelisk to Ethiopia 68 years after its removal and ultimately returned the statue of Venus of Cyrene to Libya 93 years after its removal. Chile returned cultural properties to Peru 126 years after their removal (on 16 November 2007, Chile returned to Peru 3,788 books which had been removed in 1881 during the Pacific War (1879–83) from the National Library of Peru in Lima when the city was occupied by the Chilean troops). For this case see M Hampe, 'Cómo recuperar el patrimonio documental llevado a Chile durante la Guerra del Pacifico?' [2008] *Revista Peruana de Derecho Internacional* 77.

[57] UNGA Resolution 1514 of 14 December 1960: Declaration on the Granting of Independence to Colonial Countries and Peoples.

states to their former colonies (eg from the Netherlands to Indonesia and from Belgium to Congo).[58]

It therefore seems that there are particular categories of cultural objects alienated under specific circumstances for which no time limitations apply. This principle is enshrined in law, ethics and practice (as this is derived from recent examples in the area). The categories of such objects are as follows: (i) sacred and ritual objects; (ii) national symbols; (iii) objects detached from buildings and monuments, and generally immovable property; (iv) objects belonging to an archaeological site; (v) objects belonging to a public collection; (vi) human (or ancestral) remains;[59] and (vii) objects which are inextricably linked to the identity (cultural, religious, societal or other) of a group, community or nation. These objects will have been removed illegally or unethically, meaning without the authorization or consent of the group, community or country to which they belong, or which have been acquired on the basis of exploitation of the weakness of another subject (war, hostilities, occupation, colonization, poverty, etc). These circumstances of removal should also form a prerequisite.[60]

IV. CONCLUSIONS[61]

Law (including international customary rules), ethics, practice and public feeling advocate that returns to their countries of origin of cultural treasures that have been removed either illegally or unethically at some stage have become a principle during recent years. That may be so irrespective of time limitations, depending on the case at issue (eg the significance and nature of the object, the time it was removed, the circumstances of removal). Yet it would be premature to argue that this principle would be actionable in all states or in all regional or international fora. It is, however, clear that its justifying moral and societal reasons (as well as the interests it serves for archaeology, history, research, etc) will render it even more robust in the near future.

[58] L Prott, *Commentary on the Unidroit Convention* (Leicester, Institute of Art and Law, 1997) 36. See also L Prott, 'The Ethics and Law of Returns' (2009) 61(1–2) *Museum International* 101, 103–104.

[59] Art 4.4 of the ICOM Code of Professional Ethics Museums provides that 'requests for removal from public display of human remains or material of sacred significance from the originating communities must be addressed expeditiously with respect and sensitivity. Requests for the return of such material should be addressed similarly. Museum policies should clearly define the process for responding to such requests.'

[60] Such an example is the Nazi-looted art.

[61] Many thanks to Ms Ellie Velissaropoulou for the editing of this chapter.

13

The Cultural Heritage of Mankind beyond UNESCO: The Case of International Financial Institutions

ANTONIA ZERVAKI*

I. INTRODUCTION

THE CREATION OF an international legal regime for the protection of cultural monuments, whether tangible or intangible, constitutes one of the major achievements of UNESCO. Furthermore, the organization has contributed to the construction and evolution of a broader normative framework and principles for the protection of cultural sites and monuments of universal value, establishing a delicate balance between the preservation of cultural diversity on the one hand, through the protection of local cultures and human creativity, and the linkage of cultural heritage to the interest of humanity as a whole, both in its synchronic and its diachronic dimensions, on the other.

The sophisticated and inclusive character of UNESCO's legal instruments and the increase in the number of sites and monuments inscribed on international inventories, however, create significant challenges for the contracting parties, since, in order to meet their obligations, they need considerable financial resources and expertise. UNESCO does not have the institutional and budgetary capacity to fund the preservation of these monuments on a permanent basis. The funds established by the various UNESCO conventions have limited resources. Hence, contracting parties to the UNESCO conventions undertake the core financial burden of World Cultural Heritage protection. National budgets, however, are often unable—especially during the current financial crisis—to accommodate the cost of high-standard preservation schemes.

* Department of Political Science and Public Administration, University of Athens.

The practice of recourse to international financial institutions in order to address the shortcomings in the allocation of funds for cultural heritage protection has become common both for developing and developed states during the last decades. The projects financed, not always purely cultural in nature, have a twofold character: they assist contracting states to meet their international obligations in terms of the conservation of the nominated cultural sites and monuments, and to use their cultural heritage as part of their national economic assets, serving the broader objective of economic development.

This paper focuses on the practice of two international financial institutions, the World Bank and the European Investment Bank, in relation to the financing of projects that have an impact on the cultural heritage of mankind in order to address the following questions:

1. Have the above-mentioned international financial organizations developed adequate institutional safeguards for the inclusion of World Heritage monuments in their financial agenda?
2. Is the normative character and fundamental principles of international cultural heritage protection preserved in projects implemented under international borrowing schemes?
3. Is there a need for inter-institutional arrangements (following the example of the memorandum of understanding signed by UNESCO and the World Bank) at the international level?

II. UNESCO AND THE CULTURAL HERITAGE OF MANKIND

A. The Normative Framework

UNESCO is the first international organization that has consistently contributed to the construction of the normative framework for the protection of cultural heritage through both soft and hard legalization processes.[1] It was in the organization's institutional environment that the majority of relevant international instruments were elaborated and adopted, in line with its Constitution, which provides, as one of the main purposes of the organization to, '[m]aintain, increase and diffuse knowledge . . . [b]y assuring the conservation and protection of the world's inheritance of books, works of art and monuments of history and science, and recommending to the nations concerned the necessary international conventions'.[2] Since the early 1950s, the organization

[1] 'Legalization' is defined as the 'particular form of institutionalization characterized by three components: obligation, precision and delegation'. KW Abbot, RO Keohane, A Moravsick, A-M Slaughter and D Snidal, 'The Concept of Legalization' (2000) 54 *International Organization* 401, 401. These components do not appear in a uniform way; obligation ranges from 'expressly non legal norms to binding rules (jus cogens)', precision from 'vague principles to precise, highly elaborated rules' and delegation from 'diplomacy to international courts, organization and domestic application of rules', ibid, 404.

[2] Article 1, para 2c of the UNESCO Constitution (1945) in UNESCO, *Basic Texts* (UNESCO, 2012 edn) 5.

has been associated with the implementation of existing legal instruments, as well as the elaboration and adoption of new conventions catering for the protection of tangible and intangible cultural monuments both at war and in peace, namely, the 1954 Hague Convention and its Protocols,[3] the 1970 Convention on the Illicit Trafficking of Cultural Property,[4] the 1972 World Heritage Convention,[5] the 2001 Convention on the Protection of Underwater Cultural Heritage,[6] the 2003 Convention on the Protection of Intangible Heritage[7] and the 2005 Convention on the Protection of Cultural Diversity.[8]

Its norm-generating instruments also encompass a series of relevant recommendations,[9] such as those concerning the protection of cultural and natural heritage at national level[10] and the safeguarding of traditional culture and folklore;[11] and declarations,[12] setting the principles for international cultural cooperation,[13] the protection of cultural diversity[14] and the protection of cultural heritage from intentional destruction.[15]

[3] Convention for the Protection of Cultural Property in the Event of Armed Conflict (The Hague Convention) 1954 249 UNTS 240; Protocol to the Hague Convention for the Protection of Cultural Property in the Event of Armed Conflict [1954] 249 UNTS 358; The Second Protocol to the Hague Convention for the Protection of Cultural Property in the Event of Armed Conflicts [1999] 38 ILM 769. The 1954 Convention did not originate from UNESCO; however, its implementation was closely related to the work of the organization.

[4] UNESCO Convention on the means of prohibiting and preventing the illicit import, export and transfer of ownership of cultural property (1970) 823 UNTS 231.

[5] UNESCO Convention concerning the Protection of World Cultural and Natural Heritage [1972] 1037 UNTS 151.

[6] UNESCO Convention on the Protection of Underwater Cultural Heritage [2001] 41 ILM 40.

[7] UNESCO Convention on the Safeguarding of Intangible Cultural Heritage [2003] MISC/2003/CLT/CH/14.

[8] Convention on the Protection and Promotion of the Diversity of Cultural Expressions [2005] CLT-2005/CONVENTION DIVERSITE-CULT REV.

[9] Rules of Procedure concerning Recommendations to Member States and International Conventions covered by the terms of Article IV, paragraph 4 of the Constitution, adopted by the General Conference at its 5th Session and amended at its 7th, 17th, 25th, 32nd and 35th sessions in UNESCO, *Basic Texts*, 111.

[10] Recommendation concerning the Protection at National Level of the Cultural and Natural Heritage (16 November 1972) in UNESCO, Records of the General Conference 17th Session, Paris, 17 October to 21 November 1972, vol 1 Resolutions and Recommendations (UNESCO, 1973) 146.

[11] Recommendation on the Safeguarding of Traditional Culture and Folklore (1989) in UNESCO, *Records of the General Conference, 25th Session*, Paris, 17 October—16 November 1989, *Resolutions*, vol 1 (UNESCO, 1990) 238.

[12] Multi-stage procedure for the Elaboration, Examination, Adoption and follow-up of Declarations, Charters and similar standard-setting instruments adopted by the General Conference and not covered by the Rules of Procedure concerning Recommendations to Member States and International Conventions covered by the terms of Article IV, paragraph 4, of the Constitution, adopted by the General Conference at its 33rd session in UNESCO, *Basic Texts*, 117.

[13] UNESCO Declaration of the Principles of International Cultural Cooperation (1966) in UNESCO, *Records of the General Conference, 14th Session*, Paris, 1966, *Resolutions* (UNESCO, 1967) 86.

[14] UNESCO Universal Declaration on Cultural Diversity (2001) in UNESCO, *Records of the General Conference 31st Session*, Paris, 15 October to 3 November 2001, *Resolutions*, vol 1 (UNESCO, 2001) 61.

[15] UNESCO Declaration on the Intentional Destruction of Cultural Heritage (2003) in UNESCO, *Records of the General Conference 32nd Session*, Paris, 29 September to 17 October 2003, *Resolutions*, vol 1 (UNESCO, 2004) 62.

These normative tools have created an institutional variable geometry due to their differentiated capacity to impose legally binding commitments on states, as well as in terms of the varying level of ratifications of the conventions by the latter. They have established, however, explicit and implicit standards of expected behaviour 'defined in terms of rights and obligations'[16] vis-à-vis the protection of cultural heritage of universal value. In this context, cultural heritage of universal significance is linked to specific rights and obligations of the international community in terms of protection from destruction or degradation (intentional or not) and access to the assets provided by cultural heritage (ranging from knowledge and spiritual advancement to development and quality of life).

In this context, the core ideational achievement of the UNESCO cultural protection normative framework was the progressive transition from the protection of 'cultural goods' or 'property', notions linked to private rights and the concept of *utendi et abutendi*,[17] to that of 'cultural heritage of mankind'. The linkage of cultural monuments' protection to humanity signals the shift of focus from ownership rights to the protection of cultural resources.[18] This novel perception of cultural heritage of mankind has led to the gradual detachment of the latter from the domain of 'national jurisdiction' (*domaine reservé*),[19] not in terms of the rights of ownership, but in relation to state responsibility.[20] In this way, the evolution of international institutions providing for cultural heritage protection has achieved a fine linkage of national authorities' obligations to protect significant cultural sites or monuments to the interests of the international community as a whole[21] and, according to some jurists, to the obligation *erga omnes* or *erga omnes partes* for others.[22]

[16] Using Krasner's definition of 'norms' in S Krasner, 'Structural Causes and Regime Consequences: Regimes as Intervening Variables' in S Krasner (ed), *International Regimes* (Cornell University Press, 1983) 1, 2.

[17] The concept of *abutendi* in Roman law does not necessarily mean 'misuse' but the right to use up or consume a thing. See MR Cohen and FS Cohen, *Readings in Jurisprudence and Legal Philosophy* (Beard Books, 2002) 12.

[18] J Blake, 'In Defining Cultural Heritage' (2000) 49 *International and Comparative Law Quarterly* 61, 65.

[19] F Francioni, 'The 1972 World Heritage Convention: An Introduction' in F Francioni and F Lenzerini (eds), *The 1972 World Heritage Convention: A Commentary* (Oxford University Press, 2008) 3, 4.

[20] See BT Hoffman, 'Exploring and Establishing Links for a Balanced Art and Cultural Heritage Policy' in BT Hoffman (ed), *Art and Cultural Heritage. Law Policy and Practice* (Cambridge University Press, 2006) 1, 17.

[21] F Francioni, 'Des biens culturels au patrimoine culturel: l'évolution dynamique d'un concept et de son extension' in AA Yusuf (ed), *L'action normative à l'UNESCO, Elaboration de règles internationales sur l'éducation, la science et la culture* (Editions UNESCO/Martinus Nijhoff Publishers, 2007) 231, 232.

[22] R O'Keefe, 'World Cultural Heritage: Obligations to the International Community as a Whole?' (2004) 53 *International and Comparative Law Quarterly* 189. AA Cançado Trindade, 'International Law for Humankind: Towards a New Jus Gentium, General Course of Public International Law' in *Hague Academy of International Law, Collected Courses, vol 316. 2005* (Martinus Nijhoff Publishers, 2006) 382.

In terms of the geographic and temporal compass of these rights and obligations, it should be mentioned that the concept of cultural heritage is based on the principle of equity both in its synchronic and its diachronic dimensions, that is, intra- and intergenerational equity. In the first case, cultural heritage is conceived of as a vital resource of human members of the present generation. UNESCO promotes cultural diversity and its international inventories are open to nominations from different cultures, belonging to different historic periods and representing various social realities that have existed in the past or continue to evolve. Intragenerational equity, however, is not translated solely as equal representation of existing cultural legacies in different inventories but also as equal rights over cultural expression and creativity and the outcomes (whether social or economic) thereof. Intergenerational equity, on the other hand, refers to the equal rights of different generations over cultural resources; it entails the primordial obligation to preserve the qualitative characteristics of cultural monuments in order not to impair the quantity or quality of cultural assets to be enjoyed or used by future generations.

The issue of intra- and intergenerational rights brings to the fore the relationship of cultural heritage protection to human development and environmental sustainability.[23] Human development involves the process of culture-led economic development, including economic growth and revenue generation, and the development of the so-called 'non-monetized' benefits, such as the preservation of the local social capital and cultural diversity (traditional stewardship and knowledge, oral and spiritual cultural traditions, etc) that enhances social inclusiveness.[24] On the other hand, preserving traditional knowledge and skills ensures environmental sustainability,[25] since certain manifestations of cultural heritage (either purely intangible, eg traditional farming methods, or mixed, eg cultural landscapes) may guarantee the mild exploitation of the natural environment that forms part of or confines the protected cultural sites.[26]

B. Protecting the Cultural Heritage of Universal Value in Practice

In practice, the introduction of the concept of heritage and its linkage to humanity in the UNESCO cultural protection initiatives and action was linked to a transnational public order obligation, which is evident in the reaction of

[23] The relation of culture-led activities to the implementation of the Millennium Development Goals (MDG) was emphasized in the 2010 MDG Outcome Document of the United Nations' General Assembly. According to its resolution, the General Assembly has recognized that 'all cultures and civilizations contribute to the enrichment of humankind' and emphasized 'the importance of culture for development and its contribution to the achievement of the Millennium Development Goals'. See UN Doc A/65/L.1 (17 September 2010), § 16.

[24] See UN System Task Team on the Post 2015 UN Development Agenda, 'Culture: a Driver and an Enabler of Sustainable Development, Thematic Think Piece—UNESCO', May 2012.

[25] Ibid.

[26] See T Kono, 'L'UNESCO et le patrimoine culturel immatériel du point de vue du développement durable' in Yusuf (n 21 above), 249.

the international community in several cases since the creation of the organization in the mid-1940s.

The first time the international community reacted in a coordinated way in order to safeguard cultural heritage that was threatened by human activity or natural causes was in the 1960s, when UNESCO organized two major international campaigns. The first one aimed at the relocation of a complex of Nubian monuments from the area to be flooded by the Aswan Dam (1960) and the second was the international response after the torrential rain resulting in the disastrous floods that had gravely affected, among others, the monuments and works of art of the historical cities of Florence and Venice (1966).[27] These campaigns revealed the emergence of international norms for the protection of cultural heritage in peace that extended the existing normative framework deriving from humanitarian law catering for the protection of cultural heritage at war. UNESCO's activity in this domain soon resulted in the adoption of the 1972 World Heritage Convention, which codified this normative context into concrete rules for the protection of cultural (and natural) heritage in peace.

The inclusion of the Old City of Jerusalem in the UNESCO World Heritage List in the early 1980s is probably the most illustrative example of the emergence of the organization's enhanced normative construction and its acceptance by the international community.[28] The Old City of Jerusalem was included in UNESCO's international inventory of cultural heritage of outstanding universal value despite the fact that its territorial status was still undetermined.[29] The nomination file, submitted by Jordan, was successful despite the fact that the United States opposed the decision, putting forward the argument that Jordan could not assume the responsibility stipulated in Article 26 of the World Heritage Convention.[30]

Another reaction that reveals the acknowledgement, on behalf of the international community, of the existence of certain standards of behaviour vis-à-vis the preservation of cultural heritage of universal value was the inscription

[27] See *UNESCO Courier* (1967) XXI and http://whc.unesco.org/en/activities/172/ (accessed on 9 January 2013).

[28] It should be mentioned that the effectiveness of the protection schemes implemented on-site was seriously contested due to the existing political situation and the institutional shortcomings deriving from it. See M Dumber and C Larkin, 'The Politics and the Limitations of International Agency in Contested Cities: a Study of the Role of UNESCO in Jerusalem's Old City' [2012] 38(1) *Review of International Studies* 25.

[29] No solution has been agreed by the parties involved in the dispute since the UN General Assembly Resolution 181(II) of 29 November 1947, which called for the creation of a Jewish state and a Palestinian state after the end of the British mandate and provided for the establishment of a special international regime for the City of Jerusalem but was never implemented.

[30] See CLT-82/CH/CONF.015/8, Paris, 17 January 1983, in World Heritage Committee, Report of the Rapporteur, Sixth Session, Paris, 13–17 December 1982 (UNESCO, 1983) 11. Art 26 of the World Heritage Convention refers to the conditions for international assistance, namely '[t]he World Heritage Committee and the recipient state shall define in the agreement they conclude the conditions in which a programme or project for which international assistance under the terms of this Convention is provided, shall be carried out. It shall be the responsibility of the state receiving such international assistance to continue to protect, conserve and present the property so safeguarded, in observance of the conditions laid down by the agreement.'

of the Cultural Landscape and the Archaeological Remains of the Bamiyan Valley on the UNESCO World Heritage List in 2003. In spite of the failure of the international community to prevent the Taliban regime from destroying the Buddha statues of Bamiyan Valley in Afghanistan,[31] the World Heritage Committee included the site both in the World Heritage List and in the World Heritage List in Danger, while UNESCO's General Conference adopted the Declaration concerning the Intentional Destruction of Cultural Heritage. According to the Declaration, 'intentional destruction' is defined as the

> act intended to destroy in whole or in part cultural heritage, thus compromising its integrity, in a manner which constitutes a violation of international law or an unjustifiable offence to the principles of humanity and dictates of public conscience, in the latter case in so far as such acts are not already governed by fundamental principles of international law.[32]

In this context, the Declaration recognizes individual criminal responsibility for such acts.[33]

Last but not least, the International Criminal Tribunal for the former Yugoslavia has characterized the shelling attack on the Old City of Dubrovnik, already a World Heritage site,[34] as 'an attack against the history and heritage of the region and also against the cultural heritage of mankind'.[35] The penalization of the attack reveals the degree of the embeddedness of UNESCO's normative framework by the international community and the way this is reflected on the decisions of international judicial organs.

III. MEETING THE FINANCIAL CHALLENGES OF WORLD CULTURAL HERITAGE

A. Preserving World Cultural Heritage: Think Globally, Pay Locally

Meeting the obligations set out by the various UNESCO protection schemes constitutes a highly expensive venture for states. It should be mentioned that there is no comprehensive international mechanism for supporting financially international campaigns for the safeguard of cultural heritage. In addition,

[31] F Francioni and F Lenzerini, 'The Obligation to Prevent and Avoid Destruction of Cultural Heritage: From Bamiyan to Iraq' in Hoffman (n 20 above), 28.

[32] Art II (2).

[33] According to Art VII, 'states should take all appropriate measures, in accordance with international law, to establish jurisdiction over, and provide effective criminal sanctions against, those persons who commit, or order to be committed, acts of intentional destruction of cultural heritage of great importance for humanity, whether or not it is inscribed on a list maintained by UNESCO or another international organization'.

[34] The site was inscribed on the World Heritage List in 1979 according to criteria (i), (iii) and (iv). See http://whc.unesco.org/en/list/95 (accessed on 16 August 2013).

[35] Case No IT-01-42/1-S *Prosecutor v Miodrag Jokić*, Judgment (18 March 2004) 14, §51.

UNESCO's instruments have limited financial resources that can only supplement projects financed by national budgets or other sources.

Allocating funds for World Cultural Heritage protection schemes solely from national budgets is becoming more and more difficult, taking into account

1. the high cost of monuments' and sites' preservation (ie the rehabilitation and preservation project of the Acropolis of Athens, a site inscribed on the World Heritage List in 1987[36] reached a total of approximately 40 million euro from 2000 to 2013);[37]
2. the fact that a significant number of tangible and intangible cultural monuments are situated in the developing world. In this case, national authorities face difficulties not only in allocating funds but also in terms of expertise and comprehensive management capacity, including institutional and law enforcement inadequacy at national level;[38]
3. the current economic crisis and the austerity measures implemented in countries (even in states with advanced economies) that render the allocation of national funds for the conservation of cultural heritage of outstanding universal value a very difficult, if not impossible, venture for competent state authorities;[39] and
4. the obligation undertaken by national authorities to meet the highest standards of protection and the introduction of systematic monitoring mechanisms on behalf of UNESCO's instruments.[40]

As a result, reliance on traditional re-distributional financial mechanisms has become a rare option for the state parties to UNESCO cultural protection instruments. As a response to that challenge, many states have opted for alternative sources for financing their projects, first of all by resorting to the financial mechanisms of regional organizations. European Union Member States have made extensive use of the organization's structural funds and R&D programmes,[41] while African Union Member States that are contracting par-

[36] The Acropolis of Athens was inscribed on the World Heritage List in 1987, meeting the criteria (i), (ii), (iii), (iv) and (vi) of the World Heritage Committee's Operational Guidelines. See http://whc.unesco.org/en/list/404 (accessed on 17 August 2013).

[37] The Acropolis Restoration and Conservation Project was co-financed by the EU Structural Funds. See Information Bulletin 2001 and 2011, Acropolis Restoration Service, Greek Ministry of Culture. In addition, 3.5 million euros were made available by the National Program of Public Investments. See http://www.ysma.gr/en/service (accessed on 17 August 2013).

[38] UNESCO, 'Understanding World Heritage in Asia and the Pacific. The Second Cycle of Periodic Reporting 2010–2012' [2012] *World Heritage Papers* 35, 38–39.

[39] A Zervaki, 'The International Regime for the Protection of Cultural Heritage and the Global Financial Crisis: In Search of Institutional Synergies' in E Korka (ed), *The Protection of Archaeological Heritage in Times of Economic Crisis* (Cambridge Scholars Publishing, 2014) 18; N Schlanger and K Aitchison (eds), *Archaeology and the Economic Crisis: Multiple Impacts, Possible Solutions* (Culture Lab Editions, 2010).

[40] The adoption of the periodic reporting system by the World Heritage Committee in 1998 allows for the assessment of the World Heritage Convention implementation by state parties. See http://whc.unesco.org/en/periodicreporting/ (accessed on 18 September 2013).

[41] A Zervaki, 'In Search of Resources for World Cultural Heritage Protection: Institutional Framework and Current Trends' in S Perrakis (ed), *Contemporary Protection of Cultural Goods* (forthcoming).

ties to the 1972 World Heritage Convention established the African World Heritage Fund in 2006.[42] The various Funds-In-Trust that allocate financial resources to specific countries served as an alternative option as well.[43] During the last few decades, however, a new trend has emerged in both developed and developing states: recourse to international financial institutions for the realization of large-scale restoration projects or projects implemented in different policy domains (eg transport) which may also have an impact on the management of cultural sites.

B. International Financial Institutions and the Cultural Heritage of Mankind

(i) The World Bank

The World Bank[44] provides loans and technical assistance to developing and less-developed states through its specialized institutions.[45] Despite the fact that cultural heritage protection was not one of its initial purposes, the World Bank developed its own policy towards cultural property in the 1980s. The 1986 Operational Policy Note focuses on the World Bank's policy vis-à-vis projects that may have an impact (irreversible or not) on cultural property.[46] The main preoccupation of the organization was to ensure that due concern was taken in the granting of loans so as to avoid any damage to cultural properties; at the same time, the World Bank made it clear that it wold not finance projects that 'will significantly damage non-replicable cultural property'.[47]

In the 1990s there has been an increase in the projects financed by the World Bank Group focusing on the preservation and promotion of World Cultural Heritage sites.[48] Recourse to the World Bank for that purpose became very

[42] http://whc.unesco.org/en/awhf (accessed on 18 September 2013).

[43] They consist of states' donations for specific projects, as in the case of the Flemish fund-in-trust that supports the development of World Heritage management capacity in the Arab States. See http://whc.unesco.org/en/ffit (accessed on 18 September 2013).

[44] The World Bank includes the International Bank for Reconstruction and Development (IBRD), the International Development Association (IDA) and the International Finance Corporation (IFC).

[45] IBRD provides loans to middle-income and creditworthy low-income countries, IDA provides interest-free loans and grants to governments of the poorest countries and IFC supplements the work of IBRD by promoting investments and private enterprise.

[46] World Bank Operational Policy Note OP 11.03, 'Management of Cultural Policy in Bank Financed Projects' (September 1986). According to the definition provided, '[t]he United Nations term "cultural property" includes sites having archaeological (prehistoric), paleontological, historical, religious, and unique natural values. Cultural property, therefore, encompasses both remains left by previous human inhabitants (for example, middens, shrines, and battlegrounds) and unique natural environmental features such as canyons and waterfalls' (ibid, § 1).

[47] Ibid, § 2(a).

[48] CE Di Leva, 'The World Bank's Policy on Physical Resources' in Hoffman (n 20 above), 245.

popular at that time, since the monuments listed in the World Heritage List almost doubled in the early 1990s,[49] rendering international assistance schemes (under both the World Heritage Fund and the existing Funds-In-Trust) incapable of effectively contributing to the financial burden of sound preservation and management of World Heritage sites. Additionally, most of these new inscriptions on the World Heritage inventory originated from countries that were eligible to be financed by the World Bank.

In order to administrate this new reality, the World Bank initially incorporated certain principles for cultural property protection in the environmental assessment process,[50] while in 2006 the adoption of the World Bank's Physical Cultural Resources Safeguard Policy followed.[51] These documents frame the organization's approach towards cultural monuments, applied in the following cases:

1. in projects implemented in various policy domains (ie transport, energy, sewage, irrigation systems, etc) that may have an impact on cultural sites and monuments. In this case, the applicant state should incorporate the necessary information in the environmental assessment process;
2. in projects that focus on the preservation of monuments of significant, and often of universal, value,[52] by relating them to the economic development of the region that hosts them; and
3. in the loans that finance the development of the infrastructure or services, necessary for the protection and promotion of cultural sites and monuments.

The main differences between the World Bank's approach and UNESCO's perception of cultural heritage relate to the perception of the latter by the two institutions and its impact on the development and implementation of relevant loan activities.

The World Bank is interested only in the physical monuments,[53] which are

[49] During the period 1978–89, 233 cultural sites were inscribed on UNESCO's World Heritage List, while 296 more were added in the next decade (1990–2000). See World Heritage List Statistics, available at http://whc.unesco.org/en/list/stat#s4 (accessed on 21 January 2013).

[50] The World Bank requires an environmental assessment of the projects to be financed; the environmental assessment 'takes into account the natural environment (air, water, and land); human health and safety; social aspects (involuntary resettlement, indigenous peoples, and physical cultural resources)'. See World Bank Operational Policy Note OP 4.01, 'Environmental Assessment' (January 1999, revised April 2013) § 3.

[51] World Bank Operational Policy Note OP 4.11, 'Physical Cultural Resources' (July 2006, revised April 2013).

[52] In 2010 the Bank granted a loan to the Russian Federation for the Preservation and Promotion of Cultural Heritage Project for the Russian Federation. See World Bank, 'The World Bank Continues Working Partnership with Russia for its Cultural Heritage', Press Release No 2011/224/ECA (7 December 2010).

[53] With the exception of the provisions for indigenous people, which are mainly related to their rights concerning the development processes to be supported by the Bank's institutions. The Bank recognizes that the 'identities and cultures of Indigenous Peoples are inextricably linked to the lands on which they live and the natural resources on which they depend', while, according to the performance standards of the IFC, 'the term "Indigenous Peoples" is used

referred to as 'property',[54] 'resources'[55] or 'assets'.[56] While the definition provided for the physical cultural resources resembles to the one provided for the sites protected under the World Heritage Convention,[57] there is a significant differentiation in the World Bank's perception concerning the 'utility' of cultural heritage. The World Bank recognizes the importance of physical cultural resources—at local, provincial, national and international level[58]—as 'sources of valuable scientific and historical information' and as 'integral parts of a people's identity and practices', and considers them as assets for 'economic and social development'.[59]

Despite the fact that the concept of development is not alien to the cultural heritage protection regime introduced by UNESCO, the World Bank, due to its fundamental purposes, places more emphasis on economic growth processes. It thus perceives cultural monuments as valuable assets that should be preserved and used in order to ameliorate the economic conditions of a given social group. Hence, priority is given on the capacity of states to use these resources for revenue generation, an approach which is closer to the concept of *utendi et abutendi*, emphasizing states' ability to exploit their cultural assets. The balance between sound management and overuse of states' cultural resources is delicate: extending the bearing capacity of cultural monuments may hinder the implementation of the intergenerational equity principle, since inappropriate infrastructure and excessive numbers of visitors[60] can lead to the degradation of the site; this means that future generations will not be able to benefit from the authentic qualities of the monuments or to make use of already overexploited or damaged cultural resources.

Additionally, the fact that the intangible dimension of culture is ignored also raises some questions about the impact such projects could have on: (i) the integrity of tangible cultural monuments, as conceived of by UNESCO,

in a generic sense to refer to a distinct social and cultural group possessing the following characteristics in varying degrees: self-identification as members of a distinct indigenous cultural group and recognition of this identity by others; collective attachment to geographically distinct habitats or ancestral territories in the project area and to the natural resources in these habitats and territories; customary cultural, economic, social or political institutions that are separate from those of the mainstream society or culture; or a distinct language or dialect, often different from the official language or languages of the country or region in which they reside'. See World Bank Operational Note OP 4.10, 'Indigenous Peoples' (July 2005, revised April 2013) § 2; IFC, 'Performance Standards on Environmental and Social Sustainability, Performance Standard 7' (1 January 2012) 2, § 5.

[54] World Bank Operational Policy Note OP 11.03 (n 46 above).

[55] World Bank Operational Policy Note OP 4.11 (n 51 above).

[56] Ibid.

[57] The World Bank's Physical Cultural Resources Safeguard Policy Guidebook treats the terms 'cultural heritage', 'cultural property', 'cultural assets' and 'cultural resources' as synonymous. See World Bank, 'Physical Cultural Resources Safeguard Policy—Guidebook' (March 2009), 10.

[58] World Bank Operational Policy Note OP 4.11 (n 51 above), § 1.

[59] Ibid, § 2.

[60] The challenge of managing tourism overuse and inappropriate infrastructure development for World Heritage sites remains for the World Heritage Committee and many states parties of the 1972 World Heritage Convention. See UNESCO (n 38 above), 31.

which gives great importance to the spiritual dimensions of the physical cultural objects, and its relationship to the objectives of sustainable development and intergenerational cultural continuity; and (ii) the preservation of intangible cultural heritage of universal value per se, through the implementation of large-scale investment loan projects, involving landscape alterations, undermining the spiritual link of nature and cultural heritage, or infrastructure development that would increase the number of visitors and alter the traditional production cycle and social practices of local communities.

(ii) The European Investment Bank

The European Investment Bank[61] constitutes the financing body of the European Union's policy objectives; it is a financial institution that grants loans, assists financial blending and provides advisory services to its clients, originating from EU Member States as well as a number of EU development partners.[62]

Despite the fact that culture is not included in its operational objectives[63] the European Investment Bank has developed a policy towards cultural heritage.[64] According to this policy, the European Investment Bank generally does not finance a project which threatens the integrity of cultural sites of great importance, including UNESCO World Heritage Sites. However, the organization may deviate from this general rule if certain preconditions apply.[65] One of the preconditions involves stakeholders' consultation and approval granted by the relevant authorities for the implementation of a project that will affect cultural heritage. This parameter may guarantee public participation in decision-making procedures, but it also might have negative consequences, since a standard procedure for the involvement of international bodies where the site or monument in question is under international protection is not foreseen. The case of the Elbe valley cultural landscape, a World Heritage site that was delisted due to the construction of a bridge that altered the integrity of

[61] The European Investment Bank Group consists of the European Investment Bank (EIB) and the European Investment Fund (EIF).

[62] Enlargement countries, regions that fall into the EU Neighborhood Policy and the so-called development and cooperation countries in Africa, Latin America, Asia and the Pacific.

[63] For the period 2013–15 the EIB has supported the strategic objectives of the 'Europe 2020' agenda, namely, the three dimensions of growth (smart growth, driven by a knowledge-based economy; sustainable growth, based on a resilient, green and effective economy; and inclusive growth, ensuring high employment and catering for social and territorial cohesion). Thus, the current operational objectives of the Bank include employment creation (mainly through the support of SME), cohesion among the European regions, environmental sustainability, innovation, transport and energy networks. See European Investment Bank, 'The EIB Group Operational Plan 2012–2014' (Luxembourg, February 2012).

[64] European Investment Bank, 'EIB Environmental and Social Practices Handbook' (Luxembourg, February 2010).

[65] European Investment Bank, The EIB Statement of Environmental and Social Principles and Standards (2009) 19, § 58.

the landscape, following a public consultation,[66] is illustrative; although the above-mentioned project was not financed by the European Investment Bank, this scenario could be repeated in projects submitted to the Bank as well. In this case, the needs of the present generation would probably prevail, undermining the intergenerational rights relating to the integrity of the protected cultural sites and monuments.

The European Investment Bank also provides financial or technical support for projects that aim to rehabilitate and preserve cultural sites, including those inscribed on international inventories,[67] and the development of the broader region that hosts them.[68] As in the case of the World Bank's projects, the European Investment Bank also focuses on tangible heritage and its impact on development.

The approach adopted by the latter, however, is generally closer to UNESCO's perception of the linkage between development and culture: the European Investment Bank relates culture to human development—a more comprehensive concept compared to economic growth, which is the one of the major concerns in the World Bank's projects—and balanced spatial development,[69] leaving more space for social and environmental parameters to be taken into account. According to its mission statement, the European Investment Bank finances projects with a specific objective 'to protect and improve the natural environment and to promote sustainable communities'[70] in line with the concept of intergenerational rights mentioned above. It also conceives cultural heritage as 'an instrument for . . . intercultural dialogue',[71] conforming to the intra-generational equity principle.

[66] The decision to build the bridge was taken after a local referendum. However, Dresden's City Council has stopped the project after receiving UNESCO's negative reaction and the Free State of Saxony filed a complaint to the state administrative high court. The court ruled in favour of the project and the bridge was finally constructed. See 'UNESCO Regrets Decision on Construction of Bridge that Threatens Delisting of Dresden Elbe Valley from World Heritage List', UNESCO Press Release, 15 November 2007, available at http://whc.unesco.org/en/news/396 (accessed on 17 August 2013). The site was inscribed on the World Heritage List in 2004 according to criteria (ii), (iii), (iv) and (v) and delisted in 2009. See http://whc.unesco.org/en/list/1156 (accessed on 17 August 2013).

[67] Malta Investments plc has recently signed a contract with EIB in order to implement a series of public infrastructure projects promoted by the Maltese government, including the rehabilitation of the Valetta City Gate and its ancillary urban infrastructure, a UNESCO World Heritage site. See http://www.eib.org/projects/press/2012/2012-101-eib-and-malita-investments-p-l-c-sign-eur-40-million-loan-for-parliament-building-and-the-open-air-theatre.htm (accessed on 17 August 2013).

[68] As in the case of the loan granted by the EIB to the Czech Republic in 2011 for the South Bohemia Region, where two World Heritage sites are situated: the medieval town of Český Krumlov and the village of Holašovice, famous for its baroque architecture. The project financed focused on the tourist attractiveness of the cultural sites, including the development of the transport infrastructure and the improvement of the services provided by the South Bohemia Museum. See http://www.eib.org/projects/press/2011/2011-117-czech-republic-eib-funding-to-improve-roads-and-cultural-heritage-in-south-bohemia.htm (accessed on 17 August 2013).

[69] European Investment Bank (n 64 above), 19, § 56.

[70] Ibid, 13, §10.

[71] Ibid, 19, § 56.

The European Investment Bank also takes into account the intangible cultural practices, their relationship with the physical cultural heritage and the use of the latter by the local society. It thus links the uses of physical cultural heritage to the intrinsic identity of local communities and, subsequently, to the protection of human rights, the pursuit of social cohesion, the strengthening of policies of non-discrimination, and the enhancement of the rights of minorities and indigenous peoples.[72]

IV. CLOSING REMARKS

The establishment of UNESCO in the aftermath of World War II paved the way for the construction of an international regime that created concrete standards vis-à-vis the perception and protection of cultural heritage of universal value, relating the latter to the interest of humanity as a whole. Preserving cultural heritage, however, constitutes a complex venture that requires, among others, significant financial resources. In order to meet the financial challenges of large-scale cultural projects, states have resorted to international financial institutions.

In applying for multilateral loans, borrowing states usually accommodate World Heritage preservation projects in their broader national and regional economic development agenda or rehabilitation plans. In the cases of the World Bank and the European Investment Bank, the existence of a cultural site or monument listed in one of the UNESCO's international inventories is usually highlighted in the national applications demanding financial assistance. The purpose of this emphasis is twofold: on the one hand, it seems that the international normative framework for world heritage protection has an impact on the decision-making process of the above-mentioned international financial institutions; on the other hand, cultural monuments of outstanding universal value are conceived of as revenue-generating national assets, a crucial parameter for the fulfilment of the objective of economic development, both by the applicants and the loan providers.

The main conceptual deviations from UNESCO's normative framework for cultural heritage of mankind can be summarized as follows:

1. The pre-eminent feature in both financial institutions' project development cycle is the emphasis on the objective of economic growth and the perception of cultural heritage sites or monuments as economic and social assets that may contribute to its accomplishment. UNESCO's perception of cultural heritage of mankind may not be questioned directly; in practice, however, international loan-granting processes may gradually detach the protection of the latter from the interest of the international community

[72] Ibid, 19, § 57.

as a whole and confine it to the right of a given locality of the present generation to use it for its own benefit.
2. Given the delicate balance between sound development practices and over-exploitation of the cultural environment, the prioritization of economic objectives in international loaning schemes may hinder the integrity of cultural sites or monuments, raising further questions in relation to the conformity of the projects financed with the intergenerational equity principle.
3. Both institutions focus on the physical aspects of cultural heritage. In spite of the fact that some dimensions of the immaterial elements of cultural heritage are addressed by the European Investment Bank, the projects financed take into consideration only the material dimensions of cultural monuments or sites. Marginalizing the intangible quality of culture may undermine social cohesion, sustainable development and intra-generational rights especially in relation to the promotion of cultural diversity.

Hence, this conceptual inconsistency may eventually have a significant impact on the existing UNESCO normative framework, considering: (i) the growing demand for financing projects related to World Cultural Heritage conservation and/or promotion by international loaning schemes within the framework of the World Bank or the European Investment Bank; and (ii) the fact that UNESCO does not have its own financial resources to support the protection of cultural heritage and preserve, by its own means, the fundamental corpus of principles ensuring its linkage to the rights and obligations vis-à-vis humanity as a whole.

The answer to the above-mentioned normative inconsistencies could be the institutionalization of relationships among UNESCO and international financial institutions. This development would contribute to the harmonization of standards; furthermore, it would enhance the adoption of common objectives, and promote the implementation of joint initiatives and projects. A memorandum has already been signed by the World Bank and UNESCO, in 2011.[73] This practice could be further enhanced regionally with institutions such as the European Investment Bank, but it could also lead to the conclusion of bilateral partnerships between other global financial organizations and UNESCO, in order to ensure a common perception in cultural heritage at the normative level and enhanced and coordinated support for cultural heritage protection projects, both thematically and geographically, at the operational level.

[73] Creating a concrete framework for the development of joint initiatives in the domains of culture and sustainable development. See 'World Bank and UNESCO: Expanding Opportunities for Collaboration on Culture and Sustainable Development. Memorandum of Understanding Outlines Concrete Joint Initiatives', UNESCO Press Release, 1 July 2011, http://whc.unesco.org/en/news/778 (accessed on 1 December 2013).

Section 2

Sharing the Present and Safeguarding the Future

14

Something Fishy about Fisheries: High Seas Fisheries and the Common Resource Conundrum

ROSEMARY RAYFUSE*

I. INTRODUCTION

FISH ARE A quintessential common resource. Recognized as such as long ago as the *Codex Justinianus*, their status as a common resource was immortalized in international law by Hugo Grotius who, in his famous treatise, *Mare Liberum*,[1] stated that, like the sea, their limitless character rendered them capable of possession by no one and available for exploitation by all. According to Grotius, the same principle that applied to navigation also applied to fisheries: that of freedom. Thus was born the freedom of high seas fishing, now codified in Article 87 of the 1982 Law of the Sea Convention (LOSC).[2] Unfortunately, as was also recognized long ago by none other than Aristotle: 'what is common to the greatest number has the least care bestowed upon it'.[3] In more modern times this was restated by Hardin in his 'Tragedy of the Commons', where he noted that: '[r]uin is the destination toward which all men rush, each pursuing his own best interest

* Professor, Faculty of Law, UNSW Australia (The University of New South Wales), Sydney, Australia and Con-joint Professor, Faculty of Law, Lund University, Sweden. This is an updated and expanded version of a paper presented at the ILA Regional Conference, Cape Suonio, Greece, 29 August 2013.

[1] H Grotii, *Mare Liberum sive de ivre qvod Batavis competit an Indicana commercia, dissertatio* (1608); H Grotius (trans R Van Deman Magoffin), *The Freedom of the Seas or The Right Which Belongs to the Dutch to Take Part in the East Indian Trade* (Carnegie Endowment for International Peace/Oxford University Press, 1916) 27–32 (*Mare Liberum*).

[2] 1982 United Nations Convention on the Law of the Sea, 1833 UNTS 397 (LOSC).

[3] Quoted in R De Young and S Kaplan, 'Adaptive Muddling' in R De Young and T Princen (eds), *The Localisation Reader: Adapting to the Coming Downshift* (MIT Press, 2012) 287.

in a society that believes in the freedom of the commons. Freedom in a commons brings ruin to all.'[4]

Hardin's portent of ruin seems particularly prescient in the high seas fisheries context. It is axiomatic that as a biologically renewable resource the supply of fish is potentially unlimited. To achieve this potential, all that is necessary is appropriate management of exploitation of the resource. Even Grotius acknowledged that restriction of fishing effort might be necessary if the resource were found to be exhaustible; he simply failed to conceive of it ever becoming so.[5] However, it is now a matter of historical record that by the nineteenth century the spectre of exhaustibility had reared its head and states have struggled ever since to find ways to ensure the continued viability and exploitability of fish stocks while at the same time adhering to the Grotian notion of the freedom to fish.

Despite the enclosure of vast ocean areas within exclusive economic zones under the national jurisdiction of states and the establishment of regional fisheries management organizations (RFMOs) for the management of fisheries in areas beyond national jurisdiction, the status of global marine capture fish stocks has continued to decline. According to the United Nations Food and Agriculture Organization (FAO), a staggering 87 per cent of global fish stocks are either over- or fully exploited and in need of effective management either to rebuild stocks or to prevent their decline.[6] Noting that 'the state of the world marine fisheries is worsening and has had a negative impact on fishery production', the FAO's report goes on to point out that the situation is even 'more critical for some highly migratory, straddling and other fishery resources that are exploited solely or partially in the high seas'.[7]

For better or for worse, we humans are a hopeful lot. Despite apparent evidence to the contrary, commentators have suggested that the tragedy of the commons is not inevitable.[8] Admittedly, averting a tragedy is not an easy thing, involving, as it does, significant behavioural challenges aimed at restraining both consumption and access.[9] Nevertheless, research shows that these challenges are not necessarily intractable and that human nature does not

[4] G Hardin, 'The Tragedy of the Commons' (1968) 162(3859) *Science* 1243, 1244. He later reworded this idea as '[u]nder conditions of over-population, freedom in an unmanaged commons brings ruin to all'. G Hardin, *An Ecolate View of the Human Predicament* (Environmental Fund, 1984).

[5] 'And if it were possible to prohibit any of these things, say for example, fishing, for in a way it can be maintained that fish are exhaustible, still it would not be possible to prohibit navigation, for the sea is not exhaustible by that use . . . For everyone admits that if a great many persons hunt on the land or fish in a river, the forest is easily exhausted of wild animals and the river of fish, but such a contingency is impossible in the case of the sea.' Grotius (n 1 above), 43 and 57.

[6] FAO, 'State of the World's Fisheries and Aquaculture Report 2012' (FAO, 2012). Further broken down, the report reveals that 57% are fully exploited and 30% are over-exploited.

[7] Ibid, 13.

[8] See, eg J Diamond, 'Collapse: How Societies Choose to Fail or Succeed' (Viking, 2005).

[9] E Ostrom, J Burger, CB Field, RB Norgaard and D Policansky, 'Revisiting the Commons: Local Lessons, Global Challenges' (1999) 284 *Science* 278.

necessarily lead inexorably to unsustainable outcomes.[10] Rather, researchers have concluded that the tragedy can be averted by 'specifying the conditions under which humans will behave more reasonably'.[11] While these conditions will generally vary according to the particular context, Ostrom has identified eight common conditions or themes as being conducive to the long-term survival of a regime for the management of a common property resource (a CPR institution).[12]

This paper utilizes Ostrom's conditions as a framework for assessing the efficacy of the current international legal regime for high seas fisheries in arresting what appears to be the remorseless, relentless slide into a tragedy of the high seas fisheries commons. Reluctantly, it will be concluded that, despite decades of effort, the high seas fisheries regime still does not meet the criteria for a durable CPR institution and seems unlikely to do so in the near future.

II. CLEARLY DEFINED BOUNDARIES

The first condition Ostrom identified for a durable CPR institution is the need for clear definition of both the boundaries of the resource and those who have rights to exploit it. Essentially, this condition relates to geography and participation.

In terms of geography, a number of clearly defined boundaries are identifiable. While in Grotius' time the high seas lapped at the edges of the coastal state, the post-Grotian history of the law of the sea is all about its enclosure through extensions of coastal state jurisdiction. Indeed, even in Grotius' time, state practice already included exclusive fishery zones in coastal waters. Initially claimed for the purposes of protecting the economic interests of coastal communities and their food supply, by the late nineteenth century the concept of fishery zones had become merged with that of the territorial sea and, except in cases of agreements recognizing pre-existing rights and fishing practices, it was generally accepted that states exercised fisheries jurisdiction—that is, the power to control, exclude and enforce regulations—over fisheries conducted within their territorial seas. This concept of adjacent fishery zones eventually morphed into the concept of the exclusive economic zone (EEZ). Resources within the EEZ are, from the international community's perspective, no longer common property resources. Rather, they are under the jurisdiction and con-

[10] E Ostrom, *Governing the Commons: The Evolution of Institutions for Collective Action* (Cambridge University Press, 1990).

[11] De Young and Kaplan (n 3 above). For an earlier version of the paper see R De Young, 'Tragedy of the Commons' in DE Alexander and RW Fairbridge (eds), *Encyclopaedia of Environmental Science* 601 (Kluwer Academic Publishers, 1999).

[12] Ostram (n 10 above); E Ostrom, 'The Rudiments of a Theory of the Origins, Survival and Performance of Common-Property Institutions' in DW Bromley (ed), *Making the Commons Work: Theory, Practice and Policy* (ICS Press, 1992). These conditions are neatly listed in De Young and Kaplin (n 3 above).

trol of the coastal state which determines access rights.[13] Thus, the outer limits of states' EEZs represent a clear geographical boundary with respect to the resource.

The high seas, however, remain vast, and beyond the EEZ geographical boundaries have also been defined for those fisheries resources still subject to the common property regime. These boundaries are articulated in the constitutive agreements of RFMOs established to manage fish stocks in areas like the Northwest Atlantic (NAFO),[14] the North-East Atlantic (NEAFC),[15] the South-East Atlantic (SEAFO),[16] the Western and Central Pacific (WCPFC),[17] the Eastern Pacific (IATTC),[18] the Mediterranean Sea (GFCM),[19] the Indian Ocean (IOTC[20]) and the Antarctic (CCAMLR).[21] However, despite recent developments, such as the establishment of the South Pacific RFMO (SPRFMO),[22] a number of geographic gaps still remain.[23] In addition, some RFMOs are species specific (eg tuna or salmon), regulating only particular species in a particular area, while even those that are not species specific do not necessarily manage all fish species within their regulatory area. Thus, while many geographical boundaries have been defined in the high seas fisheries context, all that is biologically relevant is not necessarily included within those boundaries.

Moreover, the ability to define clear boundaries is complicated by biological realities. Fish do not recognize arbitrary geographical limits. The extension of coastal state jurisdiction may have brought more fish under national jurisdiction, but it did not do away with the existence of straddling and highly migratory fish stocks, which migrate between areas under and areas beyond national jurisdiction or between the regulatory areas of two of more RFMOs,

[13] LOSC, Art 56.

[14] Convention on Future Multilateral Cooperation in the Northwest Atlantic Fisheries, Ottawa 24 October 1978, into force 1 January 1979, 1135 UNTS 369.

[15] Convention on Future Multilateral Cooperation in North-East Atlantic Fisheries, London, 18 November 1980, into force 17 March 1982, 1285 UNTS 129.

[16] Convention on the Conservation and Management of the Fishery Resources in the South East Atlantic Ocean, Windhoek, 20 April 2001, into force 13 April 2003, 2221 UNTS 189.

[17] Convention on the Conservation and Management of Highly Migratory Fish Stocks in the Western and Central Pacific Ocean, Honolulu 5 September 2000, into force 19 June 2004, 2275 UNTS 43.

[18] Convention between the United States of America and the Republic of Costa Rica for the Establishment of an Inter-American Tropical Tuna Commission, Washington 31 May 1949, into force 3 March 1950, 80 UNTS 3.

[19] Agreement for the Establishment of a General Fisheries Council for the Mediterranean, Rome, May 1949, into force 20 February 1952, FAO Basic Texts, Vol III, Section 7 (1977); amended Rome, 6 November 1997, into force 6 November 1997, 2275 UNTS 157.

[20] Agreement for the Establishment of the Indian Ocean Tuna Commission, Rome 25 November 1993, into force 27 March 1996, 1927 UNTS 329.

[21] Convention on the Conservation of Antarctic Marine Living Resources, Canberra, 20 May 1908, into force 7 April 1982, 1329 UNTS 47.

[22] Convention on the Conservation and Management of High Seas Fishery Resources in the South Pacific Ocean, Auckland 14 November, into force 24 August 2012, available at https://treaties.un.org/pages/showDetails.aspx?objid=0800000280363a44.

[23] Most notably in the Southwest Atlantic, the Central Arctic Ocean, the Northern Indian Ocean and the area between the South and North Pacific RFMOs.

or with the existence of discrete high seas stocks. This biological reality has implications for the second boundary—that relating to who has a right to participate in exploitation of the resource.

Article 116 of the LOSC guarantees the right of the nationals of all states to fish on the high seas. In areas under national jurisdiction, that right is circumscribed by the coastal state's rights to determine the conditions of access to fisheries.[24] This can, and has, led to imbalances in exploitation, with coastal states contesting the right of distant water fishing nations (DWFN) to fish for straddling fish stocks and highly migratory fish stocks on the high seas just outside their EEZ and DWFN complaining about excessive fishing pressure on stocks in areas under national jurisdiction. After Canada's controversial arrest of the Spanish vessel *Estai* in 1995 brought the matter to a head,[25] the 1995 UN Fish Stocks Agreement (FSA)[26] sought to overcome this difficulty and stem further attempts at 'creeping jurisdiction' by calling for conservation and management measures adopted on the high seas and by coastal states within their EEZs to be 'compatible'.[27] The FSA fails, however, to say whose measures are to be compatible with whose.[28] As the subsequent EU–Chile fisheries dispute evidenced,[29] the problem has never been fully resolved.

Perhaps more significantly, despite the best efforts of RFMOs to limit access to fisheries under their regulatory jurisdiction to the vessels of member states and cooperating non-member states, basic principles of international law, including the *pacta tertiis* rule[30] and the principle of freedom embodied in Article 116 of the LOSC, make it impossible to restrict participation in high seas fisheries. In the past few decades, attempts to more fully articulate the responsibilities incumbent on flag states have resulted in the adoption of the FAO Compliance Agreement,[31] the FSA and the FAO's Guidelines for Assessing Flag State Performance.[32] However, there remains no globally applicable sanction that would see access denied for a breach of these responsibilities. The boundary of who has the right to exploit anywhere or anytime thus remains fixed at anyone and everyone. While theoretically clear, the bound-

[24] LOSC, Arts 61 and 62.

[25] For discussion of the controversy see *Fisheries Jurisdiction* case (*Spain v Canada*) (Jurisdiction) [1998] ICJ Reports 432.

[26] 1995 Agreement for the Implementation of the Provisions of the UN Convention on the Law of the Sea of 10 December 1982 relating to the Conservation and Management of Straddling Fish Stocks and Highly Migratory Fish Stocks, 2167 UNTS 3 (FSA).

[27] FSA, Art 7.

[28] R Rayfuse, 'To Our Children's Children's Children: Achieving Compliance in High Seas Fisheries' (2005) 20(3–4) *The International Journal of Marine and Coastal Law* 509, 514.

[29] MA Orellana, 'The Swordfish Dispute between the EU and Chile at the ITLOS and the WTO' (2002) 71 *Nordic Journal of International Law* 55.

[30] Vienna Convention on the Law of Treaties, Vienna, 23 May 1969, 1155 UNTS 331, Art 34.

[31] Agreement to Promote Compliance with International Conservation and Management Measures by Fishing Vessels on the High Seas, Rome, 24 November 1993, into force 24 April 2004, 2221 UNTS 91.

[32] Adopted in 2013. See ftp://ftp.fao.org/FI/DOCUMENT/tc-fsp/2013/VolGuidelines_adopted.pdf.

ary is thus a chimera, and the efficacy of the high seas fisheries regime as a durable CPR institution fails at the first hurdle.

III. CONGRUENCE BETWEEN RULES AND LOCAL CONDITIONS

The second condition identified by Ostrom is that of congruence between rules and local conditions. This means that rules governing access and resource use should be related to local conditions. For optimum results the set of rules should be kept small and simple, so that they are easy to learn, remember, use and transmit.

In the high seas fisheries context, localization of rules is achieved through the medium of RFMOs charged with managing fisheries in particular geographical areas or particular species throughout their area of distribution. These RFMOs have adopted a plethora of measures relating to catch and effort restrictions, total allowable catches and quotas, and compliance. Over the years, these measures have become increasingly extensive and increasingly complex, governing everything from the time and manner in which offal can be discharged to requirements to 'move on' when vulnerable marine ecosystems are encountered. By way of example, the Conservation and Management Measures adopted by NAFO for 2014 extend to 113 pages,[33] while CCAMLR's Conservation Measures fill 280 pages,[34] and those adopted by the IOTC fill 227 pages.[35]

It may be true that high seas fishing is big business. However, even big business might be forgiven for being occasionally overwhelmed by the breadth, scope and detail of the measures with which fishing vessels and their flag states must comply. This is compounded by the fact that, although commonalities can be found, conservation measures often vary in critical detail as between RFMOs, thereby increasing the regulatory burden on vessels fishing in more than one RFMO area. This is not to suggest that these rules are not necessary. Indeed, given the continued decline in global fish stocks, the need for these and possibly even more rigorous measures can hardly be questioned. Rather, as may be inferred from the litany of instances of non-compliance raised in RFMO compliance committees, it is at least arguable that in some cases the number and complexity of these measures makes fulfilment of a condition requiring a small set of simple rules problematic.

[33] http://www.nafo.int/.

[34] http://www.ccamlr.org/en/document/publications/schedule-conservation-measures-force-2013/14.

[35] http://www.iotc.org/files/CMM/IOTC%20-%20Compendium%20of%20ACTIVE%20CMMs%2014%20November%202013.pdf.

IV. COLLECTIVE-CHOICE ARRANGEMENTS

The third condition identified by Ostrom is the existence of what are referred to as 'collective-choice arrangements'. The objective here is to ensure that the majority of individuals affected by the operational rules adopted are able to participate in their modification as and when necessary to ensure that the rules remain adaptable to changing circumstances. In the high seas fisheries context, this plays out in the issue of participation in RFMOs.

Article 118 of the LOSC calls upon all states fishing for the same stocks in the same areas to participate in RFMOs. The FSA goes even further and essentially tries to make participation the *sine qua non* for being able to fish.[36] Thus, in theory at least, the law makes way for all those participating in high seas fisheries to participate in rule making and modification. However, joining RFMOs is not necessarily either as easy or as appealing as it might seem. For example, the FSA requirement that a state have a 'real interest' in a fishery in order to participate effectively limits new entrants from joining in.[37] Particularly in RFMOs where quota allocation has been based on historic catch, no incentive to join has existed. On the contrary, states have often deliberately preferred to stay outside the regime. These 'free riders' are able to undermine whatever rules have been adopted. While attempts have been made to lure free riders with cooperating non-member status, that status does not necessarily bring with it the right to participate in rule making; nor, to date, has it not solved the problem of illegal, unregulated or unreported (IUU) fishing by vessels flagged in non-member flag of convenience or flag of non-compliance states.

V. MONITORING

The fourth condition identified by Ostrom as necessary for a durable CPR institution is that of monitoring. This refers to monitoring of both the condition of the resource and the activities of the exploiters. The monitors are to be accountable to the exploiters and may be 'official enforcers', or they may be the exploiters themselves. Key, however, is that all exploiters are to share equally in enforcement of the rules they have adopted.

In terms of monitoring the condition of the resource, a signal function of RFMOs is to gather data on fisheries resources for the purposes of monitoring their condition and ensuring their effective management. RFMO members are bound by extensive reporting requirements relating, inter alia, to catch and effort data, which is used by scientific committees to establish stock status

[36] FSA, Art 8.

[37] EJ Molenaar, 'The Concept of "Real Interest" and other Aspects of Cooperation through Fisheries Management Mechanisms' (2000) 15(4) *International Journal of Marine and Coastal Law* 475.

and determine total allowable catches (TACs) and quotas. Unfortunately, as the litany of calls for better compliance with reporting requirements found in RFMO reports makes clear, this data is often either incomplete or not forthcoming. To improve data acquisition, many RFMOs have adopted observer schemes whereby third party observers record catch and other scientifically relevant data. However, these schemes are not necessarily applicable to all fisheries and, if limited to catch-data recording for scientific purposes as opposed to monitoring activities for compliance purposes, their efficacy may be limited.

Moreover, as recent events in the newly established SPRFMO indicate, this data can also be misused, misconstrued or deliberately manipulated. At the first meeting of the SPRFMO in 2013 it was decided that TACs and quotas were to be set based on 2010 fishing effort levels. Data supplied by Russia indicated that it had had one vessel fishing in the area which had taken significant catches. During port inspections in third states, it was discovered that the vessel was in fact a factory freezer ship, incapable of actual fishing. It was then revealed that a significant portion of the reported catch had in fact been caught by Peruvian flagged vessels within the Peruvian EEZ and merely transhipped to the Russian flagged vessel. As a result of concerns over the data provided, the Commission decided not to allocate Russia a quota for 2013. Needless to say, Russia objected, resulting in the establishment of a review panel under the procedure for resolving disputes over objections in the SPRFMO Convention. The panel found that the lack of quota allocation had unjustifiably discriminated against Russia and that Russia could authorize its vessels to fish, although admittedly only once it was clear that the other members were not going to fill their quota and then only until the overall agreed TAC was reached.[38] While not explicitly mentioned in the decision, the point relating to manipulation of data was not lost on other members of the RFMO or on the review panel itself.

RFMOs also gather data on other aspects of fishing activities, including, in particular, compliance with their conservation measures. This information, which can come from a range of sources, including non-governmental organizations, is then reviewed by RFMO compliance committees, which, in theory, decide collectively about how to proceed in respect of transgressions. In reality, not all compliance committees are empowered to go beyond the mere receipt and review of information. Moreover, the tyranny of consensus decision-making in many RFMOs means members can block criticism of their actions, a luxury not afforded to non-members. Moreover, enforcement is not a collective effort but, rather, rests primarily with the flag state. It is true that provision for non-flag state enforcement exists in a number of bilateral treaties, in some RFMO schemes and in Articles 20–22 of the FSA. However, these schemes only operate *inter partes* or as against stateless ves-

[38] The full record of the objection, findings and recommendations and submissions to the Review Panel is available on the SPRFMO website at http://www.southpacificrfmo.org/objections/.

sels. No recognized general right of non-flag state enforcement yet exists.[39] As discussed in the following section, RFMOs have therefore adopted a plethora of measures aimed at persuading flag states (both member and non-member) to ensure that their vessels comply with international rules and at addressing the enforcement challenges posed by flag states that are either unwilling or unable to do so. Nevertheless, as evidenced by the continuing inability of RFMOs to sustainably manage many of the fish stocks under their jurisdiction, continued adherence to the principle of flag state jurisdiction represents possibly the most difficult challenge to the effective management of the high seas fisheries commons.

VI. GRADUATED SANCTIONS

Related to the fourth condition, Ostrom's fifth condition calls for those who violate operational rules to be subject to graduated sanctions, which are to be assessed by the other exploiters. In the RFMO context, there are two levels of sanction—those against the state which fails to control its vessels and those against the vessels themselves. Over the years, RFMOs have adopted increasingly complex schemes to sanction non-compliant behaviour by both members and their vessels and by vessels flagged in non-member states. Measures range from naming and shaming and/or listing on IUU vessel lists to calling for denial of port services, and, ultimately, to the retraction of an authorization to fish. Members themselves may be subject to trade-related measures, and possibly even loss of quota. These latter measures, however, are controversial in many RFMOs and are rarely resorted to. Moreover, their invocation against non-members is legally problematic. Thus, severity of sanctions can and often does simply encourage flagging out to avoid controls.

Admittedly the issue does not stop there. A natural corollary of flag state jurisdiction is flag state responsibility, which includes the obligation to apply sanctions. While no specific allusion to sanctions exists in the LOSC, the FAO Compliance Agreement requires making contravention of the Agreement an offence under national law and requires the imposition of sanctions of sufficient gravity to effect compliance and deprive offenders of the benefits accruing from their illegal activities. For serious offences, sanction must include refusals, suspension or withdrawal of the vessel's authorization to fish on the high seas.[40] The FSA goes further and seeks to ensure compliance not just with its own provisions but with measures adopted by RFMOs as well. Flag states are to enforce against their vessels wherever and whenever a violation occurs, con-

[39] R Rayfuse, *Non-Flag State Enforcement in High Seas Fisheries* (Martinus Nijhoff, 2004); R Rayfuse, 'The Anthropocene, Autopoiesis and the Disingenuousness of the Genuine Link: Addressing Enforcement Gaps in the Legal Regime for Areas Beyond National Jurisdiction' in EJ Molenaar and AG Oude Elferink (eds), *The International Legal Regime of Areas Beyond National Jurisdiction: Current and Future Developments* (Martinus Nijhoff, 2010) 165.

[40] Compliance Agreement, Art II.

duct immediate and full investigations of alleged violations, refer the matter to investigating and judicial authorities as necessary, and ensure that sanctions imposed are adequate in severity to be effective in securing compliance and discouraging violations. Sanctions are to deprive offenders of the benefits accruing from their illegal activities and include the possibility of loss of authorizations either to fish or to operate vessels, or both.[41] Nevertheless, it is trite law that a treaty is only binding on its parties. Attempts to codify the full range of flag state responsibilities binding on all states as a matter of customary international law have thus far resulted only in the adoption of 'voluntary guidelines'.[42] Despite the extensive and creative efforts of RFMOs in adopting compliance and enforcement schemes, their imperfect implementation, particularly when coupled with the ability to evade sanctions by flagging in non-member states, remains a fundamental impediment to the development of the high seas fisheries regime as a durable CPR institution.

VII. CONFLICT-RESOLUTION MECHANISMS

Ostrom's sixth condition requires the availability of easily accessible low-cost dispute settlement mechanisms and flexibility in the development and application of rules to changing circumstances. Traditionally, as the *Southern Bluefin Tuna*, *Fisheries Jurisdiction (Spain v Canada)* and *EU/Chile Swordfish* cases make clear, dispute resolution in the high seas fisheries context has been neither rapid nor cheap.[43] Nor has it been particularly successful. However, these cases represent the extreme, and states have recognized the need for more timely procedures within RFMOs themselves. Of course, many disputes or potential disputes can be resolved through diplomatic negotiation or within the context of annual discussions within RFMOs. The active involvement of RFMO secretariats in forwarding information and seeking responses to complaints in the inter-sessional period has also provided a more timely mechanism for dealing with conflicts and potential disputes.

More recently, some RFMOs have adopted dispute settlement processes specifically designed to provide prompt and accessible mechanisms to deal with disputes and resolve conflicts between the members. In particular, the convention establishing the newest RFMO, the SPRFMO, includes an innovative mechanism for resolving disputes arising from the use of the 'opt out' procedure.[44] As discussed above, this procedure was utilized for the first time in the dispute between Russia and the SPRFMO Commission regarding the refusal to grant quota to Russia. While substantively the panel's decision may

[41] FSA, Art 19.

[42] FAO Voluntary Guidelines (n 32 above), 2.

[43] R Rayfuse, 'The Future of Compulsory Dispute Settlement under the Law of the Sea Convention' (2005) 36(4) *Victoria University of Wellington Law Journal* 683.

[44] Convention on the Conservation and Management of High Seas Fishery Resources in the South Pacific Ocean (n 22 above), Art 17 and Annex II.

be open to some criticism, there is no doubt that the mechanism worked well in the procedural sense. It remains to be seen whether similar procedures can be adopted in more RFMOs, although it must be conceded that these procedures, and hence fulfilment of the condition, will always be limited by their non-applicability to non-members. Conflicts between member and non-member states, or dealing with issues beyond the limited mandate of such RFMO procedures, will remain subject to the general dispute settlement provisions set out in Part XV of the LOSC.[45] It is an open question as to whether invocation of Part XV procedures could be considered to meet the requirements of low cost, promptness and ease of availability required by this condition.

VIII. MINIMAL RECOGNITION OF RIGHTS TO ORGANIZE

The seventh condition identified by Ostrom requires that exploiters are legally able to sustain their 'ownership' of the resource through devising institutions of their choosing, and that these organizations are perceived as legitimate by the larger set of organizations in which they are nested. In the high seas fisheries context, both the LOSC and the FSA tell us that RFMOs are the international community's mechanism of choice for conserving and managing high seas fisheries resources. More than a right to organize, states are under a positive duty to do so through the establishment of appropriate regional or sub-regional fisheries organizations.[46] The legitimacy of the concept of an RFMO is therefore no longer open to question.

However, the legitimacy of the fact of an RFMO, judged by its actions, may be open to question. The presumption of legitimacy of RFMOs has been tested in recent years, with RFMOs undergoing independent review processes aimed at increasing their efficacy and thereby reinforcing their legitimacy. Nevertheless, problems still remain, with concerns being voiced in several RFMOs that their ability to agree on certain measures, such as, for example, quotas for particular fisheries in NEAFC or the adoption of marine protected areas in CCAMLR, represents a fundamental challenge to their legitimacy. With high seas fish stocks continuing to decline, challenges to the legitimacy of RFMOs may be expected to grow.

IX. NESTED ENTERPRISES

The final condition relates to resources that are part of a larger system. In such cases, durability requires that the various governance activities be organized in multiple layers of nested enterprises. There is no doubt that high seas fish resources are part of the larger corpus of maritime resources and that RFMOs

[45] Rayfuse (n 43 above).
[46] LOSC, Art 118.

are part of the broader international framework for oceans governance. RFMO members and non-members alike are bound by the obligations incorporated in the treaties to which they are party and the rules and guidelines adopted by organizations of which they are members. In theory, developments in oceans governance beyond the LOSC, including the FSA, the Compliance Agreement and the recent Port State Measures Agreement,[47] should be reflected in the measures adopted by RFMOs. In practice, this has been somewhat limited by the fact that RFMOs are autonomous entities accountable only to their members and not, except in the broadest sense, to any other organization or to the international community as a whole. This has begun to change in recent years, with the UN General Assembly taking a more active interest in reviewing the activities of RFMOs and some states taking a more proactive approach to implementing international fisheries governance mechanisms within the RFMOs of which they are members. Nevertheless, the cooperation obligations imposed on states by the LOSC and subsequent agreements remain, in large part, too general and discretionary to admit of findings of violations. Thus, while multiple layers of governance may exist, in the international context the complex patchwork of different treaty obligations complicates rather than simplifies the system.

X. CONCLUSION

When analysed against Ostrom's conditions for a durable CPR institution, the current high seas fisheries regime is found wanting in a number of respects. Importantly, the achievement of durability is hindered not only by inactivity, but by the very fundamentals of the high seas regime and its emphases on freedom and flag state jurisdiction. High seas fishing is absolutely what Hardin referred to as a 'no technical solution problem'.[48] There is no technical solution to the problem of overfishing. What is needed is, as Hardin put it, a 'change in human values or ideas or morality'.[49] In other words, we must learn to put the long-term sustainability of the resource above our short-term commercial interests. Whether this manifests itself in rejection of the notion of freedom to fish, in the modification of the rule of flag state jurisdiction or in the adoption of some other regime to better coordinate and control RFMOs remains to be seen. For now, however, the conundrum remains.

[47] Agreement on Port State Measures to Prevent, Deter and Eliminate Illegal, Unreported and Unregulated Fishing, Rome, 22 November 2009, not yet in force, available at http://www.fao.org/fileadmin/user_upload/legal/docs/2_037t-e.pdf.

[48] Hardin (n 4 above).

[49] Ibid.

15

Biodiversity, Marine Protected Areas and Areas beyond National Jurisdiction

ANTONIOS ANTONOPOULOS*

I. INTRODUCTION

THE SEA, DESPITE covering 70 per cent of the earth's surface, contains approximately 95 per cent of the biodiversity of the planet.[1] The dangers that the biodiversity and the environment face are significant and are not always assessed correctly. The first danger that comes to mind is pollution by oil, especially due to maritime accidents or accidents involving oil platforms. However, such pollution is but a minor contribution to the overall pollution of the seas.[2] That is not to say that the effects of oil pollution cannot be devastating,[3] albeit localized and able to disappear rapidly.[4] However, the operational discharges of ships collectively account for a greater amount of oil discharged into the sea.[5]

Despite the publicity, navigation is also not the major pollutant of the marine environment. Pollution through the atmosphere and from land-based sources are both major dangers for the marine environment,[6] introducing toxic substances, heavy metals and nutrients to the seas that can prove significantly

* SJD Candidate, University of Virginia School of Law; Greek State Scholarships Foundation (IKY) Scholar. Email: aa3bc@virginia.edu.

[1] F de la Calle, 'Marine Genetic Resources. A Source of New Drugs, The Experience of the Biotechnology Sector' (2009) 24 *International Journal of Marine and Coastal Law* 209, 210.

[2] C Redgwell, 'International Environmental Law' in MD Evans (ed), *International Law*, 3rd edn (Oxford, 2010) 699.

[3] See MJ Kachel, *Particularly Sensitive Sea Areas, The IMO's Role in Protecting Vulnerable Marine Areas* (Berlin/Heidelberg, 2008) 25–26.

[4] GESAMP, *Reports & Studies No 70, A Sea of Troubles* (2000) 7.

[5] GESAMP, *Reports & Studies No 75, Estimates of Oil Entering the Marine Environment from Sea-Based Activities* (2007) vii.

[6] GESAMP, *Reports & Studies No 39, The State of the Marine Environment* (1990) 88.

more harmful[7] than oil and unfortunately cannot be easily identified and addressed.[8]

There are also other risks to the marine environment than pollution. For example, marine scientific research and exploration of the deep seabed can entail a high risk to the living and biological or genetic resources.[9]

The living and genetic resources of the deep seabed, such as the microbes that can be found in the hydrothermal vents,[10] can potentially be extremely useful to biotechnology.[11] Thus, the increased interest in bioprospecting[12] for substances and processes for commercial exploitation and the manufacture of new drugs[13] is understandable. However, research and bioprospecting expeditions can prove harmful to the environment, for example by altering the conditions of the marine environment or by 'biological' pollution.[14]

Similarly, more traditional activities, such as fishing on the high seas, can have a devastating effect on the marine environment and its biodiversity. Unsustainable fishing practices are on the rise[15] and have reduced stocks of highly valuable fish to near collapse. Such a situation may have serious consequences, especially in cases where the population cannot recover fast. For example, the orange roughy is believed to live for over 150 years and does not reach sexual maturity until its third decade, and even then it does not spawn often. In addition, the practice of bottom trawling for stocks that spawn on seamount ecosystems can destroy the very seabed ecosystems that attract them, as well as eliminate whole year groups.[16]

The use of marine protected areas as tools for the protection of marine biodiversity and fisheries management has been advocated by authors and international organizations alike,[17] with the policy receiving a great boost with the Plan of Implementation of the World Summit on Sustainable Devel-

[7] Kachel (n 3 above), 27–31.

[8] D Freestone and MA Salman, 'Ocean and Freshwater Resources' in D Bodansky, J Brunnée and E Hey (eds), *The Oxford Handbook of International Environmental Law* (Oxford, 2006) 343.

[9] M Gavouneli, *Pollution from Offshore Installations* (Dordrecht, 1995) 42.

[10] JF Imhoff and M Hügler, 'Life at Deep Sea Hydrothermal Vents—Oases under Water' (2009) 24 *International Journal of Marine and Coastal Law* 202.

[11] HW Jannasch, 'Deep-Sea Hot Vents as Sources of Biotechnologically Relevant Microorganisms' (1995) 3 *Journal of Marine Biotechnology* 5.

[12] MI Jeffery, 'Bioprospecting: Access to Genetic Resources and Benefit Sharing under the Convention of Biodiversity and the Bonn Guidelines' (2002) 6 *Singapore Journal of International and Comparative Law* 747, 755.

[13] DK Leary, *International Law and the Genetic Resources of the Deep Sea* (Leiden/Boston, 2007) 159.

[14] R Warner, *Protecting the Oceans beyond National Jurisdiction, Strengthening the International Law Framework* (Leiden/Boston, 2009) 20–21.

[15] IOC/UNESCO, IMO, FAO, UNDP, 'A Blueprint for Ocean and Coastal Sustainability' (2011) 11–12, available at http://www.unesco.org/new/fileadmin/MULTIMEDIA/HQ/SC/pdf/interagency_blue_paper_ocean_rioPlus20.pdf.

[16] D Freestone, 'International Governance, Responsibility and Management of Areas beyond National Jurisdiction' (2012) 27 *International Journal of Marine and Coastal Law* 191, 193.

[17] KL Cochrane, 'Marine Protected Areas as Management Measures: Tools or Toys?' in MH Nordquist, R Long, TH Heidar and JN Moore (eds), *Law, Science & Ocean Management* (Leiden/Boston, 2007) 702–10.

opment.[18] In this sense, marine protected areas can be seen as the effective institutional arrangements necessary to support the sustainable exploitation of resources allocated on the principle of common property, as are the living resources of areas beyond national jurisdiction.[19]

II. MARINE PROTECTED AREAS UNDER THE LAW OF THE SEA CONVENTION

The basic binding instrument that provides the regulatory framework for the uses of the sea and the possible creation of marine protected areas is the 1982 United Nations Convention on the Law of the Sea (UNCLOS),[20] which aspires to be a 'constitution' for the oceans.[21] Its 320 articles, nine annexes and two implementation agreements allocate competences and provide rights and obligations for coastal states and states using the sea, striking a delicate balance between the interests of the different states.[22] The vast majority of its provisions are considered as codifying pre-existing customary rules, and those provisions considered at the time as new have now been recognized as having attained the status of customary rules,[23] with Part XI being considered an exception.

UNCLOS allocates jurisdiction to states over the water column and the seabed adjacent to their coasts, which varies from full sovereignty to limited jurisdiction on specific matters and sovereign rights for the exploitation of the resources.[24] In addition, the traditional jurisdiction of states over vessels flying their flag, exclusive[25] or concurrent, depending on where the vessel is

[18] 'Plan of Implementation of the World Summit on Sustainable Development', Report of the WSSD, UN Doc A/Conf.199/20 (2002), Resolution 2 and Annex, esp para 32. See in general U Beyerlin and M Reichard, 'The Johannesburg Summit: Outcome and Overall Assessment' (2003) 63 *Zeitschrift für ausländisches öffentliches Recht und Völkerrecht* 213.

[19] P Birnie, A Boyle and C Redgwell, *International Law and the Environment*, 3rd edn (Oxford, 2009) 732–33.

[20] United Nations Convention on the Law of the Sea, Montego Bay, 10 December 1982, 1833 UNTS 397; in force since 16 November 1994.

[21] '[E]stablishing . . . a legal order for the seas and oceans', Preamble to UNCLOS, point 4.

[22] P Allot, 'Power Sharing in the Law of the Sea' (1983) 77 *American Journal of International Law* 1.

[23] RR Churchill and AV Lowe, *The Law of the Sea*, 2nd edn (Manchester, 1999) 24; an example of a development of international law that very soon was considered as customary law is the concept of the Exclusive Economic Zone (hereinafter EEZ), see *Case concerning Continental Shelf, Tunisia/Libyan Arab Jamahiriya* [1982] ICJ Reports 100; B Kwiatkowska, *The 200-mile Exclusive Economic Zone in the New Law of the Sea* (Dordrecht, 1989) 27–37.

[24] M Gavouneli, *Functional Jurisdiction in the Law of the Sea* (Leiden/Boston, 2008) 33–58.

[25] *The Case of the SS 'Lotus', France v Turkey*, PCIJ, Series A No 10 (1927), 169; this is why states have the obligation to make sure that vessels flying their flags have to comply with the international rules on the protection of the environment. See U Jenisch, '10 Jahre Neues Internationales Seerecht—Eine Bilanz des UN-Seerechtsübereinkommens 1994–2004' (2006) 28 *Natur und Recht* 79, 85.

at each time,[26] as well as the traditional high seas freedoms, are affirmed by UNCLOS.[27]

An innovation of UNCLOS is that it is the first binding instrument to adopt a blanket obligation for the protection of the marine environment,[28] which is considered a customary obligation.[29] Part XII of the convention provides a comprehensive framework for the protection of the marine environment,[30] as an 'umbrella' convention[31]—albeit a 'non-typical' one[32]—setting the general rules and targets, while leaving the details, namely the generally recognized standards,[33] to be specified by special, technical conventions[34]— but incorporating such conventions by reference, thus making them binding on all states parties.[35]

A. In the Exclusive Economic Zone

However, UNCLOS contains only one article on the creation of marine protected areas. Article 211(6) provides for the right of a coastal state to adopt rules that go beyond the generally recognized rules and standards, if special circumstances exist, but only in respect of clearly defined areas of an exclusive economic zone (EEZ) and with the co-operation of the International Maritime Organisation (IMO).[36] In addition, coastal states are not granted any special jurisdiction for enforcement with regard to such protected areas.[37] It

[26] Gavouneli (n 24 above); N Klein, *Maritime Security and the Law of the Sea* (Oxford, 2001) 62–146.

[27] P Liacouras, 'Intelligence Gathering on the High Seas' in A Strati, M Gavouneli and N Skourtos (eds), *Unresolved Issues and New Challenges to the Law of the Sea* (Leiden/Boston, 2006) 124.

[28] C Redgwell, 'From Permission to Prohibition: The 1982 Convention on the Law of the Sea and Protection of the Marine Environment' in D Freestone, R Barnes and D Ong (eds), *The Law of the Sea, Progress and Prospects* (Oxford, 2006) 181.

[29] For example, Agenda 21, Ch 17 refers to 'International law, as reflected in the provisions of the United Nations Convention on the Law of the Sea', UN Doc A/CONF.151/26 (Vols I–III).

[30] JI Charney, 'The Marine Environment and the 1982 United Nations Conference on the Law of the Sea' (1994) 28 *International Lawyer* 879, 884.

[31] LD Guruswamy, 'Should UNCLOS or GATT/WTO decide Trade and Environment Disputes' (1998) 7 *Minnesota Journal of Global Trade* 287, 292.

[32] M Gavouneli, 'From Uniformity to Fragmentation? The Ability of the UN Convention on the Law of the Sea to Accommodate New Uses and Challenges' in Strati et al (n 27 above), 206.

[33] B Oxman, 'The Duty to Respect Generally Accepted International Standards' (1991–2) 24 *NYU Journal of International Law and Policy* 109, 109; D Vignes, 'La valeur juridique de certaines règles, normes ou pratiques mentionnées au TNCO comme "généralement acceptées"' (1979) 25 *Annuaire Français de Droit International* 712.

[34] These Conventions may be pre-existing, such as the London Convention or MARPOL 73/79, or subsequent ones (Art 237(1) UNCLOS).

[35] RR Churchill, '10 Years of the UN Convention on the Law of the Sea—Towards a Global Ocean Regime? A General Appraisal' (2005) 48 *German Yearbook of International Law* 81, 111.

[36] Art 211(6) UNCLOS.

[37] E Franckx, 'Exclusive Economic Zone, State Practice and the Protection of the Marine Environment' in E Franckx and P Gauthier (eds), *The Exclusive Economic Zone and the United*

is also evident that such special areas cannot be established in areas beyond national jurisdiction.

B. In the Area

Another article that has been interpreted as providing for the creation of marine protected areas in areas beyond national jurisdiction is Article 162(2)(x), which allows the International Seabed Authority (ISA) to 'disapprove areas for exploitation . . . in cases where substantial evidence indicates the risk of serious harm to the marine environment'.[38] The ISA has the mandate to manage the non-living resources[39] of the Area,[40] under the provisions of Part XI of UNCLOS and the 1994 Implementation Agreement[41] and the concept of 'common heritage of mankind',[42] which was proposed by Malta's representative in the UN General Assembly, Dr Arvid Pardo.[43] Interestingly enough, the concept of the Area does not include the living resources, whereas the concept of the continental shelf does include sedentary species. However, it has been shown that the mandate of the ISA is actually broader than it would appear to be, as it encompasses the protection of the environment in general[44] This

Nations Convention of the Law of the Sea, 1982–2000: A Preliminary Assessment of State Practice (Brussels, 2003) 22.

[38] Art 162(2)(x) UNCLOS; against KM Gjerde and A Rulska-Domino, 'Marine Protected Areas beyond National Jurisdiction: Some Practical Perspectives for Moving Ahead' (2012) 27 *International Journal of Marine and Coastal Law* 351, 366.

[39] According to Art 133(a) UNCLOS, '"resources" means all solid, liquid or gaseous mineral resources in situ in the Area at or beneath the seabed, including polymetallic nodules'.

[40] According to Art 1(1) UNCLOS, '"Area" means the seabed and ocean floor and subsoil thereof, beyond the limits of national jurisdiction'.

[41] Even though the Agreement Relating to the Implementation of Part XI of the United Nations Convention on the Law of the Sea, 27 July 1994, UN GA Resolution 48/263 (1994), UN Doc A/RES/48/263 is named as an 'implementation' agreement', it is in fact an amendment made to UNCLOS in order to allow for the participation of industrialized states in UNCLOS: see Art 2 of the Agreement; ED Brown, 'The 1994 Agreement on the Implementation of Part XI of the UN Convention on the Law of the Sea: Breakthrough to Universality?' (1995) 19 *Marine Policy* 5, 9–10; for a general overview of the 1994 Implementation Agreement see, among others, DH Anderson, 'Resolution and Agreement Relating to the Implementation of Part XI of the UN Convention on the Law of the Sea: A General Assessment' (1995) 55 *Zeitschrift für ausländisches öffentliches Recht und Völkerrecht* 275.

[42] R Wolfrum, 'The Principle of the Common Heritage of Mankind' (1983) 43 *Zeitschrift für ausländisches öffentliches Recht und Völkerrecht* 312; MW Lodge, 'The Common Heritage of Mankind' (2012) 27 *International Journal of Marine and Coastal Law* 733.

[43] Address by Arvid Pardo to the 22nd session of the General Assembly of the United Nations, 22 UN GAOR Annex 3 (Agenda Item 92), UN Doc A/6695 (1967); For an overview of the concept and the development of the development of the regime for deep seabed mining, see SN Nandan and MW Lodge (eds), *United Nations Convention on the Law of the Sea 1982: A Commentary, Vol VI* (Dordrecht/Boston/London, 2002) 1–70, also available at www.isa.org.jm/files/documents/EN/Pubs/Regime-ae.pdf.

[44] T Scovazzi, 'Mining, Protection of the Environment and Bioprospecting: Some Considerations on the Role of the International Sea-Bed Authority' (2004) 19 *International Journal of Marine and Coastal Law* 383, 391–96.

is a view that is supported by the International Tribunal for the Law of the Sea (ITLOS) Seabed Disputes Chamber Advisory Opinion of 2011,[45] which recognizes that the rules and regulations referred to in Article 209 UNCLOS are the international rules, regulations and procedures adopted by the ISA,[46] which seems to grant such rules and regulations the same status as the standards and regulations by the IMO.[47] In addition, UNCLOS recognizes that the ISA shall have those powers and functions as are implicit in and necessary for the exercise of those powers explicitly awarded to it.[48] This is a formal recognition of the concept of 'implied powers',[49] according to which an international organization 'must be deemed to have those powers which, though not expressly provided . . . are conferred upon it by necessary implication as being essential to the performance of its duties'.[50] International organizations have been recognized as possessing implied powers when those powers would promote their efficiency, even if they are not strictly necessary for exercising their express powers.[51] This, arguably, means that if the ISA were to assert powers that are not indispensable to its functions but were appropriate for the fulfilment of one of its purposes, such assertion would not be ultra vires.[52] However, this is not generally accepted,[53] as the general consensus is that its strictly defined mandate is to administer the resources of the Area, and thus any unrelated activity will be carried out by states without the involvement

[45] Responsibilities and Obligations of States Sponsoring Persons and Entities with Respect to Activities in the Area, Case No 17, Advisory Opinion of 1 February 2011, available at www.itlos.org/fileadmin/itlos/documents/cases/case_no_17/17_adv_op_010211_en.pdf.

[46] Ibid, para 249, 'Article 209, paragraph 2, of the Convention is based on the same approach. According to this provision, the requirements contained in the laws and regulations that States adopt concerning pollution of the marine environment from activities in the Area "undertaken by vessels, installations, structures and other devices flying their flag or of their registry or operating under their authority . . . shall be no less effective than the international rules, regulations, and procedures" established under Part XI, which consist primarily of the international rules, regulations and procedures adopted by the Authority.'

[47] See Art 211 UNCLOS, which provides for the adoption of international standards for vessel source pollution by the competent organisation, which is universally accepted as the IMO; see IMO Secretariat, 'Implications of the United Nations Convention on the Law of the Sea for the International Maritime Organisation', IMO Doc LEG/MISC/3/Rev.1; DM McRae, 'The New Oceans Regime: Implementing the Convention' (1984) 8 *Marine Policy* 83.

[48] Art 157(2) UNCLOS.

[49] MR Montaldo, 'International Legal Personality and Implied Powers of International Organisations' (1970) 44 *British Year Book of International Law* 111, 147–52.

[50] *Reparation for Injuries Suffered in the Service of the United Nations*, Advisory Opinion, [1949] ICJ Reports 182.

[51] D Akande, 'The Competence of International Organizations and the Advisory Jurisdiction of the International Court of Justice' (1998) 9 *European Journal of International Law* 437, 444.

[52] See *Certain Expenses of the United Nations*, Advisory Opinion, [1962] ICJ Reports 168; D Akande, 'International Organizations' in Evans (n 2 above), 265; against HG Schermers and NM Blokker, *International Institutional Law*, 5th edn (Leiden/Boston, 2011) para 233A, where the authors state that the implied powers 'must be *necessary* or *essential* for the organization to perform its functions' (emphasis in the original).

[53] E Egede, *Africa and the Deep Seabed Regime: Politics and International Law of the Common Heritage of Mankind* (Heidelberg/New York, 2001) 131.

of the ISA.[54] At any rate, it is not even certain that a common heritage of mankind approach to the living resources of the Area would be the appropriate solution.[55]

It is thus evident that the living resources of the areas beyond national jurisdiction are subject to the freedoms of the high seas. Thus any marine area protected only under the framework of UNCLOS would be binding only on those states that established it.[56]

C. Protection of Straddling Stocks and Highly Migratory Species

The 1995 UN Fish Stocks Agreement (the Agreement),[57] which is the second implementation agreement of UNCLOS, must also be mentioned. The Agreement helps states to fulfil their duty to co-operate under UNCLOS regarding straddling stocks and highly migratory species by providing measures to be taken and steps to be followed in order for the obligations under UNCLOS to be given effect,[58] and at the same time strengthens the broad obligations under UNCLOS.[59] Nevertheless, it is independent from UNCLOS, as states may be members of one or the other,[60] but they are also interrelated, as one can aid in the interpretation of the other.[61]

An innovation of the Agreement is that it is intended to create obligations for states that are neither a party to nor a member of a regional fisheries management organization (RFMO) with respect to the stock in question.[62] States parties to the Agreement are expected to apply the conservation measures of

[54] Churchill and Lowe (n 23 above), 239–40.

[55] N Matz-Lückm, 'The Concept of the Common Heritage of Mankind: Its Viability as a Management Tool for Deep-Sea Genetic Resources' in AG Oude Elferink and EJ Molenaar (eds), *The International Legal Regime of Areas beyond Nation Jurisdiction: Current and Future Developments* (Leiden/Boston, 2010) 61–75, especially 73–75.

[56] H Thiel, 'Approaches to the Establishment of Protected Areas on the High Seas' in A Kirchner (ed), *International Marine Environmental Law: Institutions, Implementation, and Innovations* (The Hague, 2003) 182.

[57] United Nations Agreement for the Implementation of the Provisions of the United Nations Convention on the Law of the Sea of 10 December 1982 relating to the Conservation and Management of Straddling Fish Stocks and Highly Migratory Fish Stocks, New York, 4 August 1995, 2167 UNTS 3; in force since 11 December 2001.

[58] M Hayashi, 'The 1995 Agreement on the Conservation and Management of Straddling and Highly Migratory Fish Stocks: Significance for the Law of the Sea Convention' (1995) 29 *Ocean & Coastal Management* 51, 53–54.

[59] OS Stokke, 'Managing Straddling Stocks: The Interplay of Global and Regional Regimes' (2000) 43 *Ocean & Coastal Management* 205, 208.

[60] DH Anderson, 'The Straddling Stocks Agreement of 1995—An Initial Assessment' (1996) 45 *International & Comparative Law Quarterly* 463, 467–68.

[61] D Freestone and Z Makuch, 'The New International Environmental Law of Fisheries: The 1995 United Nations Straddling Stocks Agreement' (1996) 7 *Yearbook of International Environmental Law* 3, 23.

[62] P Örebech, K Sigurjonsson and TL McDorman, 'The 1995 United Nations Straddling and Highly Migratory Fish Stocks Agreement: Management, Enforcement and Dispute Settlement' (1998) 13 *International Journal of Marine and Coastal Law* 119, 122–24.

the competent RFMO.[63] In addition states parties are to take measures in order to deter states that are not parties from undermining the effectiveness of the Agreement,[64] even including inspections on the high seas of vessels flying flags of states that are not members of the RFMO but are parties to the 1995 Agreement.[65] Thus, obligations are created for states by instruments that are *res inter alios acta*,[66] and which depart from the traditional notion of the absolute freedom of fishing on the high seas.[67]

The importance of the Agreement, despite it not containing a provision for the creation of marine protected areas, lies with the fact that it provides for concrete obligations of states to protect the marine biodiversity and ecosystems on the high seas[68] and is the first multilateral instrument to adopt the precautionary approach as a binding, substantive obligation.[69]

III. MARINE PROTECTED AREAS UNDER THE AUSPICES OF THE IMO

From its establishment, the IMO[70] assumed competences concerning the protection of the environment which were conferred on it by OILPOL.[71] In 1973, together with the adoption of MARPOL,[72] the Marine Environment Protection Committee was established,[73] which has carried out important work on marine protected areas.

[63] Art 8(3) 1995 Fish Stocks Agreement.

[64] Arts 17(4) and 33(2) 1995 Fish Stocks Agreement.

[65] Arts 21 and 222 1995 Fish Stocks Agreement.

[66] E Papastavridis, *The Interception of Vessels on the High Seas, Contemporary Challenges to the Legal Order of the Oceans* (Oxford/Portland, 2013) 199–202.

[67] P Sands and J Peel, *Principles of International Environmental Law*, 3rd edn (Cambridge, 2012) 409–10.

[68] Art 5 1995 Fish Stocks Agreement; R Barnes, 'Fisheries and Marine Biodiversity' in M Fitzmaurice, DM Ong and P Merkouris, *Research Handbook on International Environmental Law* (Cheltenham/Northampton, 2010) 547–48.

[69] S Borg, *Conservation on the High Seas, Harmonizing International Regimes for the Sustainable Use of Living Resources* (Cheltenham/Northampton, 2012) 133–35.

[70] Established as the Intergovernmental Maritime Consultative Organization, Convention of the Intergovernmental Maritime Consultative Organization, Geneva, 6 March 1948, 289 UNTS 3; in force since 17 March 1958. Its name was changed to International Maritime Organization pursuant to Resolutions A.358 (IX) of 14 November 1975 and A.371 (X) of 9 November 1977.

[71] International Convention for the Prevention of Pollution of the Sea by Oil, London, 12 May1954, 327 UNTS 3; in force since 26 July 1958; amended in 1962, 1969, 1971; NJ Healy, 'The CMI and IMCO Draft Conventions on Civil Liability for Oil Pollution' (1969–70) 1 *Journal of Maritime Law and Commerce* 93.

[72] 1973 International Convention for the Prevention of Pollution by Ships, London, 2 November 1973, 1340 UNTS 184; 1978 Protocol relating to the Convention for the Prevention of Pollution from Ships, London, 16 February 1978, 1340 UNTS 61; both instruments came into force together on 2 October 1983; since amended multiple times. See http://www.imo.org/About/Conventions/ListOfConventions/Pages/International-Convention-for-the-Prevention-of-Pollution-from-Ships-%28MARPOL%29.aspx.

[73] FL Wiswall, 'Uniformity in Maritime Law: The Domestic Impact of International Maritime Regulation' (1983) 57 *Tulane Law Review* 1208, 1220.

A. MARPOL Special Areas

MARPOL was adopted as a result of the UN Conference on the Human Environment,[74] in the sense that it was concluded based on the recommendations of the conference.[75] MARPOL is the only environmental treaty that explicitly provides for the establishment of specially protected marine areas.[76] Annexes I, II and V provide for special areas and Annex VI for emission control areas.[77] Such special areas can apply for all maritime zones, including areas beyond national jurisdiction.[78] This is made possible because the establishment of or amendment to MARPOL Special Areas is an amendment to the convention itself.[79] Thus, the protected areas derive their authority from the convention, as it is binding upon all parties thereto.[80]

However, the only available measure to be taken is the creation of special standards for the discharge of oil,[81] noxious liquid substances,[82] and garbage[83] and for the emission of SOx[84] by vessels.[85]

B. Particularly Sensitive Sea Areas

The concept of Particularly Sensitive Sea Areas (hereinafter PSSAs) was first proposed by the Swedish delegation in the International Conference on Tanker Safety and Pollution Prevention.[86] However, it was not until 1991 that the IMO adopted the first resolution on the guidelines for the establishment of a PSSA,[87] whereby it also established the Great Barrier Reef PSSA, which had

[74] UN GA Resolutions 2398 (XXIII) (1968) and 2581 (XXIV) (1969).

[75] J Roberts, *Marine Environment Protection and Biodiversity Convention, The Application and Future Development of IMO's Particularly Sensitive Sea Area Concept* (Heidelberg, 2006) 20, note 37.

[76] R Becker, 'MARPOL 73/78: An Overview in International Environmental Enforcement' (1997–98) 10 *Georgetown International Environmental Law Review* 625, 630; EJ Molenar, *Coastal State Jurisdiction over Vessel-Source Pollution* (The Hague/Boston/London, 1998) 431–35.

[77] The different annexes provide a unique regulatory system, but in essence all four provide for a type of specially protected area, see Kachel (n 3 above), 97.

[78] T Dux, *Specially Protected Marine Areas in the Exclusive Economic Zone* (Berlin, 2011) 268.

[79] Art 16 MARPOL 1973/1978.

[80] P Drankier, 'Marine Protected Areas in Areas beyond National Jurisdiction' (2012) 27 *International Journal of Marine and Coastal Law* 291, 302.

[81] Annex I, MARPOL 1973/78.

[82] Annex II, MARPOL 1973/78.

[83] Annex V, MARPOL 1973/1978.

[84] Annex VI, MARPOL 1973/1978.

[85] Gavouneli (n 24 above), 72–73.

[86] G Peet, 'Particularly Sensitive Sea Areas: A Documented History' (1994) 9 *International Journal of Marine and Coastal Law* 469, 475.

[87] IMO Resolution A.720 (17), Guidelines for the Designation of Special Areas and the Identification of Particularly Sensitive Sea Areas; see A Blanco-Bazán, 'The IMO Guidelines on Particular Sensitive Sea Areas (PSSAs), Their Possible Application to the Protection of Underwater Cultural Heritage' (1996) 20 *Marine Policy* 343.

already been recognized, in 1990.[88] The Guidelines were amended in 2001[89] and again in 2005 by the IMO Resolution A.982(24), which remains currently applicable.[90]

According to the current regulation, a PSSA is defined as 'an area that needs special protection through action by the IMO because of its significance for recognized ecological, socio-economic, or scientific attributes where such attributes may be vulnerable to damage by international shipping activities'.[91] The application for the establishment of such an area has two parts:[92] (i) the interested state(s) has to submit an application, whereby it has to show that at least one of the ecological, socio-economic or scientific and educational criteria for the identification of a PSSA is met[93] and that the area is vulnerable to impacts by international shipping;[94] and (ii) a description of the associated protective measures and the competence of the IMO to approve or adopt such measures.[95]

After the establishment of the PSSA,[96] the area and the associated protective measures are identified on charts[97] and IMO member states have to ensure that ships flying their flag abide by such measures.[98] However, apart from any jurisdiction granted by UNCLOS, coastal states and/or proposing states are not granted any additional jurisdiction to enforce them.[99]

The establishment of PSSAs is not provided in any binding instrument, and especially not in UNCLOS. Article 211(6) UNCLOS may be seen as providing at least a partial legal basis.[100] However, the two regimes are different[101] as they are based on different criteria, provide for different protective measures[102] and have different scopes of application, namely Article 211(6) relates only to pollution as defined in the Convention whereas PSSAs relate to all envi-

[88] Attached to IMO Resolution A.720 (17); see P Ottesen, S Sparkes and C Trinder, 'Shipping Treats and Protection of the Great Barrier Reef Marine Park—The Role of the Particularly Sensitive Sea Area Concept' (1994) 9 *International Journal of Marine and Coastal Law* 507; for a list of all established PSSAs, see www.imo.org/en/OurWork/Environment/PSSAs/Pages/Default.aspx.

[89] IMO Resolution A.927 (22), Guidelines for the Designation of Special Areas under MARPOL 73/78 and Guidelines for Identification and Designation of Particularly Sensitive Sea Areas.

[90] IMO Resolution A.982 (24), Revised Guidelines for the identification and designation of Particularly Sensitive Sea Areas.

[91] Ibid, para 1.1.

[92] Ibid, para 7.5.

[93] Ibid, para 4.4.

[94] Ibid, para5.

[95] Ibid, para 6

[96] Ibid, para 8.

[97] Ibid, para 9.1.

[98] Ibid, para 9.3.

[99] Ibid, para 9.2.

[100] J Roberts, 'Compulsory Pilotage in International Straits: The Torres Strait PSSA Proposal' (2006) 37 *Ocean Development & International Law* 93, 95, note 14 and the references therein.

[101] A Chircop, 'Particularly Sensitive Sea Areas and International Navigation Rights: Trends, Controversies and Emerging Issues' in I Davies (ed), *Issues in International Commercial Law* (Ashgate, 2005) 225.

[102] R Lagoni, 'Marine Protected Areas in the Exclusive Economic Zone' in Kirchner (n 56 above), 163–64.

ronmental hazards.[103] Another difference is the fact that special areas under Article 211(6) UNCLOS can only be clearly defined parts of an EEZ whereas PSSAs can cover parts of the high seas.[104]

Nevertheless, the relationship between these two regimes is close.[105] Furthermore, a combination of obligations under UNCLOS, Chapter 17 of Agenda 21[106] and the Convention on Biodiversity[107] could provide a solid legal basis for PSSAs,[108] especially since the IMO itself has recognized that the concept of PSSAs is a way to implement the Convention on Biodiversity.[109]

Arguably the greatest advantage offered by the establishment of a PSSA is the possibility of adopting associated protective measures that are not already in any instrument.[110] Further, it can be argued that protective measures might be binding even though there is no specific treaty provision they can be based on, as implementing the general obligations of Article 192 and 194(5) UNCLOS.[111] In addition, the fact that all the related resolutions are adopted by consent may signify that the states consider these resolutions as reflecting the law in this field. Therefore, they are legally binding to the extent that states had such intention.[112] The opposing view is that the outer limits of the discretion of the IMO in designating associated protective measures are the rights and obligations of states under UNCLOS and the fact that there must be a solid legal basis for such measures in a treaty document.[113] Thus, for example, mandatory pilotage schemes cannot be adopted as such a measure.[114]

[103] Dux (n 78 above), 303.

[104] R Lagoni, 'Die Errichtung von Schutzgebieten in der ausschließlichen Wirtschaftszone aus völkerrechtlicher Sicht' (2002) 24 *Natur und Recht* 121, 126; Drankier (n 80 above), 302.

[105] Comments made by the Division of Ocean Affairs and the Law of the Sea of the United Nations in connection with issues raised in document LEG 87/16/1, IMO Doc LEG 87/WP.3 (October 2003).

[106] Agenda 21: Programme of Action for Sustainable Development, UN Doc A/CONF.151/26 (Vols I–III).

[107] Convention on Biological Diversity, Rio, 5 June 1992, 1760 UNTS 79; in force since 29 December 1993.

[108] Roberts (n 75 above), 83.

[109] Report to the Commission on Sustainable Development in fulfillment of General Assembly Resolution 47/191 adopted on 22 December 1992, IMO Doc MEPC 37/INF.2 (6 February1995).

[110] KM Gjerde, 'Protecting Particularly Sensitive Sea Areas from Shipping: A Review of IMO's new PSSA Guidelines' in H Thiel and JA Koslow (eds), *Managing Risks to Biodiversity and the Environment on the High Sea, Including Tools Such as Marine Protected Areas—Scientific Requirements and Legal Aspects* (Bonn, 2001) 125–26.

[111] De La Fayette, 'The Marine Environment Protection Committee: The Conjunction of the Law of the Sea and International Environmental Law' (2001) 16 *International Journal of Marine and Coastal Law* 155, 186.

[112] Markus Detjen, The Western European PSSA—Testing a Unique International Concept to Protect Imperilled Marine Ecosystems, 30 *Marine Policy* 2006, 442, 447.

[113] See, eg IMO Resolution A.982 (24), para 7.5.2(2), where it is stated that 'if the measures are not already available in an IMO instrument, information must be provided with regard to its legal basis and/or the steps that the proposing Member Government has taken or will take to establish the legal basis'.

[114] RC Beckman, 'PSSAs and Transit Passage—Australia's Pilotage System in the Torres Strait Challenges the IMO and UNCLOS' (2007) 38 *Ocean Development & International Law* 325, 347–48.

IV. REGIONAL SEAS

Article 194(1) UNCLOS obligates states to co-operate globally and regionally for the protection of the marine environment and for setting rules to this end. Global co-operation is a reasonable requirement, since it is the only way to ensure the protection of the marine environment, especially the high seas, without hampering the rights and freedoms of all states and avoiding unilateral action.[115] Furthermore, regional co-operation ensures that the specific needs of the marine environment in the area are met, since it has different characteristics depending on the area. Thus, different solutions are needed for each area based on its ecological characteristics, its fragility, the volume of navigation, the developmental status of the coastal states.[116]

The United Nations, through its Environment Programme (UNEP),[117] has facilitated this process. The Governing Council, in its first session, decided to make the protection of the marine environment a priority[118] and in its second session it created the Regional Seas Programme.[119]

A. UNEP—Mediterranean Action Plan

The first action of the Regional Seas Programme was to create the Mediterranean Action Plan,[120] which resulted in the adoption of the Barcelona Convention[121] and two additional protocols. The system was further complemented by additional protocols on land-based sources, on special areas and on seabed operations.[122] Following the United Nations Conference on Environment and Development in Rio de Janeiro in June 1992, the Barcelona Convention was amended[123] in order to align itself with the rules articulated

[115] CO Okidi, 'Toward Regional Arrangements for Regulation of Marine Pollution: An Appraisal of Options' (1977) 4 *Ocean Development & International Law* 1, 8–12.

[116] BA Boczek, 'Global and Regional Approaches to the Protection and Preservation of the Marine Environment' (1984) 16 *Case Western Reserve Journal of International Law* 39, 52–53.

[117] UNEP was created following the Stockholm Summit. UN GA Resolution 2997 (XXVII) (1972); G Palmer, 'New Ways to Make International Environmental Law' (1992) 86 *American Journal of International Law* 259, 261.

[118] UNEP Governing Council Decision 1 E (Oceans), 12–22 June 1973; 17th Meeting, 22 June 1973.

[119] UNEP Governing Council Decision 8 (II), 11–22 March 1974; 29th Meeting, 22 March 1974.

[120] LM Alexander, 'Regional Arrangements in the Oceans' (1977) 71 *American Journal of International Law* 84, 104; for UNEP MAP see E Raftopoulos, *The Barcelona Convention and Protocols: The Mediterranean Action Plan Regime* (London, 1993); A Vallega, 'Geographical Coverage and Effectiveness of the UNEP Convention on the Mediterranean' (1996) 31 *Ocean & Coastal Management* 199.

[121] 1976 Barcelona Convention for the Protection of the Mediterranean Sea against Pollution, Barcelona, 16 February 1976, 15 ILM 1976, 290; in force since 12 February 1978.

[122] For a list of all protocols, see http://www.unepmap.org/index.php?module=content2&catid=001001001.

[123] 1995 Convention for the Protection of the Marine Environment and the Coastal Region of the Mediterranean, Barcelona, 10 June 1995, available at http://www.unepmap.org; in force

therein.[124] Also the SPA & Biodiversity Protocol was adopted in 1995,[125] which provides for the establishment of specially protected areas via a multilateral process[126] based on a number of criteria.[127]

In accordance with Article 5(1) of the protocol, special zones can be established in zones that coastal states exercise jurisdiction over and the necessary protective measures can be taken for the protection of the area.[128] An additional category of special areas, the Specially Protected Areas of Mediterranean Importance, was also created with a view to the protection of those areas that have ecosystems that can be found only in the Mediterranean,[129] and these may be situated on the high seas.[130] These areas are not unilaterally established, but they must be proposed by at least two states parties and established by a decision of the meeting of the contracting parties.[131] In addition, it is possible to include coastal zones in the specially protected areas system[132] in order to ensure integrated management and protection.[133]

One such area, situated partially on the high seas, has been identified. It is the Pelagos Sanctuary for Marine Mammals (France, Italy and Monaco), which was established in 2001 and has been fully operational since 2007, with an international management office and a permanent secretariat.[134]

B. OSPAR

Regional arrangements for the protection of the marine environment have also been created outside the UNEP framework. Of great importance here is

since 9 July 2004; see generally JJ Ruiz, 'International Law Facing Mediterranean Sustainable Development: the Revision of the Barcelona Convention and its Related Protocols' in S Belfiore, MG Lucia and E Pesaro (eds), *Regional Seas Towards Sustainable Development* (Milan, 1996) 230–55.

[124] T Scovazzi, 'The Recent Developments in the "Barcelona System" for the Protection of the Mediterranean against Pollution' (1996) 11 *International Journal of Marine and Coastal Law* 95, 95.

[125] 1995 Barcelona Protocol concerning Specially Protected Areas and Biological Diversity in the Mediterranean, 10 June 1995, 6 *Yearbook of International Environmental Law* 841; in force since 12 December 1999; see generally M Gavouneli, 'New Forms of Co-operation in the Mediterranean System' in MH Nordquist, JN Moore and S Mahmoudi (eds), *The Stockholm Declaration and Law of the Marine Environment* (The Hague/New York, 2003) 223–36.

[126] Art 9 SPA and Biodiversity Protocol (1995).

[127] T Scovazzi, 'Le Protocole Méditerranée sur les Aires Spécialement Protégées' (2003) 21 *Annuaire de Droit Maritime et Océanique* 345, 353.

[128] Art 6 SPA and Biodiversity Protocol (1995).

[129] Art 8 SPA and Biodiversity Protocol (1995).

[130] Annex I, SPA and Biodiversity Protocol (1995).

[131] Art 9 SPA and Biodiversity Protocol (1995); Scovazzi (n 127 above), 353.

[132] H Slim, 'Les Aires Spécialement Protégées en Mediterranée' (2001) 6 *Revue de l'INDEMER* 121, 129–30.

[133] VB Franch and MB Casino, 'La Protección Internacional de Zonas y Especies en la Región Mediterranéa' (1997) 13 *Anuario de Derecho Internacional* 33, 79–80.

[134] Drankier (n 80 above), 322.

the OSPAR system. It covers the North East Atlantic and the North Sea, and it was the first regional system to be created—in 1972, with the adoption of the Oslo Dumping Convention.[135] The regime was supplemented in 1974 by the Paris Convention.[136] Finally, both treaties were replaced in 1992 by the OSPAR Convention,[137] which implemented the new directions of international environmental law after the Earth Summit, such as the precautionary principle and the polluter pays principle.[138]

The OSPAR system provides for the establishment of specially protected areas that can be situated in areas beyond national jurisdiction.[139] In fact, OSPAR created a system of such protected areas, including in areas beyond national jurisdiction, in 2010, following a process that had started in 2007. There were a number of complications in the process, particularly due to the submissions of Portugal and Iceland to the Commission on the Limits of the Continental Shelf, whereby parts of the proposed specially protected areas were included in zones under their respective jurisdictions.[140] Portugal, however, co-operated, and the establishment of the protected areas and the protective and management measures were able to be adopted.[141]

It should be noted, in relation to the protective measures associated with the protected areas, that in OSPAR Annex V programmes and measures concerning fisheries and navigation are defined as being excluded from the OSPAR Commission's competences. Consequently, any relevant measure has to be put in front of the competent RFMO or the IMO for adoption under their rules, procedures and criteria.[142]

The foregoing is only a brief presentation of the main fora where there is a possibility for the establishment of marine protected areas; it is far from exhaustive. There many other regional arrangements, RFMOs, conventions and treaties, regional or sectoral, that provide for the establishment of marine

[135] 1972 Oslo Convention for the Prevention of Marine Pollution by Dumping from Ships and Aircraft, 15 February 1972, 932 UNTS 3; in force since 7 April 1974; amended by Protocol on 2 March 1983; in force since 1 September 1989.

[136] 1974 Paris Convention on the Prevention of Marine Pollution from Land-Based Sources, 4 June 1974, 13 ILM 1974, 352; in force since 6 May 1978.

[137] 1992 Convention for the Protection of the Marine Environment of the North-East Atlantic, Paris, 22 September 1992, 32 ILM 1993, 1068; in force since 25 March 1998; see generally L de La Fayette, 'The OSPAR Convention comes into Force: Continuity and Progress' (1999) 14 *International Journal of Marine and Coastal Law* 247; J Hilf, 'The Convention for the Protection of the Marine Environment of the North-East Atlantic—New Approaches to an Old Problem?' (1995) 55 *ZaöRV* 580.

[138] Sands and Peel (n 67 above), 361.

[139] D Czybulka, 'The Convention on the Protection of the Marine Environment of the North-East Atlantic' in Thiel and Koslow (n 110 above), 179.

[140] BC O'Leary et al, 'The First Network of Marine Protected Areas (MPAs) in the High Seas: The Process, the Challenges and Where Next' (2012) 36 *Marine Policy* 598; EJ Molenaar and AG Oude Elferink, 'Marine Protected Areas in Areas beyond National Jurisdiction, the Pioneering Efforts under the OSPAR Convention' (2009) 5 *Utrecht Law Review* 5.

[141] Bergen Statement, OSPAR Ministerial Meeting, 23–24 September 2010, 5, available at www.ospar.org/site/assets/files/1498/ospar_2010_bergen_statement.pdf.

[142] Drankier (n 80 above), 316–17.

protected areas, in the form of defining areas of the seas where specific activities are prohibited or creating sanctuaries for specific species.[143]

V. THE WAY FORWARD

It is thus clear that marine protected areas come in all shapes and sizes. Different organizations, with different competences and powers, based on very different legal bases, may create various marine protected areas. This could be seen as an advantage, since there is no model for a marine protected area that would be universally appropriate (this was the rationale of UNCLOS and UNEP when providing for regional marine environment protection regimes), but in fact it is not. The main problem is that none of these marine protected areas are comprehensive and multipurpose. On the contrary, as explained above, each type of marine protected area concerns only one sector of activities.

One can thus imagine a situation where a marine protected area is subject to special measures for one type of activity (eg mining) but not for fishing, which can be carried out using techniques, such as bottom trawling, that have the same devastating effect on the biodiversity of the same area. Thus, the need to establish a framework for the creation of integrated multi-purpose marine protected areas is clear.[144]

It also necessary to make sure that the required legal framework, under which it will be possible to create such marine protected areas in areas beyond national jurisdiction, which will be effective and binding upon all states and not only those members of the organization that established them, is in place.[145] This is especially important at a time when human activities in such areas are extending—in particular in the deep sea, where the environment is now recognized as being more sensitive than was hitherto thought.[146]

This is not to say that marine protected areas have to be subject to very strict rules and prohibitions, practically excluding any human activity in such area.[147] However, some unavoidable restrictions to the traditional freedoms of the high seas will be necessary. This must not be considered an insurmountable obstacle to the establishment and sound management of marine protected

[143] Ibid, 325–40.

[144] R Barnes, 'The Law of the Sea Convention and the Integrated Regulation of the Oceans' (2012) 27 *International Journal of Marine and Coastal Law* 859, 860–63.

[145] J Roberts, A Chircop and S Prior, 'Area-based Management on the High Seas: Possible Application of the IMO's Particularly Sensitive Sea Area Concept' (2010) 25 *International Journal of Marine and Coastal Law* 483, 486.

[146] AJ Davies, JM Roberts and J Hall-Spencer, 'Preserving Deep-Sea Natural Heritage: Emerging Issues in Offshore Conservation and Management' (2007) 138 *Biological Conservation* 299.

[147] C Salpin and V Germani, 'Marine Protected Areas beyond Areas of National Jurisdiction: What's Mine is Mine and What You Think is Yours is Also Mine' (2010) 19 *Review of European Community and International Environmental Law* 174, 177.

areas,[148] since these freedoms are not absolute, but in fact are subject to a number of limitations and corresponding duties that are preconditions for their exercise.[149] For example, under Article 116 UNCLOS, the high seas freedom of fishing is actually limited by the treaty obligations of the states, including those arising under Part XII UNCLOS, which provides for an overarching obligation for the protection and preservation of the marine environment and the duty to co-operate,[150] and is subject to an evolutionary interpretation.[151] This means that, since the Convention is actually a living instrument, the concept of the high seas freedoms cannot be considered static.

Another obstacle for the creation of marine protected areas in areas beyond national jurisdiction for the protection and management of living and biological resources is the ideological arguments between states about whether the concept of the common heritage of mankind should apply to such resources.[152] There are, however, ways to move forward—a pertinent example would be the situation in Antarctica, where, despite the different views of states regarding sovereignty and rights over the continent, the establishment of a regime for its protection has been established without any effect on the respective claims of states. A similar approach could be used with regard to the status of the marine living resources.[153]

From a more practical perspective, the different standards for the identification of vulnerable areas by the different organizations and treaty regimes pose yet another obstacle in the co-operation of states and international organizations in the creation and management of multi-purpose marine protected areas on the high seas. However, the United Nations and the Convention on Biological Diversity have both been working on the issue already for some time.

The General Assembly created the UN Ad Hoc Open-ended Informal Working Group in 2004.[154] Its work includes a recommendation to the General Assembly to initiate a process for the creation of a regime applicable to areas beyond national jurisdiction, including marine protected areas, under the auspices of UNCLOS,[155] which could solve the issue of the different criteria.

[148] T Scovazzi, 'Marine Protected Areas on the High Seas: Some Legal and Policy Considerations' (2004) 19 *International Journal of Marine and Coastal Law* 1, 5.

[149] D Freestone, 'Modern Principles of High Seas Governance, The Legal Underpinnings' (2009) 39 *Environmental Policy and Law* 44, 45.

[150] KM Gjerde, 'Challenges to Protecting the Marine Environment beyond National Jurisdiction' (2012) 27 *International Journal of Marine and Coastal Law* 839, 842.

[151] Ibid; A Boyle, 'Further Development of the Law of the Sea Convention: Mechanisms for Change' (2005) 54 *International & Comparative Law Quarterly* 563.

[152] T Treves, 'Principles and Objectives of the Legal Regime Governing Areas beyond National Jurisdiction' in Molenaar and Elferink (n 55 above), 17–19.

[153] D Leary, 'Moving the Marine Genetic Resources Debate Forward: Some Reflections' (2012) 27 *International Journal of Marine and Coastal Law* 435, 440–41.

[154] UN GA Resolution 59/24 (2004) Oceans and the Law of the Sea, para 73, UN Doc A/RES/59/2004.

[155] KN Scott, 'Conservation on the High Seas: Developing the Concept of the High Seas Marine Protected Areas' (2012) 27 *International Journal of Marine and Coastal Law* 849, 854.

However, until that process is complete, states and international organizations can act in accordance with the Convention on Biological Diversity, which has developed a set of scientific criteria for the identification of ecologically or biologically significant areas in open-ocean waters and deep-sea habitats.[156] These criteria can be used as a basis for a globally agreed set of criteria, including socio-economic, cultural, scientific and educational criteria, in order to overcome this fragmentation and facilitate the process of establishment of marine protected areas.[157]

One final problem, which seems to be the most difficult to overcome, is the implementation of the measures by third parties.[158] As stated above, the 1995 Fish Stocks Agreement has provisions to encourage states to become members of the competent RFMOs and has provisions for the enforcement of measures that are applicable even to ships of states that are not members, which proves that the international community has taken a step away from the absolute rule of the *res inter alios acta*. It is true that a new convention, perhaps another UNCLOS implementation agreement, with provisions similar to the ones of the 1995 Fish Stocks Agreement regarding third parties, would solve the problem,[159] even though the actual enforcement and patrolling of restricted areas may require resources that are not currently available.[160] Nevertheless, it can be argued that such marine protected areas, established for the protection of the whole international community, are a kind of objective regime, with *erga omnes* application.[161] However, this argument does not seem to be easily accepted; for example the Antarctic Treaty System may be seen as creating such a regime, whereas in fact this does not seem to be the case.[162]

VI. CONCLUSION

It is clear that the current legal framework for the establishment and management of special areas for the protection of marine biodiversity in areas beyond national jurisdiction is far from perfect. However, that does not mean that states and other stakeholders are not able to accomplish anything. As

[156] CBD COP 9 Decision IX/20 Marine and Coastal Biodiversity. It must be noted that the provisions of the CBD do not directly apply to areas beyond national jurisdiction. However, all activities under the control or jurisdiction of states parties, ie irrespective of where they are carried out, are subject to the Convention (Art 4b); T Scovazzi, 'Bioprospecting on the Deep Seabed: A Legal Gap Requiring to be Filled' in F Francioni and T Scovazzi, *Biotechnology and International Law* (Oxford/Portland, 2006) 97.

[157] Gjerde and Domino (n 38 above), 369–70.

[158] Barnes (n 68 above), 25.

[159] Gjerde and Domino (n 38 above), 371–73.

[160] N Oral, 'Protection of Vulnerable Marine Ecosystems in Areas beyond National Jurisdiction: Can International Law Meet the Challenge?' in Strati et al (n 27 above), 101.

[161] M Fitzmaurice, 'Third Parties and the Law of Treaties' (2002) 6 *Max Planck Yearbook of United Nations Law* 37.

[162] B Simma, 'The Antarctic Treaty as a Treaty Providing for an "Objective Regime"' (1986) 19 *Cornell International Law Journal* 189.

the OSPAR example shows, with co-operation between states and competent international organizations, it is possible to achieve results. Given the fact that the majority of international stakeholders are working for a common goal, it should not prove extremely difficult to achieve the necessary level of co-operation. Nevertheless, a new instrument could help remove many of the currently existing obstacles.

16

Turkish Objections to Exclusive Economic Zone Agreements Concluded by Cyprus

ERIK FRANCKX* AND MARCO BENATAR†

I. INTRODUCTION

The discovery of substantial untapped reserves[1] in the Eastern Mediterranean has spurred Cyprus into signing maritime delimitation agreements with its neighbours in an effort to create a secure legal environment for exploration and exploitation. Turkey, a fellow coastal state of the region with rights and interests of its own, has formulated a series of objections to these treaties. It is our aim to shed light on the Turkish position vis-à-vis said agreements.

After providing a background to the Cyprus exclusive economic zone (EEZ) agreements (Section II) (the texts of which are reproduced in the annexes to this chapter), we will consider the legal arguments put forward by Turkey to object to the three maritime delimitation agreements signed by Cyprus (Section III). Thereafter we will analyse these arguments, which are based on the following lines of reasoning (Section IV): the ability to establish EEZs in the Mediterranean (Section IV.A), concern for third party interests (Section IV.B) and the 'question of Cyprus' (Section IV.C). The conclusion briefly reflects on the merits of the Turkish assertions more broadly (Section V).

* Research Professor, President of the Department of International and European Law, Director of the Centre for International Law, and Vice-Dean for Internationalization of the Faculty of Law and Criminology, Vrije Universiteit Brussel. Member of the Permanent Court of Arbitration.

† Research Fellow, Max Planck Institute Luxembourg for Procedural Law. Member of the Department of International and European Law and the Centre for International Law, Vrije Universiteit Brussel. The authors would like to thank Professor Aristoteles Constantinides for his kind help in procuring secondary sources.

[1] US Geological Survey, 'Assessment of Undiscovered Oil and Gas Resources of the Levant Basin Province, Eastern Mediterranean' (2010) Fact Sheet 3014, available at pubs.usgs.gov/fs/2010/3014/ (accessed on 15 December 2013).

II. MARITIME DELIMITATION AGREEMENTS CONCLUDED BY CYPRUS

To date, Cyprus has entered into three maritime delimitation agreements with states having opposed coastlines.[2]

The first agreement, signed by Cyprus and Egypt in 2003, entered into force in 2004 (2003 Agreement).[3] This agreement is exceptional in that it effectuates EEZ delimitation in the Mediterranean. In fact, it is the first agreement of its kind in the region, where coastal states have long been hesitant to establish such zones. At the time, the treaty parties had yet to pass legislation on the EEZ. Less than a month after the entry into force of the agreement, Cyprus enacted an EEZ law.[4] It was even given retroactive effect, which does not reach as far back as the agreement's date of signature, but only a month later,[5] corresponding to the date of ratification by the Cypriot Parliament.[6] Egypt lacks specific EEZ legislation, but it did issue a declaration upon ratification of the United Nations Convention on the Law of the Sea (1982 Convention),[7] committing itself to apply Part V of the 1982 Convention pertaining to the EEZ.[8] So far, Egypt's legislative intentions have not materialized.

The agreement faithfully adheres to the delimitation method normally

[2] Cyprus is also party to an agreement affecting maritime delimitation with an adjacent state: the Treaty between the United Kingdom of Great Britain and Northern Ireland, the Hellenic Republic, the Republic of Turkey and the Republic of Cyprus concerning the Establishment of the Republic of Cyprus (adopted 16 August 1960, entered into force 16 August 1960) 382 UNTS 9. The treaty stipulates that two sovereign base areas, Akrotiri and Dhekelia, shall remain under the sovereignty of the United Kingdom (Art 1). Given that the sovereign base areas each have a coastal front, Cyprus is barred from claiming any territorial sea in the maritime zones situated between two sets of two lines starting from the territorial boundary on the coast of which the last segment indefinitely extends seaward following a certain azimuth (Annex A, s 3). The four lines and the principles on which they are grounded cannot be determined in greater detail without the published documentation of the treaty negotiations. FA Ahnish, *The International Law of Maritime Boundaries and the Practice of States in the Mediterranean Sea* (Oxford University Press, 1993) 257. The Treaty of Establishment is not further discussed in this chapter (which deals with Turkish objections to agreements signed by Cyprus) because Turkey, as a party to this treaty, does not contest it. For a critical assessment of the status of the aforementioned bases see A Pellet, 'The British Sovereign Base Areas' (2012) *Cyprus Yearbook of International Law* 57.

[3] Agreement between the Republic of Cyprus and the Arab Republic of Egypt on the Delimitation of the Exclusive Economic Zone (adopted 17 February 2003, entered into force 7 March 2004) (2003) 52 L Sea Bull 45.

[4] A Law to Provide for the Proclamation of the Exclusive Economic Zone by the Republic of Cyprus (adopted 2 April 2004, entered into force 21 March 2003) (2004) 55 L Sea Bull 22.

[5] Ibid, para 12.

[6] TC Kariotis, 'Hydrocarbons and the Law of the Sea in the Eastern Mediterranean: Implications for Cyprus, Greece and Turkey' (2011–12) 22 *Mediterranean Quarterly* 45, 47.

[7] United Nations Convention on the Law of the Sea (adopted 10 December 1982, entered into force 16 November 1994) 1833 UNTS 4.

[8] treaties.un.org/pages/ViewDetailsIII.aspx?&src=UNTSONLINE&mtdsg_no=XXI~6&chapter=21&Temp=mtdsg3&lang=en&clang=_en (accessed on 15 December 2013). The section concerning the EEZ contains the following passages:

Declaration concerning the exercise by Egypt of its rights in the exclusive economic zone

The Arab Republic of Egypt will exercise as from this day the rights attributed to it by the provisions of parts V and VI of the United Nations Convention on the Law of the Sea in the

applied in international law between states with opposing coasts, the median line.[9] Regard for third states' interests takes the form of two tripoints (points 1 and 8). Their geographic coordinates are not definitively determined; the parties and third states may change these points' location by common agreement. A party availing itself of this option is under an obligation to notify and consult the other party to the 2003 Agreement.[10]

It is patent from Map 1 that the agreement grants the island of Cyprus 'full effect'. International law lacks a clear rule on the precise impact of islands on maritime delimitation. In the present case, 'full effect' was given despite the disproportionate lengths of the Cypriot and Egyptian coasts.[11] However, if only the relevant parts of the coastlines are taken into account, ie the parts generating overlapping EEZs, the difference in length is far less pronounced. The disparity is certainly smaller than that between the Maltese and Libyan coasts, a consideration that led the International Court of Justice (ICJ) to shift the median line, moving it closer to the island of Malta.[12]

The second agreement was concluded by Cyprus and Lebanon (2007 Agreement).[13] This treaty, modelled on the 2003 Agreement, is almost its

exclusive economic zone situated beyond and adjacent to its territorial sea in the Mediterranean Sea and in the Red Sea.

The Arab Republic of Egypt will also exercise its sovereign rights in this zone for the purpose of exploring and exploiting, conserving and managing the natural resources, whether living or non-living, of the sea-bed and subsoil and the super-adjacent waters, and with regard to all other activities for the economic exploration and exploitation of the zone, such as the production of energy from the water, currents and winds.

The Arab Republic of Egypt will exercise its jurisdiction over the exclusive economic zone according to the modalities laid down in the Convention with regard to the establishment and use of artificial islands, installations and structures, marine scientific research, the protection and preservation of the marine environment and the other rights and duties provided for in the Convention.

The Arab Republic of Egypt proclaims that, in exercising its rights and performing its duties under the Convention in the exclusive economic zone, it will have due regard for the rights and duties of other States and will act in a manner compatible with the provisions of the Convention.

The Arab Republic of Egypt undertakes to establish the outer limits of its exclusive economic zone in accordance with the rules, criteria and modalities laid down in the Convention.

[The Arab Republic of] Egypt declares that it will take the necessary action and make the necessary arrangements to regulate all matters relating to its exclusive economic zone.

[9] 2003 Agreement (n 3 above), Art 1(a). The equidistance rule is an enduring feature of Cyprus's law of the sea strategy on account of its geographic condition (ie surrounded by several states with overlapping rights). A Jacovides, 'Current Issues of the Law of the Sea and their Relevance to Cyprus' in A Jacovides (ed), *International Law and Diplomacy: Selected Writings* (Martinus Nijhoff, 2011) 116.

[10] 2003 Agreement (n 3 above), Arts 1(e) and 3.

[11] T Scovazzi, 'Maritime Delimitations in the Mediterranean Sea' in JC Lloréns, AS Gil and RA Stoffels (eds), *Cursos Euromediterráneos Bancaja de Derecho Internacional*, vols VIII/IX (Tirant lo Blanch, 2009) 446.

[12] *Case concerning the Continental Shelf (Libyan Arab Jamahiriya/Malta)* (Judgment) [1985] ICJ Rep 13, para 73.

[13] Agreement between the Government of the Republic of Lebanon and the Government of the Cypriot Republic Delimiting the Exclusive Economic Zone (adopted 17 January 2007, not yet entered into force). The text is reproduced in T Scovazzi, I Papanicolopulu and G Francalanci, 'Cyprus–Lebanon (Report Number 8-19)' in DA Colson and RW Smith (eds), *International Maritime Boundaries*, vol 6 (Martinus Nijhoff, 2011) 4445, 4452–54.

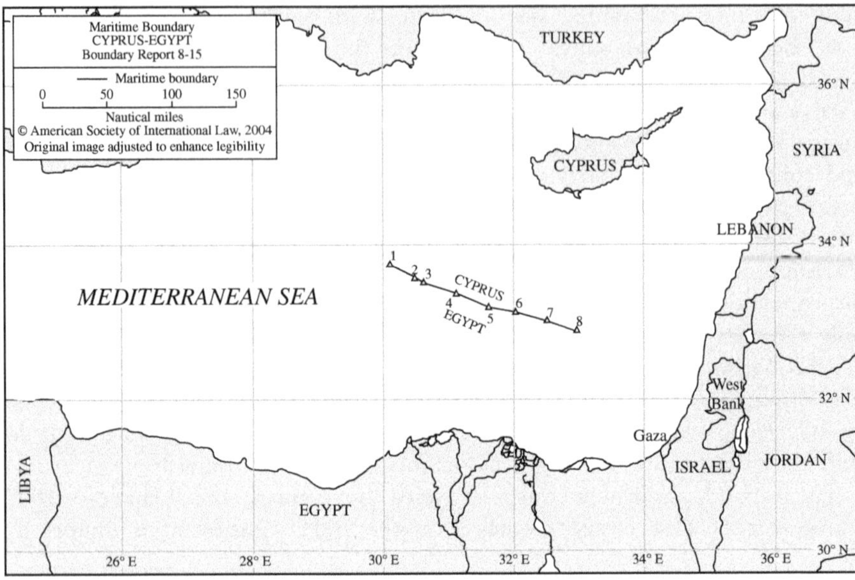

Map 1. Reproduced with the permission of the American Society of International Law. Original image adjusted to enhance legibility.

mirror image. Like Egypt, Lebanon has yet to claim an EEZ. The 2007 Agreement is similar to its 2003 counterpart when it comes to delimitation. The same basic principle, the median line, is applied. Furthermore, the parties gave all islands 'full effect': not only Cyprus, but also all small insular features off the Lebanese coast. The distance of these islands from the coastline does not exceed 10 kilometres. The resulting delimitation is an equidistant line measured from all the points which function as base points, as shown in Map 2.

The only difference between the 2003 and 2007 Agreements, which is wholly unrelated to their substance, is that the latter has not entered into force.

The third agreement was signed by Cyprus and Israel in 2010, and came into effect the subsequent year (2010 Agreement).[14] What sets this treaty apart is that, although it bears some resemblance to its predecessors, it differs on substantive points.

Turning first to the similarities, the structure of the Agreements and the number of provisions and subsections are identical. As regards delimitation, the same basic principle is applied, ie the median line, as illustrated in Map 3.

There are a number of differences. First, Israel is not bound by the 1982 Convention. As a result, the 2010 Agreement not only refers to this 'Constitution for the Oceans', but also adds a broader reference to the rules and

[14] Agreement between the Government of the State of Israel and the Government of the Republic of Cyprus on the Delimitation of the Exclusive Economic Zone (adopted 17 December 2010, entered into force 25 February 2011) (2011) 75 L Sea Bull 27.

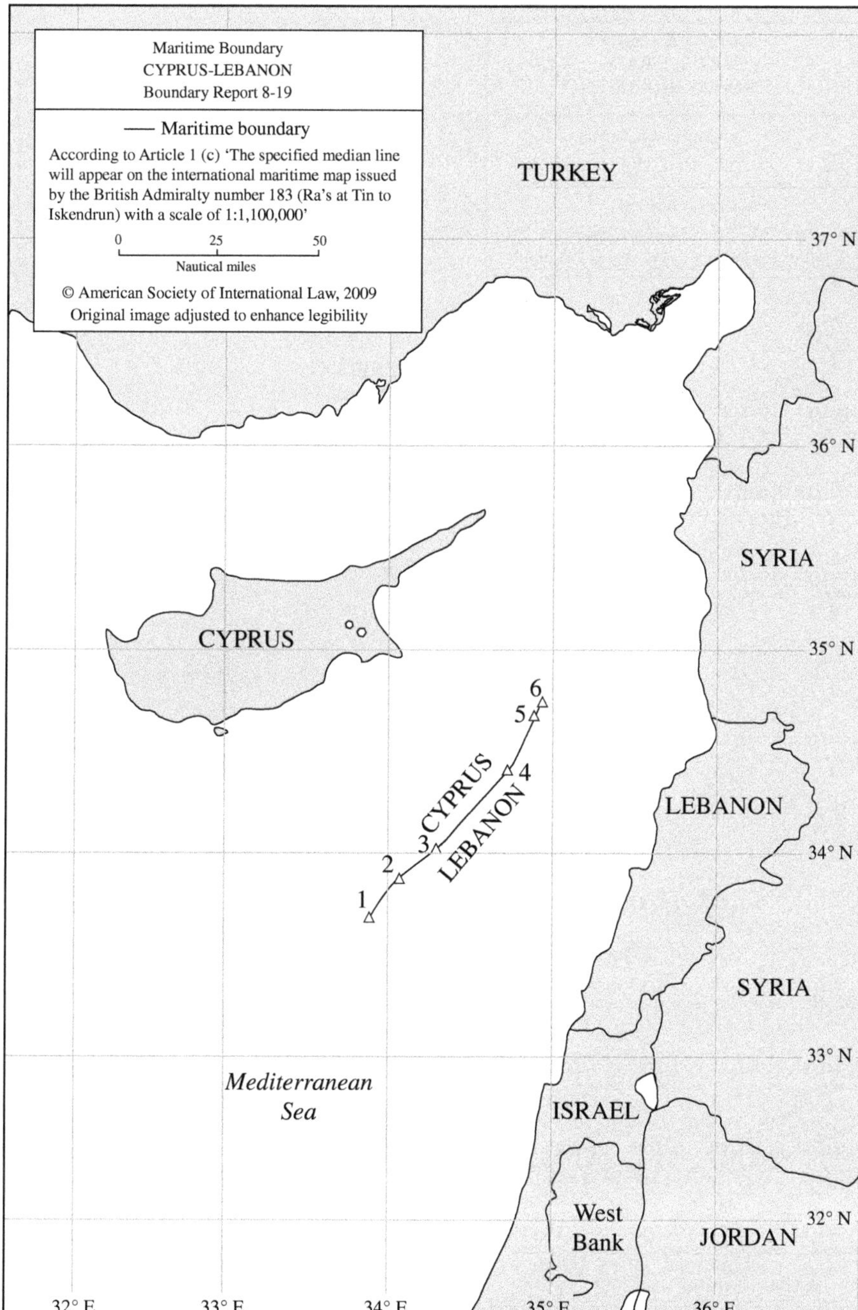

Map 2. Reproduced with the permission of the American Society of International Law. Original image adjusted to enhance legibility.

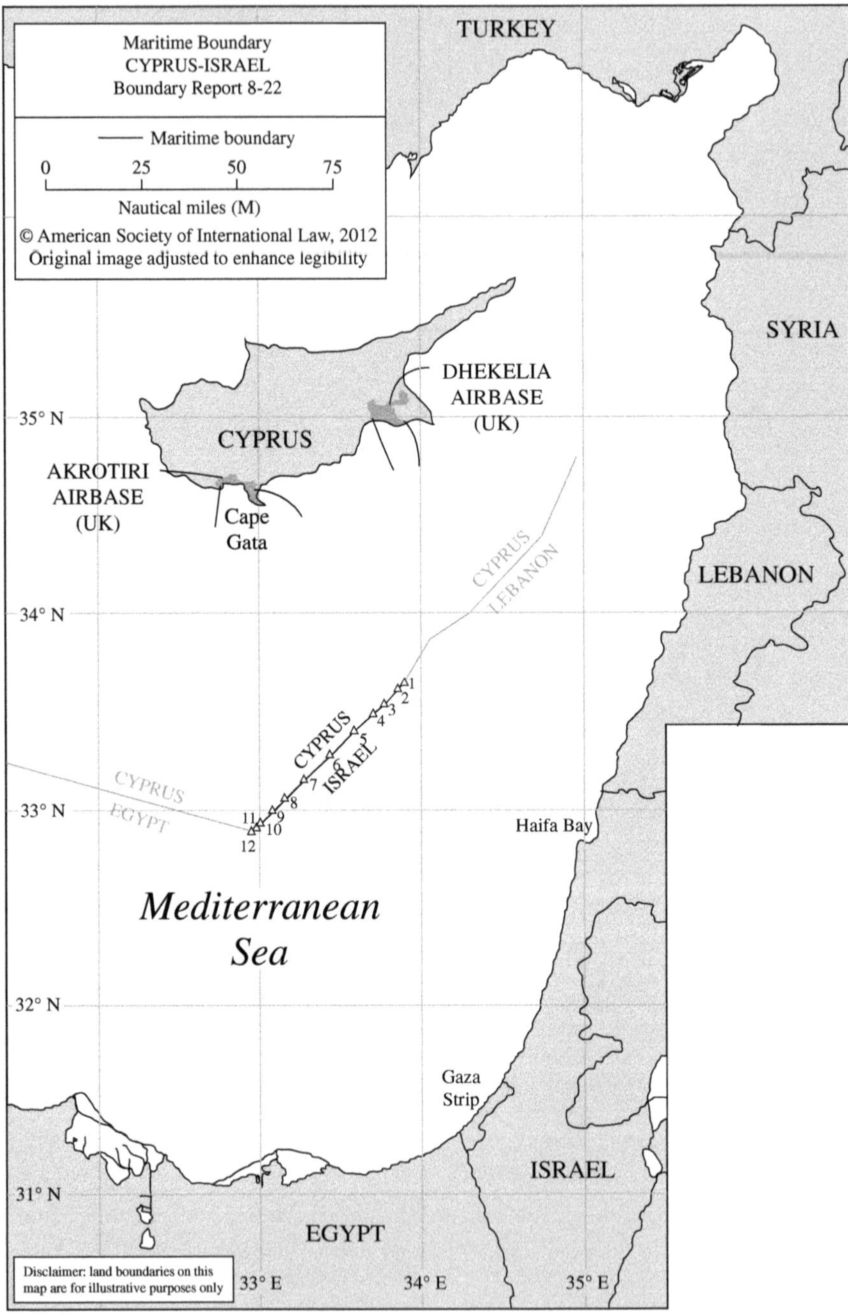

Map 3. Reproduced with the permission of the American Society of International Law. Original image adjusted to enhance legibility.

principles of the international law of the sea applicable to the EEZ concept. Secondly, the arbitration clauses incorporated in the two earlier agreements were unclear as to whether a unilateral procedure, following the exhaustion of diplomatic means, would suffice to initiate arbitral proceedings. This is not so in the 2010 Agreement, which specifies that the parties must first agree on the question to be submitted to the arbitrators and the procedural rules. This excludes ipso facto any purely unilateral measure on the part of either state to take the dispute to arbitration.[15] The third departure is the relationship between the geographic coordinates and the annexed maps. This matter is unresolved in the 2003 and 2007 Agreements, which do not indicate which of the two would prevail in case of conflict. Conversely, the 2010 Agreement stipulates that the coordinates take precedence over any map.[16]

III. THE TURKISH OBJECTIONS

In 2004, Turkey voiced its opposition to the 2003 Agreement. Despite not featuring among the signatories of the 1982 Convention,[17] it wrote a letter of protest to the Secretary-General of the United Nations. The core of the information note reads:

> The agreement signed between the Arab Republic of Egypt and the Greek Cypriot Administration of Southern Cyprus on 17 February 2003 concerning the 'Delimitation of the Exclusive Zone' has recently been published in the *Law of the Sea Bulletin* Vol. 52, page 45.
>
> It is understood from the content of the said agreement that the above-mentioned Parties delimit the EEZ through a line defined by 8 geographical coordinates in the high seas of the Mediterranean.
>
> Following a thorough examination of the said agreement, the Republic of Turkey has reached the view that the delimitation of the EEZ or the continental shelf in the Eastern Mediterranean, especially in areas falling beyond the western part of the longitude 32°16′18″, also concerns Turkey's existing ipso facto and ab initio legal and sovereign rights, emanating from the established principles of international law.
>
> It is the considered opinion of the Republic of Turkey that the delimitation of the EEZ and the continental shelf beyond the western parts of the longitude 32°16′18″ should be effected by agreement between the related states at the region based on the principle of equity.
>
> The Republic of Turkey, for the above stated legal reasons which arise from the established principles of international law, does not recognize the said agreement

[15] Ibid, Art 4(b).

[16] Ibid, Art 1(d).

[17] Information note by Turkey, concerning its objection to the Agreement between the Republic of Cyprus and the Arab Republic of Egypt on the Delimitation of the Exclusive Economic Zone (17 February 2003) (2004) 54 L Sea Bull 127.

> and reserves all its legal rights related to the delimitation of the maritime areas including the seabed and subsoil and the superjacent waters in the west of the longitude 32°16′18″.
>
> Finally, the Republic of Turkey wishes to reiterate that there is no single authority which in law or in fact is competent to represent jointly the Turkish Cypriots and the Greek Cypriots, consequently Cyprus as a whole.[18]

Turkey has also protested the 2007[19] and 2010 Agreements[20] through diplomatic initiatives. Besides opposing these bilateral treaties, Turkey has also objected to Cyprus' other hydrocarbon-related activities in the Eastern Mediterranean, such as drilling, calls for tenders and the adoption of legislation identifying oil fields.[21] These statements show that Turkey has stood by its stance first formulated in 2004. The extract quoted above thus captures the

[18] Ibid, Annex.

[19] Press release regarding the efforts of the Greek Cypriot Administration of Southern Cyprus to sign bilateral agreements concerning maritime jurisdiction areas with the countries in the Eastern Mediterranean (30 January 2007), available at www.mfa.gov.tr/_p_30-january-2007_-press-release-regarding-the-efforts-of-the-greek-cypriot-administration-of-southern-cyprus-to-sign-bilateral-agreements-concerning-maritime-jurisdiction-areas-with-the-countries-in-the-eastern-mediterranean_br___p_.en.mfa (accessed on 15 December 2013); Kariotis (n 6 above), 47; M Wählisch, 'Israel–Lebanon Offshore Oil & Gas Dispute—Rules of International Maritime Law' (2011) 15/31 *ASIL Insights* 4, fn 48, available at www.asil.org/insights/volume/15/issue/31/israel-lebanon-offshore-oil-gas-dispute-—rules-international-maritime (accessed on 15 December 2013).

[20] Turkey 'does not have any claim regarding the maritime areas subject to the said EEZ delimitation agreement. It approaches this issue within the context of the Cyprus problem.' Letter from the Permanent Representative of Turkey to the United Nations addressed to the Secretary-General (and Annex) (23 December 2010), UN Doc A/65/674–S/2010/674. See also M Leigh and C Brandsma, 'Energy Resources in the Eastern Mediterranean: Source of Cooperation or Fuel for Tension', GMF Brussels Forum Paper Series (2012) 3, available at www.gmfus.org/wp-content/blogs.dir/1/files_mf/leigh_brandsma_easternmedenergy_bf12.pdf (accessed on 15 December 2013). Lebanon, too, protested the 2010 Agreement due to its non-recognition of Israel and its view that the EEZ delimitation encroaches upon its sovereign and economic rights. See Note verbale dated 20 June 2011 from the Permanent Mission of Lebanon addressed to the Secretariat of the United Nations (2011) 76 L Sea Bull 38; A letter dated 3 September 2011 from the Minister for Foreign Affairs and Emigrants of Lebanon addressed to the Secretary-General of the United Nations concerning the geographical coordinates of the northern limit of the territorial sea and the exclusive economic zone transmitted by Israel (2011) 77 L Sea Bull 33.

[21] UNHRC, Fourth session, High-level segment, Summary record of the 5th meeting (14 March 2007), UN Doc A/HRC/4/SR.5, para 128 (Observer for Turkey); Letter from the Permanent Representative of Turkey to the United Nations addressed to the Secretary-General (27 April 2007), UN Doc A/61/885–S/2007/246; Letter from the Permanent Representative of Turkey to the United Nations addressed to the Secretary-General (23 July 2007), UN Doc A/61/1011–S/2007/456; ILC, 'Shared Natural Resources: Comments and Observations Received from Governments' (4 May–5 June 2009 and 6 July–7 August 2009), UN Doc A/CN.4/607, 19-20 (Reply from Turkey); Letter from the Permanent Representative of Turkey to the United Nations addressed to the Secretary-General (and Annex) (23 December 2010), UN Doc A/65/674–S/2010/674; Letter from the Permanent Representative of Turkey to the United Nations addressed to the Secretary-General (and Annex) (16 August 2011), UN Doc A/65/934–S/2011/526. Turkey has also reiterated its position in defence of the licences it granted to the Turkish Petroleum Corporation. See Letter from the Permanent Representative of Turkey to the United Nations addressed to the Secretary-General (and Annex) (5 September 2012), UN Doc A/66/899.

essence of the Turkish argumentation and will form the basis for our analysis of Turkey's misgivings with respect to the Cyprus EEZ Agreements.[22]

Finally, Cyprus has also expressed its legal views on these matters in a number of letters to the UN Secretary-General. Examples include refutations of Turkish objections to Cyprus' activities in the Eastern Mediterranean and disapproval of Turkey's endeavours, eg the issuance of navigational warnings, conducting seismic surveys in maritime zones claimed by Cyprus, and naval interference with foreign and Cypriot-flagged vessels engaged in the exploration and/or exploitation within said areas.[23]

Most important in the note verbale is the reference to the high seas. The parties to the 2003, 2007 and 2010 Agreements do not mention it, nor do they allude to the territorial sea (let alone the continental shelf). This omission is out of the ordinary. States generally begin with delimitation of the continental shelf—a concept that crystallized after the Second World War—before proceeding to the EEZ—a notion born out of the Third United Nations Conference on the Law of the Sea, 1973–1982. Here, the parties refrain from addressing the continental shelf, even though the non-living resources were undoubtedly the prime motive behind the three agreements. There must have been a specific reason that compelled the parties to the 2003, 2007 and 2010 Agreement to use the EEZ concept. Although the coastal state's competences in the EEZ automatically encompass those in the continental shelf in some areas—such as the Mediterranean Sea, where the maritime zones of coastal states cannot extend to a full 200 nautical miles due to overlap—the context described above suggests that the parties wanted to promote the EEZ concept's entry into the Mediterranean, where it had long been absent. For Turkey, on

[22] An elaborate information sheet is available on the website of the Turkish Ministry of Foreign Affairs, setting out its legal and political approach to the issues discussed in this chapter. See Turkish Ministry of Foreign Affairs, Maritime Delimitation & Offshore Activities in the Eastern Mediterranean. Legal & Political Perspectives. Recent Developments (21 March 2012), available at www.mfa.gov.tr/site_media/html/maritime_delimitation.pdf (accessed on 15 December 2013).

[23] Identical letters from the Permanent Representative of Cyprus to the United Nations addressed to the Secretary-General and the President of the Security Council (31 January 2007), UN Doc A/61/726–S/2007/52; Letter from the Permanent Representative of Cyprus to the United Nations addressed to the Secretary-General (15 May 2007), UN Doc A/61/913–S/2007/288; Letter from the Chargé d'affaires a.i. of the Permanent Mission of Cyprus to the United Nations addressed to the Secretary-General (6 August 2007), UN Doc A/61/1020–S/2007/474; Letter from the Permanent Representative of Cyprus to the United Nations addressed to the Secretary-General (and Annex) (14 November 2008), UN Doc A/63/554–S/2008/719; Letter from the Permanent Representative of Cyprus to the United Nations addressed to the Secretary-General (4 June 2009), UN Doc A/63/875–S/2009/291; Letter from the Permanent Representative of Cyprus to the United Nations addressed to the Secretary-General (and Annex) (15 June 2012), UN Doc A/66/851; Letter from the Permanent Representative of Cyprus to the United Nations addressed to the Secretary-General (17 October 2013), UN Doc A/68/537–S/2013/622; Letter from the Permanent Representative of Cyprus to the United Nations addressed to the Secretary-General (and Annexes) (29 October 2013), UN Doc A/68/555–S/2013/634; Letter from the Permanent Representative of Cyprus to the United Nations addressed to the Secretary-General (12 November 2013), UN Doc A/68/593–S/2013/662; Letter from the Permanent Representative of Cyprus to the United Nations addressed to the Secretary-General (5 December 2013), UN Doc A/68/644–S/2013/720.

the other hand, these waters form part and parcel of the high seas, and therefore it contests, albeit implicitly, their qualification as EEZ.

In numerous instances, Turkey invokes the longitude 32°16′18″.[24] The coordinate passes through Cape Arnauti, the westernmost point of the island of Cyprus. It can be gleaned from the Turkish line of argument that it does not accept any impact of the island upon delimitation of the western coast. Simply put, this would mean that the effect of the island on delimitation of maritime spaces west of Cyprus is entirely negated.

IV. LEGAL ANALYSIS OF THE TURKISH OBJECTIONS

An analysis of the Turkish note verbale yields three distinct objections. First, Turkey questions the capacity of coastal states in the Mediterranean to establish EEZs. Secondly, a more general problem of public international law is raised, which is the relativity of treaties and consideration for third party interests in maritime delimitation. Finally, Turkey addresses the thorny issue of Cyprus' status under contemporary international law.

A. The Exclusive Economic Zone Concept

The first argument hinges on the following quandary: can EEZs be lawfully claimed in the Mediterranean? The EEZ is first and foremost a treaty-based notion, having emerged from the negotiating tables of the Third United Nations Conference on the Law of the Sea. After 10 years of discussions, the Conference culminated in the signing of the 1982 Convention, which in Part V, entitled 'Exclusive Economic Zone', fleshes out the applicable legal regime.[25] As one of two novel maritime zones created by the 1982 Convention,[26] it is worthwhile listing the states which ratified the treaty.

[24] These coordinates were invoked most recently in Communication from the Permanent Mission of Turkey to the United Nations with reference to the Verbal Note from the Permanent Mission of Greece dated 20 February 2013 (12 March 2013), available at www.un.org/Depts/los/LEGISLATIONANDTREATIES/PDFFILES/communications/tur_note_re%20grc_12032013.pdf (accessed on 15 December 2013).

[25] 1982 Convention (n 7 above), Arts 55–75.

[26] The second new maritime zone that the 1982 Convention introduced is the Area, namely 'the seabed and ocean floor and subsoil thereof, beyond the limits of national jurisdiction'. Ibid, Art 1(1)(1). Its legal regime can be found in ibid, Part XI, Arts 133–91.

Table 1. States Parties to the United Nations Convention on the Law of the Sea*

Cyprus	Egypt	Greece	Lebanon	Israel	Syria	Turkey
Yes	Yes	Yes	Yes	No	No	No
1988	1983	1995	1995			

* Information retrieved from the United Nations Division for Ocean Affairs and the Law of the Sea. Available at http://www.un.org/Depts/los/reference_files/status2010.pdf.

To this day, three Eastern Mediterranean states have not (yet) acceded to the 1982 Convention. Once the consensus system had run its course by 1982, after a decade of intense talks, the United States insisted on holding a vote and voted against. Israel and Turkey, each for reasons of their own, followed the American lead.[27] Syria, although it did not cast a negative vote in 1982, is currently in a similar situation, because, like Israel and Turkey, it has neither signed nor ratified the Convention. Three of the four other states of the sub-region all signed the treaty in 1982 and Lebanon did so two years later, and all completed the ratification process in the 1980s (Cyprus and Egypt) or 1990s (Greece and Lebanon).

The divergent approaches among Eastern Mediterranean coastal states merits an examination of the EEZ's normative status: whilst having its basis in a treaty, has the EEZ equally become part of customary international law? Interestingly, this is one of the rare instances where conventional law gives rise to a customary rule before the convention, containing the new rule, has entered into force. The normal process is such that customary law is codified and thus poured into treaty form. Here, however, not only is treaty law converted into customary law prior to the entry into force of the convention; certain indications suggest that the normative process was ongoing before the convention had even been signed.

The EEZ concept's crystallization into custom can be traced through successive decisions of the International Court of Justice during the first half of the 1980s. In its judgment of 24 February 1982, which saw Libya and Tunisia embroiled in a dispute over the delimitation of their continental shelves in the Mediterranean Sea, the ICJ rendered a textbook example of an obiter dictum, ie an opinion that is not essential for reaching the outcome of the case:

> While it may be that Tunisia's historic rights and titles are more nearly related to the concept of the exclusive economic zone, *which may be regarded as part of modern international law*, Tunisia has not chosen to base its claims upon that concept.[28]

[27] For a list of reasons why Turkey chose not to become a party to the 1982 Convention see Y İnan and MP Gözen, 'Turkey's Maritime Boundary Relations' in M Kibaroğlu (ed), *Eastern Mediterranean: Countries and Issues* (Foreign Policy Institute Ankara 2009) 161. See also V Prescott and C Schofield, *The Maritime Political Boundaries of the World*, 2nd edn (Martinus Nijhoff, 2005) 386–88. The fourth state to vote against was Venezuela.

[28] *Case concerning the Continental Shelf (Tunisia/Libyan Arab Jamahiriya)* (Judgment) [1982] ICJ Rep 18, para 100 (emphasis added).

This passage floats somewhat adrift in a paragraph dealing with historic rights/titles and the continental shelf—the parties had not asked the ICJ to delimit their EEZs. The chronology of events is paramount, as the ICJ handed down its ruling several months before the adoption of the 1982 Convention.

It was in 1985 that the ICJ took a more pronounced position, affirming that '[i]t is in the Court's view *incontestable* that . . . the institution of the exclusive economic zone . . . is shown by the practice of States to have become a part of customary law'.[29] The novelty of the EEZ concept makes this jurisprudential development all the more significant from the perspective of international law formation.[30]

Most coastal states claim an EEZ.[31] Turkey, too, has applied this concept in the Black Sea, through municipal legislation,[32] as well as delimitation agreements with Bulgaria[33] and the USSR (as later succeeded by Georgia,[34] the Russian Federation[35] and Ukraine[36]). Notwithstanding these observations, EEZs in the Mediterranean are something of an exception. Can the region's coastal states therefore be viewed as persistent objectors to the development of the EEZ concept in this part of the world?

At the time of writing, only six countries have claimed an EEZ as such in the Mediterranean: Morocco, Syria, Cyprus, Tunisia, Libya and Lebanon.[37] Nonetheless, the trend in the Mediterranean is one of coastal states establish-

[29] *Libyan Arab Jamahiriya/Malta* (n 12 above), para 34 (emphasis added).

[30] See A Filis and R Leal-Arcas, 'Legal Aspects of Inter-State Maritime Delimitation in the Eastern Mediterranean Basin' (2013) 11 *Oil, Gas & Energy Law Intelligence* 1, 14–16.

[31] Office of Legal Affairs of the United Nations, Division for Ocean Affairs and the Law of the Sea 'Table of Claims to Maritime Jurisdiction (as of 15 July 2011)', available at www.un.org/Depts/los/LEGISLATIONANDTREATIES/PDFFILES/table_summary_of_claims.pdf (accessed on 15 December 2013).

[32] Decree by the Council of Ministers No 86/11264 (adopted 17 December 1986, entered into force on the day of publication), available at www.un.org/depts/los/LEGISLATIONANDTREATIES/PDFFILES/TUR_1986_Decree.pdf (accessed on 15 December 2013).

[33] Agreement between the Republic of Turkey and the Republic of Bulgaria on Determination of the Boundary in the Mouth Area of the Mutludere/Rezovska River and Delimitation of the Maritime Areas between the Two States in the Black Sea (adopted 4 December 1997, entered into force 4 November 1998) 2087 UNTS 5 Art 4.

[34] Exchange of Notes on the Delimitation of the Exclusive Economic Zones in the Black Sea (adopted 23 December 1986, entered into force 6 February 1987) 1460 UNTS 135; Protocol between the Government of the Republic of Turkey and the Government of Georgia on the Confirmation of the Maritime Boundaries between Them in the Black Sea (adopted 14 July 1997, entered into force 22 September 1999) (2000) 43 L Sea Bull 108 (explicitly listing as fourth and last agreement the exchange of notes).

[35] After the disappearance of the Soviet Union from the political map of the world, the Russian Federation, in a note of 17 September 1992, informed Turkey that it would continue to honour the 1986/1987 exchange of notes (ibid). As mentioned in T Scovazzi, 'Black Sea Update: The Former Republics of the Soviet Union and Turkey' in JI Charney and LM Alexander (eds), *International Maritime Boundaries*, vol 3 (Martinus Nijhoff, 1998) 2443.

[36] In a note of 30 May 1994, Ukraine also informed Turkey that it succeeds to the Soviet Union in the 1986/1987 exchange of notes (n 34 above). As mentioned in Scovazzi (ibid), 2443–44, who reproduces that note on 2445.

[37] Table of Claims to Maritime Jurisdiction (n 31 above). This list is ordered chronologically from earliest to latest.

ing zones other than those explicitly enshrined in the 1982 Convention but comparable to EEZs in functionality, such as the 'fishery zones' and 'ecological protection zones' claimed by France and more recently Italy.[38]

Table 2. Exclusive Economic Zones in the Eastern Mediterranean*

Cyprus	Egypt	Greece	Lebanon	Israel	Syria	Turkey
Yes	Yes	No	Yes	Yes	Yes	No
Leg 2004	Imp 2003		[Leg 2011]	[Imp 2011]	[Leg 2003]	

* Information retrieved from the United Nations Division for Ocean Affairs and the Law of the Sea, Table of Claims to Maritime Jurisdiction (as of 15 July 2011), available at http://www.un.org/Depts/los/LEGISLATIONANDTREATIES/PDFFILES/table_summary_of_claims.pdf.
Key: Leg = legislation; Imp = implicit; [] = information found elsewhere.

Table 2 provides an overview of EEZ claims of coastal states in the Eastern Mediterranean. Some of these states have made such claims explicitly, through promulgation of legislation, while others have done so implicitly, by agreement or, as in the case of Egypt, by declaration upon ratification of the 1982 Convention. Two states have yet to do so: Greece and Turkey. The main reason why neither state has established an EEZ in the Eastern Mediterranean is in all likelihood linked to their unresolved dispute over the Aegean Sea.

Two conclusions may be drawn from this analysis. The first is that there are no compelling reasons to doubt the customary character of the EEZ notion in contemporary international law. The number of states that have ratified or acceded to the 1982 Convention and declared an EEZ, as well as the ICJ's pronouncements in this regard, are a testament to its consolidation in custom. Secondly, the Mediterranean is not a real exception to this rule. In support of keeping EEZs out of the Mediterranean, the latter's status as a semi-enclosed sea is often emphasized.[39] The proliferation of EEZs, so the argument goes, would open Pandora's box in light of the large number of coastal states and the ensuing delimitations,[40] inexorably leading to the disappearance of the high seas. The premises of this scenario could, however, be unfounded. One can point to practice in other semi-closed seas that are far more difficult to manage at first glance, where coastal states managed to establish EEZs against the odds. The Baltic Sea is a powerful illustration. EEZ declarations were made

[38] On this divergent practice, see I Papanicolopulu, 'Mediterranean Sea' in R Wolfrum (ed), *Max Planck Encyclopedia of Public International Law* (Oxford University Press, 2012) paras 12–6, available at opil.ouplaw.com/home/EPIL (accessed on 15 December 2013); DJ Attard, 'Mediterranean Maritime Jurisdictional Claims: A Review' in J Basedow, U Magnus and R Wolfrum (eds), *The Hamburg Lectures on Maritime Affairs 2009 & 2010* (Springer, 2012) 89, 98–100, 107–12.

[39] Turkey takes the view that, under international law, EEZ or continental shelf delimitation in a semi-enclosed sea can only be undertaken through the agreement of all parties, taking into consideration the rights and interests of all those concerned. This has been stated in a number of documents submitted to the UN Secretary-General (see n 21 above).

[40] See, eg Yücel Acer, 'The Present Status of the Mediterranean Sea as to the Maritime Law' (2008) 4 *USAK Review of International Law & Politics* 119, 125, 130.

and delimitation agreements were entered into despite the prevailing cold war opposition between Eastern Bloc states and their Western counterparts. By the time of the USSR's break-up, the region had been almost entirely delimited. The Baltic Sea even preceded the North Sea, another semi-enclosed sea, which would not achieve a similar level of coverage until the 1980s. These examples demonstrate that alleged complexity should not prevent coastal states of the Mediterranean from claiming EEZs. Full EEZ coverage could even enhance governance of the Mediterranean through the benefit of having a uniform legal regime.[41]

B. The Problem of Third Parties

The question of third states arises from the essentially bilateral configuration of maritime delimitation agreements, as they only cover the parties' rights and obligations. How, then, are third states' interests protected? The *North Sea Continental Shelf* cases provide an answer.[42] The Netherlands and Denmark believed that the median line method as applied to states with opposing coasts was a rule of international law. The year of the judgment being 1969, the applicable treaty law was the body of norms that came out of the first United Nations Conference on the Law of the Sea of 1958. The solution laid down in the Convention on the Continental Shelf was the median line/equidistance principle between opposite/adjacent states.[43] These two states, with coasts facing one another in the North Sea, had proceeded to divide the sea between themselves in the form of a bilateral treaty. The Federal Republic of Germany, which was not a party to the agreement because it opposed the application of this principle, managed to take its case against the Netherlands and Denmark to the International Court of Justice. The ICJ concluded that the median line/equidistance principle was not part of pre-existing or emerging customary international law.[44]

Practice shows that states, as well as courts and tribunals, are very mindful of third parties' interests. A number of techniques are available to this end.[45] Parties can, for instance, decide not to determine the tripoints at the moment

[41] T Treves, 'The High Seas as Potential Exclusive Economic Zones in the Mediterranean' in M Kohen, R Kolb and DL Tehindrazanarivelo (eds), *Perspectives of International Law in the 21st Century. Perspectives du droit international au 21e siècle: Liber Amicorum Professor Christian Dominicé in Honour of his 80th Birthday* (Martinus Nijhoff, 2012) 175, 189.

[42] *North Sea Continental Shelf Cases (Federal Republic of Germany/Denmark; Federal Republic of Germany/Netherlands)* (Judgment) [1969] ICJ Rep 3.

[43] Convention on the Continental Shelf (adopted 29 April 1958, entered into force 10 June 1964) 499 UNTS 311 Art 6. According to these two states, no special circumstance could justify a different delimitation.

[44] *North Sea Continental Shelf* (n 42 above), para 66.

[45] For a detailed analysis of the different methods used to overcome tripoint concerns see CG Lathrop, 'Tripoint Issues in Maritime Boundary Delimitation' in DA Colson and RW Smith (eds), *International Maritime Boundaries*, vol 5 (Martinus Nijhoff, 2005) 3305.

of signing the agreement. Alternatively, they can set the tripoints while retaining the option of adjusting them upon consultation with the third state in question. It is the latter approach that was embraced in the 2003,[46] 2007[47] and 2010 Agreements.[48]

Turkey is of the opinion that its own rights have been violated. To be more precise, it considers that the zone situated to the west of longitude 32°16′18″ should not have been included in the 2003 Agreement. As in the Aegean Sea, the Turkish position is premised on islands having no effect on maritime delimitation. Therefore, Cyprus cannot generate maritime projections from its western coast. Rather, Turkey was intent on delimiting this part of the Mediterranean through a boundary agreement negotiated with Egypt.

Other states did not fail to issue rapid reactions. Cyprus replied that the Turkish argument

> is tantamount to accepting that islands and even more so a sovereign island State, in this case the Republic of Cyprus, is deprived of any maritime zones, contrary to customary international law, the [1982] Convention (articles 56, 77 and 121) and the International Court of Justice rulings.[49]

This response was followed by Greece, which, as a concerned state of the region, emphasized that delimitation should be effectuated 'in accordance with the pertinent rules of international law on the basis of the principle of equidistance/median line. This is confirmed by widespread, long-standing State practice, including the recently adopted [2003] Agreement . . .'[50]

The Turkish position would appear untenable under the law of maritime delimitation. While it is accepted that third states' interests must be taken into account in a general manner, such claims have to be reasonable, or to employ the terms of the ICJ, not 'obviously unreasonable'.[51] Even though there is no clear-cut rule stipulating the effect to be given to islands, stripping a sovereign

[46] 2003 Agreement (n 3 above), Art 1(e).

[47] 2007 Agreement (n 13 above), Art 1(e).

[48] 2010 Agreement (n 14 above), Art 1(e).

[49] Statement dated 28 December 2004 of the Position of the Government of the Republic of Cyprus with respect to the Information Note by Turkey, concerning the latter's Objection to the Agreement between the Republic of Cyprus and the Arab Republic of Egypt on the Delimitation of the Exclusive Economic Zone of 17 February 2003 (2005) 57 L Sea Bull 126. Neither Turkey's reply (Note verbale dated 4 October 2005 from the Permanent Mission of Turkey to the United Nations addressed to the Secretary-General of the United Nations (2005) 59 L Sea Bull 34) nor Cyprus's rejoinder (Note verbale dated 19 October 2006 from the Permanent Mission of the Republic of Cyprus to the United Nations addressed to the Secretary-General of the United Nations (2006) 62 L Sea Bull 164) brings new elements to bear.

[50] Note verbale dated 24 February 2005 from the Permanent Mission of Greece to the United Nations addressed to the Secretary-General of the United Nations concerning Turkey's Objection to the Agreement between the Republic of Cyprus and the Arab Republic of Egypt on the Delimitation of the Exclusive Economic Zone of 17 February 2003 (2005) 57 L Sea Bull 129.

[51] *Libyan Arab Jamahiriya/Malta* (n 12 above), para 23.

insular state of all impact on delimitation,[52] even if only in a single direction, can be qualified as a position that does not meet the test of reasonableness.[53]

C. The Cyprus Question and the Representation of its Inhabitants

The Turkish Republic of Northern Cyprus (TRNC) has been able to make its position known through the facilitation of Turkish diplomacy.[54] The TRNC argues that only a new partnership government representative of both communities living on the island could sign agreements affecting Cyprus' natural resources.[55] The Turkish and North Cypriot legal lines of argumentation do not appear to differ in any noteworthy manner.

[52] It is worth underlining the importance that the ICJ attached to the difference between Malta, as an independent state, and islands belonging to a state. *Libyan Arab Jamahiriya/Malta* (n 12 above), paras 53, 72.

[53] E Milano and I Papanicolopulu, 'State Responsibility in Disputed Areas on Land and at Sea' (2011) 71 *Zeitschrift für ausländisches öffentliches Recht und Völkerrecht* 587, 630–31, fn 142 (defining an unreasonable claim as 'manifest[ly] contrast with the basic principles applicable in the law of maritime delimitation' and listing the Turkish argument discussed above among instances of state practice lacking reasonableness). On the use of 'reasonableness' in maritime delimitation jurisprudence see O Corten, *L'utilisation du 'raisonnable' par le juge international. Discours juridique, raison et contradictions* (Bruylant, 1997) 633–38.

[54] The TRNC's views can be construed from a series of statements of TRNC government officials annexed to letters submitted by the Turkish Permanent Mission to the UN. See Letter from the Permanent Representative of Turkey to the United Nations addressed to the Secretary-General (and Annex) (2 February 2007), UN Doc A/61/727–S/2007/54; Note verbale from the Permanent Mission of Turkey to the United Nations Office at Geneva addressed to the Office of the High Commissioner for Human Rights (and Annex) (3 May 2007), UN Doc A/HRC/5/G/2, 11; Letter from the Permanent Representative of Turkey to the United Nations addressed to the Secretary-General (and Annex) (8 August 2007), UN Doc A/61/1027–S/2007/487; Identical letters from the Permanent Representative of Turkey to the United Nations addressed to the Secretary-General and the President of the Security Council (and Annex) (28 August 2007), UN Doc A/61/1033–S/2007/516; Letter from the Permanent Representative of Turkey to the United Nations addressed to the Secretary-General (and Annex) (7 September 2007), UN Doc A/61/1045–S/2007/546; Letter from the Permanent Representative of Turkey to the United Nations addressed to the Secretary-General (and Annex) (26 November 2008), UN Doc A/63/574–S/2008/741; Letter from the Permanent Representative of Turkey to the United Nations addressed to the Secretary-General (and Annex) (28 November 2008), UN Doc A/63/579–S/2008/750; Letter from the Permanent Representative of Turkey to the United Nations addressed to the Secretary-General (and Annex) (17 April 2009), UN Doc A/63/828–S/2009/216; Letter from the Permanent Representative of Turkey to the United Nations addressed to the Secretary-General (and Annex) (25 January 2011), UN Doc A/65/702–S/2011/46; Letter from the Permanent Representative of Turkey to the United Nations addressed to the Secretary-General (and Annex) (15 August 2011), UN Doc A/65/933–S/2011/523; Letter from the Permanent Representative of Turkey to the United Nations addressed to the Secretary-General (and Annex) (22 December 2011), UN Doc A/66/649; Letter from the Permanent Representative of Turkey to the United Nations addressed to the Secretary-General (and Annex) (17 October 2012), UN Doc A/67/541.

[55] Conversely, the Republic of Cyprus' position is that revenue sharing with the Turkish Cypriot community is contingent upon a political settlement of their dispute. Commentators have observed Cyprus' reticence to undertake formal negotiations in this regard. R Nathanson and R Levy, *Natural Gas in the Eastern Mediterranean: Casus Belli or Chance for Regional Cooperation?* (IEPN/INSS, 2012) 26. See also Report of the Secretary-General on the United Nations operation in Cyprus (7 January 2013), UN Doc S/2013/7, para 10; Report of the Secretary-General on

For the purpose of this analysis, it is sufficient to briefly recall some basic points about the TRNC and the Republic of Cyprus without delving into the intricacies of the conflict. The proclamation of the TRNC on 15 November 1983 was shortly followed by a UN Security Council resolution '[c]onsider[ing] the declaration . . . as legally invalid and call[ing] for its withdrawal'.[56] Only Turkey has extended recognition to the TRNC as a sovereign state.[57] The Republic of Cyprus, on the other hand, is considered by the rest of the international community to be the sole legitimate government on the island.[58] The implications of these disparate statuses are far reaching. The Republic of Cyprus, as a state, enjoys exclusive rights to the hydrocarbons within its maritime zones in accordance with the principle of permanent sovereignty over natural resources.[59] The TRNC, whether deemed a non-state or a collectively

the United Nations operation in Cyprus (5 July 2013), UN Doc S/2013/392, para 43 (noting that the offshore resources are a source of tension but could also provide an impetus for achieving a long-lasting resolution of the Cyprus question) and the following statement by the UK Minister for Europe (Mr David Lidington) to the House of Commons, reproduced in J Hartmann, S Shah and C Warbrick, 'United Kingdom Materials on International Law 2012' (2013) 83 *British Yearbook of International Law* 298, 513: 'We have repeatedly stated publicly our acceptance that the Republic of Cyprus has sovereign rights to exploit its mineral reserves within its exclusive economic zone. We think that the prospect of the greater prosperity that would flow from the successful exploitation of hydrocarbon resources in the eastern Mediterranean is one of many reasons why it is in the interests of Cyprus—all communities in Cyprus—of Turkey and of Greece to reach a settlement to the maritime disputes in that region and a final settlement to the Cyprus question, too.'

[56] UNSC Res 541 (18 November 1983), UN Doc S/RES/541, para 2. See also UNSC Res 550 (11 May 1984), UN Doc S/RES/550, paras 2–3.

[57] Some have questioned the relevance of recognition of the TRNC in the first place. See the following observations made by a former Turkish judge of the European Court of Human Rights in *Loizidou v Turkey* App No 15318/89 (ECtHR, 18 December 1996) Dissenting Opinion of Judge Gölcüklü, para 3: 'not only does northern Cyprus not come under Turkey's jurisdiction, but there is a (politically and socially) sovereign authority there which is independent and democratic. It is of little consequence whether that authority is legally recognised by the international community.'

[58] See UNSC Res 541 (n 56 above), para 7: '[The UN Security Council] [c]alls upon all States not to recognize any Cypriot State other than the Republic of Cyprus'; *Loizidou v Turkey* App No 15318/89 (ECtHR, 18 December 1996) para 44; *Cyprus v Turkey* App No 25781/94 (ECtHR, 10 May 2001) para 61.

[59] The principle is formulated in UNGA Res 1803 (XVII) (14 December 1962). Its customary status was attested to by the ICJ (*Armed Activities on the Territory of the Congo (Democratic Republic of the Congo v Uganda)* (Judgment) [2005] ICJ Rep 168, para 244). See also UNGA Res 37/253 (16 May 1983), UN Doc A/RES/37/253, para 2, in which the UN General Assembly '[a]ffirms the right of the Republic of Cyprus and its people to full and effective sovereignty and control over the entire territory of Cyprus and its natural and other resources'. Turning to the scope of the permanent sovereignty principle, it is conceptualized as a right of states but also of peoples (eg UNGA Res 1803 (XVII) (ibid) para 1: 'the right of peoples and nations to permanent sovereignty over their natural wealth and resources must be exercised in the interest of their national development and of the well-being of the people of the State concerned'). Applying the norm to the situation of Cyprus could, conceivably, be more complicated, depending on the qualification of the North Cypriot community and whether they will benefit from the oil and gas revenue. On this point, see A Skordas, 'Oil Exploitation in the Eastern Mediterranean: Cyprus, Turkey and International Law' (Woodrow Wilson International Center for Scholars, 2007), available at www.wilsoncenter.org/event/oil-exploitation-the-eastern-mediterranean-cyprus-turkey-and-international-law (accessed on 15 December 2013). See also P Athanassiou, 'State and Government Recognition and the 2011 Cyprus EEZ Demarcation and Exploration Dispute:

unrecognized state, is similar to a local de facto government,[60] having the capacity to neither (i) conclude international agreements opposable to third states[61] nor (ii) assert sovereign rights/jurisdiction at sea under customary international law.[62] Its situation should be distinguished from that of broadly (but not universally) recognized states, the treaty-making capacity of which is beyond serious dispute.[63] Bearing in mind these impediments, the 2011 continental shelf agreement[64] Turkey entered into with the TRNC lacks effect under international law.[65]

Some Reflections' [2012] *Cyprus Yearbook of International Law* 19 (assessing the legal merit of Turkey's response to Cyprus' maritime delimitation treaties and exploration contracts from the perspective of state/government recognition).

[60] F Hoffmeister, 'Cyprus' in R Wolfrum (ed), *Max Planck Encyclopedia of Public International Law* (Oxford University Press, 2012) para 29, available at opil.ouplaw.com/home/EPIL (accessed on 15 December 2013).

[61] H Dipla, 'Ressources énergétiques et limites maritimes en méditerranée orientale' (2011) 16 *Annuaire du droit de la mer* 63, 78 (noting, with reference to the rule reflected in the Vienna Convention on the Law of Treaties (adopted 23 May 1969, entered into force 27 January 1980) 1155 UNTS 331 Art 6, that the TRNC, as a non-state entity, does not possess the capacity to conclude treaties).

[62] Hoffmeister (n 60 above), para 27 (writing that 'the TRNC government cannot avail itself of any sovereign rights under the law of the sea').

[63] See also the ill-fated Annan Plan for Cyprus proposing the creation of a federal 'United Cyprus Republic', available at www.hri.org/docs/annan/ (accessed on 15 December 2013). Annex V of the Plan, comprising a list of international treaties and instruments binding on the United Cyprus Republic, includes agreements to which the TRNC is a party. This has been interpreted, at least by some, as implicit recognition of the TRNC's treaty-making capacity. K Schmalenbach, 'Article 3. International Agreements not within the Scope of the Present Convention' in O Dörr and K Schmalenbach (eds), *Vienna Convention on the Law of Treaties: A Commentary* (Springer, 2012) 66–68. For further information on international agreements submitted by the TRNC in the framework of the Annan Plan see F Hoffmeister, *Legal Aspects of the Cyprus Problem: Annan Plan and EU Accession* (Martinus Nijhoff, 2006) 168–69. It is also noteworthy that, under the Annan Plan, the proposed Constitution of the United Cyprus Republic (available at www.hri.org/docs/annan/AppendixA/FOUNDATION_AGREEMENT.pdf (accessed on 15 December 2013)) contained provisions dealing directly with law of the sea matters discussed in this piece. Art 25, para 2(b) prescribed a special majority voting procedure for '[r]atification of treaties and adoption of laws and regulations concerning the airspace, continental shelf and territorial waters of the United Cyprus Republic, including the exclusive economic zone and the contiguous zone'. Art 14 para 1(f) adds 'international navigation and the continental shelf and territorial waters' to the legislative and executive competences exercised by the federal government.

[64] Statement by Prime Minister Erdogan following the signing of continental shelf delimitation agreement between Turkey and the Turkish Republic of Northern Cyprus New York (21 September 2011), available at www.mfa.gov.tr/statement-by-prime-minister-erdogan-following-the-signing-of-continental-shelf-delimitation-agreement-between-turkey-and-the-tur.en.mfa (accessed on 15 December 2013); T Scovazzi, 'Maritime Boundaries in the Eastern Mediterranean Sea', GMF Brussels Forum Paper Series (2012) 9, available at www.gmfus.org/wp-content/blogs.dir/1/files_mf/1339504227Scovazzi_MaritimeBoundaries_Jun12.pdf (accessed on 15 December 2013). The agreement does not entirely follow the median line, but attributes a slightly larger part to Turkey. International Crisis Group, 'Aphrodite's Gift: Can Cypriot Gas Power a New Dialogue?', Europe Report N° 216 (2012) 11, available at www.crisisgroup.org/~/media/Files/europe/turkey-cyprus/cyprus/216-aphrodites-gift-can-cypriot-gas-power-a-new-dialogue.pdf (accessed on 15 December 2013).

[65] This is not to say that all actions of the TRNC government are without legal ramifications. See, eg *Loizidou v Turkey* (n 58 above), para 45: 'international law recognises the legitimacy of certain legal arrangements and transactions in such a situation, for instance as regards the regis-

V. CONCLUSION

Sometimes coastal states picture themselves in an ideal situation where adjacent or opposite states acquiesce to the full extent of their maritime claims. By way of illustration, when Belgium was preparing for negotiations with its neighbours over delimitation in the North Sea, Belgian geologists knew the continental shelf between the United Kingdom and Belgium lacked oil reserves. With a coastline measuring a meagre 64 kilometres, and concave in shape, to make matters worse, Belgium rightly considers itself a geographically disadvantaged state. In the 1980s, a suggestion gained traction among Belgian geologists to claim a zone similar to the one Germany successfully established, namely a continental shelf cutting into the middle of the North Sea. The proposal was to assert a zone starting at the Belgian coast and projecting northward, reaching the centre of the North Sea, where oil reserves were abundant, as was common knowledge at the time. After an exchange of views between geologists and legal advisers, the idea was labelled unrealistic precisely because international law did not support such a position. The plan was abandoned as a result. The Turkish position is reminiscent of this case in point. Turkey is seemingly intent on portraying an ideal situation in the Eastern Mediterranean. Yet, as we have demonstrated throughout this chapter, the three legal arguments presented by Turkey do not pass muster.

ANNEX 1: AGREEMENT BETWEEN THE REPUBLIC OF CYPRUS AND THE ARAB REPUBLIC OF EGYPT ON THE DELIMITATION OF THE EXCLUSIVE ECONOMIC ZONE[66]

The Republic of Cyprus and the Arab Republic of Egypt (hereinafter referred to as 'the two Parties')

Desiring to strengthen further the ties of good-neighbourliness and cooperation between the two countries;

Recognizing the importance of the delimitation of the exclusive economic zone for the purpose of development in both countries;

tration of births, deaths and marriages, "the effects of which can be ignored only to the detriment of the inhabitants of the [t]erritory" (see, in this context, Advisory Opinion on Legal Consequences for States of the Continued Presence of South Africa in Namibia (South West Africa) Notwithstanding Security Council Resolution 276 (1970), [1971] International Court of Justice Reports 16, p 56, para 125)'; A Cullen and S Wheatley, 'The Human Rights of Individuals in *De Facto* Regimes under the European Convention on Human Rights' (2013) 13 *Human Rights Law Review* 691, 706–11. However, the acts in question are internal and receive recognition because they benefit the civilian population. The same reasoning does not apply to international legal acts, *in casu* maritime delimitation treaties. E Milano, *Unlawful Territorial Situations in International Law: Reconciling Effectiveness, Legality and Legitimacy* (Martinus Nijhoff, 2006) 150–51.

[66] (2003) 52 L Sea Bull 45; Map 1.

Recalling the relevant provisions of the United Nations Convention on the Law of the Sea of 10 December 1982, to which the two countries are parties;

Have agreed as follows;

Article 1

(a) The delimitation of the exclusive economic zone between the two Parties is effected by the median line of which every point is equidistant from the nearest point on the baseline of the two Parties.

(b) The median line and its limits is defined by points 1 to 8 according to the list of geographical coordinates annexed to this Agreement (annex I).

(c) The median line, as determined, appears graphically on the Official Hydrographic Chart published by the British Admiralty, No 183 (Ras at Tin to Iskenderun), scale 1/1,100,000 (annex II) .

(d) At the request of either of the two Parties, any further improvement on the positional accuracy of the median line will be agreed upon by the two Parties using the same principles, when more accurate data are available.

(e) Taking into consideration article 74 of the United Nations Convention on the Law of the Sea of 10 December 1982, the geographical coordinates of points 1 and 8 could be reviewed and/or extended as necessary in the light of future delimitation of the exclusive economic zone with other concerned neighbouring States and in accordance with an agreement to be reached in this matter by the neighbouring States concerned.

Article 2

In case there are natural resources extending from the exclusive economic zone of one Party to the exclusive economic zone of the other, the two Parties shall cooperate in order to reach an agreement on the modalities of the exploitation of such resources.

Article 3

If either of the two Parties is engaged in negotiations aimed at the delimitation of its exclusive economic zone with another State, that Party, before reaching a final agreement with the other State, shall notify and consult the other Party, if such delimitation is in connection with coordinates 1 or 8.

Article 4

(a) Any dispute arising from the implementation of this Agreement shall be settled through diplomatic channels in a spirit of understanding and cooperation.

(b) In case the two Parties do not settle the dispute within a reasonable period of time through diplomatic channels, the dispute will be referred to arbitration.

Article 5

1. This Agreement is subject to ratification according to the constitutional procedures in each country.

2. This Agreement shall enter into force upon the exchange of the instruments of ratification.

DONE in duplicate at Cairo this 17th day of February 2003 in the English and Arabic languages, both texts being equally authentic. In case of differences of interpretation, the English text shall prevail.

ANNEX 2: AGREEMENT BETWEEN THE GOVERNMENT OF THE REPUBLIC OF LEBANON AND THE GOVERNMENT OF THE CYPRIOT REPUBLIC DELIMITING THE EXCLUSIVE ECONOMIC ZONE[67]

The Government of the Republic of Lebanon and the Government of the Cypriot Republic referred to hereinafter as 'the two parties',

– Desiring to strengthen the relationship of good neighbourliness and cooperation between the two states,

– In their awareness of the importance of delimiting the exclusive economic zone for the development of the two states,

– Affirming the relevant provisions of the United Nations Convention on the Law of the Sea made on the tenth of December 1982, to which the two parties are parties, have agreed to the following:

[67] Scovazzi, Papanicolopulu and Francalanci (n 13 above); Map 2.

Article 1

a. The exclusive economic zone between the two parties will be delimited on the basis of the median line such that every point along the length of it is equidistant from the nearest point on the baselines of each of the two parties.

b. The median line and its limits will be defined by the points determined from 1 to 6 set out in the list of geographical coordinates attached to this agreement as Annex 1.

c. The specified median line will appear on the international maritime map issued by the British Admiralty number 183 (Ra's at Tin to Iskenderun) with a scale of 1:1,100,000.

d. The Agreement will be made between the two parties, at the request of either of them, for any additional improvements to be made to increase the precision of locating the median line when more precise data is available pursuant to the same principles adopted.

e. Taking into account Article 74 of the United Nations Convention on the Law of the Sea made on the tenth of December 1982, the geographical coordinates of points 1 and / or 6 may be reviewed or adjusted as required in the light of future delimitation of the exclusive economic zones with other neighbouring states concerned in accordance with an agreement that may be reached regarding this matter with the neighbouring states concerned.

Article 2

In the event that there are extensions of natural resources that extend between the exclusive zone of one of the parties and the exclusive economic zone of the other party, the two parties will cooperate to reach an agreement regarding the means of utilising these resources.

Article 3

If either of the two parties enters into negotiations aiming at delimiting its exclusive economic zone with another state, this party must notify the other party and consult it before reaching a final agreement with the other state if this delimitation relates to the coordinates of Points 1 or 6.

Article 4

a. Any dispute that arises from the application of this agreement must be resolved by diplomatic means in a spirit of mutual understanding and cooperation.

b. In the event that the two parties do not reach a resolution acceptable to them by diplomatic means within a reasonable timescale, the dispute will be referred to arbitration.

Article 5

1. This agreement will be ratified in accordance with the constitutional principles adopted in each country.

2. This agreement will come into force when the two parties exchange the ratification documents.

This agreement has been issued in the City of Beirut on the seventeenth of January 2007 in two original copies in Arabic and English, each of which will have the same force of evidence, and in the event of a difference in the translation the text in English will be adopted.

ANNEX 3: AGREEMENT BETWEEN THE GOVERNMENT OF THE STATE OF ISRAEL AND THE GOVERNMENT OF THE REPUBLIC OF CYPRUS ON THE DELIMITATION OF THE EXCLUSIVE ECONOMIC ZONE[68]

The Government of the State of Israel and the Government of the Republic of Cyprus (hereinafter, each, individually, a 'Party'; jointly, the 'two Parties')

Desiring to strengthen further the ties of good-neighborliness and cooperation between the two countries;

Recognizing the importance of the delimitation of the Exclusive Economic Zone for the purpose of development in both countries;

Recalling the provisions of the United Nations Convention on the Law of the Sea of 10 December 1982, relating to the Exclusive Economic Zone;

Basing themselves on the rules and principles of international law of the sea applicable to the matter;

Have agreed as follows:

[68] (2011) 75 L Sea Bull 27; Map 3.

Article 1

(a) The delimitation of the Exclusive Economic Zone between the two Parties is effected by the median line, as such term is defined in paragraph (b) below.

(b) The median line between the two Parties and its limits are defined by points 1 to 12, in accordance with the list of geographical coordinates attached hereto as Annex I, which constitutes an integral part of this Agreement.

(c) The median line, as determined, appears graphically on the Official Hydrographic Chart published by the British Admiralty No 183 (Ra's at Tin to Iskenderun), scale 1/1,100,000 (Attached hereto as Annex II, which constitutes an integral part of this Agreement).

(d) The coordinate values of the agreed points 1 to 12 on the median line take precedence over the chart noted in paragraph (c) above, and over any other map or chart that reflects the location of the median line between the Parties.

(e) Taking into consideration the principles of customary international law relating to the delimitation of the Exclusive Economic Zone between States, the geographical coordinates of points 1 or 12 could be reviewed and/or modified as necessary in light of a future agreement regarding the delimitation of the Exclusive Economic Zone to be reached by the three States concerned with respect to each of the said points.

Article 2

In case there are natural resources, including hydrocarbons reservoirs, extending from the Exclusive Economic Zone of one Party to the Exclusive Economic Zone of the other, the two Parties shall cooperate in order to reach a framework unitization agreement on the modalities of the joint development and exploitation of such resources.

Article 3

Without prejudice to the provisions of Article 1(e), if either of the two Parties is engaged in negotiations aimed at the delimitation of its Exclusive Economic Zone with another State, that Party, before reaching final agreement with the other State, shall notify and consult the other Party, if such delimitation is in connection with coordinates 1 or 12.

Article 4

(a) Any dispute arising from the interpretation or implementation of this Agreement shall be settled through diplomatic channels in a spirit of understanding and cooperation.

(b) In the event that the two Parties do not settle the dispute within a reasonable period of time through diplomatic channels in accordance with paragraph (a) above, the dispute will be referred to arbitration. The terms of reference and the procedure of the arbitration shall be determined by the Parties, by mutual agreement, prior to the commencement of the arbitration.

Article 5

(a) This Agreement is subject to ratification according to the constitutional procedures in each country.

(b) This Agreement shall enter into force upon the exchange of the instruments of ratification.

DONE at Nicosia on the 17th of December 2010, which corresponds to the 10th of Tevet 5771, in two originals in the Hebrew, Greek and English languages, all texts being equally authentic. In case of divergence of interpretation of the texts, the English version shall prevail.

17

Towards the Acceptance of the Equidistance Rule in the Delimitation of the Continental Shelf and the Exclusive Economic Zone: The Role of International Jurisprudence

MARIA XIOURI*

I. INTRODUCTION

THE DELIMITATION OF maritime zones is an arena where international law is confronted with the infinite variety of nature and the multifaceted economic interests of states in the wealth of the sea. This struggle becomes even fiercer because of the need to delimit maritime zones with different purposes as established in the United Nations Convention on the Law of the Sea,[1] most importantly the continental shelf[2] and the exclusive economic zone (EEZ).[3] Thus, the problem arises of which method to follow in a maritime delimitation. This chapter seeks to examine the role of case law of international courts and tribunals in the establishment of a rule of international law according to which such delimitation is to be effected.

* PhD candidate, Queen Mary, University of London. Email: m.xiouri@qmul.ac.uk. This chapter is current as at 20 February 2014 and is based on a thesis submitted for the Master of Laws Degree at the Faculty of Law of the University of Athens in 2011, supervised by Professor A Bredimas and Associate Professor Ph Pazartzis. I would like to thank them, as well as Assistant Professor M Gavouneli for her helpful comments. All errors remain mine alone.

[1] Law of the Sea Convention (adopted 10 December 1982, entered into force 16 November 1994) 1933 UNTS 396 (hereinafter LOSC).

[2] See Arts 76, para 1 and 77, para 1 LOSC.

[3] See Arts 55–57 LOSC.

II. INITIAL APPROACH: EMPHASIS ON FLEXIBILITY

A. The 1958 Geneva Convention on the Continental Shelf and the *North Sea Continental Shelf* Case

In Article 6, paragraphs 1 and 2 of the 1958 Geneva Convention on the Continental Shelf,[4] the equidistance principle was established as the basic rule for the delimitation of the continental shelf, with the exception of 'special circumstances'. The International Law Commission considered such circumstances to be particular geographical features or configurations that, because of the application of the equidistance principle, might result in an unreasonable or inequitable delimitation of the continental shelf; in such a case, a delimitation otherwise than by application of the equidistance method is justified.[5]

The equidistance rule for the delimitation of the continental shelf was dealt with by an international court for the first time in the *North Sea Continental Shelf* case,[6] when Denmark, the Federal Republic of Germany and the Netherlands asked the International Court of Justice (the Court, ICJ) to declare which of the principles and rules of international law were applicable to the delimitation of the continental shelf in the North Sea. The 1958 Geneva Convention on the Continental Shelf had been ratified by Denmark and the Netherlands, but not by the Federal Republic of Germany.

In its judgment, in 1969, the Court considered the principle that a coastal state has inherent rights in the continental shelf which constitutes the natural prolongation of its land territory as the most fundamental of all the rules of law relating to continental shelf.[7] As to the equidistance rule, the ICJ declared that it was not a customary rule of international law as far as adjacent coasts are concerned.[8] It drew that conclusion based on various grounds, not all

[4] '1. Where the same continental shelf is adjacent to the territories of two or more States whose coasts are opposite each other, the boundary of the continental shelf appertaining to such States shall be determined by agreement between them. In the absence of agreement, and unless another boundary line is justified by special circumstances, the boundary is the median line, every point of which is equidistant from the nearest points of the baselines from which the breadth of the territorial sea of each State is measured.

2. Where the same continental shelf is adjacent to the territories of two adjacent States, the boundary of the continental shelf shall be determined by agreement between them. In the absence of agreement, and unless another boundary line is justified by special circumstances, the boundary shall be determined by application of the principle of equidistance from the nearest points of the baselines from which the breadth of the territorial sea of each State is measured.'

[5] See *UK/France* Arbitral Award 1977, para 70; K Ioannou and A Strati, *Law of the Sea* (in Greek; AN Sakkoulas Publications, 2000) 327.

[6] *North Sea Continental Shelf Cases (Federal Republic of Germany/Denmark; Federal Republic of Germany/Netherlands)* [1969] ICJ Reports 4. See also RY Jennings, 'The Limits of Continental Shelf Jurisdiction: Some Possible Implications of the North Sea Case Judgment' (1969) 18 *International & Comparative Law Quarterly* 819, 825

[7] Ibid, para 43.

[8] Ibid, para 81; see also E Roucounas, *Public International Law*, 3rd edn (in Greek; Nomiki Bibliothiki, 2010) 353–54.

of which seem convincing;[9] however, the most important was that when it examined the two elements of a customary rule of international law, namely state practice and *opinio juris*, it drew the conclusion that, although in certain cases the states concerned had agreed the boundaries according to the principle of equidistance, there was no evidence that they considered that they had a legal obligation to do so; thus, the element of *opinio juris* was considered to be missing.[10]

Although the Court accepted that 'no other method of delimitation has the same combination of practical convenience and certainty of application',[11] it considered that 'these factors do not suffice of themselves to convert what is a method into a rule of law'.[12] What is more, the Court went on to add that

> It would however be ignoring realities if it were not noted at the same time that the use of this method, can under certain circumstances produce results that appear on the face of them to be extraordinary, unnatural or unreasonable.[13]

In any case, the Court considered that

> delimitation is to be effected by agreement in accordance with equitable principles, and taking account of all the relevant circumstances, in such a way as to leave as much as possible to each Party all those parts of the continental shelf that constitute a natural prolongation of its land territory into and under the sea, without encroachment on the natural prolongation of the land territory of the other.[14]

Nevertheless, the Court did not make clear which these equitable principles were. It emphasized, however, that 'Equity does not necessarily imply equality. There can never be any question of completely refashioning nature . . .'[15]As to which these relevant circumstances may be, the Court enumerated among the parameters that needed to be examined:

[9] [1969] ICJ Reports paras 48–72. See analytically E Grisel, 'The Lateral Boundaries of the Continental Shelf and the Judgment of the International Court of Justice in the North Sea Continental Shelf Cases' (1970) 64 *American Journal of International Law* 562.

[10] [1969] ICJ Reports para 78. As to the element of *opinio juris* according to the judgment, see KN Guernsey, 'The North Sea Continental Shelf Cases' (2000–01) 27 *Ohio Northern University Law Review* 141.

[11] [1969] ICJ Reports para 23.

[12] Ibid, para 23. See, however, the Dissenting Opinions of Judge ad hoc Sørensen and Judges Lachs, Koretsky, Morelli and Tanaka, who considered that equidistance was customary international law or 'general law', as well as the Separate Opinion of Judge Ammoun, in which he concluded that the equidistance/special circumstances rule was applicable by virtue of equity. For an analysis of the dissenting opinions see JG Merrills, 'Images and Models in the World Court: The Individual Opinions in the North Sea Continental Shelf Cases' (1978) 41 *Modern Law Review* 638.

[13] [1969] ICJ Reports para 25.

[14] Ibid, para 101C.

[15] Ibid. However, the Court has been criticized for deciding in fact *ex aequo et bono*: W Friedmann, 'The North Sea Continental Shelf Cases—A Critique' [1970] 64 *American Journal of International Law* 229, 234; M Miyoshi, 'Considerations of Equity in Maritime Boundary Cases before the International Court of Justice' in N Ando et al (eds), *Liber Amicorum Judge Shigeru Oda* (Kluwer, 2002) 1087, 1101.

> the general configuration of the coasts of the Parties, as well as the presence of any special or unusual features; so far as known or readily ascertainable, the physical and geological structure, and natural resources, of the continental shelf areas involved.

Lastly, it included proportionality between the extent of the continental shelf areas appertaining to the coastal state and the length of its coast measured in the general direction of the coastline.[16] While, as already mentioned, 'special circumstances' function as an exception to the equidistance rule, 'relevant circumstances' are considered to be all those which lead to an equitable delimitation, not only those which function as an exception.[17]

As a conclusion, it could be said that, on the one hand, the Court did not regard equidistance as a rule of customary international law for the delimitation of the continental shelf, and considered that such customary international law constituted a delimitation according to 'equitable principles', while, on the other hand, it dissociated 'special circumstances' from their conventional application in Article 6 as an exception to equidistance and, renaming them 'relevant circumstances', declared that they were to be taken into account in any delimitation of the continental shelf.[18] In this way, it rejected the rule of equidistance as not taking proper account of the special characteristics of a delimitation, although this consideration was the exact reason for the insertion of the 'special circumstances' exception.

B. The 1982 Law of the Sea Convention

During the Third United Nations Conference on the Law of the Sea, when the concept of the EEZ emerged, the proposals for rules to govern the delimitation of the continental shelf and the EEZ were the object of exactly the same disagreements between the supporters of the equidistance principle and the supporters of the equity principle,[19] and for this reason the articles of the 1982 Law of the Sea Convention (LOSC) on the delimitation of the EEZ (Article 74) and of the continental shelf (Article 83) have the same formulation:

> The delimitation of the continental shelf (/exclusive economic zone) between states with opposite or adjacent coasts shall be effected by agreement on the basis of international law, as referred to in Article 38 of the Statute of the International Court of Justice, in order to achieve an equitable solution.

[16] [1969] ICJ Reports para 101D.

[17] C Rozakis, *In Search of Lost Time: The Law of the Continental Shelf in the ICJ Judgment on the Libya/Malta Case* (in Greek; Foundation for Mediterranean Studies, 1989) 78; RR Churchill and AV Lowe, *The Law of the Sea*, 3rd edn (Melland Schill Studies in International Law, 1999) 187.

[18] Ioannou and Strati (n 5 above), 323.

[19] R-J Dupuy and D Vignes (eds), *A Handbook on the New Law of the Sea 1* (Martinus Nijhoff Publishers, 1991) 477; T Scovazzi, 'The Evolution of International Law of the Sea: New Issues, New Challenges (2000) 286 *Recueil des Cours de l'Académie de Droit International* 39, 194, who notes that an effort to lay down clear-cut solutions would have endangered the codification of the law of the sea (ibid, 196).

As these articles are identical and dealt with in the same context, the only conclusion which can be drawn is that the principles and rules of international law on the delimitation of the continental shelf and the EEZ are the same.[20] The purpose was to allow delimitations of both continental shelves and EEZs by a single maritime boundary.[21]

It can be observed that there is no reference to equidistance, which, coupled with the 'special circumstances' clause, is preserved as a conventional rule only in Article 15 LOSC on the delimitation of the territorial sea. However, at the same time, equity is stipulated as the purpose of the delimitation and not as the rule according to which the delimitation is to be effected; moreover, there is no reference to 'equitable principles' or to the notion of 'relevant circumstances',[22] as was the approach of the ICJ in its judgment in the *North Sea Continental Shelf* case.

Given the lack of clarity in Articles 74 and 83 LOSC, the crucial role that case law would play in the development of the rules for the delimitation of maritime zones[23] hardly needs to be emphasized.

III. THE GRADUAL ACCEPTANCE OF THE PRIORITY OF THE EQUIDISTANCE METHOD

It has been observed in theory that the principle of equity,[24] which is the touchstone of the law of maritime delimitation according to Articles 74 and 83 LOSC, is not interpreted in case law in a single way. On the contrary, there are two opposite approaches: on the one hand, the 'autonomous equity', namely the equity which has an autonomous normative function, identifies the delimitation method with the result of the delimitation and rejects the obligatory nature of the equidistance method;[25] on the other hand, the 'corrective equity' which applies the equidistance method initially and subsequently takes into account relevant circumstances, in order to achieve an equitable result.[26]

[20] P Peters and G Tanja, 'Lateral Delimitation of Continental Shelf and Exclusive Economic Zone' [1984] *Il Diritto Maritimo* 472. It is thus clear that the identical text of Arts 74 and 83 LOSC is 'a somewhat emaciated and non-committal compromise text' (ibid, 472). See also L Lucchini and M Vœlckel, *Droit de la Mer*, vol II (Éditions A Pedone, 1996) 85.

[21] Churchill and Lowe (n 17 above), 195.

[22] See also MD Blecher, 'Equitable Delimitation of Continental Shelf' (1979) 73 *American Journal of International Law* 60, 65–66.

[23] Scovazzi (n 19 above), 199.

[24] It should be noted that the origin of the concept of equity can be traced back to Aristotle; see Blecher's critique (n 22 above), 87, on the use of the notion of equity in modern international law.

[25] 'La croisade contre l'équidistance', as Weil has characteristically observed: P Weil, *Perspectives du droit de la délimitation maritime* (Éditions A Pedone, 1988) 216.

[26] Ibid, 179, where Weil refers to 'équité autonome' and 'équité correctrice' respectively. See also MD Evans, *Relevant Circumstances and Maritime Delimitation* (Oxford University Press, 1989) 79–83; Y Tanaka, 'Quelques observations sur deux approches jurisprudentielles en droit de la délimitation maritime: l'affrontement entre prévisibilité et flexibilité' [2004] 2 *Revue Belge de Droit International* 419.

The origin of these approaches can be traced back to two decisions on delimitation of the continental shelf. The first, as has already been mentioned, was the ICJ judgment in the *North Sea Continental Shelf* case, in which the Court emphasized that 'there is no other single method of delimitation the use of which is in all circumstances obligatory'[27] and that consequently 'it is necessary to seek not one method of delimitation but one goal [an equitable solution]'.[28]

On the other hand, the approach of corrective equity can be traced back to the Arbitral Award in the *Case Concerning the Delimitation of the Continental Shelf between the United Kingdom and France (1977)*. Three points need to be emphasized: first of all, the Arbitral Tribunal treated the two elements of Article 6 of the 1958 Geneva Convention, namely equidistance and special circumstances, as a single rule.[29] This was a better approach than the one taken by the ICJ in the *North Sea Continental Shelf* case, which isolated the equidistance rule and ignored its exception; however, the Tribunal did not emphasize the fact that in Article 6 equidistance is the rule and 'special circumstances' its exception. Secondly, it considered that there is little difference between Article 6 and customary international law as enunciated in the *North Sea Continental Shelf* case, namely that a delimitation is to be effected according to equitable principles:

> In short, the role of the 'special circumstances' condition in Article 6 is to ensure an equitable delimitation; and the combined 'equidistance-special circumstances rule', in effect, gives particular expression to a general norm that, failing agreement, the boundary between states abutting on the same continental shelf is to be determined on equitable principles.[30]

Although the delimitation concerned states the coasts of which were opposite one another, it seems that the Arbitral Tribunal did not consider that there was a significant difference between adjacent and opposite coasts.[31] Thirdly, when drawing the delimitation line, the Arbitral Tribunal resorted to the equidistance method, modified so as to take into consideration special circumstances. It stated that

[27] [1969] ICJ Reports para 101B.

[28] Ibid, para 92. See, however, Dissenting Opinion of Judge Koretsky, para 166 and Individual Opinion of Judge Ammoun, para 56.

[29] *Case Concerning the Delimitation of the Continental Shelf between the United Kingdom of Great Britain and Northern Ireland, and the French Republic* (1977) XVIII RIAA 3, para 174.

[30] *UK/France* Arbitral Award 1977, para 70. See also DM McRae, 'Delimitation of the Continental Shelf between the United Kingdom and France: The Channel Arbitration' (1977) 15 *Canadian Yearbook of International Law* 173, 183. Nonetheless, by putting the emphasis on the geographical and other circumstances of each case (*UK/France* Arbitral Award 1977, para 70), the Tribunal, although it had taken the important step of considering Art 6 as customary international law, downgraded to a certain extent the role of equidistance: Weil (n 25 above), 161.

[31] Ibid, para 238. See also DA Colson, 'United Kingdom–France Continental Shelf Arbitration' (1978) 72 *American Journal of International Law* 96, 103.

> in a large proportion of the delimitations known to it, where a particular geographical feature has influenced the course of a continental shelf boundary, the method of delimitation adopted has been some modification or variant of the equidistance principle rather than its total rejection.[32]

Therefore, it seems that, in the end, the Arbitral Tribunal considered the function of equity as a corrective to equidistance.

However, it was mainly two developments that led to the establishment of the equidistance method in maritime delimitations, both related to the emergence of EEZ: (i) the criterion of distance as legal title to maritime zones; and (ii) the preference for a single maritime boundary, for both the continental shelf and the EEZ.

(i) First of all, it should be mentioned that the 'autonomous' notion of equity did not disappear as a result of the 1977 Arbitral Award; on the contrary, it was also supported in the continental shelf delimitation case between Tunisia and Libya (1982).[33] In this case, the ICJ decided that 'the result of the application of equitable principles must be equitable . . . It is however the result which is predominant; the principles are subordinate to the goal'.[34]Apart from the circular character of this statement, one may wonder whether it is possible to draw a delimitation line without specifying a particular method,[35] as well as whether the a priori rejection by the Court of the equidistance method is correct.[36]

Some aspects of the approach which was taken by the ICJ in the *Tunisia/Libya* case were modified by it in the *Libya/Malta* case (1985),[37] in which the applicable law was customary international law. In that case, the Court again refused the obligatory application of the equidistance rule even as a preliminary and provisional step towards the drawing of a delimitation line.[38] However, contrary to the *Tunisia/Libya* case, the Court applied the equidistance method in the delimitation phase when it drew a provisional equidistance line before taking into consideration the principle of proportionality and adjusting it in favour of Libya.[39] It seems that the Court tried to

[32] *UK/France* Arbitral Award 1977, para 249.

[33] *Case Concerning the Continental Shelf (Tunisia/Libyan Arab Jamahiriya)* [1982] ICJ Reports 18, para 110. See also DR Christie, 'From the Shoals of Ras Kaboudia to the Shores of Tripoli: the Tunisia/Libya Continental Shelf Boundary Delimitation' (1983) 13(1) *Georgia Journal of International and Comparative Law* 1, 25, who supports the view that since the Tunisia/Libya Delimitation did not involve opposite states, it cannot be said that the ICJ rejected the theory of the Arbitral Tribunal in the 1977 award between UK and France (ibid, 27).

[34] Ibid, para 70.

[35] [1982] ICJ Rep, Dissenting Opinion of Judge Oda, para 155.

[36] Ibid, Dissenting Opinion of Judge Evensen, para 15; Dissenting Opinion of Judge Gros, paras 11–12.

[37] *Case Concerning the Continental Shelf (Libyan Arab Jamahiriya/Malta)* [1985] ICJ Reports 13.

[38] Ibid, paras 43, 63. See also HL Lawrence, 'The Court Giveth and the Court Taketh Away: An Analysis of the Tunisia–Libya Continental Shelf Case' (1984) 33 International and Comparative Law Quarterly 825, 855–56.

[39] Ibid, para 73.

justify this provisional application of the equidistance method on the ground that the delimitation was between opposite coasts,[40] which differentiated it from the *North Sea Continental Shelf* case and brought it closer to the *UK v France* case. In any event, there was an implicit acceptance of the equidistance method, evidenced by its application as the first step in the delimitation phase.

As to the distance criterion, in the *Libya/Malta* case the Court went even further and established it as the only basis of legal title to the seabed and its subsoil within the limit of 200 nautical miles, in view of the emergence of the EEZ regime.[41] Moreover, it observed a connection between the legal title and the delimitation method:

> It therefore seems logical to the Court that the choice of the criterion and the method which is to employ in the first place to arrive at a provisional result should be made in a manner consistent with the concepts underlying the attribution of legal title.[42]

Thus a neutral, geometrical method, applicable to the delimitation of both maritime zones, was necessary—which was in fact no other than the equidistance line.

Thus, the end of the natural prolongation theory and the prevalence of the distance criterion permitted an important approach between the delimitation of the continental shelf and the EEZ towards the acceptance of the equidistance method as a point of departure in the delimitation process.[43]

(ii) Similarly, when the need for drawing a single boundary for more than one maritime zone arose, initially, in the period between 1984 and 1992, a trend towards the prevalence of the approach of the autonomous equity was observed.

The first case which dealt with the drawing of a single maritime boundary, both for the continental shelf and the fisheries zone, was the *Case Concerning the Delimitation of the Maritime Boundary in the Gulf of Maine Area, between Canada and USA (1984)*.[44] Both Canada and the USA were parties to the 1958 Convention on the Continental Shelf; however, as the delimitation did not concern only the continental shelf, the Chamber of the ICJ decided not to apply the Convention in that case.[45] As far as the applicable rule in such delimitation is concerned, the Chamber enunciated the 'fundamental rule', according to which the maritime delimitation between states with opposite or adjacent coasts must be effected by agreement between them or by recourse to a third party 'by the application of equitable criteria and by the use of practi-

[40] Ibid, para 62.
[41] Ibid, para 33.
[42] Ibid, para 61.
[43] Weil (n 25 above), 108.
[44] *Case Concerning Delimitation of the Maritime Boundary in the Gulf of Maine Area (Canada/United States of America)* [1984] ICJ Reports 246.
[45] Ibid, paras 124–25.

cal methods capable of ensuring, with regard to the geographic configuration of the area and other relevant circumstances, an equitable result'.[46]

As to the practical method of delimitation, the Chamber stated that such a method had to be appropriate both for the seabed and its subsoil and for the superjacent waters,[47] and must therefore be basically founded upon geography. However, it did not accept the application of equidistance as a starting point, which it considered only as a practical method,[48] though again it admitted its advantages.[49] On a practical level, however, it established one of the segments of the single boundary by drawing a provisional equidistance line and by correcting it in a second stage in order to take into consideration, inter alia, the principle of proportionality.[50] In any case, it must be noted that the search for neutral criteria applicable to both maritime zones, based mainly in geography, paved the way for the application of the equally neutral equidistance method in the delimitation of the common maritime boundary.

A similar approach was taken in the arbitral award in the case of *Delimitation of Maritime Boundary between Guinea and Guinea-Bissau (1985)*[51] and in the *Delimitation of Maritime Boundaries between Canada and France (Saint-Pierre et Miquelon case, 1992)*;[52] it should be noted that in the latter case the resulting maritime zone had 'a strange mushroom shape',[53] and was criticized by Professor Weil in his dissenting opinion as not being founded 'on the basis of law'.[54]

[46] Ibid, para 112.

[47] Ibid, para 199.

[48] Ibid, para 106. According to the Chamber 'the most that can be said is that certain methods are easier to apply and that, because of their almost mechanical operation, they are less likely to entail doubts and arouse controversy' (ibid, para 162). Contra Judge Gros, Dissenting Opinion, paras 42–44.

[49] Ibid, para 107.

[50] Ibid, para 222. See also E Decaux, 'L'arrêt de la chambre de la Cour Internationale de Justice sur l' affaire de la délimitation de la frontière maritime dans le Golfe du Maine (Canada/ États-Unis)' (1984) 30 *Annuaire Francais de Droit International* 320; AF Shelley, 'Law of the Sea: Delimitation of the Gulf of Maine' (1985) 26 *Harvard International Law Journal* 650. However, in the latter's opinion, the Chamber furthered the trend towards using equitable principles in delimitation rather than equidistance (ibid, 653).

[51] *Delimitation of the maritime boundary between Guinea and Guinea-Bissau* (1985) XIX RIAA 149; especially paras 88, 102, 111. See also E David. 'La sentence arbitrale du 14 février 1985 sur la délimitation de la frontière maritime Guinée-Guinée Bissau' (1986) 31 *Annuaire Francais de Droit International* 350, 389, who noted the subjectivity of the judgment; KA McLlarky, 'Guinea/Guinea-Bissau: Dispute Concerning Delimitation of the Maritime Boundary' (1987) 11(1) *Maryland Journal of International Law and Commerce* 93, 108.

[52] *Case Concerning the Delimitation of Maritime Areas between Canada and the French Republic* (1992) 31 ILM 1149, paras 24, 38, 40, 66–74.

[53] Ibid, Dissenting Opinion of Judge Weil, para 2. See also L de la Fayette, 'The Award in the Canada–France Maritime Boundary Arbitration' [1993] 8 *International Journal of Marine and Coastal Law* 77, 103, who noted the singularity of the geographical and political circumstances of the case.

[54] Ibid, para 2. See also K Highet 'Delimitation of the Maritime Areas between Canada and France: Court of Arbitration, June 10, 1992' [1993] 87 *American Journal of International Law*, 453, 461.

IV. EMPHASIS ON LEGAL CERTAINTY: TOWARDS THE ACCEPTANCE OF EQUIDISTANCE AS A RULE OF INTERNATIONAL LAW

Subsequently, however, there was a clearer trend in case law towards the establishment of the approach of corrective equity. The starting point of that trend was the ICJ judgment on the *Maritime Delimitation in the Area between Greenland and Jan Mayen (Denmark v Norway, 1993)*.[55] As there was no agreement between Norway and Denmark for the drawing of a single boundary, the Court examined separately the laws applicable in the continental shelf and in the fisheries zone.[56] The applicable law for the former was considered to be Article 6 of the 1958 Convention, as both states were parties to it. In this way, that judgment was differentiated from those in the *Gulf of Maine* and *Saint-Pierre et Miquelon* cases.[57] The Court considered Article 6 to be customary international law,[58] at least for the delimitation of the continental shelf of states the coasts of which are opposite each other:[59]

> If the equidistance-special circumstances rule of the 1958 Convention is, in the light of the 1977 Decision, to be regarded as expressing a general norm based on equitable principles, it must be difficult to find any material difference- at any rate in regard to delimitation between opposite coasts- between the effect of Article 6 and the effect of the customary rule which also requires a delimitation based on equitable principles.

Moreover, it went on to observe that

> Although it is a matter of categories which are different in origin and in name, there is inevitably a tendency towards assimilation between the special circumstances of Article 6 of the 1958 Convention and the relevant circumstances under customary law, and this if only because they both are intended to enable the achievement of an equitable result.[60]

Concerning the law applicable in the fisheries zone, the Court stated that the parties had not raised any objections to the drawing of the delimitation

[55] *Case Concerning Maritime Delimitation in the Area between Greenland and Jan Mayen (Denmark v Norway)* [1993] ICJ Reports 38.

[56] Ibid, para 44.

[57] Ibid, para 51.

[58] Ibid, paras 46, 51. According to MD Evans, 'Maritime Delimitation after Denmark v Norway: Back to the Future?' in GS Goodwin-Gill and S Talmon (eds), *The Reality of International Law: Essays in Honour of Ian Brownlie* (Oxford, 1999) 160, while in the *UK/France* case this reasoning was used in order to place Art 6 in the context of customary law and to justify importing the flexibility of 'equitable principles' into the article, in the *Jan Mayen* case the court used it to justify 'exporting the equidistance method into customary law'. Contra RR Churchill, 'The *Greenland–Jan Mayen* Case and its Significance for the International Law of Maritime Boundary Delimitation' (1994) 9(1) *International Journal of Marine and Coastal Law* 1, 14–16. See also JI Charney, 'Maritime Delimitation in the Area between Greenland and Jan Mayen' (1994) 88 *American Journal of International Law* 105–09.

[59] [1993] ICJ Reports para 46. See also H Dipla, 'Affaire de la délimitation maritime Groenland/Jan Mayen' [1994] 98:4 *Revue Générale de Droit International Public* 899, 909.

[60] [1993] ICJ Reports para 56.

line according to the customary rule governing the EEZ delimitation and, by emphasizing the phrase 'equitable solution' of Article 74, paragraph 1 and Article 83, paragraph 1 LOSC, stated that 'That statement of an "equitable solution" as the aim of any delimitation process reflects the requirements of customary law as regards the delimitation both of continental shelf and of exclusive economic zone'.[61] In the end, the Court drew a provisional equidistance line as a first step, which it subsequently modified in order to take into account eventual relevant circumstances,[62] such as proportionality and fair access to fisheries resources.[63]

This approach was also followed in subsequent cases in which the delimitation of single maritime boundaries for the territorial seas, continental shelves and EEZs was sought, for example in the maritime delimitation case between Eritrea and Yemen (1999),[64] in which the Arbitral Tribunal implied that this method derives its legal character from examination of the state practice and case-law.

However, it was the case concerning maritime delimitation between Qatar and Bahrain (2001)[65] which offered the Court the opportunity to bring about an important development in the law of maritime delimitation. It was the first time that the Court was asked to draw a single maritime boundary in accordance with customary international law. First of all, it should be noted that neither Bahrain nor Qatar was a party to the 1958 Convention on the Continental Shelf and LOSC was not applicable law. However, it was accepted that Articles 74 and 83 LOSC were customary international law.[66] Moreover, the Court accepted for the first time in its jurisprudence the application of equidistance as customary international law in the maritime delimitation between states the coasts of which are adjacent, as well as the equation of the applicable law in the delimitation of the territorial sea with the applicable law in the continental shelf and EEZ:

> The Court further notes that the equidistance/special circumstances rule, which is applicable in particular to the delimitation of the territorial sea, and the equitable principles/relevant circumstances rule, as it has been developed since 1958 in case-law and state practice with regard to the delimitation of the continental shelf and the exclusive economic zone, are closely interrelated.[67]

[61] Ibid, para 48.

[62] Ibid, para 53.

[63] Ibid, paras 87, 91–92. See also AG Oude Elferink, 'Maritime Delimitation between Denmark/Greenland and Norway' (2007) 38(4) *Ocean Development and International Law* 375.

[64] *Eritrea–Yemen Arbitration (Award, Phase II, Maritime Delimitation)* (1999), available at http://www.pca-cpa.org. See MD Evans, 'The Maritime Delimitation between Eritrea and Yemen' (2001) 14(1) *Leiden Journal of International Law* 141.

[65] *Maritime Delimitation and Territorial Questions (Qatar v Bahrain)* [2001] ICJ Reports 40.

[66] Ibid, para 167.

[67] Ibid, para 231. See also E Decaux, 'Affaire de la délimitation maritime et des questions territoriales entre Qatar et Bahrein' (2002) 47 *Annuaire Francais de Droit International* 177, 235.

Thus, with this judgment the law of maritime delimitation entered a phase of stabilization, at least with regard to the techniques it uses.[68]

This approach was confirmed by the ICJ in the case concerning the maritime delimitation between Cameroun and Nigeria (2002).[69] It is interesting that the Court noted that

> delimiting with a concern to achieving an equitable result, as required by current international law, is not the same as delimiting in equity. The Court's jurisprudence shows that, in disputes relating to maritime delimitation, equity is not a method of delimitation, but solely an aim that should be borne in mind in effecting the delimitation'.[70]

The same approach was followed in principle by international courts and tribunals in subsequent cases. In the *Barbados/Trinidad and Tobago maritime delimitation* case (2006),[71] the Arbitral Tribunal took a clear position in favour of the priority of equidistance in maritime delimitations, emphasizing its advantages and considered that 'a different method would require a well-founded justification'.[72] In the case concerning the delimitation of the maritime boundary between Guyana and Suriname (2007),[73] contrary to other cases, neither party considered that the provisional equidistance line constituted an equitable delimitation as required by international law, due to the geographical circumstances of the maritime area to be delimited;[74] nevertheless, the Tribunal effected the delimitation according to equidistance.

A departure from this trend may be observed in the ICJ judgment in the *Case Concerning Territorial and Maritime Dispute between Nicaragua and Honduras in the Caribbean Sea (Nicaragua v Honduras, 2007)*,[75] in which the Court stated that the equidistance method 'does not automatically have priority over other methods of delimitation and, in particular circumstances, there may be factors which make the application of the equidistance method

[68] Roucounas (n 8 above), 364.

[69] *Land and Maritime Boundary between Cameroon and Nigeria case (Cameroon v Nigeria; Equatorial Guinea intervening)* [2002] ICJ Reports 303. See also PHF Bekker, 'Land and Maritime Boundary between Cameroon and Nigeria' (2003) 97 *American Journal of International Law* 387; Y Tanaka, 'Reflections on Maritime Delimitation in the Cameroon/Nigeria Case' (2004) 53(3) *International & Comparative Law Quarterly* 369, 388; B Kwiatkowska, 'The Contribution of the 2002 (Cameroon v Nigeria: Equatorial Guinea Intervening) Land and Maritime Boundary between Cameroon and Nigeria Judgment of the International Court of Justice to Equitable Maritime Boundary Delimitation' (2005) 17 *Hague Yearbook of International Law* 95, 111–12.

[70] [2002] ICJ Reports para 294.

[71] *Arbitration between Barbados and The Republic of Trinidad and Tobago* (2006), available at http://www.pca-cpa.org.

[72] Ibid, para 306, mentioning also *Newfoundland v Nova Scotia*, Award of the Tribunal in the Second Phase, 26 March 2002, para 2.28.

[73] *Arbitration between Guyana and Suriname* (2007), available at www.pca-cpa.org, paras 342,352, 357, 377, 392.

[74] Award 2007, para 373.

[75] *Case Concerning Territorial and Maritime Dispute between Nicaragua and Honduras in the Caribbean Sea (Nicaragua v Honduras)* [2007] ICJ Reports 659.

inappropriate'.[76] However, it is notable that in that case the ICJ applied the bisector 'the line formed by bisecting the angle created by the linear approximation of coastlines' as a substitute method only after finding it 'impossible for the Court to identify base points and construct a provisional equidistance line . . . delimiting maritime areas off the Parties' mainland coasts'.[77] Indeed, it stated that in such a case 'the bisector method may be seen as an approximation of the equidistance method'.[78] This judgment has been criticized, as the view could be supported that the difficulty of identifying base points is not insurmountable, and in any case it undermines the predictability of the law of maritime delimitation.[79]

Nonetheless, the prevalence of equidistance was soon confirmed by recent decisions of international courts and tribunals. In the *Maritime Delimitation in the Black Sea case (Romania v Ukraine, 2009)*,[80] the Court, after having identified the relevant coasts, applied a three-stage methodology by drawing a provisional equidistance line between the adjacent and opposite coasts of the parties, making adjustments based on relevant circumstances in order to achieve an equitable result and assessing it on the basis of proportionality.[81]

More recently, in the *Delimitation of the Maritime Boundary between Bangladesh and Myanmar in the Bay of Bengal (2012)*,[82] the International Tribunal for the Law of the Sea (ITLOS), in its first maritime delimitation case and the first decision delimiting the continental shelf beyond 200 nautical miles,[83] noted that jurisprudence had developed in favour of the equidistance/relevant

[76] Ibid, para 272.

[77] Ibid, paras 280, 287.

[78] Ibid, para 287.

[79] Separate Opinion Judge Ranjeva, para 10; Dissenting Opinion of Judge Torres Bernárdez, para 128. See analytically Y Tanaka, 'Reflections on Maritime Delimitation in the Nicaragua/Honduras Case' (2008) 68(4) *Zeitschrift für ausländisches öffentliches Recht und Völkerrecht* 903, 928–31, 932–34.

[80] *Maritime Delimitation in the Black Sea case (Romania v Ukraine)* [2009] ICJ Reports 61.

[81] Ibid, paras 115–22. It is notable that the decision of the court in this respect was unanimous. See also CG Lathrop, 'Maritime Delimitation in the Black Sea' [2009] 103 *American Journal of International Law* 543; A Oude Elferink, 'Maritime Delimitation in the Black Sea' (The Hague Justice Portal), available at www.haguejusticeportal.net, 1–4; Y Tanaka, 'Reflections on Maritime Delimitation in the Romania/Ukraine Case before the International Court of Justice' (2009) *Netherlands International Law Review* 397, 419–20, who noted that the three-stage methodology was a variation of the corrective equity approach developed through jurisprudence; N Oral, 'International Court of Justice: Case Concerning Maritime Delimitation in the Black Sea (Romania v Ukraine)' (2010) 25(1) *International Journal of Marine and Coastal Law* 115.

[82] *Dispute Concerning Delimitation of the Maritime Boundary between Bangladesh and Myanmar in the Bay of Bengal (Bangladesh/Myanmar) (Judgment of 14 March 2012)* ITLOS Rep 2012. See I Konstantinidis, 'Dispute Settlement in the Law of the Sea, the Extended Continental Shelf in the Bay of Bengal and the CLCS: Some Preliminary Observations on the Basis of the Case Bangladesh/Myanmar before the International Tribunal for the Law of the Sea' (2011) 1(2) *Aegean Review of the Law of the Sea and Maritime Law* 267.

[83] Thus, apart from the concavity and the role of geology, a similarity of the ITLOS Decision with the *North Sea Continental Shelf* case was that the judge had to exercise 'law-making' functions in the absence of judicial precedent. See I Papanicolopulu, 'From the North Sea to the Bay of Bengal: Maritime Delimitation at the International Tribunal for the Law of the Sea' (23 March 2012), available at www.ejiltalk.org.

circumstances method[84] and followed the three-stage approach of the *Black Sea* case,[85] although Bangladesh had argued that, because of the specific configuration of its coast in the northern part of the Bay of Bengal, the Tribunal should apply the angle-bisector method.[86] Furthermore, in the view of the Tribunal, the delimitation method to be employed for the continental shelf beyond 200 nautical miles should not differ from that within 200 nautical miles and that, accordingly, the equidistance/relevant circumstances method continued to apply for the delimitation of the continental shelf beyond 200 nautical miles.[87] Therefore the ITLOS decision dispersed any fears of fragmentation of international law on maritime delimitation.[88]

Lastly, in both the maritime delimitation case between Nicaragua and Colombia (2012)[89] and that between Peru and Chile (2014)[90] the applicable law was customary international law, and the Court applied its three-stage methodology[91]—in the case between Peru and Chile, beyond the point determined by agreement between the parties.[92] The language used by the Court in the latter case is notable: at the first stage, it states that it will construct a provisional equidistance line 'unless there are *compelling reasons* preventing that', while at the third stage it states that a disproportionality test is conducted in order to assess 'whether the effect of the line . . . is such that the Parties' respective shares of the relevant area are *markedly disproportionate* to the lengths of their relevant coasts'.[93] Although the equidistance line determined only a part of the maritime boundary between the parties, it seems that the language used by the ICJ in favour of the equidistance line is stronger than in previous cases.[94]

[84] ITLOS Rep 2012, para 238.

[85] Ibid, para 240.

[86] Ibid, paras 292–93, 323–29. See also Joint Declaration of Judges ad hoc Mensah and Oxman, as well as the Joint Declaration of Judges Nelson, Chandrasekhara Rao and Cot, according to whom 'considerations of equity come into play only in the second phases of the delimitation, as they necessarily carry an important element of subjectivity'. Contra Dissenting Opinion Judge Lucky, 54–55. See, however, DH Anderson 'Delimitation of the Maritime Boundary in the Bay of Bengal (Bangladesh/Myanmar)' [2012] 106 *American Journal of International Law* 817, who supports the view that, while the Tribunal drew the equidistance line provisionally, when it adjusted it, it appeared to have adopted a different method, namely the azimuth of 215° proposed by Bangladesh as an angle bisector (ibid, 823); similarly Separate Opinion Gao, paras 53 et seq; Separate Opinion Cot, 7–9.

[87] Ibid, paras 454–55.

[88] Judge Treves, Declaration, para 2; Papanicolopulu (n 83 above).

[89] *Territorial and Maritime Dispute (Nicaragua v Colombia)* [2012] ICJ Reports 624.

[90] *Maritime Dispute (Peru v Chile)* [2014] ICJ Reports 3.

[91] [2012] ICJ Reports paras 199, 211, 216, 232.

[92] *Peru v Chile* (n 90 above), para 180.

[93] Ibid, emphasis added.

[94] See, however, the Separate (partly concurring and partly dissenting) Opinion of Judge ad hoc Orrego Vicuña (paras 28 and 34), who considered that the court in that case had not applied equity *infra legem*, as was the understanding of 1982 UNCLOS with regard to Art 74, para 1 (paras 35–37).

V. CONCLUSION

The delimitation of the continental shelf and the EEZ are the most disputed issues in the international law of the sea.[95] The law of maritime delimitation can be seen as a succession of two contrary approaches which aim to achieve an equitable solution.[96] The approach of 'autonomous' equity, which does not accept the primacy of the equidistance method, aims to ensure greater flexibility, whereas the approach of 'corrective' equity, according to which the equidistance method has to be applied in the first stage of the delimitation process and may be adjusted when this is required by relevant circumstances, aims at legal certainty. Although, in the beginning, jurisprudence tended to prefer the approach of 'corrective' equity in maritime delimitations between states with opposing coasts and the approach of 'autonomous' equity in maritime delimitations between states with adjacent coasts, since the judgments in the maritime delimitation cases between Qatar and Bahrain and between Cameroon and Nigeria, international courts and tribunals have accepted equidistance as the starting point even for delimitations between states with adjacent coasts. Thus, similarly to state practice, which is not, however, always consistent,[97] the law of maritime delimitation was developed by jurisprudence from the coexistence of the two rules in the context of LOSC—namely, the 'equidistance/special circumstances' rule, which was stipulated for the delimitation of the territorial sea, and the 'equity/relevant circumstances', rule which was stipulated for the delimitation of the continental shelf and EEZ[98]—towards their unification[99] in the approach of the equidistance/relevant circumstances rule.

Thus, equidistance can be seen as constituting the central concept of maritime delimitation and means more than just its practical advantages, namely its simplicity and its prima facie equitable character:[100] it is not only a method, but also has the value of a legal rule.[101] In any event, in most maritime delimitation decisions, the international courts or the arbitral tribunals have

[95] Scovazzi (n 19 above), 194.

[96] Tanaka (n 26 above), 454.

[97] See Tanaka (n 26 above), 448–49. See also Churchill and Lowe (n 17 above), 197; and analytically JI Charney and LM Alexander (eds), *International Maritime Boundaries*, vols I–V (Martinus Nijhoff, 1991, 1997, 2002, 2005).

[98] JP Quéneudec, 'Les Principes dégagés par le Juge et le Rôle des Circonstances Pertinentes en matière de Délimitation Maritime' in *Le Processus de Délimitation Maritime, Étude d'un Cas Fictif* (Colloque, 2003) 282.

[99] See Speech by His Excellency Judge Gilbert Guillaume, President of the International Court of Justice to the Sixth Committee of the General Assembly of the United Nations, 31 October 2001, 8–9; Quéneudec (ibid), 283; C Rozakis, 'The Greek Continental Shelf' in H Dipla and C Rozakis (eds), *Law of the Sea and its Application in Greece* (in Greek; I Sideris Publications, 2004) 224; L Lucchini, 'Le Contentieux de la Délimitation Maritime et l' Apport de la Jurisprudence' in *Le Plateau Continental dans ses Rapports avec la Zone Économique Exclusive* (Symposium International de Meknès, 2005) 28–29.

[100] Weil (n 25 above), 86; Lucchini-Vœlckel (n 20 above), vol II, 152–53.

[101] Weil (n 25 above), 302.

emphasized the role of jurisprudence for the purpose of ascertaining the rules of international law which govern the subject of maritime delimitation.[102] Judge Jennings has also described the law of maritime delimitation as 'judge-made law',[103] and Weil has stated that

> La conquête de la délimitation maritime par le droit n'est en fin de compte l'œuvre ni de la convention ni de la coutume, mais celle de la jurisprudence qui, loin d'apparaître comme une source subsidiaire du droit international, remplit ici la mission d'une source primaire et directe de droit, même si elle a choisi modestement d'en porter le credit au compte du droit coutumier.[104]

Indeed, the case law on maritime delimitations constitutes the richest contribution of the ICJ to the law of the sea, its impact consisting, on the one hand, in the clarification of rules and principles of delimitation and, on the other hand, in the unification of the rules on the delimitation of all maritime zones.[105] Thus, it might be claimed that the choice of the drafters of LOSC to leave Articles 74 and 83 vague led to the progressive development of specific methods of delimitation into rules of international law by the jurisprudence of international courts and tribunals.[106]

[102] [1984] ICJ Reports para 83; [1985] ICJ Reports para 29; [1993] ICJ Reports paras 54-55; Award 1999, para 132; [2001] ICJ Reports para 231; Award 2006, para 222; Award 2007, paras 335, 342; ITLOS Rep 2012, paras 225–26; [2012] ICJ Reports para 114; [2014] ICJ Reports paras 179–80.

[103] RY Jennings, 'What is International Law and How Do We Tell It When We See It?' (XXXVII Annuaire Suisse de Droit International, 1981) 59, 68. See also JJ Quintana, 'The International Court of Justice and the Formulation of General International Law: The Law of Maritime Delimitation as an Example' in AS Muller et al (eds), *The International Court of Justice: Its Future Role after Fifty Years* (Martinus Nijhoff, 1997) 373; Scovazzi (n 19 above), 194; L Lucchini, 'La Délimitation des Frontières Maritimes' in R Lagoni and D Vignes (eds), *Maritime Delimitation* (Martinus Nijhoff, 2006) 1, 8–9; Declaration of Judge Wolfrum in the *Bangladesh/Myanmar* case. The reasons for such an approach have been identified by Sir Hersch Lauterpacht in his classic work: H Lauterpacht, *The Development of International Law by the International Court* (Cambridge University Press, 1958]).

[104] Weil (n 25 above), 13. See also Lucchini-Vœlckel (n 20 above), vol II, 199, where there is reference to 'fonction "normative" du juge'; Ioannou and Strati (n 5 above), 325; H Thirlway, 'Judicial Activism and the International Court of Justice' in Liber Amicorum Oda (n 15 above), 75–105.

[105] See also FO Vicuña, 'The Role of the International Court of Justice and Other Tribunals in the Development of the Law of Maritime Delimitation' in *Implementation of the Law of the Sea Convention through International Institutions, Proceedings of the Law of the Sea Institute Annual Conference*, vol 23 (1990) 601–25; RR Churchill, 'The Role of the International Court of Justice in Maritime Boundary Delimitation' in AG Oude Elferink and DR Rothwell (eds), *Oceans Management in the 21st Century: Institutional Frameworks and Responses* (Martinus Nijhoff Publishers, 2004) 125–42; H Dipla, 'The Role of the ICJ and ITLOS in the Law of the Sea' in A Strati, M Gavouneli and N Skourtos (eds), *Unresolved Issues and New Challenges to the Law of the Sea* (Martinus Nijhoff Publishers, 2006) 235, 237.

[106] Scovazzi (n 19 above), 199, who considers them as rules of customary international law. See also Quintana (n 103 above), 378–79; N Ros, 'Les méthodes jurisdictionnelles de délimitation maritime' in RC Raigón and G Cataldi (eds), *L'évolution et l'état actuel du droit international de la mer: mélanges de droit de la mer offerts à Daniel Vignes* (Bruylant, 2009) 798; A Pellet, 'Article 38' in A Zimmermann et al (eds), *The Statute of the International Court of Justice—A Commentary* (Oxford University Press, 2012) 865–66.

Consequently, the fundamental issue of the law of maritime delimitation remains how to strike a balance between legal certainty, which is ensured through the application of equidistance, and flexibility, which is ensured through taking into account relevant circumstances. However, there is a trend in international case law which implies that this balance is ensured if equidistance is accepted as a rule of international law that may only be adjusted if relevant circumstances so require.

18

Collective Responsibility for Water in Central Asia

MINDIA VASHAKMADZE*

I. INTRODUCTION

WATER CONFLICTS IN Central Asia have deep historical and socioeconomic roots. After the collapse of the Soviet Union in 1991, the central system of water management disintegrated. The five Central Asian states—Kazakhstan, Kyrgyzstan, Uzbekistan, Turkmenistan and Tajikistan—need to share water resources from two major rivers flowing into the Aral Sea, Syr Darya and Amu Darya. However, there is an asymmetric regional distribution of water. The downstream countries—Uzbekistan, Kazakhstan and Turkmenistan—are dependent on water from Tajikistan and Kyrgyzstan. Most of the Syr Darya water is located within the borders of Kyrgyzstan and most of the Amu Darya is within the territory of Tajikistan. The water resources of Amu Darya and Syr Darya play a crucial role in the economic development and water supply of the entire region. However, the existing water management and irrigation systems seem to be largely outdated, and water is not used efficiently.[1] Population growth and the lack of capacity to build new water infrastructure makes access to enough safe water more questionable in the long run.[2] The shrinking of the Aral Sea, which was the result of Soviet planning and is one of the worst man-made disasters in history, has triggered considerable changes in climate conditions and has had a very negative impact on the overall environment in the region.[3] Water also

* Senior Research Fellow, Max Planck Foundation for International Peace and the Rule of Law.

[1] See, eg World Bank, 'Water Energy Nexus in Central Asia—Improving Regional Cooperation in the Syr Darya Basin' (January 2004) para 28: 'In the water sector, irrigation efficiencies have to be improved substantially . . . only 21% of the water is actually used and 79% is lost'.

[2] International Crisis Group, 'Water Pressures in Central Asia', Europe and Central Asia Report No 233 (11 September 2014) 13–17; 'Central Asian States Are World's Leading Water Wasters', available at http://www.eurasianet.org/node/70336 (last accessed on 7 October 2014).

[3] The Aral Sea was the fourth largest inland sea in the world until 1960. Syr Darya and Amu Darya supply the Aral Sea basin with water. The Soviet planners, pursuing the goal of transform-

plays a role in enduring border disputes in the Fergana Valley.[4] The International Crisis Group observed that 'Water is nearly always an element in such conflicts, whether as prime cause or conflict multiplier'.[5]

Disputes relating to the use of Syr Darya and Amu Darya remain unresolved.[6] The upstream countries (Kyrgyzstan and Tajikistan) are keen to use water to generate more hydroelectric power and attain energy self-sufficiency, while there is a need for summer irrigation in the downstream countries such as Uzbekistan and Kazakhstan (where irrigation is essential for agriculture, especially for the water-intense production of cotton). Tajikistan and Kyrgyzstan are pursuing larger energy and water projects[7] without an agreement being reached between all concerned riparian states. In particular, Uzbekistan and Kazakhstan are opposed to the construction of two large hydropower dams—Rogun in Tajikistan and Kambara-Ata in Kyrgyzstan.[8] To reduce their dependence on the upstream countries, they have developed plans to build large water reservoirs, causing further environmental concerns.[9] Thus, the states are largely focused on ensuring their 'self-sufficiency in water and energy' and pursuing 'extremely costly solutions instead of adhering to the mutual interdependence of the water system'.[10]

Although the Central Asian governments often refer to international law as an important tool for conflict resolution,[11] they have so far been unable to use the potential of this body of law to accommodate their conflicting interests. On the contrary, the riparian states are 'engaged in strategies of resource

ing the Central Asian deserts into flourishing agricultural lands, extensively diverted water from Syr Darya and Amu Darya for irrigation purposes, underestimating its long-term environmental consequences. Today, it will require consolidated international efforts to save the remaining shrinking sea. For further information see the website of the Executive Committee of the International Fund for Saving the Aral Sea at http://www.ec-ifas.org/ (last accessed on 17 January 2014).

[4] As the International Crisis Group states: 'Kyrgyzstan, Tajikistan and Uzbekistan share 3,681 km of borders, of which 961 km are disputed', Water Pressures in Central Asia (n 2 above), 9.

[5] Ibid, 10.

[6] B Pannier, 'Battle Lines Drawn in Central Asian Water Dispute', available at http://www.rferl.org/content/Battle_Lines_Being_Drawn_In_Central_Asian_Water_Dispute/1611679.html (last accessed on 28 January 2014).

[7] Rogun and Sangtuda dam projects in Tajikistan; Kambarata 1 and 2 hydroplant projects in Kyrgyzstan; the Golden Century Lake in the Kara-Kum desert in Turkmenistan.

[8] See, eg R Russel and A Erkebayev, 'Kyrgyzstan Risks Regional Water Fight, as Russia Waits in the Wings', available at http://www.washingtontimes.com/news/2012/nov/9/kyrgyzstan-risks-regional-water-fight-russia-waits/?page=all (last accessed on 14 January 2014).

[9] For example, there have been concerns in recent years that the construction of the Koksarai reservoir in Southern Kazakhstan would hinder Syr Darya's natural flow into the Aral Sea and also threaten historical monuments in the area.

[10] E Weinthal, 'Water Conflict and Cooperation in Central Asia', Human Development Report Office Occasional Paper 32 (2006) 15, discussing the Syr Daria riparian countries.

[11] See, eg the web page of the Ministry of Foreign Affairs of the Republic of Uzbekistan at http://mfa.uz/en/cooperation/aral/1406/ (last accessed on 3 October 2014). It states that Uzbekistan's position is based on the norms of international law, referring to the UNECE Convention of 1992 and the UN Watercourses Convention of 1997. However, it also emphasizes that 'Uzbekistan firmly adhere to the principle position of unacceptability of constructing hydropower facilities at the international watercourses without a preliminary endorsement by all interested countries'.

capture, by increasing their water demand without renegotiating the official agreements'.[12] The relations between Uzbekistan, Kyrgyzstan and Tajikistan are especially tense.[13] Uzbekistan periodically uses political and economic pressure on its neighbours; for example, it cut off gas deliveries to Tajikistan in 2012 and to Kyrgyzstan in 2014;[14] the Uzbek president has repeatedly warned of possible water wars in the region.[15]

Thus, the Central Asian water disputes are inextricably linked to the existing energy, agricultural and environmental controversies, as well as population growth, climate change and border conflicts. There remains potential for further, more difficult, water controversies.[16] This situation has already attracted attention of the international community.[17] However, its role remains limited.

The present chapter explores the Central Asian water controversies from an international law perspective. It argues that an increasing interdependence between the states as well as water scarcity, conflicting uses of water resources and, most importantly, their environmental and human consequences need to be addressed through enhanced cooperation. A number of questions arise in this context: how are the responsibilities for shared water resources distributed? What is the content of the obligation to cooperate? What factors induce the states to cooperate more effectively? How should the conflicts between different uses of water resources be resolved? How and to what extent are environmental and human concerns to be taken into account in the resolution of water conflicts? Does international law require an improvement in internal water management capabilities? What role do third parties play in resolving water disputes? This chapter cannot answer all these questions in a comprehensive manner; rather, it sketches relevant legal issues and attempts to enhance the basis for further, more detailed, analyses. It briefly discusses the existing legal framework for shared water management in Central Asia and emphasizes its overall ineffectiveness. It further examines whether general international law can offer some guidance to the Central Asian states in their future water sharing arrangements and cooperation strategies. It demonstrates that principles of international law may serve as a basis for designing regional water arrangements. However, they do not establish a specific frame-

[12] R Wegerich, 'Hydro-hegemony in the Amu Darya Basin' (2008) 10 *Water Policy* 71, 86.

[13] J Lillis, 'Kazakhstan and Kyrgyzstan in War of Words over Water', available at http://www.eurasianet.org/node/67317 (last accessed on 17 January 2014). 'Dammed If They Do', available at http://www.economist.com/node/21563764 (last accessed on 28 January 2014).

[14] International Crisis Group (n 2 above), 20–22.

[15] J Lilis, 'Uzbekistan Leader Warns of Water Wars in Central Asia', available at http://www.eurasianet.org/node/65877 (last accessed on 17 January 2014). See also R Nurshayeva, 'Uzbek Leader Sounds Warning Over Central Asia Water Disputes', available at http://www.reuters.com/article/2012/09/07/centralasia-water-idUSL6E8K793I20120907 (last accessed on 17 January 2014).

[16] See also Water Pressures in Central Asia (n 2 above).

[17] 'Ban Outlines UN Role in Resolving Central Asian Tensions Over Water Resources', available at http://www.un.org/apps/news/story.asp?NewsID=34291#.UT2iDzs7- (last accessed on 22 January 2014); 'Commending World Bank's Support of Tajikistan in Tackling Energy Challenges, Secretary-General Encourages Water Management Agreement in Central Asia', available at http://www.un.org/News/Press/docs/2012/sgsm14491.doc.htm (last accessed on 17 January 2014).

work for cooperation. Finally, the chapter concludes that Central Asian states bear collective responsibility for creating favourable conditions for a sustainable resolution of water controversies through regional cooperation.

II. LEGAL AND INSTITUTIONAL FRAMEWORK

Among the Central Asian states, only Uzbekistan has acceded to the 1997 UN Convention on the Law of Non-navigational Uses of International Watercourses,[18] which entered into force in 2014 and constitutes the most authoritative statement of the law of international watercourses[19] (Uzbekistan also ratified the 1992 UNECE Convention on the Protection and Use of Transboundary Watercourses and International Lakes[20]). However, the Central Asian states have concluded international agreements dealing with shared water resources at bilateral as well as regional level.[21] One of the central legal instruments concluded at the regional level constitutes the 1992 Almaty Agreement between the Republic of Kazakhstan, the Kyrgyz Republic, the Republic of Tajikistan, and the Republic of Uzbekistan on Cooperation in the Field of Joint Management of the Use and Conservation of Water Resources (the Almaty Agreement).[22] Article 1 of the Almaty Agreement states: 'Recognizing community and unity of the region's water resources, Parties have equal rights for their use and responsibility for their rational use and protection'.[23] On the basis of the Almaty Agreement, the Interstate Commission of Water Coordination (ICWC) was created.[24] It consists of the heads of the national water management authorities and facilitates regional water cooperation.

[18] The date of accession is 4 September 2007.

[19] ILM 36 (1997), 700. See Salman MA, 'The Future of International Water Law: Regional Approaches to Shared Watercourses?' in MH Arsanjani et al (eds), *Looking to the Future: Essays on International Law in Honor of W Michael Reisman* (Brill, 2011) 928: 'The wide range of endorsements of the Watercourse Convention, particularly of the International Court of Justice, is a clear recognition of the role and place of the Convention. Thus, it can be concluded that the Watercourse Convention has codified and progressively developed the principles of international water law, and it has become the principle authoritative instrument in this field.'

[20] UN Economic Commission for Europe (UNECE), Convention on the Protection and Use of Transboundary Watercourses and International Lakes (UNECE Helsinki Convention) (entered into force 6 October 1996) ILM 31 (1992) 1312.

[21] D Ziganshina, 'Procedural System of Transboundary Water Cooperation in the Aral Sea Basin' in A Kibaroglu, AJ Kirschner, S Mehring and R Wolfrum (eds), *Water Law and Cooperation in the Euphrates–Tigris Region: A Comparative and Interdisciplinary Approach* (2013) 283–86. See also L Boisson de Chazournes, 'The Aral Sea Basin: Legal and Institutional Aspects of Governance' in M Finger et al (eds), *The Multi-governance of Water: Four Case Studies* (2006) 147–71.

[22] Agreement between the Republic of Kazakhstan, the Kyrgyz Republic, the Republic of Tajikistan, Turkmenistan and the Republic of Uzbekistan on Cooperation in the Field of Joint Management of the Use and Conservation of Water Resources of Interstate Sources (signed 18 February 1992), available at http://www.icwc-aral.uz/statute1.htm (unofficial English translation) (last accessed on 17 January 2014).

[23] Ibid.

[24] For more information see http://www.icwc-aral.uz/ (last accessed on 17 January 2014).

The Almaty Agreement determines the competencies of the Commission[25] and requires states to exchange information concerning 'scientific-technical progress in water-economy, complex use and protection of water resources, common research carrying out for scientific-technical provision and expertise of water related projects'.[26]

There have been several attempts to institutionalize the water–energy link in Central Asia and to reconcile the conflicting needs of the states in more specific terms.[27] On 17 March 1998, Kyrgyzstan, Uzbekistan and Kazakhstan concluded an international treaty to arrange optimal water sharing for Syr Darya,[28] which imposes an obligation on Kyrgyzstan to release more water in summertime to be used for irrigation by downstream Uzbekistan and Kazakhstan. In return, these two countries, which are rich in oil and gas, have to pay for hydroelectricity, putting Kyrgyzstan in a position to buy oil and coal supplies from them in the winter.[29] Tajikistan also joined this agreement, which offered incentives for parties based on their respective capabilities and interests.[30] However, the agreement has not achieved its purpose—the cooperation between the states proved unsustainable because of disputes over the pricing of the electricity, coal and oil, and the lack of effective information and data sharing. In addition, the states failed to elaborate a functioning regional arrangement based on mutual interests and gains.[31]

Observers have argued that 'a credible, institutionalized and legitimate inter-

[25] Above n 22, Arts 8–11.

[26] Ibid, Art 5.

[27] On this and other related issues see also S Kushkumbayev and A Kushkumbayeva, 'Water and Energy Issues in the Context of International and Political Disputes in Central Asia', 12 (2013)*Chinese Journal of International Law* 211.

[28] Agreement between the Governments of the Republic of Kazakhstan, the Kyrgyz Republic, and the Republic of Uzbekistan on the Use of Water and Energy Resources of the Syr Darya Basin, 17 March 1998; the English translation is available at www.ce.utexas.edu/prof/mckinney/papers/aral/agreements/SyrDaryaAgr-Mar17-98.pdf (last accessed on 23 January 2014).

[29] Ibid, Art IV: 'The Naryn-Syr Darya excess power emanating from the release mode utilized on the Naryn-Syr Darya during the growing season, and the Toktogul multi-year regulated flows that exceed the needs of the Kyrgyz Republic, will be transferred to the republics of Kazakhstan and Uzbekistan in equal portions. Compensation shall be made in equivalent amounts of energy resources, such as coal, gas, electricity and fuel oil, and the rendering of other types of products (labor, services), or in monetary terms as agreed upon, for annual and multi-year water irrigation storage in the reservoirs. A single tariff policy for all types of energy resources and their transportation shall be applied for mutual settlements.'

[30] On so-called mutual gains agreements see A Grzybowski, SC McCaffrey and RK Paisly, 'Beyond International Water Law: Successfully Negotiating Mutual Gains Agreements for International Watercourses' 22 (2010) *Pacific McGeorge Global Business & Development Law Journal* 139.

[31] The World Bank Report of 2004 (para 12) stated that 'the Long Term Framework Agreement of 1998 needs to be modified to incorporate: (a) a multi-year (minimum of 10 years) perspective; and (b) explicit recognition of the obligation of the downstream riparian states to pay for the annual and multi-year water storage services, which the upstream country is obliged to provide at significant costs to its economy. This is needed to ensure equitable distribution of benefits arising from water use. The modification should also provide for a more effective mechanism for resolving disputes and disagreements adopting perhaps international arbitration procedures' (n 1 above).

preter of the rule's meaning in various instances' is missing.[32] A discussion paper on 'Strengthening the Institutional and Legal Frameworks of the International Fund for Saving the Aral Sea', issued on 31 January 2010 by UNECE, concludes that:

> despite the large number of international agreements, the current legal framework is far from perfect and requires considerable improvement. This applies to both the individual agreements and the entire system of international legal regulation of water cooperation in the region. The existing legal instruments are either of a formal or declarative nature, or simply out-dated, or are not being implemented—in whole and in part—and do not contain fully effective mechanisms to ensure compliance.[33]

It can thus be maintained that the legal framework that was created after the collapse of the Soviet Union remains somewhat fragmented; it has not proved to be a tool for effective cooperation. However, improving this legal framework does not seem to be an easy task. The states have different views not only with respect to the reasonable use of water resources, but also with respect to a possible strengthening of the institutional and legal framework for a more efficient water management.[34]

III. THE RULE OF EQUITABLE AND REASONABLE UTILIZATION

As early as 1929, the Permanent Court of International Justice emphasized that 'the community of interests in a navigable river becomes the basis of a common legal right, the essential features of which are the perfect equality of all riparian states in the use of the whole course of the river'.[35] The International Court of Justice (ICJ), referring to this principle, states in its *Gabčíkovo-Nagymaros* case of 1997: 'Modern development of international law has strengthened this principle for non-navigational uses of international watercourses as well'.[36] Some experts link this concept of 'community of interests' to the rather recent notion of 'hydrosolidarity', which emphasizes

[32] D Ziganshina, 'International Water Law in Central Asia: Commitments, Compliance and Beyond' (2009) 20 *Journal of Water Law* 96, 107; see also D Ziganshina, 'International Water Law in Central Asia: The Nature of Substantive Norms and What Flows from it', AsianSIL Working Papers 5 (2010).

[33] 'Strengthening the Institutional and Legal Frameworks of the International Fund for Saving the Aral Sea: Review and Proposals—Discussion Paper' (31 January 2010) 13, available at http://www.unece.org/ (last accessed on 17 January 2014).

[34] UNECE (The International Fund for Saving the Aral Sea), 'Report of the First Meeting of the Working Group on Strengthening Institutional and Legal Framework of IFAS and the Development of the Aral Sea Basin Programme—3' (Almaty, Kazakhstan, 10–11 December 2009) para 11: 'the proposals of national experts on the strengthening of the legal framework of cooperation were quite different, ranging from complete replacement of the legal framework to proposals to advance the existing legal framework, or to leave the existing system of agreements as it is'.

[35] *Case relating to the Territorial Jurisdiction of the International Commission of the River Oder (UK v Poland)*, 1929 PCIJ (ser A) No 23 (Sept 10), para 74.

[36] *Case Concerning the Gabčíkovo-Nagymaros Project (Hungary/Slovakia)* Judgment of 25 September 1997, para 85.

the importance of cooperation among the riparian states and their responsibility for the utilization of shared water resources.[37]

The notion of 'perfect equality of all riparian states' is to be translated into a workable treaty arrangement. The related rule of equitable and reasonable utilization is also open-textured; however, the 1997 UN Convention,[38] the 1992 UNECE Convention, the Helsinki Rules (not legally binding)[39] and the international jurisprudence[40] confirm its legal significance. The most authoritative statement of this rule is reflected in the 1997 UN Convention, which determines that 'watercourse states shall in their territories utilize an international watercourse in an equitable and reasonable manner', and imposes an obligation on states to take into account the interests of the watercourse states, 'consistent with the adequate protection of the watercourse'.[41] Paragraph 2 of Article 5 states that the

> watercourse states shall participate in the use, development and protection of an international watercourse in an equitable and reasonable manner. Such participation includes both the right to utilize the watercourse and *the duty to cooperate* in the protection and development thereof.[42]

The International Law Commission (ILC) commented in this context that 'a watercourse state has the right, within its territory, to a reasonable and equitable share, or portion, of the uses and benefits of an international watercourse'.[43] Article 6 contains a non-exhaustive list of criteria that must be taken into consideration by the watercourse states to ensure an equitable and reasonable utilization of shared water resources.[44] This notion seems to have attained a rather complex character and covers concerns related to environmental protection, human rights and sustainable development. Accordingly,

[37] P Wouters, S Vonogradov and BD Magsig, 'Water Security, Hydrosolidarity and International Law: A River Runs Through It…' [2009] *Yearbook of International Environmental Law* 134. See also AK Gerlak, RG Varady and AC Haverland, 'Hydrosolidarity and International Water Governance' (2009) 14 *International Negotiation* 311.

[38] Convention (n 19 above).

[39] 'The Helsinki Rules on the Uses of the Waters of International Rivers', Report of the Committee on the Uses of the Waters of International Rivers (International Law Association, 1967). See also Committee on Water Resources, 'Water Resources Law—Fourth Report' in ILA Report of the Seventy-First Conference (Berlin 2004) 2004 (Berlin Rules), Art 12–13.

[40] *Case Concerning the Gabčíkovo-Nagymaros Project* (n 36 above), para 78. The Court confirms that the States have a 'basic right to an equitable and reasonable sharing of the resources of an international watercourse'.

[41] Art 5 (n 19 above).

[42] Emphasis added.

[43] 'Draft Articles on the Law of the Non-navigational Uses of International Watercourses and Commentaries thereto and Resolution on Transboundary Confined Groundwater 1994' [1994] II-ii *Yearbook of the International Law Commission* 97.

[44] They include: geographic, hydrographic, hydrological, climatic, ecological and other factors of a natural character; the social and economic needs of the watercourse states; the population dependent on the watercourse in each watercourse state; the effects of the use of the watercourses in other watercourse states; existing and potential uses of watercourses; conservation, protection, development and economy of use of the water resources and the costs of measures taken to that effect; the availability of alternatives, of comparable value, to a particular planned or existing use.

the boundaries and content of the right of equitable utilization depend on the circumstances of a particular case and need to be specified in respective inter-state arrangements.

The relationship between the rule of equitable utilization and the no-harm rule, which is another guiding norm enshrined in the 1997 Convention and is closely linked to a due diligence obligation of states to protect and preserve watercourse ecosystems, seems to be an uneasy one.[45] According to the no-harm rule, the states shall take 'all appropriate measures to prevent the causing of significant harm to other watercourse states'.[46] The state practice demonstrates that the rules of equitable utilization and no harm may indeed conflict with each other. As Salman indicates,

> lower riparian (states) tend generally to favour the no harm rule, as it protects their existing uses; whereas upper riparians tend, by and large, to favour the principle of equitable and reasonable utilization because it provides them with a fair share even if that may impact downstream riparians.[47]

McCaffrey argues that

> if state A's hydroelectric use conflicts with state B's agricultural use, the conflict is not to be resolved solely by applying the 'no-harm' rule of Article 7, but rather through reference to the 'package' of articles setting forth the principles of equitable utilization and 'no-harm'.

He continues:

> in actual disputes, it seems probable that the facts and circumstances of each case, rather than any a priori rule, will ultimately be the key determinants of the rights and obligations of the parties. Difficult cases . . . will be resolved by cooperation and compromise, not by rigid insistence on rules of law.[48]

Thus, the rule of equitable utilization only offers a general framework for accommodating existing water controversies in Central Asia. At the same time, it does not impose substantial legal constrains on the states' freedom of action and can be broadly interpreted by them. As already emphasized above, there are no effective compliance mechanisms and a legitimate rule interpreter in Central Asia to remedy this situation. The water dispute in the region can indeed be resolved only through negotiations and enhanced cooperation.

[45] SC McCaffrey, 'The Contribution of the UN Convention on the Law of the Non-navigational Uses of International Watercourses' (2001) 1 *International Journal of Global Environmental Issues* 250, 256–57: 'This standard takes into account the sensitivity of the ecosystem as well as the capability of the state involved to protect it'.

[46] Convention (n 19 above), Art 7, para 1.

[47] Salman (n 19 above), 917.

[48] McCaffrey (n 45 above), 255.

IV. THE ROLE OF VITAL HUMAN NEEDS AND ENVIRONMENTAL PROTECTION

Local communities in the Central Asian states are directly affected by water controversies and the ensuing ecological situation in the region.[49] Population growth, water scarcity, climate change and environmental problems also create much insecurity for current and future generations with respect to their free access to freshwater. Paragraph 2 of Article 10 of the 1997 UN Convention refers to the necessity to take into account 'vital human needs' while resolving conflicts between different uses of an international watercourse.[50] The ILC explains this rule by stating that 'special attention is to be paid to providing sufficient water to sustain human life, including both drinking water and water required for the production of food in order to prevent starvation'.[51] Scholars conclude that 'apportionment on the basis of needs is . . . justified . . . from the point of view of the expected result, namely, optimal utilization'.[52] The status and content of a right to water[53] and its impact on the law of international watercourses nevertheless remains debatable; however, some writers commenting on the draft convention argued that it does not go far enough in incorporating human rights considerations into its text.[54]

Inefficiency of water use in Central Asia, which directly affects human conditions in the region, is far reaching and cannot be satisfactorily resolved without effectively addressing the critical state of domestic water infrastructures. The question as to whether the states bear an obligation to improve their national water management capacities should remain open. However, this seems to be a necessary precondition for effective water management (though not yet a requirement of international law). The creation of an effective regional water management mechanism may indeed require the implementation of reforms in domestic water sectors, the strengthening of the states' capabilities to protect the water resources and their ecosystems, and the creation of accountability mechanisms based on enhanced public involvement in decision-making. The

[49] The President of Kazakhstan emphasized in his recent statement: 'To our neighbors and brothers who are "sitting" on the upper reaches of these rivers, we send another "fraternal signal" that we—Kazakhstan and Uzbekistan on the Amu-Darya and Turkmenistan, located downstream—most of all perceive the shortage of water; each person feels it, because this is their life; this is the life of millions of people', available at http://www.inform.kz/rus/article/2492724 (last accessed on 17 January 2014).

[50] 'In the event of a conflict between uses of an international watercourse, it shall be resolved with reference to articles 5 to 7, with special regard being given to the requirements of vital human needs.'

[51] 'Draft Articles' (n 43 above), 110.

[52] E Benvenisti, 'The Role of International Law: Equity and the Apportionment of Shared Water Resources' in AM Rabello (ed), *Aequitas and Equity* (Hebrew University 1997) 269, 280.

[53] See the Committee on Economic, Social and Cultural Rights, 'General Comment 15, The Right to Water (Twenty-ninth session, 2003)', UN Doc E/C.12/2002/11 (2002).

[54] E Benvenisti, 'Collective Action in the Utilization of Shared Freshwater: The Challenges of International Water Resources Law' (1996) 90 *American Journal of International Law* 384, 406–08.

right to public participation is not yet widely recognized in international treaties; however, it is gaining increasing recognition.[55]

An effective protection of vital human needs is also inextricably linked to the environmental protection of the shared water resources. The states have to take environmental protection into consideration under customary international law. This is what the Permanent Court of Arbitration concluded in its *Kishenganga* case between Pakistan and India (2013). The court emphasized that 'hydro-electric projects . . . must be planned, built and operated with environmental sustainability in mind'.[56] In its decision on the *Pulp Mills on the River of Uruguay* of 2010, the ICJ recognized the customary nature of environmental impact assessment.[57] These conclusions are, in principle, also applicable to the Central Asian context. Environmental considerations limit the respective states' freedom of action. In particular, the obligation to assess environmental impact and preserve the integrity of ecosystems plays a crucial role in this context.

It can be observed that environmental considerations indeed play a substantial role in Central Asian water controversies. One example is the controversy between Tajikistan and Uzbekistan over the construction of the Rogun dam in Tajikistan. Uzbekistan requested an independent assessment of the Rogun construction and its environmental consequences. However, it rejected the World Bank report, which largely endorsed the dam's construction.[58] This case shows that such controversial issues can only be resolved by negotiation in good faith. The assistance provided by third parties may play an important role. International institutions may[59] to a certain degree facilitate the depoliticization of a dispute by issuing authoritative assessments and recommendations.[60] Their

[55] See Berlin rules, Art 18 (n 39 above).

[56] Permanent Court of Arbitration, *Indus Waters Kishenganga Arbitration (Pakistan v India)*, Partial Award, 18 February 2013, para 454.

[57] *Pulp Mills on the River Uruguay (Argentina v Uruguay)*, Judgment [2014] ICJ Reports 14, para 204: 'In this sense, the obligation to protect and preserve, under Article 41 *(a)* of the Statute, has to be interpreted in accordance with a practice, which in recent years has gained so much acceptance among States that it may now be considered a requirement under general international law to undertake an environmental impact assessment where there is a risk that the proposed industrial activity may have a significant adverse impact in a transboundary context, in particular, on a shared resource. Moreover, due diligence, and the duty of vigilance and prevention which it implies, would not be considered to have been exercised, if a party planning works liable to affect the regime of the river or the quality of its waters did not undertake an environmental impact assessment on the potential effects of such works.'

[58] World Bank, 'Key Issues for Consideration on the Proposed Rogun Hydropower Project', draft for discussion (17 June 2014), available at http://www.worldbank.org/content/dam/World bank/Event/ECA/central-asia/WB%20Rogun%20Key%20Issues.pdf (last accessed on 3 October 2014).

[59] 'World Bank Discloses Next Round of Interim Rogun Assessment Studies', available at http://www.worldbank.org/en/news/press-release/2013/10/01/world-bank-discloses-next-round-of-interim-rogun-assessment-studies (last accessed on 22 January 2014).

[60] 'Commending World Bank's Support of Tajikistan in Tackling Energy Challenges, Secretary-General Encourages Water Management Agreement in Central Asia' (n 17 above). UN Secretary-General expressed his believe that the results of the World Bank's assessment of the planned Rogun hydropower project would provide 'informed guidance in the decision-making

impact may, however, remain limited in practice when perceived national security interests are at stake, as demonstrated by Uzbekistan's negative reaction[61] to the World Bank's report and its continued rejection of the construction of the Rogun dam by adhering to its 'principle position of unacceptability of constructing hydropower facilities at the international watercourses without a preliminary endorsement by all interested countries'.[62]

V. REQUIREMENT OF COOPERATION

The Central Asian states are strongly interdependent,[63] and an optimal utilization of regional water resources cannot be achieved without effective cooperation and a more integrated approach to shared water problems. However, the legal scope of the duty to cooperate remains rather obscure. Article 8 of the 1997 Convention establishes a general obligation to cooperate, which is closely linked to the rule of equitable utilization. According to this provision, 'Watercourse states shall cooperate on the basis of sovereign equality, territorial integrity, mutual benefit and good faith in order to attain optimal utilization and adequate protection of an international watercourse'. This may result in the 'establishment of joint mechanisms and commissions . . . to facilitate cooperation on relevant measures and procedures'.[64] The ILC did not further qualify the duty to cooperate. Rather, it came to the conclusion that 'a general formulation would be more appropriate, especially in view of the wide diversity of international watercourses and the uses thereof'.[65] Article 24 of the Convention envisages the establishment of joint management mechanisms. Regarding this, the ILC stated that 'states should consider establishing joint management mechanisms in order to attain maximum possible benefits'. Another central document of the law of international watercourses—the UNECE Convention on the Protection and Use of Transboundary Watercourses and International Lakes—also contains provisions on

process on the project. That, in turn, should entail constructive dialogue on water and energy issues between the riparian States in Central Asia.'

[61] Water Pressures in Central Asia (n 2 above), 18–19.

[62] Above n 11 (on the webpage of the Ministry of Foreign Affairs).

[63] See the web page of the Ministry of Foreign Affairs of the Republic of Uzbekistan (n 11 above): 'It is an open secret that Amudarya and Syrdarya rivers—the two major transboundary rivers of Central Asia have historically been a common good and the source of life for the nations of the region'.

[64] According to para 2 of Art 8 of the UN Watercourse Convention: 'In determining the manner of such cooperation, watercourse States may consider the establishment of joint mechanisms and commissions, as deemed necessary by them, to facilitate cooperation on relevant measures and procedures in the light of experience gained through cooperation in existing joint mechanisms and commissions in various regions'. See also Art 5, para 2, which enshrined the obligation to 'participate in the use, development and protection of an international watercourse', which 'includes both the right to utilize the watercourse and the duty to cooperate in the protection and development thereof' (n 19 above).

[65] Commentary on Art 8 in 'Draft Articles' (n 43 above), 106.

cooperation, requesting parties to cooperate through bilateral and multilateral agreements.[66]

The practice of states indicates that joint management mechanisms have indeed been established in a wide range of cases.[67] International law favours institutionalized cooperation. However, it does not seem to require a specific form of institutionalized cooperation among riparian states; it may also take other, relatively non-institutionalized, forms. The ICJ has contributed very little to the clarification of substantive obligations of states to cooperate. In its case concerning pulp mills on the Uruguay River, the ICJ found there to be a violation of procedural obligations by Uruguay, which failed to consult with Argentina as determined by the respective international treaty of 1975 prior to authorizing and constructing the pulp mills.[68] At the same time, the court maintained that the procedural obligations had to be separated from the substantive obligations, which required cooperation between the two states as well as the monitoring and prevention of pollution of the river. The court did not address the legal character of cooperation in more specific terms.

In the Central Asian context, the experts emphasize the importance of the respective states' efforts to establish 'a sound procedural system of cooperation to facilitate their interactions over shared waters'.[69] This should, however, be directed at enhancing the effectiveness of cooperation by shifting the focus of the involved states to their mutual gains stemming from regional cooperation. The Central Asian states have created a number of joint institutions, such as the Interstate Commission of Water Coordination and the International Fund for Saving the Aral Sea.[70] Within this rather fragmented institutional framework, they interact on regional water issues. However, the underlying problem is a lack of effective cooperation among the states (in particular, the unwillingness or inability of states to reach a long-term and mutually acceptable compromise). The regional cooperation/negotiations are not bringing sustainable results.[71] Thus, the most challenging question in this context remains how

[66] UNECE Helsinki Convention (n 20 above), Art 2(6): 'The Riparian Parties shall cooperate on the basis of equality and reciprocity, in particular through bilateral and multilateral agreements, in order to develop harmonized policies, programmes and strategies covering the relevant catchment areas, or parts thereof, aimed at the prevention, control and reduction of transboundary impact and aimed at the protection of the environment of transboundary waters or the environment influenced by such waters, including the marine environment'.

[67] See, eg Wouters, 'Sovereignty Revisited—Examining the Rules of International Law that Govern Transboudary Water Resources with a Focus on Upstream/Downstream State Practice—Possible Lessons Learned for Euphrates–Tigris' in Kibaroglu et al (n 21 above), 384–95.

[68] *Pulp Mills* (n 57 above).

[69] Ziganshina (n 21 above), 282.

[70] For details see the website of the Executive Committee of the International Fund for Saving the Aral Sea at http://www.ec-ifas.org/ (last accessed on 17 January 2014). For other institutional aspects of governance see also Boisson de Chazournes (n 21 above).

[71] Camm, 'Tajikistan: Water Conference Produces Platitudes, Few Concrete Ideas', available at http://eurasianet.org/node/67415 (last accessed on 17 January 2014).

to use incentives to induce the states to cooperate more effectively in reaching a mutually acceptable regional arrangement.[72]

VI. CONFLICTING WATER NEEDS

International law attempts to strike a balance between different uses of water resources. According to Article 10 of the 1997 UN Convention, 'in the absence of agreement or custom to the contrary, no use of an international watercourse enjoys inherent priority over other uses'. In case of conflicts, the states must observe the no-harm rule. However, the scope of this rule and the consequences of its violation are not clearly defined. The ILC concluded that 'the fact that an activity involves *significant harm* would not of itself necessarily constitute a basis for barring it'.[73] The ILC further emphasized: 'it is not intended to guarantee that in utilizing an international watercourse *significant harm* would not occur. It is an obligation of conduct, not an obligation of result.'[74]

In *Pulp Mills*, the ICJ did not find that Uruguay, committing certain procedural violations by failing to consult the other party, was under a duty not to construct the pulp mills. In *Lake Lanoux Arbitration*,[75] the tribunal concluded that the French action (diverting a river shared with Spain) did not contravene any rules of international law. At the same time, the tribunal emphasized that the states have a duty to seek to enter into comprehensive agreements to resolve any problems that may arise in their relations. According to this ruling,

> Consultations and negotiations between the two states must be genuine, must comply with the rules of good faith and must not be mere formalities. The rules of reason and good faith are applicable to procedural rights and duties relative to the sharing of the use of international rivers; and the subjecting by one state of such rivers to a form of development which causes the withdrawal of some supplies from its basin, are not irreconcilable with the interests of another state.[76]

The tribunal also stated that 'the rule that states may utilize the hydraulic power of international watercourses only on condition of a prior agreement between the interested states cannot be established as a custom, even less as a general principle of law'.[77] At the same time,

[72] The World Bank, in para 25 of its 2004 report, attempted to elaborate on the possible gains to Uzbekistan in participating in the arrangements proposed by this institution. They included, among others, a less expensive and more reliable electricity supply and a stable supply of irrigation water in summer (n 1 above).

[73] 'Draft Articles' (n 43 above), 103. Emphasis added.

[74] Ibid, emphasis added.

[75] *Lake Lanoux Arbitration, France v Spain* (Arbitral Tribunal 16 November 1957) (1957) 12 RIAA 281, 24 ILR 101. Emphasis added.

[76] Ibid, para 7.

[77] Ibid, para 13.

> according to the rules of good faith, the upstream state is under the obligation to take into consideration the various interests involved, to seek to give them every satisfaction compatible with the pursuit of its own interests, and to show that in this regard it is genuinely concerned to reconcile the interests of the other riparian state with its own.[78]

That does not mean, however, that Spain could have 'invoke[d] a right to insist on a development of Lake Lanoux based on the needs of Spanish agriculture'.[79] However, the environmental considerations pointed out above impose certain constrains on state's freedom of action in similar situations. In *Kishenganga*, the Court of Arbitration declared that the states are required to take environmental protection into account while pursuing their hydroelectric projects.[80]

It can be maintained that general international law does not prohibit the use of water resources as a strategic resource influencing economic or other interests of another riparian state. In Central Asia too, the water of international rivers constitutes a strategic resource and the related disputes are politicized. However, this does not relieve the states of their basic legal obligations; they have to take into account important concerns of other riparian states, such as environmental protection of the ecosystems of international rivers and the essential role of limited water resources in the promotion of human development in this region. Moreover, the states have a duty to act in good faith while negotiating and concluding water management and sharing agreements.

VII. CONCLUSION

This chapter has demonstrated that the Central Asian states are strongly interdependent in many respects. The conclusion at which the ICJ arrived in its *Gabčíkovo-Nagymaros* case is very much applicable to the Central Asian region and its main rivers too. The court stated that 'The Danube has always played a vital part in the commercial and economic development of its riparian states, and has underlined and reinforced their interdependence, making international co-operation essential'.[81] The Central Asian states will need to improve their cooperation to achieve a mutually acceptable utilization of regional rivers, which is directly linked to the prevention of further environmental disasters and human suffering. This would require the consolidation of the institutional framework and the elaboration of more substantial treaty norms, which reinforce a regional system of environmental protection and utilization of Syr Darya and Amu Darya. A need to improve domestic water management systems, which is necessary for the promotion of human development in the region, and the corresponding duties of the riparian states should

[78] Ibid, para 22.
[79] Ibid, para 24.
[80] *Indus Waters Kishenganga Arbitration* (n 56 above), para 454; see also para 449.
[81] Above n 36, para 17.

also be reflected in a regional arrangement. The duty to cooperate will remain unfulfilled if the states do not manage to enter into genuine negotiations, which constitute the core of the obligation to cooperate. Entering into negotiations without any intention of reaching a mutually acceptable resolution of water disputes would deprive such negotiations of any sense and purpose. Only a results-driven negotiation process offering incentives and gains to the parties involved would increase the probability of achieving mutually acceptable solutions. It should seek to establish an integrated regional framework and enshrine a burden-sharing mechanism based on the capacities and resources of the riparian states. It should also reflect the interests of the directly affected communities in the region to whom Syr Darya and Amu Darya provide an indispensable lifeline.

19

International Law, Governance and Trade of Water Services

ANDREIA COSTA VIEIRA*

I. INTRODUCTION

THE INTERNATIONAL COMMUNITY is facing a global water crisis. The liberalization of water services has been suggested by some neoliberal institutions as a way of dealing with such a crisis.[1] At the same time, the international scenario has been framed by a social phenomenon called 'governance'; this water governance takes into consideration both institutional and normative pluralism. Moreover, water has been recognized by the United Nations General Assembly as a human right. Thus, conflicts of interests may arise between the human right to water and free trade.

In this chapter, the world's water crisis is first briefly analysed. Next, the elements of international trade and economic law that have been introduced as a potential solution to this crisis are presented and the liberalization process of water services that has been occurring in some countries is remarked upon. Finally, a pluralistic solution to the water crisis will be presented, from integrated water management through water governance to sustainable development and the protection of human rights.

II. A WATER CRISIS

Water has been one of the main concerns on the international relations agenda. Pollution, scarcity, imprudent waste, public health and sanitation, bad water

* PhD in International Law, University of São Paulo, Brazil; Visiting Fellow at the Lauterpacht Centre for International Law—University of Cambridge, UK (2013); LLM in International Law, University of Nottingham, UK; Professor of International Law and Lawyer in Brazil. Email: andreiacostavieira@usp.br; andreia.vieira@fgv.br.

[1] J Budds and G McGraham, "Are the Debates on Water Privatization Missing the Point? Experiences from Africa, Asia and Latin America" [2009] *Environment and Urbanization* 91.

services management and interstate water disputes are some of the main concerns of what has been termed a 'water crisis'.

The United Nations World Water Development Report (2009) contains a subchapter entitled 'A Global Water Crisis', which points out that, although environmental concerns about water resources have to be taken into consideration, they are not the core issue of this water crisis. The report calls attention to the increase in consumption, mainly in the most industrialized, richest and most populated nations in the world.[2]

In 2009, the International Water Management Institute published a report in which it stressed the scarcity of water in many different regions in the world and it identified two different kinds of scarcity: economically water-scarce basins and physically water-scarce basins. Economically water-scarce basins are due to a lack in infrastructure investment, which causes unequal water distribution. Physically water-scarce basins are due to a lack of water resources in the territory considered or overpopulation compared to the availability of water in an area.[3]

Some have said that the Middle East region has been running out of water since 1970.[4] This concern has been reiterated by others who have affirmed that all water available in the Middle East comes from underground sources and that the region's underground water has been consumed at a rate far above its capacity to recharge.[5]

In Africa, the scenario is no different. Egypt uses the Nile to its maximum capacity. Libya has run out of surface water and has been using the Nubian Aquifer beyond its capacity to recharge. The same has happened in Chad, Sudan and Kenya, while in South Africa, the richest country in that continent, about 15 million people do not have enough access to a basic amount of fresh water.[6]

It is the same story in China. Climate changes and overpopulation, in addition to industrialization and high consumption, have been critical factors in causing a water crisis there.[7]

India is one of the countries that has felt this water crisis the most. In most parts of the country, water mining takes place at twice the rate of natural

[2] WWAP, 'WWDR3—Water in a Changing World' (World Water Assessment Programme, 16 March 2009), available at http://www.unesco.org/new/en/natural-sciences/environment/water/wwap/wwdr/wwdr3-2009/ (accessed on 3 August 2013).

[3] International Water Management Institute (IWMJ), *Water for Food, Water for Life. A Comprehensive Assessment of Water Management in Agriculture* (Earthscan Publications, 2007).

[4] T Allan, 'Virtual Water: a Long Term Solution for Water Short Middle Eastern Economies?' paper presented at the 1997 British Association Festival of Science, Water and Development Session, Leeds, 9 September 1997, 3.

[5] M Barlow and T Clarke, *Blue Gold. The Battle Against Corporate Theft of the World's Water* (Earthscan Publications, 2002) 19.

[6] Ibid, 51. According to the World Health Organization, a basic amount of fresh water would be 40 liters per person per day.

[7] PH Gleick et al, 'The World's Water 2008–2009: The Biennial Report on Freshwater Resources' (Pacific Institute, 2008) 79.

recharge and aquifer waters have been dropping by one to three metres per year. Moreover, water pollution and bad sanitation, combined with overpopulation, have been the main causes of disease in India.[8]

Water scarcity has also troubled Europe. In 2000, Spain had to buy bulk water that was shipped in from France, while at the same time a pipe was being built from Barcelona to Montpellier, France, for water to be supplied from that region.[9] England's 33 major waterways have lost volume because of water overuse and England has had to buy water from Scotland in periods of shortage. In the Netherlands and Germany, salmon disappeared in 1958 due to pollution and loss of volume of the Rhine river. In fact, 90 per cent of the Rhine river original flood plains has been lost to industrial development. The fisheries of the Danube river have also been harmed over the last 25 years due to increased pollution and dams.[10]

Attention has also been focused on Australia, which suffered a long period drought in the 1990s and 2000s, which lasted for more than 12 years in many parts of the country.[11]

There are also concerns of a water crisis in the USA. Like other states, California has had to deal with long periods of drought, and has often had to buy water from Canada in order to supply its agriculture.[12] In 1999, under the NAFTA disputes procedures, Sun Belt, a Californian company, raised a complaint against the Canadian province of British Columbia for being in breach of a public procurement contract, which consisted of a sale of bulk water that was to be shipped from Canada to California. The dispute was not resolved under the NAFTA arbitration procedures but was solved diplomatically.[13]

In Latin America, many places have also faced water scarcity. Mexico has had concerns with pollution of the Rio Colorado and periods of drought, most of them involving the United States as an upstream co-riparian, which has used the Rio Colorado waters for irrigation and industrial matters, causing pollution and salinization of the river waters in the Mexican territory.[14] Due to scarcity, Peru has one of the highest prices per cubic metre of water on the continent, and Honduras has maintained its water supply through the bulk shipping of water for quite a long time.[15]

Argentina has faced long financial crises, which have been 'remedied' with

[8] Barlow and Clarke (n 5 above), 24.

[9] PH Gleick et al, 'The World's Water 2002–2003: The Biennial Report on Freshwater Resources' (Pacific Institute, 2002) 44.

[10] Barlow and Clarke (n 5 above), 31.

[11] Gleick et al (n 7 above).

[12] CG Caubet, 'Domínio da água ou direito à água? Rivalidades nas relações internacionais do século XXI' in S Nasser and F Rei (eds), *Direito Internacional do Meio Ambiente* (Atlas, 2006) 178.

[13] Information available at http://www.naftaclaims.com/disputes_canada_sunbelt.htm (accessed on 7 August 2013).

[14] Trade and Environment Database (TED), American University, Washington, DC, available at http://www.american.edu/TED/SUPER.HTM (accessed on 7 August 2013).

[15] Barlow and Clarke (n 5 above).

the privatization of public services, and the privatization of its water services has left many Argentines with very high water bills to pay for poor-quality water.[16] The same happened in Uruguay until 2004, when the country renationalized the water services that had previously been privatized,[17] and Bolivia faced a serious supply crisis in 2000 due to extremely high water prices after the privatization of its water services. However, Bolivia also renationalized the administration of water services after 2005.[18]

Brazil contains 12–18 per cent of all fresh water available in the world, but is also suffering a water crisis itself, due to bad public administration and poor infrastructure investments that are failing to balance the unequal natural distribution of its water sources with the unequal distribution of population in its regions and the unequal income distribution of its population.[19]

Due to all these concerns, water has been termed 'the blue gold'[20] and has attracted attention from the private sector, which has suggested the private management of water services in order to deal with this water crisis.

III. INTERNATIONAL TRADE AND LIBERALIZATION OF WATER SERVICES—A SOLUTION TO THE WATER CRISIS?

In the 1980s and 1990s, the IMF and the World Bank promoted the privatization of public services by granting credits and investments that were conditional on it.

The IMF, the World Bank and the General Agreement on Tariffs and Trade (GATT, signed in 1947) became the three pillars of the international economy and trade after the Second World War, forming the so-called Bretton Woods system. In 1995, a World Trade Organization (WTO) was created by the Marrakesh Agreement. Many multilateral treaties that had been negotiated during the Uruguay Round were brought into force. Among them were an updated General Agreement on Tariffs and Trade (GATT 1994) and the General Agreement on Trade in Services (GATS).

GATS comprises a set of clauses that promote trade liberalization in services in a bottom-up negotiation manner—that is, what is not included in the countries' specific list of negotiations will not be brought to negotiation.[21] The definition of trade in services is set in Article 1(2) and covers cross-border supply, consumption abroad, commercial presence and presence of natural

[16] D Azpiazu et al, 'Água potable y saneamiento en Argentina. Privatizaciones, crisis, inequidades y incertidumbe future' (2005) 22(59) *Cuadernos del Cendes* 47.

[17] See D Hall et al, 'Making Water Privatization Illegal—New Laws in Netherlands and Uruguay' (Public Services International Research Unit, 2004).

[18] Caubet (n 12 above), 173.

[19] See CEM Tucci et al, 'Relatório Nacional sobre o Gerenciamento da Água no Brasil' (Instituto de Pesquisas Hidráulicas, 2000).

[20] See Barlow and Clarke (n 5 above).

[21] U Celli, *Comércio de Serviços na OMC. Liberalização, Condições e Desafios* (Juruá, 2009).

persons. GATS excludes only services supplied in the exercise of governmental authority, that is, 'any service which is supplied neither on a commercial basis, nor in competition with one or more service suppliers' (GATS, Article 1(3)(a) and (b)).

In 1936, in the middle of the Great Depression, Keynes advocated in favour of a welfare state, as opposed to the classic economic theories of free trade.[22] After the Second World War, a Keynesian model of state intervention was developed, together with the concept of free trade. These were enshrined in the preamble of GATT 1947:

> The Parties . . . [r]ecognizing that their relations in the field of trade and economic endeavor *should be conducted with a view to raising standards of living, ensuring full employment and a large and steadily growing volume of real income and effective demand, developing the full use of the resources of the world* and expanding the production and exchange of goods (emphasis added).

During the Uruguay round of multilateral trade negotiations, Keynesian principles were also introduced in some of the agreements negotiated, such as the Marrakesh Agreement (preamble), GATT 1994 (Article XX) and GATS. GATS Articles XIV 'General Exceptions' and XIV bis 'Security Exceptions' allow countries to keep a degree of flexibility in their policies to enable them, when necessary, to introduce measures to protect human, animal or plant life or health or any other value enshrined in the two articles.

Liberal economic theories were also raised in the middle of the world economic crisis of the 1970s, driven by the thoughts of exponential economists such as Hayek.[23]

After this neoliberal awakening, the IMF and the World Bank promoted free trade through promotion of the liberalization of public services. Public water services were privatized in many countries.[24]

However, is privatization of water services the proper way to deal with the contemporary concerns of a world water crisis?

In 1989, water services were privatized in Great Britain based on arguments of efficiency and investment. According to the British government, competition was the key for development in the water sector. The 1989 Water Act transferred the property of the infrastructure and management of all water services in the country to the private sector. By 2008, water services tariffs had increased by about 39 per cent over and above the general rate of inflation; the water quality did not follow the same trend.[25] According to the UK

[22] See JM Keynes, *The General Theory of Employment, Interest and Money* (Palgrave Macmillan, 1936).

[23] See FA Hayek, "The Theory of Money and Economic Fluctuations", in *Money, Capital & Fluctuations: Early Essays* (Routledge, 1984).

[24] J Budds and G McGranahan, 'Are the Debates on Water Privatization Missing the Point? Experiences from Africa, Asia and Latin America' [2003] *Environment & Urbanization* 91.

[25] See D Hall and E Lobina, 'Water Privatization' (Public Services International Research Unit, 2008).

Consumer Council for Water, efficiency and productivity are not expressions to be used with regard to water services in Great Britain.[26]

In the 1990s, Argentina privatized its water services in most parts of the country, in accordance to the neoliberal requirements of the IMF and the World Bank, which conditioned the granting of credits upon the privatization of public services. Since then, tariffs have risen according to the dollar exchange rate and many consumers have not been able to pay their water bills. Investments were not made according to the initial contracts and the high water tariffs were not followed by good quality water in most places.[27]

The IMF and the World Bank's requirements also brought about privatization of water services in Bolivia in 1999. Water tariffs doubled in less than a year, and consumers had no access to tap water. In 2000, a civil protest in the region of Cochabamba manifested as strikes and resulted in imprisonments and deaths. However, the legislation that had authorized the privatization of the counrty's water services was abolished and the water services was returned to public control.[28]

In Uruguay, also due to the IMF and the World Bank's requirements, water services were privatized in 1992. Poor water quality, high tariffs and inaccessibility to water services raised protests all over the country. In 2004, the Uruguay Constitution was changed in order to prohibit private property and management of water services and to sustain a human right to water.[29]

Privatization of water services has also taken place in 14 countries in Africa, under the auspices of the IMF and the World Bank, and the same sorts of claims have been raised in these countries. In South Africa, the Constitution of which guarantees a right to water, many have felt the impact of water restrictions.[30]

In the United States, most of the federate states and/or municipalities have public ownership and management of water services, though in some regions there are public–private partnerships. In some cities, such as Atlanta (Georgia), Pekin (Illinois) and Dayton (Ohio), water services were privatized but, due to public complaints, were returned to public ownership.[31]

Most of Brazil's water services are publicly owned and run. However, some concession agreements have raised concerns, such as the one signed in 2000 privatizing the water services in Manaus, the capital city of the Amazonas State, which comprises predominantly Amazon forest and river. Water prices

[26] Consumer Council for Water, 'Complaint Handling in the Water Industry in England and Wales, April 2010–March 2011', available at http://www.ccwater.org.uk/upload/pdf/Complaint_Handling_in_the_Water_Industry.pdf (accessed on 9 July 2013).

[27] See Azpiazu et al (n 16 above).

[28] Caubet (n 12 above), 173.

[29] See Hall et al (n 17 above).

[30] Budds and McGranahan (n 24 above), 106.

[31] See AA Craig, 'Water Privatization Trends in the US' (2009) 33 *William & Mary Environmental Law and Policy Review* 785.

have increased since this privatization took place and many complaints of inaccessibility to water services have being brought by citizens of Manaus.[32]

Two countries that have always been mentioned as successful cases of privatization of water services are France and Chile.

The water services in France have been in private hands since the nineteenth century. Most of the water companies that have won private water contracts in countries in Africa and Latin America are based in France. Although water has been privately owned in France for historical reasons,[33] recent public concerns have changed this scenario. In 2000, the city of Grenoble won a court battle to cancel the contract with Lyonnaise des Eaux, taking the water services into public ownership.[34] In Paris, in 2010, due to very high tariffs charged by the private water companies and to a recent claim for water as a public good, water services became public and their management was taken over by the municipality.[35]

The water services in Chile were privatized in the 1990s and this privatisation of public services was successful. Despite many claims from human rights groups,[36] the private water services have public approval in Chile, mainly due to good quality water guaranteed by a previous regulation related to environmental and social concerns.[37]

IV. INTERNATIONAL TRADE LAW AND WATER GOVERNANCE: TOWARDS SUSTAINABLE DEVELOPMENT AND PROTECTION OF HUMAN RIGHTS

In 1968, Hardin published an article entitled 'The Tragedy of the Commons', wherein he advised that

> Therein is the tragedy. Each man is locked into a system that compels him to increase his herd without limit—in a world that is limited. Ruin is the destination towards which all men rush, each pursuing his own best interest in a society that believes in the freedom of the commons. Freedom in a commons brings ruin to all.[38]

Some matters, such as environmental protection, population growth and public health, need prohibitive and adjudicative legislation, that is, the state's intervention. Too much freedom in these areas could bring ruin to all.

[32] A Olivier, 'Water Tariff Increase in Manaus (Brazil): An Evaluation of the Impact of Households', Working Paper DT/2006-10 (Institute de Recherche pour le development, 2006).

[33] B Barraqué, 'Politiques de l'eau em Europe' (1995) 45(3) *Revue Française de Science Politique* 420.

[34] Barlow and Clarke (n 5 above), 189.

[35] See <http://www.paris.fr/politiques/les-politiques-parisiennes/l-eau/rub_9706_stand_82999_port_24008 (accessed on 5 August 2013).

[36] Barlow and Clarke (n 5 above), 73.

[37] V Foster, 'Ten Years of Water Service Reform in Latin America: Toward an Anglo-French Model', Water Supply and Sanitation Sector Board Discussion Paper Series 3 (World Bank Group, 2005) 21.

[38] G Hardin, 'The Tragedy of the Commons' (1968) 162(3859) *Science* 1243.

In general, public services and public policies should not be left in the invisible hands of the market.[39] One should not expect a social vision from the market, since the market's vision is towards profit. That is the market's *anima*. It is not the sum of individual wills that form a collective will.[40] There must be regulatory instruments to promote a social attitude.

A great awareness towards sustainable development grew in the 1990s. Since this concept was publicized in the Brundtland Report in 1987,[41] it became a maxim in many international treaties and agendas worldwide. According to the report, 'Sustainable development is development that meets the needs of the present without compromising the ability of future generations to meet their own needs'. There are three core dimensions in this concept—human needs, environmental protection and economic development—which are linked by the principle of intergenerational solidarity.

The 1992 Rio Declaration on Environment and Development, the 2002 Johannesburg Plan of Implementation and the 2012 Rio +20 report 'The Future We Want'[42] (the 2012 Rio Report) stress the sustainable development basis for public policies management. The 2012 report stresses the importance of trade as an engine for development and sustained economic growth, as well as a free trade multilateral market to stimulate development worldwide (Principle 281).

On the other hand, some multilateral treaties, such as GATT (Article XX) and GATS (Article XIV), establish exceptions to free trade measures, such as measures that are necessary for the protection of human, animal and plant life or health, and measures that are related to the protection of exhaustible natural resources.

Moreover, the preamble of the WTO Marrakesh Agreement recognizes that the parties' relations in the field of trade and economic endeavour should be conducted with a view to raising standards of living while, at the same time, allowing for the optimal use of the world's resources in accordance with the objective of sustainable development, seeking both to protect and preserve the environment and to enhance the means for doing so in a manner consistent with their respective needs and concerns at different levels of economic development.

In the 2012 Rio Report, sustainable development is linked directly to water services. From Principle 119 onwards, the document emphasizes that water is at the core of sustainable development, and it underlines the importance of water and sanitation within the three dimensions of sustainable development. It reaffirms the 2002 Johannesburg Plan of Implementation regarding halving the proportion of people without access to safe drinking water and basic

[39] See E Ostrom, *Governing the Commons: The Evolution of Institutions for Collective Action* (Cambridge University Press, 1990).
[40] C Derani, *Direito Ambiental Econômico* (Max LImonad, 1997) 64.
[41] UN Doc A/42/427 (1987).
[42] UN Doc A/CONF.216/16 (2012).

sanitation by 2015, as well as integrated water resource management and water efficiency plans to ensure sustainable water use (Principle 120).

Principle 121 of the 2012 Rio Report reaffirms commitments regarding the human right to safe drinking water and sanitation.

This Principle is a confirmation of the human right to water recognized by the General Assembly of the United Nations (GA) in 2010.[43] The 2010 GA Resolution confirms that all people have the right of access to drinking water, in a quality and quantity that satisfies their basic needs.

In 2002, the Economic, Cultural and Social Committee of the United Nations interpreted paragraphs 11 and 12 of the 1966 UN Covenant on Economic Social and Cultural Rights in such a way as to say that the recognition of the right of everyone to an adequate standard of living also means a right to water, comprising availability, quality and access to drinking water.[44]

The 2012 Rio Report also points out that the progressive realization of access to safe and affordable drinking water and basic sanitation for all is a necessary step for the eradication of poverty and to protect human health (Principle 120). In order to achieve this goal, Principle 120 stresses the importance of improving the implementation of integrated water management at all levels as appropriate.

However, there remains a question of what 'the implementation of integrated water management at all levels as appropriate' means. This language is too broad to mean how to eradicate poverty and protect human health through the realization of access to safe and affordable drinking water and basic sanitation. In fact, 'the implementation of integrated water management at all levels as appropriate' means a pluralism: a normative pluralism, an institutional pluralism and an actors' pluralism, all interconnected.

In a contemporary international agenda, the idea of pluralism goes together with the notion of governance. Contemporary international law has been shaped by the influence of governance in order to make it suitable for contemporary international needs. Moreover, some scholars have pointed out that the contemporary water crisis is due to a governance crisis, and only a 'governance structure' is capable of finding solutions.[45]

Governance is a product of globalization. Jürgen Habermas offers a concept of globalization that is quite inclusive:

> By globalization is meant the cumulative process of a worldwide expansion of trade and production, commodity and financial markets, fashions, the media and computer programs, news and communications networks, transportation systems and flows of migration, the risks generated by large scale technology, environmental damage and epidemics, as well as organized crime and terrorism.

[43] UN GA Doc A/64/L.63/Rev.1.

[44] Ibid, Comment 15—ECOSOC.

[45] See P Rogers and A Hall, 'Effective Water Governance', TEC Background Papers 7 (Global Water Partnership, 2003); Castro (n 48 below).

> These processes enmesh nation-states in the dependencies of an increasingly interconnected world society whose functional differentiation effortlessly bypasses territorial boundaries.[46]

The process of globalization has changed the world structure. It has made states become interconnected and interdependent. In the absence of a world government, this interdependency of states has been structured by elements of world governance.

Andrew Hurrel remarks that governance is a variety of processes that coordinate social systems through different actors, different rules and different activities, but all of them are interdependent with regard to cooperation.[47]

States continue to be the main actors, but they are not alone. International organizations, non-governmental organizations and their rule-making procedures have also been important in the development of contemporary international law. These non-state rules have been termed soft law and have connections with the politics of soft power,[48] which means power and norms that do not have binding effects but that influence and make changes happen.

Therefore the concept of water governance should be subject to the pragmatic pluralism that is inherent in all spheres of society and knowledge, since the management of water resources is not only in public hands.[49]

On the other hand, this contemporary construction of water governance does not mean that water services should be left solely in the private sector's hands. In many circumstances, the involvement of the private sector is inevitable. Nevertheless, 'the implementation of integrated water management at all levels as appropriate' means that efficiency of water governance comprises joint efforts from the public sector, the private sector and civil society.

The United Nations adopted the Convention on the Law of Non-navigational Uses of Watercourses in 1997. The 1997 Convention entered into force in August 2014, but it was considered a customary international law by the International Court of Justice in the *Gabčíkovo-Nagymaros* case in 1997, since it upholds the principle of equitable and reasonable use of transboundary water resources by co-riparian states.[50] An integrated water management would mean cooperation and fairness with regard to the use of transboundary watercourses, considering the needs of both upstream and downstream co-riparian states.

In 2004, the International Law Association adopted the Berlin Rules on Water Resources, which was the most complete document ever published on

[46] J Habermas, *The Divided West* (Polity Press, 2006) 175.

[47] A Hurrel, *On Global Order: Power, Values, and the Constitution of International Society* (Oxford University Press, 2007) 95.

[48] See JS Nye, *Bound to Lead: the changing nature of American Power* (Basic Books, 1990).

[49] JE Castro, 'Water Governance in the Twentieth-First Century' (2007) 10(2) *Ambiente e Sociedade* 99, 102.

[50] *Gabčíkovo-Nagymaros Project (Hungary v Slovakia)*, Judgment [1997] ICJ Reports 7.

freshwater and became a standard for the construction of domestic legislation.[51] It summarizes contemporary customary international law related to freshwater resources.

Many non-governmental organizations have water concerns as their foundation cause. The World Water Council—a non-governmental entity—was founded in Marseille, France, in 1996, and became the organizer of the World Water Forums that have taken place every three years since 1997. The World Water Forums have become the most important events for water governance, and have produced interstate ministerial declarations, focusing on issues related to water governance, water security and integrated water management. In 2009, the World Water Forum recognized the right to fresh water. In 2010, the UN General Assembly recognized the human right to water.[52]

Other international non-governmental organizations that have, inter alia, been important actors in the international water agenda are the Global Water Partnership and the World's Water Pacific Institute.[53]

Individuals have also played important roles in the consolidation of water rights. The population protests in South Africa, Bolivia and Uruguay have brought changes in their domestic Constitutions with regard to water rights. Protests in some US cities and in Paris have returned the water services to public ownership. All these popular movements have had their own voices in the consolidation of the right to water. Individuals have participated in numerous World Water Forums as representatives of local communities or local river basins. This is a consequence of globalization and dynamic contemporary international law that has been shaped by global governance.

V. CONCLUSION

The IMF, the World Bank and the private sector have suggested private management of water services as a solution to the water crisis. However, many states' policies have demonstrated that whenever water services are in private hands, social and environmental concerns are not at stake, since the market aims at profit and the market's tariffs will always be determined by the market's main interests. Apart from a few exceptions, the liberalization of water services has not been a solution for the water crisis. Instead, public management of water services has replaced private services even in countries such as France, where the water market has been in private hands for almost two centuries. Social and environmental claims of a human right to water have returned water services to public ownership.

[51] The original text of the Berlin Rules is available at http://www.internationalwaterlaw.org/documents/intldocs/ILA_Berlin_Rules-2004.pdf (accessed on 6 August 2013).

[52] Information available at http://www.worldwatercouncil.org/ (accessed on 6 August 2013).

[53] Information available at http://www.pacinst.org/ (accessed on 6 August 2013).

This new human right to water is a claim that is accommodated perfectly within the new phenomenon of global governance. Water governance comprises the implementation of integrated water management at all levels. As has been demonstrated, efficient water governance entails joint efforts from the public and private sectors, as well as from civil society and individuals, in accordance with the objective of sustainable development.

Part III

Towards a New Order for International Investment and Trade

Section 1

International Arbitration at a Crossroads

20

The Rule of Law in International Investment Arbitration

AUGUST REINISCH*

I. INTRODUCTION

THE RULE OF law in international law in general, and in international investment arbitration in particular, can be studied from different perspectives. The notion itself is not sufficiently clear. A number of books have been written about the subject and it is evident that the rule of law, 'prééminence du droit', 'Rechtsstaatlichkeit' and similar notions are very often intrinsically linked to the various national legal systems from which they come.[1] For present purposes, reference to some of the aspects highlighted in the UN definition of the rule of law in the Secretary-General's 2004 Report[2] seem to be a very useful starting point. In particular, the demands of equal enforcement and independent adjudication of legal rules and principles,

* Professor of International Law, University of Vienna, Austria.

[1] HJ Berman, *Law and Revolution. The Formation of the Western Legal Tradition* (1985); I Brownlie, *The Rule of Law in International Affairs: International Law at the Fiftieth Anniversary of the United Nations* (1998); TRS Allan, *Constitutional Justice: A Liberal Theory of the Rule of Law* (2003); P Craig, *Formal and Substantive Conceptions of the Rule of Law: and Analytical Framework* (2005); J Waldron, *The Law* (1990); D Dyzenhaus, *Recrafting the Rule of Law: The Limits of Legal Order* (1999); R Grote, 'Rule of Law, Rechtsstaat and "Etat de droit"' in C Starck (ed), *Constitutionalism, Universalism and Democracy* (1999) 269–306; M Koskenniemi, *The Gentle Civilizer of Nations: The Rise and Fall of International Law* (2001) 1870–1960; P Allott, *Towards the International Rule of Law: Essays in Integrated Constitutional Theory* (2005); T Bingham, *The Rule of Law* (2011); I Flores and K Himma (eds), *Law, Liberty and the Rule of Law* (2013).

[2] See 'Report of the Secretary-General on the Rule of Law and Transitional Justice in Conflict and Post-Conflict Societies', S/2004/616 (23 August 2004) para 6 ('The "rule of law" is a concept at the very heart of the Organization's mission. It refers to a principle of governance in which all persons, institutions and entities, public and private, including the State itself, are accountable to laws that are publicly promulgated, equally enforced and independently adjudicated, and which are consistent with international human rights norms and standards. It requires, as well, measures to ensure adherence to the principles of supremacy of law, equality before the law, accountability

as well as fairness in the application of the law, legal certainty, the avoidance of arbitrariness and procedural and legal transparency, seem to be particularly relevant for investment arbitration.

International investment law and, especially, its protection standards can be regarded as an expression of the rule of law; at the same time, the rule of law requires that international investment arbitration itself conforms to the basic principles of a law-abiding system. While the former perspective will be mentioned only briefly, the latter aspect will be outlined in the following preliminary reflections in more detail.

II. INTERNATIONAL INVESTMENT ARBITRATION AS AN EXPRESSION OF THE RULE OF LAW

There is a widespread assumption that the rule of law is supposed to be guaranteed by investment standards, in particular by the obligation of fair and equitable treatment. In fact, fair and equitable treatment can be regarded as an enhanced version of international law standards preventing denial of justice[3] or, put in a positive way, demanding due process and a fair trial.[4] The

to the law, fairness in the application of the law, separation of powers, participation in decision-making, legal certainty, avoidance of arbitrariness and procedural and legal transparency').

[3] See J Paulsson, *Denial of Justice in International Law* (2005); SM Schwebel, *Justice in International Law: Further Selected Writings* (2011); F Francioni, 'Access to Justice, Denial of Justice and International Investment Law' (2009) 20 *European Journal of International Law* 729; M Paparinskis, *The International Minimum Standard and Fair and Equitable Treatment* (2013).

[4] In various investment cases, a number of elements have been developed by arbitral tribunals to evidence fair and equitable treatment. Among them is a procedural requirement of due process, which is often phrased in language that closely resembles the international minimum standard of due process. See, eg *Waste Management, Inc v United Mexican States*, Case No ARB(AF)/00/3, ICSID Additional Facility Award of 30 April 2004, para 98 ('the minimum standard of treatment of fair and equitable treatment is infringed by conduct attributable to the State and harmful to the claimant if the conduct is arbitrary, grossly unfair, unjust or idiosyncratic, is discriminatory and exposes the claimant to sectional or racial prejudice, or involves a lack of due process leading to an outcome which offends judicial propriety—as might be the case with a manifest failure of natural justice in judicial proceedings or a complete lack of transparency and candour in an administrative process. In applying this standard it is relevant that the treatment is in breach of representations made by the host State which were reasonably relied on by the claimant'). Recently, it seems that this more limited interpretation, inspired by what is known in investment law as the *Neer* standard (*LFH Neer and Pauline Neer (USA) v United Mexican States* (1926) IV RIAA 60), prevails over a broader reading of fair and equitable treatment in cases like *MTD Equity v Chile*, ICSID Case No ARB/01/7, Award, 25 May 2004, para 113 ('Fair and equitable treatment should be understood to be treatment in an even-handed and just manner, conducive to fostering the promotion of foreign investment. Its terms are framed as a pro-active statement—"to promote", "to create", "to stimulate"—rather than prescriptions for a passive behavior of the State or avoidance of prejudicial conduct to the investors') and *Técnicas Medioambientales Tecmed, SA v United Mexican States*, ICSID Case No ARB(AF)/00/2, Award, 29 May 2003, para 154 (fair and equitable treatment standard protects 'basic expectations' of investors 'that the host State acts in a consistent manner, free from ambiguity and totally transparent.').

See, in general, R Dolzer, 'Fair and Equitable Treatment: A Key Standard in Investment Treaties' (2005) 39 *International Lawyer* 87; C Schreuer, 'Fair and Equitable Treatment in Arbitral Practice' (2005) 6 *The Journal of World Investment & Trade* 357; J Tudor, *The Fair and Equita-*

law on expropriation also embraces rule of law principles. Neither customary international law nor international investment agreements (IIAs) generally prohibit takings. Rather, they usually permit them if certain basic rule of law requirements, such as public interest, due process, non-discrimination and compensation, are complied with.[5] Also, almost all IIAs unequivocally require that expropriations be carried out in compliance with due process of law[6] and—another rule of law requirement—in a non-discriminatory fashion.[7]

ble Treatment Standard in the International Law of Foreign Investment (2008); K Yannaca-Small, 'Fair and Equitable Treatment Standard: Recent Developments' in A Reinisch (ed), *Standards of Investment Protection* (2008) 111–30; UNCTAD, *UNCTAD Series on Issues in International Investment Agreements, vol 3. Fair and Equitable Treatment* (1999); S Vascannie, 'The Fair and Equitable Treatment Standard in International Investment Law and Practice' (1999) 70 *British Year Book of International Law* 99. See also, in particular, SW Schill, 'Fair and Equitable Treatment under Investment Treaties as an Embodiment of the Rule of Law', IILJ Working Paper 2006/6 (Global Administrative Law Series), available at http://www.iilj.org; SW Schill, 'Fair and Equitable Treatment, the Rule of Law and Comparative Public Law' in SW Schill, *International Investment Law and Comparative Public Law* (2010) 151–83; JR Picherack, 'The Expanding Scope of the Fair and Equitable Treatment Standard: Have Recent Tribunals Gone too Far?' (2008) 9(4) *Journal of World Investment & Trade* 255; C Schreuer, 'Fair and Equitable Treatment in Arbitral Practice' (2005) 6(3) *Journal of World Investment & Trade* 357; R Klager, 'Fair and Equitable Treatment: A Look at the Theoretical Underpinnings of Legitimacy and Fairness' (2010) 11(3) *Journal of World Investment & Trade* 435.

[5] See, eg Art 13(1) Energy Charter Treaty 1994 ('Investments of Investors of a Contracting Party in the Area of any other Contracting Party shall not be nationalized, expropriated or subjected to a measure or measures having effect equivalent to nationalization or expropriation (hereinafter referred to as "Expropriation") except where such Expropriation is: (a) for a purpose which is in the public interest; (b) not discriminatory; (c) carried out under due process of law; and (d) accompanied by the payment of prompt, adequate and effective compensation'). See also R Dolzer, 'Indirect Expropriations: New Developments?' (2002) 11 *NYU Environmental Law Journal* 64; U Kriebaum, 'Regulatory Takings: Balancing the Interests of the Investor and the State' (2007) 8 *Journal of World Investment & Trade* 717; A Reinisch, 'Expropriation' in P Muchlinski, F Ortino and C Schreuer (eds), *The Oxford Handbook of International Investment Law* (2008) 407–58; A Reinisch, 'Legality of Expropriations' in A Reinisch (ed), *Standards of Investment Protection* (2008) 171–204; MW Reisman and RD Sloane, 'Indirect Expropriation and its Valuation in the BIT Generation' [2003] *British Year Book of International Law* 115; UNCTAD, *Taking of Property* (2000).

[6] See, in addition, the specifications in Art 13(2) ECT ('The Investor affected shall have a right to prompt review, under the law of the Contracting Party making the Expropriation, by a judicial or other competent and independent authority of that Contracting Party, of its case, of the valuation of its Investment, and of the payment of compensation, in accordance with the principles set out in paragraph (1)'); Art 5(3) Austria/Georgia BIT (2001) ('Due process of law includes the right of an investor of a Contracting Party which claims to be affected by expropriation by the other Contracting Party to prompt review of its case, including the valuation of its investment and the payment of compensation in accordance with the provisions of this Art by a judicial authority or another competent and independent authority of the latter Contracting Party'). See also *ADC Affiliate Limited and ADC & ADMC Management Limited v Republic of Hungary*, ICSID Case No ARB/03/16, Award, 2 October 2006, para 435 ('Some basic legal mechanisms, such as reasonable advance notice, a fair hearing and an unbiased and impartial adjudicator to assess the actions in dispute, are expected to be readily available and accessible to the investor to make such legal procedure meaningful. In general, the legal procedure must be of a nature to grant an affected investor a reasonable chance within a reasonable time to claim its legitimate rights and have its claims heard. If no legal procedure of such nature exists at all, the argument that "*the actions are taken under due process of law*" rings hollow').

[7] See *Mike Campbell (Pvt) Ltd and Others v Zimbabwe*, Decision of 28 November 2008, SADC (T) Case No 2/2007, 53 ('In examining the effects of Amendment 17 on the applicants,

The primary assumption is that, through the acceptance of these and other investment disciplines, like full protection and security or the non-discrimination requirements of national treatment and most-favoured-nation (MFN) treatment,[8] host states will attract more foreign investors, since the assurance of compliance with certain minimum treatment standards will increase their willingness to invest in a foreign legal system, which exposes them to various aspects of not only economic, but also political risk.[9] While this supposed causal relationship often underlies the thinking of treaty-makers,[10] the jury is still out whether and to what extent legal security in the form of enhanced protection through IIAs actually leads to increased investment activities.[11]

it is clear to us that those effects have had an unjustifiable and disproportionate impact upon a group of individuals distinguished by race such as the Applicants. We consider that the differentiation of treatment meted out to the Applicants also constitutes discrimination as the criteria for such differentiation are not reasonable and objective but arbitrary and are based primarily on considerations of race. The aim of the Respondent in adopting and implementing a land reform programme might be legitimate if and when all lands under the programme were indeed distributed to poor, landless and other disadvantaged and marginalized individuals or groups'). See also AFM Maniruzzaman, 'Expropriation of Alien Property and the Principle of Non-Discrimination in International Law of Foreign Investment: An Overview' (1998) 8 *Journal of Transnational Law and Policy* 57; A Reinisch, 'Is Expropriation Ripe for Codification?—The Example of the Non-discrimination Requirement for Lawful Expropriations' in AK Bjorklund and A Reinisch (eds), *International Investment Law and Soft Law* (2012) 271–304.

[8] See A Reinisch, *Standards of Investment Protection* (2008); R Dolzer and C Schreuer, *Principles of International Investment Law*, 2nd edn (2012) 130–215.

[9] N Rubins and NS Kinsella, *International Investment, Political Risk and Dispute Resolution* (2005).

[10] Agreement between the Republic of Austria and the Great Socialist People's Libyan Arab Jamahiriya for the promotion and protection of investments, Preamble, 7 January 2004, 2333 UNTS 411 (2005) ('Recognizing that the promotion and protection of investments will strengthen the readiness for such investments and thereby make an important contribution to the development of economic relations'); United Kingdom of Great Britain and Northern Ireland and Benin—Agreement for the promotion and protection of investments, Preamble, 27 November 1987, 1556 UNTS 183 (1990) ('Recognising that the promotion and reciprocal protection under international agreement of such investments is likely to encourage individual investment initiatives and will increase prosperity in both states'); Treaty between the Federal Republic of Germany and the Republic of Ghana for the encouragement and reciprocal protection of investments, Preamble, 24 February 1995, German Federal Law Gazette II 1997/48, 2055 ('Recognizing that the encouragement and contractual protection of such investments are apt to stimulate private business initiative and to increase the prosperity of both nations'). Preamble of the ICSID Convention ('considering the need for international cooperation for economic development, and the role of private international investment therein'). According to the Report of the Executive Directors on the Convention, 'adherence to the Convention by a country would provide additional inducement and stimulate a larger flow of private international investment into its territories, which is the primary purpose of the Convention'. 1 ICSID Reports 25.

[11] See M Hallward-Driemeier, 'Do Bilateral Investment Treaties Attract FDI? Only a Bit . . . and They Could Bite', World Bank Policy Research Working Paper No 3121 (2003); J Salacuse and NP Sullivan, 'Do BITs Really Work? An Evaluation of Bilateral Investment Treaties and their Grand Bargain' (2005) 46 *Harvard International Law Journal* 67; E Neumayer and L Spess, 'Do Bilateral Investment Treaties Increase Foreign Direct Investment to Developing Countries?' (2005) 33 *World Development* 1567; T Büthe and H Milner, 'The Politics of Foreign Direct Investment into Developing Countries: Increasing FDI through Policy Commitment via Trade Agreements and Investment Treaties?', available at www.duke.edu/~buthe/downloads/ButheMilner_FDI_27sep07.pdf (accessed on 22 January 2014); J Tobin and S Rose-Ackerman, 'Foreign Direct Investment and the Business Environment in Developing Countries: the Impact of Bilateral Investment Trea-

For present purposes, an additional assertion is more interesting. It has been argued that compliance with treaty-based standards will not only work in favour of the direct beneficiaries of IIA standards, ie investors from the other contracting parties, but will also have a positive spill-over effect on the general rule of law climate in host states.[12] In the long run, the argument goes, it will not be tenable that only foreign investors benefit from the investment standards inspired by the rule of law, but the usually constitutional law-based requirement of equal treatment will push towards all (including domestic) actors enjoying the same level of treatment that is based on the rule of law.

While it will certainly require much additional empirical evidence as to what extent investment law disciplines actually enhance the rule of law in host countries as a result of an expected spill-over effect, the present reflections turn towards the rule of law aspects of investment arbitration and the broader system of international investment law itself. In a way, this change of perspective resembles the development in other areas of international law, where the question 'quis custodied ipsos custodes'[13] has been increasingly raised, asking whether the systems intended to safeguard certain core values comply with those values themselves.[14]

ties', Yale Law School Center for Law, Economics and Public Policy Research Paper No 293; KP Gallagher and MBL Birch, 'Do Investment Agreements Attract Investment? Evidence From Latin America' (2006) 7 *Journal of World Investment & Trade* 961; T Büthe and HV Milner, 'The Politics of Foreign Direct Investment Into Developing Countries: Increasing FDI Through International Trade Agreements?' (2008) 52 *American Journal of Political Science* 741; KP Sauvant and LE Sachs (eds), *The Effect of Treaties on Foreign Direct Investment: Bilateral Investment Treaties, Double Taxation Treaties and Investment Treaties* (2009); UNCTAD, *The Role of International Investment Agreements in Attracting Foreign Direct Investment to Developing Countries* (2009); A Berger, M Busse, P Nunnenkamp and M Roy, 'Do Trade and Investment Agreements Lead to More FDI? Accounting for Key Provisions Inside the Black Box', Kiel Working Paper 1647 (2010); M Busse, J Koeniger and P Nunnenkamp, 'FDI Promotion Through Bilateral Investment Treaties: More Than a Bit?' (2010) 146 *Review of World Economics* 147; A Berger, M Busse, P Nunnenkamp and M Roy, 'Attracting FDI Through BITs and RTAs: Does Treaty Content Matter?' (2012) 75 *Columbia FDI Perspectives*; KP Sauvant and J Reimer (eds), *FDI Perspectives: Issues in International Investment* (2012); O de Schutter, JFM Swinnen and J Wouters (eds), *Foreign Direct Investment and Human Development: The Law and Economics of International Investment Agreements* (2013).

[12] See R Dolzer, 'The Impact of International Investment Treaties on Domestic Administrative Law' (2006) 37 *New York University Journal of International Law and Policy* 953, 971; G van Harten and M Loughlin, 'Investment Treaty Arbitration as a Species of Global Administrative Law' (2006) 17 *European Journal of International Law* 121; S Montt, *State Liability in Investment Treaty Arbitration. Global Constitutional and Administrative Law in the BIT* (2009).

[13] ('Who guards the guardians?') Decimus Junius Juvenal, Satires VI, 347. See also MH Arsanjani, 'Claims against International Organizations—*Quis custodiet ipsos custodes*' (1980/81) 7 *Yale Journal of World Public Order* 131, addressing problems of the responsibility of international organizations; DP Forsythe, 'Who Guards the Guardians: Third Parties and the Law of Armed Conflict' (1976) 70 *American Journal of International Law* 41, on the system of protective powers under the Geneva Conventions.

[14] A Reinisch, 'Securing the Accountability of International Organizations' (2001) 7 *Global Governance* 131; WE Holder, 'Can International Organizations be Controlled—Accountability and Responsibility' (2003) 97 *American Society of International Law Proceedings* 231; FD Berman, MN Shaw and AHA Soons, *Accountability of International Organisations: International Law Association Committee Report* (2004); R Wilde, 'Enhancing Accountability at the International

III. THE RULE OF LAW IN INTERNATIONAL INVESTMENT ARBITRATION

The emphasis on the rule of law in investment arbitration requires a closer scrutiny of this particular form of dispute settlement which has flourished over the past two decades. Rule of law issues in investment arbitration include: the independence and impartiality of arbitrators; the question of what is required for parties to have a 'fair trial' before an investment tribunal, such as the right to be heard, procedural fairness and equality of arms; access to justice, given the financial implications for developing countries and small- and medium-size enterprises; and the adequacy of the control system, be it International Centre for Settlement of Investment Disputes (ICSID) annulment or set-aside procedures before domestic courts. In other words, the central issue is whether the current system of investment arbitration meets the requirements of the rule of law.

The following considerations briefly touch upon some of the issues raised above. The analytical framework of whether the adjudicatory system of investment arbitration conforms to rule of law requirements will be considerations of due process/absence of denial of justice under general international law, as well as the more specific procedural guarantees contained in human rights treaties. A set of similarly worded fair trial guarantees that are often built upon customary international law principles developed in the field of denial of justice[15] are enshrined in human rights instruments, such as the Universal Declaration of Human Rights,[16] the International Covenant on

Level: The Tension Between International Organization and Member State Responsibility and the Underlying Issue at Stake' (2005–06) 12 *ILSA Journal on International and Comparative Law* 395; R Wolfrum and U Deutsch (eds), *The European Court of Human Rights Overwhelmed by Applications: Problems and Possible Solutions* (2007); R Wilde, 'Understanding the International Territorial Administration Accountability Deficit: Trusteeship and the Legitimacy of International Organizations' (2008) 12 *International Peacekeeping: The Yearbook of International Peace Operations* 93; M Parish, 'An Essay on the Accountability of International Organizations' (2010) 7 *International Organizations Law Review* 277; J Wouters, E Brems, S Smis and P Schmitt (eds), *Accountability for Human Rights Violations by International Organisations* (2010); A Nollkaemper and D Jacobs, 'Shared Responsibility in International Law: a Conceptual Framework'(2012–13) 34 *Michigan Journal of International Law* 359; M Evans and P Koutrakos, *The International Responsibility of the European Union* (2013).

[15] See J Paulsson, *Denial of Justice in International Law* (2005) 133.

[16] Art 10 Universal Declaration of Human Rights, GA Res 217(III), UN GAOR, 3d Sess, Supp No 13, UN Doc A/810 (1948) 71 ('Everyone is entitled in full equality to a fair and public hearing by an independent and impartial tribunal, in the determination of his rights and obligations and of any criminal charge against him').

Civil and Political Rights[17] and the European Convention on Human Rights (ECHR).[18]

A. Independence and Impartiality of Arbitrators

One of the core aspects of the right to a fair trial/due process is the requirement that claims must be determined by independent and impartial adjudicators. This prerequisite of most human rights instruments[19] has a functional equivalent in various arbitration rules,[20] can be enforced through various arbitrator challenge procedures[21] and is ultimately guaranteed by annulment proceedings under the ICSID Convention and residual local court control in non-ICSID cases, which can also make the lack of independence and impartiality a ground for annulment or set-aside/non-recognition of awards.[22]

In investment arbitration practice, arbitrator challenges have increased dramatically over recent years.[23] While it is obvious that law firms have discovered

[17] Art 14, para 1 International Covenant on Civil and Political Rights, 19 December 1966, 999 UNTS 171 (1976) ('All persons are equal before the courts and tribunals. In the determination of any criminal charge against him, or of his rights and obligations in a suit at law, everyone shall be entitled to a fair and public hearing by a competent, independent and impartial tribunal established by law').

[18] Art 6, para 1 European Convention on Human Rights, European Convention for the Protection of Human Rights and Fundamental Freedoms (adopted 4 November 1950, entered into force 3 September 1953) 213 UNTS 221 ('In the determination of his civil rights and obligations or of any criminal charge against him, everyone is entitled to a fair and public hearing within a reasonable time by an independent and impartial tribunal established by law').

[19] All the human rights instruments cited above speak of 'independent and impartial tribunals'.

[20] See, eg Art 6(7) UNCITRAL, Arbitration Rules as revised in 2010, UN Doc A/Res/65/22 (2010) ('independent and impartial arbitrator'); Art 14(1) ICSID Convention, Convention on the Settlement of Investment Disputes between States and Nationals of Other States, 18 March 1965, 575 UNTS 159 ('Persons . . . of high moral character and recognized competence in the fields of law, commerce, industry or finance, who may be relied upon to exercise independent judgment').

[21] Art 57 ICSID Convention ('A party may propose to a Commission or Tribunal the disqualification of any of its members on account of any fact indicating a manifest lack of the qualities required by paragraph (1) of Article 14'); Art 12(1) UNCITRAL Arbitration Rules (n 20 above) ('Any arbitrator may be challenged if circumstances exist that give rise to justifiable doubts as to the arbitrator's impartiality or independence').

[22] Although the ICSID Convention does not make the lack of independence and impartiality an express ground for annulment, cases where arbitrators have acted in such a way may be challenged under 'serious departure from a fundamental rule of procedure'. See C Schreuer, L Malintoppi, A Reinisch and A Sinclair, *The ICSID Convention. A Commentary*, 2nd edn (2009) 983–86; Art 52(1) ICSID Convention ('Either party may request annulment of the award by an application in writing addressed to the Secretary-General on one or more of the following grounds: (a) that the Tribunal was not properly constituted; (b) that the Tribunal has manifestly exceeded its powers; (c) that there was corruption on the part of a member of the Tribunal; (d) that there has been a serious departure from a fundamental rule of procedure; or (e) that the award has failed to state the reasons on which it is based').

[23] See L Malintoppi, 'Independence, Impartiality and Duty of Disclosure of Arbitrators' in Muchlinski et al (n 5 above), 789–829; A Sheppard, 'Arbitrator Independence in ICSID Arbitration' in C Binder, U Kriebaum, A Reinisch and S Wittich (eds), *International Investment Law for the 21st Century: Essays in Honour of C Schreuer* (2009) 131–56; N Rubins and B Lauterburg, 'Independence, Impartiality and Duty of Disclosure in Investment Arbitration' in C Knahr,

arbitrator challenges to be another playing field that they can try out, it is not clear whether the suggested lack of independence and impartiality of arbitrators is indeed a systemic problem. The fact that relatively few challenges are upheld in the ICSID system and that a higher number of challenges are upheld by appointing authorities like the Permanent Court of Arbitration[24] or the International Chamber of Commerce, often in decisions without giving reasons,[25] is inconclusive as such. While it has been critically noted that the ICSID arbitrator challenge system which gives the non-challenged arbitrators the power to rule on challenges of their co-arbitrators[26] may be inspired by a misguided *esprit de corps* in many rejections,[27] it could also mean that the often detailed reasoning demonstrates the spuriousness of the grounds invoked by challenging parties. The relatively more frequent findings of a lack of independence and impartiality of arbitrators in systems where the determination is made by arbitration institutions could indicate a greater awareness of the actual existence of bias and dependence, whereas it could also reflect a more cautious approach resulting in many arbitrator disqualifications simply in order to avoid any further discussion even where no actual lack of independence and impartiality can be recognised.

In general, it appears that arbitrator disqualifications occur more frequently in situations where a lack of formal independence is evident through some, often very loose, relationship between an arbitrator's law firm and a corporate affiliate of one of the parties than in situations where even serious concerns exist about the impartiality of 'repeat appointments' with a track record of deciding certain issues always in favour of claimants or respondents.[28]

Clearly this area of impartiality and independence is a crucial one from a rule of law perspective, and it will require further efforts to ensure that

C Koller, A Reinisch and W Rechberger (eds), *Investment and Commercial Arbitration—Similarities and Divergences* (2010) 153–80; A Reinisch and C Knahr, 'Conflict of Interest in International Investment Arbitration' in A Peters, L Handschin and D Hoegger (eds), *Conflict of Interest in Governance—An Interdisciplinary Outlook on the Global, Public, Corporate and Financial Sphere* (2012) 103–24.

[24] Art 13(4) UNCITRAL Arbitration Rules (n 20 above).

[25] Rubins and Lauterburg (n 23 above), 153, 161.

[26] Art 58 ICSID Convention ('The decision on any proposal to disqualify a conciliator or arbitrator shall be taken by the other members of the Commission or Tribunal as the case may be, provided that where those members are equally divided, or in the case of a proposal to disqualify a sole conciliator or arbitrator, or a majority of the conciliators or arbitrators, the Chairman shall take that decision. If it is decided that the proposal is well-founded the conciliator or arbitrator to whom the decision relates shall be replaced in accordance with the provisions of Section 2 of Chapter III or Section 2 of Chapter IV').

[27] JP Commission, 'Precedent in Investment Treaty Arbitration. A Citation Analysis of a Developing Jurisprudence' (2007) 24(2) *Journal of International Arbitration* 129–58; JB Simmons, 'Valuation in Investor-State Arbitration: Toward a More Exact Science' in JN Moore (ed), *International Arbitration: Contemporary Issues and Innovations* (2013) 53–114, at 113.

[28] H Kuo, 'The Issue of Repeat Arbitrators: Is it a Problem and how Should the Arbitrations Institution Respond' (2001) 4(2) *Contemporary Asia Arbitration Journal* 247; D Kapeliuk, 'The Repeat Appointment Factor: Exploring Decision Patterns of Elite Investment Arbitrators' (2010–11) 96 *Cornell Law Review* 47.

the adjudicators live up to the lofty standards of 'high moral character and recognized competence in the fields of law, commerce, industry or finance, [exercising] independent judgment'[29] and that the users of the system will continue to have confidence in having their cases heard by independent and impartial decision-makers.

B. Basic Procedural Fairness

The fair and efficient settlement of disputes requires a thorough and precise scrutiny of the allegations raised by claimants, as well as of the defences put forward by respondents. The principle of the equality of arms has long been considered to be a cornerstone of the arbitral process[30] and it is equally required under many human rights treaties.[31] In this respect, it is relevant that human rights bodies have held that removing disputes from the jurisdiction of courts is in conformity with the right of a fair trial as long as such alternative dispute settlement systems as arbitration respect the basic premises of due process.[32] The annulment and set-aside grounds for arbitral awards that have resulted from proceedings that did not conform to basic fair trial

[29] Art 14(1) ICSID Convention.

[30] N Blackaby, C Partasides, A Redfern and M Hunter, *Redfern and Hunter on International Arbitration*, 5th edn (2009) 6.11 et seq; T Wälde, '"Equality of Arms" in Investment Arbitration: Procedural Challenges' (2011) 1 *Transnational Dispute Management*.

[31] *Weiss v Austria*, Communication No 1086/2002, 24 May 2002, UN Doc CCPR/C/77/D/1086/2002, para 9.6; *Frank v Jamaica*, Communication No 223/1987, 4 April 1989, UN Doc CCPR/C/35/D/223/1987, para 10.4; *Rowe and Davis v United Kingdom*, Application No 28901/95, 16 February 2000, ECHR, paras 59–66; *Ernst and Others v Belgium*, Application, No 33400/96, 15 July 2003, ECHR, paras 60, 61; Human Rights Committee, 'General Comment 32, Right to Equality Before Courts and Tribunals and to a Fair Trial (Article 14)', 23 August 2007, UN Doc CCPR/C/GC/32. See also M Nowak, *UN Covenant on Civil and Political Rights. CCPR Commentary* (2005) 321; P van Djik, F van Hoof, A van Rijn and L Zwaak (eds), *Theory and Practice of the European Convention on Human Rights* (2006) 580.

[32] See *Deweer v Belgium,* ECtHR, 27 February 1980, Series A, No 35, para 49 ('In the Contracting States' domestic legal systems a waiver of this kind is frequently encountered both in civil matters, notably in the shape of arbitration clauses in contracts'); *Lithgow and Others v United Kingdom*, ECtHR 8 July 1986, Series A, No 102, para 201 ('the word "tribunal" in Article 6 para 1 (art 6-1) is not necessarily to be understood as signifying a court of law of the classic kind, integrated within the standard judicial machinery of the country (see, inter alia, the Campbell and Fell judgment of 28 June 1984, Series A No 80, p 39, para 76); thus, it may comprise a body set up to determine a limited number of specific issues, provided always that it offers the appropriate guarantees'); *Kolgu v Turkey*, ECtHR, 27 August 2013, Application No 2935/07, para 40 ('As regards the merits, the Court recalls at the outset that Art 6 of the Convention does not preclude the setting up of arbitration tribunals in order to settle disputes between private entities. Indeed, the word "tribunal" in Article 6 is not necessarily to be understood as signifying a court of law of the classic kind, integrated within the standard judicial machinery of the country; thus, it may comprise a body set up to determine a limited number of specific issues, provided always that it offers the appropriate guarantees').

considerations also evidence the importance of complying with such a rule of law inspired concept.[33]

Assessing the overall quality of investment arbitration as regards compliance with fair trial requirements is difficult. Whether reliable empirical findings can be made is questionable. However, it appears an important field of inquiry, that is worthwhile taking up. In the absence of reliable assessments, many generalizations of 'insiders' such as individual arbitrators and counsel may be based on anecdotal experience, and their reliability is likely to be precarious as well.

Nevertheless, it appears plausible to assert that, in general, the time and effort spent by investment panels in solving complex cases is usually much greater compared to domestic courts. Legal and factual issues are regularly scrutinized in a particularly thorough fashion, and tribunals generally address all aspects of a dispute in much more detail.[34] In this context, a special role is performed by counsel of the parties, who often prepare very elaborate submissions that deal with many aspects of a claim in minute detail. As a result, investment awards and decisions usually contain a comprehensive discussion of all aspects of a dispute, and this usually ensures that all party submissions are fairly adjudicated.

Of course, this thoroughness is inversely related to the time efficiency of investment proceedings. Some cases can go on for months, and sometimes years, and that in itself causes fair trial problems. However, it is hard to argue that investment tribunals would not fully address all aspects of investment disputes.

C. Access to Investment Arbitration

Access to dispute settlement systems is an important element of a fair trial/due process. This notion clearly underlies the customary international law concept of denial of justice which may occur not only when court or administrative proceedings fall short of international standards, but equally where no rem-

[33] See, in particular, Art 52(1)(d) ICSID Convention ('Either party may request annulment of the award by an application in writing addressed to the Secretary-General on one or more of the following grounds: . . . (d) that there has been a serious departure from a fundamental rule of procedure'); on this notion see most recently *Victor Pey Casado and President Allende Foundation v Republic of Chile*, ICSID Case No ARB/98/2, Decision on Annulment, 18 December 2012, para 73 (fundamental rules 'include the right to be heard, the fair and equitable treatment of the parties, proper allocation of the burden of proof and absence of bias'). See also Art 34(2)(a)(ii) UNCITRAL Model Law on International Commercial Arbitration (1985), with amendments as adopted in 2006, UN Doc A/Res40/72 (1985) and UN Doc A/Res61/33 (2006). See also N Blackaby, C Partasides, A Redfern and M Hunter, *Redfern and Hunter on International Arbitration*, 5th edn (2009) 10.50 et seq.

[34] A remarkable development has taken place in this regard, and one need only compare the length of the early ICSID cases of the 1980s with the most recent ones.

edies are available.[35] It is also enshrined in human rights instruments, albeit sometimes implicitly. Thus, human rights bodies had to clarify that access to justice is inherent in a fair trial.[36]

In the field of investment arbitration, a number of problems have been noted with regard to the general accessibility of this form of dispute settlement. As a matter of law, only investors covered by IIAs, providing for investor-state dispute settlement, or having entered into a contractual relationship with a host state containing an arbitration clause, will be able to access investment arbitration;[37] in the case of treaty arbitration, host states will only have a limited possibility to raise (counter-)claims.[38] Additionally, the high cost of investment arbitration often implies that not all investors will be (financially) able to institute investment arbitration in order to vindicate their rights; similarly, the (regularly non-refunded) costs of defending investment claims often lead to a serious financial burden even on successful respondent states.[39]

Limiting the cost of investment arbitration has been recognized as an important desideratum by many, though it remains unclear how to reach this goal.[40] Clearly arbitration costs are also a function of the thoroughness of the adjudicatory process, and the length and level of detail with which claims

[35] J Paulsson, *Denial of Justice in International Law* (2005) 134 et seq.

[36] For Art 6 ECHR see *Golder v United Kingdom*, ECtHR Application No 4451/70, ECtHR 21 February 1975, Series A No 18, [1975] ECHR 1, para 36; *Waite and Kennedy v Germany*, ECtHR, Application No 26083/94, 18 February 1999, para 50.

[37] On the distinction between treaty and contract arbitration see J Crawford, 'Treaty and Contract in Investment Arbitration' (2008) 24 *Arbitration International* 351; BM Cremades and DJA Cairns, 'Contract and Treaty Claims and Choice of Forum in Foreign Investment Disputes' in N Horn (ed), *Arbitrating Foreign Investment Disputes* (2004) 325–51; Y Shany, 'Contract Claims vs Treaty Claims: Mapping Conflicts between ICSID Decisions on Multisourced Investment Claims' (2005) 99 *American Journal of International Law* 835.

[38] P Lalive and L Halonen, 'On the Availability of Counterclaims in Investment Arbitration' (2011) 2 *Czech Yearbook of International Law* 141; Y Kryvoi, 'Counterclaims in Investment Arbitration' (2012) 21(2) *Minnesota Journal of International Law* 216; AK Bjorklund, 'Role of Counterclaims in Rebalancing Investment Law' (2013) 17(4) *Lewis & Clark Law Review* 461; G Carducci, 'Dealing With Set-Off Counterclaims in International Commercial and Investment Arbitration' (2013) 3 *Yearbook on International Arbitration* 173; AK Hoffman, 'Counterclaims in Investment Arbitration' (2013) 28(2) *ICSID Review* 438.

[39] Recently, investment tribunals have appeared to be more willing to depart from the tradition of having each party bear its own costs and splitting the costs of the proceedings and move towards a 'loser pays' system. See *Plama Consortium Ltd v Republic of Bulgaria*, ICSID Case No ARB/03/24, Award, 27 August 2008, paras 321–23; *Europe Cement Investment and Trade SA v Turkey*, ICSID Case No ARB(AF)/07/2, Award, 13 August 2009, paras 182–86; *Gemplus SA, SLP SA, Gemplus Industrial SA de CV v The United Mexican States*, ICSID Case No ARB(AF)/04/3, Award, 16 June 2010, paras 17–27; JY Gotanda, 'Consistently Inconsistent: The Need for Predictability in Awarding Costs and Fees in Investment Treaty Arbitrations' (2010) 28 *ICSID Review* 420; RH Kreindler, 'The Final Rulings on Costs: Loser Pays All?' (2010) 1 *Transnational Dispute Management*.

[40] Some have suggested that only sole arbitrators should be appointed in order to reduce costs. However, given that the costs of the tribunal are usually a minor element of the total arbitration costs, including the parties' representation costs, it would appear that this would hardly lead to a significant reduction of arbitration costs.

are scrutinized should not be reduced merely for efficiency and cost-saving purposes.

D. Consistent Outcomes of Investment Decisions

Much has been written about the problem of inconsistent awards and the general 'absence . . . of a rule of *stare decisis* in the ICSID arbitration system'.[41] This is, of course, a feature shared with most other international dispute settlement systems.[42] The absence of a system of binding precedent must also be regarded from the perspective of the rule of law and its inherent demands of predictability as well as equal treatment. This, in turn, has often led to a de facto case law in many forms of dispute settlement under international law.[43]

It is a basic requirement of the rule of law that equal cases should be decided equally. So far, it is clear that a number of crucial issues in investment law have not been consistently interpreted. These areas range from the meaning of an umbrella clause[44] to the notion of an 'investment' under Arti-

[41] *Amco v Indonesia*, ICSID Case No ARB/81/1, Decision on Annulment, 16 May 1986, para 44. Art 53(1) ICSID Convention, stating that an 'award shall be binding on the parties', has been generally interpreted as excluding a system of binding precedent in ICSID arbitration. See Schreuer et al (n 22 above), 1101; more specifically, Art 1136 (1) NAFTA ('An award made by a Tribunal shall have no binding force except between the disputing parties and in respect of the particular case'). See also in general Commission (n 27 above); G Kaufmann-Kohler, 'Arbitral Precedent: Dream, Necessity, or Excuse' (2007) 23(4) *Arbitration International* 357; A Bjorklund, 'Investment Treaty Arbitral Decisions as *Jurisprudence Constante*' in C Picker, I Bunn and D Arner (eds), *International Economic Law: The State and Future of the Discipline* (2008) 265; A Reinisch, 'The Role of Precedent in ICSID Arbitration' [2008] *Austrian Arbitration Yearbook* 495; C Schreuer and M Weiniger, 'A Doctrine of Precedent' in Muchlinski et al (n 5 above), 1188–1206; L Reed, 'The De Facto Precedent Regime in Investment Arbitration: A Case for Proactive Case Management' (2010) 25(1) *ICSID Review* 95.

[42] Art 59 Statute of the International Court of Justice ('The decision of the Court has no binding force except between the parties and in respect of that particular case'). Art 33(2) Statute of the International Tribunal for the Law of the Sea, Annex VI to the United Nations Convention on the Law of the Sea (UNCLOS), 10 December 1982; in force 16 November 1994 ('The decision shall have no binding force except between the parties in respect of that particular dispute').

[43] See RY Jennings, 'The Judiciary, International and National, and the Development of International Law'(1996) 45 *International & Comparative Law Quarterly* 9; M Shahabuddeen, *Precedent in the World Court* (1996); R Bhala, 'The Precedent Setters: De facto stare decisis in WTO Adjudication' (1999) 9 *Journal of Transnational Law & Policy* 1.

[44] See S Alexandrov, 'Breaches of Contract and Breaches of Treaty—The Jurisdiction of Treaty-based Arbitration Tribunals to Decide Breach of Contract Claims in SGS v Pakistan and SGS v Philippines' (2004) 5 *The Journal of World Investment and Trade* 555; C Schreuer, 'Travelling the BIT Route: Of Waiting Periods, Umbrella Clauses and Forks in the Road' (2004) 5 *The Journal of World Investment and Trade* 231; A Sinclair, 'The Origins of the Umbrella Clause in the International Law of Investment Protection' (2004) 20 *Arbitration International* 411; T Wälde, 'The "Umbrella" Clause on Investment Arbitration—A Comment on Original Intentions and Recent Cases' (2005) 6 *The Journal of World Investment and Trade* 183.

cle 25 ICSID Convention,[45] the interpretation of what amounts to a state of necessity[46] and the reach of MFN clauses.[47] As important and irritating as these inconsistent interpretations are, one should not overlook the fact that in many fields investment tribunals have actually consolidated the law in quite a remarkable fashion and contributed to the specification of the meaning of often vague treatment standards contained in IIAs.[48] They have done so by paying respect to earlier investment awards, taking their reasoning into account without adhering to a system of actual precedent. Rather, tribunals tend to treat preceding interpretations as more or less persuasive evidence[49]

[45] See S Manciaux, 'The Notion of Investment: New Controversies' (2008) 9(6) *Journal of World Investment & Trade* 443; Schreuer et al (n 22 above), 128; A Reinisch, 'From the Perennial Issue of the Notion of Investment Pursuant to Article 25 ICSID Convention and Narrow Dispute Settlement Provisions to Further Clarifications of Substantive Standards of Protection—ICSID Arbitration in 2009' (2010) 10 *The Global Community Yearbook of International Law and Jurisprudence* 749; P-E Dupont, 'The Notion of ICSID Investment: Ongoing Confusion or Emerging Synthesis' (2011) 12(2) *Journal of World Investment & Trade* 245; R Dolzer and C Schreuer, *Principles of International Investment Law* (2012) 44 et seq.

[46] See W Burke-White and A von Staden, 'Investment Protection in Extraordinary Times: Interpreting Non-precluded Measures Provisions' (2007) 48 *Virginia Journal of International Law* 307; A Reinisch, 'Necessity in International Investment Arbitration—An Unnecessary Split of Opinions in Recent ICSID Cases?' (2007) 8 *Journal of World Investment and Trade* 191; S Schill, 'International Investment Law and the Host State's Power to Handle Economic Crises' (2007) 24(3) *Journal of International Arbitration* 265; M Waibel, 'Two Worlds of Necessity in ICSID Arbitration: CMS and LG&E' (2007) 20 *Leiden Journal of International Law* 637; AK Bjorklund, 'Emergency Exceptions: State of Necessity and *Force Majeure*' in Muchlinski et al (n 5 above), 495; J Alvarez and K Khamsi, 'The Argentine Crisis and Foreign Investors: A Glimpse into the Heart of the Investment Regime' (2009) 1 *Yearbook on International Law and Policy 2008–2009* 379; C Binder, 'Changed Circumstances in International Investment Law: Interfaces between the Law of Treaties and the Law of State Responsibility with a Special Focus on the Argentine Crisis' in C Binder, U Kriebaum, A Reinisch and S Wittich (eds), *International Investment Law in the 21st Century, Essays in Honour of C Schreuer* (2009) 608; AK Bjorklund, 'Economic Security Defenses in International Investment Law' (2009) 1 *International Investment Law and Policy Yearbook* 479.

[47] E Gaillard, 'Establishing Jurisdiction Through a Most-Favoured-Nation Clause' (2005) 233(105) *New York Law Journal*; Z Douglas, 'The MFN Clause in Investment Arbitration: Treaty Interpretation Off the Rails' (2011) 2(1) *Journal of International Dispute Settlement* 97; J Maupin, 'MFN-Based Jurisdiction in Investor-State Arbitration: Is There any Hope for a Consistent Approach?' (2011) 14(1) *Journal of International Economic Law* 157; M Paparinskis, 'MFN Clauses and International Dispute Settlement: Moving Beyond Maffezini and Plama' (2011) 26 *ICSID Review* 14–58; S Schill, 'Allocating Adjudicatory Authority: Most-Favoured-Nation Clauses as a Basis of Jurisdiction—A Reply to Zachary Douglas' (2011) 2(2) *Journal of International Dispute Settlement* 353.

[48] With regard to the fair and equitable treatment standard see *Suez, Sociedad General de Aguas de Barcelona SA, and InterAgua Servicios Integrales del Agua SA v The Argentine Republic*, ICSID Case No ARB/03/17, Decision on Liability, 30 July 2010, para 189 ('In interpreting this vague, flexible, basic, and widely used treaty term, this Tribunal has the benefit of decisions by prior tribunals that have struggled strenuously, knowledgeably, and sometimes painfully, to interpret the words "fair and equitable" in a wide variety of factual situations and investment relationships. Many of these cases arose out of Argentina's economic crisis of 2001–2003. Although this tribunal is not bound by such prior decisions, they do constitute "a subsidiary means for the determination of the rules of [international] law"').

[49] See in general HP Glenn, 'Persuasive Authority' (1987) 32 *McGill Law Journal* 261.

of the interpretation and specification of the law,[50] which they will adhere to in order to build a *jurisprudence constante*.[51]

In this softened version of an emerging case law, investment arbitration contributes to core aspects of the rule of law, ie that like cases should be decided in a like way and that a consistent interpretation of the same treaty standards enhances the certainty and predictability of adjudicatory outcomes.[52]

E. Transparency

An issue linked to the consistency of dispute settlement outcomes is the problem of transparency in investment law.[53] Transparency is usually seen as the opposite of the prevailing notion that arbitration ensures confidentiality of

[50] See, eg *ADC Affiliate Limited and ADC & ADMC Management Limited v Republic of Hungary*, ICSID Case No ARB/03/16, Award, 2 October 2006, para 293 ('It is true that arbitral awards do not constitute binding precedent. It is also true that a number of cases are fact-driven and that the findings in those cases cannot be transposed in and of themselves to other cases. It is further true that a number of cases are based on treaties that differ from the present BIT in certain respects. However, cautious reliance on certain principles developed in a number of those cases, as persuasive authority, may advance the body of law, which in turn may serve predictability in the interest of both investors and host States').

[51] See, eg *Société Générale de Surveillance SA v Republic of the Philippines*, ICSID Case No ARB/02/6, Decision on Jurisdiction, 29 January 2004, para 97 ('In the Tribunal's view, although different tribunals constituted under the ICSID system should in general seek to act consistently with each other, in the end it must be for each tribunal to exercise its competence in accordance with the applicable law, which will by definition be different for each BIT and each Respondent State. Moreover there is no doctrine of precedent in international law, if by precedent is meant a rule of the binding effect of a single decision. There is no hierarchy of international tribunals, and even if there were, there is no good reason for allowing the first tribunal in time to resolve issues for all later tribunals. It must be initially for the control mechanisms provided for under the BIT and the ICSID Convention, and in the longer term for the development of a common legal opinion or *jurisprudence constante*, to resolve the difficult legal questions discussed by the SGS v Pakistan Tribunal and also in the present decision'); *AES Corporation v The Argentine Republic,* ICSID Case No ARB/02/17, Decision on Jurisdiction, 26 April 2005, para 33 ('From a more general point of view, one can hardly deny that the institutional dimension of the control mechanisms provided for under the ICSID Convention might well be a factor, in the longer term, for contributing to the development of a common legal opinion or *jurisprudence constante*, to resolve some difficult legal issues discussed in many cases, inasmuch as these issues share the same substantial features').

[52] See *Saipem SpA. v The People's Republic of Bangladesh*, ICSID Case No ARB/05/07, Decision on Jurisdiction, 21 March 2007, para 67 ('The Tribunal considers that it is not bound by previous decisions. At the same time, it is of the opinion that it must pay due consideration to earlier decisions of international tribunals. It believes that, subject to compelling contrary grounds, it has a duty to adopt solutions established in a series of consistent cases. It also believes that, subject to the specifics of a given treaty and of the circumstances of the actual case, it has a duty to seek to contribute to the harmonious development of investment law and thereby to meet the legitimate expectations of the community of States and investors towards certainty of the rule of law').

[53] See C Knahr, 'Transparency, Third Party Participation and Access to Documents in International Investment Arbitration' (2007) 23 *Arbitration International* 327; A Asteriti and C Tams, 'Transparency and Representation of the Public Interest in Investment Treaty Arbitration' in S Schill (ed), *International Investment Law as Comparative Public Law* (2010) 787–816, at 795 et seq.

the dispute settlement process. In commercial arbitration, confidentiality of the fact that a dispute has arisen all the way to the resulting solution by a binding award is normally highly valued, and is often a reason to opt for this alternative to ordinary judicial proceedings.[54] In investment arbitration one party is normally a state, the actions of which are scrutinized, and that those actions are usually not merely 'commercial' ones but rather involve the exercise of governmental authority, implies that there is a public interest in the 'quasi-judicial review' of investment disputes by arbitration panels.[55] Thus, the public has a legitimate interest in knowing what investment disputes are about and how they are resolved.[56] This has led a number of investment tribunals to acknowledge that there is no 'general principle of confidentiality' in investment arbitration.[57]

The recognition of this interest has led to multiple adaptations of the investment dispute settlement system in practice, ranging from tailor-made specific permissions to parties to make certain documents publicly available in the recognition of an 'overall trend in [investment arbitration] towards transparency'[58] to more information about the existence of investment disputes,[59]

[54] S Kouris, 'Confidentiality: Is International Arbitration Losing One of Its Major Benefits?' (2005) 22 *Journal of International Arbitration* 127.

[55] G Van Harten and M Loughlin, 'Investment Treaty Arbitration as a Species of Global Administrative Law' (2006) 17 *European Journal of International Law* 121; WW Burke-White and A von Staden, 'Private Litigation in a Public Law Sphere: The Standard of Review in Investor-State Arbitrations' (2010) 35 *Yale Journal of International Law* 283-346.

[56] See also Art 1(4)(a) UNCITRAL Rules on Transparency in Treaty-based Investor-State Arbitration, pre-release version (effective date: 1 April 2014), available at http://www.uncitral.org/uncitral/en/uncitral_texts/arbitration/2014Transparency.html, acknowledging '[t]he public interest in transparency in treaty-based investor-State arbitration'.

[57] See *SD Myers Inc v Canada*, Procedural Order No 16, 13 May 2000, para 8; *Metalclad Corporation v Mexico,* Case No ARB(AF)/97/1, Award, 30 August 2000, para 13. See also Notes of Interpretation of Certain Chapter 11 Provisions, NAFTA Free Trade Commission, 31 July 2001, para 1 ('Nothing in the NAFTA imposes a general duty of confidentiality on the disputing parties to a Chapter 11 arbitration').

[58] *Biwater (Gauff) Tanzania Ltd v United Republic of Tanzania*, ICSID Case No ARB/05/22, Procedural Order No 3, 29 September 2006, para 122. See also C Knahr and A Reinisch, 'Transparency versus Confidentiality in International Investment Arbitration—The *Biwater Gauff* Compromise' (2007) 6 *The Law and Practice of International Courts and Tribunals* 97.

[59] ICSID regularly publishes a short description of disputes pending before it. See Regulation 22(1) ICSID Administrative and Financial Regulations, ICSID Convention, Regulations and Rules ICSID/15 (April 2006) 51 ('The Secretary-General shall appropriately publish information about the operation of the Centre, including the registration of all requests for conciliation or arbitration and in due course an indication of the date and method of the termination of each proceeding'). See also Art 2 UNCITRAL Rules on Transparency in Treaty-based Investor-State Arbitration 2013 (n 56 above) ('Once the notice of arbitration has been received by the respondent, each of the disputing parties shall promptly communicate a copy of the notice of arbitration to the repository referred to under article 8. Upon receipt of the notice of arbitration from the respondent, or upon receipt of the notice of arbitration and a record of its transmission to the respondent, the repository shall promptly make available to the public information regarding the name of the disputing parties, the economic sector involved and the treaty under which the claim is being made').

public arbitration hearings[60] and a tendency to make investment awards more generally publicly available.[61] However, other tools have been used in order to allow the public interest to be satisfied not only through receiving information, but also by being expressed on certain matters under consideration in investment arbitration, mainly through the instrument of amicus curiae submissions—a tool that was developed in WTO dispute settlement[62] and has found its way into investment arbitration.[63]

From another perspective, transparency is a practical tool to enable investment tribunals to adjudicate in a consistent manner.[64] Only when 'precedents' are known and available can they be taken into account. Thus, the publication

[60] Art 6(1) UNCITRAL Rules on Transparency in Treaty-based Investor-State Arbitration 2013 (n 56 above) ('Subject to article 6, paragraphs 2 and 3, hearings for the presentation of evidence or for oral argument ("hearings") shall be public').

[61] Regulation 22(2) ICSID Administrative and Financial Regulations (above n 59) ('If both parties to a proceeding consent to the publication of: (a) reports of Conciliation Commissions; (b) arbitral awards; or (c) the minutes and other records of proceedings, the Secretary-General shall arrange for the publication thereof, in an appropriate form with a view to furthering the development of international law in relation to investments'). See the much further reaching publication demands of Art 3(1) UNCITRAL Rules on Transparency in Treaty-based Investor-State Arbitration 2013 (n 56 above) ('Subject to article 7, the following documents shall be made available to the public: the notice of arbitration, the response to the notice of arbitration, the statement of claim, the statement of defence and any further written statements or written submissions by any disputing party; a table listing all exhibits to the aforesaid documents and to expert reports and witness statements, if such table has been prepared for the proceedings, but not the exhibits themselves; any written submissions by the non-disputing Party (or Parties) to the treaty and by third persons, transcripts of hearings, where available; and orders, decisions and awards of the arbitral tribunal').

[62] See PC Mavroidis, 'Amicus Curiae Briefs Before the WTO: Much Ado About Nothing' in A von Bogdandy, Y Mény and PC Mavroidis (eds), *European Integration and International Co-Ordination: Studies in Transnational Economic Law in Honour of Claus-Dieter Ehlermann* (2002) 317–30; JB Cawley, 'Friend of the Court: How WTO Justifies the Acceptance of the Amicus Curiae Brief from Non-Governmental Organizations' (2004) 23(1) *Penn State International Law Review* 47; J Durling and D Hardin, 'Amicus Curiae Participation in WTO Dispute Settlement: Reflections on the Past Decade' in R Yerxa and B Wilson (eds), *Key Issues in WTO Dispute Settlement: the First Ten Years* (2005) 221–31; CL Lim, 'The Amicus Brief Issue at WTO' (2005) 4(1) *Chinese Journal of International Law* 85; R Howse, 'Membership and its Privileges: The WTO, Civil Society, and the Amicus Brief Controversy' in R Howse (ed), *The WTO System: Law, Politics & Legitimacy* (2007) 273–91.

[63] The 2006 amendment to the ICSID Rules of Procedure has inserted a new rule 37(2)m which expressly provides for the filing of *amicus curiae* briefs. See A Parra, 'The New Amendments to the ICSID Regulations and Rules and Additional Facility Rules' (2004) 3 *The Law and Practice of International Courts and Tribunals* 181; see also Art 4(1) and (3) UNCITRAL Rules on Transparency in Treaty-based Investor-State Arbitration 2013 (n 56 above) ('1. After consultation with the disputing parties, the arbitral tribunal may allow a person that is not a disputing party, and not a non-disputing Party to the treaty ("third person(s)"), to file a written submission with the arbitral tribunal regarding a matter within the scope of the dispute . . . 3. In determining whether to allow such a submission, the arbitral tribunal shall take into consideration, among other factors it determines to be relevant: (a) Whether the third person has a significant interest in the arbitral proceedings; and (b) The extent to which the submission would assist the arbitral tribunal in the determination of a factual or legal issue related to the arbitral proceedings by bringing a perspective, particular knowledge or insight that is different from that of the disputing parties').

[64] See n 43 above.

of dispute settlement outcomes is an important prerequisite to ensuring predictability and certainty of investment arbitration—crucial rule of law values.

IV. CONCLUSION

The settlement of investment disputes between private parties and host states through arbitration is a relatively young form of dispute settlement that has only recently produced a wealth of cases. Whether it will lead to a sustainable, long-term alternative to the resolution of such disputes by national courts or by inter-state dispute settlement mechanisms inspired by the traditional diplomatic protection paradigm will also depend upon whether it will be able to accommodate and integrate demands of the rule of law in its various procedural aspects.

21

Three Pillars of International Public Policy

GEORGIOS PETROCHILOS*

I. INTRODUCTION

1. The topic must strike one as odd: surely, one would think, there are more than three pillars to public policy. I will readily agree with the proposition that there must be—indeed, there are, as a matter of fact—many more than three strands of public policy. But the question is whether we can identify three absolutely essential, core principles that underpin the whole establishment of the practice of international commercial arbitration—in other words, whether we can identify the pillars of the edifice.

In order to do so, one must establish two propositions:

- that arbitral tribunals sitting in an international commercial dispute have a duty, or at the very least a right, to resort to a conception of public policy that is different from, or even contrary to, the domestic law (or laws) that they must apply; and
- that, although by definition public policy purports to protect only essential interests—be they political, social or economic—there are some interests that are more essential than others.

II. FOUNDATION FOR APPLICATION OF INTERNATIONAL PUBLIC POLICY BY ARBITRAL TRIBUNALS

2. The first question is why and how an arbitrator should have a duty to defend any public policy to start with. After all, it is plain, on the authority

* Head, International Arbitration Group, Freshfields Bruckhaus Deringer LLP, Paris. The views set out in this chapter are the author's alone and do not represent those of his firm or colleagues. This chapter is the slightly edited text of a lecture given at the ILA Regional Conference, Athens, 30 August 2013.

of both European courts (which is beyond criticism), that arbitrators do not engage the international responsibility of the state in which they sit and whose legal order is called upon to supervise them.[1] Arbitrators do not have the forum in the traditional conception that judges of state courts do.

3. A conclusion that might at first be drawn from this is that arbitrators have no duty, possibly not even a right, to apply any public policy other than the public policy of the seat of the arbitration and of the law applicable to the merits of the case (which is typically the law chosen by the parties in their agreement as the proper law of the contract). As the Caribbean Court of Justice put it, 'there is no universal standard of public policy'.[2] In that view, an arbitral tribunal is purely instrumental—a services provider the functions of which are tightly circumscribed by domestic law, and domestic law only. They would comply with national law not because they function as organs of a national legal order, but purely in order to comply with their mandate from the arbitrants to produce a valid award.

4. To illustrate the consequences of that view, suppose that an arbitral tribunal faces an interdiction to continue with the arbitration from the controlling courts of the seat of the arbitration, as, for example, occurred in the *Himpurna v Indonesia*[3] case. In the domestic-law approach, the tribunal must heed that interdiction to the letter—no matter how patently irregular, unreasonable, politically motivated and legally groundless it may appear to the tribunal to be.

5. As a further illustration, suppose that the law applicable to the merits condones a contract for corruption of local officials: then the tribunal would be compelled to apply the law as it finds it and hold the contract valid. Conversely, if the law applicable to the merits requires the tribunal to set aside the parties' agreement as ostensibly invalid, the tribunal should also apply the law as it finds it, even if it is persuaded that the purported invalidity is a sham—a political device targeting the particular contract rather than a law of general application.

6. Shocking as these outcomes may appear, one view holds that it is not for arbitrators to substitute their own views of justice and morality for those of applicable laws, however odious those may appear to be to most reasonable observers. Rather, if a result that is produced by an odious law is unacceptable to other legal systems, they will operate their own public policy to refuse the enforcement of arbitral awards applying such laws. This view proceeds on the premise that in commercial matters there are no higher principles of international law that seek to correct, or to set aside altogether, applicable

[1] See Case C-102/81 *Nordsee Deutsche Hochseefischerei GmbH v Reederei Mond Hochseefischerei Nordstern AG & Co KG* [1982] ECR I-1095, para 13; *KR v Switzerland* (App No 10881/84) (1987) 51 DR 83.

[2] *BCB Holdings Limited and Belize Bank Limited v Attorney General of Belize* [2013] Caribbean Court of Justice 5, para 23 (Appellate Jurisdiction).

[3] See *Himpurna California Energy Limited (Bermuda) v Republic of Indonesia* (2000) 25 YCA 186, para 11.

domestic law. The premise, therefore, is that international law operates on a separate plane, and it could apply in commercial matters only as part of the applicable domestic law—for example, through an international convention incorporated into national law or as a rule of customary international law that is also a part of national law.

7. The contrary view holds that arbitrators are not merely services providers, but rather have a 'transnational' public policy to defend—being the sum total of fundamental norms on which consensus may be said to exist in the international community. This is said to be not international law per se, but, rather, a broader body of common law applicable in international trade and commerce. Professor Lalive expounded on this notion in a seminal paper in 1986,[4] which has been subsequently endorsed by the House of Lords and the Institut de Droit International.[5]

8. The retort would be that it is not the function of international law to correct bad deals. If two parties agreed to submit their contract or their arbitral process to the law of an idiosyncratic, retrograde or arbitrary state, did they not do so in exercise of their freedom of choice—which is itself recognized by international law? Should we not respect their agreement—which is also a principle recognized by international law? Should we not respect the fact that the choice of law or the choice of arbitral seat also had a price, which was reflected in the economic bargain that the parties struck? These are legitimate questions to ask, but ultimately, I submit, they miss the point. The point is not about using international law as a device to alter the bargain of the parties. Rather, it is about the proper function of international law in commercial and economic matters.

9. There exists today a body of international economic law that, for present purposes, is for the most part codified in four principal sources:

- First, there are almost 3,000 investment treaties. They are, as the *Mondev* tribunal rightly held, evidence of *opinio juris*,[6] even if they are not subscribed in exactly the same terms by all members of the international community of states. These treaties reflect certain core principles—notably about the permissible limits of expropriatory conduct, the need to accord fair and equitable treatment, the observance of commitments freely given to investors, the need for (physical and legal) protection and security to investments, and the prohibition of unjustified discrimination. This body

[4] P Lalive, 'Transnational (or Truly International) Public Policy and International Arbitration', *Comparative Arbitration Practice and Public Policy*, ICCA Congress Series No 3 (1986) 257.

[5] See *Kuwait Airways Corp v Iraqi Airways Company and ors* [2002] UKHL 19, para 115; Institut de Droit International, 'Resolution on Arbitration Between States, State Enterprises, or State Entities, and Foreign Enterprises' (1990) 63ii *Annuaire de l'Institut de Droit International* 324, Art 2.

[6] See *Mondev International Ltd v USA* (ICSID Case No ARB(AF)/99/2), 11 October 2002, para 111.

of law concerns of course investments and their treatment by states and state entities.

- Secondly, in matters concerning the arbitral process and the control of arbitral proceedings, we have the Model Law on International Commercial Arbitration[7] and the Arbitration Rules[8] that have been prepared under the auspices of the United Nations (ie UNCITRAL) on the basis of consensus within the United Nations.
- Thirdly, there are a number of specialized treaties—notably on the corruption of state officials,[9] the protection of cultural heritage objects,[10] and the trade in illicit substances and armaments[11]—which may be relevant to discrete issues arising in a commercial arbitration.
- Finally, there are obligatory (Chapter VII) Security Council Resolutions which may be relevant in the case. One example is the invalidity of a transaction prohibited by UN sanctions.[12] Another example is the invalidity of title acquired through unlawful occupation of territory.[13]

10. The rules set out in these sources are not a reflection of any one tribunal's individual perception of justice and morality, nor are they the product of a comparative study of domestic legal systems by an individual tribunal. Rather, they are rules of international law, or the product of international conferences widely subscribed by the international community of states. As such, they do reflect a certain *opinio juris*. In other words, the proper measure of whether a principle commands consensus in the international community is whether it is endowed with the status of a rule—and that is not a subjective test but, rather, an objective one.

11. Of course, not all such rules are entitled to the status of public policy. Some rules are more important than others, and only the basic precepts reflected in the most fundamental of rules can be said to embody public policy. But that is always the problem with public policy: to deduce from discrete rules the broader but basic purpose—the basic policy—that such rules purport to give effect to. That, of course, is an exercise in judgement, and as such it is

[7] UNCITRAL Model Law on International Commercial Arbitration, 1985 (UN Doc A/40117, Annex I), as amended in 2006 (UN Doc A/61/17, Annex I).

[8] UNCITRAL Arbitration Rules, 1976 (UN Doc A/31/98, Annex I), as revised in 2010 (UN Doc A/65/17, Annex I).

[9] Eg OECD Convention on Combating Bribery of Foreign Public Officials in International Business Transactions (17 December 1997; in force 15 February 1999) (1998) 37 ILM 1.

[10] Convention for the Protection of Cultural Property in the Event of Armed Conflict (14 May 1954; in force 7 August 1956) 249 UNTS 240; Convention Concerning the Protection of World Cultural and Natural Heritage (23 November 1972; in force 17 December 1975) 1037 UNTS 151.

[11] United Nations Convention against Illicit Traffic in Narcotic Drugs and Psychotropic Substances (20 December 1988; in force 11 November 1990) UNTS No 27627; Arms Trade Treaty (2 April 2013; not in force).

[12] See, eg UN Security Council Resolutions Nos 1737 (2006), 1747 (2007), 1803 (2008) and 1929 (2010) on the Iran sanctions.

[13] See, eg UN Security Council Resolution No 660 (1990) on Iraq's occupation of Kuwait, UN Doc S/RES/660, para 3.

subjective. As the Swiss Tribunal fédéral put it in a decision in 2006, '[t]he fleeting character of public policy may be inherent to the concept, due to its excessive generality'.[14]

12. If the relevant sources of international law—treaty based, customary or part of mandatory Security Council Resolutions—are part of the applicable domestic law, their application by an arbitral tribunal is self-evident, and the matter then is one of duty, not mere entitlement. But even if they are not part of applicable domestic law, an arbitral tribunal is entitled—though perhaps not obligated—to observe them. The ICC tribunal in the *Westinghouse v Philippines* case[15] put it as follows: '[Unlike a state court, an arbitral tribunal] has to take into consideration the requirement of international public policy that might, in certain circumstances, require the consideration of other provisions than those of the governing law'.

13. Saying that international law does not apply on the commercial plane is not a good objection: if a principle is relevant to the case, it is obvious that international law does apply, or else the principle would not be relevant in the first place. And if international law does apply, it is not a good objection either to say that an arbitral tribunal cannot access international law. After all—as originally stated—an arbitral tribunal, unlike a domestic court, has no local sovereign to whom it owes exclusive allegiance.

14. I am aware of the riposte that allowing arbitrators to overrule applicable domestic law may expose their awards to be set aside, eg on grounds of non-compliance with local public policy, and thus, the argument goes, the whole idea of an international public policy may lead to complete nullities and monumental wastes of money and time. That is not a bad point. It puts the finger on a key choice. If arbitrators are to follow applicable domestic law even where it contravenes international law, they may produce awards that are perfectly good locally—within the confines of the jurisdiction of the relevant domestic law—but not in any other country that respects international law as part of its public policy. By contrast, if arbitrators observe international law, disregarding national law if need be, and run the risk of annulment of their award, it is possible that other jurisdictions will nevertheless regard the award as standing, refusing to recognize the annulment, by the application (again) of public policy. The decisions of the Amsterdam Court of Appeal and the English Court of Appeal in the *Yukos/Rosneft* saga[16] illustrate this point well. The courts refused to recognize a Russian court annulment of an arbitral award on the grounds of systematic and pervasive interference by

[14] *Tensaccia SpA v Freyssinet Terra Armata RL*, 132 ATF III 389 (2006), s 2.1.

[15] ICC Case No 6401/1991 (1992) 7(1) Mealey's International Arbitration Report 31.

[16] See *Yukos Capital SARL v OAO Rosneft*, 28 April 2009 (Amsterdam Court of Appeal), discussed critically by AJ van den Berg, (2010) 27(2) *Journal of International Arbitration* 179; *Yukos Capital SARL v OJSC Rosneft Oil Company* [2012] EWCA Civ 855.

the Russian government in judicial business in politically sensitive cases. The English court stated the position as follows:

> [J]udgments are recognisable and enforceable in other nations only to the extent that they have observed what we would call substantive or natural justice, what in the United States is called due process, and what internationally is more and more being referred to as the rule of law.[17]

15. I should add, in closing on this point, that the approach I have just outlined does not seek to disregard the fundamental principles of morality and justice that are accepted in domestic legal systems. It is clear that they, too, form part of public policy, and this has been recognized in too many national court decisions to warrant specific reference. But such principles are for domestic courts, not arbitral tribunals, to enforce in exercising control over arbitral awards. Put otherwise, I submit that the only proper warrant for an arbitral tribunal to overrule or qualify the application of a domestic law rule that would otherwise be applicable is if there is a contrary rule of international law reflecting international public policy.

16. I now come to the three principles of public policy which I submit are essential—above all others—to an effective system of international commercial arbitration.

III. RESPECT FOR THE AGREED FORUM

17. The first principle is respect for arbitration as the agreed forum. The premise of this principle is that arbitration is the normal method for the resolution of international commercial disputes—not a *juridiction d'exception* or a derogation from the jurisdiction of state courts, but an equal and equally reliable forum. Another way of putting this is to say that arbitral tribunals may be relied upon to identify the law and the facts, adjudicate fairly, apply mandatory rules and produce a judicial decision rather than a commercial settlement clothed in the form of an arbitral award. And that is, of course, international arbitration as practised in many—though perhaps not all—jurisdictions of the world.

18. Because arbitration is consistent with the parties' needs and expectations in international commerce, agreements for submission to arbitration benefit from a number of important rules which in their totality reflect the principle of respect for the agreed forum. I have singled out three as cardinal. First, the rule that a domestic court may have jurisdiction to compel arbitration by assisting in the constitution of the tribunal where not to do so would condone the international delict of denial of justice. Such occurrences are obviously very rare, but there is one case which stands out, *Israel v National Iranian*

[17] [2012] EWCA Civ 855, para 87.

Oil Company.[18] The dispute concerned an oil pipeline supplying Iranian oil to Israel, which was disrupted some years after the Iranian revolution. The contract provided for purely ad hoc arbitration: no arbitral institution, no arbitration rules and no arbitral seat were agreed. Israel sued and NIOC defaulted in the proceedings. There being no agreed seat, arbitration law or arbitration rules, there was no obvious mechanism to constitute an arbitral tribunal in circumstances of a defaulting respondent. The Paris Court of Appeal, to which Israel resorted, accepted to appoint an arbitrator in the stead of NIOC. The Cour de cassation approved the lower court in a decision of February 2005. It reasoned as follows:

> The impossibility for a party to have access to a forum, be it an arbitral forum, . . . and thus to exercise a right that is part of international public policy under basic rules of arbitration law and Art 6(1) of the ECHR, constitutes a denial of justice—and this establishes the jurisdiction of the French court to assist in the constitution of the arbitral tribunal, provided there is a link with France.[19]

19. This ruling was codified in the recent modifications to French arbitration law (1505(4) CPC).[20] Also, the Tribunal fédéral of Switzerland, where the tribunal which was eventually constituted fixed its seat, recently accepted that the French courts had properly exercised jurisdiction.[21]

20. Secondly, the rule of separability of the arbitration agreement. This is codified in the UNCITRAL Model Law[22] and Arbitration Rules[23]—and, indeed, in every domestic statute and set of Arbitration Rules of which I am aware. The rule provides that the invalidity of an arbitration agreement will not be presumed to follow from the invalidity of the main agreement of which the arbitration agreement typically forms a part; rather, the invalidity will need to be specifically demonstrated in respect of the arbitration agreement itself.

21. A very good illustration of this is the decision of a distinguished tribunal in the ICSID case of *Niko Resources v Bangladesh*, where it was held that corruption in the procurement of a public contract may affect the validity of the main agreement (though ultimately, on the facts of that case, it did not) but it will not be assumed to affect the validity of the arbitration clause in the agreement and it will have to be specifically demonstrated (which it had not been).[24] By application of the same principle, the English High Court also upheld a series of awards issued in relation to contracts of guarantee which,

[18] CA Paris, 29 March 2001, *National Iranian Oil Company (NIOC) v Etat d'Israël* (2002) 129 JDI 498.

[19] Cass Civ 1ère, 1 February 2005, [2005] Rev Arb 693, (2005) 30 YCA 125, para 2.

[20] See French Code of Civil Procedure, Art 1505(4).

[21] See *Etat d'Israël v National Iranian Oil Company* (2013) 31(2) ASA Bulletin 383.

[22] UNCITRAL Model Law, Art 16(1).

[23] UNCITRAL Rules, Art 23(1).

[24] See *Niko Resources Ltd v People's Republic of Bangladesh and ors* (ICSID Case No ARB/10/11 and ICSID Case No ARB/10/18), Decision on Jurisdiction, 19 August 2013, paras 446 and 464.

it was commonly accepted, were invalid due to failure to register them with the Chinese authorities, as was required by Chinese law.[25]

22. The third aspect of the principle of respect for access to the agreed forum is the approach taken in all recent cases involving corrupt contracts which were submitted to arbitration. The initial approach, reflected in an ICC award given by Judge Lagergren as sole arbitrator in 1963, was altogether to decline jurisdiction to hear a claim relating to a corrupt contract—one that the arbitrator held was 'contrary to good morals and to international public policy common to the community of nations'.[26] But all more recent decisions, culminating in the well-known *World Duty Free v Kenya* case,[27] have held that the tribunal does have jurisdiction—unless it can be specifically shown that the arbitration agreement would not have been obtained had it not been for corruption—if only to hold the substantive agreement invalid on grounds of illegality.[28]

IV. PROHIBITION OF CORRUPT CONTRACTS

23. These cases are a segue to the second principle, which relates to the prohibition of corrupt contracts. There is an important distinction here, and it is one that the *Niko v Bangladesh*[29] decision brings to the fore well. One category of corrupt contracts—by far the largest category—are contracts which are lawful in their purpose (eg the provision of a public service or public procurement) but unlawful as to the manner in which they were obtained, that is, by corrupting public officials. Here, the function of international law is to defer to the public policy of the state concerned—very much as explained by the ICJ in an unrelated context in the *Guardianship of Infants Convention* case[30] and very much as provided for under Article V(2)(b) of the New York Convention of 1958.[31] In other words, the function of international law is to cross-refer to domestic law and to allow it fully to develop its consequences.

24. An altogether separate, and different, category is contracts of corruption, where the contract has corruption as its very purpose. There, as the *Niko*

[25] See *Emeraldian Limited Partnership v Wellmix Shipping Limited and ors* [2010] EWHC 1411 (Comm).

[26] ICC Case No 1110/1963 (1994) 10(3) Arbitration International 227, para 20.

[27] *World Duty Free Company Limited v The Republic of Kenya* (ICSID Case No Arb/00/7) 4 October 2006, paras 157 and 164–65.

[28] For a monograph-length treatment see R Kreindler, *Competence-Competence in the Face of Illegality in Contracts and Arbitration Agreements* (2013; reprinted from (2012-III) 361 RdC).

[29] See n 24 above.

[30] *Case Concerning the Application of the Convention of 1902 Governing the Guardianship of Infants* [1958] ICJ Reports 55.

[31] Convention on the Recognition and Enforcement of Foreign Arbitral Awards (10 June 1958; in force 7 June 1959) 330 UNTS 3, Art V(2)(b): 'Recognition and enforcement of an arbitral award may also be refused if the competent authority in the country where recognition and enforcement is sought finds that . . . the recognition or enforcement of the award would be contrary to the public policy of that country'.

decision makes plain, it is a 'principle of international public policy' that 'the prohibition of bribery overrides the general principle of party autonomy'.[32] That is to say, the parties are not able to ratify the contract after the corruption came to the fore and in this way to salvage it from invalidity. International law will not allow ratification of the contract, which will remain ab initio invalid, even if applicable domestic law says otherwise. In that regard, the *Niko* decision follows the 1996 award in ICC Case 7664 (*Frontier AG v Thomson CSF*)[33] very closely, and that approach is also mirrored in the decision of the English court in the *Hilmarton* case.[34]

V. FAIRNESS OF PROCESS AND INDEPENDENCE/ IMPARTIALITY OF ARBITRATORS

25. The UNCITRAL Model Law on International Arbitration, the UNCITRAL Arbitration Rules and the 1958 New York Convention require, in plain and mandatory terms, that arbitrators be independent and impartial.[35] This is both fundamental and elementary, for two distinct reasons:

- First, because it is unthinkable that a partial or non-independent tribunal will hear the parties in equality, conduct the process fairly and decide with an open mind—and these rules are, in the words of UNCITRAL, the *Magna Carta* of arbitration;[36] and, in the words of the International Court of Justice, 'requirements of good administration of justice'.[37]
- The second reason is that the appearance of independence and impartiality of arbitrators is ultimately what gives confidence in the fairness of the entire process—and such confidence is in itself a public good.

26. It should therefore come as no surprise that it has been held that independence and impartiality form parts of the international public policy of the community of nations.[38]

[32] Above n 24, para 434.

[33] ICC Case No 7664/1996, reported by A Sayed, *Corruption in International Trade and Commercial Arbitration* (2001), 51, 119, 248, 290, 353 and 565, cited with approval in *Niko v Bangladesh* (n 24 above), para 119.

[34] See *Omnium de Traitement et de Valorisation SA v Hilmarton Ltd* [1999] 2 Lloyd's Rep 223. Although the contract was technically contrary to Algerian law (which prohibited contracts for intermediation in public procurement), Swiss law contained no such prohibition, and it was not the case that the object of the contract was corruption of public officials.

[35] UNCITRAL Model Law, Art 12; UNCITRAL Rules, Art 12; New York Convention, Art V(1)(b).

[36] Analytical commentary on draft text of a model law on international commercial arbitration: report of the Secretary-General, UN Doc A/CN.9/264, (1985) 16 UNCITRAL YB 104, 124.

[37] *Application for Review of Judgment No 158 of United Nations Administrative Tribunal* [1973] ICJ Reports 166, 179.

[38] See, eg Tribunal fédéral, *Club Atlético de Madrid SAD (Spain) v Sport Lisboa e Benfica—Futebol SAD (Portugal), Fédération Internationale de Football Association—FIFA (Switzerland)* (2010) 28 ASA Bulletin 511, (2010) 35 YCA 614, s 7.

27. It is true that all domestic laws require that arbitrators be impartial and independent. However, in practice not all laws espouse the same conception of independence and impartiality.[39] Does international law set some limits beyond which domestic law cannot venture? I should think yes. And I should think that, in due course, with the development of practice, those limits will emerge in rather clear guidelines.

28. In that connection, it has been said, as we heard from Lord Mance yesterday, that the very idea of appointment of arbitrators by parties may be antithetical to independence and impartiality. The argument is that a party in litigation is focusing its energies on winning the case—not on appointing an impartial and independent arbitrator. This discussion is raging in the field of investment arbitration,[40] where issues fall within generally narrow compasses and where decisions are public, neither of which is true in commercial arbitrations. Nevertheless, the argument about the principle of party appointment has been made for all types of cases, and logically applies to all types of cases. In my view, while it is of course difficult to deny that party appointments are made tactically—with a view to winning the case—it does not and cannot follow that parties appoint partial or non-independent arbitrators. Parties, or at least properly advised parties, are thinking of effective arbitrators, by which I mean arbitrators that are—in addition to being competent—philosophically inclined to understand, and possibly espouse, the type of case that the party appointing them will be advancing in the arbitration. A partial or dependent arbitrator is the very contrary: a cause for embarrassment and the least likely person to be effective.

[39] See S Luttrell, *Bias Challenges in International Commercial Arbitration: The Need for a 'Real Danger' Test* (2009) 63–185; K Daele, *Challenge and Disqualification of Arbitrators in International Arbitration* (2012), 269–453.

[40] See notably N Ziadé, 'L'éthique et l'arbitrage en matière d'investissement: grandeur et misère de la fonction d'arbitre' [2012] *Revue de l'Arbitrage* 307.

22

Abuse of Rights in Modern International Investment Arbitration: The Rule of Law Revisited? The Practitioner's View

STRATIS G GEORGILAS*

I. INTRODUCTION

ONE OF THE problems an international lawyer in practice is likely to encounter is the dishonest client. There are clients whose case would involve previous dishonesty. Some dishonesty is relatively venial; other dishonesty is more serious.[1] What I propose to analyse is how the World Court, along with other international tribunals, deal with litigants who seem to employ a particular type of dishonesty, namely 'abusive practices', especially in investment proceedings, under the prism of the rule of (international) law. In this context, one should be mindful that the rule of law is a rule of integrity,[2] one of the most powerful words or expressions today,[3] and that, in Tom Bingham's words, 'observance of the rule of law is quite as important on the international plane as on the national, perhaps even more so'.[4]

* Barrister, LLM (i) (Cantab, Hughes Hall), G-H Chambers, Head of Chambers, Athens. Email: www.ghlaw.co.gr. 2014 ©. I am indebted to J Crawford (Cantab), Chr Greenwood (Cantab & ICJ) and V Lowe (Cantab & Oxon). I wish to thank Sofia Roma, apprentice at G-H Chambers, for her research assistance. The usual disclaimer applies.

[1] To paraphrase Lord Reed's lecture (University of Edinburgh, 26 October 2012), available at http://www.supremecourt.gov.uk/docs/speech-121026.pdf (last accessed on 12 October 2014).

[2] Lord Neuberger MR, 'The Tyranny of the Consumer and the Rule of Law', paper presented at the 25th Annual Bar Conference, 6 November 2010.

[3] BZ Tamanaha, *On the Rule of Law* (Cambridge University Press, 2004) 3.

[4] T Bingham, *The Rule of Law* (Allen Lane, 2010) 110.

The rule of law mirrors the history of efforts to restrain unchecked sovereign power, which is still present in many states today.[5] According to some, not least James Crawford, doubt should be cast on whether the cardinal legal value of the rule of law can be sought even in principle within the premises of international law, since it is predicated on domestic law only.[6] However, international practice has undergone a substantial change: the UNSC first used the phrase in the operative paragraph 2 of SC Resolution 1040 (1996) in support of the UNSG efforts to promote 'the rule of law in Burundi'. Of paramount significance, states expressly reaffirmed their commitment to 'an international order based on the rule of law and international law' at the UN World summit in 2005.[7] The maxim is found no less than 12 times in the resulting resolution, including in the first section on 'values and principles', as well as, inter alia, under the heading of investments.[8] State practice has steadily endorsed it. As Arthur Watts described it, 'the transition from the establishment of international order by the hegemonic power of one or a few states to the full establishment of the international rule of law is a still-continuing process'.[9]

With the current state of international affairs, the sovereign independence of states is indeed balanced, if not curtailed, by the international rule of law.[10]

II. DOGMATIC UNDERPINNINGS

Eminent legal authorities, like Westlake, maintain that the prohibition of employing abusive practices, which spread into international law from Roman law, is incorporated within the customary law of nations.[11] This has never been contradicted, as Hersch Lauterpacht acknowledges.[12] Lauterpacht adds that there is no better evidence of the legal conviction of states than those international acts and agreements where states formulate the law to be fol-

[5] N Politis, 'Le Problème des Limitations de la Souveraineté et la Theorie de l' Abus des Droits dans les Rapports Internationaux' (1925) 1 *Revue Critique de Jurisprudence Belge* 5. S Chesterman, 'An International Rule of Law?', available at http://ssrn.com/abstract=1081738 (accessed on 12 October 2014) 38.

[6] J Crawford, 'International Law and the Rule of Law' (2003) 24 *Adelaide Law Review* 3, 5; J Waldron, 'Are Sovereigns Entitled to the Benefit of the International Rule of Law?' (2011) 22 *European Journal of International Law* 315.

[7] UN DOC A/RES/60/1, available at http://www.un.org/summit2005 (accessed on 12 October 2014) § 134.

[8] S Beaulac, 'An Inquiry into the International Rule of Law', EUI No 2007/14, 28.

[9] (1993) 36 GYIL 15, 45.

[10] Morin spoke of an emerging international rule of law: JY Morin, 'L'État de Droit: Emergence d' un Principe du Droit International' (1995) 255 *Revue Critique de Jurisprudence Belge* 9, 27. See also I Brownlie, *The Rule of Law in International Affairs* (Brill 1998). For a quite novel approach, E Benvenisti, 'Sovereigns as Trustees of Humanity: On the Accountability of states to foreign Stakeholders' (2013) 107 *American Journal of International Law* 295.

[11] John Westlake (1828–1913) Whewell Professor or International Law at Cambridge. See *International Law*, vol i, 2nd edn (1910–13) 13.

[12] H Lauterpacht, *Private Law Sources and Analogies of International Law* (reprint, Lawbook Exchange, 2002) 27.

lowed by international judicial tribunals.[13] He also suggests that there is no need to resort to rules of an extraneous system of law so long as other avenues are open.[14] His insight is of particular merit should title of jurisdiction include, say, the United Nations Convention on the Law of the Sea (signed more than 20 years after his death), in Article 300 of which the doctrine of abuse of rights is expressly incorporated.[15] A state upholding its obligation to act in good faith and the corresponding right of others to rely on the former's conduct is bound by its own act. This affirmation of the duty to act in good faith,[16] and therefore the prohibition of abusing one's rights, rests well on general international law.

III. THE CASE LAW OF THE WORLD COURT

International society no longer seems to tolerate the unchecked use of rights without regard to its social consequences. There is no legal right, however well established, which could not, in some circumstances, be refused enforcement on the ground that it has been abused.[17]

Indeed, in May 1926, the Permanent Court of International Justice was cautious when it held that German acts of alienation did not overstep the limits of normal administration of public property. In a much quoted passage,[18] it found that

> Only a misuse of this right [Germany's right to dispose of state property situated in Upper Silesia] could endow any act of alienation with the character of a breach of Germany's international obligations on the matter . . . *Such misuse cannot be presumed and it rests with the party who states that there has been such misuse to prove his statement.*[19]

[13] Ibid, 60.

[14] Ibid, 85.

[15] Being mindful of Art 18 of VCLT 1969, it is suggested that a signatory enjoys a fairly large margin of discretion in terms of compliance with the Treaty in question before the moment of ratification and, allegedly, 'the only possible way to claim a violation of a signed treaty is by having recourse to the theory of abuse of rights or to the disregard of the principle of good faith . . . need to be assessed to a large extend in concreto taking into account circumstances varying from one situation to another and not easily established', O Corten and P Klein (eds), *The Vienna Conventions on the Law of Treaties, A Commentary,* vol I (Oxford University Press, 2011) 376.

[16] H Lauterpacht, *The Development of International Law by the International Court* (Cambridge University Press, 2010) 172. See also AC Kiss, *L'Abus de Droit en Droit International* (LGDJ, 1952). JF O' Connor, *Good Faith in International Law* (Dartmouth, 1991). R Kolb, *La bonnefoi en droit international public* (Presses universitaires de France, 2000).

[17] Lauterpacht, ibid 164. G Schwarzenberger, 'Uses and Abuses of the "Abuse of Rights" in International Law' (1956) 42 *Grotius Society Transactions* 147, 157–58. GDS Taylor, 'The Content of the Rule against Abuse of Rights in International Law' (1972–573) 46 *British Year Book of International Law* 323. M Byers, 'Abuse of Rights: An Old Principle, A New Age' (2002) 47 *McGill Law Journal* 389.

[18] *Certain German Interests in Polish Upper Silesia*, Series A, No 7 (1926) 30.

[19] Ibid, emphasis added.

A clear affirmation of this finding is found in the *Free Zones* case,[20] where the court, while upholding the legality of French fiscal legislation applied in the territory of the Free Zones, as in any other part of France, nevertheless emphasised that 'a reservation must be made as regards the case of abuse of a right, an abuse which, however, cannot be presumed by the Court'.[21]

On similar issues, the court held[22] that a state is estopped from relying on its own non-fulfilment of an international obligation.[23] Hence, the result of a clear and unequivocal representation of one litigant, on which his adversary was entitled to rely and actually did rely, constitutes a substantial change in the latter's position[24] which is of enormous legal significance. In a rather implicit acknowledgement of the principle of good faith, the court acceded to a request when the respondent's declaration, the court's title of jurisdiction, expired while the application was in process of drafting and a few days before it was filed.[25] Finally, one notable exposition and application of the *alter* Janus face, namely the 'clean hand principle', is found in the opinions rendered by the court in the *Diversion of Water from the Meuse*, particularly in the individual opinion appended by Judge Hudson and the dissenting opinion issued by Judge Anzilotti.[26]

As Judge Greenwood puts it, even in a system that has no precedent, most tribunals will not seek to diverge with earlier findings, unless compelled to do so; in a way, he continues, tribunals take some comfort in knowing that the principles they are looking at have been applied in a certain way by previous tribunals in similar circumstances.[27] The case law of the International Court of Justice (ICJ) follows this pattern.

Right from its early days,[28] the ICJ clearly endorsed the principle prohibiting abuse of rights in the frequent affirmation of the duty of states to act in good faith when exercising their legitimate rights. The court was of the opinion that 'Article 4 of the Charter does not forbid the taking into account

[20] Series A/B, No 46 (1932) 167.

[21] Ibid.

[22] *Chorzow Factory—Indemnity; Jurisdiction*, Series A, No 9 (1927) 31.

[23] Affirmed in the *Danzig Railway Officials*, Series B, No 15 (1928) 27.

[24] *Serbian Loans*, Series A, No 20 (1929) 39. Affirmed in *Eastern Greenland*, Series A/B, No 53 (1933) 69.

[25] *Pajzs, Csaky, Esterhazy*, Series A/B, No 68 (1936) 41, 65. Rosenne argues that, in principle, this finding is applicable also to the case in which a declaration is denounced while the application is in process of drafting, 'unless the argument could be sustained that there was an element of mala fides or abuse of rights in the filing of the denunciation', S Rosenne, *The Law and Practice of the International Court 1920–2005* (Martinus Nijhoff, 2006) 941.

[26] Quoted by SM Schwebel, *Justice in International Law* (Cambridge University Press, 2011) 297–98.

[27] Quoted by N Gallagher, 'The Rule of Law and Investment Protection' in R McCorquodale (ed), *The Rule of Law in International and Comparative Context* (British Institute of International and Comparative Law, 2010) 139. An echo of Shahabudeen's views can be clearly identified thereto: M Shahabudeen, *Precedent in the World Court* (Cambridge University Press, 1996).

[28] *Conditions of Admission to Membership in the United Nations* [1948] ICJ Reports 63.

of any factor which is possibly, reasonably and in good faith to connect with the conditions laid down in that Article'.[29]

In a given case where the ICJ was asked to apply the principle of the general direction of the coast for the purpose of determining the baseline of territorial waters, it held[30] 'one cannot confine oneself to examining one sector of the coast only, *except in a case of manifest abuse*'.[31]

It also upheld the principle *ex injuria jus non oritur*, a special manifestation of the prohibition to employ abusive practice, holding that 'The principle ex injuria jus non oritur is sustained by the Court's findings that the legal relationship created by the 1977 Treaty is preserved and cannot in this case be treated as voided by unlawful conduct'.[32]

It was again Judge Lauterpacht who stated in his separate opinion that

> [A]n Administering state which consistently sets itself above the solemnly and repeatedly expressed judgment of the Organization, in particular in proportion as that judgement approximates to unanimity, may find that it has overstepped the imperceptible line between impropriety and illegality, between discretion and arbitrariness, *between the exercise of the legal right to disregard the recommendation and the abuse of that right*, and that it has exposed itself to consequences legitimately following as a legal sanction.[33]

One has to note the forceful language used by Judge ad hoc Van Den Wyngaert in *Arrest Warrant of 11 April 2000 (Democratic Republic of the Congo v Belgium)*, who dissented on the ground that 'The Congo did not come to Court with clean hands. In blaming Belgium for investigating and prosecuting allegations of international crimes that it was obliged to investigate and prosecute itself, The Congo *acts in bad faith*.'[34]

At the jurisdiction and admissibility phase, the World Court has been asked many times to pronounce that a party has been practising an abuse of rights or has not been acting in good faith. An application that was properly filed and presented, within the framework of that party's right to have recourse to the World Court in the circumstances of the case, was not declared an abuse of process.[35] An objection to the admissibility of an application was also dismissed. In an almost identical fashion, the court found the application to be properly submitted, namely within the framework of the remedies open

[29] Ibid, emphasis added. Judge Azevedo invoked the doctrine of abuse of rights, too, [1948] ICJ Reports 79–80. The very same applies in the Dissenting Opinion of Judge Alvarez in *Competence of the General Assembly for the Admission of a State to the United Nations* [1950] ICJ Reports 15.

[30] *AngloNorwegian Fisheries Case* [1951] ICJ Reports 142.

[31] Ibid, emphasis added.

[32] *Gabčíkovo-Nagymaros Project* [1997] ICJ Reports 7. Judge Weeramantry's Separate Opinion treated the principle of abuse of rights as a 'well-established area of international law', available at http://www.icj-cij.org/docket/files/92/7383.pdf (accessed on 12 October 2014).

[33] *Voting Procedure on Questions relating to Reports and Petitions concerning the Territory of South-West Africa, Advisory Opinion* [1955] ICJ Reports 67, emphasis added.

[34] [2002] ICJ Reports 137, emphasis added.

[35] *Arbitral Award of 31 July 1989* [1991] ICJ Reports 53, 63.

to the applicant. Such conduct does not amount to an abuse of process.[36] As to whether raising preliminary objections constitutes a per se abuse of the respondent's right, the World Court was adamant and, *in casu*, declined to accept so. It reiterated previous case law and held that

> the Court must, in each case submitted to it, verify whether it has jurisdiction to deal with the case and, if necessary, whether the Application is admissible and as such objections are raised by the respondent may be useful to clarify the legal situation. As matters now stand, the preliminary objections presented by Yugoslavia have served that purpose.[37]

The World Court gives full effect to the intention of the parties. It interprets their intention in accordance with the paramount principle of good faith in a fair and reasonable manner. The doctrine of abuse of rights is an instrument that is wielded with restraint by the judiciary. In a broader sense, good faith cannot be easily reconciled with an absolute form of sovereignty advanced by some states. Consequently, the main function of the prohibition to employ abusive practices is that of a safety valve to be kept in reserve.

IV. THE TREATIFICATION OF RIGHTS IN FOREIGN INVESTMENT DISPUTES AND THE RULE OF LAW

In the present form of our international society, each international situation is capable of being determined as a matter of law.[38] In particular, a dramatic and rapid change has taken place in the international legal investment landscape.

International protection afforded to foreign investors who are presenting all kind of grievances is of an unprecedented magnitude.[39] Prior to 1959, international investment protection essentially rested on general international law. This does not hold true nowadays, since 'treaties have become the fundamental source of international law in the area of foreign investment'.[40] This treatification has paved the way to the firm establishment of the rule of law in the respective international investment regime, for a clear, recognizable and identifiable system has been developed. Indeed, some legal instruments—the Energy Charter Treaty being a leading example—refer expressly to the rule of law. Accordingly, remedies provided by other bilateral and multilateral investment treaties (BITs and MITs) ensure that the treatment of foreign investment is subject to the rule of law. Moreover, since the state has been 'dethroned

[36] *Phosphate in Nauru* [1992] ICJ Reports 240, 255.

[37] *Application of the Genocide Convention, Preliminary Objections* [1996-II] ICJ Reports 595, 622.

[38] RY Jennings and A Watts, *Oppenheim's International Law*, 9th edn (Longman, 1992) 12–13.

[39] T Weiler, *The Interpretation of International Investment Law* (Martinus Nijhoff, 2013), esp Chapter 7.

[40] JW Salacuse, 'The Treatification of International Investment Law' (2007) 13 *Law & Business Review of the Americas* 155, 157.

from its status as the sole subject of international law',[41] a recognised legal regime governing the relationship between investors and states has surfaced. Effectively, a rule of law system has emerged.[42] Here, the role of international law is, inter alia, to reinforce the rule of law internally. There seems to be a presumption against the foreign investor's intentions of promoting public good. Practice has shown that this presumption does not necessarily comport with reality. As the Minister for Finance of Uruguay allegedly put it, upon signing the USA–Uruguay BIT, 'We are not doing it for them, we are doing it for us'.[43] Alas, some governments eagerly deploy the powers of the state especially in investment disputes. The *Barcelona Traction* case was triggered by the then Franco-ruled government of Spain against a foreign utility investor, while Josef Stalin's keen personal 'interest' in the *Lena Goldfield* case is well known and well documented.[44]

No state has ever suggested, directly or indirectly, that its practice contravenes or even disregards the international rule of law. No state practice to this effect can be traced. On the contrary, case law proves that the plethora of states refers to the rule of law as a defence for actions under scrutiny. The international community now pays much closer attention than it did in the past to the ethical standards necessary to ensure that the rule of law is observed in the settlement of international disputes.[45]

It is common knowledge to international lawyers that the mere existence of recourse to an impartial international judicial tribunal, applying known legal rules in order to determine the law and resolve legal disputes, is a condition *sine qua non* for the existence of the international rule of law. Should one pay closer attention to the so-called institutionalized investment arbitration, one could easily face the 'shaping of the rule' characteristic of the prohibition to employ *mala fides* practice. Its antonym, *bona fides*, constitutes a preliminary assessment of a state's practice, with a special value when the settlement mechanism is instituted. Despite its high degree of subjectivity[46] and relativity,[47] flexibility is this principle's main advantage. It is widely acknowledged that prohibition of abuse should promote the cause of justice, and therefore the

[41] Schwebel (n 26 above), 137, 140, identifying a reshape of the body of general international law, 141.

[42] Gallagher (n 27 above), 139.

[43] Quoted by JW Salacuse, *The Law of International Investment Treaties* (Oxford University Press, 2010) 114.

[44] T Wälde, '"Equality of Arms" in Investment Arbitration' in K Yannaka-Small (ed), *Procedural Challenges in Arbitration under International Investment Agreements* (Oxford University Press, 2010) 163.

[45] Judge Buergenthal expressed a wish to this effect, 'The Proliferation of Disputes, Dispute Settlement Procedures and Respect for the Rule of Law' (Geneva, 21–22 April 2006).

[46] M Sornarajah, *The International Law on Foreign Investment* (Cambridge University Press, 2007) 93–94.

[47] The doctrine of clean hands 'is not an absolute one': C Amerasinghe, *Diplomatic Protection* (Oxford University Press, 2008) 222.

rule of law. After all, the rule of law includes an implied clause that it should not be abused.[48]

All contracting states, whether under the The International Centre for Settlement of Investment Disputes (ICSID) regime, the Energy Charter Treaty or any BIT in force, are under a general obligation to ensure, in good faith, that the convention's object and purpose are not frustrated.[49] Quite recently, in *Micula et al v Romania*, it was held that

> Good faith is a standard that is flexible. A requirement of good faith is prevalent in all fields of the law and will arise in various matters, such as . . . the prohibition to abuse rights, and the protection of legitimate expectations. As such, it eludes any strict definition. However, as a minimum, good faith would require that any party would not consciously conduct itself in such a way that should contradict the implications of that party's earlier behaviour, a concept akin to the prohibition of estoppel.[50]

Even consent to arbitral jurisdiction may not be withheld arbitrarily, while state parties to a BIT must consider recourse to ICSID in good faith.[51] A quite common condition for the institution of arbitral investment protection proceedings is that an amicable settlement has been attempted through consultations or negotiations to be undertaken in good faith.[52]

V. THE TRIBUNALS' CASE LAW IN INVESTMENT ARBITRATION

The scope and margin of the prohibition to employ abusive practices that is presented before arbitral tribunals is surprising.

In *Gardella v Ivory Coast*[53] the issue was, inter alia, about the law applicable to contractual issues against the background of general international law. The tribunal decided that 'it is necessary to have regard to the principle of good faith'.[54] Full credit has to be given to the tribunal in *Duke Energy v*

[48] E De Brabandere, 'Good Faith, Abuse of Process and the Initiation of Investment Treaty Claims' (2012) *Journal of International Dispute Settlement* 3 609, 612, citing *Action Ltd v Czech Republic,* Award of 15 April 2009, § 107.

[49] D Draguiev, 'Bad Faith Conduct of States in Violation of the "Fair and Equitable Treatment" Standard in International Law and Arbitration' (2014) 5 *Journal of International Dispute Settlement* 273.

[50] ICSID Case No ARB/05/20, Award of 11 December 2013, 831, available at http://www.italaw.com/sites/default/files/case-documents/italaw3036.pdf (accessed on 12 October 2014), an annulment request pending.

[51] Eg the Netherlands–Yugoslavia BIT of 1976. In *MCI Power v Ecuador* it was held that Ecuador has not acted in bad faith when refusing to sign an arbitration agreement, quoted by KJ Vandervelde, *Bilateral Investment Treaties* (Oxford University Press, 2010) 211. U Topkan 'Abuse of the Right to access ICSID Arbitration' (2014) 28 *ICSID Review* 627.

[52] For the ICSID regime see, inter alia, C Schreuer, *The ICSID Convention—A Commentary* (Cambridge University Press, 2001) 239. Recommendations of conciliators must be considered in good faith.

[53] 1 ICSID Reports 283.

[54] Ibid, 287.

Ecuador,[55] where it was held that it had 'a duty to contribute to the harmonious development of investment law and thereby promote certainty in the rule of law'.[56] The very same applies in *Daimler v Argentina*,[57] where the tribunal acknowledged that 'it is a fundamental principle of the rule of law that "like cases should be decided alike", unless a strong reason exists to distinguish the current case from previous one'.[58]

At the *jurisdiction and admissibility* phase, in *SPP v Egypt*,[59] the tribunal held that jurisdictional instruments are to be interpreted objectively and in good faith, and jurisdiction will be found to exist if—but only if—the force of the arguments militating in favour of it is preponderant. In *Tradex v Albania*,[60] the consent clause was subject to the condition that the dispute 'cannot be settled amicably'. The tribunal found that Tradex sent five letters over four months to the competent Albanian Ministry, with none of them eliciting a reply or resulting in any action. Consequently, these letters were held to be a sufficient effort of good faith to reach an amicable settlement. In *Arif v Moldova*,[61] the tribunal rejected a respondent's argument that it had not had a fair opportunity to engage in settlement discussions at any time after the dispute had actually matured and that the claimant did not pursue in good faith the negotiations he had started.[62] In *Abaclat v Argentina*,[63] the tribunal rightly pointed out that

> the theory of abuse of rights is an expression of the more general principle of good faith . . . a fundamental principle of international law, as well as investment law. As such, the tribunal hold that the theory of abuse of rights is, in principle, applicable to ICSID proceedings.[64]

In *Malicorp v Egypt*,[65] the tribunal attached a considerable weight to the principle of good faith where a concession has been granted as a result of error, fraud or corruption and the state requests the tribunal to decline jurisdiction because of the violation of the principle.[66] In *Phoenix Action v Czech Republic*,[67] the tribunal emphasised the need to preserve the system of direct legal access to investment arbitration from abuses, with good faith operating as a safeguard against abusive uses.[68] Again, in *Arif v Moldova*,[69] the tribunal

[55] Award of 18 August 2008.
[56] Ibid, § 117.
[57] Award of 22 August 2012.
[58] Ibid, § 52, citing *Suez, Sociedad v Argentina*.
[59] 3 ICSID Reports 143, Award of 14 April 1988.
[60] Decision on Jurisdiction of 24 December 1996.
[61] Award of 8 April 2013.
[62] Ibid, § 340.
[63] Award of 4 August 2011.
[64] Ibid, § 646.
[65] Award of 7 February 2011.
[66] Ibid, § 115.
[67] Award of 15 April 2009.
[68] Ibid, §§ 142–44.
[69] Award of 8 April 2013.

found that there are temporal limitations on a jurisdictional argument based on the illegality of an investment, where the legality of the investment has been accepted and acted upon in good faith by both parties over a period of time.[70] In *Atlantic Triton v Guinea*,[71] the tribunal addressed a claim by Guinea for damages from Atlantic Triton for having instituted abusive proceedings to obtain provisional measures and rejected it.[72] In *CMS Gas Transmission Company v Argentina*,[73] it was held that the plea of necessity invoked by Argentina under customary international law should be subject to judicial review. Accordingly, the tribunal's review of Argentina's plea was not limited merely to whether the exception was invoked in good faith.[74]

Regarding the merits, in *Saabi v Senegal*,[75] the tribunal held that the correct approach, as with any other agreement, was an interpretation consistent with the principle of good faith and 'the interpretation must take into account the consequences which the parties must reasonably and legitimately be considered to have envisaged as flawing from their undertakings'.[76]

In *Inceysa v El Salvador*,[77] the tribunal held that one supreme principle was that of good faith, which means the absence of deceit. It found the claimant to be in violation of the principle of good faith by submitting false information during the process of bidding for the contract that was the basis of the dispute.[78] In *Fraport v Philippines*,[79] the tribunal held that legal violations made by the investor in good faith, such as where the law was not clear or the legal violation was not central to the profitability of the investment, should not result in a loss of treaty protection.[80] In *Tecmed v Mexico*,[81] the tribunal found that the denial to renew a permit necessary to operate a solid waste disposal facility violated the obligation of good faith, which requires reasonableness, consistency and transparency.[82] In *Siemens v Argentina*,[83] the tribunal did not endorse an argument to the effect that the structure of the state does not permit it to fulfil its undertakings, for such contention was found to run counter to the principle of good faith, underlying fair and equitable treatment.[84] On the other hand, in *Encana v Ecuador*,[85] the tribunal held that an executive agency of a state does not repudiate an obligation

[70] Ibid, § 376.
[71] 3 ICSID Reports 17, Award of 21 April 1986.
[72] Ibid, 19.
[73] Award of 25 September 2007.
[74] Ibid, § 120.
[75] 2 ICSID Reports 205, Award of 25 February 1988.
[76] Ibid, 206.
[77] Award of 2 August 2006.
[78] Ibid, § 244.
[79] Award of 16 August 2007.
[80] Ibid, § 396.
[81] Award of 29 May 2003.
[82] Ibid, § 154.
[83] Award of 6 February 2007.
[84] Ibid, § 308.
[85] Award of 3 February 2006.

merely by contesting its existence, as long as it submits its actions to judicial review in good faith and honours the decisions of the courts in performing that review.[86] In *Parkerings—Companiet v Lithuania*,[87] the tribunal seemed to acknowledge that the state's conduct may have violated its duty of good faith under the contract and that its failure to disclose might have breached the contract. Interestingly enough, in *Middle East Cement Shipping & Handling Co SA v Egypt*,[88] the ICSID Tribunal held that a state may treat foreign investment unfairly and inequitably without necessarily acting in bad faith.[89] In *Autopista Concessionada v Venezuela*[90] and *Tokios Tokeles v Ukraine*,[91] both tribunals reached the conclusion that an abuse of rights exists when establishing a corporation for the sole purpose of gaining access to an international arbitration. The very same was held in *Phoenix Action v Czech Republic*,[92] where the tribunal found that when restructuring a corporation for already existing disputes of a domestic character, eg a Czech citizen selling shares to a company incorporated in Israel, the latter owned by the vendor's spouse, an abusive practice exists. It was also followed in *Pac Rim Cayman LLC v El Salvador*,[93] where altering the nationality of a corporation, having assessed that a dispute already exists or foreseeing that a particular dispute is utterly possible, was also held to be abusive, but was distinguished both in *Aquas de Tunari v Bolivia*,[94] when restructuring took place for a legitimate purpose (in this case, avoiding double taxation), and in *Mobil v Venezuela*,[95] where it was justified for protection against onerous national measures on future disputes.

VI. CONCLUDING REMARKS

No modern award has in fact found a state to have acted in bad faith towards an investor, for states can offer public policy as a justification. However, tribunals will eventually have to tackle the issue in the very near future. Caution should be taken, however, for, as Amerasinghe described it,

> The temptation to overemphasise the interest of the individual and to ignore those of the respondent state, on the basis that it is the alien (or the national abroad) that requires as much protection as he can get or protection at any cost, is to be avoided.[96]

[86] Ibid, § 192–94.
[87] Award of 11 September 2007.
[88] Award of 12 April 2002.
[89] Ibid, § 116.
[90] Award of 27 September 2001.
[91] Award of 19 April 2004.
[92] Award of 15 April 2009.
[93] Award of 1 June 2012, § 299.
[94] Award of 21 October 2005.
[95] Award of 10 June 2010.
[96] Above n 46, 344.

The inappropriate liberation of adjudicators from the restraints imposed by general international law might be one of the most serious threats to the legitimacy of the rule of law of the BIT generation.[97] Secondly, certain key BIT clauses have been applied in dissimilar and sometimes contradictory ways, without proper justification[98] After this litany of criticisms, the lately proclaimed self-consciousness of tribunals' role to uphold the rule of law and determine whether the claimant has been denied justice by measures so void of reason that they breathe bad faith or trying to uphold his own rights still remains a quite subjective test. Applying a principle in practice is the safest route to a better future, should one follow precedent.

The effect of the abuse of rights prohibition can be summarized in that, as a rule, meets the question of curving the effect of a right of a less compelling legal merit. By necessary implication, this function forms an integral part of the substance of the rule of law, for the core value of prohibition from one abusing (one's own) rights is inextricably linked with the international rule of law. As Judge Greenwood put it,

> There had to be limits laid down by the law in the exercise of power, including some form of a doctrine of abuse of rights . . . War is the antithesis of the rule of law . . . The reality is that the rule of law in international society cannot be separated from the rule of law within the state . . . To me, respect of the rule of law is fundamental for preserving peace.[99]

Still, what Hersch Lauterpacht observed some 50 years ago retains its value, namely

> The determination of the point at which the exercise of a legal right has degenerated into abuse of a right is a question which cannot be decided by an abstract legislative rule but only by the activities of Courts drawing the line in each particular case.[100]

[97] S Montt, *State Liability in Investment Treaty Arbitration* (Hart Publishing, 2009) 153.

[98] Ibid, 140. Fortier identifies lack of transparency and consistency in arbitral decision making as major flaws, LY Fortier, 'Investment Protection and the Rule of Law' in R McCorquodale (n 26 above), 126, 129. See also A Bianchi, 'Adhocism and the Rule of Law' (2002) 13 *European Journal of International Law* 263.

[99] 'The Rule of Law in International Society', The First Milon Kumar Banerji Memorial Lecture, 16 January 2013), available at http://www.youtube.com/watch?v=JNaup3oQzxM (accessed on 12 October 2014).

[100] Lauterpacht (n 16 above), 162.

23

Abstract Interpretations in International Investment Law

FRIEDRICH ROSENFELD*

I. INTRODUCTION

INTERNATIONAL INVESTMENT LAW is currently witnessing a paradigmatic shift towards more normative control:[1] states use various techniques in order to limit the indeterminacy of international investment law.[2] One of these techniques—designated as 'abstract interpretations'—shall be examined in the present chapter. An 'abstract interpretation' will be defined as the determination of a norm's legal content that is made (i) without reference to concrete facts and (ii) with binding force for all subjects to which the norm applies. Mechanisms that have been used in recent practice to obtain such abstract interpretations include state–state arbitral proceedings as well as authoritative interpretation mechanisms (see Section II).

The normative framework for abstract interpretations is still largely unexplored. In the present chapter, it is argued that abstract interpretations have elements which are analytically similar to law making. It is submitted that

* Dr Friedrich Rosenfeld practises arbitration with Hanefeld Rechtsanwälte in Hamburg. He is Global Adjunct Professor at NYU Law in Paris, Visiting Professor at the International Hellenic University in Thessaloniki and Lecturer at Bucerius Law School in Hamburg. This chapter was finalised during a stay as Global Hauser Fellow from Practice and Government at NYU School of Law in 2014. The author wishes to thank Professor Franco Ferrari and Dr Tillmann Rudolf Braun, MPA (Harvard), Berlin, for valuable comments on previous versions of this chapter. The standard disclaimers apply.

[1] See A van Aaken, 'Control Mechanisms in International Investment Law', University of St Gallen Law School, Working Paper No 2013-23 (December 2013) 1–35; JW Yackee, 'Controlling the International Investment Law Agency' (2012) 53 *Harvard Journal of International Law* 391, 434 et seq; W Alschner, 'The Return of the Home state and the Rise of "Embedded" Investor-State Arbitration' in S Lalani and R Polanco (eds), *The Role of the State in Investor-state Arbitration*, (Brill, 2014) 192 et seq.

[2] A related technique is the trend to draft norms of international investment law not as standards, but as rules. See F Rosenfeld, 'The Trend from Standards to Rules in International Investment Law and its Impact upon the Interpretive Power of Arbitral Tribunals' (2014) *American Society of International Law Proceedings* 191–93.

authoritative interpretation mechanisms may lawfully render such abstract interpretations, whereas arbitral tribunals may generally not. The key consideration supporting this distinction is that authoritative interpretation mechanisms are composed of state representatives who act on the basis of joint agreement. Arbitral tribunals, in contrast, are composed of private actors who decide in contentious proceedings. Standard arbitration clauses may not be interpreted as conferring jurisdiction to render abstract interpretations (see Section III).

The conclusion to be drawn is that a higher degree of determinacy of international investment law can only be achieved on the basis of agreement and not in contentious proceedings. It is submitted that this result is in line with the general framework of public international law. Thus, the decision to refine the normative content of international investment law is a prerogative of states and not an obligation (see Section IV).

II. THE NOTION OF ABSTRACT INTERPRETATIONS

A. Definition

For the purposes of the present chapter, an 'abstract interpretation' is defined as the determination of a norm's legal content that is made (i) without reference to concrete facts, and (ii) with binding force for all those subjects to which the norm applies. Three elements characterize abstract interpretations under this definition.

First, abstract interpretations are geared towards determining the meaning of a norm.[3] The determination of a norm's meaning differs from the creation of a norm in that it is governed by the criteria set forth in Article 31 et seq of the Vienna Convention on the Law of Treaties (VCLT). The possible outcomes of this interpretive process are a priori determined by the interpretive scope of a norm. Notwithstanding the aforesaid, even norm interpretation may involve certain creative elements. This will be explained in greater detail below.[4]

Secondly, abstract interpretations are not related to concrete facts. When a decision-making body renders an abstract interpretation, it refrains from determining the 'consequences, which the law attaches to the occurrence of a given fact'.[5] Instead, it merely determines a norm's meaning with the view to

[3] *Cf Case Concerning a Boundary Dispute between Argentina and Chile Concerning the Delimitation of the Frontier between Boundary Post and Mount Fitzroy*, RIAA, Vol. XXII (1994), 75 (C-121): 'Interpretation is a legal operation designed to determine the precise meaning of a rule'. See also *Case Concerning the Factory at Chorzow, Dissenting Opinion of Judge Ehrlich (Jurisdiction)*, 1927, PCIJ, Series A, No 9, 39: 'Interpretation constitutes the process of "determining the meaning of a rule" while application is the process of "determining the consequences which the rule attaches to the occurrence of a given fact"'.

[4] See below, p 337.

[5] See *Case Concerning the Factory at Chorzow, Dissenting Opinion of Judge Ehrlich (Jurisdiction)* (n 3 above), 39.

being applied in the future to circumstances that are typically as yet unknown.[6] This differs from concrete interpretations, which are made with the purpose of being immediately applied to a limited set of concrete facts.

Thirdly, abstract interpretations have binding force for all those subjects to which the norm applies. This element of generality distinguishes abstract interpretations from concrete interpretations as rendered by arbitral tribunals to resolve concrete disputes. When an arbitral tribunal renders a concrete interpretation to resolve a concrete dispute, this only binds the parties in the judged matter (*res judicata*). With regard to other parties and matters, concrete interpretations may, or may not, have persuasive authority. This means that concrete interpretations may only augment the argumentative burden in subsequent proceedings.[7] Unlike abstract interpretations, they are not binding.

The above definition is subject to the following caveat: it is not suggested that it would be impossible to conceive of abstract interpretations with different effects, such as mere *inter partes* binding force for the two states involved in the arbitration. Yet the latter forms of abstract interpretations have little practical value for the purpose of controlling the normative content of international investment law.[8] For this reason, they will not be addressed in the present chapter.

B. Examples

Two mechanisms have been used in recent practice in order to obtain abstract interpretations: authoritative interpretation mechanisms (see (i) below) and state–state arbitral tribunals (see (ii) below). As set forth below, authoritative interpretation mechanisms have proven to be a successful means of obtaining abstract interpretations whereas state–state arbitral proceedings have not.

(i) Authoritative Interpretation Mechanisms

Authoritative interpretation mechanisms are non-adjudicatory decision-making bodies that exist under some international investment agreements. Their purpose is to render binding interpretations of the respective investment

[6] Even where abstract interpretations are rendered in reaction to concrete circumstances, they will nevertheless also apply to future, as yet unknown, circumstances.

[7] M Jacob, 'Precedents: Lawmaking through International Adjudication' (2011) 12(5) *German Law Journal* 1005, 1015. See also ibid, 1019, confirming that 'there is a fundamental difference between something being binding . . . and something imposing a burden'.

[8] For details, see also below p 336.

agreement.[9] State representatives render these interpretations on the basis of joint agreement.[10]

Authoritative interpretation mechanisms are increasingly gaining in importance in international investment law. Current drafts for future European investment agreements, for example, envisage the establishment of such a mechanism.[11] The most prominent existing authoritative interpretation mechanism is the North American Free Trade Agreement (NAFTA) Free Trade Commission, which is composed of ministerial representatives of party states.[12] The NAFTA Free Trade Commission has a specific mandate to render binding interpretations of the NAFTA that are not related to any concrete facts.[13] It has made use of its interpretive powers in order to clarify the normative content of NAFTA provisions. Among others, it determined in 2001 that the obligation under Article 1105 NAFTA to grant investments fair and equitable treatment and full protection and security prescribes the customary international law minimum standard of treatment.[14]

This interpretation of the NAFTA Free Trade Commission fulfils all three elements of an abstract interpretation as defined in the present chapter. First, it was geared towards determining the meaning of the obligation under Article 1105 NAFTA to grant investments fair and equitable treatment and full protection and security. Secondly, it was rendered without reference to any concrete factual setting. Thirdly, it had binding force for all subjects to which Article 1105 NAFTA applies.[15] Authoritative interpretation mechanisms have thus proven to be successful in obtaining an abstract interpretation of international investment law. The same does not hold true for state–state arbitral proceedings.

(ii) State–State Arbitral Proceedings

Unlike authoritative interpretation mechanisms, state–state arbitral tribunals are composed of private actors who render decisions in contentious proceed-

[9] E Pan, 'Authoritative Interpretation of Agreements: Developing More Responsive International Administrative Regimes' (1997) 38 *Harvard International Law Journal* 503, 517 et seq. See also Art XXIX of the IMF Articles of Agreement; Art IX WTO Agreement; G Kaufmann-Kohler, 'Interpretive Powers of the Free Trade Commission and the Rule of Law' in E Gaillard and F Bachand (eds), *Fifteen Years of NAFTA Chapter 11 Arbitration* (Juris, 2011) 175, 179 et seq; A Roberts, 'Power and Persuasion in Investment Treaty Interpretation: The Dual Role of states, (2010) 104 *American Journal of International Law* 179, 180 et seq.

[10] *Cf* Pan (ibid), 517; Kaufmann-Kohler (ibid), 176.

[11] See, eg Consolidated CETA Text (26 September 2014), available at http://trade.ec.europa.eu/doclib/docs/2014/september/tradoc_152806.pdf (accessed on 2 October 2014).

[12] *Cf* Kaufmann-Kohler (ibid), 176 et seq. See also Art 2001 NAFTA.

[13] Art 1131, para 2 NAFTA reads: 'An interpretation by the Commission of a provision of this Agreement shall be binding on a Tribunal established under this Section'.

[14] Free Trade Commission Clarifications Related to NAFTA Chapter 11 (31 July 2001), available at http://www.worldtradelaw.net/nafta/chap11interp.pdf (accessed on 2 October 2014).

[15] See n 38 below.

ings on the sole basis of jurisdictional consent.[16] The majority of international investment treaties contain state–state arbitration clauses providing for such consent. Their origins date back from times when investor disputes were still resolved exclusively on the inter-state level. Among others, many friendship, commerce and navigation treaties contain state–state arbitration clauses.[17] While it has been argued that the emergence of investor-state arbitration in the twentieth century created a distinct jurisdictional track that has reduced the scope of state–state arbitration,[18] scholars such as Anthea Roberts are currently predicting a re-emergence of state–state arbitration.[19]

The potential use of state–state arbitration proceedings as a mechanism to obtain abstract interpretations came to the fore in the recent case of *Ecuador v United States*.[20] In this case, Ecuador sought a binding interpretation confirming that the obligation under Article II(7) of the US–Ecuador bilateral investment treaty (BIT) to provide effective means of asserting rights and claims is equivalent to the prohibition of a denial of justice as it exists under customary international law.[21] Ecuador's decision to initiate these state–state arbitral proceedings was prompted by a prior arbitral award in *Chevron Corp and Texaco Petroleum Co v Republic of Ecuador*. In this award, the arbitral tribunal had interpreted Article II(7) of the US–Ecuador BIT as an independent treaty obligation that goes beyond the standard under customary international

[16] On state–state arbitration, see A Roberts, 'State–State Investment Treaty Arbitration: A Hybrid Theory of Interdependent Rights and Shared Interpretive Authority' (2014) 55(1) *Harvard International Law Journal* 1 et seq; A Mitchell and J Munro, 'State–State Dispute Settlement under the Trans-Pacific Partnership Agreement' in T Voon (ed), *Trade Liberalisation and International Co-Operation* (Elgar, 2013) 156 et seq; C Lo, 'Between State–State Dispute Settlement and Investor-State Arbitration under BITs' (2013) 6(1) *Contemporary Asia Arbitration Journal* 1 et seq; M Potestà, 'State-to-State Dispute Settlement Pursuant to Bilateral Investment Treaties: Is There Potential?' in N Boschiero et al (eds), *International Courts and the Development of International Law* (Springer, 2013) 753 et seq.

[17] See A Newcombe and L Paradell, *Law and Practice of Investment Treaties* (Oxford University Press, 2009), 4 et seq.

[18] M Reisman, for example, argues that many bilateral investment treaties have set up a two-track jurisdictional structure. The inter-state arbitral track would cover cases such as the non-enforcement of a final award or disputes when one state purports to denounce a treaty. See M Reisman, Expert Opinion in *The Republic of Ecuador v The United States of America*, PCA Case No 2012-5, 24 April 2012, paras 16 et seq, available at http://www.pca-cpa.org/showpage.asp?pag_id=1455 (accessed on 2 October 2014).

[19] See A Roberts, 'State–State Investment Treaty Arbitration: A Hybrid Theory of Interdependent Rights and Shared Interpretive Authority' (n 16 above), 1 et seq.

[20] Request of the Republic of Ecuador to the United States of America Pursuant to Article VII of the Treaty between the United States of America and the Republic of Ecuador concerning the Encouragement and Reciprocal Protection of Investment. For other state–state arbitrations in the field of international investment law that did not concern abstract interpretations see *Italian Republic v Republic of Cuba*, Interim Award, 15 March 2005, available at http://www.italaw.com/sites/default/files/case-documents/ita0434_0.pdf (accessed on 2 October 2014); *Italian Republic v Republic of Cuba*, Final Award, 15 January 2008, available at http://www.italaw.com/sites/default/files/case-documents/ita0435_0.pdf (accessed on 2 October 2014). See also *Chile v Peru*, reported in *Empresas Lucchetti, SA v Republic of Peru*, ICSID Case No ARB/03/04, Award, 7 February 2005, para 7.

[21] Ibid, para 15.

law.[22] Ecuador considered this interpretation to be flawed and approached the United States in order to reach agreement on how to interpret the effective means provision. When the United States showed no satisfactory reaction, Ecuador initiated the state–state arbitral proceedings.[23]

Similar to the interpretation of the NAFTA Free Trade Commission, the award sought by Ecuador would have fulfilled all elements of an abstract interpretation. First, Ecuador made clear that it only desired an interpretation, ie the determination of the meaning of Article II(7) US–Ecuador BIT. Secondly, Ecuador's request was not related to any facts. And thirdly, only an award with binding force for all subjects to which Article II(7) US–Ecuador BIT applies would have been of benefit to Ecuador.[24] Ecuador made clear that it wished to have legal certainty with the view to future investment proceedings by US investors. An award with a merely inter-state binding effect would have failed to attain this goal.[25] The arbitral tribunal, however, denied its jurisdiction and Ecuador did not obtain the desired abstract interpretation.[26]

III. THE NORMATIVE FRAMEWORK FOR ABSTRACT INTERPRETATIONS

The observation that only authoritative interpretation mechanisms and not arbitral tribunals have rendered abstract interpretations gives cause to examine the normative framework for abstract interpretations in greater detail.

[22] *Chevron Corp and Texaco Petroleum Co v Republic of Ecuador*, PCA/UNCITRAL, Partial Award on the Merits, 20 March 2011, para 262.

[23] Request of the Republic of Ecuador (n 20 above), para 13. The United States alleged that they had not taken any view with regard to Ecuador's request for interpretation. Cf *The Republic of Ecuador v The United States of America* (n 18 above), Statement of Defense of Respondent United States of America, 7.

[24] Ecuador made clear that it sought a binding award as opposed to an advisory opinion. See *The Republic of Ecuador v The United States of America* (n 18 above), Counter-Memorial of Claimant Republic of Ecuador on Jurisdiction, para 112.

[25] *Chevron Corp and Texaco Petroleum Co v Republic of Ecuador* (n 22 above), para 219. In the view of Ecuador, persuasive authority for its position already existed. Among others, Ecuador had adduced the following cases in support of its position in the *Chevron* case: *Duke Energy Electroquil Partners & Electroquil SA v Republic of Ecuador*, ICSID Case No ARB/04/19, Award, 18 August 2008; *Occidental Exploration and Production Company v The Republic of Ecuador*, LCIA Case No UN3467, Final Award, 1 July 2004; *Noble Ventures, Inc v Romania*, ICSID Case No ARB/01/11, Award, 12 October 2005.

[26] According to public information, the award was rendered on 29 September 2012. *Cf* http://www.italaw.com/cases/1494 (accessed on 2 October 2014).

A. Abstract Interpretations Have Elements That Are Analytically Similar to Law Making

The starting point for the analysis is the thesis that abstract interpretations have elements that are analytically similar to law making.[27] Abstract interpretations and the sources of law set out in Article 38 of the Statute of the International Court of Justice share certain common characteristics: they regulate a form of social behaviour that is typically not limited to a concrete set of already existing facts, they have binding effects for others and a compliance deficit may trigger a sanction.[28] When the NAFTA Free Trade Commission determines with binding force that Article 1105 NAFTA prescribes the customary international law minimum standard, this therefore has effects comparable to creating a more refined norm.[29] In a similar vein, the interpretation sought by Ecuador in the US–Ecuador arbitration would have had effects similar to creating a more refined provision of the US–Ecuador BIT.

Admittedly, abstract interpretations still consist in determining the meaning of a previously set norm as opposed to creating a new norm. As has been set out above, this process is guided by the formal criteria for the ascertainment of normative content set out in Article 31 et seq VCLT and the possible outcomes are a priori limited by the interpretive scope of the respective norms.[30] Yet interpretation may nevertheless involve certain creative elements which are analytically similar to law making.[31] These creative elements exist due to the indeterminacy of legal norms.[32] In order to overcome this indeterminacy, decision-makers who interpret legal norms have to make a choice. Kelsen has observed in this regard that interpretation is not merely a cognitive exercise, but may involve an 'act of will'.[33]

In the case of abstract interpretations, the creative exercise of determining a norm's legal content has a permanent effect. The one-time exercise of an act of will with binding force thus limits the possibility of exercising multiple acts of will in light of concrete facts in the future. If, for example, the NAFTA Free Trade Commission determines that Article 1105 NAFTA reflects

[27] This is not to suggest that concrete interpretations contain no elements of law making. However, there are different degrees of such law making. *Cf* A von Bogdandy and I Venzke, 'Beyond Dispute: International Judicial Institutions as Lawmakers' (2011) 12(5) *German Law Journal* 979, 983. See also D Kennedy, *A Critique of Adjudication* (Harvard University Press, 1997), 23 et seq.

[28] *Cf* also Pan (n 9 above), 530, on law making by authoritative interpretation mechanisms.

[29] *Cf* also Roberts (n 9 above), 200 et seq, on the lacking distinction between interpretation and modification in general. *Cf* also C Brower, 'Why the FTC Notes of Interpretation Constitute a Partial Amendment of NAFTA Art 1105' (2005–06) 46 *Virginia Journal of International Law*, 347, 358 et seq.

[30] See above, p 332.

[31] See also M Koskenniemi, *From Apology to Utopia* (Cambridge University Press, 2006), 590.

[32] HLA Hart, *The Concept of Law*, 3rd edn (Oxford University Press, 2012) 257.

[33] H Kelsen, *Pure Theory of Law* (Lawbook Exchange, 2009) 354. *Cf* also von Bogdandy and Venzke (n 27 above), 984 et seq.

the standard of customary international law, there is no more room to argue differently in future arbitrations.

It would be wrong to conclude from the above observations that abstract interpretations can never be legal. As masters of the treaties, states are in a position to delegate certain law-making functions to other entities. However, there are good reasons to assume that states have delegated such law-making powers only to authoritative interpretation mechanisms and not to arbitral tribunals.

B. States Have Delegated Law Making Powers to Authoritative Interpretation Mechanisms

Authoritative interpretation mechanisms may lawfully render abstract interpretations. This follows from two considerations: first, the wording of investment agreements with authoritative interpretation mechanisms provides a clear legal basis for such abstract interpretations. Article 1131 NAFTA, for example, explicitly provides that an interpretation by the Free Trade Commission shall be binding on tribunals.[34] Likewise, Article X.27 of the draft Comprehensive and Economic Trade Agreement (CETA) reads in relevant part:

> Where serious concerns arise as regards matters of interpretation that may affect investment, the Committee on Services and Investment may, pursuant to Article X.42(3)(a), recommend to the Trade Committee the adoption of interpretations of the Agreement. An interpretation adopted by the CETA Trade Committee shall be binding on a Tribunal established under this chapter. The CETA Trade Committee may decide that an interpretation shall have binding effect from a specific date.[35]

Such wording expresses the clear intent to delegate certain law making powers to authoritative interpretations mechanisms.

Secondly, the decisions of authoritative interpretation mechanisms may constitute a 'subsequent agreement' in the sense of Article 31(3)(a) VCLT. This has been acknowledged in the recent report of the International Law Commission on Treaties over Time.[36] Article 31(3)(a) VCLT requires that any such subsequent agreement between the parties regarding the interpretation or application of a treaty be taken into account. It acknowledges the binding force of subsequent agreements.[37]

[34] Art 1131(2) NAFTA. See also Art 2001(2)(c) NAFTA.

[35] Consolidated CETA Text (n 11 above).

[36] International Law Commission, 65th session, Geneva, 6 May–7 June and 8 July–9 August 2013, 'First Report on Subsequent Agreements and Subsequent Practice in Relation to Treaty Interpretation', UN Doc A/CN.4/660, para 88.

[37] See also *Case Concerning Kasikili/Sedudu Island (Botswana v Namibia)* [1999] ICJ Reports 1045, para 49 (Judgment, 13 December 1999), ruling that 'an agreement as to the interpretation of a provision reached after the conclusion of the treaty represents an authentic interpretation by the parties which must be read into the treaty for purposes of its interpretation'.

Arbitral practice has confirmed the binding effect of authoritative interpretations in various cases.[38] One exception was the award on damages in *Pope & Talbot Inc v Government of Canada*.[39] In this case, the arbitral tribunal struggled to determine the effects of an authoritative interpretation for its award on damages and did not consider itself bound by it. However, the arbitral tribunal's approach resulted from the exceptional situation that an authoritative interpretation was made after the arbitral tribunal had rendered its award on liability.[40] The overall authority of authoritative interpretation mechanisms to render abstract interpretations has not been questioned by this exceptional case.[41]

C. States Have Not Delegated Similar Law Making Powers to Arbitral Tribunals

Similar considerations do not hold true for arbitral tribunals. An arbitral award is rendered in contentious proceedings and not on the basis of a subsequent agreement in the sense of Article 31(3)(a) VCLT. Accordingly, a third party effect of arbitral awards may not be grounded upon the rationale enshrined in Article 31(3)(a) VCLT.

Moreover, standard arbitration clauses provide no sufficient basis to support the proposition that arbitral tribunals have jurisdiction to render abstract interpretations as defined in the present chapter. This becomes clearer if one considers the above-mentioned *Ecuador v United States* case.[42] The arbitration clause relied upon by Ecuador provided that '[a]ny dispute between the

[38] *Mondev International Ltd v United States of America*, Award, ICSID Case No ARB (AF)/99/2, 11 October 2002, paras 100 et seq; *ADF Group v United States of America*, Award, ICSID Case No ARB (AF)/00/1, 9 January 2003, para 177; *Methanex Corporation v United States of America*, UNCITRAL, Final Award of the Tribunal on Jurisdiction and Merits, 3 August 2005, Part IV.C, para 20; *United Parcel Service of America Inc v Government of Canada*, UNCITRAL, Award on the Merits, 22 November 2002, para 42; *Merrill & Ring Forestry LP v Government of Canada*, UNCITRAL (ICSID Administered), Award, 31 March 2010, para 190; *Loewen Group, Inc and Raymond L Loewen v United States of America*, Award, ICSID Case No ARB(AF)/98/3, 26 June 2003, para 126; *Waste Management, Inc v United Mexican States*, Award, ICSID Case No ARB(AF)/00/3, 30 April 2004, paras 89 et seq. See, however, *Pope & Talbot Inc v Government of Canada*, Award in Respect of Damages, 31 May 2002, paras 17 et seq.

[39] *Pope & Talbot* (ibid), paras 17 et seq.

[40] This has nevertheless received increasing criticism. See, eg *Mondev International* (n 38 above), para 106, referencing the criticism of the United States

[41] If at all, the award in *Pope & Talbot* (n 38 above) shows that there is a need for procedural safeguards, including rules on the interplay of abstract interpretations with concrete cases rules on transparency. On procedural safeguards see Roberts (n 9 above), 183; R Dolzer and C Schreuer, *Principles of International Investment Law* (Oxford University Press, 2012) 33; UNCTAD, 'Reform of Investor-State Dispute Settlement: In Search of a Roadmap' (June 2013) 6, fn 22, available at http://unctad.org/en/PublicationsLibrary/webdiaepcb2013d4_en.pdf (accessed on 2 October 2014); Kaufmann-Kohler (n 9 above), 194; M Ioannidis, 'A Procedural Approach to the Legitimacy of International Adjudication: Developing Standards of Participation in WTO Law' (2011) 12(5) *German Law Journal* 1175, 1179.

[42] Above n 20.

Parties concerning the interpretation or application of the Treaty which is not resolved through consultations or other diplomatic channels' may be submitted to arbitration.[43] To reach the conclusion that this arbitration clause conferred jurisdiction to render an abstract interpretation, one would have to overcome a number of obstacles.

Above all, it would need to be established that a purely abstract interpretive dispute over a BIT provision is covered by the arbitration agreement. While the wording of Article VII of the US–Ecuador BIT makes a broad reference to disputes about the 'interpretation or application' of BIT provisions, it contains no sufficient indication that a purely abstract interpretive dispute is covered by this provision.[44] The consideration of the context and the object and purpose is not very enlightening, either. There is notably no evidence suggesting that both Ecuador and the United States shared an interest in abstract interpretations which had potentially far-reaching implications for future facts that could not yet be anticipated. It is noteworthy in this context that in the *Ecuador v United States* case the existence of a dispute as such was already contested, as the United States had not reacted to the interpretive request of Ecuador.[45]

Even assuming that abstract disputes were covered by the arbitration clause in Article VII of the US–Ecuador BIT, it would need to be established that the parties intended an arbitral award containing an abstract interpretation to have binding force for subsequent tribunals. The wording of the arbitration clause did not allow for such conclusion. Neither is there a doctrine of binding precedent in arbitration or a general principle according to which every state–state award would automatically create obligations for third parties. Instead, one may find many similarly worded investor-state arbitration clauses.[46] To assume that all these arbitral clauses confer jurisdiction to render

[43] Treaty between the United States of America and the Republic of Ecuador concerning the Encouragement and Reciprocal Protection of Investment, available at http://www.state.gov/documents/organization/43558.pdf (accessed on 3 November 2013).

[44] To assume that interpretive disputes are not covered by Art VII of the US–Ecuador BIT does not render this provision void. In most cases, arbitral tribunals interpret the law before applying it to concrete facts. At the same time, there are cases where arbitral tribunals apply the law without interpreting it. This alone justifies the use of the wording 'interpretation or application'.

[45] Ecuador argued that the United States refused to enter into a discussion on the interpretation of the bilateral investment treaty in a situation where a response was called for. *Cf* Request of the Republic of Ecuador (n 20 above), para 14. The United States, in contrast, argued that it had not taken any position and cannot be compelled to take a position on Ecuador's interpretation. *Cf The Republic of Ecuador v The United States of America* (n 18 above), 2 et seq. On this question, see also the expert opinions by Prof Michael Reisman, Prof Christian Tomuschat, Prof Alain Pellet, Prof Stephen McCaffrey and Prof CF Amerasinghe, available at http://www.pca-cpa.org/showpage.asp?pag_id=1455 (accessed on 2 October 2014).

[46] Art IX of the Treaty between the United States of America and the Republic of Poland concerning Business and Economic Relations with Protocol and Four Related Exchanges of Letters, signed 21 March 1990 at Washington, for example, allows investors to assert proceedings concerning the interpretation or application of an investment agreement. The provision reads as follows: 'For purposes of this Article, an investment dispute is defined as a dispute involving (a) the interpretation or application of an investment agreement between a Party (including any agency or instrumentality of such Party) and a national or company of the other Party; (b) the interpretation or application of any investment authorization granted by a Party's foreign

abstract interpretations with general binding force would be at odds with the decentralized, non-hierarchical structure of investment arbitration.

Finally, jurisprudence provides hardly any support for interpreting standard arbitration clauses as a basis for an arbitral tribunal's jurisdiction to render abstract interpretations. One even finds significant resistance against the permissibility of such abstract interpretations. In the *Case concerning the Northern Cameroons*, for example, the International Court of Justice held that courts may 'pronounce judgment only in connection with concrete cases' and that they 'are not there to make legal pronouncements in abstracto'.[47] In a similar vein, the Anglo-Italian Conciliation Commission held in the *Dual Nationality* case that

> [a]n interpretation, according to which the Commission would also have the faculty to interpret the Peace Treaty in an abstract and general manner, with obligatory effect for all future cases, would run the risk, because it is abusive, of ending in a judgment blemished by excess of power (it would create rules of law, which is not a jurisdictional function, but a legislative function).[48]

Arguably, the weight of this jurisprudence is weakened to some extent by the existence of courts such as the European Court of Justice, of which the authority to render abstract interpretations under Article 267 Treaty on the Functioning of the European Union (TFEU) is widely acknowledged.[49] However, leaving aside the intricate question of whether states are entitled to delegate similar law-making functions to an arbitral tribunal, one would at least expect significantly clearer language than that used in a standard arbitration clause to actually express such intent. The jurisprudence of the Iran–United States Claims Tribunal does not lead to a different conclusion. While the Iran–United States Claims Tribunal had jurisdiction over certain

investment authority to such national or company; or (c) an alleged breach of any right conferred or created by this Treaty with respect to an investment.'

[47] *Case concerning the Northern Cameroons (Cameroon v United Kingdom)*, Preliminary Objections, Judgment of 2 December 1963 [1963] ICJ Reports 15, 33–34: 'The function of the Court is to state the law, but it may pronounce judgment only in connection with concrete cases where there exists at the time of the adjudication an actual controversy involving a conflict of legal interests between the parties. The Court's judgment must have some practical consequence in the sense that it can affect existing legal rights or obligations of the parties, thus removing uncertainty from their legal relations.' For a different position, see *Case concerning certain German Interests in Polish Upper Silesia (The Merits), Germany v Poland*, Publications of the Permanent Court of International Justice No 7, 18.

[48] *Cases of Dual Nationality*, Anglo-Italian Conciliation Commission, XIV UN Rep Int'l Arb Awards 34. For a different position, see *The Question whether the re-evaluation of the German Mark in 1961 and 1969 constitutes a case for application of the clause in article 2 (e) of Annex I A of the 1953 Agreement on German External Debts*, Decision of 16 May 1980, XIX UN Rep Int'l Arb Awards 67, 89, emphasizing the applicant's 'right to an authoritative interpretation'.

[49] Art 267 TFEU provides: 'The Court of Justice of the European Union shall have jurisdiction to give preliminary rulings concerning: (a) the interpretation of the Treaties; (b) the validity and interpretation of acts of the institutions, bodies, offices or agencies of the Union'. See also M Broberg and N Fenger, *Preliminary References to the European Court of Justice* (Oxford University Press, 2009) 441 et seq.

interpretive disputes, these decisions provided 'merely interpretive guidance'[50] and always implied some elements of concreteness.[51] Moreover, the institutional setting of the Iran–United States Claims Tribunal was different from that of investment arbitration.

IV. CONCLUDING REMARKS

The conclusion to be drawn from the above observations is that a higher degree of determinacy may only be achieved on the basis of joint agreement, but not in contentious proceedings before a state–state arbitral tribunal. Is this a shortcoming of international investment law? Would it be better to achieve more determinacy at every price?

From a policy perspective, there are certainly manifold reasons that may justify a preference for a higher degree of determinacy. Above all, legal norms are a form of social control, which only functions when said norms are intelligible and capable of being obeyed.[52] Opaque norms without clear normative content, in contrast, are unable to perform this form of social control. A minimum degree of determinacy is also required in order to guarantee the legitimacy of the system of investment protection.[53] Excessively broad standards may be perceived as leaving too much discretion to arbitral tribunals. To the extent that this leads to inconsistent and flawed decisions, the trust in the system of investment protection risks being undermined. Moreover, indeterminate norms may trigger high costs but little benefit for the actors who have to apply this norm in practice.[54] It would be undesirable if these actors had to invest high transaction costs in order to obtain information about the content of legal norms.[55] The alternative of acting on the basis of incomplete information, however, would produce distorted outcomes.[56] From Ecuador's perspective, it would, for example, have been a waste of resources to act on

[50] See, eg *United States of America v The Islamic Republic of Iran*, Iran–US Claims Tribunal, Case A/17, Decision No DEC.37-A17-FT (18 June 1985) (C-152), reprinted in 8 Iran USCTR 189.

[51] *Cf* Roberts (n 16 above), 56.

[52] Hart (n 32 above), 207.

[53] *Cf* J Hueckel, 'Rebalancing Legitimacy and Sovereign in International Investment Agreements' (2012) 61 *Emory Law Journal* 601, 605. *Cf* also C Knahr and A Reinisch, 'Transparency versus Confidentiality in International Investment Arbitration—The Biwater Gauff Compromise' (2007) 6 *The Law and Practice of International Courts and Tribunals* 97, 111, claiming that a higher degree of predictability will ensure the confidence in the system.

[54] *Cf* also C-S Zoellner, 'Transparency: An Analysis of an Evolving Fundamental Principle in International Economic Law' (2005–06) 27 *Michigan Journal of International Law* 579, 586 et seq.

[55] Kaplow argues that a standard is more costly than a rule since it requires individuals to get information about the content of the norm that is already answered in case of a rule: L Kaplow, 'Rules versus Standards: An Economic Analysis' (1992) 42 *Duke Law Journal* 557, 569.

[56] On the economic analysis of law see, eg L Kaplow, 'Fairness versus Welfare' (2001) 114 *Harvard Law Review* 961; H Eidenmüller, *Effizienz als Rechtsprinzip [Efficiency as Legal Principle]*, 2nd edn (Mohr-Siebeck, 1995); R Cooter and T Ulen, *Law and Economics*, 4th edn (Pearson Addison Weasley, 2004).

the assumption that the effective means obligation under the US–Ecuador BIT sets a higher threshold than customary international law if indeed this assumption proved to be incorrect. Conversely, it would have been inefficient to act on the assumption that the effective means obligation is equivalent to customary international law and to pay damages in case this assumption proved to be incorrect.

However, the above policy considerations should not lead to the oversimplified conclusion that a high degree of legal determinacy is always good and should be achieved at every price. Prominent scholars such as Martti Koskenniemi have correctly observed that some degree of legal indeterminacy is a central aspect of international law's acceptability.[57] This is due, among others, to what HLA Hart has described as two 'human handicaps', ie the 'relative ignorance of fact' and the 'relative indeterminacy of aim'.[58] The term 'relative ignorance of fact' refers to the dilemma that human beings cannot anticipate all future circumstances and developments where a norm will be applied in practice. In a complex world, this is impossible. The 'relative ignorance of fact' brings with it the 'relative indeterminacy of aim'. To put it in simple terms: since human beings cannot anticipate every future constellation in detail, they are often unable to formulate precise aims.[59] A certain degree of legal indeterminacy accommodates these constraints since it leaves the possibility of an informed choice: a flexible norm grants decision-makers discretion to consider information that was unavailable or that could not be anticipated when creating this norm.[60] Admittedly, decision-makers rendering abstract interpretations may dispose of more information than norm creators. The difference, however, is only a matter of degree. After all, it should not be forgotten that the factual settings in which a norm will be applied are subject to change.[61]

In light of the above, it makes sense that abstract interpretations may only be rendered on the basis of joint agreement and not in contentious proceedings. The decision to refine the normative content of international investment law is a prerogative of states and not an obligation.[62]

[57] Koskenniemi (n 31 above), 590. See also K Kress, 'Legal Indeterminacy' (1989) 77 *California Law Review* 283 et seq.

[58] Hart (n 32 above), 127.

[59] See also Koskenniemi (n 31 above), 590.

[60] *Cf* Hueckel (n 53 above), 626. See also M Koskenniemi, 'The Fate of Public International Law: Between Technique and Politics' (2007) 70 *Modern Law Review* 1, 9.

[61] Koskenniemi (n 31 above), 596. See also Kaplow (n 55 above), 568 et seq.

[62] *The Republic of Ecuador v The United States of America* (n 18 above), 3.

Section 2
International Trade in Transformation

24

Regionalism and the Constitutionalization of the WTO

DENCHO GEORGIEV*

I. INTRODUCTION

LEGALLY, CONTEMPORARY REGIONAL groupings are most often based on free trade areas or customs unions, ie on regional trade agreements, as described in Article XXIV of the General Agreement on Tariffs and Trade (GATT) and also in Article V bis of the General Agreement on Trade in Services (GATS). The GATT and the GATS are two of the most important agreements on which the WTO (World Trade Organization) is built. Hence, for regionalism, the fundamental theoretical question from the point of view of international law is that of the relationship between such regional trade agreements (RTAs), on the one hand, and WTO law, on the other hand. More specifically, the question arises of which of the two, in case of a conflict between them, 'prevails', to use the language of the Vienna Convention on the Law of Treaties.

In spite of its importance, this question has not attracted much academic attention. An attempt to explain the legal relationship between the WTO and RTAs under Article XXIV GATT was to describe them as *inter se* modifications of the GATT and to conclude that their relationship with the WTO was of a 'constitutional' character, from which a primacy of the WTO over RTAs was derived.[1] Moreover, in line with views that RTAs undermine the multi-

* Burgas Free University, Vice-President of the Bulgarian Association of International Law, former Bulgarian Ambassador to the WTO.

[1] T Cottier and M Foltea, 'Constitutional Functions of the WTO and RTAs' in L Bartels and F Ortino (eds), *Regional Trade Agreements and the WTO Legal System* (2006) 43–76.

lateral trading system[2] and proposals for reform of the WTO,[3] the primacy of the WTO over RTAs was suggested as a feature of a future constitutionalization of the WTO.[4]

In this chapter I first explore the current relationship between the WTO and RTAs from the point of view of general international law as codified in the Vienna Convention on the Law of Treaties (VCLT)[5] and from the point of view of WTO law[6] itself, and then to look at the future of the WTO and the proposals for its constitutionalization.

II. THE RELATIONSHIP BETWEEN TREATIES ON THE SAME SUBJECT MATTER IN GENERAL INTERNATIONAL LAW

Both the WTO Agreements and RTAs are international treaties, and the key legal question for the relationship between such international treaties is which of them applies or 'prevails' in case of conflicts between them. Under general international law there is no a priori primacy between treaties; they basically have equal standing. What general international law provides for, however, are 'rules of application', which contain provisions on the conditions for priority in certain cases. One such rule of application—which, as I shall demonstrate, is quite obviously applicable in this case—is Article 30(2) of the VCLT, which reads that '[w]hen a treaty specifies that it is subject to, or that it is not to be considered as incompatible with, an earlier or later treaty, the provisions of that other treaty prevail'.

Although the general heading of Article 30 is 'Application of successive treaties relating to the same subject matter', its second paragraph applies to 'earlier or later' treaties, which means that it applies not just to subsequent treaties but to all treaties relating to the same subject matter which include a 'conflict clause'.[7] The paragraph contains the basic rule of Article 30, and commentators point out that the other rules of this article 'are intended to be residuary rules—that is rules which will operate in the absence of express treaty provisions regulating priority'.[8] The special rapporteur and subsequently expert-consultant at the Vienna Conference, Sir Humphrey Waldock, confirmed to the conference that 'the rules in paragraphs 3, 4 and 5 were

[2] J Bhagwati, *Termites in the Trading System. How Preferential Agreements Undermine Free Trade* (2008).

[3] P Sutherland et al, *Report on the Future of the WTO; Addressing Institutional Challenges in the New Millennium* (2004) 23, para 84.

[4] See also T Cottier, 'Towards a Five Storey House' in C Joerges and E-U Petersmann (eds), *Constitutionalism, Multilevel Trade Governance and International Economic Law* (2011) 495–532.

[5] 1155 UNTS I-18232, 331, available at https://treaties.un.org/doc/Publication/UNTS / Volume%201155/volume-1155-I-18232-English.pdf.

[6] WTO legal texts and documents available at http://docsonline.wto.org.

[7] In the sense used by the UN International Law Commission in its report on fragmentation: UNGA Doc A/CN.4/L.682, 13 April 2006, para 252.

[8] I Sinclair, *The Vienna Convention on the Law of Treaties*, 2nd edn (1984) 97.

thus designed essentially as residuary rules'.[9] Hence the other rules of Article 30 need to be read as applicable only in case there is no conflict clause in the respective treaties which provides for priority. Since, as we shall see, WTO agreements do contain conflict clauses on the relationship with RTAs, as foreseen in Article 30(2), paragraphs 3, 4 and 5 of Article 30 VCLT are inapplicable.

RTAs do relate to the 'same subject matter' as some of the WTO Agreements, and in particular two of the most fundamental agreements annexed to the Agreement Establishing the WTO: the GATT and the GATS. In the first case, the 'same subject matter' is 'tariffs and trade', and in the second case it is 'trade in services'. The rule of Article 30(2) VCLT is therefore relevant for the relationship between RTAs and the WTO agreements.

Article 30(2) VCLT provides that a treaty may specify that it 'is subject to' or that it is 'not to be considered as incompatible with' another treaty, the effect in both cases being the same: priority of the other treaty. Thus the VCLT imposes a reading of the expression 'not to be considered as incompatible with' which goes significantly beyond its ordinary meaning. A simple straightforward reading would suggest that 'not incompatible with' means that the two treaties are compatible with each other and that therefore neither of them has priority over the other. Article 30(2) VCLT, however, explicitly provides that the 'other treaty' has to 'prevail'. This means that if, in a conflict rule, a treaty provides for its own compatibility with another treaty, that other treaty is not to be considered as simply compatible with it but shall have primacy over the treaty which contains this conflict rule. The application of this provision is not a matter of discretion for those applying it but an obligatory rule of application (contained in Section 2 'Application of Treaties' of Part III 'Observance, Application and Interpretation of Treaties' of the VCLT) which has to be respected whenever the question of the relationship, ie conflict between treaties on the same subject matter, arises and whenever a conflict rule providing for compatibility is included in the respective treaty.

III. THE CONFLICT CLAUSES FOR RTAS IN THE WTO AGREEMENTS

The question now is whether RTAs or the WTO Agreements contain 'conflict clauses' which specify their legal relationship, as envisaged in Article 30(2) VCLT. Such conflict clauses are indeed included in Article XXIV:5 GATT and Article V:1 GATS. The chapeau of Article XXIV:5 GATT states: 'Accordingly, the provisions of this Agreement shall not prevent, as between the territories of contracting parties, the formation of a customs union or of a free trade area or the adoption of an interim agreement necessary for the formation of a

[9] Ibid. The residuary character of Art 30 VCLT is also confirmed by the report of the UN International Law Commission on fragmentation (n 7 above), para 251.

customs union or of a free trade area'. Article V:1 GATS states: 'This Agreement shall not prevent any of its Members from being a party to or entering into an agreement liberalizing trade in services between or among the parties to such an agreement'.

The language used in these provisions ('shall not prevent') is not identical to that of Article 30(2) VCLT, but it seems impossible to conceive these words in the GATT and the GATS as meaning anything different from 'not to be considered as incompatible with' in the VCLT. If we accept that the words 'shall not prevent' in the conflict clause of Article XXIV:5 were intended to mean compatibility between the GATT and RTAs, then, as has been shown above, this is exactly the case envisaged by Article 30(2) VCLT, where priority is provided for the 'other treaty'—in this case, for RTAs.

It should be noted that the conflict rules contained in Article XXIV:5 GATT and Article V:1 GATS are not unconditional. The texts of the chapeaus with the expression 'shall not prevent' in the texts of the GATT and the GATS are followed by the words 'Provided that . . .', and subparagraphs (a)–(d) of Article XXIV:5 GATT and (a) and (b) of Article 5 GATS contain certain requirements which constitute the conditions for the priority of RTAs over the GATT/GATS. For the legal relationship between WTO law and RTAs, this means that if these requirements are not met, the respective RTA cannot be seen as prevailing over WTO law, especially with respect to third parties. If it cannot be demonstrated that the requirements are not met, then the primacy of the respective RTA over the WTO Agreements follows from Article 30(2) VCLT and Articles XXIV:5 GATT and V:1 GATS. It is important to identify the WTO provisions containing these requirements—the conditions over which RTAs cannot prevail—in order to clarify more specifically over what in the WTO Agreements RTAs have priority.

In the conflict clause, grammatically, the subject of the sentence in the chapeau of Article XXIV:5 is 'the provisions of this Agreement', which means that it is all of the provisions of the GATT over which customs unions and free trade areas will 'prevail' (except the provisions constituting the conditions themselves).

The word 'accordingly' refers to the previous paragraph 4,[10] which contains the motives for giving RTAs that specific status with respect to the GATT. These motives per se do not formulate the conditions which RTAs must fulfil, but only clarify why closer integration is 'desirable' and what their purpose 'should' be. This wording shows that it is not requirements that are formulated here but only motivations and purposes.

The basic requirement of Article XXIV:5 GATT is that duties and other

[10] 'The contracting parties recognize the desirability of increasing freedom of trade by the development, through voluntary agreements, of closer integration between the economies of the countries parties to such agreements. They also recognize that the purpose of a customs union or of a free trade area should be to facilitate trade between the constituent territories and not to raise barriers to the trade of other contracting parties with such territories.'

regulations of commerce shall not be higher or more restrictive than prior to the formation of the respective RTA. For free trade areas, this applies to each single duty or measure. For customs unions, the requirement is that duties and regulations shall not 'on the whole' be higher or more restrictive. So, for customs unions, Article XXIV:6 provides that increases of duties on imports into the customs union and compensatory adjustments have to be negotiated as modifications of schedules pursuant to Article XXVIII. Interim agreements leading to the formation of a customs union or a free trade area must include a plan and a schedule for the formation of the RTA within a 'reasonable period of time', which, according to paragraph 3 of the GATT 1994 Understanding on the Interpretation of Article XXIV, can be longer than 10 years only in exceptional cases that need to be explained to the Council for Trade in Goods.

What does this basic WTO requirement for RTAs mean for the legal relationship between the WTO Agreements and RTAs in terms of priority under the VCLT? It means that if RTA parties raise their duties and other barriers to trade without initiating negotiations with affected third parties under Article XXVIII for the modification of their GATT schedules, their RTA cannot have primacy over the GATT. If such negotiations are initiated and the procedures of Article XXVIII are followed by the RTA parties, it should be considered that the requirements of Article XXIV:6 have been followed and hence that the RTA has priority over the GATT. If the negotiations do not result in an agreement on compensatory adjustments, under Article XXVIII GATT customs union parties are nevertheless free to modify their schedules and then affected third parties can withdraw equivalent concessions. In that case (and also in case they missed the deadlines for withdrawing equivalent concessions), these third parties cannot claim priority of other GATT provisions over the RTA.

The basic central requirement of not raising, or not raising on the whole, barriers to trade concerns third party rights, ie the rights of other WTO Members who are not parties to the respective RTA. The priority of RTAs over the GATT affects their rights with respect to RTA parties not only under the most favoured nation (MFN) and non-discrimination clauses (which concern most directly duties and trade barriers that cannot be raised), but also under all other GATT provisions in case of conflicts between the RTA and the GATT. This follows from the formulation of the conflict clause in the chapeau of Article XXIV:5, which speaks of 'the provisions of this agreement', ie of all, not just some, of the GATT provisions.

I describe the requirement of Article XXIV:5 which follows immediately after the words 'provided that' as 'basic', since it contains the central and essential condition for the priority of RTAs over the GATT. In addition to this, however, RTAs, in order 'to be consistent with Article XXIV', as has been agreed in the GATT 1994 Understanding, must also satisfy the provisions of the next three paragraphs of that Article: paragraph 6 (on the increases of duties), which was discussed above, paragraph 7 (on the providing of information, on consultations and on recommendations) and paragraph 8 (on the definitions of a customs union and a free trade area). From the point of view of the priority of RTAs over the GATT, the GATT 1994 Understanding does not introduce any new conditions in addition to paragraph 5, but confirms the substantive logical link of other provisions of Article XXIV to the basic requirement of paragraph 5 and further clarifies and specifies the requirement in paragraphs 2–11 of the Understanding.

The requirements contained in Article XXIV:7 are procedural. Subparagraph (a) provides that RTA parties 'shall promptly notify the CONTRACTING PARTIES and shall make available to them such information regarding the proposed union or area as will enable them to make such reports and recommendations to contracting parties as they may deem appropriate'. This obligation to notify and make available the required information can be seen as a condition for the priority of an RTA over all other GATT provisions. Consequently, if an RTA has not been notified to the WTO, RTA parties cannot avail themselves of the priority of their RTA over the GATT in dispute settlement with third parties.

Subparagraph 7(b) envisages the possibility of recommendations which can be made

> *after* having studied the plan and schedule included in an interim agreement referred to in paragraph 5 in consultation with the parties to that agreement and taking due account of the information made available in accordance with the provisions of subparagraph (a)

and

> *if* . . . the CONTRACTING PARTIES *find* that such agreement is not likely to result in the formation of a customs union or of a free trade area within the period contemplated by the parties to the agreement or that such period is not a reasonable one (emphases added).

The obligation for RTA parties, and thus a requirement for their RTA, is that they then 'shall not maintain or put into force, as the case may be, such agreement if they are not prepared to modify it in accordance with these recommendations'. This means that approval of RTAs by WTO bodies (ie the Committee on Regional Trade Agreements or the Council for Trade in Goods) is not a condition for the validity and primacy of RTAs over the GATT before there is a positive finding that the respective RTA does not comply with the requirements.[11] If there is no such positive finding of inconsistency with Article XXIV:5–8 and no recommendation, there cannot be any obligations for

[11] Such a positive finding of inconsistency with the requirements of Art XXIV, paras 5–9 can also precede or be contained in an approval of GATT-inconsistent RTAs under Art XXIV, para 10 ('The CONTRACTING PARTIES may by a two-thirds majority approve proposals which do not fully comply with the requirements of paragraphs 5 to 9 inclusive, provided that such proposals lead to the formation of a customs union or a free trade area in the sense of this Article'). The primacy of such RTAs over the GATT would in these cases follow from their very approval under para 10.

the parties to the RTA to fulfil. Hence, in case there is no explicit recommendation, RTAs must be presumed to be GATT-consistent and to have priority over the GATT.[12]

This presumption of consistency of RTAs with the WTO can be challenged[13] in WTO dispute settlement procedures, following paragraph 12 of the GATT 1994 Understanding on Article XXIV.[14]

The definitions in paragraph 8 of a customs union and of a free trade area, through their so-called internal trade requirement,[15] provide for the elimination of duties and other restrictive regulations of commerce between the constituent customs territories. Externally, for customs unions only, the members of the union apply the same duties and other regulations of commerce to the trade of territories not included in the union. The definitions, however, do not provide in their internal trade requirement for the elimination of all duties but stipulate that duties and other restrictive regulations of commerce between the constituent customs territories have to be eliminated with respect to '*substantially* all the trade' (emphasis added). In a similar way, externally, for customs unions, not 'the same' but 'substantially the same' duties and other regulations of commerce must be applied by each of the members of the union to the trade of territories not included in the union.

In subparagraphs 8(a)(i) and 8(b), the 'other regulations of commerce' which have to be eliminated on 'substantially all the trade' are specified by the text 'except, where necessary, those permitted under Articles XI, XII, XIII, XIV, XV and XX'. This means that restrictions permitted under these articles can, but need not, be eliminated between RTA parties. It does not mean, however, that all other restrictions, including such permitted by other GATT provisions, must necessarily be eliminated between RTA parties: if some (such as those under Article XIX or XXI) are not eliminated, this can be justified by the discretion of the parties to eliminate not all, but substantially all, restrictive measures. From the point of view of the conditions for the primacy of RTAs over the GATT, however, when assessing whether such restrictive regulations

[12] Following some members' views that failure by the GATT and WTO bodies to reject RTAs 'did not imply acceptance nor did it constitute a legal finding of GATT consistency with Article XXIV', the panel report in *Turkey—Textiles* (WT/DS34/R, paras 9.712ff) considered it erroneous to interpret the absence of challenges in the GATT or WTO 'as tantamount to its tacit acceptance by contracting parties'. For the validity of RTAs and their primacy over the GATT, however, such acceptance is not needed and the absence of acceptance does not imply inconsistency with the requirements of Art XXIV, paras 5–8.

[13] The challenge itself, however, cannot overturn the presumption, as proposed by JHJ Bourgeois and S Chobanova, 'RTAs under WTO Law and under Public International Law' in Bulgarian Association of International Law (2013) *Studies on International Law*, vol 8, 61–70. To overturn the presumption, a positive decision in WTO dispute settlement would be necessary.

[14] 'The provisions of Articles XXII and XXIII of GATT 1994 as elaborated and applied by the Dispute Settlement Understanding may be invoked with respect to any matters arising from the application of those provisions of Article XXIV relating to customs unions, free trade areas or interim agreements leading to the formation of a customs union or free trade area.'

[15] JH Mathis, *Regional Trade Agreements in the GATT/WTO: Article XXIV and the Internal Trade Requirement* (2002).

are eliminated on substantially all the trade, those permitted under Articles XI–XV and XX should not be taken into account.

There has never been agreement among WTO Members on how the requirements for 'substantially all the trade' and 'substantially the same duties and other regulations of commerce' should be interpreted, and this has been one of the main reasons for the inconclusive reviews under Article XXIV:7 GATT. The two major opposing approaches in the interpretation of the internal trade requirement were a 'quantitative' one (that it is sufficient that a certain percentage of the trade between the participants is covered) and a 'qualitative' one (that no sectors—or, at least, no major sectors—of trade are excluded). The approach of the (then) European Communities was 'quantitative': that the volume of liberalized trade should reach at least 80 per cent of total trade.[16] The 'qualitative' approach (of the US and others) was that 'the percentage of trade covered, even if it were established to be 90 per cent, was not . . . the only factor to be taken into account'[17] and that the exclusion of a whole sector, no matter what percentage of trade involved, is contrary to the spirit of Article XXIV and the GATT.[18]

In the Uruguay Round, the 'substantially all trade' requirement was not specified further. The preamble of the GATT 1994 Understanding recognizes that the contribution of RTAs to the expansion of world trade 'is increased if the elimination between the constituent territories of duties and other restrictive regulations of commerce extends to all trade, and diminished if any major sector of trade is excluded'. From this wording, however, it is not possible to derive an argument in favour of the 'qualitative' approach since it does not formulate a formal normative requirement, nor even a recommendation, but just an evaluation of a possible contribution to the increase of world trade which RTA parties can make if they so wish.

In *Turkey—Textiles*, the Appellate Body did not attempt to formulate a more specific standard for the internal trade requirement. It only noted that 'it is clear . . . that "substantially all the trade" is not the same as all the trade, and also that "substantially all the trade" is something considerably more than merely some of the trade'. It agreed that 'the terms of sub-paragraph 8(a)(i) offer "some flexibility" to the constituent members of a customs union when liberalizing their internal trade in accordance with this subparagraph', yet it cautioned 'that the degree of "flexibility" that sub-paragraph 8(a)(i) allows is limited by the requirement that "duties and other restrictive regulations of commerce" be "eliminated with respect to substantially all" internal trade'.[19] This seems to be quite correct, because otherwise the Appellate Body would 'add to or diminish the rights and obligations in the covered agreements', thereby infringing Article 3(2) of the WTO Dispute Settlement Understanding

[16] GATT Doc L/778, 20 December 1957, para 30, 28–29.
[17] GATT Doc L/1235, 4 June 1960, para 48, 12.
[18] *GATT Analytical Index—Guide to GATT Law and Practice* (2012), 825.
[19] WTO Appellate Body Report, *Turkey—Textiles*, WT/DS34/AB/R, para 48.

(DSU). The formation of RTAs is a right of WTO Members, and the standards on 'substantially all' and 'substantially the same' duties and regulations of commerce, as established by Article XXIV:8(a) and (b) GATT, have granted RTA parties a margin of discretion: a 'degree of flexibility', as the Appellate Body describes it. This margin of discretion is granted to RTA parties, not to WTO bodies or its dispute settlement system, and it would be diminished if, for example, the Appellate Body were to adopt an approach which the RTA parties do not share. Neither the panels nor the Appellate Body, or the Dispute Settlement Body, can change the standard itself by establishing the margin of discretion because this would limit the flexibility of RTA parties and thus 'add to or diminish' their rights and obligations.[20] What the WTO dispute settlement system can do is only decide in specific disputes whether the degree of 'flexibility' granted to RTA parties by the internal trade requirement has been overstepped and the elimination of duties in their RTA cannot reasonably be conceived as covering substantially all trade.

In the GATS, the basic requirements for integration agreements, and thus for their primacy over the GATS, are similar to those in Article XXIV of the GATT. They are contained in Article V on Economic Integration and Article V bis on Labour Markets Integration Agreements.

The conflict clause for the relationship with RTAs is contained in the chapeau of Article V.1, which reads: 'This Agreement shall not prevent any of its Members from being a party to or entering into an agreement liberalizing trade in services between or among the parties to such an agreement.' The requirements—ie conditions for the priority of such an agreement over the GATS—include 'substantial sectoral coverage' and

> absence or elimination of substantially all discrimination . . . between or among the parties, in the sectors covered ..., through . . . elimination of existing discriminatory measures, and/or . . . prohibition of new or more discriminatory measures, either at the entry into force of that agreement or on the basis of a reasonable time-frame, except for measures permitted under Articles XI, XII, XIV and XIV bis.

A note on 'substantial sectoral coverage' specifies that '[t]his condition is understood in terms of number of sectors, volume of trade affected and modes of supply. In order to meet this condition, agreements should not provide for the a priori exclusion of any mode of supply'. Thus, on modes of supply, an approach was adopted which seems similar to the 'qualitative' interpretation of the 'substantially all trade' requirement in Article XXIV GATT. It should

[20] The standard itself cannot be changed by other WTO bodies either. For a change of the standard, a change in the agreements themselves is necessary. The penultimate paragraph of the preamble of the Understanding on the Interpretation of Article XXIV of the GATT 1994, which states: 'Convinced also of the need to reinforce the effectiveness of the role of the Council for Trade in Goods in reviewing agreements notified under Article XXIV, by clarifying the criteria and procedures for the assessment of new or enlarged agreements, and improving the transparency of all Article XXIV agreements', does not represent such a change, nor does it empower the Council for Trade in Goods to 'clarify' the criteria. It only states that the purpose of the clarifications, which follow in the body of the text of the Understanding, is to reinforce the Council's role.

be noted, however, that this requirement is limited only to the modes of supply and cannot be extrapolated generally to the requirement for 'sectoral coverage', which specifies only that it should be 'substantial'. The condition is not coverage of 'substantially all' sectors but merely 'substantial sectoral coverage', 'understood in terms of numbers of sectors', which arguably is considerably less than 'substantially all'. Thus the standard of the 'internal trade requirement' in the GATS for RTAs on services is set considerably lower than that for goods in the GATT.

Alongside these basic requirements in paragraph 1 of Article V GATS, which represent the conditions which have to be fulfilled for the primacy of RTAs on services over the GATS, the paragraphs which follow contain specifications and clarifications referring to these conditions. Thus paragraph 2 specifies that when 'evaluating whether the conditions . . . are met, consideration may be given to the relationship of the agreement to a wider process of economic integration or trade liberalization among the countries concerned'.

Paragraph 3 concerns the participation of developing countries in RTAs, providing for 'flexibility . . . in accordance with the level of development of the countries concerned', regarding the basic requirements and with particular reference to the absence or elimination of substantially all discrimination, 'both overall and in individual sectors and subsectors'.

The purpose of these two paragraphs is obviously not to tighten but, on the contrary, to increase the flexibilities and discretion of RTA parties under the conflict clause of paragraph 1.

Paragraphs 4 and 5 contain the requirement that services RTAs should not raise the overall level of barriers to third parties and specify the procedures for raising specific barriers. Unlike the requirements for goods RTAs in Article XXIV:5 GATT, however, the requirement in Article V:4 GATS not to 'raise the overall level of barriers to trade in services' is not formulated as a basic requirement, contained in the conflict clause of paragraph 1 itself, linked immediately to the words 'provided that', but outside the sentence of the conflict clause. What follows from this is that if RTA parties have gone through the procedures of Article XXI for raising specific barriers, then a complaining third party cannot be entitled to more than withdrawing 'substantially equivalent benefits', as provided for in Article XXI:4(b), and cannot profit from a priority of other GATS rules over the RTA. Generally, one could conclude that the raising of specific services barriers should follow the procedures provided for in Article V GATS, but it cannot be a ground for not recognizing the priority of the RTA over all other GATS provisions. In dispute settlement, a claim that the overall level of barriers has been raised cannot be accepted as a ground for not recognizing the primacy of the RTA over the GATS unless that claim has been raised in the WTO examination of the RTA under paragraph 7 and unless it has been substantiated in procedures under paragraph 5 for the specific increases of barriers which have raised the overall level.

Similarly, the provision of paragraph 6 (which entitles juridical persons of other WTO Members, engaged in substantive business operations in the territory of the parties, to treatment under the RTA) does not constitute a condition for the primacy of RTAs over the GATS. What follows from the inclusion of this provision in Article V GATS is only that, although it is not a condition for the priority of integration agreements on services over the GATS, in case of violations by the RTA parties, the infringing measures can be challenged through WTO dispute settlement.

Paragraph 7, similarly to Article XXIV:7 GATT, contains the requirement to 'promptly notify' services integration agreements to the WTO and procedures for examination of such services RTAs, and provides for the possibility for recommendations. As in the GATT, the obligations to notify and make available the required information can be seen as conditions for the priority of a services RTA over all other GATS provisions.

Alongside the economic integration agreements in Article V, the GATS provides in Article V bis for another type of RTAs which establish full integration of labour markets. Such RTAs exempt citizens of parties from requirements concerning residency and work permits, and must be notified to the WTO. The note on 'full integration' specifies that '[t]ypically, such integration provides citizens of the parties concerned with a right of free entry to the employment markets of the parties and includes measures concerning conditions of pay, other conditions of employment and social benefits'. It appears that in the conflict clause of Article V bis it is the word 'full' that describes the 'internal' requirement, unlike in the GATT and elsewhere in the GATS, where the formulation 'substantial' is used.

The general conclusion which can be made from the analysis of the conflict clauses contained in Article XXIV:5 GATT and Articles V and V bis GATS is that there is priority of RTAs over all other provisions of the GATT and the GATS except over the conflict clauses containing the conditions for priority, and unless there is a positive finding by WTO bodies on the inconsistency of the RTA with the provisions of these clauses.

The priority of RTAs over the other WTO Agreements can be derived from their link to the GATT or the GATS. The understandings, protocols, decisions, etc enumerated in the GATT 1994 are integral parts of it and, therefore, the reference to 'the provisions of this Agreement' in the conflict clause of Article XXIV:5 GATT has to be read as a direct reference to the provisions of these instruments as well. The other Multilateral Agreements on Trade in Goods, together with the GATT 1994, are included in Annex 1A to the Marrakesh Agreement Establishing the WTO and, as stipulated in its Article II:2, are integral parts of it. Some of them, in their names or texts, refer explicitly to GATT 1994 provisions. The name of the antidumping agreement, for instance, is Agreement on Implementation of Article VI of the General Agreement on Tariffs and Trade 1994, and that of the customs valuation agreement is Agreement on Implementation of Article VII of the General Agreement on Tariffs and Trade 1994. Others refer to GATT provisions in their texts (eg on definitions and coverage in Article 1 of the Agreement on Rules of Origin). If provisions of these agreements are based on GATT 1994 provisions, over which RTAs have priority, this priority should also apply over the respective provision in the multilateral trade agreement. If, for example, a provision from a multilateral trade agreement is not applicable in a situation unless a GATT 1994 provision is applicable as well, which would normally be the case, then the priority of an RTA over the GATT 1994 provision would also apply over the respective multilateral agreement.

The priority of RTAs over the GATT and the related Multilateral Agreements on Trade in Goods in Annex 1A of the WTO Agreements is not affected by the priority of these Agreements over the GATT 1994, as stipulated in the general interpretative note to Annex 1A of the Marrakesh Agreement,[21] because it concerns only the relationship between them and the GATT and not the relationship with non-WTO treaties, such as RTAs. Their relationship to RTAs is a different one, which depends, on the one hand, on their specific link to the GATT and, on the other hand, on the relationship of the GATT to RTAs.

IV. THE RELATIONSHIP BETWEEN WTO LAW AND RTAS IN WTO BODIES

In the WTO, the question of the legal relationship between the WTO and RTAs has not yet been approached from the point of view of general international law, based on Article 30(2) VCLT and the conflict clauses of Articles XXIV:5 GATT and V and V bis GATS. Rather, the focus of the WTO Committee on RTAs has been on WTO compatibility and on conformity with Article XXIV GATT for the purposes of paragraph 7 reviews. In these reviews, some third parties have been trying to contest the conformity of RTAs with GATT requirements, especially with the internal trade requirement. In the history of the GATT, the European Communities, which themselves were an RTA, were the principal users of Article XXIV, and the US played a leading role in the contestations of the RTAs of the European Communities in the reviews. As mentioned, these reviews were not conclusive because of the differences of opinion on the internal trade requirement. In WTO accession negotiations, some WTO Members were trying to 'multilateralize' the tariff preferences granted by RTA parties to each other by pressing for inclusion of comparable MFN concessions in their accession schedules. In trade policy reviews, the WTO Secretariat explored whether the RTAs of some WTO Members

[21] 'In the event of conflict between a provision of the GATT 1994 and a provision of another agreement in Annex 1A to the Agreement Establishing the WTO (referred to in the agreements in Annex 1A as the "WTO Agreement"), the provision of the other agreement shall prevail to the extent of the conflict.'

give rise to trade diversion, with a view to encouraging them to lower their applied MFN tariff rates in order to ensure cheaper imports.

At the first Ministerial Conference of the WTO in Singapore, ministers stated that they 'reaffirm the primacy of the multilateral trading system, which includes a framework for the development of regional trade agreements' and renewed their 'commitment to ensure that regional trade agreements are complementary to it and consistent with its rules'.[22] This was a political declaration, which does not modify the GATT 1994 texts and cannot be seen as replacing or changing the conflict rules of Articles XXIV:5 GATT or V:1 and V bis GATS to mean that the WTO agreements have legal priority over RTAs.

Nevertheless, in dispute settlement, the panel in *Turkey—Textiles* based its legal conclusions on the primacy of the WTO over RTAs, as reiterated in the Singapore Declaration,[23] and derived third party rights from an incorrect reading of Article XXIV:5 GATT. When, in the same case, the report was appealed, the Appellate Body did not refer either to a primacy of the WTO over RTAs or to the Singapore Declaration. However, although it did not agree with the panel's reasoning, it upheld its main conclusions. The interpretation it gave of Article XXIV:5 GATT ignored its meaning as a conflict clause and introduced the additional condition that RTA measures which were otherwise inconsistent with the GATT would be considered GATT-consistent only if the formation of the RTA 'would be prevented' without them. The Appellate Body interpreted the text of the GATT that 'the provisions of this Agreement shall not prevent . . . the formation of a customs union' to mean that measures which are allowed upon the formation of a customs union, although otherwise not GATT-consistent, can be justified 'only to the extent that the formation of the customs union would be prevented' as a result of their introduction.[24] Thus we see a semantic mistake, whereby the subject of the sentence, 'the provisions of this Agreement', ie the provisions of the GATT itself (which do not prevent the formation of RTAs), is substituted by GATT-inconsistent measures without which the formation of the customs union would be prevented. With this interpretation, the WTO Appellate Body did not properly construe the ordinary meaning of the text of Article XXIV:5 GATT, thereby changing the rights and obligations provided in the GATT, contrary to Article 3(2) of the DSU. Instead of enforcing the conflict rule of Article XXIV:5 GATT, the Appellate Body misinterpreted it and, without explicitly introducing the legal primacy of the GATT over RTAs, formulated a new, very broad and open-ended condition which allowed for the introduction of primacy of the WTO over RTAs through the back door.

It should be emphasized that these GATT/WTO practices cannot change the legal validity and applicability of the conflict clause in Article XXIV:5 and the priority of RTAs, which follows from Article 30(2) VCLT. From the point of

[22] WTO, WT/MIN(96)/DEC, para 7.
[23] WTO, WT/DS34/R (31 May 1999) para 9.184.
[24] WTO, WT/DS34/AB/R (22 October 1999), paras 45–46, 58–59.

view of Article 30(2) VCLT, such a change would only be possible by means of changing the conflict clause in the WTO agreements through modification or amendment. Another way of reversing the legal relationship between RTAs and the WTO Agreements could be by including a conflict clause in RTAs that provides for WTO priority. What the effect of such a clause in RTAs on third party rights would be would depend on its wording. Since the conflict clause of Article XXIV:5 provides for RTA priority over all GATT provisions other than those of Article XXIV itself, an RTA conflict clause on WTO priority in order to avoid a circular—and thereby nullifying—effect would have to list the WTO provisions which would have priority and from which third parties could derive rights.

V. DOES A WTO PRIMACY FOLLOW FROM A CONSTITUTIONAL RELATIONSHIP WITHIN THE WTO?

It should be noted that the existence per se of requirements for WTO consistency (ie conditions for the priority of RTAs over WTO agreements) in the conflict clauses of WTO Agreements cannot change the legal relationship between the WTO and RTAs as separate international treaties from one under international law into some other type of relationship for which the rule of Article 30(2) VCLT would not apply. There has been an attempt to present the relationship between the WTO and RTAs not as one based on international law but, because of the requirements formulated in Article XXIV:5 GATT, as a different kind of relationship, that is hierarchical and 'constitutional' in character.[25] In this view, RTAs are not international treaties separate from the WTO but *inter se* modifications of WTO Agreements between only some of the Members of the WTO; therefore, Article 41 VCLT ('Agreements to modify multilateral treaties between certain of the parties only') applies.[26] The argument is that, under the WTO, 'as a multilateral treaty defining terms and conditions for the deviation of non-discriminatory rights and obligations . . . a constitutional and hierarchical relationship between WTO rules and RTAs emerges under Article 41 VCLT' and 'RTAs are subject to the conditions of WTO law . . . in the same way as legislation, in a domestic context, is subject to requirements of constitutional law'.

This approach, deriving primacy of the WTO over RTAs from a mere analogy with domestic constitutional law, is flawed: first, because RTAs are not part of the legal system of the WTO and, second, because *inter se* modifi-

[25] Cottier and Foltea (n 1 above), 56–57.

[26] Views based on the assumption that Art 41 VCLT applies to the legal relationship between WTO and RTAs have also been expressed by Mathis (n 15 above), 271–84, and J Pauwelyn, *Conflict of Norms in International Law: How the WTO Law Relates to other Rules of International Law* (2003) 303ff. On the view that Art 41 VCLT does not apply to RTAs see D Georgiev, 'The World Trade Organization and International Economic Integration: Legal Aspects' in MJ Jovanovic (ed), *International Handbook on the Economics of Integration*, vol I (2011) 145ff.

cations of international treaties under Article 41 VCLT do not necessarily result in a hierarchical or constitutional relationship between the initial and the modified treaties.

RTAs do not belong to the system of the WTO—unlike the agreements attached to the Agreement Establishing the WTO: the 'multilateral' agreements (the GATT 1994 Agreements, the GATS, the TRIPS, the DSU, the TPRM) and the 'plurilateral' ones—and are hence not based on the WTO. RTAs are not mentioned in Article II ('Scope of the WTO') of the Agreement Establishing the WTO alongside 'multilateral' and 'plurilateral' agreements, and RTAs are not covered by the provisions outlining the system of WTO law and establishing its hierarchy. RTAs are not mentioned in Article X ('Amendments') of the WTO Agreement, nor are they mentioned in Article XXX GATT ('Amendments'). Moreover, there are no indications that the WTO Agreement, RTA parties or other WTO Members perceive RTAs as *inter se* GATT 'modifications' in the sense of Article 41 VCLT and not as separate international agreements. The only provisions in the WTO which describe the legal relationship between RTAs and the WTO Agreements are the ones in Article XXIV GATT and Articles V and V bis GATS. Notifications under Article XXIV:7(a) GATT do not refer to the respective RTAs as GATT *inter se* modifications.

As for the argument that RTAs are modifications of the WTO and are based on it in the same way as a national legislation is based on a domestic constitution, it should be noted that modifications of treaties under Article 41 VCLT do not necessarily create a hierarchical relationship and primacy of the original treaty over the modified one. That an analogy between Article 41 VCLT and the primacy of national constitutions over legislation is quite mistaken becomes obvious if the question is posed whether, following the logic of this analogy, an original domestic constitution should necessarily have primacy over a modified one. Hence, Article 41 VCLT on *inter se* treaty modifications is not relevant for the relationship between the WTO and RTAs.

Generally speaking, the primacy of the rules of one legal system over the rules of another is established by each legal system for itself, in the same way as each legal system establishes the relationships between different categories of its own rules: by allocating them a place within its own hierarchy of norms. In domestic law, for example, the primacy of international law over provisions of domestic law cannot be deduced solely from the obligatory character of international agreements for the states parties to them, ie from the principle of *pacta sunt servanda*, or from other rules of general international law.[27] The rules establishing the place of international law in the domestic legal

[27] *Cf* E-U Petersmann, *International Economic Law in the 21st Century: Constitutional Pluralism and Multilevel Economic Governance of Interdependent Public Goods* (2012), 81, who considers that Art 27 VCLT ('[a] party may not invoke the provisions of its internal law as justification for its failure to perform a treaty') contains a 'claim' by international law for primacy over domestic law and that this 'claim' 'must remain subject to constitutional restraints' by domestic law.

hierarchy, given their importance, are normally included in the 'constitution' of the national legal system. Such rules are, for example, the constitutional provisions giving direct effect or primacy to ratified international treaties or to general international law over domestic legislation. On the other hand, conflict rules in private international law are usually not regarded as 'constitutional'.

The question itself about the relationship between the WTO and RTAs can be considered 'constitutional' in the sense that the answer to it is based on some 'constitutional' rules. Within general international law, it is the rules of the Vienna Convention that play such a 'constitutional' function with respect to separate international agreements, such as the WTO or its Agreements, on the one hand, and RTAs, on the other hand. Article 5 VCLT confirms explicitly that it applies 'to any treaty which is the constituent instrument of an international organization and to any treaty adopted within an international organization without prejudice to any relevant rules of the organization'.

Within parts of international law, within its branches and 'regimes', there can be legal systems with their relatively autonomous 'legal orders', and a 'constitutionalization' could involve the establishment of legal hierarchies, separated to some extent from international law. Similarly to states, international institutions and RTAs can establish their own autonomous 'legal orders', relatively separate from international law. Such is the case of the EU, which is an RTA (even though it is much more than just an RTA).

As for the WTO, although it has its own 'integrated and distinctive legal order',[28] its law is not separated from the legal system of international law to a degree which would exclude the application of general international law. Article 3(2) DSU explicitly stipulates that the dispute settlement system of the WTO serves to 'clarify the existing provisions of those agreements in accordance with customary rules of interpretation of public international law'. These customary rules are codified in the Vienna Convention. In its very first report, the WTO Appellate Body stated that the GATT is not to be read in 'clinical isolation' from public international law and drew attention to the rules of interpretation of the VCLT.[29]

The conclusion can be drawn that, as Article 41 VCLT is inapplicable to the legal relationship between the WTO Agreements and RTAs, and as there is no 'constitutional' separation of the WTO from general international law as codified in the Vienna Convention, the conflict clauses of Article XXIV GATT and Articles V and V bis GATS that establish this relationship have to be interpreted in the light of Article 30(2) VCLT. Therefore, the legal relationship between the WTO and RTAs cannot be regarded as 'constitutional' and no WTO primacy could be derived from it.

[28] P Lamy, 'The Place of the WTO and its Law in the International Legal Order' (2007) 17 *European Journal of International Law* 971.

[29] In *US—Gasoline*, WTO, WT/DS2/AB/R, 17.

VI. REGIONALISM AND THE PRIMACY OF EU LAW OVER NATIONAL LAW

What is the experience in the EU with the constitutionalization of legal hierarchies and with regionalism in multilevel economic governance, and what could be relevant for the WTO from this experience?

The principle of the primacy of European Community law over the law of the Member States was not spelled out in the treaties establishing the Communities but was formulated in 1964 by the European Court of Justice (the Court). When we look at the substantive grounds[30] on the basis of which the Court formulated this principle and when we compare these grounds with the system of WTO law, key differences emerge. Unlike EU law, WTO law does not constitute a legal system meant to become part of the legal systems of WTO Members (or of the legal systems of their RTAs). Moreover, there is no limitation of sovereignty or transfer of powers on the part of Members to the WTO: on the contrary, the WTO system was meant to be and was shaped as 'member driven'.

In the European Union, primacy of EU law over the law of the Member States was not the result of a 'constitutionalization'. Actually, developments went in the opposite direction, as the primacy of the law of the then European Community brought about constitutional problems in the Member States and contributed to the perception of a need for constitutionalization at the level of the Community. The supranational model adopted in the Community—where legally binding decisions by non-elected representatives of the national executive branches, taken by majority vote behind closed doors, had direct effect on individuals at national level and primacy over acts of national parliaments and even over national constitutions—generated a deficit of legitimacy which needed to be overcome by constitutionalization.

This deficit was felt in particular with respect to fundamental rights. The European Court of Justice developed its doctrine that fundamental rights form an integral part of the general principles of law which are protected by the Court,[31] that these principles are part of EU law and that the Court was bound to draw inspiration from the constitutional traditions common to the Member States.[32] In 1974, the German Federal Constitutional Court, in its *Solange-I* decision,[33] held that, as long as the European Community did not possess a catalogue of fundamental rights, equivalent to that in the Federal Constitution, provisions of Community law which collided with German fundamental constitutional rights would not be applicable in Germany. In 1977, a Joint Declaration by the European Parliament, the Council and the Commission stressed

[30] Case 6/64 *Costa v Enel* [1964] ECR 585, 593.
[31] Case 11/70 *Internationale Handelsgesellschaft* [1970] ECR 1125.
[32] Case 4/73 *J Nold v Commission* [1973] ECR 491.
[33] *Internationale Handelsgesellschaft v Einfuhr- und Vorratsstelle für Getreide und Futtermittel*, 29 May 1974, BVerfGE 37, 271ff.

'the prime importance they attach to the protection of fundamental rights, as derived in particular from the constitutions of the Member States'.[34] The final result of these developments, after the failed attempt at explicit constitutionalization of the European Union, was that a catalogue of fundamental rights was embodied in the Charter of Fundamental Rights of the EU which, with the Lisbon Treaty, was given 'the same legal value as the Treaties'.[35] Fundamental rights, 'as they result from the constitutional traditions common to the Member States', were given constitutional status as 'general principles of the Union's law'[36] and were thus accorded standing as primary EU law and primacy over secondary legislation enacted by the institutions.

In the European Union the constitutional importance of the question of primacy of EU law over the law of the Member States was acknowledged with the Treaty establishing a Constitution for Europe, which contained a clause on 'Union law' stipulating that 'the Constitution and law adopted by the institutions of the Union in exercising competences conferred on it shall have primacy over the law of the Member States'.[37] After the Constitutional Treaty was rejected in the referenda in France and the Netherlands, this clause, alongside with much of other constitutional terminology, was not reproduced in the Lisbon Treaty. Instead, in its Declaration concerning primacy annexed to the Final Act, the Intergovernmental Conference recalled

> that, in accordance with well settled case law of the Court of Justice of the European Union, the Treaties and the law adopted by the Union on the basis of the Treaties have primacy over the law of Member States, under the conditions laid down by the said case law.[38]

Not including a primacy clause in the treaties was an indirect confirmation of the constitutional importance of such a clause: as constitutionalization was not generally acceptable, some concepts essentially associated with it had to be given up, including this one.

Another aspect of the constitutional developments in the EU that is relevant for this inquiry is its regional policy. It was first introduced in the treaties establishing the Communities under the heading 'economic and social cohesion' with the Single European Act in 1986 with the aim of reducing disparities between the various regions and the backwardness of the least favoured regions. Thus it became one of the forms of positive integration accompanying market liberalization in the Internal Market as an area without internal frontiers in which all barriers to the free movement of goods, persons, services and capital were lifted. In the Treaty on the Functioning of the European Union, 'Economic, Social and Territorial Cohesion' was included as one of the Union's internal policies. The EU supports the achievement of the objectives of its

[34] [1977] OJ C103/1.
[35] Art 6(1) TEU [2008] OJ C115/19.
[36] Art 6(3) TEU.
[37] Art I-6 of Part I, Title I [2004] OJ C310/12.
[38] Declaration No 17 [2008] OJ C115/344.

regional policy through its structural funds, including the Regional Development Fund, the Cohesion Fund and other financial instruments. For the period 2007–13, regional policy was the second largest item in the Union's budget.

One of the conclusions which can be drawn from the experience of the EU is that primacy does not follow implicitly from some inherently 'constitutional' character of the relationship between levels of multilevel economic governance. On the contrary, if it is not shaped with due regard to constitutional values, principles and rights, and especially if introduced in combination with majority decision making and direct effect for individuals, it can lead to fundamental problems of legitimacy. Another conclusion which can be drawn from the experience of the EU with regionalism is the importance of positive integration aimed at 'reducing disparities between the levels of development of the various regions and the backwardness of the least favoured regions', resulting from negative integration through complete market liberalization and the lifting of all trade and other barriers.

VII. PRIMACY OF THE WTO OVER RTAS AND PROSPECTS FOR THE CONSTITUTIONALIZATION OF THE WTO

Having shown the current state of the law—with primacy of RTAs over WTO law—and the constitutional importance of the legal relationship between different layers of international multilevel economic governance, we can now turn to the question of whether this state of affairs should be changed, ie whether it would be better to reverse the relationship existing now in positive[39] WTO law and to give precedence of the WTO over RTAs through constitutionalization.

With this in view, I will first examine some of the arguments of opponents of RTAs, who tend to see them as 'stumbling' rather than 'building' blocks of the international trading system, and then look at some of the visions promoting a constitutionalization of the WTO, with primacy of WTO law over RTAs.

A. Stumbling or Building Blocks?

The basic economic argument expressed by opponents of RTAs is that of trade diversion, as first elaborated by Jacob Viner in 1950. The logic of this argument is that, because of MFN duties and other trade barriers, consumers would buy at higher prices from less efficient producers within an RTA instead of buying from more cost-effective producers from markets not included in the RTA. From the point of view of the interests of the respective economy, this

[39] Cottier, for instance, while agreeing that in terms of 'positive law' RTAs are not part of the WTO legal system, expressed the opinion that primacy of the WTO over RTAs would be justified in view of 'general welfare' (in a panel discussion on 'RTAs in the WTO and in International Law' at the 75th Conference of the International Law Association in Sofia, Bulgaria).

could, indeed, be seen as a cost which would need to be balanced with some other benefits from the RTA. From the point of view of the economic welfare of a country, participation in an RTA would be economically effective if there are positive balances not only between the trade creation and the trade diversion effects of the RTA, but, more importantly, between the country's own export interests and those of its RTA partners, between its gains, on the one hand, and the adjustment costs necessitated as a result of the elimination of trade barriers within the RTA, on the other hand, etc. Such balances of interests, both between different economies and within each of them, may be easier to achieve in an RTA than in multilateral WTO negotiations because deeper economic integration provides for more possibilities than mere trade liberalization. Deeper integration involves not only negative integration through the lifting of trade barriers but also positive integration in the form of common legal regimes, policies, various forms of redistribution, etc. If the economy of a customs territory can achieve a better balance of its different—economic and other—interests by participating in an RTA rather than through multilateral WTO negotiations, then from the point of view of its own interests the RTA would obviously be the better choice.

This does not mean that all RTAs actually concluded under Article XXIV GATT or V GATS are per se of equal interest to all their parties or that there is a positive balance of the interests of all individual participants in every RTA. After the conclusion of an RTA, that balance may turn out to be different from what parties had expected if they had wrongly assessed the real consequences of the conclusion of the RTA, if they had ceded to political pressures from hegemonic powers, etc. The same is also true, however, for multilateral negotiations in the WTO. There is, for example, the view that not all developing countries were fully aware of what they were signing up to in the Uruguay Round. At the same time, if it is clear that a proposed RTA or a provision in an RTA is not in the interest of a party, eg if hegemonic powers are trying to impose one-sided provisions for RTAs, of unequal interest to the different participants, there is no obligation to accept such provisions or join such RTAs.

Some advocates of a constitutionalization of the WTO, who argue in favour of its primacy over RTAs, seem to associate general economic welfare with the interests of third parties.[40] Here one should bear in mind that the basic condition for the WTO conformity of RTAs—that of not raising trade barriers to third parties—does account for such interests. Going beyond this by 'multilateralizing' (eg by exempting from liberalization some tariff items, where trade diversion occurs and which would be of interest to third parties, by means of the 'substantially all trade' flexibility or by lowering the MFN tariff to zero) would be tantamount to granting a concession to third parties without getting something in return, ie giving third parties a free ride. If general economic welfare is associated with more world trade, then it should be recognized

[40] Cottier and Foltea (n 1 above), 64; *cf* n 39 above.

that RTAs, the very purpose of which is free trade, do make a contribution to world trade through their internal trade and are thereby building blocks of the international trading system.

Hence the conclusion can be made that economically, both in the interests of RTA parties and for general welfare, MFN liberalization is not better than the conclusion of RTAs. Even the Sutherland Report of 2004 on the future of the WTO, which is strongly opposed to RTAs and other preferential trade agreements, admits that the economic debate whether RTAs are building or stumbling blocks is inconclusive.[41]

It seems, therefore, that the principal accent of RTA opponents is placed not so much on economic considerations as on considerations which can be described as systemic, organizational, political, institutional and, in this sense, constitutional. A major argument of RTA opponents is that RTAs undermine and erode—like termites[42]—the MFN principle which is central to the international trading system and that, therefore, the WTO needs to assert itself over RTAs.

While it is true that RTAs are not in line with the MFN principle in the GATT and the WTO—RTAs were meant by definition to be exceptions to this central principle—it is also true, as has been argued above, that they may offer broader possibilities, economically or otherwise, for better solutions from the point of view of the balance of interests of RTA parties, compared to possible MFN liberalization through WTO negotiations. A better balance of interests may be achievable in RTAs through deeper positive integration, including 'WTO-plus' provisions. So what is important constitutionally for each individual country is its ability and freedom to assess the balance of its interests on its own, choose accordingly what it considers better, and join or not join any MFN or RTA trade liberalization scheme. This freedom is a legal right under WTO law and, at the same time, a political and moral responsibility of the state[43] (or customs territory) towards its own citizens, including a responsibility to compensate for the costs of trade liberalization. Priority of the WTO over RTAs would limit this freedom by restricting existing possibilities for deeper positive integration and is arguably not a better constitutional solution. Plans for a constitutionalization of the WTO, which propose a shift away from what some call the mantras of sovereignty and member-driven governance by introducing binding decisions by weighted majority voting, can have the same effect—or purpose—of limiting the freedom of WTO Members to join (or not to join) MFN or RTA liberalization schemes which meet (or

[41] Above n 3.

[42] Above n 2.

[43] Pope Francis sees the economic imbalance between the prosperity of a few separating them from the majority as 'the result of ideologies which defend the absolute autonomy of the marketplace' and speaks of a 'right of states, charged with vigilance for the common good, to exercise . . . control': Francis, *Evangelii Gaudium. Apostolic Exhortation* (2013) 47.

do not meet) their own interests and to shape such schemes to their mutual advantage.

Limiting that freedom (ie the sovereignty) of the states by giving the WTO, with its central principle of MFN, legal primacy over RTAs through a constitutionalization of the WTO, could be considered better and justified only if it can be convincingly demonstrated that such loss of freedom of the state is adequately compensated. There would have to be, for example, constitutional guarantees for a fairer and more equitable distribution of the benefits of trade liberalization and of globalization in general, as well as of the burdens and costs, such as poverty, loss of jobs, disparities of levels of development, inequalities between and within economies and between citizens of different economies, and environment-related problems. The concerns about the inequalities and injustices on which trade and trade liberalization are based and which they generate go to the heart of the most fundamental problems of globalization. Although we do not need to discuss recipes for their solution here, these are concerns and problems in the light of which questions such as whether MFN liberalization is better than regional integration and whether and how multilevel economic governance should be constitutionalized have to be approached.

A key question about a constitutionalization of the WTO from this point of view is whether the MFN principle alone can guarantee a fair and equitable distribution between trading partners of the costs and benefits of trade liberalization. If that is the case, then introducing primacy of the GATT/WTO over RTAs as part of a future constitutionalization of global economic governance could understandably be considered justified and acceptable.

MFN treatment, however, although central to the international trading system, enshrined as it is in the very first provision of Article I of the GATT, was never meant to guarantee such a fair and equitable distribution of the benefits and costs of trade liberalization, or general economic welfare and justice. What it does guarantee is only the equality of customs treatment of goods imported from or exported to any country enjoying that treatment. The 'embedding'[44] of market liberalization with the aim of achieving greater economic equality and justice is assumed to be the primary responsibility of each individual economy and government, so the response to globalization 'must start at home'.[45] It should be obvious, however, that the domestic embedding within economies cannot account for the disparities and inequalities between economies. These inequalities need to be tackled, and an embedding can only be effective at the appropriate higher international level, eg through

[44] In the sense of the term as used by J Ruggie, 'International Regimes, Transactions and Change: Embedded Liberalism in the Post War Economic Order' (1982) 36 *International Organization* 379.

[45] *Cf* International Labour Office, *A Fair Globalization: Creating Opportunities for All* (2004) xi, 54ff; M Bacchetta and M Jansen, *Making Globalization Socially Sustainable* (ILO/WTO, 2011); D Ben-David et al, *Trade, Income Disparity and Poverty* (WTO, 1999).

trade negotiations, where each individual country is in a position to act and undertake obligations and give concessions based on the assessment of costs and benefits to itself and of the balance between its own export and other interests and those of its trading partners. In the WTO, such embedding can take the form of exceptions to and limitations of the principle of MFN, such as the 'enabling clause' and Generalized System of Preferences schemes, and exceptions for developing countries to the rules of WTO Agreements. Article XXIV of the GATT on RTAs is one of those exceptions which can help the embedding of liberalized markets through deeper economic integration, including positive integration. It is not by asserting MFN treatment over other rules in the GATT but by embedding it, by supplementing and limiting it, eg through exceptions, that a balance of interests between different participants in the international trading system could be achieved.

Although central to the international trading system, MFN treatment has never been explicitly formulated in the legal texts as a principle and has never been meant to have a constitutional status with primacy over other rules. If we want to bring more economic equality and economic justice into the international trading system, and thereby into globalization, it would necessarily be by embedding, and possibly limiting, the central principle of MFN through other arrangements, not by asserting it and giving it legal primacy.

B. Primacy of WTO Law and Visions for its Constitutionalization

Having seen that MFN liberalization is not per se 'better' than RTAs, we can now turn to some of the visions for a constitutionalization of multilevel economic governance and their relevance for the legal relationship between the WTO and RTAs. Can these visions, or approaches, which seem to refer implicitly to a non-existent just, or at least better, global society of more general welfare, justify and legitimize primacy of the WTO over RTAs?

I have identified three approaches to the constitutionalization of multilevel economic architecture which explicitly, although in different ways, provide for some form of primacy of a global law.

(i) The 'Five Storey House'

The first approach I want to examine associates the constitutionalization of the WTO specifically with its legal primacy over RTAs.[46] Its advocates look for a framework for constitutionalizing global economic governance that goes 'beyond international law' and leaves behind 'the mantras of traditional perceptions of sovereignty, independence and self-determination'.[47] A hierarchical

[46] Cottier and Foltea (n 1 above).
[47] Cottier (n 4 above), 496, 497.

structure of a five-storey house is proposed, with the global level, including the WTO, at the top, followed by the regional, national, subnational and local levels. Supremacy of global law is foreseen as 'the rule' and the 'organizing principle', with exceptions only for human rights and fundamental values.[48]

As distributive justice is seen not as a shared but as a conflicting value on which there is no agreement in international law,[49] this proposal does not foresee or seek special constitutional solutions at the highest global level for problems of distributive justice or of the inequalities between economies. On the contrary, its author seems to be looking at ways of restricting existing forms of embedding, such as RTAs and other preferential agreements. Thus it seems that with this constitutional proposal one would have to rely on the assumption 'that economic growth, encouraged by a free market, will inevitably succeed in bringing about greater justice and inclusiveness in the world'.[50]

The main thrust of the proposal seems to be the enhancing of global trade governance through the primacy of higher over lower storeys and a radical change of the paradigm of WTO decision making from consensus to weighted majority voting.[51] The resulting limitation of the freedom of WTO Members would not be compensated by constitutionally guaranteed and effective mechanisms of embedding of market liberalization at the global level. This approach to the constitutionalization of multilevel economic governance cannot therefore justify a primacy of the WTO over RTAs.

(ii) Constitutional Rights to Trade

Another approach to the constitutionalization of global economic governance advocates a 'human rights approach to trade' and respect for 'constitutional pluralism',[52] which can be understood as implying recognition of the primacy of human rights, if acknowledged constitutionally, at any level. The author of this approach calls for a 'cosmopolitan paradigm change'[53] involving a transition from the 'state-centered' Westphalian system to a 'citizen-oriented' system of international economic law whereby the mutual obligations between states would be transformed into citizens' rights and human rights of private parties with a new higher, 'constitutional', rank. Thus private 'rights to import and export', as in the 2001 WTO protocol on the accession of China and as derived from other WTO provisions, would acquire the status of human rights and

[48] Ibid, 525.

[49] Ibid, 522.

[50] An opinion which was described by Pope Francis as a 'trickle-down' theory 'which has never been confirmed by the facts', expressing 'a crude and naïve trust in the goodness of those wielding economic power and in the sacralized workings of the prevailing economic system' (n 43 above), 46.

[51] Cottier (n 4 above), 531; Cottier and Foltea (n 1 above), 74.

[52] Petersmann, 'The Future of International Economic Law: A Research Agenda' in Joerges and Petersmann (n 4 above), 540.

[53] Petersmann (n 27 above), 20.

primacy because of their 'constitutional dimension'.[54] Accordingly, although this approach sees the WTO and RTAs as 'competing fora for constitutional reforms',[55] it could be concluded that the result of converting WTO law into private 'rights to trade' with a higher, 'constitutional', rank would have the net effect of giving primacy of WTO law over the law of RTAs.

The proponent of this approach focuses on individual freedom 'as the ultimate goal of economic life and the most efficient means of realizing general welfare'.[56] His view is that the GATT 1947 paradigm of 'embedded liberalism' has 'entailed far reaching policy failures'.[57] Thus he seems to attach less importance to values other than individual freedom, such as equality or solidarity, possibly on the assumption that they would be a consequence of individual freedom.

The focus of this project on the constitutionalization of individual rights to trade, combined with a 'respect for constitutional pluralism' and with a rejection of embedding and redistribution, is likely to have the effect of guaranteeing and upgrading only existing economic rights and risks consolidating the existing and generating new economic and social inequalities, and leading to more disparities and segregation. Therefore this vision of a constitutionalization of the WTO does not seem to provide a better alternative to the primacy of RTAs over the WTO and cannot justify a restriction of the freedom of WTO Members to choose deeper economic integration.

(iii) Solidarity as a Condition for the Democratic Legitimacy of Constitutionalization

Another project to consider is a 'narrative from the perspective of a constitutionalization of international law' in which 'the European Union can be understood as an important step on the path towards a politically constituted world society'.[58] The proponent of this project sees three components of a democratically constituted global polity: first, an association of legal persons (hence, logically, states, but also other formations, such as the EU or RTAs), granting its free and equal citizens equal private and civic autonomy; second, a bureaucratic organization, securing decision-making powers for collective action; and third, 'civic solidarity as the medium of integration within and across state borders which is a necessary condition for joint political will

[54] Ibid, 126.

[55] E-U Petersmann, 'The WTO and Regional Trade Agreements as Competing Fora for Constitutional Reforms: Trade and Human Rights' in Bartels and Ortino (n 1 above), 281–312.

[56] Ibid, 283.

[57] E-U Petersmann, 'Multilevel Trade Governance in the WTO Requires Multilateral Constitutionalism' in Joerges and Petersmann (n 4 above), 5.

[58] Habermas, 'The Crisis of the European Union in the Light of a Constitutionalization of International Law' (2012) 23 *European Journal of International Law* 335, 336; see also J Habermas, *Zur Verfassung Europas. Ein Essay* (2011).

formation, and hence for both the communicative generation of democratic power and the legitimation of public authority'.[59]

What is noteworthy in this constitutionalizational project is the crucial role of solidarity as a necessary condition for the democratic legitimacy of public authority at the supranational level and, one could conclude, for the legitimacy of constitutionalization, including such a feature of constitutionalized public authority as 'the subordination of the Nation-states under supranational law'.[60]

The author of this approach does not regard the existing state of the EU as a model for the constitutionalization of international law. He states that the EU 'can be understood as an important step towards a politically constituted world society', obviously if it itself undergoes that kind of constitutionalization and if it meets the conditions for solidarity, which he associates with 'distributive justice', 'redistribution of burdens across national borders',[61] the elimination of social inequalities between states and with guarantees at the higher constitutional level for what the German Federal Constitution calls 'uniformity of living standards'.[62] He says that '[a] Europe-wide civic solidarity cannot emerge if social inequalities between Member States become permanent structural features along the fault lines separating poor from rich nations'.[63]

Indeed, although the Treaty on the EU, perceived as the EU's current constitution, proclaims that the Union 'shall work for' a 'social market economy',[64] and although it provides for redistribution through its regional, cohesion and other policies with the 'aim' of 'reducing the disparities between the levels of development of the various regions',[65] it does not guarantee economic or social equality throughout the Union in the way this is done, for example, with respect to the 'uniformity of living standards' in the taxation provisions of the German Constitution[66] for its federal territory. On the contrary, while imposing social, fiscal, economic and other standards through the primacy of EU law over that of Member States, the Union leaves them without important means and instruments for effectively achieving those standards and for embedding market liberalization within the Internal Market.

Thus this approach does not regard the primacy of supranational law as a means to achieving a constitutionalized world society; on the contrary, it defines solidarity as a condition for the democratic legitimacy of constitutionalization. Consequently, such an approach to multilevel economic governance

[59] See Habermas (2012) (ibid), 339.
[60] Ibid.
[61] Ibid, 347.
[62] Ibid, 348.
[63] Ibid.
[64] Art 3(3) TEU.
[65] Art 174 TEU.
[66] Art 106(3) of the *Grundgesetz*.

can serve as a justification for the introduction of the primacy of WTO law over RTAs but only if and after this condition of solidarity is fulfilled.

VIII. CONCLUSION

The more general conclusion that could be drawn about regionalism and the constitutionalization of the WTO is that introducing a primacy of WTO law over RTAs or other aspects of constitutionalization (such as binding decisions, adopted by majority voting), which limit the freedom of WTO Members to conclude or shape, in their mutual interests, their RTAs or other trade liberalization schemes, cannot be justified and considered as democratically legitimate as long as it is the individual WTO Members who have the responsibility for meeting the costs of globalization and for bearing the burdens of the embedding of the liberalization of markets in their economic and social systems.

A future constitutionalization of the WTO, involving the primacy of its law over that of WTO Members and/or over their RTAs, could be considered justifiable and legitimate[67] only if that burden is shifted to the global level of the WTO in the form of constitutional guarantees for more social justice and more equality between economies (eg through global taxation and redistribution mechanisms), ensuring a reduction of economic and social disparities at the global level. As such a legitimation of a future constitutionalization of the WTO appears quite utopian, the current primacy of RTAs over WTO law will remain a matter of legitimate interests for RTA parties.

[67] On the role of the concept of legitimacy for change in international law see Georgiev, 'Politics or Rule of Law: Deconstruction and Legitimacy in International Law' (1993) 4 *European Journal of International Law* 1.

25

OPEC Production Quotas and the World Trade Organization

PAOLO DAVIDE FARAH* AND ELENA CIMA†

I. INTRODUCTION

WITH MORE IMPORTANCE being given to the climate change debate, energy has slowly come to attract increasing attention throughout the world. The energy sector can be roughly divided

* West-Virginia University, John D Rockefeller IV School of Policy and Politics, Department of Public Administration and College of Law (WV, USA). Research Scientist and Principal Investigator at gLAWcal—Global Law Initiatives for Sustainable Development (United Kingdom). Double PhD in International Law at Aix-Marseille University (France) and at Università degli Studi di Milano (Italy). LLM College of Europe, Bruges (Belgium), JD in International and European Law, Paris Ouest La Defense Nanterre (France). Visiting Scholar (2011–12) at Harvard Law School, East Asian Legal Studies—EALS (USA) and IIEL Fellow (2004–05) at Georgetown University Law Center (USA). EU Commission Marie Curie Fellow at Tsinghua University School of Law, Center for Environmental, Natural Resources & Energy Law (THCEREL) in Beijing. Earlier drafts of this chapter were presented at the ILA—International Law Association Annual Conference, ILA Hellenic Regional Conference 2013, 'Imperium Iuris: Governance, Trade, Resources', Cape Sounion, Athens, Greece, 31 August 2013 and at the 'Workshop on Sustainable Energy Investments', hosted at Tsinghua University, Center for Environmental, Natural Resources, and Energy Law (THCEREL), School of Law on the 11 December 2012 in the Framework of the EU Commission Seventh Framework Program FP7-PEOPLE-2010 Marie Curie IRSES, EPSEI Project 'Evaluating Policies for Sustainable Energy Investments: Towards an Integrated Approach on National and International Stage'. An extended version of this chapter was first published in September 2013 in *Journal of International Economic Law* 16(3): 707–40. The chapter is the result of the joint research of the authors, as shown in Sections 1 and 6. Paolo Davide Farah focused on Sections 3., 4.1, 5, 5.2. and 5.3, Elena Cima on Sections 2, 4, 4.2 and 5.1.

† PhD Candidate at the Graduate Institute of International and Developments Studies, Geneva, LLM Yale Law School 2014; LLB University of Milan 2010. The research leading to these results has received funding from the People Programme (Marie Curie Actions) of the European Union's Seventh Framework Programme (FP7/2007–13) under REA grant agreement No 269327 Acronym of the Project: EPSEI (2011–15) entitled 'Evaluating Policies for Sustainable Energy Investments: Towards an Integrated Approach on National and International Stage', University of Turin—Dipartimento di Giurisprudenza.

into renewable energy, on the one hand, and fossil fuels, on the other. The former category is at the core of all the main international agreements regarding climate change and current environmental concerns: the increasing exploitation of renewable energy sources has become an urgent matter, and a possible route to reach this goal is to facilitate trade and exchange in renewable energy goods, services and technologies through trade liberalization.[1] Another possible route to achieve the global goal of reducing CO_2 emissions and protect the environment requires a reduction in the use of fossil fuels, such as coal and oil. As far as petroleum is concerned, the relevant market is predominantly controlled by a few actors, gathered in the Organization of Petroleum Exporting Countries (OPEC),[2] which set prices and quotas as they please.

OPEC clearly seems to have the freedom and power to control and set the world price for oil, and has done so undisturbed—by cutting prices or imposing quotas according to its members' specific needs—for half a century. The environmental concerns and the 'climatic emergency' that have affected the world in the last decade certainly represent a new challenge for OPEC. This freedom implies that we cannot predict the way OPEC will react to the existing climatic regime and the growing demands of the international community, whether by decreasing its quotas in order to limit supply, taking full advantage of the residual oil demand and boost prices, or deciding not to reduce the production ceiling to curtail the accelerated price decline that was recently announced. This situation creates uncertainty and instability in the energy market, and prevents complete and fair competition for alternative sources. Moreover, it seems largely inconsistent with the principles of the WTO, which has always treated quotas strictly. How does OPEC control oil prices? What is the relationship between OPEC and the WTO? And what would be the result of a WTO dispute concerning OPEC's production quotas? In the next sections we will try to shed light on all these issues.

This chapter analyses OPEC's production quotas compliance with the

[1] T Cottier, O Nartova and SZ Bigdeli (eds), *International Trade Regulation and the Mitigation of Climate Change: World Trade Forum* (Cambridge University Press, 2009); J Watson, *The WTO and the Environment: Development of Competence beyond Trade* (Routledge, 2012); H Hohmann (ed), *Agreeing and Implementing the Doha Round of the WTO* (Cambridge University Press, 2008); G Biglaiser and JK Horowitz, 'Pollution Regulation and Incentives for Pollution-Control Research' (1995) 3 *Journal of Economics and Management Strategy* 663, 663–84; W Antweiler, BR Copeland and MS Taylor, 'Is Free Trade Good for the Environment?' (2001) 91 *American Economic Review* 877, 877–901; MA Cole and RJR Elliott, 'Determining the Trade–Environment Composition Effect: The Role of Capital, Labor and Environmental Regulations' (2003) 46 *Journal of Environmental Economics and Management* 363; M David and B Sinclair-Desgagné, 'Environmental Regulation and the Eco-Industry' (2005) 28 *Journal of Regulatory Economics* 141; J Ederington and P McCalman, 'Endogenous Firm Heterogeneity and the Dynamics of Trade Liberalization' (2008) 74 *Journal of International Economics* 422; Z-X Zhang, *Liberalizing Climate-Friendly Goods and Technologies in the WTO: Product Coverage, Modalities, Challenges and the Way Forward* (FEEM Working Paper No 102, 2010).

[2] The Organization of Petroleum Exporting Countries (OPEC) was founded on 14 September 1960 in Baghdad. It now includes 13 member countries, with Qatar, Indonesia, Libya, United Arab Emirates (UAE), Algeria, Nigeria, Ecuador and Angola having joined its founding members (Iran, Iraq, Kuwait, Saudi Arabia and Venezuela).

rules and principles established by the WTO. International institutions and agreements—such as the WTO and its framework—are designed to provide the stability and predictability necessary for economic growth, but OPEC's monopoly and control over oil prices undermines the stability and transparency of the market for oil. Challenging this monopoly is necessary to level the playing field where all energy sources compete. As OPEC's production quotas are being questioned here, a WTO dispute involving quotas will be used for comparison.

II. OPEC'S CONTROL OF OIL PRICES

Petroleum is the largest primary commodity of international trade in terms of both volume and value. For all countries—whether they are oil producing and exporting or oil consuming and importing—political stability and economic survival depend to a large extent on the availability and affordability of oil in the international market place. During the first half of the twentieth century, the US—where oil was first found and the first wells were drilled at the end of the nineteenth century—was the world's dominant oil producer. After the Second World War, in which the US provided two-thirds of the oil to its allies, its dominance began to fade, mainly because other oil-producing countries, in the wake of renewed nationalism, started claiming the resources as their own.[3] As a result, in September 1960, representatives of five of the world's leading oil-producing nations—Iran, Iraq, Kuwait, Saudi Arabia and Venezuela[4]—met in Baghdad and formed the Organization of Petroleum Exporting Countries.[5] The initial goal of OPEC was to protect the collective bargaining power of these oil-producing nations from protectionism and the coordinated operations of the world's largest oil corporations. In the first years following its creation, OPEC did not show remarkable results, mainly because in the majority of the countries belonging to the organization (the exception being Iran) the oil reserves actually belonged by contract to the oil companies, and there was a surplus of oil in the world market. By the end of the 1960s, however, the situation had changed drastically. The oil countries started setting the

[3] In fact, the main oil companies were American, British and Dutch, but they were mainly operating overseas. There was no common identity between the countries these companies belonged to and the countries where oil was discovered and produced.

[4] On OPEC, in general, see D Yergin, *The Prize. The Epic Quest for Oil, Money & Power* (Free Press, 1991); D Yergin, *The Quest. Energy Security and the Remaking of the Modern World* (The Penguin Press, 2011); G Brown (ed), *Opec and The World Energy Market: A Comprehensive Reference Guide*, 2nd edn (Longman, 1993); AL Danielsen, *The Evolution of OPEC* (Harcourt Brace Jovanovich, 1982); ALP Burdett (ed), *OPEC: Origins & Strategy, 1947–1973* (Archive Editions, 2004); R El Mallakh (ed), *OPEC: Twenty Years and Beyond* (Westview Press, 1982); I Seymour, *OPEC: Instrument of Change* (St Martin's Press, 1981); DA Rustow and JF Mugno, *OPEC: Success and Prospects* (New York University Press, 1976).

[5] The specific event that triggered the creation of OPEC was when Exxon cut 14 cents a barrel, probably the most famous price cut in the history of oil.

price at which oil would be sold, causing a major shift in power, from the oil companies to the oil-exporting countries.[6] OPEC was now able to control the world oil market, and its price-fixing manoeuvres, which were always triggered by political needs, caused the two 1970s oil shocks.[7] The factors that initially held back the explosive force of OPEC were vanishing: demand was higher than supply and oil companies were gradually squeezed out.[8] However, at the beginning of the 1980s, the production of non-OPEC countries overtook OPEC production. By 1986, oil prices had fallen and OPEC countries needed to regain control of the market by increasing their share. This was achieved by introducing a system of production quotas, which brought prices back up and remains in place today.[9]

III. OPEC AND THE WTO

OPEC and the WTO are seen by the general public as widely differing organizations. First of all, they differ in terms of the reasons—the philosophies, even—that inspired their creation.[10] The WTO is inspired by the belief that free trade is the only viable way to improve the general global well-being because it inevitably brings net mutual gains for all countries.[11] OPEC, on

[6] The event that marked this shift in the balance of powers was the increase in the price posted by Libya in 1970. The country obtained a 30-cent increase in the posted price and increased its share of profit from 50 to 55 per cent. Yergin, *The Prize* (n 4 above), 556–62.

[7] The first oil shock, the 1973 Arab embargo, was triggered by the hostility between Israel and the Arab regions, and took place during the war of Yom Kippur—the fourth of the Arab–Israeli wars. For the first time, oil-exporting countries decided to use oil as a real weapon. They increased the posted price by 70 per cent, up to USD 5.11 a barrel. Moreover, they agreed to an embargo, cutting production by 5 per cent in the first month, and continud to cut it by 5 per cent in each succeeding month. The embargo to the United States was total, as a reaction to the US support of Israel. The second oil shock, in 1978–79, stemmed from the Iranian revolution. Iran stopped its production and the oil shortage, which was initially compensated for by increased production in other OPEC countries, deepened, as Iran was the second largest world producer of oil.

[8] The exclusion of foreign oil companies happened through a process of nationalization. By the 1970s, concessions in Iran and Iraq had already been wiped out. By the end of the decade, even the remaining great concessions—in Kuwait, Saudi Arabia and Venezuela—were terminated. In 1974, Kuwait acquired a 60 per cent participation in Kuwait Oil Company, established in 1934 by British Petroleum and Gulf. The following year, the country took over the remaining 40 per cent of the company and no links were left with the founders. The same happened to Aramco, the Arab–American oil company which included Exxon, Chevron, Mobil and Texaco. Last, in 1976, nationalization occurred in Venezuela as well.

[9] The control of prices—pushing them up and then down—according to OPEC's needs and interests is nothing new in the oil sector. The exact same strategy had been used less than a century before by the largest and most powerful oil company of the nineteenth century: Rockefeller's Standard Oil. Whenever new oil reserves were discovered and new companies gained market shares, Standard Oil—when it could not buy them out—would lower prices to eliminate the competition and then increase them once again as demand rose.

[10] MG Desta, 'The Organization of Petroleum Exporting Countries, the World Trade Organization and Regional Trade Agreements' (2003) 37(3) *Journal of World Trade* 523.

[11] See JH Jackson, WJ Davey and AO Sykes, *Legal Problems of International Economic Relations*, 5th edn (Thomson West, 2008); AO Sykes, 'Comparative Advantage and the Normative Economics of International Trade Policy' (1998) 1 *Journal of International Economic Law* 57.

the other hand, focusing on the specific case of oil, reached the conclusion that free trade would lead to wasteful competition among producers, while government control is the only viable and beneficial option. Consequently, even the goals of the two organizations differ strongly. The goal of the WTO is clearly and explicitly declared in the Preamble to the Agreement establishing the Organization:

> raising standards of living, ensuring full employment and a large and steadily growing volume of real income and effective demand, and expanding the production of and trade in goods and services, while allowing for the optimal use of the world's resources in accordance with the objective of sustainable development[12]

The goal pursued by OPEC, on the other hand, is the opposite, as set out in Article 2 of its Statute: 'the coordination and unification of the petroleum policies of Member Countries and the determination of the best means for safeguarding their interests, individually and collectively' by 'ensuring the stabilization of prices in international oil markets'.[13] Needless to say, the means through which the WTO and OPEC plan on achieving their respective goals are also different. The former tries to achieve trade liberalization by setting rules that eliminate or reduce trade barriers. It does so by dealing with all possible barriers: (i) tariffs; (ii) non-tariff barriers, such as quotas, licences, standards and regulations; and (iii) subsidies. The latter, on the other hand, aims to stabilize oil prices on the global market and, as will be shown later, does so by restricting oil production whenever oil prices fall below a certain threshold.

Gradually, OPEC members have started joining the WTO.[14] This, of course, opens the door to potential conflicts. A country that is a member of both organizations needs to comply with all their rules. The practice of production quotas often conducted by OPEC countries might not be entirely consistent with the WTO framework, and this might create the opportunity for challenging such measures.

IV. HISTORY OF CASES AGAINST OPEC

Historically, OPEC members have influenced oil prices in two main ways: direct price setting—from 1973 to 1985—and restriction of supplies—since 1985.[15] It is thus fair to say that the organization controls the world price of oil by controlling its production.[16] Whenever the price falls below the price range approved by OPEC itself, supply is restricted, through what we could

[12] Preamble to the Agreement establishing the World Trade Organization.

[13] OPEC Statute, Art 2.

[14] Angola, Ecuador, Indonesia, Kuwait, Nigeria, Qatar, Saudi Arabia, UAE and Venezuela.

[15] R Mabro, *OPEC and The Price of Oil* (Oxford Institute for Energy Studies, 1992) 16; Desta (n 10 above), 533. Yergin, *The Prize* (n 4 above); Brown (n 4 above); Seymour (n 4 above).

[16] S Soft, *Carbonomics—How to Fix the Climate and Charge it to OPEC* (Diamond, 2008) 75.

define as production quotas. Now, the question is: are these production quotas adopted in violation of the WTO framework? Before addressing this issue, we thought it might be useful to provide the reader with an overview of the actions adopted by the US against OPEC and all the attempts made to challenge its measures.

A. US Domestic Cases Concerning OPEC

The global energy crisis and dramatic peak in world oil prices of the 1970s were generally attributed to the practices of price fixing conducted by OPEC members.[17] It is no surprise, then, that American firms would challenge such practices under US antitrust law because of the damage they caused to their workers and consumers.[18] In particular, two disputes are worth mentioning: *International Ass'n of Machinists & Aerospace Workers (IAM) v OPEC*[19] and *Prewitt Enterprises, Inc v OPEC.*[20]

The former is a private antitrust case, filed in 1978 in the Central District of California. The plaintiff, the International Association of Machinists and Aerospace Workers, claimed that OPEC's production quotas and price-setting activities were damaging its members. The plaintiff claimed such practices violated Section 1 of the Sherman Act,[21] and asked for injunctive and monetary relief. The court granted judgment in favour of the defendant,[22] based on the fact that foreign nations are not 'persons', as required by the Sherman Act, and therefore could not be sued. The court also stressed that such nations are actually immune under the Foreign Sovereign Immunities Act, reaffirming the principle of the state's sovereignty over its own natural resources, which

[17] Yergin, *The Prize* (n 4 above); M Leigh, 'International Association of Machinists and Aerospace Workers v Organization of Petroleum Exporting Countries' (1982) 76(1) *The American Journal of International Law* 160; L Crocker, 'Sovereign Immunity and the Suit Against OPEC' (1980) 12 *Case Western Reserve Journal of International Law* 215.

[18] S Waller, 'Suing OPEC' (2002) 64 *University of Pittsburgh Law Review* 105, 106; SA Broome, 'Conflicting Obligations for Oil Exporting Nations?: Satisfying Membership Requirements of both OPEC and the WTO' (2006) 38 *George Washington International Law Review* 410; A Ajomo, 'An Appraisal of the Organization of the Petroleum Exporting Countries (OPEC)' (1977) 13 *Texas International Law Journal* 11; F Mirvahabi, 'Claims to the Oil Resources in the Persian Gulf: Will the World Economy be Controlled by the Gulf in the Future?' (1976) 11 *Texas International Law Journal* 75; MR Joelson and JP Griffin, 'The Legal Status of Nation-State Cartels Under United States Antitrust and Public International Law' (1975) 9 *International Law* 617; AC Udin, 'Comment, Slaying Goliath: The Extraterritorial Application of U.S. Antitrust Law to OPEC' (2001) 50 *American University Law Review* 1321; GM King, 'Comment, Cartel Pricing in the International Energy Market: OPEC in Perspective' (1975) 54 *Oregon Law Review* 643.

[19] *International Ass'n of Machinists & Aerospace Workers, ('IAM') v Organization of Petroleum Exporting Countries ('OPEC')*, 477 F Supp 553 (CD Cal 1979).

[20] *Prewitt Enters, Inc v OPEC*, No CV-00-W-0865-S, 2001 WL 624789 (ND Ala 22 March 2001).

[21] Section 1 of the Sherman Act provides that: 'Every contract, combination in the form of trust or otherwise, or conspiracy, in restraint of trade or commerce among the several States, or with foreign nations, is declared to be illegal'.

[22] See n 19 above.

have no commercial nature.[23] Moreover, in the view of the court, the plaintiff failed to demonstrate a clear and substantial link between the price-setting activities performed by OPEC members and the rise in world oil prices. On appeal, the Ninth Circuit[24] affirmed the dismissal but on different grounds.[25] The dismissal was based on the Act of State Doctrine, according to which 'a United States court will not adjudicate a politically sensitive dispute which would require the court to judge the legality of the sovereign act of a foreign state'.[26]

The second suit was filed in 2001 by a gas station operator, on behalf of all US private entities that purchased petroleum in the US market starting from 1999. The claim was that, once again, OPEC's production quotas and price-fixing practices violated Sections 1 and 2 of the Sherman Act. This time, the plaintiff did not ask for damages, but just for injunctive relief. This case was decided on appeal, where the Eleventh Circuit affirmed that the court could not establish jurisdiction over OPEC.

B. US Cases Concerning OPEC and WTO

Many doubts surround the possibility for the US to ask foreign countries to abide by US laws, since this kind of approach would systematically clash with the principle of sovereign states, one of the pillars of public international law and international relations. The situation is, of course, different if an international organization is involved. As already mentioned, a number of OPEC members have individually joined the WTO, and are therefore subject to its principles and rules.[27] Thus, it is perfectly acceptable for the WTO to ask its members to comply with its own agreements.

Moving from the national to the international arena, the first international attempts to 'bust up' the OPEC cartel occurred once again in the US.[28] The first move was made by Representative Peter DeFazio, who, on 13 March 2000, introduced a resolution urging President George W Bush to 'file a complaint at the World Trade Organization against oil-producing countries for violating trade rules that prohibit quantitative limitations on the import or export of resources or products across borders.'[29] Moreover, the US congressman asked for the approval of a bill which would require the United States Trade Rep-

[23] Waller (n 18 above), 8.

[24] See n 19 above.

[25] Leigh (n 17 above).

[26] See n 19 above, 1358.

[27] Broome (n 18 above), 410.

[28] The expression 'bust up' the cartel is taken from Office of Senator Frank R Lautenberg, "Busting Up the Cartel: The WTO Case against OPEC" (2004), available at http://lautenberg.senate.gov/documents/foreign/OPEC%20Memo.pdf (the Lautenberg Report), which will be discussed further on in this paragraph.

[29] HR Con Res 276, 106th Cong (2000). In 2011, DeFazio renewed his attempt by sending a letter to President Obama asking 'to bring a dispute in the WTO against members of the Organ-

resentative to initiate trade disputes in front of the WTO Dispute Settlement Body against all those OPEC countries that are also members of the WTO.[30] This attempt was unsuccessful, but it was to DeFazio's credit that the first steps had been taken in that direction. His attempts were then followed in 2004 by Senator Frank R Lautenberg, who released a report entitled *Busting Up the Cartel: The WTO Case against OPEC*.[31] The report represents the first document where legal ground for a case against OPEC in front of the WTO is provided. Of course, it only addresses those OPEC countries that are also members of the WTO, since they are the only ones that are bound by WTO commitments. The report, which will be analysed further in the following section, suggests how OPEC practices—namely, production quotas aimed at setting oil prices—violate WTO obligations and how none of the exceptions provided for in the agreements apply to this specific case.[32] In addition to the report, Senator Lautenberg subsequently introduced the 2008 OPEC Accountability Act,[33] which had a similar objective to the bill introduced by DeFazio,[34] which was never enacted.

V. POSSIBLE TREATMENT OF OPEC PRODUCTION QUOTAS UNDER THE WTO FRAMEWORK

As already mentioned, the Lautenberg Report is the first document providing a legal analysis of the reasons why OPEC production quotas are inconsistent with the WTO framework. We thus decided to use the report as a starting point to evaluate whether a country desiring to challenge these measures in front of the Dispute Settlement Body (DSB) would have a winning case. In particular, the Lautenberg Report examines the compliance of OPEC's production quotas with Article XI of the General Agreement on Tariffs and Trade (GATT)[35]—on quantitative restrictions—and their possible justification under Articles XI:2 and XX. The exact same provisions are at the core of a a recent Appellate Body report, *China—Measures Related to the Exportation*

ization of Petroleum Exporting Countries (OPEC) for manipulating the supply and price of oil at the expense of US consumers and our economic recovery'.

[30] See Library of Congress, Summary & Status for the 107th Congress: House Concurrent Resolution 276. See also Broome (n 18 above), 411.

[31] The Lautenberg Report (n 28 above).

[32] See Broome (n 18 above), 412; T Carey, 'Cartel Price Controls vs Free Trade: A Study of Proposals to Challenge OPEC's Influence in the Oil Market through WTO Dispute Settlement' (2009) 24(4) *American University International Law Review* 785, 795–96.

[33] See OPEC Accountability Act, S 2976, 110th Cong (2008).

[34] The similarity lies in the fact that this Act also requires the USTR to first initiate consultations with countries that are members of both OPEC and the WTO, and, if consultations fail, requires the USTR to request a WTO dispute settlement panel to judge the case.

[35] The General Agreement on Tariffs and Trade (GATT) was adopted in 1948 and, because of the failure of the International Trade Organization (ITO), was the only multilateral instrument governing international trade from 1948 until the World Trade Organization (WTO) was established in 1995.

of Various Raw Materials (hereinafter *China—Raw Materials*).[36] The latter concerns China's use of certain export restraints—including quotas—on the exportation of several raw materials.[37] This is why we decided to use the interpretation given by the Panel and the Appellate Body in the *China—Raw Materials* case as the starting point for our study on OPEC.[38]

Before starting our analysis, we should briefly mention the non-inclusion of energy in the WTO framework. The word 'energy' does not appear in any agreement signed within the framework of the WTO.[39] A reason for this may be that most oil producers and exporters[40] were not involved in the negotiation process of the GATT and, at the same time, when OPEC was established in 1960, four of OPEC's five founders were not members of the GATT.[41] Furthermore, the driving force behind the GATT was countries' desire to gain market access for those products they had a surplus of, and none of the contracting parties had a surplus in petroleum. Although progress has been made and the WTO system appears to be more flexible towards the energy issue, many problems remain unsolved. Even though the provisions contained in the WTO Agreements—at least some of them—can apply to energy goods and services, as they do to any goods or services, it is also true that these rules might prove to be inadequate and certainly their application will not be easy.[42]

[36] WTO Panel Report, 'China—Measure Related to the Exportation of Various Raw Materials' ('China—Raw Materials'), WT/DS394/R, WT/DS395/R and WT/DS398/R, adopted 5 July 2011; WTO Appellate Body Report, 'China—Measure Related to the Exportation of Various Raw Materials' ('China—Raw Materials'), WT/DS394/AB/R, WT/DS395/AB/R and WT/DS398/AB/R, adopted 30 January 2012.

[37] Bauxite, coke, fluorspar, magnesium, manganese, silicon carbide, silicon metal, yellow phosphorus and zinc. Quotas are not the only measures at stake in this dispute. The complainants—US, EU and Mexico—identified four types of restraints that China imposes on the exportation of these raw materials: export duties, export quotas, export licensing and minimum export price requirements. WTO Panel Report, 'China—Raw Materials' (ibid), para 2.

[38] This dispute does not deal directly with energy or renewable energy goods or services; nevertheless, it is not entirely unrelated. Dozens of vital green technologies depend on critical raw materials derived from rare earth minerals, 90 per cent of which are produced in China, and China uses different measures to restrict exports of these materials. See B Naughton, *The Chinese Economy—Transition and Growth* (The MIT Press, 2007) 29.

[39] The Havana Charter initially contained some provisions related to the matter, but none of these were then included in the GATT. The Havana Charter was signed by 53 countries on 24 March 1948 and was supposed to be the charter of the ITO. However, the Charter never came into force and during the same year the international community adopted the GATT, which consists of the fourth chapter of the Havana Charter. See Y Selivanova, *Energy Dual Pricing in WTO Law: Analysis and Prospect in the Context of Russia's Accession to the WTO* (Cameron May, 2008) 3–4.

[40] Even though some countries that are now quite rich in oil (such as Norway and the United Kingdom) were founders of the GATT, their oil wealth was discovered years later.

[41] Desta (n 10 above), 529.

[42] Gabrielle Marceau gave an effective example of this inadequacy during the Trade, Energy and Environment Conference, which took place at the WTO on 22–23 October 2009. She started off with the example of fuels and subsidies. Fuels produced from agriculture might actually fall under both the Agreement on Subsidies and Countervailing Measures (ASCM) and the Agreement on Agriculture (AoA). Subsidies are treated quite differently in the two texts: the ASCM, for example, completely prohibits export subsidies, while the AoA does not necessarily; the latter

A. General Elimination of Quantitative Restrictions: GATT Article XI:1

Quotas are just one of many possible ways to restrict the market and create obstacles to international trade flows. In particular, they can be listed among the so-called non-tariff barriers—in contrast to the other main method of restraint, tariffs—which can be described as non-tax measures adopted in international trade relations in order to narrow the amount of imported/ exported commodities.[43] Quotas, unlike tariffs, are prohibited in the WTO system,[44] through GATT Article XI:1, entitled 'General Elimination of Quantitative Restrictions', which reads as follows:

> No prohibitions or restrictions other than duties, taxes or other charges, whether made effective through quotas, import or export licenses or other measures, shall be instituted or maintained by any contracting party on the importation of any product of the territory of any other contracting party or on the exportation or sale for export of any product destined for the territory of any other contracting party.

According to the Lautenberg Report, OPEC's production quotas violate this provision.[45] There is no doubt that such measures qualify as 'quantitative restrictions', since they are specifically designed to control the supply of oil on global markets and have the practical effect of reducing the amount of oil available on such markets.[46] However, even though production quotas can be considered as quantitative restrictions, a WTO Panel or Appellate Body might reject the claim that they fall within the scope of Article XI:I because the latter refers specifically to measures 'instituted or maintained . . . on the importation . . . or on the exportation'. OPEC's production quotas cannot technically qualify as 'export quotas' and therefore, if we follow a strict interpretation of the provision, they do not constitute a violation of Article XI:I.[47] WTO case law shows a general approach of WTO bodies to give a quite broad

also provides flexibilities for green subsidies, while the category of non-actionable subsidies within the ASCM lapsed in 2000.

[43] Apart from quotas, non-tariff barriers include standards and technical regulations, which are regulated by the Agreement on Technical Barriers to Trade and the Agreement on Sanitary and Phytosanitary Measures. For a broad analysis of all types of barriers to trade, see in general Jackson et al (n 11 above), 339; AF Lowenfeld, *International Economic Law* (Oxford University Press, 2003) 68–93; P Picone and A Ligustro, *Diritto dell'Organizzazione Mondiale del Commercio* (CEDAM, 2002) 175–99.

[44] The reason why tariffs are generally preferred lies in the fact that they are more visible, do not need a licence to administer, do not require government funds and give only a limited amount of protection, so that if a foreign-based industry is efficient enough, it will still be able to export to the tariff-imposing country. Another advantage of tariffs is that they are easily negotiable by the various states at the international level, through mutual concessions. Jackson et al (n 11 above).

[45] The Lautenberg Report (n 28 above), 8.

[46] See Broome (n 18 above), 414; Desta (n 10 above), 534.

[47] See Broome (n 18 above), 416; Broome noted that the effect of production quotas on exports is merely incidental, and this material distinction would likely be appreciated by any panel or appellate body. Broome's analysis goes even deeper: the author even states that, since we are talking about production quotas, we need to look at oil before production—in which state oil cannot be considered as a product, which excludes it from the applicability of the GATT as a whole. See also Carey (n 32 above), 801.

interpretation of this provision.[48] The Panel, in *China—Raw Materials*, clarified that the term 'restrictions' encompasses all those measures that create uncertainties and affect investment plans, restrict market access for imports or make importation prohibitively costly, concluding that the term needs to be interpreted quite broadly.[49] Even on other occasions, the Panel focused on the effects of the measure and reached the conclusion that, whether it restricted exports directly or indirectly, through a limitation of the production, was irrelevant.[50] The Panel once even stated that the discipline of Article XI:1 extends to restrictions of a '*de facto* nature'.[51] This approach is perfectly in line with the interpretation generally given to WTO basic principles. Article XI, together with Articles I, II and III, contains one of the main principles of the GATT and the WTO and, as such, needs to be interpreted broadly so as to encompass as many measures as possible.[52]

B. Essential and Temporary Measures to Prevent a Critical Shortage: GATT Article XI:2

As far as the *China—Raw Materials* dispute is concerned, China did not deny the presence of quotas within its market, but rather tried to convince the Panel

[48] Besides, the 2010 WTO Annual Trade Report states that, economically, a production quota in a country that mainly exports the concerned products produces the same effects as an export quota and therefore should be treated accordingly. WTO, 'World Trade Report 2010: Trade in Natural Resources' (2010).

[49] WTO Panel Report, 'China—Raw Materials' (n 36 above), para 7.206. See WTO Panel Report, 'Colombia—Indicative Prices and Restrictions on Ports of Entry', WT/DS366/R, adopted 27 April 2009, para 7.240; WTO Panel Report, 'India—Quantitative Restrictions on Imports of Agricultural, Textile and Industrial Products' ('India—Quantitative Restrictions'), WT/DS90/R, adopted 6 April 1999, para 5.128. On another occasion, in 'Japan—Trade in Semi-Conductors', the Panel even declared that Art XI does not just refer to laws and regulations but rather extends to a much broader array of measures. It also found that a number of Japanese measures and requirements 'constituted a coherent system restricting the sale for export of monitored semi-conductors at prices below company- specific costs to markets other than the United States' and thus was inconsistent with Art XI:1. WTO Panel Report, 'Japan—Trade in Semi-Conductors', BISD 35S/116, adopted 4 May 1988.

[50] WTO Panel Report, 'Japan—Trade in Semi-Conductors' (ibid), 114–17. See also Carey (n 32 above), 800, 801. However, the Appellate Body in 'China—Raw Materials', gave a more narrow interpretation of the term, pointing out that the terms 'prohibition' and 'restriction' in Art XI:1, are both qualified by the word 'export.' WTO Appellate Body Report, 'China—Raw Materials' (n 36 above), para 321.

[51] WTO Panel Report, 'Argentina—Measures Affecting the Export of Bovine Hides and the Import of Finished Leather', WT/DS155/R, adopted 19 December 2000, para 11.17.

[52] This can be linked to the way Art III has been often read and interpreted by the WTO. In particular, 'Japan—Alcoholic Beverages' is interesting reading. The Appellate Body stated that 'the broad and fundamental purpose of Article III is to avoid protectionism', thus giving this provision an interpretation that goes beyond its wording to the general objective and purpose of protecting free trade. Since Art XI, exactly like Art III, expresses one of the main principles of the Agreement, nothing stops us from applying the same reasoning to this provision. WTO Appellate Body Report, 'Japan—Taxes on Alcoholic Beverages' ('Japan—Alcoholic Beverages'), WT/DS11/AB/R, adopted 4 October 1996. See RJ Girouard, 'Water Export Restrictions: A Case Study of WTO Dispute Settlement Strategies and Outcomes' (2003) 15 *Georgetown International Environmental Law Review* 247, 257. See also Broome (n 18 above), 414, 415.

(unsuccessfully) that its measures were justified because they fell under the scope of Article XI:2(a). This provision excludes the applicability of the first paragraph of Article XI to those prohibitions or restrictions that are 'temporarily applied to prevent or relieve critical shortages of food stuffs or other products essential to the exporting contracting party'. When analysing this provision, two fundamental elements need to be discussed: the essential and temporary natures of the measure. The Panel stressed that the essentiality of the measure needs to be assessed in relation to the specific characteristics of the country concerned.[53] Secondly, the measure needs to be temporary, meaning that such exception cannot be used to justify long-term measures aimed at addressing an inevitable depletion of a finite resource.[54] Finally, China had to prove that the measure was adopted to deal with a 'critical shortage'. Finding that China failed to prove both these two last requirements—the temporary nature of a measure aimed at addressing a critical shortage—the Panel rejected China's defence under Article XI:2(a) and the Appellate Body upheld its conclusions.[55]

Turning to OPEC production quotas, they would encounter the exact same problem. While the essential nature of the measures adopted by oil-exporting countries could be recognized, the same cannot be said about the other two requirements: the quotas, which were initially meant to be an emergency measure and therefore temporary, have become a constant. Moreover, the OPEC should prove the existence of a critical shortage, as well as the direct link between the measure and the need to prevent such shortage, which could prove to be hard, considering that OPEC countries have never hidden their real purpose—the control of world oil prices.

C. The Conservation of Exhaustible Natural Resources: GATT Article XX(g)

The GATT allows members to deviate from its core principles in a series of circumstances, listed in Article XX, provided the measure at stake falls under one of the subparagraphs and it is not 'applied in a manner which would con-

[53] WTO Panel Report, 'China—Raw Materials' (n 36 above), para 7.276.

[54] Ibid, para 7.305. The 'temporary nature' requirement is used to distinguish this exception from the one provided for in Art XX(g), also related to the conservation of exhaustible natural resources, which allows long-term measures.

[55] Despite upholding the Panel's conclusions, the Appellate Body gave a fairly different interpretation of the term 'temporary'. The Appellate Body agrees with the Panel that Art XI:2(a) requires a 'fixed time-limit' for the application of the measure. However, it disagrees that 'temporary' must necessarily refer to a time limit fixed in advance. WTO Appellate Body Report, 'China—Raw Materials' (n 36 above), para 331. Moreover, the Appellate Body stressed the fact that the three requirements set out in Art XI:2(a) need to be read together to define the scope of the provision: 'whether a shortage is "critical" may be informed by how "essential" a particular product is. In addition, the characteristics of the product as well as factors pertaining to a critical situation, may inform the duration for which a measure can be maintained' (para 328).

stitute a means of arbitrary or unjustifiable discrimination between countries where the same conditions prevail, or a disguised restriction on international trade', according to the chapeau.[56] In particular, paragraph (g) proves to be particularly useful when dealing with energy, as it refers to measures 'relating to the conservation of exhaustible natural resources if such measures are made effective in conjunction with restrictions on domestic production or consumption'.

There is no doubt that petroleum qualifies as a natural resource. In fact, on one occasion,[57] the Appellate Body, rejecting the complainants' arguments that the concept of 'exhaustible natural resources' under Article XX(g) applied only to 'finite resources such as minerals, rather than biological or renewable resources', stated that 'Article XX(g) is not limited to the conservation of "mineral" or "non-living" natural resources . . . Living resources are just as "finite" as petroleum, iron ore, and other non-living resources'.[58]

The real question here is whether these measures are 'relating to the conservation of exhaustible natural resources'. For a measure to be considered 'relating to', it needs to exhibit a 'substantial relationship' with the conservation of exhaustible natural resources, and cannot merely be 'incidentally or inadvertently aimed at' the conservation of exhaustible natural resources.[59] In *China—Raw Materials*, China tried to justify its measure by arguing that it represents the recognition of each state's 'sovereign rights over their own natural resources'.[60] The recognition of such sovereignty represents one of the core principles of public international law.[61] OPEC countries might use the exact same argument to justify the Organization's production quotas. The Organization has always been very clear as to what are the reasons underlying its practices, namely the need to control world oil prices, and its supply restrictions are directly triggered by falls in global oil prices, while the conservation of natural resources has never been mentioned. However, OPEC might argue that the world is heavily dependent on oil, and therefore market stability—

[56] In particular, in 'US—Gasoline', the Appellate Body found that any defence under Art XX needs to be structured in the following way (the so-called two-tier test): first, the country needs to prove that the measure falls under the scope of one of the subparagraphs (letters a–j); secondly, the measure needs to be consistent with the chapeau of the article. WTO Appellate Body Report, 'United States—Standards for Reformulated and Conventional Gasoline' ('US—Gasoline'), WT/DS2/AB/R, adopted 29 April 1996.

[57] WTO Appellate Body Report, 'US—Shrimps', WT/DS58/A8/R.

[58] Ibid, para 5.57. See also Broome (n 18 above), 424; Desta (n 10 above), 536; Carey (n 32 above), 894.

[59] WTO Panel Report, 'US—Gasoline', WT/DS2/R, adopted 29 January 1996, para 6.39; WTO Appellate Body Report, 'US—Gasoline' (n 56 above), para 19. The Panel recalled the ruling in the *Herring and Salmon* case (BISD 355/98), where it was established that a measure 'had to be *primarily aimed* at the conservation of an exhaustible natural resource to be considered as "relating to" conservation within the meaning of Article XX:(g)'.

[60] WTO Appellate Body Report, 'US—Shrimps' (n 57 above), para. 7.364.

[61] D Nincic, *The Problem of Sovereignty in the Charter and in the Practice of the United States* (1970) 268–69; FX Perrez, 'The Relationship between "Permanent Sovereignty" and the Obligation Not to Cause Transboundary Environmental Damage' (1996) 26 *Environmental Law* 1187, 1192.

which the Organization seeks through its practices—is absolutely necessary to ensure the availability and maintenance of oil reserves.[62] If it is true that the Panel might take this argument into account, we cannot forget that Article XX contains exceptions, not principles, and the WTO has always proved to adopt a very textualist and narrow approach when interpreting exceptions.[63] The Panel adopted this kind of approach in *China—Raw Materials*, rejecting China's defence on the ground that China could not prove the 'relation' between its measures and the 'conservation of exhaustible natural resources', nor the fact that the quotas were 'made effective in conjunction with restrictions on domestic production or consumption'.[64] We do not see why the same approach should not be kept in a dispute involving OPEC's production quotas, and such a textualist approach would be very likely to reject a potential defence under Article XX(g).

VI. CONCLUSIONS

The purpose of the World Trade Organization—the reason why it was initially established—is the protection of free trade among Member States and the increase in trade liberalization. This is exactly why the provisions of all WTO Agreements which further develop this basic principle, such as GATT Articles I, III and—particularly relevant for our discussion—XI, receive a very broad interpretation by the WTO Dispute Settlement Bodies. In contrast, exceptions—though they exist—are interpreted and applied very strictly. This is exactly the approach followed by the Panel and the Appellate Body in the *China—Raw Materials* dispute, and in several disputes concerning the environment.

From this perspective, we have tried to show how, if production quotas established by OPEC were to be challenged in front of the WTO and if the Panel—as it should—gave the same interpretation of WTO provisions—broad when it comes to principles and strict when it comes to exceptions—OPEC measures would be found to be inconsistent with such agreements. Interestingly, though, no one has ever challenged OPEC's measures. This might be

[62] See Broome (n 18 above), 427.

[63] See J Pauwelyn, 'Squaring Free Trade in Culture with Chinese Censorship: The WTO Appellate Body Report on "China—Audiovisuals"' (2010) 11(1) *Melbourne Journal of International Law* 119. JY Qin, 'Pushing the Limits of Global Governance: Trading Rights, Censorship and WTO Jurisprudence—A Commentary on the China–Publications Case' (2011) 10 *Chinese Journal of International Law* 271, 292; JY Qin, 'The Challenge of Interpreting "WTO-PLUS" Provisions' (2010) 44(1) *Journal of World Trade* 127, 132.

[64] With reference to the definition of 'in conjunction', the Appellate Body reversed the interpretation of the Panel. The latter concluded that Art XX requires the quantitative restriction to be primarily aimed at making the restrictions on domestic production or consumption effective, while the Appellate Body declared that it is necessary for the trade restriction to operate jointly with the restrictions on domestic production or consumption to satisfy such condition. WTO Appellate Body Report, 'China—Raw Materials' (n 36 above), para 356.

because of political reasons rather than mere juridical ones. However, if a country broke the spell and tried to 'bust up' the cartel, challenging its practices in front of the WTO, the Panel would be forced to apply the same provisions it had to apply in the cases related to renewable energy or even to raw materials. How would the Panel interpret these provisions? Would it do it consistently and coherently with its previous judgments? Will political considerations be taken into account or will it limit itself to a pure juridical approach? It would be extremely interesting to see how the Panel would act when challenged with such controversial problems. The WTO might not be ready to further open its mind towards the need to protect our environment. However, this does not mean that it might not be ready to expand the value of free trade to lands where such value is not yet completely embraced.

26

The Role of the WTO in Addressing Regulatory Pricing Policies in the Energy Sector

ILARIA ESPA*

I. INTRODUCTION

ENERGY ISSUES ARE increasingly being discussed within the World Trade Organization (WTO). Many factors have contributed to ignite the debate on what should be the role of the WTO in promoting trade in energy goods and services and, more generally, global energy governance:[1] (i) the prominence acquired by energy security issues in a context of heavily geographically concentrated energy resources, on the one hand, and universal need for access to such resources, on the other hand;[2] (ii) the gradual liberalization of energy markets;[3] (iii) the recent accession of major energy-producing

* Marie Curie (COFIT) Senior Research Fellow, World Trade Institute, University of Bern.

[1] The former WTO Director-General Pascal Lamy repeatedly advocated a strengthened role of the WTO in energy governance on several occasions, such as during the speech 'Energy, Trade and Global Governance' at the conference 'Global Challenges at the Intersection of Trade, Energy and the Environment' organized at the Graduate Institute of International and Development Studies on 22–23 October 2009 and the intervention on 'Energy Policy and the WTO' held at the Workshop on 'The Role of Intergovernmental Agreements in Energy Policy' organized by the Energy Charter Secretariat on 29 April 2013 at the WTO.

[2] P Lamy, 'Energy, Trade and Global Governance' in J Pauwelyn (ed), *Global Challenges at the Intersection of Trade, Energy and the Environment* (Center for Economic Policy Research, 2010) 15.

[3] The energy sector has been characterized by the existence of natural monopolies and the prominent role of state-owned enterprises: T Cottier et al, 'Energy in WTO Law and Policy' in T Cottier and P Delimatsis (eds), *The Prospects of International Trade Regulation: From Fragmentation to Coherence* (Cambridge University Press, 2011) 211. Accordingly, it has been traditionally regulated through a 'sovereignty-based approach': J Pauwelyn, 'Global Challenges at the Intersection of Trade, Energy and the Environment: An Introduction' in Pauwelyn (ibid), 2–3. The major changes in the structure of the energy industry have made it possible to subject energy goods and services to standard trading and market rules. N Mizulin, 'EC Experience in Creating an Internal Energy Market: Lessons for the WTO' in Pauwelyn (ibid), 71.

countries, such as Saudi Arabia[4] and the Russian Federation,[5] and the prospective accession of several big suppliers of primary energy supplies, such as Kazakhstan, Azerbaijan, Algeria, Libya, Iran, Iraq and Sudan; and (iv) the climate change impacts of trade-related measures used by governments within the framework of their energy policies.[6]

Against this backdrop, the question arises as to whether the WTO rulebook has the potential to address emerging energy concerns at the crossroads of trade, energy and climate change.[7] WTO rules do in fact apply to energy goods and services, but they were not originally drafted for this purpose.[8]

This chapter aims to contribute to this debate by focusing on the specific issue of dual pricing. Dual pricing schemes are regulatory pricing policies widely used by governments of energy-producing countries with the aim of creating a wedge between the domestic price of energy resources and their international price.[9] They can be implemented through price ceilings or sales of energy inputs by state-trading enterprises (STEs) at preferential rates,[10] or by means of export tariffs.[11] Dual pricing and export tariffs, however, have conventionally been addressed separately despite their fundamental comparability in terms of economic effects and underlying rationales. In particular, they have been addressed under the General Agreement on Tariffs and Trade

[4] WTO, 'Report of the Working Party on the Accession of the Kingdom of Saudi Arabia', WT/ACC/SAU/61 (1 November 2005); WTO, 'Protocol on the Accession of the Kingdom of Saudi Arabia', WT/L/627 (11 November 2005).

[5] WTO, 'Report of the Working Party on the Accession of the Russian Federation', WT/ACC/RUS/70 (17 November 2011); WTO, 'Protocol on the Accession of the Russian Federation', WT/MIN(11)/24WT/L/839 (17 December 2011).

[6] The energy sector is responsible for two-thirds of global greenhouse gas emissions: International Energy Agency (IEA), 'Redrawing the Energy Climate Map: World Energy Outlook Special Report' (2013) 15, available at http://www.iea.org/publications/freepublications/publication/WEO_Special_Report_2013_Redrawing_the_Energy_Climate_Map.pdf (accessed June 2014).

[7] For an overview of the energy-relevant issues covered, to a greater or a lesser extent, by WTO rules and the potential problems arising out of the interpretation and the application of such rules to energy see Pauwelyn (n 2 above), 1–9.

[8] G Marceau, 'The WTO in the Emerging Energy Governance Debate' in Pauwelyn (ibid), 25. Since its early decades, the multilateral trading system served as a negotiating forum for the progressive reduction of import tariffs on a most-favoured nation (MFN) basis with the aim of improving market access for foreign exporters: JH Jackson, *World Trade and the World of GATT* (Bobbs-Merill, 1969). This strong focus on market access has determined a 'marginality' of energy issues, much more affected by export barriers. In the words of Professor Joost Pauwelyn, 'When it comes to energy . . . import restrictions is not the issue (few countries impose import duties on oil). Rather, what matters is "production management" and price stability . . . for energy exporters, and access to foreign supplies (or production, export and transit restrictions) for energy importers. Consequently, in a GATT club worried about "how can I export more", the central question of "how can I import more" (or can I maximise the return on my energy resources) was not addressed': Pauwelyn (n 2 above), 3–4.

[9] Y Selivanova, *Energy Dual Pricing in WTO Law: Analysis and Prospects in the Context of Russia's Accession to the WTO* (Cameron May, 2008) 5–7.

[10] V Pogoretskyy, 'Energy Dual Pricing in International Trade: Subsidies and Anti-dumping Perspectives' in Y Selivanova (ed), *Regulation of Energy in International Trade Law: WTO, NAFTA and the Energy Charter* (Wolters Kluwer, 2011) 183.

[11] Selivanova (n 9 above), 6.

(GATT) as measures affecting trade in goods despite being functionally equivalent to subsidies imposed on the consumption of fossil fuels.[12]

This chapter is organized as follows: Section II will explore the effects and the rationale of dual pricing practices, and to what extent they can be implemented through export tariffs. Section III will assess the adequacy of the relevant GATT rules and the 'WTO-plus' obligations[13] that large energy-producing countries have assumed on the use of dual pricing and/or export duties on primary energy products in the context of their WTO accession. Section IV will discuss first-best and second-best options to tackle dual pricing policies more effectively and coherently. Section V will provide some concluding remarks.

II. EFFECTS AND RATIONALE OF DUAL PRICING PRACTICES: HOW MUCH COMPARABILITY WITH EXPORT TAXES?

Energy dual pricing is a 'two-tier pricing policy whereby a government or a public monopoly keeps domestic prices for energy low comparatively with export or world prices'.[14] In other words, the domestic price of primary energy products is artificially regulated at a below-market level so as to create a price differential between domestic prices and the prevailing international prices. Although governments usually stress the safety net rationale of dual pricing practices,[15] these schemes do not solely target low-income households but are most often applied across all sectors of the economy (ie including energy-intensive manufacturing sectors).[16] For this reason, two main aspects related to dual pricing have caused particular concern: first, the unfair advantages they confer by providing cheaper energy inputs to domestic downstream producers, thus distorting the competition with foreign industrial consumers of energy;[17] secondly, the negative climate change effects they produce by encouraging the excessive consumption of fossil fuels domestically.[18] Both aspects arise from

[12] I Espa and S Rolland, 'Subsidies, Clean Energy and Climate Change' (2015), E15 Initiative (International Centre for Trade and Sustainable Development (ICTSD) and World Economic Forum) 3–7.

[13] WTO-plus obligations are commitments that exceed the obligations arising out of multilateral WTO Agreements, which are negotiated by acceding members with existing WTO members: H Horn et al, 'Beyond the WTO? An Anatomy of EU and US Preferential Trade Agreements' (2010) 33(10) *The World Economy* 1567.

[14] V Pogoretskyy, 'The System of Energy Dual Pricing in Russia and Ukraine: The Consistency of the Energy Dual Pricing System with the WTO Agreement on Anti-Dumping' (2009) 10(4) *Global Trade and Customs Journal* 313.

[15] IEA et al, 'The Scope of Fossil Fuel Subsidies in 2009 and a Roadmap for Phasing Out Fossil-Fuel Subsidies' (2010) 11–13, available at http://www.oecd.org/env/cc/46575783.pdf (accessed September 2014).

[16] Pogoretskyy (n 10 above), 186–88.

[17] Selivanova (n 9 above), 6.

[18] By altering the terms of competition between fossil fuels and renewable energy, dual pricing policies discourage investment in cleaner forms of energy. Espa and Rolland (n 12 above), 6–7.

the fact that dual pricing schemes are functionally equivalent to consumption subsidies.

Governments may induce an artificial decline in domestic prices compared to world prices through price controls or ceilings, through sales of energy inputs by STEs at preferential rates or by imposing export tariffs. Export taxes have in fact the same economic effect as more 'conventional' dual pricing policies implemented in the domestic market, namely they reduce the domestic price of the product affected by the restriction. This effect results out of the implementation of a price on exports (so-called price effect), which induces a contraction in the volume of exports (so-called trade effect) causing a diversion onto the domestic market (so-called supply-side effect).[19] Because of their similar economic effects, export taxes also more or less openly benefit domestic downstream processing sectors such as de facto dual pricing policies.[20] However, they often purport to raise government revenues, especially in energy-rich countries that are heavily dependent on the exportation of energy resources.[21]

III. RELEVANT WTO DISCIPLINES

As measures affecting trade in energy goods, dual pricing schemes are conventionally addressed under the GATT despite the paucity of the relevant rules contained in this WTO agreement. Major energy-producing countries acceding to the WTO after its entry into force have therefore been required to undertake additional commitments in their accession protocols in the attempt to fill the gaps of existing disciplines. The same holds true in the case of export taxes. As a result of this exercise, WTO rules relevant to dual pricing are overall very fragmented. The fragmentation of these rules therefore limits their effectiveness in tackling distortive government practices leading to excessive consumption of fossil fuels.

A. GATT Provisions Relevant to Dual Pricing

In the GATT, the only provision addressing the issue of price controls is Article III:9 on maximum price control measures. It reads as follows:

[19] R Piermartini, *The Role of Export Taxes in the Field of Primary Commodities* (WTO, 2004) 3–5.

[20] Export restrictions have often been contested as practices that unfairly encourage the export of value-added products through the inducement of a dual pricing regime on raw materials to the benefit of domestic producers, causing a 'deterioration of the terms of competition'. See, eg 'Report of the Ad-hoc Working Group on Defining Critical Raw Materials' (30 July 2010) Annex V, 130 and 209, available at ec.europa.eu/enterprise/policies/raw-materials/files/docs/annex-v_en.pdf (accessed November 2013.

[21] M Radetzski, *A Handbook of Primary Commodities in the Global Economy* (Oxford University Press, 2010) 71.

> The contracting parties recognize that internal maximum price control measures, even though conforming to the other provisions of this Article, can have effects prejudicial to the interests of contracting parties supplying imported products. Accordingly, contracting parties applying such measures shall take account of the interests of exporting contracting parties with a view to avoiding to the fullest practicable extent such prejudicial effects.

Article III:9 does not contain a substantive obligation. Rather, it is a general provision formally requiring that a member pays due regard to the interests of exporting members prior to applying the measure. Moreover, its wording refers specifically to importing countries implementing pricing policies which could potentially harm the interests of exporters, and does not mention the reverse situation.

To the extent that dual pricing is implemented through the sale of energy inputs by STEs at preferential rates, Article XVII GATT may apply.[22] Article XVII:1, in particular, states:

> (*a*) Each contracting party undertakes that if it establishes or maintains a State enterprise, wherever located, or grants to any enterprise, formally or in effect, exclusive or special privileges, such enterprise shall, in its purchases or sales involving either imports or exports, act *in a manner consistent with the general principles of non-discriminatory treatment* prescribed in this Agreement for governmental measures affecting imports or exports by private traders.
>
> (*b*) The provisions of subparagraph (*a*) of this paragraph shall be understood to require that such enterprises shall, having due regard to the other provisions of this Agreement, make any such purchases or sales *solely in accordance with commercial considerations*, including price, quality, availability, marketability, transportation and other conditions of purchase or sale, and shall afford the enterprises of the other contracting parties adequate opportunity, in accordance with customary business practice, to compete for participation in such purchases or sales.
>
> (*c*) No contracting party shall prevent any enterprise (whether or not an enterprise described in subparagraph (*a*) of this paragraph) under its jurisdiction from acting in accordance with the principles of subparagraphs (*a*) and (*b*) of this paragraph (emphasis added).

[22] Art XVII of the GATT is relevant to dual pricing inasmuch as the enterprise selling energy resources to domestic consumers at preferential rates can be qualified as a state trading enterprise (STE). Although no specific definition of STEs is included in Art XVII, various guiding instruments, such as the WTO Background Paper on STEs and the Uruguay Round Understanding on the Interpretation of Article XVII GATT, suggest that a determination in this respect should be made on a case-by-case basis having regard to two fundamental criteria: (i) the level of government ownership and its ability to exercise control over a given enterprise; and (ii) the ability of a given enterprise to influence trade flows based on the exclusive or special privileges granted to it: WTO, 'Operations of State Trading Enterprises as They Relate to International Trade', Background Paper by the Secretariat G/STR/2 (26 October 1995), para 95; Understanding on the Interpretation of Article XVII GATT of the GATT, available at http://www.wto.org/english/docs_e/legal_e/08-17_e.htm (accessed September 2014). In addition, the indication that a given enterprise is a state trading enterprise within the meaning of Art XVII could be indicated in WTO members' accession documents or in the notifications to the WTO Council for Trade in Goods in accordance with Art XVII:4 (a) GATT: Pogoretskyy (n 10 above), 193–96.

Based on existing WTO jurisprudence, Article XVII:1 requires that STEs act in accordance with the principle of non-discrimination.[23] However, it is not clear from the text of the provision whether Article XVII:1 is meant to cover both standards of the non-discrimination principle (that is, the most-favoured nation clause and the national treatment requirement). Although in *Korea—Various Measures on Beef* the Panel seemed to suggest that this may be the case,[24] the negotiating history of Article XVII indicates that it was intended to cover cases of discrimination between different WTO members only (ie the MFN standard).[25] Under this scenario, Article XVII would not capture the practice of dual pricing inasmuch as the use of different prices in export and domestic markets does not entail MFN violations.[26] Even admitting that Article XVII covers the national treatment requirement, moreover, it is uncertain to what extent this would ensure an adequate regulation of dual pricing: the national treatment rule as laid down in Article III GATT applies in fact uniquely to imports,[27] while the practice of dual pricing affects the export side.

B. 'WTO-plus' Commitments on Dual Pricing Undertaken by Newly Acceding Energy-Producing Members

The issue of dual pricing was specifically addressed during the accession negotiations of the first energy-producing countries that joined the WTO, although with mixed results. Saudi Arabia undertook, in its working party report, legally binding commitments on energy dual pricing, but they are quite limited in scope as they cover only natural gas and natural gas liquids (NGLs, ie waste products associated with the extraction of natural gas and used as inputs to produce fertilizers):

> In response to concerns expressed by a member of the Working Party, the representative of Saudi Arabia stated that producers/distributors of NGLs in Saudi Arabia would operate, within the relevant regulatory framework, on the basis of normal commercial considerations, *based on the full recovery of costs and a*

[23] GATT Panel Report, 'Canada—Administration of the Foreign Investment Review Act (FIRA)', BISD 30S/140 (7 February 1984); WTO Appellate Body Report, 'Canada—Measures Relating to Exports of Wheat and Treatment of Imported Grain', WT/DS276/AB/R (27 September 2004).

[24] WTO Panel Report, 'Korea—Measures Affecting Imports of Fresh, Chilled and Frozen Beef', WT/DS161/R, WT/DS169/R (10 January 2001), para 753. However, on that occasion the Panel was concerned with the case of an STE detaining an import, not an export, monopoly.

[25] Pogoretskyy (n 10 above), 197–98.

[26] Moreover, it is noteworthy that, according to the Ad Note to Art XVII:1 of the GATT, '[t]he charging by a state enterprise of different prices for its sales of a product in different markets is not precluded by the provision of this article, provided that such different prices are charged for commercial reasons, to meet conditions of supply and demand in export markets'. In other words, a given STE may still charge different prices in different foreign markets as long as this is justified by commercial reasons.

[27] S Defilla, 'Energy Trade under the ECT and Accession to the WTO' (2003) 21 (4) *Journal of Energy and Natural Resources Law* 431.

> *reasonable profit*. He confirmed that his Government's policy was to ensure that these economic operators, in respect of their supplies of NGLs to industrial users, would fully recover their production and investment costs (fractionation, overheads, financing charges, transportation, maintenance and upgrade of fractionation and distribution infrastructure) and make a profit in the ordinary course of business.[28]

This commitment is not simply a reiteration of existing requirements set out in Article III:9. It constitutes a WTO-plus obligation inasmuch as Saudi Arabia agreed to fix prices in a manner that permits the full recovery of costs and a reasonable profit.[29] In addition, Saudi Arabia committed to:

> apply its price regulations and profit controls in a WTO consistent fashion taking into account the interests of exporting WTO members as provided for in Article III:9 of the GATT 1994 and in Article VIII of the General Agreement on Trade in Services (GATS) [as well as to] *publish the price and profit controls of goods and services* listed in Annex A, as well as any modifications or additions, in the official gazette.[30]

The level of commitment agreed upon by the Russian Federation on dual pricing in its working party report is also limited to the pricing of natural gas, but is much more ambiguous. On the one hand, Russia seems to claim the legitimacy of its dual pricing policies as generally considered:

> the representative of the Russian Federation stated that underground resources within the territory of the Russian Federation, including subsoil domain and mineral resources contained therein, energy and other resources, were the property of the State. The Russian Federation exercised its sovereign rights over the resources. He added that the current practice of regulation of energy and natural gas prices in the Russian Federation was not different from similar practices of many WTO members, who continued to regulate energy prices. Similar to the practice of other countries, energy and natural gas price regulation in the Russian Federation was aimed at prevention of abuse of monopoly position and protection of consumers' interests from monopoly price increases.[31]

On the other hand, with respect to the regulation of natural gas prices, Russia expressed its intention to modify state regulation of gas prices and develop market-pricing principles for the domestic gas market,[32] and clarified that:

> the basic principle of price-setting was to ensure economically viable production and recovery of costs, including, inter alia, the cost of production, overheads, financing charges, transportation, maintenance and upgrade of extraction and distribution

[28] 'Report of the Working Party on the Accession of the Kingdom of Saudi Arabia' (n 4 above), para 33 (emphasis added).

[29] P Milthorp and D Christy, 'Energy Issues in Selected WTO Accession' in Selivanova (n 10 above), 275.

[30] 'Report of the Working Party on the Accession of the Kingdom of Saudi Arabia' (n 4 above), para 37 (emphasis added).

[31] 'Report of the Working Party on the Accession of the Russian Federation' (n 5 above), para 123.

[32] Ibid, para 120.

infrastructure, investment in the exploration and development of new fields done or planned, and reasonable profits.[33]

However, similar to Saudi Arabia, the Russian Federation agreed that 'upon accession, producers/distributors of natural gas in the Russian Federation would operate, within the relevant regulatory framework, on the basis of normal commercial considerations, based on recovery of costs and profit'.[34]

In light of the constellation of WTO-plus obligations undertaken by newly acceding WTO members on dual pricing, it is clear that the incumbent WTO membership insisted on requesting that energy-producing countries undertake additional commitments in the absence of substantive and effective rules on dual pricing in the GATT. In this perspective, and in light of the numerous energy-producing countries currently negotiating their accession to the WTO, it is reasonable to assume that the practice of dual pricing would then be specifically addressed within many more accession packages. However, as in the cases of Saudi Arabia and the Russian Federation, it is also likely that energy-endowed countries would tend to negotiate narrowly tailored commitments on energy pricing. Hence, the WTO regulation of dual pricing policies would appear rather fragmented, resulting from the varying country-specific commitments assumed by new WTO members in their accession protocols.

C. Article XI:1 GATT and Existing WTO-plus Obligations on Energy Export Taxes

Tackling the use of export taxes in the energy sector is very important inasmuch as WTO members can de facto implement dual pricing policies by arbitrarily raising export tariffs that privilege domestic consumption over foreign consumption. Several WTO instruments control the use of export taxes. Under the GATT, in particular, any export 'prohibitions or restrictions other than duties, taxes or other charges, whether made effective through quotas . . . export licences or other measures' is outlawed. While WTO members are pre-empted from introducing quantitative forms of export restrictions on energy products,[35] they remain free to use export 'duties' or 'taxes'[36] as per Article XI:1. Yet, the GATT does not envisage a mandatory

[33] Ibid, para 126.

[34] Ibid, para 132.

[35] Existing WTO jurisprudence concerning quantitative forms of export restrictions has consistently interpreted Art XI:1 in a broad manner: I Espa, 'Energy Export Restrictions in the WTO between Resource Nationalism and Sustainable Development' in F Seatzu, A Bonfanti and F Romanin Jacur (eds), *Natural Resources Grabbing: Erosion or Legitimate Exercise of State Sovereignty?* (Brill, 2015) 361, 366–67.

[36] The admissibility of export duties or taxes under Art XI:1 stems from the fundamental choice of 'tariffs' over quantitative restrictions as the lawful means of restricting imports and exports in the GATT. Tariffs are in fact more transparent and predictable in their effects: J Bonarriva et al, 'Export Controls: An Overview of their Use, Economic Effects, and Treatment

mechanism for scheduling binding levels of export duty concessions similar to the one described for import tariffs under Article II:1(b).[37]

Against this general background, some members acceding to the WTO after its entry into force have undertaken specific obligations on the use of export duties within their protocols of accession and the associated working party reports.[38] The Russian Federation is the only major energy-exporting country among them to have assumed substantial commitments in the energy sector. In particular, the Russian Federation created a new 'Part V' on export duties within its GATT Schedule of Concessions as admitted by Article II:1(a) GATT, and it bound therein over 700 tariff lines, including many primary energy products.[39] By doing so, the Russian Federation reserved its right to renegotiate and/or modify these commitments in accordance with the GATT rules, including the rules on deconsolidation of scheduled concessions under Article XXVIII GATT and the general exceptions recognized under Article XX GATT.[40] The legal technique chosen by the Russian Federation to incorporate its export duty commitments seems to be directly related to the far greater scope of such commitments in the energy sector compared to any other large exporter acceding to the WTO in the energy sector.[41] Saudi Arabia's specific obligations, in contrast, consist of refraining from imposing export duties on a very restricted set of products, not including any energy products.[42] This means that Saudi Arabia remains free to apply export taxes on any energy products, including those products already subject to specific dual pricing commitments, without any upper bound limit.[43] The same holds true for any original WTO member bound exclusively by GATT obligations.

in the Global Trading System', Office of Industries Working Papers 16 (US International Trade Commission, August 2009).

[37] WTO members are nevertheless allowed to negotiate and schedule export concessions by terms of Art II:1(a) GATT and Art XXVIII *bis* GATT: Espa (n 35 above), 368.

[38] Nine of the 31 countries that have acceded to the WTO to date have agreed to adopt WTO-plus commitments on export duties (Mongolia, Latvia, Croatia, China, Saudi Arabia, Vietnam, Ukraine, Montenegro and the Russian Federation).

[39] 'Report of the Working Party on the Accession of the Russian Federation' (n 5 above), para 638.

[40] J Qin, 'Reforming WTO Discipline on Export Duties: Sovereignty over Natural Resources, Economic Development and Environmental Protection' (2012) 46(5) *Journal of World Trade* 1160.

[41] Exceptional WTO-plus commitments on the use of export duties have also been undertaken by China in its Protocol of Accession in the form of a general elimination obligation with only limited flexibilities: 'Protocol on the Accession of the People's Republic of China', WT/L/432 (23 November 2014) para 11.3. While this obligation also includes all energy products, it has limited relevance, as China is the largest world importer of primary energy products: Espa (n 35 above), 375–77.

[42] Saudi Arabia agreed not to impose any export duty on iron and steel scrap: 'Report of the Working Party on the Accession of Saudi Arabia' (n 4 above), para 184, incorporated into the Accession Protocol by virtue of para 315.

[43] As Saudi Arabia acceded to the WTO before the Russian Federation, the narrowly tailored WTO-plus obligations on export taxes may reflect concerns over the adjustability of these commitments when contained in specific provisions of an accession protocol and/or Working Party report: Qin (n 40 above), 1157–58.

IV. OPTIONS FOR REINFORCING THE TREATMENT OF ENERGY DUAL PRICING IN THE WTO LEGAL FRAMEWORK

The panorama of WTO disciplines relevant to various dual pricing policies is highly fragmented and overall deficient, at least when assessed from an energy-specific perspective. The attempts to compensate for the shortcomings of existing GATT disciplines through the negotiation of WTO-plus obligations in the accession protocols of new energy-producing members have produced mixed results, with large suppliers abiding by narrowly tailored commitments with a view to defending their key economic interests.

In light of the above, it is noteworthy that, in the context of the WTO Doha negotiations, the Negotiating Group on Rules has discussed possible avenues to rethink existing WTO rules on subsidies in the attempt to adequately tackle market-distorting dual pricing practices.[44] Some WTO members advocated, in particular, an amendment to the WTO Agreement on Subsidies and Countervailing Measures (ASCM) so as to include dual pricing within the category of prohibited subsidies.[45] According to these proposals, Article 3.1 ASCM should also outlaw 'the provision, by the virtue of government action, of goods to domestic production on terms and conditions more favourable than those generally available for such goods when destined for export'.[46]

However, this formulation does not seem to cover the use of export tariffs as instruments to implement dual pricing. The issue of export taxes was in fact dealt with separately by the Doha Negotiating Group on Non-Agricultural Market Access (NAMA), reflecting the explosion of attention towards the proliferation of such measures in other sectors.[47] The latest proposal for reforming WTO disciplines on export taxes,[48] in particular, endorsed a 'negotiating option'[49] for the purpose of stimulating a greater level of commitment on the part of WTO members, according to which 'WTO members should undertake to schedule export taxes on non-agricultural products in their Schedules of Concessions and bind the export taxes at a level to be negotiated'.[50]

[44] A Yanovich, 'WTO Rules and the Energy Sector', in Selivanova (n 10 above), 22.

[45] United States Proposal, 'Expanding the Prohibited "Red Light" Subsidy Category', WTO/RL/GEN/94 (16 January 2006); European Union Proposal, 'Submission of the European Communities on Subsidies', WTO/TN/RL/GEN/135 (24 April 2006).

[46] Ibid.

[47] I Espa, 'The "Rhetoric" of Proliferation of Mineral Export Restraints and WTO Under-Regulation' (2013) 2(2) *Bocconi Legal Papers* 185.

[48] 'EC Revised Submission on Export Taxes', TN/MA/W/101 (17 January 2008). This proposal is currently inserted into the fourth revision of draft modalities for non-agricultural market access.

[49] The expression 'negotiating option' borrows from Bin Gu, who saw it as opposed to a 'judicial option' consisting of a *revirement* of the Appellate Body's approach to the applicability of Art XX for violations of para 11.3 of China's Accession Protocol: B Gu, 'Mineral Export Restraints and Sustainable Development—Are Rare Earths Testing the WTO's Loopholes?' (2011) 14(4) *Journal of International Economic Law* 781.

[50] 'EC Revised Submission on Export Taxes' (n 48 above), para 9. Special flexibilities are envisaged for least developed countries, which would be requested to 'schedule export taxes but [at the same time] maintain these export taxes unbound for a certain number of tariff lines (the number is to be negotiated), in reflection of their specific developmental interests and concerns'.

This proposal aimed at encouraging WTO members to negotiate export duty concessions in an 'appropriate part' of their schedules on a systematic basis, as allowed by Article II:1(a) GATT and Article XXVIII bis GATT.

The Doha proposals on dual pricing and export taxes would ensure the general applicability of, respectively, ASCM and GATT rules to dual pricing schemes functionally equivalent to subsidies and export tariffs adopted to implement dual pricing policies, while avoiding the fragmentation inherent to the negotiation of multiple country-specific (and presumably narrowly tailored) WTO-plus commitments by current and prospective WTO members. Regrettably, however, they have not progressed beyond the proposal stage as their destiny is tied to the future of the Doha Negotiations.

While a system-wide reform remains a first-best solution to fill the regulatory gaps in relevant WTO disciplines, existing provisions may in the interim provide a sufficient basis to address dual pricing policies. As to ASCM disciplines in particular, their applicability may be ensured inasmuch as dual pricing schemes could be considered to constitute a 'subsidy' within the meaning of the Agreement.[51] Under Article 1 ASCM, a 'subsidy' must: (i) provide a contribution by a government or any public body within the territory of a member under Article 1.1(a)(1) or any form of income or price support in the sense of Article XVI GATT as per Article 1.1(a)(2); and (ii) confer a benefit to the recipient under Article 1.1(b). Moreover, it must be 'specific' within the meaning of Article 2 ASCM.

Many authors have argued that dual pricing may fulfil the first definitional element, either by qualifying as a governmental provision of goods under Article 1.1(a)(1)(iii) ASCM or by being considered equivalent to a form of governmental entrustment or direction to private enterprises to sell energy inputs to domestic users at a price that is below market prices under Article 1.1(a)(1)(iv) ASCM.[52] Finding the existence of a 'benefit' also seems to be possible in principle, although the identification of the relevant product market and the proper price benchmark may entail a complex economic analysis.[53] While the existence of different prices for the domestic and export markets arguably improves the competitive position of the recipients in comparison to what would have happened under market conditions, according to Article 14(d) ASCM a benefit is bestowed insofar as the provision of goods occurs at a less than adequate remuneration, to be measured on the basis of 'prevail-

[51] Many authors have addressed the issue of compatibility of dual pricing policies with the ASCM, reaching different conclusions. Eg S Ripinsky, 'The System of Gas Dual Pricing in Russia: Compatibility with WTO Rules' (2004) 3(3) *World Trade Review* 463; J Selivanova, 'World Trade Organization Rules and Energy Pricing: Russia's Case' (2004) 38(4) *Journal of World Trade* 559; Pogoretskyy (n 10 above), 202–12. It is interesting to note, however, that '[t]he SCM Agreement has been the principal instrument used to evaluate the WTO compliance of dual-pricing policies of acceding energy-producing countries': Marceau (n 8 above), 36.

[52] For an overview of the arguments and a discussion of the possible legal difficulties in defending such claims see Espa and Rolland (n 12 above), 5–6.

[53] Pogoretskyy (n 10 above), 203–08.

ing market conditions . . . in the country of provision . . . (including price, quality, availability, marketability, transportation and other conditions of purchase or sale)'. In the case of energy dual pricing, however, domestic market conditions would not be of use as a benchmark for the purpose of determining the existence of a benefit. According to the Appellate Body Report in *US—Softwood Lumber IV*, an alternative cross-border benchmark for the determination of adequate remuneration could be considered when there is no 'adequate' domestic market because the government plays a predominant role in the supply of the goods.[54] This circumstance may be considered to apply in the case of dual pricing practices, and alternative benchmarks may include proxies construed on the basis of the world price for similar goods[55] or production costs, or the 'prices for the same inputs in economies at a similar stage of development with a similar resource base'.[56]

Dual pricing schemes falling within the ASCM definition of 'subsidy' would moreover need to be 'specific' within the meaning of Article 2 ASCM unless they constitute a prohibited subsidy under Article 3 ASCM.[57] Dual pricing schemes do not currently fall under the category of prohibited subsidies, nor do they fulfil the de jure specificity criterion, as they often apply equally to all sectors to the general benefit of the domestic manufacturing sector and not of specific enterprises, groups of enterprises, industries or groups thereof, or specific sectors, as required under Article 2 ASCM.[58] Yet dual pricing could arguably be considered a de facto specific subsidy under Article 2.1(c) to the extent that low energy prices confer a disguised advantage to certain enterprises or industries due to their particular needs (eg energy-intensive sectors such as fertilizers).[59] In *US—Softwood Lumber IV*, the panel interpreted the de facto specificity test rather smoothly by saying that the specificity requirement is met when the subsidized good is particularly useful only for certain enter-

[54] WTO Appellate Body Report, 'United States—Final Countervailing Duty Determination with Respect to Certain Softwood Lumber from Canada', WT/DS257/AB/R (19 January 2004) para 90. For the Appellate Body, the role of the government is predominant when 'it effectively determines the price at which the private suppliers sell the same or like products': ibid, paras 87–96 and 101.

[55] However, in the case of energy resources such as natural gas or electricity, there is no such price due to the market configuration. It is not clear to what extent the price benchmark could be identified based on the price of similar goods as determined in local/regional markets: Pogoretskyy (n 10 above), 207. Possibly to solve this problem, some authors have suggested that export prices could constitute the benchmark: Marceau (n 8 above), 36.

[56] Selivanova (n 9 above), 123.

[57] Provided they fall within the definition of subsidy under Art 1 ASCM, subsidies that are de jure or de facto contingent on export performance (Art 3.1(a) ASCM) or on the use of domestic goods over imported goods (Art 3.1(b) ASCM) fall under the category of prohibited subsidies and are deemed to be specific within the meaning of Art 2 ASCM: PC Mavroidis, *Trade in Goods* (Oxford University Press, 2012), 549.

[58] Selivanova (n 51 above); R Quick, 'Export Taxes and Dual Pricing: How Can Trade Distortive Government Practices Be Tackled?' in Pauwelyn (n 2 above), 195; 'Report of the Working Party on the Accession of the Kingdom of Saudi Arabia' (n 4 above), paras 29–33; 'Report of the Working Party on the Accession of the Russian Federation' (n 5 above), paras 124–33.

[59] Pogoretskyy (n 10 above), 210–12.

prises.[60] This approach seems to leave quite a significant margin of manoeuvre to WTO dispute settlement bodies.

Provided these premises are correct, WTO members suffering the adverse effects produced by energy dual pricing schemes could challenge such practices before the WTO dispute settlement bodies under the ASCM or decide to impose a countervailing duty unilaterally. This scenario would arguably have a deterrent effect on WTO members and possibly contribute to raising the level of ambition of the accession negotiations of prospective energy-producing members. Moreover, it would be in line with the sentiment of some WTO members, as emerged during the Doha Round negotiations on Rules.

Finally, while leaving aside the question of whether this approach could also be applicable to address dual pricing policies when implemented through export tariffs,[61] it is noteworthy that the solution proposed in the latest Doha proposal on export taxes has already been implemented in the context of Russia's accession to the WTO. Hence, should export tariffs continue to be addressed separately by means of specific accession protocol provisions, existing regulatory gaps could at least partially be filled by reproducing the Russian model in the accession negotiations of major energy-exporting countries to the WTO, with a view to reassuring prospective members about the flexibility of their obligations on export duties and thus stimulating the maximum level of commitment on the part of these countries. The consolidation of such a model could then serve as a basis for the negotiation of export duty commitments on a more general level, with all countries progressively incorporating export duty concessions into their GATT schedules in accordance with the spirit of Articles II:1(a) and XXVIII GATT.

V. CONCLUSIONS

This chapter aimed at contributing to the emerging debate on trade and energy by focusing on the specific issue of dual pricing policies, including those implemented through export tariffs. It has shown that the current configuration of WTO rules applicable to dual pricing policies may not prove adequate to effectively address the increasingly varied panorama of distortive government practices pursued to privilege domestic over foreign consumption of energy products. GATT rules are in fact overall deficient, while the panorama of relevant WTO-plus obligations on dual pricing and export taxes, addressed as separate issues, consists of a network of narrowly tailored commitments, with the only exception being the export duty concessions negotiated by the Russian Federation on a wide range of primary energy products. Moreover, in the case of certain energy-producing countries, such as Saudi Arabia, export

[60] WTO Appellate Body Report (n 54 above).

[61] The status of export restraints under the ASCM is unclear: Espa and Rolland (n 12 above), 5–6.

duty commitments contradict the 'correspondent' commitments on energy dual pricing, thus undermining the overall effectiveness of WTO disciplines to tackle these practices.

From this perspective, this chapter has examined first-best and second-best options for reinforcing the treatment of energy dual pricing in the WTO legal framework. The former category consists of the solutions put forward so far in the context of the Doha Round, aimed at designing a broader, system-wide reform of relevant ASCM (for dual pricing policies) and GATT (for export taxes) rules generally applicable to any primary commodity. The analysis of these proposals has shown, in particular, that these options do not set forth new disciplines as such, but build on existing WTO provisions in an attempt to clarify that the measures at issue fall within their scope of application. Hence, in the case of the ASCM, the incorporation of dual pricing among the prohibited subsidies indirectly indicates that the Agreement should be interpreted as applying to dual pricing policies. In the case of export taxes, the solution of negotiating export duty concessions in GATT schedules of concessions gives full implementation to the mechanism already envisaged by GATT provisions, albeit not mandatorily. Based on these considerations, the chapter indicates second-best solutions, which do not require the reform of existing WTO rules but could serve as interim steps to better tackle dual pricing policies, at least in the energy sector.

In conclusion, although not specifically drafted with energy in mind, the current WTO rulebook already potentially contains solutions that could effectively address dual pricing policies and export tariffs. However, inasmuch as such issues continue to be addressed separately, the importance of strengthening WTO rules with respect to both practices cannot be underestimated: the protectionist goal of privileging domestic over foreign consumption of energy products can in fact be pursued alternatively by dual pricing policies implemented in the domestic market and the levying of export taxes, and both distortive practices must thus be tackled specifically to achieve effective energy governance.

27

Legitimate Countermeasures in International Trade Law and their Illegality in International Investment Law

JUNIANTO JAMES LOSARI* AND
MICHAEL EWING-CHOW†

I. INTRODUCTION

THE DEFENCE OF countermeasures is well accepted in public international law as a part of customary international law (CIL). Even so, the legitimacy of unilateral countermeasures as a response to a breach of an international obligation has always been a problem in international law. Lawyers have attempted to understand and limit the unilateral actions of states by suggesting many requirements, such as those found in the Draft Articles on State Responsibility (ILC Articles).[1] Under Article 22 of the ILC Articles, although State B may breach its international obligation against State A, the wrongfulness of the breach can be precluded if State B can demonstrate that its act constitutes a legitimate countermeasure taken against a breach done earlier against it.

Without a universal governance system controlling the enforcement of states' obligations, states traditionally had very few options other than to use power or even coercion against the breach of international obligations. The

* Research Fellow, Centre for International Law (CIL) (www.cil.nus.edu.sg).

† Associate Professor, National University of Singapore, WTO Chair, Head Trade/Investment Law and Policy, Centre for International Law (CIL) ((www.cil.nus.edu.sg).

This article was presented at the 2013 ILA Regional Conference in Greece. It has been published as JJ Losari and M Ewing-Chow, 'A Clash of Treaties: The Lawfulness of Countermeasures in International Trade Law and International Investment Law' (2015) 16 *Journal of World Investment and Trade* 274–313.

[1] International Law Commission, 'Draft Articles on Responsibility of States for Internationally Wrongful Acts with Commentaries' (2001) II(2) *Yearbook of International Law Commission* (ILC Articles and Commentary).

relatively recent rise of dispute settlement mechanisms (DSMs) seems to offer a solution to this conundrum of getting states to comply with international obligations. In reality, however, some states have, for a variety of reasons, not complied even with binding and final DSM decisions. For these states, it may be that countermeasures are a last resort for the injured state to encourage compliance from the breaching states.

The law on countermeasures has probably been most defined by public international law relating to the use of force. Indeed, the ILC Articles limit the use of force as countermeasures.[2] However, some recent cases in the field of international economic law have emphasized the need to resolve the issue of countermeasures and the tensions when dealing with economic countermeasures.[3]

In World Trade Organization (WTO) law, countermeasures are formally incorporated in the Understanding on Rules and Procedures Governing the Settlement of Disputes (DSU) of the WTO.[4] Non-compliance with a ruling of the Dispute Settlement Body (DSB) may lead to the suspension of concessions or other WTO obligations (hereinafter referred to as countermeasures).[5]

The use of countermeasures is not explicitly provided for in most investment agreements. Nevertheless, at least one arbitral tribunal has accepted countermeasures as a defence under CIL applicable to an investment agreement.[6] In doing so, it relied heavily on the ILC Articles and past cases[7] to determine the legitimacy of the countermeasure.[8]

There is a close relation between countermeasures in international trade law and those in investment law. Countermeasures deemed to be legitimate under WTO law may affect the interests of private individuals, including those of foreign investors. In such a situation, if there is an investment agreement between the two disputing WTO members, an investor of one of the members impacted by a trade countermeasure may bring a claim of violation of the investment agreement against the other member.

The likelihood of such a situation is not remote, considering how closely trade and investment are interrelated in this globalized world through the global value chains (GVCs). Goods are moved across borders, often between subsidiaries of multinational companies (MNCs). This happened in the sugar

[2] Ibid, Art 50(1).

[3] *Archer Daniels Midland Company and Tate & Lyle Ingredients Americas, Inc v Mexico* [2007] ICSID ARB(AF)/04/5, Award (*ADM v Mexico*); *Corn Products International, Inc v Mexico* [2008] ICSID ARB(AF)/04/1, Award; *Cargill, Inc v Mexico* [2009] ICSID ARB(AF)/05/2, Award.

[4] 1994 Dispute Settlement Rules: Understanding on Rules and Procedures Governing the Settlement of Disputes, Annex 2, 1869 UNTS 401, 33 ILM 1226 (WTO DSU).

[5] Ibid, Art 22(1)–(2).

[6] *ADM v Mexico* (n 3 above), [111], [121].

[7] *Case Concerning the Gabčíkovo-Nagymaros Project (Hungary/Slovakia)* [1997] ICJ, Judgment, ICJ Reports 7; *Portuguese Colonies case* [*Cysne*] [1930] UNRIAA, vol II (Sales No 1949.V.1), [1035]–[1052]; *Portuguese Colonies case* [*Naulilaa*] [1928] UNRIAA, vol II (Sales No 1949.V.1), [1025]–[1026].

[8] *ADM v Mexico* (n 3 above), [121], [125].

war between Mexico and the United States (US), where Mexico claimed that their measures affecting American investors were legitimate countermeasures against a prior breach by the US of its trade obligations under the North American Free Trade Agreement (NAFTA).[9] While this concerned the NAFTA, the legitimacy of countermeasures taken under the bigger trade regime of the WTO as a legitimate defence before an investor-state arbitration tribunal may be similarly called into question. A negative response to this question may create a clash between the two regimes, namely by significantly restricting states' options to enforce their legitimate trade interests, as well as removing the value of countermeasures as an effective tool to ensure compliance in the WTO.

This chapter is a continuation from the analysis that was conducted by one of the authors in his previous paper on convergence and divergence between trade and investment law.[10] This chapter seeks to explore this issue in greater detail, and will be done in the following sequence. Section II will briefly describe the defence of countermeasures in public international law. Section III will analyse countermeasures in international trade law, specifically in WTO law. Section IV will analyse the defence of countermeasures in international investment law by probing through arbitral awards that have dealt with the matter. Section V will explore the interaction of countermeasures in international trade law and in international investment law, and provide recommendations thereof. Section VI will conclude.

II. COUNTERMEASURES IN INTERNATIONAL LAW

In CIL, the defence of countermeasures precludes the wrongfulness of an internationally wrongful act by a state taken as a response to a prior internationally wrongful act. A lawful countermeasure should only seek for cessation and/or to obtain reparation for the injury caused.[11] Countermeasures are historically unilateral actions,[12] which may be taken by a state at its own risk and may incur responsibility if it is later found that the measure is not legitimate.[13] The coverage of countermeasures is very limited to preclude wrongfulness only against the wrongdoer.[14] The measure must be temporary, and may not affect

[9] 1993 North American Free Trade Agreement, 32 ILM 289 and 605, entered into force on 1 January 1994; for further discussion on the convergence between the two fields see A Antoni and M Ewing-Chow, 'Trade and Investment Convergence and Divergence: Revisiting the North American Sugar War' (2013) 1(1) *Latin American Journal of International Trade Law* 321; J Kurtz, 'The Use and Abuse of WTO Law in Investor-State Arbitration: Competition and its Discontents' (2009) 20(3) *European Journal of International Law* 749.

[10] Ibid, Antoni and Ewing-Chow.

[11] ILC Articles and Commentary (n 1 above), 75.

[12] The defence was formerly known as 'reprisals'.

[13] D Harris, *Cases and Materials on International Law*, 7th edn (Thomson Reuters, 2010) 460–61.

[14] ILC Articles and Commentary (n 1 above), Art 49(1).

the following obligations: (i) the obligation to refrain from the threat or use of force; (ii) obligations for the protection of fundamental human rights; (iii) obligations of a humanitarian character prohibiting reprisals; and (iv) obligations under peremptory norms of general international law.[15]

According to the International Court of Justice (ICJ) in *Gabčíkovo-Nagymaros*, a legitimate countermeasure has to fulfil several prerequisites, including: (i) taken in response to a previous international wrongful act of another state;[16] (ii) directed against that state;[17] (iii) taken after a prior call upon the offending state and prior offer to negotiate;[18] and (iv) proportionate.[19] The ILC Articles provide two other conditions, namely: (i) temporary, only during the existence of the wrongful act;[20] and (ii) not imposed when the dispute is pending before a court or tribunal.[21]

These requirements for a legitimate defence of countermeasures under CIL are important for our further analysis of this defence in international trade law and international investment law regimes.

III. COUNTERMEASURES IN INTERNATIONAL TRADE LAW

A. WTO DSU as *Lex Specialis*

For the purpose of this discussion, international trade law hereinafter refers specifically to the regime of the WTO, which has an established system requiring pre-authorization of countermeasures.

The WTO DSU, one of the cornerstones of the 1994 Marrakesh Agreement Establishing the WTO,[22] applies to disputes brought pursuant to the consultation and dispute settlement provisions of the agreements listed in Appendix 1 of the DSU:[23] (i) multilateral agreements on trade in goods; (ii) the General Agreement on Trade in Services (GATS);[24] (iii) the Agreement

[15] Ibid, Art 50(1).

[16] Ibid, 130 [3].

[17] Ibid, 76; *Gabčíkovo-Nagymaros* (n 7 above), [83]; *Cysne* (n 7 above), [1056]–[1057].

[18] ILC Articles and Commentary (n 1 above), Art 52(1)(a) and (b), p 136[4]–[6]; *Naulilaa* (n 7 above), [1027]–[1028]; *Gabčíkovo-Nagymaros* (n 7 above), [84].

[19] ILC Articles and Commentary (n 1 above), Art 51, p 130; *Gabčíkovo-Nagymaros* (n 7 above), [85]–[87]; *Naulilaa* (n 7 above), [1028]; *Air Services Arbitration Case (France v United States)* [1978] 18 RIAA 416, [83].

[20] ILC Articles and Commentary (n 1 above), Arts 49(2) and 53, p 131[7], [9]; *Gabčíkovo-Nagymaros* (n 7 above), [87].

[21] ILC Articles and Commentary (n 1 above), Arts 50(2)(a) and 52(3)(b), p 133[12], 136[8]; *Air Services Arbitration* (n 19 above), [84]–[89], [95]–[96].

[22] 1994 Marrakesh Agreement Establishing the World Trade Organization, 1867 UNTS 154, 33 ILM 1144, entered into force on 1 January 1995.

[23] WTO DSU (n 4 above), Art 1(1).

[24] 1994 General Agreement on Trade in Services, Annex 1B, 1869 UNTS 183, 33 ILM 1167, entered into force on 1 January 1995.

on Trade-Related Aspects of Intellectual Property Rights (TRIPS);[25] and (iv) plurilateral trade agreements. Further, the WTO DSU does not allow WTO members to resort to rules of countermeasures under CIL, ie unilateral countermeasures.[26]

B. Requirements for a Lawful Trade Countermeasure

The DSU allows WTO members to take countermeasures against a breach of the WTO law (trade countermeasures) as authorized by the DSB. The DSU imposes several requirements for a legitimate trade countermeasure.

(i) Proper Subject

Article 22.3(a) of the DSU provides a general principle that the complaining WTO member should first seek suspension of concessions or other obligations with respect to the same sector(s) as that in which the Panel or the Appellate Board (AB) has found a violation or other nullification or impairment. For example, for a violation of tariff of health products, the complaining WTO member must also suspend concessions on the sector of goods under the GATT. Only when this is not practicable or not effective does Article 22.3(b) of the DSU allow the complaining member to suspend concessions or other obligations in other sectors under the same agreement (cross-sector retaliation). If this is not practicable or effective, and the circumstances are serious enough, then Article 22.3(c) of the DSU allows the member to suspend concessions or other obligations under another covered agreement (cross-agreement retaliation), for example the GATS.

The cases in Table 1 demonstrate that most of the countermeasures taken were the imposition of additional duties that deviate from the existing schedule of the retaliating member. The other countermeasures were suspensions of obligations under the TRIPS. Normally, the relevant suspended obligation is the protection of intellectual property rights owned by nationals of the non-complying state. In *EC–Banana III (Ecuador)*, Ecuador proposed to take countermeasures by suspending obligations under Article 14 of the TRIPS regarding the protection of rights of performers, producers of phonograms (sound recordings) and broadcasting organizations,[27] by allowing copies of phonograms to be made in Ecuador without the consent of the right hold-

[25] 1994 Agreement on Trade-Related Aspects of Intellectual Property Rights, Annex 1C, 1869 UNTS 299, 33 ILM 1197, entered into force on 1 January 1995.

[26] *US—Section 301–310 of the Trade Act 1974* [2000] Panel Report, WT/DS152/R, [7.38]–[7.39].

[27] Ibid, [144].

Table 1. Examples of Trade Countermeasures taken in the WTO

Case	Initial violation	Approved countermeasures			Status of sanction
		Same sector	Same agreement	Other sector and agreements	
US—Upland Cotton[a]	Subsidies on cotton (GATT and SCM Agreement)	Imposition of additional custom duties under Agreement on Trade in Goods (Annex 1A) on medical products, food, and arms		GATS Horizontal and/or sectoral concessions and obligations for all sectors in Brazil's schedule under the GATS, including: business services; communication services; construction and related engineering services, etc TRIPS: copyright and related rights; trademarks; industrial designs; patents; and protection of undisclosed information	Both parties concluded a mutual framework agreement to resolve the issue. The US provided certain payment to Brazil
US—Gambling[b]	Limitations on market access in gambling and betting services those are not specified in its Schedule (Article XVI GATS)	Not practicable and may impair the limited entertainment options in Antigua	Not practicable due to the risk of economic disruption	TRIPS: copyright and related rights, trademarks, industrial designs, patents, and protection of undisclosed information	The DSB authorized Antigua to take countermeasures according to the Decision of Arbitrators, eg in respect of IP rights
EC—Bananas III (Ecuador)[c]	Tariff quota reallocation (Article XIII:1 GATT and the chapeau of Article XIII:2 GATT) Export certificate requirement (Art. I:1 GATT) Import licensing procedures (Article III:4 GATT and Article II and XVIII GATS)	Suspension of tariff concessions under the GATT (not including investment goods or primary goods used as inputs in manufacturing and processing industries)		GATS with respect to wholesale trade services in the principal distribution services; TRIPS: section 1, Article 14, sections 3 and 4	The DSB authorized Ecuador to take countermeasures equivalent to US$ 201.6 million. The case went through two compliance panels, and eventually the parties reached a mutually agreed solution in 2012

[a] *United States—Subsidies on Upland Cotton* [2004] Panel Report, WT/DS267/R and Corr.1, Add.1, Add.2 and Add.3, [2005] WT/DS267/AB/R, [2009] WT/DS267/ARB/2 (*US—Upland Cotton*).
[b] *United States—Measures Affecting the Cross-Border Supply of Gambling and Betting Services* [2007] Decision of the Arbitrators (Art 22.6 DSU), WT/DS285/ARB (*US—Gambling*).
[c] *European Communities — Regime for the Importation, Sale and Distribution of Bananas* [2000] Decision of the Arbitrators (Art 22.6 DSU), WT/DS27/ARB/ECU (*EC—Bananas III (Ecuador)*).

ers in the country of production.[28] This is an example where the retaliations authorized by the WTO cover fields that directly affect individuals.

(ii) Level of Countermeasure

Article 22.4 of the DSU requires the level of countermeasures to be equivalent to the level of nullification or impairment. In practice, the level of suspension is limited to the harm suffered by the complaining member. The 'equivalent' requirement is fulfilled when the level is 'equal to or below the level of nullification or impairment sustained'.[29] This requirement is somewhat similar to the requirement of proportionality in CIL. If there is disagreement as to the level of a countermeasure, it may be brought to arbitration,[30] which will assess the proportionality of the countermeasure before it is authorized and implemented. During the course of the arbitration, countermeasures should not be carried out.

(iii) Non-retroactive Remedies

Since the main objective of the WTO dispute settlement is 'to secure the withdrawal of the measures' found to be illegal,[31] the remedies granted under the system are merely prospective,[32] or limited to the harm that occurs after a WTO member fails to implement a panel or AB report within a reasonable period of time. This is clearly a deviation from CIL that allows for retroactive remedies, and that reparation must wipe out, as far as possible, all the consequences of the illegal act and re-establish the situation that would have existed if that act had not been committed.[33]

[28] Ibid, [155].

[29] *United States—1916 Act [EC]* [2004] Decision of the Arbitrators (Art 22.6 DSU), WT/DS136/ARB, ¶5.21.

[30] WTO DSU (n 4 above), Art 22.6.

[31] Ibid, Arts 3.7 and 19.1.

[32] *United States—Import Measures on Certain Products from the European Communities* [2000] Panel Report, WT/DS165/R, [6.106].

[33] *Chorzow Factory Case (Germany v Poland)* [1928] PCIJ, Ser A, No 17, [47]; *Military and Paramilitary Activities in and against Nicaragua (Nicaragua v US)* [1986] ICJ, Merits, ICJ Reports 14, [114]; *Reparations for Injuries Suffered in the Service of the United Nations* [1949] ICJ, Advisory Opinion, ICJ Reports 174, [184].

(iv) Prior Authorization from the DSB

Articles 3.7 and 22.2 of the DSU allow members to take countermeasures on a discriminatory basis vis-à-vis the other member, subject to authorization by the DSB. According to Article 22.6 of the DSU, the DSB (which consists of all WTO members) is supposed to grant authorization for countermeasures within 30 days of the expiry of the reasonable period of time unless all members decided by consensus to reject the request (negative consensus rule).

Within the WTO regime, the potential issue of DSB-authorized countermeasures interfering with private rights of investor has been identified in the past, particularly in the discussion of the *EC–Banana III (Ecuador)* arbitrators during the Article 22.6 DSU proceeding. The discussion recognizes that countermeasures of the GATS would affect service suppliers who are commercially present in the territory of the member taking countermeasures and could lead to conflicts with rights to, for example, equal treatment embodied in national legislation or international treaties.[34] Similarly, countermeasures under the TRIPS may interfere with private rights owned by natural or legal persons.[35] While there is an awareness of the problem, the arbitrators left the resolution of the problem entirely to the prerogatives of the member implementing the countermeasures.[36] This in itself does not resolve the problems that may arise from legitimate trade countermeasures, as can be seen further below.

IV. COUNTERMEASURES IN INTERNATIONAL INVESTMENT LAW

In international investment law, the defence of countermeasures is never mentioned explicitly in investment treaties. At the same time, not many cases have dealt with this issue, perhaps because it has rarely been put as a defence. Nevertheless, there are several NAFTA Chapter 11 cases that may provide some guidance on how arbitral tribunals view this defence.

The most prominent cases are those arising from a set of strikingly similar facts in the sugar war between Mexico and the US, dealing with the imposition of tax on beverages containing high-fructose corn syrup (HFCS) by Mexico.[37] Despite the similar set of facts, the tribunals have different analyses, as elaborated below.

[34] *EC—Bananas III (Ecuador)* (see note c to Table 1 above), [113], [157].

[35] Ibid, [157].

[36] Ibid, [158].

[37] *ADM v Mexico* (n 3 above); *Corn Products v Mexico* (n 3 above); *Cargill v Mexico* (n 3 above).

A. The Facts of the US–Mexico Sugar War

The sugar war involved three dispute settlement forums, the WTO DSB (two different cases),[38] a NAFTA Chapter 19 tribunal[39] and NAFTA Chapter 11 investor-state arbitration tribunals. The underlying reason for the dispute was the disagreement between Mexico and the US on the American sugar import quotas allocated to Mexico under the NAFTA.[40]

Mexico sought to clarify the uncertainties created by the exchange of letters between the countries regarding the quota by resorting to the dispute settlement mechanism established under NAFTA Chapter 20. However, the US had not formally established its panel roster and refused to cooperate in composing the panel.[41] As there was no automaticity in panel formation, no NAFTA Chapter 20 panel could be formed.

Failing to settle the dispute through NAFTA, Mexico initiated an antidumping investigation of American exports of HFCS to Mexico and decided to impose provisional duties in 1997 and definitive duties in 1998. The US successfully challenged these duties before the NAFTA tribunals[42] and the WTO, and Mexico was obliged to withdraw the duties.[43]

In 2002, the Mexican Congress, stating that it was 'committed to protecting the domestic sugar industry',[44] introduced a series of measures to 'stop the displacement of domestic cane sugar by imported HFCS and soft drinks and syrup sweetened with HFCS'. These were: (i) a 20 per cent tax on the transfer and importation of soft drinks using any sweetener other than cane sugar (soft drinks tax); (ii) a 20 per cent tax on the commissioning, mediation, agency, representation, brokerage, consignment and distribution of soft drinks using any sweetener other than cane sugar (distribution tax); and (iii) a number of bookkeeping requirements for taxpayers subject to the soft drink tax and the distribution tax.

These measures were challenged before the WTO.[45] The dispute was eventually resolved in 2006, when the US and Mexico agreed to achieve free trade in HFCS by 2008, as well as to repeal the Mexican measures as of 2007.[46] However, a number of American investors in Mexico also filed investment disputes against Mexico under the investor-state dispute settlement mechanism

[38] *Mexico—Anti-Dumping Investigation of High Fructose Corn Syrup from the United States* [2000] Panel Report, WT/DS132/R (*Mexico—Corn Syrup*); *Mexico—Taxes on Soft Drinks* [2005] Panel Report, WT/DS308/R and [2006] Appellate Body Report, WT/DS308/AB/R.

[39] *Review of the Final Determination of the Antidumping Investigation on Imports of High Fructose Corn Syrup, Originating from the United States of America* [2001] MEX-USA-98-1904-01 (*Antidumping Determination on HFCS*).

[40] Antoni and Ewing-Chow (n 9 above), 321.

[41] Ibid, 327.

[42] *Antidumping Determination on HFCS* (n 39 above).

[43] *Mexico—Corn Syrup* (n 38 above).

[44] *ADM v Mexico* (n 3 above), [80].

[45] Ibid, Panel and Appellate Body Reports.

[46] *ADM v Mexico* (n 3 above), [97]; *Cargill v Mexico* (n 3 above), [124].

established under NAFTA Chapter 11, seeking damages for their losses during the period when the measures were in place. In the arbitration proceedings, Mexico attempted to justify its measures by claiming that they constituted legitimate countermeasures against the US for the latter's violation of NAFTA Chapter 7 and 20 obligations.[47]

B. Contextualizing the NAFTA Dispute Settlement Bodies

Under the NAFTA, parties to the agreement can request for the establishment of a tribunal or a panel under different chapters, and in this analysis of countermeasures in investment law, Chapter 11 and 20 are particularly relevant.

The Chapter 11 panel's competence is limited to a claim of breach of an obligation under Section A of Chapter 11 and NAFTA Articles 1502(3)(a) and 1503(2). On the other hand, the Chapter 20 panel's competence is broader and encompasses disputes between the parties regarding the interpretation or application of NAFTA,[48] though it cannot address disputes arising from Chapter 11.

The issue of countermeasures is also regulated within NAFTA Article 2019, ie non-implementation/suspension of benefits. To a certain extent, countermeasures under this provision are similar to that of the WTO DSU. They can be taken only after there is a finding of inconsistency with NAFTA obligations. However, there is no requirement to obtain an authorization. Only if one of the disputing parties disagrees with the level of a proposed countermeasure can the Free Trade Commission establish a panel to determine whether the level of the countermeasure is manifestly excessive. In a way, there remains a check and balance mechanism to ensure that countermeasures are not taken abusively.

As a NAFTA Chapter 20 panel could not be formed in the Mexico sugar war cases, Mexico could not invoke the defence of countermeasures regulated by Chapter 20. In addition, there was no initial finding of a breach by the US of its NAFTA obligations.

C. Countermeasures Analysis by Investor-State Arbitration Tribunals

The tribunals in the three cases about Mexico's tax measures on soft drinks dealt in different ways with Mexico's claims that the measures were countermeasures taken in response to the alleged breach of the US's obligations under the NAFTA. The awards were issued in the following order, *ADM v Mexico* (2007), *Corn Products v Mexico* (2008) and *Cargill v Mexico* (2009).

[47] *ADM v Mexico* (n 3 above), [110]; *Cargill v Mexico* (n 3 above), [379]; *Corn Products v Mexico* (n 3 above), [144].

[48] NAFTA (n 9 above), Art 2004.

The tribunal in *Cargill v Mexico* actually considered only the previous award of *ADM v Mexico*, as the award in *Corn Products* was not publicly released in time.

Below, we assess the tribunals' awards in relation to a discussion on the availability of the defence of countermeasures.

As mentioned earlier, NAFTA Chapter 11 does not explicitly provide for the defence of countermeasures. Although it is provided for in NAFTA Chapter 20, in all three cases Mexico argued that the defence arises from CIL.[49] We will analyse both types and how they fit into Chapter 11.

(i) Countermeasures under CIL

All tribunals dealt with the question of whether a state can raise this defence for breach of its NAFTA Chapter 11 obligations. The tribunal in *ADM v Mexico* found that, although not explicitly provided in Chapter 11, countermeasures are available by incorporation from CIL. It opined that, since Chapter 11 did not specifically prohibit the use of countermeasures, the question about the availability of such a defence was a question of CIL.[50]

Although the tribunals in *Corn Products v Mexico* and *Cargill v Mexico* did not explicitly mention their position regarding the availability of this defence under Chapter 11, they strongly believed that countermeasures could not be applied under Chapter 11 to preclude wrongfulness.[51] In *Corn Products v Mexico*, the tribunal opined that 'there is no room for a defence based upon the alleged wrongdoing not of the claimant but of its State of nationality, which is not a party to the proceedings'.[52] It supported this argument with lengthy discussion regarding the nature of the rights and obligations which arise under Chapter 11, as discussed further below. The tribunal in *Cargill v Mexico* took this approach and decided similarly.[53]

The *Corn Products* and *Cargill* tribunals' analyses lead us to an assessment of the rights under NAFTA Chapter 11. This is particularly important because, under the ILC Articles, it is recognized that countermeasures may not preclude wrongfulness against third parties, especially if they have individual rights.[54] However, the term 'individual rights' was not defined further.

In *ADM v Mexico*, this issue was addressed in one of the requirements for legitimate countermeasures, namely non-impairment of individual substantive rights of claimants. Although claimed to be derived from CIL,[55] the require-

[49] *ADM v Mexico* (n 3 above), [110]; *Cargill v Mexico* (n 3 above), [379]; *Corn Products v Mexico* (n 3 above), [158].

[50] *ADM v Mexico* (n 3 above), [120].

[51] *Corn Products v Mexico* (n 3 above), [191]; *Cargill v Mexico* (n 3 above), [430].

[52] *Corn Products v Mexico* (n 3 above), [161].

[53] *Cargill v Mexico* (n 3 above), [422]–[429].

[54] ILC Articles and Commentary (n 1 above), Art 49.

[55] *ADM v Mexico* (n 3 above), [133].

ment is not present in either *Gabčíkovo-Nagymaros* or the ILC Articles.[56] The tribunal examined whether NAFTA Chapter 11 provides a self-contained mechanism endorsing substantive and procedural rights for qualified investors, and whether such rights are independent from the rights of the NAFTA member states.[57]

For this evaluation, the tribunal considered three theories: (i) the traditional derivative theory—'when investors trigger arbitration proceedings against a State, they are in reality stepping into the shoes and asserting the rights of their home State'; (ii) an intermediate theory—'investors are vested only with an exceptional procedural right to claim state responsibility under Section B before an international arbitral tribunal';[58] and (iii) a direct theory—'investors ... are vested with direct independent rights and that they are immune from the legal relationship between the member States'.[59]

The tribunal adopted the intermediate theory,[60] and Mexico supported this by citing NAFTA jurisprudence, scholarly writings and the position of the member states in their intervention in other NAFTA Chapter 11 proceedings.[61] Specifically, the tribunal in *Loewen Group, Inc & Raymond v United States of America*[62] opined that Chapter 11 provides what in origin are the rights of the member states regarding the treatment of their national's investment. The specific words of the tribunal were: 'claimants are permitted for convenience to enforce what are in origin the rights of Party states'.[63]

The intermediate theory was viewed as one that respected the traditional structure of international law and the object and purpose of Chapter 11.[64] The tribunal viewed Section A of Chapter 11 as substantive obligations which were inter-state instead of accruing individual rights.[65] It opined that the proper interpretation of the NAFTA would not lead to an approach where investors are granted individual rights. It distinguished the structure of NAFTA Chapter 11 and human rights treaties.[66] The former only granted a procedural right of action under Section B of Chapter 11—which would not otherwise exist under international law— and simply complemented the promotion and protection of aliens under CIL.[67] With this theory, since individuals do not have rights

[56] Ibid, [126].
[57] Ibid, [161].
[58] Ibid, [163].
[59] Ibid, [166].
[60] Ibid, [171].
[61] Ibid, [167].
[62] *Loewen Group, Inc & Raymond v United States of America* [2003] ICSID Case No ARB (AF)/98/3, Award.
[63] Ibid, [233].
[64] *ADM v Mexico* (n 3 above), [168].
[65] Ibid, [168].
[66] See also A Gourgourinis, '"Investors" rights *qua* Human Rights? Revisiting the "Direct"/"Derivative" Rights Debate' in M Fitzmaurice and P Merkouris (eds), *The Interpretation and Application of the European Convention of Human Rights: Legal and Practical Implications* (Martinus Nijhoff Publishers, 2013) 147–82.
[67] Ibid, [171], [173]–[174].

under NAFTA, the defence of countermeasures may preclude wrongfulness of violations under Chapter 11.

In *Corn Products v Mexico*, a different analysis emerged. Citing the commentary to Article 49 of the ILC Articles, the tribunal highlighted that countermeasures cannot affect the rights of a party other than the state responsible for the prior breach.[68] The tribunal found that, under Chapter 11, an investor has rights of its own, distinct from those of the state of its nationality.[69] The tribunal also found that the conferral of procedural rights on investors in Chapter 11 implies the parties' intention to also confer substantive rights. Otherwise, a procedural right to institute proceedings to enforce rights which were not theirs would be counterintuitive.[70]

The tribunal opined that the fiction in the notion of diplomatic protection did not need to continue because in investor-state arbitration the state of nationality did not control the conduct of the case, nor received any payment of compensation.[71] It cited *Republic of Ecuador v Occidental Exploration and Production Co*, whereby the Court of Appeal for England and Wales found that investors under both the NAFTA and bilateral investment treaties were asserting rights of their own rather than exercising a mere procedural power to enforce the rights of their state.[72]

The tribunal in *Cargill v Mexico* also believed that it would be a fiction to say that investors' rights under NAFTA Chapter 11 are the rights of the state.[73] The tribunal agreed that the rights of investors under Chapter 11 were derived from the agreement of the state parties, and may be dependent on the continuation of that agreement. However, it drew an analogy to the origin of the rights of individuals within a municipal legal system that may be found in the act of a soverign but did not negate the existence of such rights. Further, the tribunal refused the classification of procedural and substantive rights. For the tribunal, what matters is the fact that the investor institutes the claim, calls a tribunal into existence, and is the named a party in the proceedings and award.[74]

[68] *Corn Products v Mexico* (n 3 above), [164].
[69] Ibid, [165].
[70] Ibid, [169].
[71] Ibid, [173].
[72] Ibid, fn 72, citing *Republic of Ecuador v Occidental Exploration and Production Co* [2005] EWCA Civ 1116, [2006] QB 432 (*Occidental v Ecuador*), [14.22]; see also M Paparinskis, 'Investment Treaty Arbitration and the (New) Law of State Responsibility' (2013) 24(2) *European Journal of International Law* 617; TR Braun, 'Globalization-driven Innovation: The Investor as a Partial Subject in Public International Law—An Inquiry into the Nature and Limits of Investor Rights', Jean Monnet Working Paper Series 04/13 (2013) 26.
[73] *Cargill v Mexico* (n 3 above), [386].
[74] Ibid, [426].

(ii) Countermeasures under NAFTA Chapter 20

Article 31(1) of the Vienna Convention on the Law of Treaties 1969 (VCLT)[75] clearly obliges tribunals who are interpreting a treaty to look at the context of the treaty. The context of Chapter 11, in the broader sense, also includes the general framework of the NAFTA as a free trade agreement (FTA) providing the right to countermeasures under Article 2019 NAFTA. This context was raised by the claimants and Mexico in both *ADM v Mexico* and *Cargill v Mexico*.

In *ADM v Mexico*, the claimants argued that the right to countermeasures under CIL for violations of NAFTA provisions had been waived by the NAFTA parties because the NAFTA was *lex specialis*.[76] The NAFTA regulates the existence of an internationally wrongful act under the FTA and its legal consequences, as well as its own dispute settlement mechanism under NAFTA Chapters 19 and 20.[77]

NAFTA Chapter 20 provides that countermeasures can be taken only in a situation of non-compliance with a decision rendered in a Chapter 20 state-to-state arbitration,[78] and in this case such a decision did not exist.[79] Mexico responded to the claimants' arguments by stating that a party 'cannot be bound by a *lex specialis* that has proved impossible to invoke',[80] referring to the refusal of the US to cooperate in the composition of a panel. This position arguably has its legal basis in Article 52(4) of the ILC Articles, which provides that the *lex specialis* rule (pending dispute before a tribunal) does not apply if the breaching state failed to implement the dispute settlement procedures in good faith, ie the US's refusal to provide a roster of panelists to establish a Chapter 20 panel.

Unfortunately, this argument was never addressed by the tribunal in *ADM v Mexico*. Instead, it dismissed the *lex specialis* argument[81] and ruled that CIL should continue to govern all matters not covered by Chapter 11, including countermeasures.[82]

In *Cargill v Mexico,* Mexico raised this concern when the tribunal assessed the nature of the rights of investors under Chapter 11. Mexico challenged the tribunal's belief that investors had rights[83] by arguing that such conception would undermine Article 2019 of the NAFTA, which allows a party to take

[75] 1969 Vienna Convention on the Law of Treaties, UN Doc A/Conf.39/27/1155 UNTS 331/8 ILM 679, entered into force on 27 January 1980.

[76] ILC Articles and Commentary (n 1 above), Art 51.

[77] *ADM v Mexico* (n 3 above), [113]–[114]; *Cargill v Mexico* (n 3 above), [395]–[396].

[78] This was also acknowledged by the tribunal in *ADM v Mexico* (n 3 above), [122], but it considered that the default regime under CIL applied to the situation in the case (presumably the tribunal referred to Chapter 11).

[79] Ibid, [115].

[80] Ibid; *Cargill v Mexico* (n 3 above), [397], [400]–[401].

[81] Ibid, [117].

[82] Ibid, [119].

[83] *Cargill v Mexico* (n 3 above), [426].

countermeasures, and in general could constrain states' basic rights under international law and endow investors with greater rights than states.[84] The tribunal noted Mexico's argument, but opined that it could be addressed by the fact that there is always a range of possible countermeasures to be adopted that may not affect investors[85] without considering the reality where GVCs have become a norm, thus any trade countermeasures could affect investors.

NAFTA Article 1115 provides, '*[w]ithout prejudice to the rights and obligations of the Parties under Chapter Twenty* (Institutional Arrangements and Dispute Settlement Procedures), this Section establishes a mechanism for the settlement of investment disputes' (emphasis added). NAFTA Article 1112 also provides that, in the case of inconsistency between Chapter 11 with another NAFTA chapter, the other chapter shall prevail. If these were taken into account, it would be clear that states' rights to take countermeasures under Chapter 20 will prevail over its obligations under Chapter 11. Otherwise, there would be ongoing tension in the agreement itself. If legitimate trade countermeasures under the NAFTA could preclude wrongfulness under Chapter 11, logically, other trade countermeasures incorporated by CIL should have the same effect, at least under the NAFTA framework.

V. RESOLVING THE TENSION ON COUNTERMEASURES BETWEEN TRADE AND INVESTMENT LAW

Of all issues addressed by the investment tribunals above, the biggest issue is whether defence of countermeasures is available under NAFTA Chapter 11. Absent the defence, WTO members may not be able to take legitimate trade countermeasures that impact investors. This section proposes several ways to resolve the tension between the two regimes.

A. Revisiting the Nature of Individual Rights in International Investment Law

In the past, the right of the individual under international law is enforced through the doctrine of diplomatic protection. Under this doctrine, an injury to an individual by a foreign state is actionable by the individual's state of nationality.[86] In diplomatic protection, Vattel opined that the rights and obligations of the protection of citizens were state rights, not individual rights.[87]

[84] Ibid, [391]–[392].

[85] Ibid, [428].

[86] K Parlett, *The Individual in the International Legal System* (Cambridge University Press 2011) 47.

[87] E de Vattel (edited by B Kapossy and R Whatmore), *The Law of Nations or, Principles of the Law of Nature Applied to the Conduct and Affairs of Nations and Sovereigns* (first published in 1758; Liberty Fund, 2008), bk II, ch VI, 298, [71].

In the nineteenth and early twentieth centuries, various arbitrations had taken place relating to disputes over claims relating to the imposition of excessive customs duties,[88] treatment of nationals (arrest or imprisonment),[89] expropriation of property[90] and breach of contract by a state.[91] The procedures used in these arbitrations suggested that the claims were inter-state claims.[92] The state of nationality had control over the claims throughout the whole procedure,[93] was entitled to receiving payment of the awards[94] and received legally binding decisions on an inter-state basis.[95] The exception at that time was the Central American Court of Justice, which gave individuals exclusive control of claims.[96] Even so, the court did not treat the individuals as having any direct rights from international law, but merely a procedural right.[97]

The Permanent Court of International Justice (PCIJ) affirmed the doctrine of diplomatic protection in the *Mavrommatis* case as a right of a state to ensure respect for the rules of international law.[98] Furthermore, in *Chorzów Factory*, the PCIJ indirectly affirmed that in a diplomatic protection claim the rights at issue are states' rights, not individual rights.[99]

After 1945, in *Interhandel*, the ICJ affirmed the doctrine of diplomatic protection as expounded by the PCIJ in *Mavrommatis*. The ICJ mentioned that the state had 'adopted the cause of its national' whose rights had been violated.[100] In this sense, there was recognition for the right of the individual over his/her property under national law. This was made clearer in *La Grand*, when the ICJ proclaimed that individuals can have rights created by international treaties if the state parties intended to confer it, as could be indicated in the text of the treaty.[101] This is again confirmed in *Avena v Mexico*,[102] where the court found that Article 36(1) of the Vienna Convention on Con-

[88] *Great Britain–France* [1842] in A de Clerq (ed), *Recueil des Traités de la International Arbitrations*, vol V, 4936; *Great Britain–Portugal* [1842] in ibid, 4979.

[89] *Great Britain–Peru* [1864] in JB Moore, *History and Digest of the International Arbitrations to which the United States has been a Party*, vol v (Government Printing Office, 1898) 4967; *Spain–US* [1870] in ibid, vol II, 1007; *Great Britain–Colombia* [1872] in ibid, vol II, 2050.

[90] *Great Britain–Russia* [1902] IX UNRIAA 51.

[91] *US–Paraguay* [1859] in Moore (n 89 above), vol II) 1485; *Great Britain–US* [1863] in Moore (n 89 above), vol I) 237.

[92] Parlett (n 86 above), 53.

[93] *US–Great Britain* [1794] Moore (n 89 above), vol I, 271, 277, and 322.

[94] *US–Great Britain* [1853] Moore (n 89 above), vol I, 391, 406.

[95] Parlett (n 86 above), 58–59.

[96] '1907 Convention for the Establishment of a Central American Court of Justice' (1908) 2 *American Journal of International Law* 231, Art 2.

[97] Parlett (n 86 above), 65.

[98] *Mavrommatis Palestine Concessions* [1924] PCIJ, Judgment No 2, PCIJ Reports, Ser A, No 2, 12.

[99] *Chorzow Factory* (n 33 above), 26–28.

[100] *Interhandel (Switzerland v United States)* [1959] ICJ, Preliminary Objections, ICJ Reports 6, 27.

[101] *LaGrand (Germany v United States)* [2001] ICJ, Judgment, ICJ Reports 466, 492–94 [77].

[102] Ibid, 492-4, ¶77; *Avena and other Mexican Nationals (Mexico v United States)* [2004] ICJ, Judgment, ICJ Reports 12, 36 [40].

sular Relations (VCCR) confers rights to individuals. Nevertheless, in neither case did the ICJ opine about the nature of the individual rights, ie whether they were independent or dependent on the state parties.

The advent of the human rights movement and international investment law requires us to rethink what the recognition of individual right means. We argue that 'individual rights' should be unpacked in today's context. Individuals may have a right that is separate from states' rights, arising from contracts with states (including concession contracts), inalienable human rights and constitutional rights. This is clear in both international law and domestic law. Conversely, in the case of investment rights found inside international investment agreements (IIAs), whether bilateral investment treaties (BITs) or investment chapters in FTAs, we suggest that these benefits are connected to the rights of the home states and not severable independent rights.

The classification of either substantive right or procedural right as argued by some of the NAFTA tribunals is not useful in trying to understand the nature of these rights. Rovine, in his concurrence of the *ADM v Mexico* tribunal, specifically mentioned that the ILC Articles 'do not distinguish between procedural rights that may be superseded by countermeasure, and substantive rights that may not'.[103] Instead, in relation to countermeasures, one should assess the nature of individual right as meant in Article 49 of the ILC Articles.

We believe that when referring to 'individual rights', the ILC Articles refer to independent individual rights without attachment to the rights of states, such as inalienable human rights. This is supported by the fact that the ILC Articles clearly foresee this possibility that companies may lose business or even go bankrupt because of certain countermeasures, without necessarily stating that such collateral effects may affect the legitimacy of countermeasures.[104]

When it referred to third parties, it mentioned third states that basically have their own independent rights. Third-party individuals do not always have the same right as states. Except for human rights, third-party individuals have no independent individual rights and only derive those rights from treaties.

Some international agreements may provide that certain individuals may have an access to international tribunals to bring a direct claim against a state.[105] This is evident in some international human rights treaties[106] as well as some IIAs with investor-state dispute settlement (ISDS) clauses. However, we suggest that this access does not mean that the rights are independent. We suggest that individuals may enjoy rights under CIL and treaties, but the rights granted may still be dependent or independent of the state parties, depending on the intention of the states.

[103] *ADM v Mexico*, Concurring Opinion of Arthur W Rovine, Issues of Independent Investor Rights, Diplomatic Protection and Countermeasures (21 November 2007) [4].

[104] ILC Articles and Commentary (n 1 above), 130[5].

[105] Parlett (n 86 above), 47; Harris (n 13 above), 628.

[106] Convention for the Protection of Human Rights and Fundamental Freedoms, signed on 4 November 1950, and its protocols ETS 5, 213 UNTS 221, Art 34.

The reasoning of the tribunal in *Corn Products* and *Cargill* that the direct enforcement mechanism in ISDS provisions indicates the desire of the states to grant independent individual rights to investors, separate from those of the states,[107] appears to make a leap of logic.

First, this reasoning is not supported by customary rules of interpretation. According to Article 31 of the VCLT, in interpreting a treaty, one should look into the ordinary meaning of the text in its context, and in the light of its object and purpose. The ICJ in *Avena* and *La Grand* also ruled that the text of the treaty demonstrates the intention of the parties.[108]

No IIA declares that the rights of the investors are independent of the state parties. Most IIAs provide for the ability of states—the masters of the treaty— to amend[109] or terminate[110] IIAs, and this may suggest that the rights therein are not intended to be independent. Investors are merely beneficiaries of the treaties. It is the right of states to have their citizens protected when investing abroad and their obligation to provide such protection to the citizens of the other parties. The individual rights of investors to be protected as obtained through IIAs remain revocable by the master of treaties, namely the states. The rights are fully dependent on the state parties.[111]Absent the treaty, no such right exists. Simply, the rights are anchored in the investment treaties they stem from.[112]

Even the so-called procedural rights—direct access to international arbitration through an ISDS clause— can be modified. For example, unilateral denunciations of the Convention on the Settlement of Investment Disputes between States and Nationals of Other States by several countries may affect the procedural rights of investors.[113] Treaties can also be amended with the consent of all the parties without the consent of the investor.

Furthermore, this is different from rights arising from concessions contracts entered into between a state and a private investor. In such a contract, both parties have their own respective rights and obligations. Private investors have

[107] Z Douglas, *The International Law of Investment Claims* (Cambridge University Press, 2009) 167–84; Braun (n 72 above), 36–37; AK Bjorklund, 'Private Rights and Public International Law: Why Competition Among International Economic Law Tribunals is Not Working' (2007–08) 59(2) *Hastings Law Journal* 241, 265; *Corn Products* (n 3 above), [173]; *Cargill* (n 3 above), [426]; *Occidental v Ecuador* (n 72 above), [14.22].

[108] *La Grand* (n 101 above), [77]; *Avena* (n 102 above), 40.

[109] VCLT (n 75 above), Arts 39–41.

[110] Ibid, Arts 54–64.

[111] A Newcombe and L Paradell, *Law and Practice of Investment Treaties: Standards of Treatment* (Kluwer Law International, 2009) 511, [10.19].

[112] FG de Cossio, 'Investment Protection Rights: Substantive or Procedural', available at http://208.56.169.136/PDF/arbitraje/Investor%20Rights%20Procedural%20or%20Substantive.pdf, 10.

[113] See also C Screuer, 'Consent to Arbitration' (2005) 2(5) *TDM* 7; C Schreuer, 'Denunciation of the ICSID Convention and Consent to Arbitration' in M Waibel et al (eds), *The Backlash against Investment Arbitration: Perceptions and Reality* (Kluwer Law International, 2010) 353, 358; compare with A Mezgravis and C González, 'Denunciation of the ICSID Convention: Two Problems: One Seen and One Overlooked' (2012) 7 *TDM* 1, 5–10; VCLT (n 75 above), Art 70(1)(b).

rights in the contract and can enforce the contract before tribunals, including arbitration if the terms of the contract provides for such. Only in this case do investors enjoy independent rights, and countermeasures cannot preclude wrongfulness arising thereof.

By finding that the investor has no independent right under IIAs, the tension of legitimate trade countermeasures in investment law may be resolved. The Commentary to Article 22 of the ILC Articles provides that indirect or consequential effects on countermeasures on third parties which do not involve an independent breach of any obligation to those third parties will preclude wrongfulness.[114]

B. Issuance of Joint Interpretation of the Treaty by the State Parties

If decoding the nature of individual right in international investment law fails to solve the tension between trade and investment regimes, and it is still believed that investment treaties confer individual rights, we will need an alternative solution—the issuance of a joint interpretation by state parties.[115] It is incomprehensible that legitimate trade countermeasures, especially ones that have been authorized by the WTO, can be considered illegitimate or even inadmissible before an arbitral tribunal established under either the NAFTA or other IIAs. Allowing such a paradox to continue will restrict states' options of countermeasures, and even discredit the effectiveness of such mechanism to ensure compliance in the WTO DSM.

In the case of NAFTA, this tension can probably be solved by having the NAFTA Free Trade Commission (FTC)[116] issue a binding interpretation of NAFTA Chapter 11 under Article 1131 NAFTA. The FTC can state that 'Nothing in Chapter 11 of the NAFTA may prohibit a Party to take measures in accordance with Article 2019 of the NAFTA or WTO DSU Article 22'. This type of clause may address the issue better because the tribunal needs not to go through the analysis of what constitutes 'individual rights' in Article 49 of the ILC Articles.

Newer IIAs, such as Article 40 of the ASEAN Comprehensive Investment Agreement,[117] also allows a request for a joint interpretation of any provision of the agreement from the member states.[118]

Although most BITs do not have such a mechanism, as mentioned above, Article 31(3)(a) of the VCLT makes it possible for treaty parties to issue a joint interpretation which shall be taken into account by tribunals as highly per-

[114] ILC Articles and Commentary (n 1 above), 75.

[115] See M Ewing-Chow and JJ Losari, 'Which is to be the Master?: Extra-Arbitral Interpretative Procedures for IIAs' (2014) 11(1) *TDM* 1–20.

[116] NAFTA (n 9 above), Art 2001.

[117] 2009 ASEAN Comprehensive Investment Agreement, entered into force on 29 March 2012.

[118] See also Art 15.21 of the 2003 Singapore–United States FTA, 19 USC 3805, entered into force on 1 January 2004.

suasive evidence.[119] Nonetheless, this mechanism still pleads for a question to be answered: which provision should be interpreted to clarify the relationship between trade countermeasures and investment countermeasures? Since no BIT contains a provision on countermeasures, we suggest a joint interpretation on provisions regarding instituting a claim before investor-state arbitration. The joint interpretation may include a clause such as, 'An investor may bring a claim against the breach of this agreement subject to legitimate trade countermeasures'.

This may seem to be an oversimplification of joint interpretation, and we do recognize that if the joint interpretation in effect amends the treaty, it will have to go through a certain procedure, as required by the BIT itself. However, we argue that it does not amend the BIT but merely restates the CIL position on state responsibility.[120]

We also note that an issue may arise as regards the willingness of the treaty parties to issue this type of joint interpretation, especially given that the area of countermeasures remains less clear. Because the question arising from the existing disputes actually raises an important concern for the trade interests of these states, we believe that there is some merit in considering that a joint interpretation will be possible.

C. Write into BITs and IIAs a Clause that Exempts WTO Authorized Countermeasures

An alternative to the creation of a body is to amend IIAs by including a clause that recognizes the right of parties to take countermeasures, specifically legitimate trade countermeasures, such as those authorized by the WTO. This is especially useful for the parties who are members of the WTO or are parties of certain FTAs. The clause could be formulated as follows:

> Nothing in this agreement shall prevent a Contracting Party from taking a trade countermeasure that has been authorized by the Dispute Settlement Body of the World Trade Organization [or the authorized body of the relevant FTA] against the other Contracting Party, despite the fact that the countermeasure may have effects on investments of nationals or companies of the other Contracting Party under this agreement.

There are in fact several BITs which implicitly provide the possibility of raising legitimate trade countermeasures in IIAs. For example, Article 3(5) of the 2002 Thailand—Russia BIT provides:

[119] For further reading see A Roberts, 'Power and Persuasion in Investment Treaty Interpretation: The Dual Role of States' [2010] 104 *American Journal of International Law* 179.

[120] This is especially true in the case of ICSID Arbitration: where the parties to the BIT do not agree on the applicable law, Art 42(1) of the ICSID Convention shall apply, namely international law, including CIL.

> Nothing in this Agreement shall oblige the Contracting Parties to grant to investor and investment of each other the treatment under this Article which is more favourable, than the treatment that they will grant to each other pursuant to the obligations under the Agreement Establishing the World Trade Organization (WTO) of April 15, 1994, including obligations under General Agreement on Trade in Services (GATS) and also under any other multilateral arrangement concerning the treatment of investments which both Contracting Parties are parties to.

We acknowledge that amending an IIA is not simple. Where an IIA does not specify the procedure to amend, Article 39 of the VCLT provides that it can be done by an agreement between the parties. This may not necessarily be difficult to achieve, especially when both treaty parties are members of the WTO, because there is greater interest for their potential future legitimate trade countermeasures to be recognized in the investment regime.

An amendment may need to be made long before any countermeasures are imposed. Otherwise, the party subject to the countermeasures may be reluctant to agree to the amendment, especially when its affected investor has lobbied the government regarding the negative impacts that he or she may suffer. The other difficulty is the requirement to obtain ratification, which will involve the legislative branches of the parties. Where political interest is at play, this is not an easy task.

Alternatively, where the parties cannot agree to amend, state parties may simply terminate the existing treaty and redraft a new treaty. However, this will be subject to the termination clause of each treaty. Even in this situation, consent by both parties is needed in the process, and the ratification process may pose an extreme political challenge to them both.

VI. CONCLUSION

This chapter has highlighted the prominent tension arising between the two regimes of trade and investment law. It is hard to discern that a legitimate trade countermeasure—that has gone through assessment of a dispute settlement body and been authorized— can lead to an investment claim against the state. This issue is in fact becoming very imminent, especially with the number of BITs that have been concluded amongst states during the last 50 years and the increasing number of IIAs and FTAs with investment chapters that have been concluded or are currently being negotiated, coupled with the intrinsically close relationship between the two regimes—not to mention the rising number of GVCs where investors have their operations in various different parts of the world. All these factors demonstrate the high likelihood of a similar case to the sugar war arising in the future.

We note that the central issue in this tension is the nature of rights of individual under IIAs. This is critical to determine whether countermeasures can preclude wrongfulness under the IIAs. It is important to understand the nature of individual rights of third-party individual, as raised by the ILC Articles, and the authors believe that such rights should be independent individual rights. If countermeasures affect the independent third-party individual right, they cannot preclude wrongfulness.

In order to understand the nature of rights of investors in IIAs, we should interpret the IIAs based on its plain reading, object and purpose, as well as its context, including its general framework (in the case of FTAs) and general international law those are applicable to the agreements at the same time, and how it relates to other agreements. Even though textual reading of some IIAs may imply that they confer rights to investors, in reality the rights are not independent from the state parties. This is clearly shown from the fact that state parties may revoke the treaty, thereby no rights of investors are left and they cannot even complain regarding such revocation. This is different from individual rights in human right treaties, or even in concession contracts entered by an investor and a state, where the individuals do enjoy independent rights.

We have recommended several ways to resolve the tension, including by 1) revisiting at our understanding of the nature of rights of individuals; 2) issuance of joint interpretation by state parties, and 3) amendment of investment agreements. The first suggestion may depend on an appropriate investment tribunal being given a relevant case. There is no guarantee that the relevant tribunals will adopt such a theory and interpretation method. Meanwhile the second and third suggestions will require further actions by state parties of IIAs, each requiring different political actions and may have their own difficulties. However, once taken, these two ways can ensure that if such tensions will arise exist in the future cases, that international investment law will respect legitimate trade countermeasures.

28

Duplicating the Trade Law 'Spaghetti Bowl'? Increasing Regionalization and Overlap of Investment Treaties—a Review of State Practice

WOLFGANG ALSCHNER*

I. INTRODUCTION

INVESTMENT LAW IS currently experiencing a turn towards regionalization.[1] While the annual numbers of newly concluded bilateral investment treaties (BITs) have recently dropped to pre-1990 levels, states are increasingly signing regional treaties to protect foreign investment.[2] About every fourth international investment agreement (IIA) negotiated in 2012 was a regional one.[3] These treaties take the form of comprehensive economic partnership agreements like North American Free Trade Agreement (1992) (NAFTA), which combine trade liberalization with investment protection (abbreviated here as preferential trade and investment agreements (PTIAs)) or may be concluded as self-standing investment treaties, such as the trilateral investment treaty between China, Japan and South Korea (2012). Well-known regional integration efforts, like the ASEAN Comprehensive Investment Agreement (2009) or ongoing inter-regional negotiations, such as the Transpacific

* Graduate Institute of International and Development Studies, Geneva, Switzerland. This chapter was inspired by the preparatory work to UNCTAD's *World Investment Report* 2013. The views expressed in this chapter are those of the author alone.

[1] H El-Kady, 'An International Investment Policy Landscape in Transition: Challenges and Opportunities' (2013) 10 *TDM*; W Alschner, 'Regionalism and Overlap in Investment Treaty Law: Towards Consolidation or Contradiction?' (2014) 17 *Journal of International Economic Law* 271.

[2] UNCTAD, *World Investment Report 2013: Global Value Chains: Investment and Trade for Development* (United Nations, 2013) 101.

[3] Ibid.

Partnership (TPP), are further cases in point. Accordingly, UNCTAD concludes that 'the balance is gradually shifting from bilateral to regional treaty making'.[4]

The regionalization of investment treaty law poses both threats and opportunities, as recognized by UNCTAD in the 2013 edition of its *World Investment Report*. On the one hand, regionalism presents an opportunity to consolidate investment treaties and reduce the field's complexities. 'With thousands of treaties, many on-going negotiations and multiple dispute-settlement mechanisms, today's IIA regime has come close to a point where it is too big and complex to handle for governments and investors alike.'[5] Regionalization could remedy some of these challenges by replacing several BITs with one regional IIA.[6] On the other hand, regionalism may also exacerbate existing problems, 'leading to a multiplication of treaty layers, making the network of international investment obligations even more complex and prone to overlap and inconsistency'.[7] Based on a small sample of agreements reviewed, UNCTAD concludes that regionalism is currently geared towards adding to rather than replacing existing investment treaties.

Taking UNCTAD's work a step further, this chapter reviews a wider array of state practice in order to determine whether the regionalization of IIAs leads to a consolidation or a parallelism of treaty layers. It finds first that approaches towards regionalization differ. Some countries use regionalism to consolidate their treaty networks, while others add a parallel layer of investment protection. These strategies differ not only between states, but also within one country's treaty network. Confirming UNCTAD's research, most countries tend to use regionalism for creating parallel treaty layers rather than to consolidate their treaty networks, resulting in increased overlap, complexity and fragmentation. However, regionalism may still lead to a significant consolidation of IIAs. If the EU Commission is successful with its current strategy of phasing out intra-EU BITs (BITs between two EU members) and a replacement of extra-EU BITs (BITs between an EU member and a third country) with EU-led IIAs, then we will observe a drastic consolidation of the number of BITs, potentially reducing their numbers by half.

Secondly, the trend towards parallel treaty layers may be a result of both rational choice and bounded rationality. On the one hand, treaty parallelism may be a rational choice as some countries sign regional treaties to set a minimum standard of investment protection, which they further deepen or broaden in existing or future bilateral treaties. In these cases, consolidation is undesirable and parallelism and differentiation are necessary evils to achieve

[4] UNCTAD, *World Investment Report 2012: Towards a New Generation of Investment Policies* (United Nations, 2012) 86.

[5] UNCTAD, *World Investment Report 2011: Non-Equity Modes of International Production and Development* (United Nations, 2011) xvii.

[6] UNCTAD, *World Investment Report 2013* (n 2 above), 107.

[7] Ibid, 105.

policy objectives specific to a particular governance level. On the other hand, some parallelism may result from bounded rationality, as countries underestimate the costs and overestimate the benefits of overlapping treaty layers. In light of the latter, there may be further room for consolidation where there is no rational justification for parallel treaty layers.

Thirdly, although treaty overlap entails a number of risks, such as parallel proceedings and inconsistent treaties, consolidation is not the only policy response available. International trade law demonstrates that overlapping layers of treaties can co-exist without undermining one another. Countries continue to engage in multilateral rule-making and dispute settlement at the WTO, complementing regional integration efforts. Hence, parallelism is not a problem per se as long as the ensuing spaghetti bowl of overlapping agreement is properly managed.

II. ACCOMMODATING REGIONALISM: AN OVERVIEW OF STATE PRACTICE

Countries around the world have signed close to 2900 BITs to attract and protect foreign investment.[8] The recent proliferation in regional investment adds another treaty layer to this existing network of BITs. The question arises how countries accommodate this turn towards regionalism. Does regionalism lead to a consolidation or multiplication of treaty layers? This section illustratively reviews, region-by-region, how states have responded to existing or foreseeable treaty overlaps arising from the current trend towards regionalism. Given the myriad of regional integration initiatives, this account cannot be comprehensive; instead, it focuses on the countries that have been most active in recent regional investment treaty-making.

A. Africa

The largest regional investment treaty in Africa is the COMESA Common Investment Area (CCIA), which was signed in 2007 and spans all the way from Egypt to Swaziland along the East African coast, comprising 19 member countries. It overlaps with 24 BITs concluded among its member states. CCIA Article 32 partly addresses this overlap with BITs. It affirms the rights and obligations under existing BITs (paragraph 1) and allows members to conclude new BITs that conform to the principles, objective and terms of the CCIA (paragraph 2). In addition, Article 32 mandates that the terms of the CCIA prevail over such new (but not existing!) BITs in case of any inconsistency. Put differently, existing BITs are left unregulated by the CCIA.

[8] UNCTAD, *World Investment Report 2013* (n 2 above), 101.

The other large African integration project, the Southern African Development Community (SADC), passed a Protocol on Finance and Investment in 2005 the investment provisions of which also overlap with 16 existing BITs. Article 26 of the Protocol affirms the right of members to conclude BITs with third countries but is silent on the issue of existing agreements among its members. Silence is an anomaly among the reviewed agreements.

Aside from overlapping BITs and PTIAs, Africa is particularly prone to overlap among competing regional investment treaties as many states are members to intersecting regional groupings. In Northern Africa, Arab countries, such as Egypt, Libya and Sudan, are members of both the Unified Agreement for the Investment of Arab Capital and COMESA. In Southern Africa, countries such as Mauritius, Malawi, Seychelles and Zambia are members of both COMESA and SADC. The latter two treaties differ in their integration depth. A Mauritian company can, for instance, sue Mauritius for a failure to comply with the COMESA treaty, but not for a failure to live up to its SADC obligation.[9]

B. Middle East and Central Asia

Another area where regionalism has a long history is the Middle East.[10] The Unified Agreement for the Investment of Arab Capital in the Arab States was concluded in 1980 under the umbrella of the Arab League. Since then, overlaps have arisen with subsequent BITs, eg the Kuwait–Egypt BIT (2001), and may, at some point, arise with sub-regional integration projects like the Gulf Cooperation Council, which has yet to pass a long-envisaged common investment protection code.[11] The purpose of the Unified Agreement, as stated in the preamble and Article 3, is to set a regional 'minimum standard', allowing countries to go beyond it in investments laws or bilateral agreements. Hence, Arab countries openly endorse the possibility of parallelism. Nevertheless, by setting up the Arab Investment Court, which Arab countries can refer to for their investment dispute settlement also under bilateral agreements,[12] the Unified Agreement also created an instrument for harmonization and uniform application of overlapping treaties. The Unified Agreement is currently under revision. A new draft text was adopted in 2013.[13]

[9] G Erasmus, 'The COMESA Court of Justice: Regional Agreements Do Protect Private Parties', Trade Brief (tralac, 2013).

[10] See generally H El-Kady, 'The Proliferation of International Trade and Investment Arrangements in the Arab World: Key Issues and Challenges' (2006) 3 *African Technology Development Forum Journal* 48.

[11] MR Hassanien, *United States Bilateral Free Trade Agreements: consistencies Or Conflicts with Norms in the Middle East?* (Kluwer Law International, 2010) 85.

[12] Art 30 of the Unified Agreement; see also W Ben Hamida, 'First Arab Investment Court Decision, The' (2006) 7 *Journal of World Investment & Trade* 699, 709–10.

[13] UNCTAD, *World Investment Report 2013* (n 2 above), 105.

Overlap is also present in Central Asia, where different economic integration projects intersect. Kazakhstan, Kyrgyzstan, Tajikistan and Uzbekistan are party to both the Economic Cooperation Organization and the Eurasian Economic Community. In addition, some BITs and PTIA also connect individual countries in the region, increasing treaty overlap further.[14] The case of Central Asia also shows that overlap does not necessarily translate into deeper economic integration. While bilateral relationships in the region are governed by, at times, as many as five overlapping free trade agreements, the depths of these agreements remain shallow.[15]

C. South and East Asia

Investment treaty-making in South East Asia has followed a peculiar path. While in the rest of the world BITs predate the move towards regionalism, in South East Asia regionalism predated BITs. ASEAN was created in 1967 to sooth political tensions between its original members (Indonesia, Malaysia, Philippines, Singapore and Thailand). Starting in the late 1970s, ASEAN developed a more pronounced orientation towards economic integration and in 1987, three years after Brunei had joined the organization, the first regional investment treaty was signed.[16] In the 1990s, Cambodia, Lao, Vietnam and Myanmar joined the organization and, in 1998, a new Framework Agreement on the ASEAN Investment Area was concluded which contained an action plan to enhance investment protection and liberalization in the region. Investment integration efforts culminated in 2009 with the conclusion of the ASEAN Comprehensive Investment Agreement (ACIA), which entered into force in 2013.[17]

Catching up with the law-making at the regional level, ASEAN member countries began to conclude bilateral investment treaties among themselves, starting in 1990. Today, the ACIA overlaps with 26 BITs of ASEAN member states. Fourteen of these were concluded with Cambodia, Lao, Vietnam and Myanmar before they joined the organization. Of the remaining 12, only four

[14] For instance, Kyrgyzstan–Uzbekistan and Turkmenistan–Uzbekistan have also signed BITs among themselves.

[15] J Pauwelyn and W Alschner, 'Forget about the WTO: The Network of Relations between Preferential Trade Agreements (PTAs) and "Double PTAs"' in A Dür and M Elsig (eds), *Trade Cooperation—The Purpose, Design and Effects of Preferential Trade Agreements* (Cambridge University Press, 2015).

[16] Agreement among the Government of Brunei Darussalam, the Republic of Indonesia, Malaysia, the Republic of the Philippines, the Republic of Singapore and the Kingdom of Thailand for the Promotion and Protection of Investments Manila, 15 December 1987, available at http://www.asean.org/news/item/agreement-among-the-government-of-brunei-darussalam-the-republic-of-indonesia-malaysia-the-republic-of-the-philippines-the-republic-of-singapore-and-the-kingdom-of-thailand-for-the-promotion-and-protection-of-investments-manila-15-december-1987-2 (last accessed on 19 August 2013).

[17] For an account of ASEAN's investment policy developments see http://www.asean.org/communities/asean-economic-community/category/asean-investment-area-aia-council (last accessed on 19 August 2013).

have entered into force.[18] Even though the parallelism between regional and bilateral treaties developed organically, the ASEAN members did make a conscious choice to leave these treaties in place at the conclusion of the ACIA. In Article 44, the ACIA provides that 'Nothing in this Agreement shall derogate from the existing rights and obligations of a Member State under any other international agreements to which it is a party'.

A similar acceptance of overlapping treaties was also adopted in the treaty practice of ASEAN and its members with third countries in the region (also known as ASEAN+), resulting in what is also referred to as Asia's noodle bowl.[19] ASEAN is party to three free trade agreements (FTAs) with comprehensive investment chapters or side-agreements in East and South-East Asia: the ASEAN–China FTA, the ASEAN–Korea FTA (AKFTA) and the ASEAN–Australia–New Zealand Free Trade Area (AANZFTA).[20] These three agreements overlap with 21 BITs concluded by ASEAN member states and also exist in parallel to eight PTIAs concluded individually by ASEAN members.

Two types of references to existing overlapping agreements are found in these three ASEAN+ treaties that are largely similar, yet differ in one important aspect. Whereas, the ASEAN–China Investment Agreement in Article 23 affirms the continued validity of 'rights and obligations of a Party under any other international agreements to which it is a party', AKFTA (Article 23(1)) and AANZFTA (Chapter 18, Article 2(2)) only reaffirm existing rights and obligations arising from 'agreements to which the Parties are party'. Depending on the interpretation adopted, this may be a distinction without a difference or a conscious effort to affirm only the superiority of agreements to which all the contracting parties are party (eg the WTO Agreement). In any event, the two latter agreements contain more explicit overlap clauses. AKFTA (Article 23(2)) provides that existing and future investment obligations that are more favourable to an investor shall remain unaffected by the agreement. Concerning future treaties, AANZFTA explicitly allows parallelism. Article 2(4) in Chapter 18 states that

> [n]othing in this Agreement shall prevent any individual ASEAN Member State from entering into any agreement with any one or more ASEAN Member State and/or Australia and/or New Zealand relating to trade in goods, trade in services, investment, and/or other areas of economic cooperation.

Hence, all ASEAN+ agreements endorse the parallel existence of bilateral treaties, but differ in the way that overlap is addressed.

[18] These four agreements are the Indonesia–Thailand BIT (1998), Indonesia–Singapore BIT (2005), Indonesia–Malaysia BIT (1994) and Philippines–Thailand BIT (1995).

[19] 'The Noodle Bowl: Why Trade Agreements Are All the Rage in Asia', *The Economist*, 3 September 2009, available at http://www.economist.com/node/14384384 (last accessed on 19 August 2013).

[20] The ASEAN–Japan FTA (2003) only contains a negotiation mandate for investment provisions. Negotiations on an investment agreement to supplement the ASEAN–India FTA (2009) were reportedly concluded in December 2012, but no agreement has been signed yet.

How complicated overlap practice can be in South East Asia is perhaps best illustrated by the investment relationship between China and Singapore, which is governed by three overlapping agreements. The China–Singapore FTA incorporates, *mutatis mutandis*, the ASEAN–China FTA investment provisions. At the same time, it does not mention the China–Singapore BIT, which was signed in 1985 and is still in force.[21] In sum, ASEAN members and their treaty partners seem to generally endorse the existence of parallel treaties by reaffirming the continued validity of existing agreements in various ways.

Apart from the ASEAN-led developments, further regional investment law-making has occurred between China, Japan and South Korea. In May 2012 the three countries signed a trilateral investment agreement, which overlaps with three BITs currently in force among them. The agreement is probably the most explicit and forceful example of states choosing parallelism rather than a phasing out of their existing BITs. Article 25 reaffirms existing BITs and clarifies that

> [i]t is confirmed that, when an issue arises between an investor of a Contracting Party and another Contracting Party, nothing in this Agreement shall be construed so as to prevent the investor from relying on the bilateral investment agreement between those two Contracting Parties which is considered by the investor to be more favorable than this Agreement.

This clarification sheds light on one of the policy reasons behind parallelism: to offer the maximum of protection to foreign investors.

The challenges of overlapping treaties in South East Asia are likely to increase further in light of ongoing negotiations. In November 2012, negotiations began on a Regional Comprehensive Economic Partnership Agreement (RCEP) involving ASEAN, Australia, China, India, Japan, New Zealand and South Korea.[22] Similarly, the inter-regionally negotiated TPP will also overlap with existing ASEAN treaties and BITs. If the current practice of duplication continues, the RCEP and the TPP would add a third and even a fourth layer of investment disciplines to the region.

D. Americas

In North America, regionalization began in 1988, when Canada and the US signed an FTA, which included a rudimentary investment chapter. This agreement was superseded four years later when Mexico, Canada and the US

[21] The China–Singapore FTA merely provides in Art 112: '1. The Parties affirm their existing rights and obligations with respect to each other under existing bilateral and multilateral agreements to which both Parties are parties, including the WTO Agreement. 2. In the event of any inconsistency between this Agreement and any other agreement to which both Parties are parties, the Parties shall immediately consult with each other with a view to finding a mutually satisfactory solution.'

[22] UNCTAD, *World Investment Report 2013* (n 2 above), 103.

concluded the NAFTA. Interestingly, the Canada–United States FTA seems to have been merely suspended (rather than terminated) by the conclusion of the NAFTA.[23] In contrast to its predecessor, the NAFTA includes a fully-fledged investment chapter (Chapter 11) with investor-state dispute settlement. Subsequently, investment treaty regionalism spread to South and Central America. In 1994, the Mercosur countries signed the Protocol of Colonia and the Protocol of Buenos Aires. However, since these two agreements never entered into force, the degree of regional investment integration in South America has remained limited. Chile and Peru have individually concluded several PTIAs with countries around the region. Especially for Chile, this has resulted in a number of overlaps with prior BITs. The Chile–Peru FTA (2006), for example, overlaps with a prior BIT (2000), with the former prevailing over the BIT to the extent of any inconsistency.[24] In contrast, Chile has refrained from including investment standards in some of its other PTAs, like the Chile–Panama FTA (2006), which instead refers to an existing BIT.[25] One may wonder whether these two very different approaches adopted by Chile in the same year are the result of a careful strategy of differentiation vis-à-vis its treaty partners or occurred more haphazardly.

The same is not true for Central America. There, starting in the late 1990s, Costa Rica, Nicaragua, El Salvador, Guatemala and Honduras (together as Central America, or only the latter three as the Northern Triangle) began to conclude PTIAs with other countries of Latin America, such as the Dominican Republic, Panama, Mexico and Colombia, but also with the United States. Since Central American countries had been less active in prior investment treaty-making, the overlap with BITs and existing PTIAs ensuing from this regionalization was rather limited. Where it occurred, however, it was addressed in very different ways. In the case of the Dominican Republic–Central American FTA (DR–CAFTA), overlap with bilateral treaties was dealt with like in the ASEAN context, by affirming existing obligations.[26] In contrast, the recently concluded Central America–Mexico FTA took a different route and terminated pre-existing, bilateral FTAs rather than opting for parallel treaties.[27] The latter agreement is a prime example of states using regionalization to consolidate existing treaties and to start their investment relations on a clean slate.

Other regional developments are also noteworthy. The Caribbean Community is a regional grouping of 15 island states. While the organization

[23] NAFTA itself does not contain a clause formally terminating the prior FTA. The US implementation legislations considered the Canada–US Trade Agreement as being merely suspended: see s 107 of the North American Free Trade Agreement Implementation Act, 8 December 1993, HR 3450 (103rd), available at www.gpo.gov/fdsys/pkg/BILLS-103hr3450enr/pdf/BILLS-103hr3450enr.pdf (last accessed 28 September 2014).

[24] See Art 19.2 of the Chile–Peru FTA (2006).

[25] See ch 9 of the Chile–Panama FTA (2006) referring to the Chile–Panama BIT (1996).

[26] See Art 1.3, CAFTA–DR (2004).

[27] See Art 21.7, Central America–Mexico FTA (2011).

signed a PTIA with Costa Rica in 2004, no overlap with existing BITs could be identified. Finally, Chile, Costa Rica, Colombia, Mexico and Peru have signed a framework agreement setting up the Pacific Alliance, which will eventually encompass an investment protection treaty.[28] It remains to be seen how the Pacific Alliance will deal with existing investment agreements among its members.

E. Europe

Regionalism and overlap are also on the rise in Europe. Not only does the region host three organizations active in the conclusion of IIAs—the EU, the European Free Trade Association (EFTA) and the Central European Free Trade Agreement (CEFTA)—but it also comprises the largest network of BITs, heightening the potential of treaty overlap. However, the three organizations deal with treaty overlap in very different ways.

Beginning with CEFTA, which today comprises Albania, Bosnia and Herzegovina, Macedonia, Moldova, Montenegro, Serbia and Kosovo, the 2006 CEFTA treaty opts for a coexistence with BITs concluded among its member states. CEFTA Article 30 read together with Annex 6 lists existing BITs and affirms the rights and obligation contained therein.

Moving to EFTA, a number of PTIAs signed by EFTA overlap with BITs concluded between its member states and third countries. The EFTA–Ukraine FTA (2005), which contains an investment chapter, for instance, exists in parallel to the Switzerland–Ukraine BIT (1995).[29] Importantly, however, neither that FTA nor the EFTA–Colombia FTA (2008) contains an investor-state arbitration provision. This diminishes their relevance from the perspective of investors. The latter agreement even goes a step further and insulates itself from the Colombia–Switzerland BIT (2006), which exists in parallel, by providing in Article 5.7 that:

> The provisions of this Chapter shall be without prejudice to the rights and obligations of the Parties under other international agreements, to which Colombia and one or several EFTA States are parties. It is understood that *any dispute settlement mechanism in an investment protection agreement to which Colombia and one EFTA State are parties is not applicable to alleged breaches of this Chapter.* (emphasis added)

In contrast, the EFTA–Singapore FTA (2002) contains a fully fledged investor

[28] See the Pacific Alliance presentation leaflet, available at alianzapacifico.net/wp-content/uploads/2013/07/ABC-ALIANZA-DEL-PACIFICO-PRENSA-INGLES.pdf (last accessed 28 September 2014).

[29] Art 4.1(3) of the EFTA–Ukraine FTA (2005) stipulates: 'The provisions of this Chapter shall be without prejudice to the interpretation or application of the rights and obligations under any other international agreement relating to investment or taxation to which Ukraine and one or several EFTA States are parties.'

state arbitration clause while coexisting with the Singapore–Switzerland BIT (1978), which does not contain an arbitration provision. The Switzerland–Liechtenstein–Iceland–South Korea investment treaty (2005), which has an investor-state arbitration clause, adopts yet a different mechanism to manage the overlap with the Switzerland–South Korea BIT (1971). In Article 27 it states that

> [a]s long as it is in force or remains effective, this Agreement replaces and suspends the 'Agreement between the Government of the Swiss Confederation and the Government of the Republic of Korea concerning the Encouragement and Reciprocal Protection of Investments' of 7 April 1971.

Switzerland has thus adopted a 'belts and suspenders' strategy, making sure that investment protection is secured without risking unpredictable parallelism of treaties. Taken together, we clearly see that EFTA states have taken a proactive step towards managing overlapping treaty layers in a tailor-made and highly sophisticated manner.

Finally, with respect to treaty overlap in the EU context, it is best to distinguish between two categories of parallelism. On the one hand, EU law contains investment protection standards, which overlap with the around 190 BITs signed among EU member states typically before their accession to the EU (intra-EU BITs).[30] On the other hand, EU members have notified 1401 BITs with non-EU countries (extra-EU BITs) to the EU Commission, which may overlap with future EU investment treaties.[31] Both of these existing and potential overlaps are likely to be met with consolidation efforts.

First, with respect to extra-EU BITs, the entry into force of the Lisbon treaty in 2009 marked a shift in the competency over foreign investment policy-making from EU member states to the EU.[32] Since then, the Commission has begun formulating a comprehensive new EU investment policy.[33] IIA nego-

[30] EU Commission, 'Bilateral Investment Treaties between EU Member States (intra-EU BITs)', available at ec.europa.eu/internal_market/capital/analysis/monitoring_activities_and_analysis/index_en.htm (last accessed 28 September 2014).

[31] EU Commission, List of the bilateral investment agreements referred to in Article 4(1) of Regulation (EU) No 1219/2012 of the European Parliament and of the Council establishing transitional arrangements for bilateral investment agreements between Member States and third countries [2013] OJ C131/02; see also 'Getting to Grips with the EU's Approach to BITs', *GAR News*, 8 August 2013, available at http://globalarbitrationreview.com/news/article/31796/getting-grips-eus-approach-bits/?utm_medium=email&utm_source=Law+Business+Research&utm_campaign=2956183_GAR+Briefing&dm_i=1KSF,1RD07,9GPMS6,69TE0,1 (last accessed on 19 August 2013)

[32] See Art 188C(1) of the Treaty of Lisbon (Art 207(1) of the Treaty on the Functioning of the European Union). See also M Burgstaller, 'Investor-State Arbitration in EU International Investment Agreements with Third States' (2012) 39 *Legal Issues of Economic Integration* 207; A Reinisch, 'The Future Shape of EU Investment Agreements' (2013) 28 *ICSID Review* 179.

[33] Communication from the Commission, 'Towards a Comprehensive European International Investment Policy', COM(2010)343 final (Brussels, 7 July 2010), available at trade.ec.europa.eu/doclib/html/147884.htm (last accessed on 19 August 2013). See generally, UNCTAD, *Investment Policy Monitor* No 3, 7 October 2010, 7; UNCTAD, *Investment Policy Monitor* No 5, 5 May 2011, 8–9.

tiations have already been launched with a number of countries, including the United States, Canada, Japan and ASEAN, with more in the pipeline.[34] At the same time, member states will be able to continue signing BITs for a transition period under an interim arrangement.[35] Importantly, however, the regulation setting up this arrangement makes clear that BITs by member states with third countries 'will be progressively replaced by agreements of the Union relating to the same subject matter'.[36] This is a significant development, as EU member BITs with third countries comprise almost half of the BIT universe. The regionalization of EU investment policy-making is thus likely to translate into a consolidation rather than a duplication of existing BIT networks.

Secondly, with respect to intra-EU BITs, the question of overlap is more problematic. Like in the ASEAN case, European countries have signed BITs among themselves prior to their accession to the European Union. Intra-EU BITs involving Central and Eastern European member states are thus particularly common. The legal relationship between EU law and these intra-EU BITs is complex.[37] While both bodies of law seek to protect investment, they do so in very different ways and in varying degrees of specificity, leading tribunals and academic commentators to question whether they govern the 'same subject matter' for the purpose of general international law conflict rules.[38] Nevertheless, it is undisputed that both EU law and investment law may govern the same investment transaction and may be simultaneously applicable in an investment dispute, which gives rise to questions of consistency and fragmentation where the two bodies of law provide for different solutions to the same legal prob-

[34] EU press release, 'The EU's Bilateral Trade and Investment Agreements—Where Are We?', 1 August 2013, available at http://europa.eu/rapid/press-release_MEMO-13-734_en.htm (last accessed on 19 August 2013).

[35] EU press release, 'Q&A: EU Gives Greater Clarity to EU Investment Rules', MEMO/12/977, 12 December 2012, available at http://europa.eu/rapid/press-release_MEMO-12-977_en.htm (last accessed on 19 August 2013). The interim arrangement is based on EU Commission Procedure 2010/0197/COD, 'Proposal for a Regulation of the European Parliament and of the Council Establishing Transitional Arrangements for Bilateral Investment Agreements between Member States and Third Countries', COM(2010)344 final (Brussels, 7 July 2010). The adoption of the proposal was delayed after a close vote in the International Trade Committee and required further parliamentary debate. See European Parliament, 'Resolution on the Future European International Investment Policy', 2010/2203(INI) (6 April 2011), available at www.europarl.europa.eu/sides/getDoc.do?type=TA&language=EN&reference=P7-TA-2011-141 (last accessed on 19 August 2013).

[36] EU Regulation No 1219/2012 of 12 December 2012 establishing transitional arrangements for bilateral investment agreements between Member States and third countries [2012] OJ L351/40, recital 5.

[37] T Eilmansberger, 'Bilateral Investment Treaties and EU Law' (2009) 46 *Common Market Law Review* 383; M Burgstaller, 'European Law and Investment Treaties' (2009) 26 *Journal of International Arbitration* 181; A Reinisch, 'Articles 30 and 59 of the Vienna Convention on the Law of Treaties in Action: The Decisions on Jurisdiction in the *Eastern Sugar* and *Eureko* Investment Arbitrations' (2012) 39 *Legal Issues of Economic Integration* 157; J Kleinheisterkamp, 'Investment Protection and EU Law: The Intra- and Extra-EU Dimension of the Energy Charter Treaty' (2012) 15 *Journal of International Economic Law* 85.

[38] See, eg Eilmansberger (n 37 above), 400.

lem.[39] The European Commission is concerned that these intra-EU BITs (i) challenge the supremacy of EU law, (ii) lead to discrimination between intra-EU investors and a fragmentation of the internal EU capital market, and (iii) undermine the exclusive jurisdiction of the European Court of Justice over EU law.[40] As a result, the Commission has approached EU member states with a view to starting a process of terminating all intra-EU BITs.[41] Since opinions on the utility of leaving intra-EU in place diverge among member states,[42] this process is likely to be cumbersome. If successful, however, the EU is likely to become the new avant-garde in dealing with vertical investment treaty overlap. Not only is the existence and the potential of treaty overlap arguably greatest in numerical terms in the EU context, but the region also features the most targeted efforts to manage this overlap.

F. Inter-regional Treaties

Aside from strictly regional integration efforts, the number of inter-regional treaties is also on the rise. On the one hand, this concerns bilateral PTIAs that connect two countries on different continents, which overlap with existing BITs. Here, state practice is similarly diverse, ranging from an earlier BIT's termination,[43] suspension[44] or incorporation[45] to the parallel existence[46] of BITs and bilateral PTIAs.

On the other hand, plurilateral inter-regional investment agreements also exist or are being negotiated, and these will add yet another layer of treaty protection to bilateral and intra-regional treaties. The two most important existing agreements in this respect are the Energy Charter Treaty and the

[39] Kleinheisterkamp (n 37 above), 89–94, 98–103.

[40] N Lavranos, 'Bilateral Investment Treaty (BITS) and EU Law', SSRN Scholarly Paper ID 1683348 22–25 (Social Science Research Network, 2010), available at http://papers.ssrn.com/abstract=1683348 (accessed on 19 August 2013). See also kluwerarbitrationblog.com/blog/2010/09/28/the-european-commissions-opposition-to-intra-eu-bits-and-its-impact-on-investment-arbitration/$ (last accessed on 19 August 2013).

[41] EU Commissioner Karel De Gucht stated, during a hearing at EU Parliament on 22 May 2013, that: 'The Commission agrees that bilateral and investment treaties (BITS) between EU Member States do not comply with EU law . . . Commission officials have therefore initiated informal discussions with [the EU Member States] with a view to reaching agreement on the joint termination of all these agreements within an agreed time frame. Several Member States have already agreed bilaterally to terminate their agreements, and the Commission has encouraged them to proceed with doing so. However, in those cases where Member States are not willing to terminate agreements, the Commission is ready to play its role as a guardian of the Treaties so as to ensure compliance with EU law.' Available at www.europarl.europa.eu/sides/getDoc.do?pubRef=-//EP//TEXT+CRE+20130522+ITEM-019+DOC+XML+V0//EN (last accessed on 19 August 2013).

[42] Kleinheisterkamp (n 37 above), 99.

[43] Chile–South Korea FTA (2003), Art 21.4, terminating the Chile–South Korea BIT (1996).

[44] Canada–Peru FTA (2008), Art 845, suspending the Canada–Peru BIT (2006). See also Panama–United States FTA (2007), Art 1.3(2) or Morocco–United States FTA (2004), Art 1.2(3).

[45] Japan–Peru FTA (2011), Art 2(3) incorporates the Japan–Peru BIT (2008).

[46] China–Peru FTA (2009) exists parallel to the China–Peru BIT (1994).

Organization of the Islamic Conference (OIC) Investment Agreement. Even though the Energy Charter is by definition limited to the energy sector, its investment protection obligation closely follows the generic language of BITs, giving rise to overlap issues. Interestingly, Article 16 of the Energy Charter treaty regulates this overlap with existing or subsequent investment treaties not by adopting a *lex specialis* approach (giving priority to the more special agreement, eg for energy the Energy Charter) or a *lex posterior* approach (giving priority to the later agreement in time), but by letting the provision which is the most favourable to the investor prevail to the extent of a normative conflict. Rather than being sector-specific, the OIC Agreement is of universal application. It aims to set a minimum standard of protection in OIC states, and in Article 18 allows two or more contracting states to enter into a more preferential agreement.

Apart from these existing inter-regionals treaties, several more high-profile negotiations are ongoing. First, after adopting a statement on 'Shared Principles for International Investment' in April 2012, the EU and US launched negotiations of a Transatlantic Trade and Investment Partnership in 2013. The agreement will replace nine BITs already in force between the US and EU countries.[47] Secondly, negotiations for a TPP are well advanced. Once concluded, the TPP will overlap with at least 47 IIAs.[48] It remains to be seen what overlap arrangement will be chosen. Thirdly, ongoing negotiations in Africa, including among COMESA, SADC and the East African Community, to join their free trade and investment areas are likely to further increase the overlap between different treaty layers in Africa.[49] With these and other initiatives under way, we will see either a new wave of treaty overlap or the significant consolidation of the IIA universe.

G. Conclusion: Towards Consolidation or Fragmentation?

In a prior quantitative study, I found that, on a global scale, 'every fourth investment agreement overlaps with another investment agreement'.[50] The (albeit less comprehensive) qualitative review of state practice in this chapter confirms the widespread occurrence of parallel treaty layers and adds a number of important nuances. First, the way countries deal with treaty overlap arising from regionalization differs starkly between countries. On the one hand, some countries chose to consolidate overlapping treaties either de facto by incorporation or suspension or *de jure* by termination. On the other hand,

[47] This number diverges from UNCTAD, *World Investment Report 2013* (n 2 above), 107 because of the accession of Croatia to the EU in the meantime.

[48] UNCTAD, *World Investment Report 2012* (n 4 above), 85.

[49] For more information see the Tripartite website at www.comesa-eac-sadc-tripartite.org/ (last accessed 16 August 2013).

[50] Alschner (n 1 above), 276.

some countries leave their overlapping treaties in simple coexistence, either by staying silent on the question or by explicitly or implicitly affirming the continued validity of parallel treaty layers. The EU, for example, uses regionalism as an opportunity to consolidate existing treaty networks; in South East Asia, in contrast, regionalization goes hand in hand with an increase in overlap and parallelism.

Secondly, we observe varying approaches in handling overlap also within countries. Chile is a case in point, at times duplicating and at times consolidating its treaty network. Similarly, EFTA states seem to tailor-make their approach to overlap in light of different negotiation partners.

Thirdly, two somewhat opposing trends seem to emerge from this review of state practice. On the one hand, UNCTAD is correct in asserting that regionalization does not translate into an unequivocal move towards the consolidation of IIAs.[51] Countries across the globe opt for parallel treaty layers instead of termination, suspension or incorporation. On the other hand, while the majority of countries favour parallelism, around half of all BITs may nevertheless be consolidated through regionalism if the EU indeed achieves the termination of intra- and extra-EU BITs.

Hence, regionalism may lead to both a significant consolidation of the BIT universe, possibly reducing the number of BITs to half of their number today, and an increasingly complex IIA universe marked by the parallelism of different treaty layers.

III. WHY DO COUNTRIES OPT FOR PARALLEL TREATY LAYERS?

The preference in many countries for coexisting BITs and regional PTIAs is puzzling, because parallel treaty layers pose several risks. First, overlapping treaties are prone to increase contracting states' exposure to investment claims by potentially allowing an investor to challenge a state measure twice under two parallel treaties, opening the doors for double recovery.[52] Indeed, there is a clear incentive on the side of foreign investors to use overlapping investment treaties to their advantage by exploiting the opportunities of parallel arbitration claims or access to more favourable treaties.[53] Secondly, parallel treaties may contain contradicting rights and obligations, making it difficult or even impossible for a state to comply with all its treaty commitments simultaneously. Finally, parallel treaty layers raise transaction costs and hamper predictability, since it will often be unclear for both states and investors which

[51] UNCTAD, *World Investment Report 2013* (n 2 above), 105.

[52] See also ibid, 106.

[53] See *CME Czech Republic BV v The Czech Republic*, UNCITRAL and *Ronald . Lauder v The Czech Republic*, UNCITRAL. See also F De Ly et al, 'Who Wins and Who Loses in Investment Arbitration—Are Investors and Host States on a Level Playing Field: The Lauder/Czech Republic Legacy' (2005) 6 *Journal of World Investment & Trade* 59.

treaty governs an investment relationship until an arbitral tribunal is able to address the issue.

Two explanations may account for why, in spite of these risks, we observe a general embracement of parallelism. First, countries may opt for parallelism out of rational choice. These countries consider that they cannot achieve a stated objective by relying solely on one treaty layer. After carefully and comprehensively analysing benefits and risks, they opt for parallelism. Secondly, policy-makers may act on bounded rationality. Because of cognitive constraints, they may underestimate the risks and overestimate the benefits of parallel treaty layers. While it is beyond this chapter to empirically investigate which explanation is predominant, we will discuss them in turn, starting with the latter.

If countries act on bounded rationality, they may not sufficiently reflect on the risks arising from unconsolidated treaty overlap when they sign new regional investment treaties. Were they to do so, they would consolidate parallel treaties. The history of international investment law is characterized by an overly optimistic estimation of the benefits of BITs coupled with a poor assessment of their potential risks.[54] Countries tend to gain a realistic understanding of the latter only 'when the claims hit', ie when they themselves are facing actual claims from investors.[55] Indeed, today investment treaty parallelism is not yet widely acknowledged as a source of concern outside of the EU. There the debate is fuelled, at least in part, by the increased invocation of IIAs by intra-EU investors, in circumvention of the parallel EU legal order.[56] It may thus not be a coincidence that the region currently most affected by overlap is also the region where consolidation efforts are most overtly discussed. Elsewhere, the risks brought about by overlapping IIAs may not receive adequate attention until parallel proceedings are launched and conflicts between treaties arise.

Cognitive shortcuts may also be at play when countries let more tangible small short-term costs outweigh more serious, yet also more intangible, long-term costs. Treaty consolidation creates short-term costs since terminating parallel existing agreements requires consensus among the contracting parties.[57] Such consensus may be easily obstructed if investors of either side perceive, whether justified or not, that they could lose some investment

[54] LN Skovgaard Poulsen, 'Sacrificing Sovereignty by Chance: Investment Treaties, Developing Countries, and Bounded Rationality', PhD thesis, London School of Economics and Political Science (2011); LN Skovgaard Poulsen, 'Bounded Rationality and the Diffusion of Modern Investment Treaties' (2013) 58 *International Studies Quarterly* 1.

[55] LN Skovgaard Poulsen and E Aisbett, 'When the Claim Hits: Bilateral Investment Treaties and Bounded Rational Learning' (2013) 65 *World Politics* 273.

[56] LE Peterson, 'Intra-EU Treaty Claims Continue to Proliferate', *IA Reporter*, 19 January 2014.

[57] Of course, investment treaties can also be denounced unilaterally, but this will trigger the treaties' survival clause, locking in protection for existing investments for a period of up to 20 years. See W Alschner, A Berdajs and V Lanovoy, 'Legal Basis and Effect of Denunciation under International Investment Agreements' (Graduate Institute of International and Development Studies, 2010), available at graduateinstitute.ch/files/live/sites/iheid/files/sites/ctei/shared/

protection if the earlier treaty is terminated. Current negotiations over the phasing out of intra-EU BITs are a case in point, with member states and academics disagreeing on the need for BIT protection in addition to EU law.[58] Upon careful assessment, however, these short-term costs, which are only incurred once, may be easily outweighed by the long-term costs arising from the various risks discussed above.

If bounded rationality is a major explanation for unconsolidated treaty overlap, states should carefully reconsider the need for parallel treaty layers. There may yet be considerable room for further treaty consolidation. If, however, parallelism is a rational choice, there would be little potential for further consolidation. Under this second explanation, countries opt for parallelism after a careful and informed cost–benefit analysis, because consolidation is undesirable.

Parallelism may be a rational choice where parallel treaty layers complement each other. For instance, a BIT may contain an investment protection standard which does not exist in the regional treaty. The Japan–South Korea BIT (2002), for instance, contains an additional pre-establishment national treatment commitment (Article 2(1)) and more extensive performance requirements (Article 9) as compared to the overlapping trilateral China–Japan–South Korea investment treaty. In that case, consolidation through the termination of the BIT would reduce the level of investment protection and liberalization, and may hence be undesirable.

Consolidation is also not desirable where countries seek to tailor their investment policy to the specific needs of a bilateral investment relationship while still participating in regional investment rule-making. Some regional treaties are signed to set a regional minimum standard of investment protection either explicitly, like the Unified Agreement on Arab Capital, or implicitly, like the ACIA, allowing countries to go beyond this level in bilateral treaties (see Section II above). Following the logic that one size may not fit all, states can then tailor their BITs to their negotiating partners and the specific level of political risk, independence of the judiciary or outward/inward investment flows and stocks involved.

This latter rational choice explanation may account for some of the variation we observe in practice. Politically like-minded countries of a similar level of development may be more inclined to take the risk of cutting back on complementarity, opting for a one-size-fits all approach to avoid the risks of parallelism. Especially in the EU, where countries, at least in theory, could compensate for any loss of intra-EU investment protection ensuing from BIT terminations through an increase in the standards of protection under EU law,

CTEI/Law%20Clinic/UNCTAD%20-%20International%20Investment%20Treaties%20Denunciations%20%28final%20-%20June%29.pdf.

[58] For differing assessments, see C Söderlund, 'Intra-EU BIT Investment Protection and the EC Treaty' (2007) 24 *Journal of International Arbitration* 455, 464; Reinisch (n 37 above), 178; Kleinheisterkamp (n 37 above), 99–100.

this may be a feasible option. In contrast, in more heterogeneous regions, the setting of regional minimum standards which co-exists with more tailor-made bilateral relationships may be preferred to consolidation. In that sense, it is not surprising that in South East Asia or the Middle East countries of different levels of development opt for both regional standard setting through PTIAs and increased bilateral protection where warranted through BITs.

Which explanation, rational choice or bounded rationality is more prevalent in explaining treaty overlap is an empirical question that would benefit from further research. As this preliminary account has made clear, answering this question will help to assess the potential for further consolidation where treaty overlap cannot be justified on rational grounds.

IV. MANAGING THE 'SPAGHETTI BOWL'

Whatever the explanation for the current prevalence of unconsolidated overlap may be, some overlap is here to stay and so are the risks associated with it. To maximize the positive effects of complementarity without having to accept the risks resulting from parallelism, states have to manage the co-existence of parallel treaty layers. That such coordination of vertically overlapping treaties is possible can be seen from investment law's neighbouring field—international trade law.

International trade law is famous for its 'spaghetti bowl' of overlapping trade agreements.[59] Yet, in spite of the parallelism between the World Trade Organization (WTO) and the more than 250 FTAs in force,[60] the world trading system is still functioning fairly well. While the recent surge in FTAs demonstrates that countries are turning increasingly to regional treaties to go further and deeper in their economic integration,[61] the WTO is far from losing its role in multilateral rule-making and dispute settlement. The international minimum standard of trade liberalization continues to be set at the multilateral level. The recent success of the Bali WTO Ministerial Conference and the adoption of the Trade Facilitation Agreement are proof of the WTO's continuous role in multilateral rule-making.[62] Moreover, the fear of crowding

[59] See, eg K Bagwell and RW Staiger, 'Will Preferential Agreements Undermine the Multilateral Trading System?' (1998) 108 *The Economic Journal* 1162; A Panagariya, 'The Regionalism Debate: An Overview' (1999) 22 *World Economy* 455; J Pauwelyn, 'Editorial Comment: Adding Sweeteners to Softwood Lumber: The WTO–NAFTA "Spaghetti Bowl" Is Cooking' (2006) 9 *Journal of International Economic Law* 197.

[60] For up-to-date numbers of FTAs between WTO members in force, see the WTO Regional Trade Agreement database, available at rtais.wto.org/UI/PublicAllRTAList.aspx (last accessed 28 September 2014).

[61] WTO, 'World Trade Report 2011: The WTO and Preferential Trade Agreements: From Coexistence to Coherence' (WTO, 2011), 56.

[62] 'Days 3, 4 and 5: Round-the-clock Consultations Produce "Bali Package"', *WTO News*, 5–7 December 2013, available at www.wto.org/english/news_e/news13_e/mc9sum_07dec13_e.htm, (last accessed 28 September 2014).

out the WTO's role in dispute settlement has not materialized. As the 2011 World Trade Report finds, WTO members continue to have frequent recourse to the WTO dispute settlement mechanism to solve disputes with their FTA partners.[63] Tactical forum shopping remains rare, and highly contentious disputes are resolved through multijurisdictional amicable settlements.[64]

The Appellate Body (AB) has done its share to manage the overlap between FTAs and the WTO. On the one hand, it has been keen to preserve the multilateral bargain and the non-discrimination principle. It held that Brazil's exemption for Mercosur countries from its health-motivated ban of retreaded tyres to be inconsistent with General Agreement on Tariffs and Trade (GATT) Article XX[65] and struck down a US safeguard measure that investigated but subsequently exempted imports from FTA partners from its application.[66] On the other hand, the AB also affirmed and strengthened member states' rights to conclude FTAs eg by extending the scope of the GATT, Article XXIV defence beyond most-favoured nation violations[67] or by leaving open the possibility that a dispute settlement clause in an FTA may be a 'legal impediment' to a WTO proceedings.[68]

A look at international trade law thus shows that a lack of consolidation is not a problem per se, as long as the spaghetti bowl of overlapping treaty layers is properly managed through complementary treaty design and purposeful coordination.[69] Applied to the investment law context, some comfort can be drawn from the fact that, even without consolidation, regionalism is not bound to exacerbate existing problems. Provided that states and arbitral tribunals carefully manage treaty overlap through complementary agreements and coordination between governance layers, similar to what is done in international trade law, a side-by-side of bilateral and regional investment treaty layers can work without running the risk of worsening existing complexities and inconsistencies.

[63] WTO, World Trade Report 2011 (n 61 above), 176.

[64] W Alschner, 'Amicable Settlements of WTO Disputes: Bilateral Solutions in a Multilateral System' (2014) 13 *World Trade Review* 65.

[65] Appellate Body Report, 'Brazil–Measures Affecting Imports of Retreaded Tyres', WT/DS332/AB/R, adopted 17 December 2007.

[66] For instance, Appellate Body Report, 'United States–Definitive Safeguard Measures on Imports of Certain Steel Products', WT/DS248/AB/R, WT/DS249/AB/R, WT/DS251/AB/R, WT/DS252/AB/R, WT/DS253/AB/R, WT/DS254/AB/R, WT/DS258/AB/R, WT/DS259/AB/R, adopted 10 December 2003.

[67] Appellate Body Report, 'Turkey–Restrictions on Imports of Textile and Clothing Products', WT/DS34/AB/R, adopted 19 November 1999.

[68] Appellate Body Report, 'Mexico—Tax Measures on Soft Drinks and Other Beverages, WT/DS308/AB/R', adopted 24 March 2006, para 54.

[69] See also Alschner (n 1 above), 285–98.

V. CONCLUSION

Regionalization of investment treaties is on the rise. Ever more BITs tend to overlap with regional agreements concluded to protect foreign investment. This chapter has reviewed state practice and shown that countries deal with this overlap in different ways. Some use regionalism to consolidate their IIA network. If the EU were to consolidate its extra- and intra-EU BITs successfully, the global number of BITs could be reduced to almost half of its number today. Most countries, however, opt for parallel layers of bilateral, regional and inter-regional treaties.

UNCTAD found that such

> Parallelism is also at the heart of systemic problems of overlap, inconsistency and the concomitant lack of transparency and predictability arising from a multi-faceted, multi-layered IIA regime. It adds yet another layer of obligations and further complicate countries' ability to navigate the complex spaghetti bowl of treaties and pursue a coherent, focused IIA strategy.[70]

While it is true that consolidation is desirable wherever possible, it sometimes makes sense for countries to leave parallel treaty layers in place to achieve complementary policy objectives. Importantly, the choice for or against consolidation should be driven by a careful assessment of costs and benefits rather than by cognitive shortcuts and bounded rationality.

Where parallel treaty layers exist, states and arbitral tribunals must carefully manage the ensuing overlap to avoid the pitfalls of parallelism mentioned in UNCTAD's 2013 World Investment Report. Trade law's experience shows that a co-existence of multiple treaty layers has its challenges, but also that these challenges can be managed. If investment law is to duplicate trade law's spaghetti bowl, it should not only reproduce complexities that are already existing in trade law, but also develop similar strategies to manage the challenges arising from regionalism and overlap.

[70] UNCTAD, *World Investment Report 2013* (n 2 above), 106–07.

29

Most-Favoured Nation and National Treatment in the EU and US Regional Trade Agreements—Tools for Equal or Discriminatory Treatment?

MAGDALENA SLOK-WODKOWSKA*

I. INTRODUCTION

According to the WTO database, the European Union is a party to over 40 regional trade agreements (RTAs) notified to the WTO, while the United States has notified only 14 of them. It results from a completely different attitude towards regional, WTO-extra integration. It is probably also because the aims of the EU and the US RTAs are different. Moreover, the degree of integration in the RTAs varies by region and time of conclusion. There are also various standards of treatment granted in these RTAs.

The most popular standards of treatment—national treatment (NT) and most-favoured nation treatment (MFN)—have been used for centuries to combat discrimination in economic relations. Both NT and MFN are also bases of the WTO legal system, as they are core clauses of the General Agreement on Tariffs and Trade (GATT) and the General Agreement on Trade in Services (GATS). Therefore, clauses related to treatment included in RTAs strongly influence economic cooperation between partners who are at the same time WTO members and overlap with the WTO law.

A vivid discussion has been going on for years about a competitive thesis concerning regional economic integration, which is often called 'preferential

* University of Warsaw. This project is funded by National Science Centre of Poland on the basis of the decision N DEC-2013/09/B/HS4/01488.

discrimination': on the one hand, it permits countries to integrate more deeply, which is positive to international trade, while on the other hand it helps to raise barriers to 'troublesome' countries.[1] This chapter is intended as a modest contribution to the discussion.

The aim of this chapter is to analyse standards of NT and MFN in the RTAs concluded by the EU and the US as two major trading forces of the world. It may be of particular importance especially in the context of a future trade and investment partnership agreement between those two regions. I will concentrate on the various types of wording of different clauses, differences between them and their development, as well as their scope, as it may show both a degree of integration as well as influencing trade between partners.

In my view, the structure of clauses is influenced strongly by the character and type of a particular agreement. It is impossible to discuss clauses related to treatment in these agreements without an analysis of the agreements themselves, especially in the case of the EU, which has a broad variety of RTAs, with different objectives and very different scopes of application. Therefore, in the first part of the chapter I will briefly describe and compare RTAs concluded by the EU and the US. I believe that this is essential for any further analysis. In the next part I will analyse NT and MFN clauses separately in relation to goods and services included in RTAs.

II. CHARACTERISTICS OF EU AND US REGIONAL TRADE AGREEMENTS

The EU itself is a regional trade agreement in the meaning of the WTO law—according to Article XXIV GATT, as it is a customs union, and Article V GATS—and required notification under Article XXIV GATT after conclusion of the treaty establishing the European Economic Community. In addition, the Union and its predecessors—the European Economic Community and the European Community—have always been strong proponents of regional integration and have had a long history of establishing free trade agreements.

This is the first significant difference between the attitudes of the EU and the US towards RTAs. The US has been quite reluctant to engage in economic integration outside the WTO framework. The US's first RTA was concluded in 1985 with Israel and the second was concluded in 1987 with Canada (replaced in 1992 by the North American Free Trade Agreement—NAFTA). Clearly, the US had a negative attitude towards regional integration in addition to the GATT.

It is also quite clear that the US reversed its practice after 2000. Between 2000 and 2007, the US concluded a further 12 regional trade agreements. All of them are called 'free trade agreements' and, besides the liberalization of

[1] See RH Snape, 'History and Economics of GATT's Article XXIV' in K Anderson and R Blackhurst (eds), *Regional Integration and the Global Trading System* (Harvester, 1993) 278.

trade in goods, they also cover trade in services, with further chapters related to intellectual property and public procurement. These were notified to the WTO as economic integration agreements (EIAs).

The US's agreements are listed in Table 1.

Table 1. RTAs concluded by USA

Signatory	Type of agreement	Year signed	EIA (Y/N)	MFN—goods	MFN—services	NT—goods	NT—services
CAFTA–DR[a]	FTA	2004	Y	N	Y	Y=GATT	Y
Israel	FTA	1985	N	N	N	N	N
NAFTA	FTA	1992	Y	N	Y	Y=GATT	Y
Jordan	FTA	2000	Y	N	N	Y=GATT	Y
Chile	FTA	2003	Y	N	Y	Y=GATT	Y
Singapore	FTA	2003	Y	N	Y	Y=GATT	Y
Australia	FTA	2004	Y	N	Y	Y=GATT	Y
Morocco	FTA	2004	Y	N	Y	Y=GATT	Y
Bahrain	FTA	2005	Y	N	Y	Y=GATT	Y
Colombia	FTA	2006	Y	N	Y	Y=GATT	Y
Oman	FTA	2006	Y	N	Y	Y=GATT	Y
Peru	FTA	2006	Y	N	Y	Y=GATT	Y
Panama	FTA	2007	Y	N	Y	Y=GATT	Y
South Korea	FTA	2007	Y	N	Y	Y=GATT	Y

Data concerning US free trade agreements comes from: http://www.ustr.gov/trade-agreements/free-trade-agreements.

[a] Dominican Republic–Central America–United States Free Trade Agreement.

It is also worth noting that all of them except the one with Canada are still in force. The US is currently negotiating only two new agreements, though both of them should be crucial to international economic relations—a Trans-pacific Partnership and a Transatlantic Trade and Investment Partnership—a long-awaited trade agreement with the EU.

The situation of the EU agreements is entirely different, and not only because of their sheer number. The EU has concluded different types of agreements, depending on their time of conclusion and scope, and, above all, the degree of integration proposed by the EU. Some of them are no longer in force due to further accession of the other party to the EU.

Most of them have been concluded as association agreements (AAs), which are a special kind of international treaty concluded by the EU (and formerly by the EEC and EC) with especially close partners on a specially designed legal basis—this is currently Article 217 of the Treaty on the Functioning of the European Union. As the European Court of Justice explained in the *Demirel* judgment, AAs create 'special, privileged links with non-member country which must, at least to a certain extent, take part in the Community system'.[2]

Although AAs cover a very broad range of issues, they always have a trade part, which includes a free trade agreement (FTA), but they also cover trade in services and other trade-related issues.[3] In consequence, AAs can be qualified as EIAs within the meaning of WTO law. The first such agreement was concluded in 1963 with Turkey, and was a basis for a customs union formed in 1995.

It should be noted that the association agreements of the EU can be grouped in a number of types. First, there are agreements concluded with potential candidate countries. The current generation of such agreements are stabilization and association agreements (SAAs). The second group are Euromediterranean agreements, which are with North African countries, the majority of which are former colonies of the EU members. The newest AAs have recently been signed with Eastern Partnership states, creating deep and comprehensive FTAs (DCFTAs). Special ties link the EU with the Africa, Caribbean, Pacific (ACP) group of countries, as they cooperate on the basis of the Cotonou Convention, which was signed in 2000 with the intention of it being supplemented by economic partnership agreements (EPA), concluded separately with smaller groups of states, thus establishing FTAs and EIAs.

Table 2. RTAs concluded by EU

Signatory	Assoc'n agree't	Type of agreement	Year signed	EIA T/N	MFN—goods	MFN—services	NT—goods	NT—services
Albania	Y	SAA	2006	Y	N	Y	N	Y
Algieria	Y	Euromediterranean	2002	N*	N	Y = GATS	N	Y
Bosnia & Hercegovina	Y/N	Interim SAA	2008	N	N	N	N	N
Cameroon	Y/N	interim EPA	2009	N	Y asymmetric	N	Y	N
CARIFORUM	Y/N	EPA	2008	Y	Y asymmetric	Y	Y	Y
Central America	Y	FTA/ Association Agreement	2012	Y	N	N	N	Y
Chile	Y	FTA/ association	2002	Y	N	N	Y	Y
Columbia & Peru	N	FTA	2012	Y	N	N	Y	Y

[2] C-12/86 *Meryem Demirel v Stadt Schwäbisch Gmünd* [1987] ECR I-3719, para 9.

[3] See H Horn, P Mavroidis, A Sapir, 'Beyond the WTO? An anatomy of EU and US preferential trade agreements', *The World Economy* 33(11).

Eastern & Southern Africa	Y/N	interim EPA	2009	N	Y asymmetric	N	Y	N
Egypt	Y	Euro-mediterranean	2001	N*	N	Y= GATS	N	N
Georgia	Y	Association/ DCFTA	2014	Y	N	Y	N	Y
Israel	Y	Euro-mediterranean	1995	N*	N	Y= GATS	N	N
Ivory Coast	Y/N	interim EPA	2009	N	Y asymmetric	N	Y	N
Jordan	Y	Euro-mediterranean	1997	N*	N	Y	N	Y
Korea	N	FTA	2010	Y	N	Y	Y	Y
Lebanon	Y	Euro-mediterranean	2002	N*	N	Y= GATS	N	N
Macedonia	Y	SAA	2000	Y	N	Y	N	Y
Mexico	N	FTA	2000	Y	Y	Y	Y	Y
Moldova	Y	Association/ DCFTA	2014	Y	N	Y	N	Y
Montenegro	Y	SAA	2010	Y	N	Y	N	Y
Morocco	Y	Euro-mediterranean	1996	N*	N	Y= GATS	N	N
Pacific countries	Y/N	interim EPA	2009	N	Y asymmetric	N	Y	N
Palestinian Authority	Y	Euro-mediterranean	1997	N	N	N	N	N
Serbia	Y	SAA	2008	Y	N	Y	N	Y
Singapore	N	FTA	-	Y**	N	N	Y	Y
South Africa	N	Trade Development and Cooperation	1999	N	N	Y= GATS	N	N
Tunisia	Y	Euro-mediterranean	1995	N*	N	Y= GATS	N	N
Turkey	Y	Custom Union	1996	N	N	N	N	N
Ukraine	Y	Association/ DCFTA	2014	Y	N	Y	Y	Y

*Agreements cover services but are not notified as EIAs.
**Notified to the WTO only as an early announcement.

The agreements listed in Tables 1 and 2 are the main body of the analysis, but other agreements negotiated and signed by the EU are used as a comparison.[4]

The agreements negotiated and signed by the EU and the US vary significantly. The EU RTAs types are far more complex, while the US RTAs are very similar to one another, being simply FTAs or EIAs. The EU AAs are not only broader in scope but also differ because of the different goals they are meant to achieve. Despite all the differences, the US and the EU have similar partners in their RTAs. Of the 20 states which have established FTAs with the US, 15 also have FTAs in force with the EU, although eight of them entered into force as recently as 2013. Two are about to sign RTAs.

III. NATIONAL TREATMENT AND MOST-FAVOURED NATION TREATMENT—CHARACTERISTICS OF CLAUSES

There is no doubt that both the MFN and NT clauses are essential elements of the WTO legal system. It should be noted, though, that they were both also present in trade agreements long before the WTO, and even the GATT, had been established. Both types of clauses were also classified as standards of international economic law by G Schwarzenberger,[5] though he played down the NT standard compared to an MFN. He defined MFN as treatment 'on a footing not inferior to that of the most favoured third state'.[6] NT is much younger, as states were interested in diminishing tariffs rather than in lifting discrimination against foreigners. Schwarzenberger defines NT as a standard the objective of which is to grant internal parity of partners—in other words, equality of treatment between nationals and foreigners.[7] The essence of both the MFN and NT standards lies in a *tertium comparationis* (international in the case of MFN, internal in the case of NT.

Despite being known and used for such a long time, and despite a number of attempts at unifying the standards of MFN, there is no one, commonly agreed clause stipulating MFN or NT. Both standards have nevertheless been highly globalized through the GATT and subsequently through other WTO agreements. Both clauses are a central part of the agreements and are the basis of the international trading system. They also became the benchmark for any

[4] The analysis does not cover RTAs which are no longer in force, with too close partners (European Economic Area and Switzerland) and mini-states.

[5] G Schwarzenberger, 'The Province and Standards of International Economic Law' (1948) 2 *International Law Quarterly* 409; id, *International Law and Order* (Stevens & Son, 1971) 157; id, *The Frontiers of International Law* (Stevens & Sons, 1962) 220; id, *The Principles and Standards of International Economic Law* (Hague Academy of International Law, 1966) 67.

[6] G Schwarzenberger, 'The Most-Favoured-Nation Standard in British Practice' [1945] *British Yearbook of International Law* 96.

[7] Schwarzenberger, 'The Province and Standards' (n 5 above) 410.

other MFN or NT granted, especially in RTAs.[8] As both the EU and the US are active and important members of the WTO, MFN and NT clauses in the RTA agreements should always be assessed in relation to the GATT's clauses. They are significant only if they bring added value to the existing clause from the GATT, which is especially important in relation to goods, as both of the relevant GATT clauses have a very broad scope of application.

IV. MOST-FAVOURED NATION CLAUSES IN RELATION TO GOODS

Probably because of the very broad and unconditional scope of the GATT's MFN clause, additional MFN treatment is rarely granted in regional trade agreements concluded by the EU or the US in relation to goods. This could also be because preferential agreements are an exception from the GATT's MFN, and Article XXIV enables the granting of exceptional preferences that are stronger than MFN only for establishing a free trade area or a customs union (CU). Further, as establishing an FTA or a CU means that there are no duties between partners, there should be no space for any further preferences there. It should be noted here, however, that, because of the different scopes of FTAs, which in fact rarely cover all trade between parties of the FTA, there is a margin where an MFN could also be used.

Nevertheless, the term MFN, when referring to the GATT clause itself, is often used to describe rates of tariffs levied according to the GATT's Article I, mainly as a benchmark for further preferences.[9] It is also often used in provisions concerning suspension of preferential treatment.[10] In this meaning, it is more a symbol of worse treatment,[11] contrary to preferential treatment on the basis of an RTA.

MFN treatment in relation to goods is not granted in any of the US agreements. It is also absent in the majority of EU RTAs. The most significant exceptions here are EPAs concluded by the EU with ACP countries. In all of these EPAs, including interim EPAs, which only cover trade in goods, there is a clause similar to the MFN included,[12] though it is called 'more favorable treatment'.

[8] Almost all partners of the RTAs with the EU and all of the US's partners are WTO member states.

[9] See the US agreements, eg Art 308 of the NAFTA agreement or Art 5.10 of the US–Singapore Agreement.

[10] Eg Art 38 of the EU–Albania Agreement, Art 3.1 of the EU–South Korea Agreement or Art 7.1 of the US–Singapore Agreement.

[11] See J Baghwati, *Termites in the Trading System, How Preferential Agreements Undermine Free Trade* (Oxford University Press, 2008) 14; R Hudec, *Essays on the Nature of International Trade* (Cameron May, 1999) 312.

[12] Art 19 of the UE–CARIFORUM agreement and of the EU–Cameroon agreement, Art 17 of the EU–Ivory Coast Agreement, Art 16 of the EU–Pacific countries agreement and of the EU–Eastern & Southern Africa agreement.

The clauses are asymmetric—the obligations of the EU and its ACP partner are different. They oblige the EU to grant better treatment if it gave such to any other partner, but only if these preferences arise from another free trade agreement. The EPAs were probably designed to exclude any other, more developed and tighter modes of cooperation, especially customs unions. It also leaves some space for interpretation, whether other types of agreements concluded by the EU, such as association agreements with an FTA component or DCFTAs, are FTAs in the meaning of the EPAs' MFN clause. Such controversies might be even stronger if we take into account that in almost all EPA agreements the clauses refer to an FTA, whereas the EU–Cameroon Agreement refers to an economic integration agreement. On the other hand, in the MFN clause of the EU–CARIFORUM Agreement in relation to trade in services there is a reference to the conclusion of an EIA.

A relevant obligation of the ACP partners is limited only to FTAs concluded with a 'major trading partner', defined subsequently in the very same article as 'a country or territory accounting for a share of world merchandise exports above 1%' or, in the case of a group of countries or territories, above 1.5%. Concluding an FTA with such a partner does not lead to providing any preferences automatically. It only obliged an ACP partner to enter into consultation with the EU. Although asymmetry here clearly arises from the fact that the main goal of the agreements is the development of a weaker partner, it is perceived as being detrimental to an ACP partner.[13] It can also be seen as inconsistent with the WTO enabling clause, as it triggers a conclusion of the south–south free trade agreements with partners such as Brazil.[14] It should, however, be noted that this quasi-MFN does not necessarily mean that additional preferences are automatically granted. We can assume that the EU, following its declared values, will enable a weaker ACP partner to offer some additional preferences to another developing country even if that developing country is a major trading partner.

The only MFN clause that can be found in the EU RTAs in relation to trade in goods is very classic in its form, but extremely narrow in its scope: the MFN clause in Annex 2-C to the EU–South Korea FTA is limited only to the production of cars. It specifies that the preferential treatment concerns only internal taxation and emissions standards. It shows that the MFN can be used to tackle problems with standardization and non-tariffs barriers—the most important problems facing modern international trade. Here, though, the very narrow scope of application enables the parties to precisely define and also predict potential preferences. No similar clause was included in the most similar FTA concluded by the EU—the recently signed EU–Singapore Agreement.

[13] C Chase, 'MFN in the CARIFORUM–EC Economic Partnership Agreement: Policy Blunder or Legal Inconsistency?' (2011) *Legal Issues of Economic Integration* No 2, 190.

[14] Ibid, 192.

V. NATIONAL TREATMENT IN RELATION TO TRADE IN GOODS

As can be seen in Tables 1 and 2, contrary to the MFN clause, despite its presence in the GATT, NT is relatively often used or at least mentioned in the RTAs concluded both by the EU and by the US.

NT is mentioned in all of the US RTAs except the one with Israel. The relevant clause is very similar in all of them. They directly refer to the GATT's clause as a benchmark, invoking both the clause and its interpretative notes. Although NT is granted *mutatis mutandis* here, it is doubtful that it really changes the scope of application of the GATT's clause.

The US clauses,[15] in their second paragraphs, refer to the regional level of government, which is value added compared to the universal wording of the clause used in the GATT. It concretizes an obligation of NT to regional level, stating that regional authorities should treat other party nationals as these from other parts of the country. It practically restricts the national treatment to central level, as regional authorities are free to discriminate between their regional goods and those from abroad as long as they treat goods from other states and those from other parts of their own state in the same discriminatory manner.

The standard clause used in the US agreement also includes, in an annex, a list of exceptions from NT. The compliance of such a regulation with WTO law might be questionable, although an analysis of these exceptions enables the assumption that all these exceptions are designed in accordance with the GATT's Article XX or arise directly from the WTO legal system.

In the NT clauses of the US agreements, additional clarification was made that the NT should be granted by any level of government or authority to 'like, directly competitive or substitutable domestic goods'. The last statement might be difficult to interpret because, on one hand, according to the same article in an FTA, it should be read exactly the same way as Article III of the GATT. On the other hand, in GATT Article III we find only 'like' product, which is explained in some WTO panel and Appellate Body (AB) judgments as the same as 'directly competitive or substitutable'—though the actual meaning and interrelation between 'like' and 'directly competitive' might be controversial.[16] Therefore, when the words 'like', 'competitive' and 'substitutable' are used in a provision, such a discussion becomes moot.

One agreement concluded by the EU strongly resembles the US clause: the EU–Peru and Colombia Agreement, where not only has Article III of the GATT been referred to, but also its interpretative notes, which should be applied *mutatis mutandis* to the agreement. The clause also includes a clari-

[15] All agreements except the US–Australia FTA.

[16] R Hudec, '"Like Product": The Differences in Meaning in GATT Articles I and III', in T Cottier and P Mavroidis (eds), *Regulatory Barriers and the Principle of Non-Discrimination in World Trade Law* (University of Michigan Press 2000) 101–23; available also at: http://worldtradelaw.net/document.php?id=articles/hudeclikeproduct.pdf.

fication mentioned above (ie referring to like, competitive and substitutable goods), which is normally used in the US agreements. As Peru and Colombia both established free trade agreements with the US long before they established the one with the EU, this is probably a direct influence of the US standard clause.

Among the 29 of the EU agreements taken into account, only 10 contain NT clauses in relation to trade in goods. Besides the EU–Peru and Colombia Agreement, mentioned above, among these agreements are all EPAs and interim EPAs concluded with ACP countries. The newly signed agreement with Ukraine also contains such a clause, although it has not been used in subsequent DCFTAs. The wording in all of these clauses is very similar and is obviously inspired by Article III, paragraphs 1, 2 and 4 of the GATT. The scope and listed internal measures are exactly the same. Paragraph 1 of the relevant NT clauses in the EPAs and interim EPAs mirrors Article III, paragraph 2 of the GATT and concerns internal taxation; paragraph 2 mirrors Article III, paragraph 4; and paragraph 3 mirrors Article III, paragraph 1. Exceptions are also the same and cover internal subsidies and public procurement, as well as trade defence instruments.

The differences in wording are not significant, apart from one exception. Article 18, paragraph 6 of the interim EPA concluded with Eastern & Southern Africa stipulates that African states, especially those which are least developed countries, can depart from the NT obligation 'to promote the establishment of domestic production and protect infant industry'. The decision is taken by an EPA committee, but some exceptions are listed directly in Annex III to the interim EPA.

Besides the EU EPAs in which ACP countries are signatories, only two other agreements contain very similar clauses: Article 13 of the decision establishing free trade area with Mexico and Article 77 of the EU–Chile Association Agreement, which has wording that mirrors Article III of the GATT exactly.

The actual meaning of these clauses in both the EU EPAs and the American agreements is debatable, with unclear added value. On the one hand, the inclusion of such clauses may be seen as a step forward in regional trade agreements and proof of the growing significance of non-tariff measures in international trade. On the other hand, almost all partners of the EU in these agreements are WTO member states, which are obliged to grant NT for exactly the same measures on the basis of the GATT. The difference comes from the different legal bases and, in consequence, potentially different systems of enforcement and dispute settlement.

It is worth highlighting that no NT clause in relation to trade in goods has been included in the EU agreement with the only non-WTO member or observer—Lebanon. The same objective seems to be attained in this agreement through different clauses that prohibit quantitative restrictions and discrimination, even though the full NT is absent.

Another agreement of the EU is the one with South Korea. This also directly refers to the GATT and the fact that NT should be granted in accordance with the GATT. 'Non-tariff measures' are especially highlighted here, and it is confirmed that they should be a subject of NT. The agreement also contains another specific provision that might be classified as an NT clause. It requires that both partners grant NT in the access to public participation in the decision-making process for issuing technical standards. NT should be granted to 'economic operators and other interested persons'. It proves how important technical measures have become to international trade in goods.

VI. MOST-FAVOURED NATION CLAUSES IN RELATION TO TRADE IN SERVICES

Most-favoured nation clauses are more often used in relation to trade in services than in relation to trade in goods. It is probably because of this that they can have different scopes of application than liberalization under the auspices of the WTO. It is easier to grant additional preferences here, and to grant preferences that can potentially expand thanks to the MFN clause. On the one hand, services are much less liberalized then trade in goods, while on the other hand there are much fewer agreements, especially among those concluded by the EU that cover trade in services and have been notified to the WTO as EIAs.

However, the real assessment of the legal meaning of these provisions is extremely complicated. Because of the nature of MFN clauses both in the GATS and in RTAs, the actual meaning might be hidden in annexed lists of exceptions and will therefore not be easy to grasp.[17] It is equally true for agreements concluded by the EU and the US.

Among the EU RTAs, not all of those covering trade in services and other aspects of economic integration have been notified as EIAs. None of the association agreements concluded with Mediterranean states have been, although all of them cover trade in services. It is probably because of this that almost all of them invoke directly commitments from Article II of the GATS and they are not aimed to broaden its scope. Such invocation can be found in the EU–Morocco, EU–Israel, EU–Tunisia, EU–Egypt and EU–Lebanon agreements.

One of the agreements between the EU and the Mediterranean states that has not been notified under Article V of the GATS is the one with Jordan. This agreement includes a classic (in wording and content) MFN clause in relation to a right of establishment. The clause is asymmetric. According to Article 30 of the agreement, the EU grants MFN treatment to the establishment of a company within a member state territory as well as MFN treatment to an established company. It also encompasses branches. On its part, Jordan

[17] For more comments see P Latrille and J Lee, 'Services Rules in Regional Trade Agreements, How Diverse and How Creative as Compared to the GATS Multilateral Rules?', Staff Working Paper (WTO, 2012) 23.

agrees to grant, in relation to the right of establishment, and to companies and branches, not only MFN but also national treatment—whichever is the better. (Note that a combined MFN and NT clause is sometimes used in EU agreements.) There is, however, a list of exceptions from that treatment in the annex. The agreement has not been notified to the WTO, probably because the text was agreed before Jordan acceded to the WTO in 2000. The agreement gave both parties the time and opportunity to include all preferences in Jordan's accession documents and list of Article II exceptions.

The combined MFN and NT clause, which was probably taken from investment treaties, where such clauses are often used, was used for the first time in an RTA in the EU–Jordan Agreement, then developed in other agreements concluded shortly after it. The wording is more preferable to foreigners, because they can be entitled to better treatment then nationals on the basis of MFN. A very similar combined clause was used in the EU–Algeria Agreement in relation to commercial presence—both the establishment thereof and their subsidiaries (Article 32 of the agreement). However, the clause is not reciprocal: it is only Algeria that is obliged to grant MFN or NT to the EU's companies and their subsidies or branches. In this agreement, in its Article 30, the GATS MFN clause related to supply of services has simply been broadened to include Algeria, which was not a WTO member state at the time of the conclusion of the Association Agreement with the EU. In the EU–Algeria Agreement, a similar clause has been used in relation to a maritime transport.

SAAs all include clauses very similar to the one from the EU–Algeria Agreement, although with some very significant changes. They are also combined clauses, related to the right of establishment and treatment of companies after establishment, but the clause is reciprocal. Some of these clauses (eg in the EU–Albania and EU–FYROM Agreements) enable the Balkan party to suspend NT treatment, with conservation of the MFN treatment, due to development needs. This is the only exception from the reciprocity here.

In every SAA the combination of MFN and NT is granted in relation only to commercial presence (which can be compared to a mode 3 of services from the GATS), but there is also a possibility of widening the scope of the clause so that it also covers the self-employed. Such a decision would be taken by the Stabilization and Association Council a few years after entry into force of a given agreement (five years in the cases of FYROM and Albania, four years for Serbia and Montenegro). No such a decision has yet been taken.

The clauses granting NT and MFN in SAAs are supplemented by additional provisions which enable parties of the agreements to introduce additional requirements to the other party concerning the establishment and operation of a company, which are justified by legal or technical differences. This seems to be a crucial provision, as it may serve as a legal basis for introducing measures which may seriously impair market access. On the other hand, it constitutes an exception only from NT. Both parties still cannot discriminate against third countries.

The EU agreement with South Africa resembles the agreements concluded with the Mediterranean states (perhaps because it was concluded at the same time). It also has not been notified under GATS, Article V, but this is because no additional preferences, as defined in Article V, were granted and the ultimate aim of the provisions is simple confirmation of the previous commitment to the GATS.

Combined MFN and NT clauses have also been used in all three newly signed agreements with Eastern Partnership countries—Moldova, Georgia and Ukraine. MFN and NT, whichever is the better, is granted for the establishment, as well as operation of, an established subsidiary, branch or representative office of a judicial person of the other partner. These clauses are limited by scope to operations in the fields listed in the annexes, which play a crucial role here.

A completely different MFN clause has been included in the EU–CARIFORUM Agreement. This is the only full EPA that has been concluded so far, but, on the basis that in every interim EPA we can find like provisions in relation to trade in goods, we can assume that, in potential EPAs concluded in the future, the MFN clause in relation to goods will be similar. Like the MFN clause in relation to trade in goods, the MFN clause in relation to trade in services is asymmetric. Although the EU party is obliged to grant MFN after granting similar preferences to any other partner, the developing states that comprise CARIFORUM are obliged to reciprocity only in the case of concluding an FTA with a major trading economy (defined in the same way as in relation to trade in goods); in other cases they must enter into consultations. There are two separate MFN clauses related to trade in services. Article 70 covers commercial presence (here the term 'establishment' has not been used), while Article 79 covers supply of services. The scope of the MFN clause is, however, limited to the lists of commitments included in Annex IV to the agreement.

The MFN clause in relation to trade in services in the EU–Mexico Agreement has a quite complicated structure. First of all, it refers to 'less favourable treatment', which is forbidden, rather than to 'more favourable treatment', as in the majority of agreements. It is clearly linked with an obligation stated in paragraph 3 of the MFN clause,[18] which obliges a party to enter into negotiations in order to grant preferences in case of entering into another economic integration agreement. Paragraph 2 explicitly excluded from the MFN all agreements concluded before issuing the decision on liberalization that had been notified under Article V of the GATS. The scope of the MFN is also limited and covers only mutual recognition accorded to service suppliers. This means that it can potentially broaden the scope of services liberalized.

Other agreements concluded by the EU with American countries do not include MFN treatment in relation to trade in services. Instead, they refer to lists of commitments and NT. This could be explained by the fact that they

[18] Art 5 of the Decision 2/2001.

are all cross-regional agreements, concluded by parties with strong and close partners in their regions, with whom they have close economic relations. The same technique was used in the recently signed EU agreement with Singapore.

The only other agreement which includes an MFN also in relation to trade in services is the EU–South Korea Agreement. Here, MFN has been granted in relation to supply of services and suppliers. However, other agreements of both partners of a 'significantly higher level' have been excluded from the MFN, as well as agreements concluded before the EU–Korea Agreement entered into force. The 'significantly higher level' has not been defined, but we can assume that it refers to some future agreements with important and closer partners, with whom the party is more closely integrated. The scope of the MFN clause has been limited to services, which were liberalized in the agreement.

The usage of MFN clauses in the US agreements is far less complicated and miscellaneous than in the EU. Twelve RTAs concluded by the US that cover services have been designed in a similar manner. All of them include two separate MFN clauses in relation to trade in services—one to supply of services and the other to investments and investors. They are all so-called NAFTA-type agreements,[19] as NAFTA was the first one and became a pattern for others. The wording of the clause in each agreement is classic, as it simply provides that one party should accord treatment that is no less favourable than treatment accorded to any third party. There are no exceptions, nor the asymmetry that can be found in the RTAs concluded by the EU. The actual meaning and economic importance here depends not on the wording but on the exceptions from the MFN treatment, which are usually listed in annexes, as well as the lists of concessions, as the scope of the MFN is related to the scope of concessions. The only US RTA which covers trade in service and does not include an MFN clause is the US–Jordan Agreement. This only refers to the GATS MFN clause and the way that the GATS list of exceptions is to be understood in the agreement.

VII. NATIONAL TREATMENT IN RELATION TO TRADE IN SERVICES

A variety of NT clauses can be found in relation to trade in services. First, it must be observed that the majority of the EU RTAs and all of the US RTAs do not follow the GATS model of liberalization of trade in services. They usually do not refer to the GATS modes, preferring to grant preferences and preferential treatment (understood as an NT) to supply of services (both the US and the EU), investments and investors (usually but not exclusively the US), and right to establishment (the EU). Such constructions make an NT a

[19] Typology after Latrille and Lee (n 17 above).

central clause and the most important preference of the chapters concerning trade in services.

Construction used in the US RTAs is based on the lists on concessions and list of areas where supply of services and investment have been liberalized. NT clauses play a central role there, and granting NT to certain services or types of investments is a key element of liberalization.

Therefore, we find NT clauses in all 13 US EIAs, even in the US–Jordan Agreement, in which the wording of the clause is different than in the other US RTAs. What is more, its importance is even greater, as it is practically the only hard obligation that can be found in Article 3 of this agreement—the sole article directly concerning trade in services.

All other agreements contain two separate clauses—one referring to services suppliers and the other to investments and investors. In all other US RTAs, the NT clauses are extremely simple in wording and refer only to 'like circumstances'. In relation to services suppliers, no limitations are included, while in relation to investors and investments, the scope of application is explicitly stated within an article. It refers to acquisition, expansion, management, conduct, operation and sale or other disposition of investments. In the US–South Korea Agreement there is a separate chapter concerning financial services that also includes an NT clause. In some of the agreements (eg NAFTA, US–Morocco, US–CAFTA–DR, US–South Korea, US–Bahrain) there is a 'regional level' clause, which is the same as can be found in relation to trade in goods in the US RTAs.

While the US has created its own family of NAFTA-type agreements, the majority of the EU RTAs do not belong to any agreement family.[20] As a consequence, in the majority of the EU RTAs liberalization of trade in services is not described by modes. Usually RTAs contain separate provisions concerning services and services suppliers (mode 1 and partly mode 2 of services' supply) and establishment (which is close to the GATS mode 3, ie commercial presence). Only two of the EU RTAs have been classified as GATS-like—the agreements with Mexico and with Chile.

The GATS-like construction of these agreements also influences the wording of the NT clauses. The EU–Chile Agreement and Decision 2/2001 of the EU–Mexico Joint Council both contain an NT clause which exactly mirrors Article XVI of the GATS. It should be noted, though, that the EU–Chile Agreement comprises two NT clauses in relation to trade in services. There is a separate clause, with exactly the same wording, granting NT to establishment. The same separate clauses have been used in the EU–CARIFORUM Agreement and recently concluded agreement with Central America. Also, the not yet signed agreement with Ukraine replicates this model. The agreement with South Korea is based on the same model, though, as well as granting NT for establishment, it also covers investors.

[20] Latrille and Lee (ibid).

In relation to services, unlike an NT clause replicated from the GATT, repeating clauses from the GATS has legal significance. In all of the above-mentioned agreements, the key element of liberalization of services is a broader list of commitments compared to the GATS commitments. In such a situation the scope of NT is also broadened—it might be used, for example, in a wider variety of services and situations.

Slightly different clauses have been used in the EU–Peru and Colombia Agreement. Here, we also have two separate articles—one related to a right to establishment and investors and the other to services and services suppliers. Both articles contain three analogical provisions—one for each party to the agreement. The wording is precise in defining the scope of application, but does not contain any additional explanations. As a result, it mirrors only the first paragraph of Article XVI of the GATS, concentrating mainly on the scope of concessions made by parties in annexes to the agreement.

A question may arise whether such a change and lack of interpretative paragraph in the EU–Colombia and Peru Agreement really influences its actual legal meaning. In my view, it does not. If we use GATT's Article III as a comparison, it is obvious that 'treatment less favourable' refers to both factual and legal treatment. Also, the answer to the question of whether formally different treatment conforms with that provision is, in my view, affirmative. There are situations where formally identical treatment of domestic and foreign services and suppliers may not be possible. The decisive factor should be the actual market access for foreigners.

Another group of EU agreements that include an NT clause are the SAAs. All of them, except an interim SAA with Bosnia and Herzegovina, have been notified to the WTO as EIAs, and all contain chapters related to cross-border supply of services and establishment, but none of them contain a pure NT clause in these areas.

All SAAs and all DCFTAs with Eastern Partnership countries contain a clause related exclusively to the establishment and operation of subsidiaries and branches of companies. The clause stipulates that parties grant each other treatment no less favourable than that accorded by a partner to their own companies (branches or subsidiaries) or to any company of any third country, whichever is the better. It combines MFN and NT in one clause (as described above).

What distinguishes SAA from other EU RTAs, including recent DCFTAs, is the fact that they do not contain a specific list of commitments. Therefore the scope of NT for establishment is very broad and may be applied to all sectors. This could be explained by the purpose of SAAs, which is full membership in the EU of a non-EU party. The same model has been used in the past in the European agreements. The right to establishment has been limited only by the legal and technical differences between partners.

Contrary to establishment, the right to provide services has not been granted in European agreements in the past or in SAAs. They all contain chapters related to the supply of services, but without granting NT treatment. NT treatment was granted only in explicitly specified sectors—in maritime transport (operating of ships) in the EU–Albania, EU– Serbia and EU–Montenegro agreements. The three partners should grant NT also to EU members' nationals in relation to real estate acquisition, but Albania should do it in accordance with its GATS list of concessions. This difference is because, of the three, only Albania is a WTO member state. The above-mentioned concessions relating to supply of services are not included in the EU–FYROM Agreement, perhaps because this SAA was signed a few years earlier.

On the other hand, recent DCFTAs with Eastern Partnership countries contain an NT clause related to market access for service suppliers. Its wording, as in many other EU agreements, mirrors the GATT clause. The reason for such a deep commitment is that it has a limited scope. National treatment is granted only to those sectors and suppliers that have been explicitly granted market access in the annexes. This could be a sign of a new tendency in the EU agreements, but is also proof of deeper relationships with these partners.

As was mentioned above, although agreements with Mediterranean states have not been notified as EIAs to the WTO, they all comprise chapters concerning trade in services. They all prohibit discrimination based on nationality in relation to workers and working conditions, but the clauses stipulating it do not have the characteristics of NT clauses. Nonetheless, two of the agreements—with Algeria and Jordan—contain combined MFN/NT clauses identical to those in SAAs.

Separate clauses granting NT in relation to maritime transport services are quite common in EU AAs. A few other agreements also contain such clauses, such as the EU–Peru and Colombia Agreement, the EU–Central America Agreement, Decision 2/2002 of EC–Mexico Joint Council and the EU–South Korea Agreement.

In agreements with Central America and South Korea, there are NT clauses in relation to some aspects of telecommunication services. In agreements with South Korea and Mexico, there are NT granted for financial services.

VIII. CONCLUSIONS

The worlds of the US and EU RTAs are completely different. The US has concluded much fewer agreements, which are at the same time much more unified. The EU RTAs vary a lot with regard to the time they were signed and the partners involved, while the US RTAs are very similar to each other. The US RTAs also seems to be very economy oriented, while the EU RTAs cover a very broad range of issues, sometimes not related to trade matters. The majority of the FTAs concluded by the EU are parts of broader association agreements.

The analysis of clauses show that they are not so discriminatory as it may first appear. In the majority of agreements concluded by both analysed parties, the NT and MFN clauses repeat the obligations from the GATT and GATS or explicitly invoke them to confirm the ongoing obligation to grant national treatment. Some added value might be found in a clarification made by the US RTAs that national treatment concerns both like and directly competitive products. The GATS NT and MFN clauses may differ from those of RTAs by the scope in the latter being defined in annexes. In the US agreements, lists of exceptions from both standards are also used.

There are also a few important questions on how the wording of such clauses implies dispute settlement. Does it change jurisdiction? Who should settle a dispute on a basis of a clause from the RTA that simply repeats a relevant GATT or GATS obligation? Should the interpretation of the WTO panels and AB be used to interpret the wording of a clause that mirrors the one from the GATT or GATS?

There is one clear example of using MFN, or rather 'more favoured nation', as a tool for discrimination—the EPAs and interim EPAs concluded by the EU with ACP countries. This clearly entitles the EU to obtain better treatment than that obtained on the basis of the WTO law, but also better than that obtained on the basis of a given RTA. It is also a type of MFN that is unknown in the modern world—nonreciprocal, conditional and, in some cases, dependent on the result of negotiations.

As a final remark, there is some similarity between the clauses used in the EU RTAs with American states and the corresponding clauses from the US RTAs. This might be treated as a prediction for how NT and MFN clauses in the future Transatlantic Trade and Partnership Agreement may look. In my view, it is likely that, if the parties decide to include any of them, they will be similar to the pattern used by the US—with precise wording and the detailed scope in relation to services being defined in annexes and recalling the GATT's NT in relation to goods.

30

Recent Trends of Common Commercial Policy of the European Union: From Global to Regional (and Back?) in the Governance of International Economic Order

CHIARA CELLERINO*

I. INTRODUCTION

INTERNATIONAL TRADE GOVERNANCE has traditionally aspired to the creation of a multilateral global trade system. Following the summit at Los Cabos (Mexico) on 18–19 June 2012, the G20 leaders reaffirmed 'the importance of an open, predictable, rules based, transparent multilateral trading system and . . . committed to ensure the centrality of the WTO'. On the same occasion, they confirmed their commitment to 'open trade and investment, expanding markets and resisting protectionism in all its forms, which are necessary conditions for sustained global economic recovery, jobs and development'.[1]

In fact, the bite of the financial crisis that started in 2008 triggered protectionist attitudes and the flourishing of 'buy national' or WTO-inconsistent measures to support export in several countries. Furthermore, the stalling of WTO Doha round of negotiations undermined the confidence in the success of a multilateral global trading scheme. Against this background and, according to some authors, in reaction to the slow pace of the multilateral agenda, some

* Research Fellow in European Union Law at University of Genoa, PhD (University of Udine), LLM (Columbia University).

[1] G20 Leaders Declaration, Los Cabos, 18–19 June 2012, available at http://www.consilium.europa.eu/uedocs/cms_Data/docs/pressdata/en/ec/131069.pdf, paras 26–27.

players have started boosting bilateral/regional approaches to liberalization as alternative avenues for achieving economic gains from improved international trade liberalization.[2]

In this context, some features of the recently negotiated European Union's comprehensive bilateral/regional free trade agreements (FTAs) deserve particular analysis—not only because the content of such agreements reflects a new approach in European common commercial policy that is strikingly different to those used in the past, but also because they raise some issues as regards their impact on European legal order and on the future of multilateral trade system in general.

In this chapter I offer an overview of some significant features of the new generation EU-negotiated FTAs, looking at the new competences conferred upon the European Union by the Lisbon Treaty in the common commercial policy domain. I also provide some insights on the effects of such agreements on European Union legal order, focusing on the possibility of invoking their direct applicability before European and Member State courts. I then make some critical considerations on issues of European governance connected to their conclusion, before presenting some closing remarks.

II. COMMON COMMERCIAL POLICY IN CONTEXT

Common commercial policy is one of the few areas where the European institutions were entrusted with external competences since the very establishment of the EEC. The endowment of a common commercial policy was in fact conceived as a natural complement to the internal market.[3] With the Treaty of Lisbon, such competence has been placed under the broader umbrella of the European Union external action: Articles 206–07 TFEU (formerly Articles 131–34 TEC) now belong to Part V TFEU, encompassing all competences characterized by 'external contents', such as development cooperation (Articles 208–11 TFEU), economic, financial and technical cooperation with third countries (Articles 212–13 TFEU) and humanitarian aid (Article 214 TFEU).

[2] In the last few decades, a large number of scholarly writings have analysed the rationale behind the proliferation of free trade agreements, their (reportedly negative) impact on the multilateral system and on the principle of non-discrimination, and the ways for the WTO to face this phenomenon. See, eg R Baldwin and P Low (eds), *Multilateralizing Regionalism, Challenges for the Global Trading System* (Cambridge University Press, 2009); LE Rakman, 'The Proliferation of Free Trade Agreements: Bane or Beauty?' (2008) 42 *Journal of World Trade* 367; T Cottier, 'The Challenge of Regionalization and Preferential Relations in World Trade Law and Policy' (1996) 1 *European Foreign Affairs Review* 149; F Shoneveld, 'The EEC and Free Trade Agreements, Stretching the Limits of GATT Exceptions to Non-discriminatory Trade?' (1992) 26 *Journal of World Trade* 59. For further references see also P Mavroidis, 'Always Look at the Bright Side of Non-delivery (WTO and Preferential Agreements, Yesterday and Today)' (2011) 10 *World Trade Review* 375, who advocates a more 'no-harm' policy approach to such agreements, and id, *Preferential and Trade Agreements: A Law and Economics Analysis* (Cambridge University Press, 2014).

[3] R Baratta, 'La politica commerciale comune dopo il Trattato di Lisbona' [2012] *Diritto del commercio internazionale* 403.

Moreover, the general objectives of European external action, such as those provided by Articles 3.5 and 21 TEU, apply to common commercial policy.[4]

The inherently external nature of this competence rests on the fact that its domain 'relates to trade with non-member countries, not to trade in the internal market'. More precisely, as recently clarified by the Court of Justice, 'only those acts of the European Union with a specific link to international trade are capable of falling within the field of the common commercial policy'.[5] In this perspective, it comes as no surprise that, according to Article 207 TFEU, the scope of common commercial policy includes, for example, the regulation of tariff rates, export policy, measures to protect trade in the event of dumping or subsidies, the conclusion of tariff and trade agreements.[6] Yet the Court of Justice has always purported an extensive notion of this competence, not limited to traditional aspects of liberalization of trade, but also including 'more elaborate means devised with a view to furthering the development of international trade', such as international agreements that comprehensively regulate the world market for certain products,[7] international agreements setting production standards that bear a positive effect on the environment[8] or, more recently, agreements that extend internal market conditions for the provision of certain services to third countries.[9]

As the Court of Justice puts it, common commercial policy is the result of a 'combination and interaction of internal and external measures': sometimes agreements are concluded to implement a policy fixed in advance by European institutions; sometimes European commercial policy is shaped by international agreements binding the EU.[10] In this regard, the participation of the European Union to the legal framework deriving from the WTO agreements is particularly explanatory. It is worth recalling that, when the Community was originally established, the General Agreement on Tariffs and Trade (GATT) had been in place for about 10 years. Member States were therefore bound by such multilateral regime when they concluded the Treaty of Rome establishing the European Economic Community (TEEC) and desired to

[4] See A Dimopoulos, 'The Effects of the Lisbon Treaty in the Principles and Objectives of the Common Commercial Policy' (2010) 15 *European Foreign Affairs Review* 153.

[5] Case C-414/11 *Daiichi Sankyo and Sanofi-Aventis Deutschland* [2013] ECR I-0000, paras 50–52; Case C-137/12 *Commission v Council* [2013] ECR I-0000, paras 56–58; Case C-411/06 *Commission v Parliament* [2009] ECR I-7585, paras 71–72.

[6] For further analysis on the type of measures falling within the scope of common commercial policy, also in combination with Art 352 TFEU, see P Koutrakos, 'Legal Basis and Delimitation of Competences' in M Cremona and B De Witte (eds), *EU Foreign Relations Law, Constitutional Fundamentals* (Oxford University Press, 2008) 171.

[7] Opinion 1/78 on the International Agreement on Natural Rubber [1979] ECR 2871.

[8] Case C-281/01 *Energy Star* [2002] ECR I-12049. See also Case C-70/94 *Werner* [1995] ECR I-3189; Case C-83/94 *Leifer* [1995] ECR I-3231; Case C-124/95 *Centro-Com* [1995] ECR I-81.

[9] Case C-137/12 *Commission v Council* (n 5 above). On the phenomenon of 'exporting' the internal market standards through multilateral conventions see M Cremona, 'The Single Market as a Global Export Brand: Exporting the Single Market (2010) 21 *European Business Law Review* 663.

[10] Opinion 1/75 [1975] ECR 1355.

observe the undertakings provided therein, in accordance with the obligations under Article XXIV GATT. In order to reassure their international partners that the establishment of the Community would not jeopardize the principles agreed upon within the GATT, the funding Treaties contained two important provisions: on the one hand, a clear statement that rights and obligations arising from agreements concluded before the entry into force of such treaty, and in particular multilateral agreements concluded with the participation of Member States, are not affected by the provisions of the treaty ((former) Article 234 TEEC, then (former) Article 307 TEC and today Article 351 TFEU); and on the other hand, and more interestingly for this analysis, a provision seeking adherence of the European Union's objectives in the implementation of common commercial policy to the same aims and objectives as those pursued within the WTO agreements ((former) Article 110 TEEC, then (former) Article 131 TEC and today Article 206 TFEU).

In order to implement the conferral of competences and powers previously exercised by Member States in the area governed by the GATT, the European institutions de facto replaced the Member States within the GATT framework, appearing in tariff negotiations and as a party to agreements concluded within the GATT on behalf of the Member States.[11] With the negotiation of the Marrakesh agreements of 1994, the Community formally became a party to the newly established WTO by concluding such agreements together with the Member States.[12] This also explains why Article 206 TFEU contains an explicit reference to the fact that, with the establishment of a custom union, the European Union shall contribute to 'the harmonious development of world trade, the progressive abolition of restrictions on international trade and on foreign direct investment, and the lowering of customs and other barriers'. Such provision reflects the openness of the European internal market to trade with the rest of the world, in line with the liberalization spirit that characterizes the multilateral system, and ideally with requirements set out in Article XXIV GATT. In this vein, therefore, the participation of the European Union to such multilateral legal framework shapes the orientation of its common

[11] Joined Cases 21–24/72 *International Fruit Company NV and others v Produktschap voor Groenten en Fruit* [1972] ECR 1219, paras 10–18.

[12] See Council Decision (EC) 94/800 concerning the conclusion on behalf of the European Community, as regards matters within its competence, of the agreements reached in the Uruguay Round multilateral negotiations (1986–1994) [1994] OJ L336/1 and Opinion 1/94 [1994] ECR I-5267. According to Art IX, para 1, of the Agreement establishing the World Trade Organization, the European party enjoys a 'multiple' vote, equal to (but not higher than) the number of its Member States which are members of the WTO. After Lisbon, despite the conferral of exclusive competence to the European Union in most aspects of international trade, Member States have continued to be part of the WTO as well as the European Union, and no withdrawal from their partnership nor change in the decision-making rule mentioned in Art IX of the Agreement establishing the World Trade Organization has been negotiated so far. However, with the entry into force of the Lisbon Treaty as of 1 December 2009, the Union has succeeded the (former) European Community in all its legal position within the WTO. See Verbal note from the Council of the European Union and the Commission of the European Communities of 30 November 2009, WT/L/779.

commercial policy as a whole, although an express reference to compliance with the WTO framework is lacking in the Treaties.[13]

Article 206 TFEU does not impose on the European Union a legal obligation to liberalize trade unilaterally, nor to mirror internal trade liberalization in the external sphere.[14] Rather, the use of words such as 'contribute', 'harmonious' and 'progressive' seems to suggest that liberalization is an objective of common commercial policy, but room for political discretion in the choice of relevant means to realize it in trade negotiation rests upon European institutions, as also allowed under the same WTO framework.[15] This is at least the construction we should accept if we want to support a strong political EU actorship at global level, coherent with its internal policies, in furtherance of the general objectives set in Articles 3 and 21 TEU, including not only development of third countries and their inclusion in global economy, but also the 'protection of [European] citizens' (Article 3.5 TEU) and the development of a 'highly competitive social market economy' (Article 3.3 TEU).[16]

It should be remembered that, besides the multilateral dimension within the WTO, the European Union pursues liberalization on two additional axes: at the unilateral level, through the 'generalized system of preference' on non-reciprocal basis,[17] and at the bilateral or regional level, through the conclusion of free trade agreements with single or groups of third countries. In the present chapter the features of the latter dimension of liberalization shall be investigated.

III. THE NATURE AND SCOPE OF COMMON COMMERCIAL POLICY COMPETENCE: FROM ROME TO LISBON

The common regulation of trade aspects with the rest of the world at European level was traditionally conceived in the context of the operation of the internal

[13] P Fois, 'Sulle pretese novità del regionalismo internazionale contemporaneo' [2012] *Rivista di diritto internazionale* 5.

[14] Case C-51/75 *EMI v CBS UK* [1976] ECR 811, para 17.

[15] See M Krajewski, 'The Reform of Common Commercial Policy' in A Biondi, P Eeckhout and S Ripley (eds), *EU Law after Lisbon* (Oxford University Press, 2012) 295. A more strict interpretation of this provision is suggested by Dimopoulos (n 4 above), 160–61, who argues that, with the Treaty of Lisbon, the introduction of the word 'shall' in Art 206 TFEU in principle prohibits the European institutions from adopting restrictive measures and stepping back from the existing level of liberalization, save exceptions based on the pursuit of Art 21 TEU objectives.

[16] On possible conflicts among general objectives in external action see Krajewski (ibid); Dimopoulos (ibid). On values and objectives in common commercial policy in general see J Larik, 'Much More Than Trade: The Common Commercial Policy in a Global Context' in M Evans and P Koutrakos (eds), *Beyond the Established Legal Orders. Policy Interconnections between the EU and the Rest of the World* (Hart Publishing, 2011) 13; M Cremona, 'Values of EU Foreign Policy' in Evans and Koutrakos (ibid), 275.

[17] Council Regulation (EC) 732/2008 applying a scheme of generalised tariff preferences from 1 January 2009 and amending regulations (EC) 552/97, (EC) 1933/2006 and Commission Regulations (EC) 1100/2006 and (EC) 964/2007 (GSP Regulation) [2008] OJ L211/1, and subsequent amendments.

market and, more precisely, for the defence of the common interests of the European Union, 'within which the particular interests of the Member States must endeavour to adapt to each other'.[18] In this vein, since the very beginning it became clear that the defence of EU common interest in international trade matters was incompatible with the affirmation of Member States' concurrent powers in this field: as the Court of Justice affirmed in its Opinion 1/75, with reference to the conclusion of an international agreement regarding export credits, any unilateral action on the part of the Member States would lead to disparities and distortion of competition between undertakings of the various Member States in external markets, and therefore compromise the smooth functioning of intra-Community trades. Such distortion could only be eliminated by means of a 'strict uniformity' of international trade regulation in all Member States, ie with an a priori EU exclusive competence in the field of common commercial policy.[19]

The scope of the EU exclusive competence in common commercial policy has changed throughout the treaty reforms, also as a reaction to landmark decisions of the Court of Justice on the matter. In particular, exclusivity had been acknowledged with reference to the international trade of goods. However, with the emergence of a wider trade agenda in the Uruguay Round, involving issues beyond those traditionally dealt with by the old GATT, such as trade of services and trade-related aspects of intellectual property, the Court of Justice ruled, in its Opinion 1/94, that the (former) Community was deprived of fully exclusive competence in the latter two areas, for which competence had to be partly shared with the Member States.[20] This vertical fragmentation

[18] Opinion 1/75 [1975] ECR 1355.

[19] Ibid, para 45. See Baratta (n 3 above), 403. As clarified by the Court of Justice, however, common commercial policy does not preclude Member States from adopting autonomous indirect taxation measures applicable to third countries' products, Joined Cases C-228 to 234/90, C-339/90 and C-353/90 *Simba SpA and others v Ministero delle finanze* [1992] ECR I-3713, paras 16–19. On links between internal market harmonization and uniformity in the external sphere see M Cremona, 'The External Dimension of the Single Market: Building (on) the Fundations' in C Barnard and J Scott (eds), *The Law of the Single European Market* (Hart Publishing, 2002) 351 at 374.

[20] Opinion 1/94 (n 12 above). In particular, the Community was held to have exclusive competence as regards trade of goods and cross-border trade of services, ie mode 1 under Art 1(2), GATS; by contrast, it was held to lack exclusive competences as regards provision of services through consumption abroad, commercial presence and the presence of natural persons, ie modes 2–4 under Art 1(2) GATS, as well as for trade-related aspects of intellectual property. Authors have not been tender in commenting on the said opinion of the Court, which purported an inward-looking definition of common commercial policy, detached from the actual agenda that was taking shape in international trade negotiations. For extensive consideration see, *ex multis*, P Pescatore, 'Opinion 1/94 on "Conclusion" of the WTO Agreement: Is There an Escape from a Programmed Disaster?' (1999) 36 *Common Market Law Review* 387; J Martín y Pérez de Nanclares, 'La competencia de la CE para celebrar el acuerdo de la OMC (Comentario al dictamen del TJCE 1/94, Acuerdo OMC, de 15 de noviembre de 1994)' [1995] *Revista de Instituciones Europeas* 593; J Bourgeois, 'L'avis de la Cour de justice des Communautés européennes à propos de l'Uruguay Round : un avis mitigé [1994] *Revue du marché unique européen* 11; N Emiliou, 'The Death of Exclusive Competence?' (1996) 21 *European Law Review* 294; G Tognazzi, 'Il parere n. 1/94: nuovi sviluppi in tema di relazioni esterne della Comunità europea' [1996] *Diritto comunitario e degli scambi internazionali* 75.

of competence triggered the reform of the relevant provision of the Treaties introduced in Amsterdam and, more decisively, in Nice: Member States agreed to transfer additional portions of competences to the European institutions in matters of trade in services and commercial aspects of intellectual property in order to endow the (former) Community with a clear legal basis for negotiations in the WTO.[21] However, some ambiguity on the exclusivity of such competence remained in the text of the Treaties, also because of the safeguard clause provided in former Article 133(5) TEC.[22] Furthermore, carve-outs of shared competence were expressly maintained under former Article 133(6) TEC as regards the so-called 'sensitive services' (ie cultural, audiovisual, educational, social and health services), as well as for transport services, which are still excluded from the common commercial policy domain today. The Court of Justice shed some light on those provisions in its Opinion 1/08, where it clarified, inter alia, that all modes of provision of services under Article 1.2 of the General Agreement on Trade in Services (GATS) were to be included in the Community competence pursuant to Article 133(5) TEC, save the exception of 'sensitive services', which fell under the shared competence of the Community and Member States pursuant to Article 133(6) and therefore required the joint participation of Community and Member States in the relevant agreement. Moreover, in case of horizontal agreements affecting all service sectors, an additional legal basis would be required in order to cover transport services.[23]

The Treaty of Lisbon has significantly improved the blurred legal framework outlined above. First, it definitely resolves the issue of the nature of common commercial policy by listing it among the a priori exclusive competences of

[21] M Cremona, 'A Policy of Bits and Pieces? The Common Commercial Policy after Nice' [2001] *Cambridge Yearbook of European Legal Studies* 61.

[22] Art 133(5) TEC, as reformed by the Nice Treaty, provided that: 'This paragraph shall not affect the right of the Member States to maintain and conclude agreements with third countries or international organisations in so far as such agreements comply with Community law and other relevant international agreements'. On the legal framework post-Nice see Cremona (ibid); J Helikoski, 'The Nice Reform of Art 133 EC on the Common Commercial Policy' (2002) 1 *Journal of International Commercial Law* 1; HG Krenzler and C Pitschas, 'Progress or Stagnation? The Common Commercial Policy after Nice' (2001) 6 *European Foreign Affairs Review* 291; C Hermann, 'Common Commercial Policy After Nice: Sisyphus Would Have Done a Better Job' (2002) 39 *Common Market Law Review* 7; D Diverio, 'Competenze comunitarie e accordi di servizi' [2002] *Diritto del commercio internazionale* 235; RL Arcas, 'Exclusive or Shared Competence in the Common Commercial Policy: From Amsterdam to Nice' (2003) 30 *Legal Issues of European Integration* 3; P Koutrakos, '"I Need to Hear You Say It": Revisiting the Scope of the EC Common Commercial Policy' (2003) 22 *Yearbook of European Law* 407; M Krajewski, 'Of Modes and Sectors—External Relations, Internal Debates and the Special Case of (Trade in) Services' in M Cremona (ed), *Developments in EU External Relations Law* (Oxford University Press, 2008) 188.

[23] Opinion 1/08 [2008] ECRI-11129, paras 131–51. For further consideration see M Cremona, 'Balancing Union and Member States Interests: Opinion 1/08, Choice of Legal Base and the Common Commercial Policy under the Treaty of Lisbon' (2010) 35 *European Law Review* 678; L Mola, 'Il Parere 1/08 della Corte di giustizia sulle modifiche agli impegni specifici allegati al GATS: status quo ante Trattato di Lisbona e prospettive in merito alla conclusione di accordi commerciali sui servizi' [2010] *Diritto comunitario e degli scambi internazionali* 675.

the Union under Article 3(1)(e) TFEU. Secondly, Article 207(1) TFEU clarifies the scope of such competence as including, without further qualification:

> tariff rates, the conclusion of tariff and trade agreements relating to trade in goods and services, and the commercial aspects of intellectual property, foreign direct investment, the achievement of uniformity in measures of liberalization, export policy and measures to protect trade such as those to be taken in the event of dumping or subsidies.[24]

Member States are therefore precluded to exercise concurrent external competences as regards international trade matters mentioned in Article 207 TFEU. A significant exception remains the transport sector, according to the exclusion provided under Article 207(5) TFEU. In principle, the European Union should therefore be able to conclude a wide range of trade agreements without the mixed participation of Member States, unless provisions on transport services and non-commercial aspects of intellectual property are included.[25] It is, however, doubtful whether clauses on criminal enforcement of intellectual property rights would be enough to trigger the mixed participation of the Member States when they are merely supplementary to the main purpose of the agreement. In this regard, a recent ruling of the Court of Justice held that provisions on seizure and confiscation measures contained in the European Convention on the Legal Protection of Services based on, or consisting of, conditional access would not impinge on the exclusive competence of the Union to conclude the convention pursuant to common commercial policy legal basis, as such criminal law provisions were merely ancillary to achieve the primary objective of the convention. Therefore the European Union had the competence to conclude such convention alone.[26]

It could be questioned whether a similar reasoning could be applied by analogy in other cases where clauses on cultural, political or other types of

[24] On the reform of common commercial policy introduced by the Lisbon Treaty see PC Muller-Graff, 'The Common Commercial Policy enhanced by the Reform treaty of Lisbon?' in A Dashwood and M Maresceau (eds), *Law and Practice of EU External Relations* (Cambridge University Press, 2008) 188; Baratta (n 3 above), 403; Krajewski (n 15 above), 292; Dimopoulos (n 4 above), 153; A Dimopoulos, 'The Common Commercial Policy after Lisbon: Establishing Parallelisms between Internal and External Economic Policy' [2008] *Croatian Yearbook of European Law and Policy* 102; Larik (n 16 above), 13; M Bronckers, 'Common Commercial Policy' in C Tobler (ed), 'The Lisbon Treaty' (Europa Institute of Leiden University, 2008) 46; F Hoffmeister, 'The European Union's Common Commercial Policy a Year after Lisbon—Sea Change or Business as Usual?' in P Koutrakos (ed), *The European Union's External Relations a Year After Lisbon*, CLEER Working Paper 2011/3; GV Puig and B Haddab, 'The Common Commercial Policy after Lisbon: An Analysis of the Reforms' (2011) 36 *European Law Review* 289; E Cannizzaro, 'Artt 206, 207 TFUE' in A Tizzano (ed), *Trattati dell'Unione europea* (Giuffrè, 2014) 1701.

[25] However, in those areas where the Union does not have harmonization powers, such as those listed in Art 6 TFEU, the exercise of common commercial policy competences on the external sphere 'shall not affect the delimitation of competences between the Union and the Member States, and shall not lead to harmonisation of legislative or regulatory provisions of the Member States', according to Art 207(6) TFEU. See Krajewski (ibid) 155.

[26] Case C-137/12 *Commission v Parliament* (n 5 above), paras 70–72. See also Case C-377/12 *Commission v Council,* not yet published.

non-commercial cooperation are included in trade agreements, sometimes deliberately to justify the mixed participation of Member States in normative areas where the Union lacks exclusive competences. Should we accept this construction, a number of (true or) 'false' mixed agreements might cease to exist in the future. However, it is not obvious that such clauses can be considered 'ancillary' to the main purpose of horizontal trade agreements, and practice does not seem to support this view; for example, the decision regarding the conclusion of the EU–Korea FTA was adopted on grounds of three different legal bases, reflecting the commercial, transport and cultural cooperation aspects of the agreement, although cultural cooperation is dealt with in a protocol, and is certainly not the core of the FTA.[27] In these cases, different criteria seem to have prevailed on the 'centre of gravity' test in the choice of legal basis, although such practice is at odds with the settled case law of the Court of Justice. In any case, a 'safe' solution for Member States not to disappear from international negotiations of horizontal trade agreements would certainly be the inclusion of transport issues in the agenda.

The above does not resolves all definitional problems under Article 207 TFEU, as Member States' interests in some sectors are still safeguarded by way of different procedural requirements (unanimity vote) for the conclusion of relevant agreements (Article 207(4) TFEU). Furthermore, the scope of the new exclusive competence in the field of foreign direct investments is still to be defined and will probably need some clarification by the Court of Justice.[28]

[27] Council Decision on the signing, on behalf of the European Union, and provisional application of the Free Trade Agreement between European Union and its Member States, of the one part, and the Republic of Korea, of the other part [2010] OJ L127/1.

[28] Request for an Opinion submitted by the European Commission pursuant to Article 218(11) TFEU (Opinion 2/15) [2015] OJ C363/18. It is not possible to deal here with the issues raised by the scope of the new competence at stake. For extensive consideration see F Ortino and P Eeckhout, 'Towards an EU Policy on Foreign Direct Investments' in Biondi et al (n 15 above), 292; Krajewski (n 15 above); M Krajewski, 'External Trade Law and the Constitutional Treaty: Towards a Federal and More Democratic Common Commercial Policy' (2005) 42 *Common Market Law Review* 91; NJ Calamita, 'The Making of Europe's Investment Policy: Uncertain First Steps' (2012) 39 *Legal Issues of Economic Integration* 301; A Dimopoulos, 'The Compatibility of EU Investment Agreements with EU Law' (2012) 39 *Legal Issues of Economic Integration* 447; JA Bischoff, 'Just a Little Bit of "Mixity"? The EU's Role in the Field of International Investment Protection Law' (2011) 48 *Common Market Law Review* 1527; RV Puig, 'The Scope of the New Exclusive Competence of the European Union with Regard to "Foreign Direct Investment"' (2013) 40 *Legal Issues of Economic Integration* 133; J Ceyssens, 'Towards a Common Foreign Investment Policy? Foreign Investment in the European Constitution' (2005) 32 *Legal Issues of Economic Integration* 259; L Mola, 'Which Role for EU in the Development of International Investment Law?', Working Paper 26/08 (Society of International Economic Law, 2008); T Eilmansberger, 'Bilateral Investment Treaties and EU Law' (2009) 46 *Common Market Law Review* 383; MR Mauro, 'Accordi internazionali sugli investimenti e Unione europea' [2010] *Studi sull'integrazione europea* 403; A Perfetti, 'La tutela dei valori non commerciali nella politica dell'Unione europea in materia di investimenti? [2011] *La Comunità internazionale* 247; F Marrella, 'Unione europea e investimenti esteri' in SM Carbone (ed), *L'Unione europea a vent'anni da Maastricht, verso nuove regole, XVII Convegno SIDI Genova 31 maggio–1 giugno 2012* (Editoriale Scientifica, 2013) 107. For the position of the Commission on these issues see Communication of the Commission, 'Towards a Comprehensive European International Investment Policy', COM(2010)343 final. On the pragmatic way the European institutions are approaching the progressive transfer of competences in

It is not even clear whether the exclusive competence at stake would cover investments in the transport sector. In this regard, practice so far developed is not offering much help in defining the boundaries of European foreign investment competence, as FTAs including investment chapters are being negotiated (and will probably be concluded) as mixed agreements (see Section IV below). The definition of its scope will likely become clearer in the future, with the negotiations of the first stand-alone bilateral investment treaties (BITs) from the European Union.[29]

IV. THE 'GLOBAL EUROPE' STRATEGY: FROM GLOBAL TO REGIONAL

Before the entry into force of the Lisbon Treaty, a significant change had already occurred in the conduction of European common commercial policy. In 2006, the European Commission (the Commission) spelled out its new overarching strategy, 'Global Europe: Competing in the World', in order to identify the role of common commercial policy in the implementation of the Lisbon agenda for jobs and sustainable growth.[30] In particular, without denying the centrality of multilateral commitment, a major emphasis was placed on the importance of devoting diplomatic efforts to the bilateral and regional dimensions, promoting the conclusion of new comprehensive bilateral/regional FTAs which would establish preferential free trade and investment 'corridors' between the European Union and its commercial partners. The new generation of FTAs would be based on reciprocity, would be comprehensive in scope and would aim at the highest possible degree of liberalization in most economic sectors, including services and investments (see Section V below). This should also ensure their compatibility with the WTO.[31]

this field from the Member States to the European Union see Regulation (EU) 1219/2012 establishing transitional arrangements for bilateral investment agreements between member states and third countries [2012] OJ L351/40.

[29] See Regulation (EU) 912/2014 of 23 July 2014, establishing a framework for managing financial responsibility linked to investor-state dispute settlement tribunals established by international agreements to which the European Union is party, [2014] OJ L251/121.

[30] Communication from the Commission, 'Global Europe: competing in the world', COM(2006)567 (Global Europe Strategy).

[31] In order to be WTO compatible, FTAs should first and foremost comply with requirements set by Art XXIV GATT and Art V GATS. By providing comprehensive liberalization for goods and services (the latter is less comprehensive when based on a positive list approach, such as in the case of the EU–Korea FTA), it seems likely that such agreements will generally meet the 'substantial trade' and 'substantial sectoral coverage' requirements provided for custom unions and free trade areas to maximize trade creation as opposed to trade diversion within the WTO. However, such provisions have substantially remained unenforced, save for a general exercising of transparency regarding the existence and content of such agreements (facilitated by the WTO transparency mechanism for regional trade agreements, established in 2006). Resort to the WTO dispute settlement mechanism may occur if a third country claims a violation of relevant WTO obligations on the side of one of the parties of the relevant FTA (see, eg the *Turkey—textile imports* case, WT/DS34/AB/R). However, this has hardly happened in WTO case law. In principle, Member States should instead be barred by European law from starting a claim before WTO in

From a political-economic standpoint, this shift in European policy is reportedly justified by the need to neutralize potential trade diversion resulting from FTAs between third countries, and in particular by the United States' active agenda on 'competitive liberalization', which, from about 2000, started to use FTAs more aggressively as an alternative to multilateral liberalization. Additionally, the EU needed to forge strategic links with countries or regions experiencing rapid economic growth as a tool to boost the competitiveness and growth of European industry.[32] The Commission also considers that such bilateral tools go further and faster in promoting openness and integration of markets, and tackle issues that would not be ready for multilateral discussion. In this latter respect, the new strategy does not depart from the traditional Commission's rhetoric of mutual complementarity between multilateralism and regionalism in trade relations.[33]

Besides, the EU has always pursued foreign policy interests through the conclusion of preferential trade agreements of different kinds with third countries, also with a view to pursuing development cooperation or stabilization and security aims.[34] Suffice it to recall the free trade agreements concluded with southern Mediterranean countries (Algeria, Egypt, Israel, Jordan, Lebanon, Morocco, Occupied Palestinian Territory, Tunisia) and those with some developing countries (Chile, Mexico, South Africa), the stabilization and association agreements with the Western Balkans countries (Albania, Bosnia and Herzegovina, Croatia, Former Yugoslav Republic of Macedonia, Montenegro, Serbia), the economic partnership agreement with the 78 ACP countries (in the framework of Cotonou Agreements), and the European free trade association and customs unions with Andorra, San Marino, Turkey, Iceland, Liechtenstein, Norway and Switzerland. As a result of numerous bilateral and regional preferential trade agreements and unilateral schemes, including the generalized system of preferences for developing countries, in 2010 the most-favoured nation (MFN) regime applied to only ten industrialized countries importing into the European Union, ie Australia, Canada, Taiwan, Hong Kong, China, Korea, Japan, New Zealand, Singapore and the United States.[35]

this regard, in compliance with the principle of mutual cooperation in external relations and by virtue of the exclusive conferral of competences in common commercial policy.

[32] S Woolcock, 'European Union Policy Towards Free Trade Agreements', ECIPE Working Paper No 3 (ECIPE, 2007).

[33] M Cremona, 'Rhetoric and reticence: EU external commercial policy in a multilateral context' (2001) 38 *Common Market Law Review* 359. Despite the tension between the two schemes, the substantial moratorium on the enforcement of Art XXVI GATT and V GATS at the WTO level eased the proliferation of bilateral/regional agreements witnessed in the recent years. On this topic see Mavroidis (n 2 above), and the literature quoted therein.

[34] P Koutrakos, *The External Relations of the European Union, Legal and Constitutional Foundations* (Oxford University Press, 2004) 347.

[35] Representing more than half of European imports. See Commission staff working document, 'Trade as a Driver of Prosperity—Accompanying Document to the Communication Trade, Growth and World Affairs Trade Policy as a Core Component of the EU's 2020 Strategy', COM(2010)612. As is shown below, some of them have just signed, or are about to sign, new generation FTAs with the European Union based on the Global Europe strategy.

As regards exports, the European Union had preferential access only to a limited number of countries in the world, the remainder of European export taking place on an MFN basis.[36] The reason for such imbalance is because numerous preferential trade relations between European Union and third countries are not based on reciprocal commitments. The most prominent example of non-reciprocity was the (former) Lomé Convention with ACP countries, which raised multiple claims of incompatibility with the WTO framework from several WTO members.[37]

In this respect, the Global Europe strategy differs from past approaches since the European Union uses FTAs in a more 'offensive' way. The key criteria outlined by the Commission for selecting the new generation FTAs partners are particularly indicative of the change of approach, seeing preferential trade relations not solely as an 'altruistic' tool of commercial policy. More precisely, future commercial partners are chosen by the Union on the basis of (i) market potential, with reference to economic size of the market and growth perspectives, and (ii) the level of protection against European exports, with reference to both tariffs and non-tariff barriers to trade (NTBs).

On those grounds, the first far-reaching FTA based on the Global Europe strategy was concluded in 2009 with Korea, followed in 2010 by an agreement with the Andean Community (Colombia, Peru and Ecuador).[38] Political agreement on the key elements of a comprehensive economic and trade agreement (CETA) with Canada was reached at the end of 2013. This agreement was the first to include an investment chapter negotiated by the European Union, followed by the FTAs with Singapore and Vietnam, respectively finalized in 2014 and 2015. Negotiations are still ongoing with ASEAN, USA, Japan, India and Mercosur. In the case of Japan and ASEAN, negotiating directives conferred before the entry into force of the Lisbon Treaty were integrated afterwards, in order to allow discussions on investment chapters.[39] An update of the free trade agreements with southern Mediterranean countries is also on the agenda of the Commission. With reference to China, due to the opportunities and risks it represents for the European economy, the European Council has authorized the Commission to negotiate the first stand alone treaty on invest-

[36] COM(2010)612 (ibid).

[37] For a full account of the relationship of the European Union with ACP countries, as evolved from the Youndé through the Lomé and Cotonou Agreements, and its compatibility with WTO framework, see, among many, L Bartels, 'The Trade and Development Policy of the European Union' in Cremona (n 22 above), 128; A Abass, 'The Cotonou Trade Regime and WTO Law' (2004) 10 *European Law Journal* 439; S Bartelt, 'ACP–EU Development Cooperation at a Cross Roads? One Year after the Second Revision of the Cotonou Agreements (2012) 17 *European Foreign Affairs Review* 1.

[38] Contacts are being maintained among the parties for the possible accession of other members of the Andean Community to the same agreement (Bolivia). For an updated account of trade negotiations currently in place see the Commission document 'Overview of FTA and Other Trade Negotiations', available at http://trade.ec.europa.eu/doclib/docs/2006/december/tradoc_118238.pdf.

[39] 'EU and Canada Conclude Negotiations on Trade Deal', press release, 18 October 2013, available at http://europa.eu/rapid/press-release_MEMO-13-913_en.htm.

ments.[40] Russia and the Gulf Cooperation Council also represent interesting opportunities for European exports, but talks were only at the informal level at the time of writing.[41]

V. THE NEW GENERATION FTAS: THE MODEL AGREEMENT WITH KOREA…

Each agreement has a different content and different political-economic justifications, which influence its provisions and the results of negotiations. Some common features can, however, be fleshed out based on the model EU–Korea FTA. As already mentioned, the starting point of these agreements is that they are based on the principle of 'reciprocity' in market access and aim for the highest degree of liberalization in the trade of goods, services and investments.

As regards trade in goods, the agreements are not limited to the traditional clauses on national treatment and market access through the reduction or abolition of duties. The European Union also fights the imposition of export duties in third countries, which are not outlawed by the GATT (see Article 2.11 of the EU–Korea Agreement).[42] Furthermore, the EU–Korea FTA goes into detail about the discipline of respective systems of trade remedies, imposing common standards for anti-dumping and countervailing duties, as well as for the activation of the safeguard clause (Chapter 3), tackles technical barriers to trade (TBT) and sanitary and phytosanitary (SPS) barriers, protection of intellectual property rights (IPR), and provides trade and custom facilitation mechanisms, such as an important prohibition of pre-shipment inspections (Article 6.10). A full protocol of the agreement is also devoted to mutual administrative assistance in custom matters.

In this context, special attention is paid by the European Union to NTBs to the trade of goods, which are nowadays considered among the most obstructive obstacles to international commerce due to the general decrease in tariff barriers under the WTO's aegis in the last few decades. In particular, while reaffirming the commitments under the TBT and SPS agreements, more detailed provisions are also in existence. For example, the EU–Korea FTA includes a rule aimed at ensuring proportionality and necessity in the imposition of marking and labelling rules. In addition, it seems noteworthy that sectoral TBT disciplines are incorporated in four separate annexes, relating, respectively, to consumer electronics (Annex 2-B), automotive (Annex 2-C), pharmaceuticals and medical devices (Annex 2-D), and chemicals (Annex 2-E). Regulatory harmonization of standards is provided in certain cases, based

[40] 'EU investment negotiations with China and ASEAN', Press Release 18 October 2013, available at http://europa.eu/rapid/press-release_MEMO-13-913_en.htm.

[41] 'Overview of FTA and Other Trade Negotiations' (n 38 above).

[42] See F Hoffmeister, 'The Deep and Comprehensive Free Trade Agreements of the European Union—Concept and Challenges' in M Cremona and T Tackas, 'Trade Liberalization—New Directions in the Low Politics of EU Foreign Policy', EUI Working Paper 2014/1, 15.

on acceptance of international standards or mutual recognition.[43] Special cooperation mechanisms are also provided for the development of SPS standards among the parties, although such provisions are not subject to the dispute settlement mechanisms provided by the agreement (see below).

The provisions regarding IPR are a fundamental complement to the liberalization of the trade of goods. One of the most comprehensive chapters on the EU–Korea FTA is dedicated to IPR. The Agreement on Trade-Related Aspects of Intellectual Property Rights requires the parties to apply a number of international conventions and introduce provisions for criminal sanctions for IPR violations. Furthermore, it breaks new ground in the protection of geographical indications, through the establishment of a common register for wines and spirits and other agri-food products, which can be considered as a 'pilot' precedent for future multilateral solutions.[44]

Moving now to services and investments, the agreements aim at liberalizing cross-border provision of services and establishment in the widest possible range of sectors.[45] Depending on whether the negotiation mandate was given before or after the entry into force of the Lisbon treaty, agreements may also include investment protection clauses. This was not the case for Korea and the Andean Community, but occurred in the EU–Canada CETA, EU–Singapore FTA and EU–Vietnam FTA. However, when investment protection clauses are lacking, market access to some types of foreign direct investments is nevertheless guaranteed through the provisions regarding trade in services and establishment (see, for example, chapter 7 of the EU–Korea FTA). In particular, Article 7.9 of the EU–Korea FTA expressly defines an investor as 'any person that seeks to perform or performs an economic activity through setting up an establishment'. The notion of establishment is defined in the following terms:

> i) the constitution, acquisition or maintenance of a juridical person [including capital participation in a juridical person with a view to establishing or maintaining lasting economic links] ii) the creation or maintenance of a branch or representative office within the territory of a Party for the purpose of performing an economic activity.

Foreign direct investments consisting in establishment are therefore granted market access through the prohibition of a number of practices generally used by countries to curtail the commercial presence of foreign investors (Article 7.11). Similar prohibitions also apply to cross-border provision of services (Article 7.5), which might qualify as foreign direct investments in some circum-

[43] B Rigod, 'TBT-Plus Rules in Preferential Trade Agreements' (2013) 40 *Legal Issues of Economic Integration* 247.

[44] European Parliament, DG for External Policies, Policy Department, 'An Assessment of the EU–Korea FTA' (2010), available at http://www.europarl.europa.eu/RegData/etudes/etudes/join/2010/133875/EXPO-INTA_ET(2010)133875_EN.pdf.

[45] In the case of the EU–Korea FTA, a positive list approach is adopted. Exceptions regard audiovisual services, national maritime cabotage, domestic and international air services, their selling and marketing, related reparations and maintenance services, and CRS services (Art 7.4).

stances. Additionally, in service sectors which the parties commit to liberalize, a national treatment standard is accorded to establishments and investors of the other party 'with respect to all measures affecting establishment' (Article 7.12), and to service suppliers 'with respect to all measure affecting cross-border supply of services' (Article 7.6). The said provisions shall not limit investors' rights deriving from existing or future international agreements relating to investments (BITs) between Member States and Korea (Article 7.15).

Public procurement, capital movement competition rules and sustainable development are also dealt with in the agreements.

Implementation of these FTAs is usually ensured by an institutional framework based on a number of working groups and committees to monitor and promote its proper execution.[46] In addition, a transparent EU/state dispute settlement mechanism is usually provided. In the case of the EU–Korea FTA, the latter has been considered the 'most substantial breakthrough' in the agreement.[47] It is based on the WTO dispute settlement model, providing for mandatory consultation, preference for mutually agreed solutions, the possibility of resorting to arbitration with reduced procedural time-frames for the issuance of the settlement award (120–50 days, or 60–75 days in case of urgency), temporary remedies in cases of non-compliance, including the possibility of temporarily reverting MFN tariffs in certain cases, and arbitral review of compliance measures (Articles 14 ff). Hearings of arbitration panels are open to public and the submission of *amicus curiae* briefs is possible.

With reference to the relationship between such bilateral dispute settlements and the jurisdiction of the WTO dispute settlement body, the EU–Korea FTA provides an exclusivity clause that precludes concomitant dispute settlement proceedings in order to avoid duplications (Article 14.19).[48] In case of the provisions of an FTA being identical to WTO obligations, subsequent proceedings are allowed only if the selected forum fails to give redress for procedural or jurisdictional reasons. Needless to say, such issues may only arise if one of the parties chooses not to abide by the dispute settlement clauses of the FTA and seeks review under the WTO settlement provisions. However, the full compatibility of such clause with the compulsory and exclusive jurisdiction of the WTO dispute settlement body could probably be questioned. Social and environmental clauses are also subject to a panel dispute, but the rulings are not binding in this case. Moreover, an innovative mediation mechanism has been included for non-tariff measures, issuing a non-binding advisory opinion to solve the market access problems.

[46] In the EU–Korea FTA, legitimate exceptions to its proper implementation can relate to security or balance of payments reasons (Art 15.8), whereas the ordinary public policy purposes listed in Art XX GATT allow national rules to derogate only from goods-related measures (Art 2.15).

[47] 'An Assessment of the EU–Korea FTA' (n 44 above).

[48] See recently L Zoppo, 'Considerazioni sul concorso delle giurisdizioni internazionali: i modelli di conflitto e le modalità di coordinamento' [2014] *Rivista di diritto internazionale* 88.

VI. ...AND THEIR EFFECTS IN EUROPEAN LEGAL ORDER

Pursuant to Article 216(2) TFEU, international agreements concluded by the Union bind European institutions as well as Member States. Yet, according to well-established case law,

> the Court can examine the validity of Community legislation in the light of an international treaty only where the nature and the broad logic of the latter do not preclude this and, in addition, the treaty's provisions appear, as regards their content, to be unconditional and sufficiently precise.[49]

In this regard, the Court of Justice (the Court) has been generally reluctant to get involved in the judicial review of European measures—including its international agreements—with WTO undertakings, unless the *Fediol* and *Nakajima* exceptions apply.[50] This reluctance is justified by the following reasoning: requiring European judicial organs to police WTO compliance would deprive the European Union's legislative or executive powers of the room to enter into temporary negotiated arrangements under the WTO framework, room that is instead enjoyed by other contracting parties that do not allow judicial review of their domestic law rules against WTO commitments.[51] The Court therefore focuses on the general characteristics of the WTO agreements, in order to argue that they are not conceived at international level as intended to confer rights upon the individuals that they can enforce before European and domestic courts. Accordingly, the Court of Justice also rejected damages actions of exporters suffering the consequences of a WTO dispute settlement body authorized cross-sector retaliation, due to European Union's failure to bring its measures into WTO conformity in the *Bananas* dispute, as the award of damages was perceived by the Court as an indirect policing of European Union legislative powers vis-à-vis WTO obligations.[52]

[49] Case C-308/06 *Intertanko* [2008] ECR I-4057, para 45; Case C-366/10 *Air Transport Association of America* [2011] ECR I-0000, paras 73 ff. On this topic see B Bonafé, 'Direct Effect of International Agreements in the EU Legal Order: Does it Depend on the Existence of an International Dispute Settlement System?' in E Cannizzaro, P Palchetti and R Wessel (eds), *International Law as the Law of the European Union* (Brill, 2012) 229.

[50] Such exceptions refer to cases in which: (i) the Union intended to implement a particular obligation assumed in the context of the WTO; and (ii) the Union measure refers expressly to the precise provisions of the WTO agreements. In such cases, the court has to review the legality of the European measure in question in the light of the WTO rules.

[51] Case C-149/96 *Portugal v Council* [1999] ECR I-8395, paras 42–52; Case C-377/02 *Van Parys* [2005] ECR I-1465. On the effects of WTO agreements in US legal order see G Gattinara, 'The Relevance of WTO Settlement Decisions in the US Legal order' (2009) 36 *Legal Issues of Economic Integration* 285.

[52] Joined Cases C-120 and 121/06 *FIAMM & Others v Council and Commission* [2008] ECR I-6513. For a detailed consideration see M Dani, 'Remedying European Legal Pluralism: The FIAMM and Fedon Litigation and the Judicial Protection of International Trade Bystanders' (2010) 21 *European Journal of International Law* 303; P Mavroidis, 'It's All Right, I'm only Bleeding (A Comment on the Fedon Jurisprudence of the Court of First Instance)', STALS Research Paper no 11/2008; M Bronckers and S Goelen, 'Financial Liability of the EU for Violation of WTO Law: A Legislative Proposal Benefiting? Innocent Bystander?' (2012) 39 *Legal Issues of Economic Integration* 399; A von Bogdandy, 'Legal Effects of WTO Decisions within the European Union

Nevertheless, the Court took an opposite view with reference to effects in domestic legal orders of other bilateral or multilateral trade agreements concluded by the European Union with third states, such as free trade association with EFTA countries,[53] cooperation agreements with neighbouring countries[54] and the conventions with ACP countries.[55] In these cases, the Court of Justice policed Member States' action vis-à-vis the legal obligations provided in such agreements as an integral part of European law to which Member States must abide, in view of the direct applicability of their provisions.[56] The existence in the same agreements of an institutional EU/state framework for consultations and negotiations in their implementation did not preclude the possibility of their provisions being directly applicable by the judges of the Member States. In particular, in the *Kufberger* case regarding the application of the association agreement between the former Community and its Member States and Portugal (not then a member) in the import of port wine, the Court affirmed that:

> The fact that a court of one of the parties applies to a specific case before it a provision of the agreement involving an unconditional and precise obligation and therefore not requiring any prior intervention on the part of the joint committee does not adversely affect the powers that the agreement confers on that committee'.[57]

The Court tried to give some explanations to the contradictory solutions adopted in the mentioned cases. In particular, in *Portugal v Council*, it clarified that

> the agreement establishing the WTO, including the annexes is still founded, like GATT 1947, on the principle of negotiations with a view to 'entering into reciprocal and mutually advantageous arrangements' and is thus distinguished, from the viewpoint of the Community, from the agreements concluded between the Community and non-member countries which introduce a certain asymmetry of obligations, or create special relations of integration with the Community, such as the agreement which the Court was required to interpret in *Kupferberg*.[58]

The fact that such bilateral agreements had the political purpose of establishing preferential trade relations, also on a non-reciprocal basis, in order to integrate the third country with the European Union, was seemingly an important element for granting direct applicability, as allegedly opposed to

Law: A Contribution to the Theory of the Legal Acts of International Organizations and the Action for Damages under Article 288(2) EC' (2005) 39 *Journal of World Trade* 45.

[53] Case C-104/81 *Kupferberg* [1982] ECR 3641, regarding association with Portugal; Case C-13/08 *Stamm* [2008] ECR I-11087, regarding association with Switzerland.

[54] Case C-18/90 *Bahia Kziber* [1991] ECR I-199, regarding the cooperation agreement with Morocco.

[55] Case C-87/75 *Bresciani* [1976] ECR 129, regarding the application of the Youndé Convenion.

[56] The Court of Justice may also intervene, in certain cases, through infringements proceedings against Member States breaching European Union negotiated agreements. See the comprehensive review of the case law on the topic by M Mendez, 'The Enforcement of EU Agreements: Bolstering the Effectiveness of Treaty Law?' (2010) 47 *Common Market Law Review* 1719.

[57] *Kufberger* (n 53 above), para 20.

[58] *Portugal v Council* (n 51 above), para 42.

the principle of negotiations for 'mutually advantageous solutions' enshrined in the WTO system.

A question now arises on which of the above-mentioned lines of case law are applicable to the new generation FTAs. On the one hand, they establish bilateral preferential relationships, the effectiveness of which depends also on their judicial enforcement.[59] On the other hand, they are based on reciprocal commitments and provide inter-party dispute settlement mechanisms which offer flexible tools to settle quarrels on a mutually satisfactory basis. The answer to the above question seems easier than expected: parties to such agreements expressly excluded their capability to create rights and obligations directly in the parties' legal order: Article 14.17 EU–Korea FTA provides that: 'any ruling of the arbitration panel shall be binding on the Parties and shall not create any rights or obligations for natural or legal person'. A fortiori, the full agreement does not seem intended to create rights and obligations that are directly applicable in domestic courts. The EU–Canada CETA, in the provisional draft text, is even more eloquent on the issue, stating that:

> nothing in this Agreement shall be construed as conferring rights or imposing obligations on persons other than those created between the Parties under public international law, nor as permitting this Agreement to be directly invoked in the domestic legal systems of the Parties. No Party may provide for a right of action under its domestic law against the other Party on the ground that a measure of the other Party is inconsistent with this Agreement (Article 14.15).

It is therefore clear that the new FTAs are not intended to be directly enforced in domestic courts and, a fortiori, the Court of Justice will not assess the validity of European measures vis-à-vis their provision. It is true that, according to the *Merck Genéricos* judgment, Member States' judges would retain the freedom to recognize direct effects, according to conditions set under national law, on those provisions of the relevant agreements that do not fall under the exclusive competence of the European Union.[60] However, with the mentioned widening of competences transferred to the European Union in the common commercial policy domain, this room for national courts is significantly reduced since the Lisbon Treaty. Such a direct enforcement by domestic courts would in fact impinge on European exclusive competence in common commercial policy, and would reduce the room for manoeuvre of European institutions in negotiating mutually satisfactory solutions with trading partners in the implementation of such agreements.

At the same time, it is not clear how the lack of direct applicability of such agreements copes with the existence of investor-state dispute settlement mechanisms, which will very likely be included in future EU-negotiated FTAs

[59] Their aim is expressly to 'establish a free trade area' (see Art 1 of the EU–Korea FTA). Additionally, most of their provisions are clear, precise and unconditional, like other bilateral agreements enforced by the Court of Justice in the past.

[60] Case C-431/05 *Merck Genéricos* [2007] ECR I-9, para 47.

containing investment chapters. In fact, such tribunals are created for direct use by enterprises and individuals whose rights under the relevant FTA have been breached by the EU or by the Member States. In this regard, enforcement of arbitral awards within the EU shall probably need to be regulated by legislation to be implemented at the EU level, in order to overcome the lack of direct applicability of the agreement as a whole. This will also lead the EU to assume a competence, that of procedural law of arbitration, which has traditionally been jealously preserved by Member States, as demonstrated by the continuing exclusion of arbitration by the Brussels I Regulation (recast). A number of open questions and delicate legal issues need to be addressed in the coming years.

VII. SOME INTERNAL GOVERNANCE CONSIDERATIONS

Having clarified the issues above, it is clear that the new generation FTAs are capable of impacting considerably on the competing conditions of European industry at the European level. Inevitably, the European market has both defensive and offensive interests in liberalization. In the case of Korea, for example, the automotive, textile and consumer electronics sectors bore defensive interests from the importation of competing Korean products, yet they did not succeed in blocking the liberalization measures in the agreement, especially as regards TBT. This was mainly due to the incapability of the sectors to gather a uniform position vis-à-vis the European institutions. By contrast, the pharmaceuticals and chemical industries unanimously welcomed the TBT measures in the agreement, being keen to exploit their comparative advantage in the Korean market. By the same token, European up-market production, services and agriculture gain significant benefits from the liberalization.

That said, some critical considerations are worth making with regard to the decision-making process leading to the conclusion of such agreements by the European Union and its aptitude to reflect the relevant interests of European industry. The decision-making process has been recently amended by the Lisbon Treaty through a stronger parliamentary involvement both as regards informational obligations during the negotiation procedure (Article 218(10)) and concerning the approval for conclusion of the agreements (Article 218(6) TFEU). The room for parliamentary manoeuvre is somehow constrained by the fact that it is only asked for approval or rejection, without any chance to amend the agreement negotiated by the Commission and approved by the Council. Yet this has not prevented the Parliament from gaining a significant role in external relations since the entry into force of the Lisbon Treaty, when it repeatedly refused to approve international agreements, including agreements in the common commercial policy domain. This happened recently in the case of the Anti-Counterfeiting Trade Agreement between European Union and its Member States and Australia, Canada, Japan, Korea, Mexico, Morocco and

New Zealand.[61] In addition, the Parliament was very active in the elaboration of Regulation 511/2011 on the implementation of the safeguard clause contained in the EU–Korea FTA, governing the use of such bilateral trade defence instrument, and succeeded in amending several aspects of the Council version of the regulation. The increased participation of the Parliament offers to stakeholders an opportunity to get indirectly involved in the decision-making process through representation of their own interests. In addition, one should consider that stakeholders are involved by the Commission in the early preparatory phase of discussion about launching trade negotiations, when the Commission holds public consultations with civil society in order to gather information relevant to the perspective content of the possible agreement.[62]

At the same time, the qualified majority voting for most of the trade agreements impedes single governments in having their national industry interests fully reflected in the agreements. The industrial structures of single Member States in fact differ significantly from one another. As a consequence, whereas the positive effects of FTAs are shared by the internal market as a whole, the negative effects of liberalization hit on the industry of some Member States much more heavily than on others, depending on their industrial structure. This, of course, is the price that must be paid for having common policies set at the European level. By the same token, the need to preserve the balance of the internal market precludes the possibility, invoked by the European Parliament, of having regional safeguard measures in place.[63] In this respect, the disparities generated by the different impacts of the same agreement on the economies of single Member States might be in conflict with the principles of economic, social and territorial cohesion of the European Union, as enshrined in Article 174 TFEU. The Court has already ruled that such provisions 'merely lay down a programme, so that the implementation of the objective of economic and social cohesion must be the result of the policies and actions of the Community and also of the Member States'. Agreements cannot be reviewed against these objectives.[64] However, financial measures

[61] E Baroncini, 'L'Unione europea e la procedura di conclusione degli accordi internazionali dopo il trattato di Lisbona' [2013] *Cuadernos de Derecho Transnacional* 5; M Cremona, 'The EU's Regulatoy Policy, Democratic Accountability and the ACTA: A Cautionary Tale' in Cremona and Tackas (n 42 above), 55.

[62] In most cases, the Commission then starts an informal dialogue with the country concerned on the content of a future negotiation, which is known as a scoping exercise. This is important to assess whether the countries have similar enough interests to achieve an agreement. Also of importance in the preparation for negotiation is the conduction by the Commission of an impact assessment of the deal both for the Union and for the other country. When the Commission is persuaded of the opportunity to proceed with the third country concerned, it requests authorization from the Council to open negotiations. The Council can then issue the relevant 'negotiating directives'. See Commission DG Trade, 'Trade Negotiations Step by Step', available at http://trade.ec.europa.eu/doclib/docs/2012/june/tradoc_149616.pdf.

[63] Proposal for a regulation of the European Parliament and of the Council implementing the bilateral safeguard clause of the EU-Korea Free Trade Agreement 2010/0032(COD)—07/09/2010, text adopted by Parliament, partial vote at 1st reading/single reading.

[64] *Portugal v Council* (n 51 above), 86.

aimed at compensating particularly fragile industry sectors in some Member States are possible and should be evaluated carefully.[65]

Some additional points can be made: first, European institutions, acting as a federal state government in the field of common commercial policy, should intensify their efforts in order to preliminarily assess the 'general interest' of European industry, resisting the 'political temptation' of reaching partnerships at any cost. In order to do so, impact assessments and the democratic involvement of stakeholders are certainly important tools, even though deviations from socially optimal solutions may still occur, as seen in the case of the EU–Korea FTA. Secondly, a more structured common industrial policy at the European level could help European institutions to make more strategic and aware choices in the negotiations of free trade agreements. The opportunity of a stronger competence of the European Union, which today is limited to supporting competence under Article 6 TFEU, in developing and programming European industrial priorities should be assessed also in terms of economic models, which are left to other fields of research to investigate.[66] It seems reasonable, however, to argue that some more strategic links between commercial and (improved) industrial policy at the European level could be of help in allowing European institutions to act more effectively in trade negotiations in the interests of European citizens.

VIII. CONCLUDING REMARKS

Bilateral/regional approaches to trade liberalization have traditionally been considered to be in conflict with the multilateral method pursued at the WTO level, as they erode the principle of non-discrimination, might hide protectionism by a closely integrated group and tend to isolate weaker economies. Yet the WTO framework is not itself closed to bilateral/regional methods, provided that certain conditions are met. Moreover, as suggested by some scholars, a number of factors in recent years have contributed to make this tension less acute: the general reduction of MFN tariffs resulted in a reduction of trade diversion created by FTAs. Empirical research also showed the overall positive implications on welfare deriving from such agreements. Furthermore, their new comprehensive content reaches out to areas that are outside the WTO mandate.[67] In this perspective, the extension of European FTAs' scope to NTBs, services and investments fosters their vocation to create building

[65] See, eg Regulation (EC) No 852/95 of 10 April 1995 on the grant of financial assistance to Portugal for a specific programme for the modernization of the Portuguese textile and clothing industry [1995] OJ L86/10.

[66] The original lack of competence of the former EEC in this field was due to the neo-liberal rationale behind the creation of the common market, relying on the free interplay of market forces for the benefit of economic development. See G Scalese, 'Art 173 TFUE' in Tizzano (n 24 above), 1562.

[67] Mavroidis (n 2 above).

blocks, rather than stumbling blocks, of the multilateral system. At the same time, some EU-negotiated innovative solutions in areas such as IPR and NTB support the idea that these FTAs should be brought into the multilateral discussion as possible platforms on which to gather further international consensus and push forward the multilateral agenda. From an EU point of view, however, it seems clear that regional as well as multilateral solutions are equally acceptable in order to further the liberalization objectives mentioned in Article 206 TFEU. This 'mutual complementarity' approach seems to converge with some recent WTO studies, according to which, despite the tendency of countries (and European Union) to form new large blocs (so-called 'mega-regions'), trade among and outside these areas remains central, and therefore cooperation at the multilateral level remains crucial.[68] With this in mind, we should strive for European FTAs to be as comprehensive and trade creating as possible. We cannot exclude that 'competitive liberalization' will ultimately trigger political economy interests that bring governments back to the table of multilateral negotiations.

[68] L Fontagné, J Fouré and Alexander Keck, 'Simulating World Trade in the Decades Ahead: Driving Forces and Policy Implications', WTO Working Paper ERSD/2014/05, 15.

Index

www.ingramcontent.com/pod-product-compliance
Ingram Content Group UK Ltd.
Pitfield, Milton Keynes, MK11 3LW, UK
UKHW021238300926
15471UKWH00013B/390